Jeremiah O'Connell

Catholicity in the Carolinas and Georgia

Leaves of its history

Jeremiah O'Connell

Catholicity in the Carolinas and Georgia
Leaves of its history

ISBN/EAN: 9783742837660

Manufactured in Europe, USA, Canada, Australia, Japa

Cover: Foto ©Lupo / pixelio.de

Manufactured and distributed by brebook publishing software (www.brebook.com)

Jeremiah O'Connell

Catholicity in the Carolinas and Georgia

CATHOLICITY

IN THE

CAROLINAS AND GEORGIA:

LEAVES OF ITS HISTORY.

BY

REV. DR. J. J. O'CONNELL, O.S.B.

THE HISTORY OF CATHOLICITY IN THE UNITED STATES, BOTH BEFORE AND AFTER THE WAR OF INDEPENDENCE, RE-ASSERTS THE PROOFS OF THE DIVINE ORIGIN OF THE CHRISTIAN RELIGION.—See pp. ii., seq.:

THE ESTABLISHMENT AND PRESERVATION OF CATHOLICITY IN THE CAROLINAS AND GEORGIA, ARE AMONG THE NOBLEST TRIUMPHS OF THE CHURCH IN THE REPUBLIC.—See pp. 32, seq.:

A. D. 1820. - - - A. D. 1878.

NEW YORK:
D. & J. SADLIER & CO., 31 BARCLAY
MONTREAL: 275 NOTRE DAME

NIHIL OBSTAT.

P. HERMAN WOLFE, Prior,

Benedictine Monastery of St. Mary's Help,

Censor Theologicus.

IMPRIMATUR.

✠ J. J. KEANE, D. D.,

Bishop of Richmond, Administrator Apostolic of North Carolina.

Copyright, 1879, by D. & J. Sadlier & Co.

J. M. J.

TO THE

IMMACULATE VIRGIN MARY,

MOTHER OF GOD,

PATRONESS OF THE CHURCH, DESTROYER OF ALL HERESIES,
AND HELP OF CHRISTIANS,
WHOM NONE EVER INVOKED IN VAIN,

THIS VOLUME IS DEDICATED,

WITH

THE MOST PROFOUND HUMILITY AND CONFIDENCE,

BY

HER UNWORTHY BUT DEVOTED, CLIENT,

J. J. O'CONNELL.

THANKS.

The author returns sincere thanks to the following persons, for materials furnished, and courtesies and favors extended to him during the preparation of this work:

His Grace Most Rev. James Gibbons, D.D., Baltimore, Md.
Rt. Rev. P. N. Lynch, D.D., Charleston, S. C.
Rt. Rev. William H. Gross, D.D., Savannah, Ga.
Rt. Rev. Abbot Wimmer, O.S.B., St. Vincent's, Pa.
Very Rev. James A. Corcoran, D.D., Philadelphia, Pa.
Very Rev. Herman Wolf, O.S.B., St. Mary's Help, N. C.
Very Rev. D. J. Quigley, Charleston, S. C.
Rev. Edward Quigley, Buffalo, N. Y.
Rev. Thomas Quigley, Henry, Ill.
Rev. C. J. Croghan, Charleston, S. C.
Rev. H. P. Northrop, Charleston, S. C.
Rev. Father Butler, S.J., Augusta, Ga.
Rev. C. C. Prendergast, Augusta, Ga.
Rev. J. J. Reilly, Newbern, N. C.
Rev. J. B. White, Raleigh, N. C.
Rev. P. J. Ryan, Washington, D. C.
Rev. Joseph Keller, O.S.B., Santa Clara, Cal.
Rev. J. M. Folchi, S.J., Santa Clara, Cal.
Rev. Father Oswald Moosmuller, O.S.B., Skiddaway, Ga.
Rev. Mother Mary Baptist Lynch, Valle Crucis, S. C.
Sister Mary Antonia O'Connell, Charleston, S. C.
Brother Philip Canady, O.S.B.
James McMahon, Esq., Brooklyn, N. Y.
Richard H. Clark, LL.D., New York.
Hon. M. P. O'Connor, Charleston, S. C.
William G. Kennedy, Esq., Sumter, S. C.
John Phelan, Esq., Charlotte, N. C.
Benedictine Community, St. Mary's Help, N. C.

AUTHORS.

The following works were consulted in compiling this treatise. A general acknowledgment of indebtedness is gratefully tendered, special quotations having been omitted in the interests of conciseness and simplicity:

Bishop England's Works.
Darras' "Church History."
Spalding's "Life of Archbishop Spalding."
Clark's "Lives of Deceased Bishops of the United States."
Murray's "Popular History of the Catholic Church in the United States."
John Gilmary Shea's works.
McGee's "Catholic History of North America."
Brownson's "Life of Gallitzin."
De Courcy's "Catholic Church in the United States;" translated by Shea.
Byrne's "Irish Immigration to the United States."
Felton's "History of the Church in New England."
Butler's "Lives of the Saints."
The American Catholic Quarterly Review.
"Faith of Our Fathers," by Archbishop Gibbons.
Cardinal Wiseman's Lectures.
Gury's "Moral Theology."
Archbishop Kenrick's "Theology."
Works of Archbishop Hughes.
Works of Father Faber.
Works of Rev. T. Burke, O.P.
Dr. Spalding's "Miscellanea."
The Catholic World.
Metropolitan.
Decrees of the Councils of Baltimore.
Wheeler's "History of North Carolina."
Gibbs' "Documentary History of South Carolina."
McCall's "History of Georgia."
Catholic Magazine.
"Catholic Almanac."
New York Tablet.
New York Freeman's Journal.
Catholic Review.
Files of Catholic journals, and many other sources.

PREFATORY EPISTLE

TO

JAMES McMAHON, Esq.,

BROOKLYN, N. Y.

My Dear and Esteemed Friend:

To you and to a learned Benedictine father, hidden in monastic seclusion, is the reader indebted for whatever pleasure or edification he may derive from the perusal of this volume.

In your zeal for the circulation of Catholic literature, by which the interests of religion are so eminently promoted, you suggested the work, and your disinterested co-operation alone facilitated the publication.

"Catholicity in the Carolinas and Georgia" is the title of the volume. The subject is old, but the book is new, if such be possible in the nineteenth century. Slavery, like another wall of China, isolated the Church in the Southern States from the world abroad, and during a century *she sat in darkness and in the shadow of death.* The learning of her Bishops, like a lightning flash, was the only ray that rent the universal gloom. Eminent writers, who fluently related the progress of the Faith in America, slightly noticed its existence in the South, or barely recognized it in a line or two, like the epitaph on a tomb. To narrate the means and manner of the establishment of the Church, her progress, and unostentatious triumphs, in the face of appalling difficulties and disheartening obstacles, and to preserve the memory of the great and good men, whom God raised up and fitted for the work, is the object of the writer. The salvation of souls, the edification of the faithful, and the good of religion, all conducing to the honor and glory of God, are primary and impelling motives.

Things should be called by their proper names. I have discarded the name of history,—rather a pretentious title, and demanding a fulness of detail impossible under existing difficulties. Most of the records of the diocese perished with the *U. S. Catholic Miscellany* in the conflagration of Charleston; the parochial registers were, in some instances, destroyed during the civil war; the few imperfect fragments that escaped are void of interest for the generality of readers, and would scarcely repay the labor of antiquarian research and a literary pilgrimage. Valuable information furnished by friends, a life of forty years amid the scenes described, a participation in missionary labors, the living traditions of the people, and a good memory should suffice to render an ordinary person competent for the performance of a labor of love. Few of any important events in the history of the Church in these States since its introduction are unknown to the writer. There are still many living witnesses of all he relates. Having used all due diligence in collecting materials and ascertaining dates, he is not responsible for inaccuracies or grave omissions, if such there be.

I claim a margin for slight errors of date; they are unavoidable under present circumstances. When unconnected with questions of national interest, or do not imperil the succession to the throne of a country, or a bishop's chair, they are not a fundamental defect, and will entirely fade away and disappear under the ponderous tread of time. Within a few years it will crowd into a narrow compass the most important events and distinguished names, designating the Battle of Waterloo, the abolition of domestic slavery, the Vatican Council, the Russo-Turkish war, or the principal historical events of the nineteenth century,—the Emperor Napoleon, Pius IX., Archbishop Carroll, and a few other distinguished persons,—cotemporaries. My industry secures commendable accuracy, and I cannot be much at fault in this particular.

While all the faithful, from Leo XIII. to the humblest Catholic negro, are not indifferent to aught that concerns our holy religion, yet a peculiar merit of this treatise is its local interest. The plan embraces *the establishment of Catholicity in the Carolinas and Georgia; the formation of missions, churches, and institutes; the early priests; their privations, sufferings, and fidelity; the first Catholics who were benefactors to religion, and conspicuous for piety;* all, as one body, planting the Cross and preserving the Faith, despite of the difficulties that obstructed the first announcement of the Gospel in the Gentile world. This ranks among the noblest triumphs of the Church in the Republic, and gives evidence of Divine aid, plain as the finger of God on the tablets of the Hebrew law-giver.

I do not intend to record the names of all deserving Catholics on the first missions; it would be impossible,—only such as presented themselves more readily to my memory; the others are written in the Book of Life. Nor were all these faultless. Like monuments in a city of the dead, I do not claim that the just only die, while the impious live on forever. In the main they were good, strong in faith, and generous beyond their means; their declining days were consoled by the mercy in which they had hoped during life. The record is intended to be a means of preserving the Faith among their descendants. Each chapter bears evidence of this leading intention. Like an army roll, the humble and the more distinguished are placed side by side on the record. They fell at different times during the conflict, and went to receive their reward. Brave, and generous, and true, they never faltered. The banner of the Cross was borne gallantly through war and pestilence, incendiarism and persecution, and planted on the soil; the name of Catholicity is now firmly fixed thereon, like the title to the Cross; the efforts of man and the power of Satan can never detach it. The earth was moistened by the blood of martyrs, the sweats of confessors, the tears of missionaries, and baptismal water from the brow of infants, flowing abroad like the rivers of Paradise, and refreshing the barren waste with the dews of Heaven's grace.

When the Books of the Law were restored on the return of the Children of the Captivity, and read in the hearing of the repenting sons of Judah, they wept for their infidelity, and bound themselves and their offspring, by an oath, to future obedience. A loiterer, on entering a Catholic cemetery, was startled at reading, in the necrology of the silent tomb, the name of his ancestor. A living voice spoke to him from the cold, gray slab. He listened to it, like the fiery zealot on the road to Damascus, fell on his knees, and rose a convert. *The stones of the streets cry alarm*, graves have tongues, and tombs preach the faith of those whose lips are sealed by the icy finger of death. If, unhappily, a descendant of one here mentioned lose the Faith, perhaps the page will mantle his brow with shame, and smite his heart with sorrow for his degeneracy, and lead him back to be numbered once more among the worthy sons of

> "That few; that gallant few;
> That noble band of brothers."

In this interest I have woven into the thread of the narrative moral reflections and doctrinal explanations, that the reader may acquire a knowledge of the Faith while perusing a chapter of its history. I wish to please and to teach as a companion, but not as a pedantic moralist. The points were frequently the topics of familiar conversation on the missions and by the firesides of the laity. Where the validity of the Sacraments, articles of faith, and essential discipline are not concerned, freedom of opinion is granted. Such questions can only be closed by Papal authority. I have sedulously adhered to the common teaching of the fathers, without intending to decide a disputed point definitely, limit the license granted by the Church, or forestall her infallible decision. The views expressed with regard to the local administration of ecclesiastical matters are the common opinions of the faithful, both clergy and laity; they are not presented for the presumptuous purpose of instructing the superior wisdom of the learned hierarchy.

I was reluctantly compelled to use the first person; the absence of any written records of domestic facts,—of an authority under which sensitiveness may find shelter from publicity,—left no alternative. An humble sharer in the labors of the missions for many years, while detailing my own, I have described those of others; and at a sacrificing of personal feeling, the plan will be more agreeable to most readers, on account of the personal character impressed on the narrative. Popular opinion, and the voice of the public press, demand this open, candid form, which accords best with the spirit of the age in which we live.

Devoted to my religion with the intensity of honest feeling and rational conviction, I am, however, convinced that many differ with me in their belief. I entertain no ill-will, hatred, or malice against my brother man of any other creed; I cherish charity for all. While condemning prejudice or injustice, and all the other sad consequences of error, I have abstracted from the individual, whom I regard as probably the victim of invincible error, and for whose salvation I would readily lay down my life. I am a citizen of the United States, and sincerely attached to her form of government. Forbidden by my profession, and incapacitated by my position in society, from participating in the angry strife of politics which led to the disruption of the Government, I took no share in accelerating that measure, though one of the greatest sufferers by its disaster. Believing, in common with others at the time, the political doctrine of States' rights to be just and in accordance with the Constitution, I conformed to the then state of things, and discharged the duties of a citizen conscientiously under the short-lived administration. Public men and measures I have criticised whenever their acts overstepped their legitimate bounds, interfered with the rights of conscience, or militated against the interests of religion. I have, like all the writers of the day, described them, but in milder terms. The facts have already passed into history, and have acquired their just proportions, independently of the commentaries of the writer. I have cautiously avoided retailing the frailties of my fellow-man, assailing individual character, or invading the sanctity of private life. The happiness of mankind, the good of religion, and the welfare of society suffer by the wanton exposure of human frailties. I have omitted facts and suppressed names in these interests.

The biographies are dispersed through the several chapters; necessity suggested the arrangement, and it will be found to strengthen, rather than interrupt, the thread of the narrative, by supplying historical details. Whatever of missions, faith, and order illumine the vast realm of the Church, radically exist in each individual bishop. WHEREVER THERE IS A BISHOP, THERE IS ALSO THE CHURCH. This honorable distinction was conferred by popular acclamation on every priest on our missions. *There goes the Catholic Church!* was the expression, accompanying the finger of scorn, that often pointed at the lone, friendless man who trod the streets of the city, like paths of the desert, companionless, without sympathy, without place of worship. The priests were the only ecclesiastical body. Like the prophet in the wilderness, he was the *one only Catholic Church* in the vicinity. The history of the church or station was that of the priest; his life and manners marked the establishment and progress of the Faith in the locality. In his absence there was no mission, no church, and nothing left to be placed on record. Repetitions will be met, and they are unavoidable in the plan; the same clergymen having labored on various missions, encountering the same difficulties, with but slight modification. But they are of advantage, because saving the reader the inconvenience of making frequent references. The style is simple,— the writer's usual mode of speaking when his theme is religion,— to him the sole of objects of interest in human life. On a revision there is scarcely a sentence which he could not involve in a more polished form,—liable, on a second examination, to further alteration. The change may contribute more to a literary reputation, but would be of doubtful advantage to the popularity of the work among the generality of readers. I rest contented if I have succeeded in making myself understood, the sole use and chief excellence of language. An incorrect date, an awkward sentence, misplaced commas, or error of facts will elude the vigilance of the most cautious writer. These and other faults will be met, for nothing human is perfect. Mistakes will be cheerfully corrected in a future edition, and the more accurate information is earnestly solicited.

My desire is to see it not only on the shelves of the library, but in the hands of the laity, also encouraging them to emulate the example of their ancestors in maintaining and practising the Faith planted in their midst by the labors of so many illustrious bishops and zealous priests, who needed only the tomahawk of the Huron, or the club of the Cherokee to raise them to the eminence of Father Jogues and Bishop Juarez in the annals of the Church.

Writers who crave indulgence from the public for their literary productions betray weakness, and exhibit profound ignorance of human nature. The individual may possess kind and gentle feelings and a sympathy with his race, but the public rarely or never; they are victims of the passions of the hour. The dying gladiator in vain turned a last, lingering look for pity to the assembled intelligence, refinement, and beauty of Rome. They bid him perish, and the first people in the metropolis of the world gloated, with fixed gaze, on his dying agony.

Critics whose motives are selfish have ridiculed and held up to public scorn the noblest productions of the human mind. Archbishop Hughes justly remarked, "that it was a poor book indeed which could not be criticised." It is as difficult a task for an author to write a book that will please all his readers as for a rich man to make a will that will suit all his heirs. To one who has breasted for nearly sixty years the rough current of human life, the opinions of man are a matter of slight importance. I have labored to be in accordance with the teachings of the Church, and have consulted able theologians and the most approved authors. The terms, "saint," "martyr," and other similar expressions are merely superlatives, used in the common acceptation, and not in the sense in which they are applied by the Church to the servants of God in her Pontifical decrees, or in a process of canonization. I am not aware that the book contains anything contrary to sound Catholic doctrine. I submit it to the judgment of the Holy Catholic Church and her illustrious head, Leo XIII. My highest honor is to be an obedient son of the one true Faith. I may err; but, with God's grace, a heretic I never can be.

    Believe me always,
     My Dear Mr. McMahon,
      Yours devotedly in Jesus and Mary,

        J. J. O'CONNELL.

Benedictine House of St. Mary's Help, Gaston Co., N. C.,
 Feast of the Nativity of St. John the Baptist, 1878.

TABLE OF CONTENTS.

	PAGE
APPROBATION	ii
DEDICATION	iii
THANKS	v
AUTHORS	vii
PREFATORY EPISTLE TO JAMES MCMAHON	ix
INTRODUCTION	21

CHAPTER I.
Bishop England.. 37

CHAPTER II.
Bishop England (continued)—Very Rev. Richard Swinton Baker, Administrator............................. 80

CHAPTER III.
Rt. Rev. I. A. Reynolds, D.D., and Rt. Rev. P. N. Lynch, D.D.. 105

CHAPTER IV.
Missions in the City of Charleston........................ 137

CHAPTER V.
Beaufort and its Missions................................. 168

CHAPTER VI.
Columbia, S. C... 196

CHAPTER VII.
Columbia, S. C. (continued).............................. 230

CHAPTER VIII.
Columbia, S. C. (continued).............................. 263

CHAPTER IX.
Columbia and its Missions............................... 291

CHAPTER X.
Columbia and its Missions—Chester, Yorkville, Spartanburg, Anderson, Laurens, Newberry, Pendleton, Walhalla, Tunnel Hill, etc............................. 319

CHAPTER XI.
Columbia and its Missions—Greenville, Chick Springs, Merrittsville, Williamston, etc........................... 356

CHAPTER XII.
Vicariate of North Carolina—Wilmington, New Berne, Raleigh, Fayetteville, etc............................. 395

CHAPTER XIII.
Charlotte, Salisbury, Morgantown, Swannanoa, Asheville, etc. 424

CHAPTER XIV.
Benedictine Parish—Institute of St. Mary of Help, Gaston and Cabarrus Counties............................ 467

CHAPTER XV.
Savannah and other Missions............................. 500

CHAPTER XVI.
Savannah and Augusta................................... 536

CHAPTER XVII.
Columbus, Central Georgia, East Florida, and Alabama..... 569

CHAPTER XVIII.
Macon, Milledgeville, Atlanta, etc...................... 594

CATHOLICITY

IN THE

CAROLINAS AND GEORGIA.

CATHOLICITY

IN THE

CAROLINAS AND GEORGIA.

INTRODUCTION.

Population—A Free Church in a Free Country—The American Church, proof of the Divine origin of Christianity—Figures—Name and faith unchangeable—Great Ireland—A Catholic Republic in the Middle Ages—The keys of the Kingdom of Heaven—The American Catholic Church—Christianity triumphs in the desert—Early Martyrs—Indian Knownothings—Trees and rocks and streams preach Catholicity—Puritan Missionaries—The Defender of the Faith—Paradise Lost—Ezekiel's Vision—The Amphitheatre and Tyburn—St. Ignatius and Archbishop Plunket—The Code of Draco and England—The Shrine of Alfred the Great, and St. Louis—But one Catholic Church open in America for a Century—Chains and Slavery—The establishment of the United States and its Constitution the work of the Catholics in a great measure—The Jesuits lay the foundation of Catholicity—Archbishop Carroll—Irish Immigration builds the Church—Growth—Councils—Devotion to the See of Peter—A Cardinalate and a Primate—A Storm—Vandalism—A Sad Scene—The Mystery of Iniquity triumphant—The Slavery War—Peace and Prosperity procured for the Church—The last of Protestantism—False blame—Catholicity and Christianity one and the same—A tribute—Summary—Cotton States in the background—All prose and no poetry—Facts stranger than fiction.

THERE are to-day sixty millions of Catholics in America about eight of whom inhabit our portion of the continent, the United States, with his Eminence Cardinal McCloskey at the head, Archbishop Gibbons as Primate, and a brilliant array of Archbishops, Bishops, Priests, and Religious, conspicuous for learning, piety, and zeal, and millions of devout generous Catholics living under a free government, the best under the sun; the Church in the United States is the fairest portion of our Lord's inheritance on earth; a claim recognized by the saintly Pius IX., when he declared this the only country in which he felt that he was really Pope. The population grafted on a Celtic element of four millions, and inspired with all its energy and activity, have made this country the terror of her enemies, the admiration of mankind, the refuge and shelter of the oppressed of all nations, the vindication of the inalienable rights of man, the downfall of tyranny, the sanctuary of the Faith.

Her triumph is the reassertion of the Divine origin of the Christian religion. There was nothing of prejudice, of wealth, of learning and philosophy, of penal enactments, of civilization, of barbarism, of open violence and hidden stratagem, of persecution and blandishment, that obstructed the first announcement of the Gospel, which was not arrayed against her, resisted her every step; *all fought against her from her very youth.* With means equally inadequate, she surmounted all difficulties and the greater one still of a sham Christianity, that concocted a universal conspiracy against the truth, confounded right and wrong, and cast doubt and uncertainty on all revealed and many natural truths, inducing a universal scepticism, which has at last divided men into two grand classes—the infidel and the Catholic.

Many a time at the point of the sword, the tomahawk of the savage, the pen of the reviler, the torch of the incendiary, the ravages of infuriated mobs, was she commanded, like her Divine Founder, to come down from the Cross or change her title; strong and vigorous, she was now too old to change her manners, on which the persecution of eighteen centuries had made no impression; threats could not intimidate, disaster dismay, or prosperity relax. Three times had she reconverted the world and restored society; she gave to heaven every saint that ever entered its portals. She carried in her hands the destinies of the human race, the chalice of salvation; the mysteries of redemption, the unsealed book of the Gospels, and the rod of Aaron. Her lips touched with fire utter the truths taught by the patriarch, the prophet, and the Son of God: on her finger is the Apostle's ring, and in her soul all that God ever revealed to man. Creation found its explanation in her existence, revelation its meaning, doubt and difficulty their solution, the human race its end; and all the external works of the invisible and everlasting God, their harmony and import, the ark of the deluge, she knows no shipwreck. Like the tabernacle in the desert borne in safety by the priestly tribe to the extreme shore of time, she will be incorruptible until restored to her Divine Founder; the same stroke that annihilates the world will transfer her to her house in the Paradise of God, where she had her origin.

Whether found in the eternal fitness of things, or inherited from the sire of our race, the gift of calling things by their proper names is inherent to man. The Church of to-day, as in the time of St. Augustine, must be called Catholic; all the effects of heresy and the combined action of the human race could not change nor transfer it to any other body. Knownothingism, the last violent effort of Protestantism to destroy the Church, vindicated its title to this name in asserting that Catholicity was a foreign religion and a recent importation into the United States.

Bishop Lynch, in a learned discourse delivered some years ago, startled America, when he affirmed that there was a pre-Columbian history of the continent in the archives of the Church. The statement was confirmed by subsequent research; and now the theme is familiar to the juveniles of a country school.

America, called GREAT IRELAND, was discovered by St. Brendan in the sixth century. Archbishop Williams and other prelates of the New England Sees can claim their descent from Bishops John and Eric and many missionary priests, who during the middle ages, erected Cathedrals, founded monasteries, ruled and governed the Church of God, watered the soil with their blood, and established a Catholic republic in Vinland, before a Puritan had set foot on Plymouth Rock. There was a Catholic republic in America before a Plantaganet or a Tudor wielded the sceptre of Alfred, before the dalmatic of St. Edward became the coronation robe of an apostate, or the title of Defender of the Faith was perverted to give plausibility to the greastest falsehood ever uttered by Satan on earth. America was concealed like the hiding-place of the prophets, until the increasing numbers of the human family required broader possessions; the Father of Mercies, as he had given the keys of the kingdom of heaven to Peter, placed in the hands of a lay Pontiff of Catholicity the keys of the western ocean the intrepid mariner unlocked the gates.

Accompanied in a second voyage, by Father Boyle, twelve priests, one hundred and fifty Catholics, on the Feast of the Epiphany, 1494, he planted the Cross on the shores of this long-lost part of the globe, the Sacrifice of Calvary was renewed, the vision of the prophet fulfilled, the Continent consecrated to Catholicity, the Church established, and the star of empire rested in the West. Perhaps the interruption of the sessions of the Council of the Vatican, prevented the Father from returning by his pathway, under the heaven-sanctioned invocation of his name. Many a wandering tribe roamed the vast extent of the New World. In a high degree they possessed all the virtues and vices of the barbarian—cruelty and clemency, courage and cunning, disorder and law, agriculture and hunting, manufacture and indolence. They were corrupted to the core. The religion superstition and pure devil worship; the women were slaves and the social state polygamy. The Franciscan, the Dominican, the Jesuit, and other priests accompanied the several expeditions. Missionary centres were formed and within a century, the arts of civilized life were practised, schools were established, nations and tribes were converted, fine fields of agriculture spread out far and wide: the *Gloria in Excelsis* was heard in the primeval forests; monasteries, convents, and churches studded the country from Labrador to the Halls of Montezuma. The Church regained as much there as she had lost in Central and Western Europe by the agency of immoral kings and the ravages of the thirty years' war. The Church hailed a new empire, heaven new tongues and tribes and peoples, and civilization a boundless domain.

It was not an easy victory; the new soil drank deeply of the blood of martyrs. The *Secti sunt, occisi sunt* of St. Paul seemed the prophecy of the manner of their death, and applies equally to the apostles of America and the prophets of Israel. Some were cast away at sea, some were drowned in rivers, others were tortured at the stake, others clubbed to death, many, overpowered by weariness, hunger, and sickness, sank down in the pathless wilds to the sleep that knows no waking. The Church, like the mother of sorrows standing at the foot of the Cross, mourned over the sufferings of her children, whilst she rejoiced at their glory. Father Jogues and Lallemant, Corpa, Cancer, Martinez, the unburied bones of Bishop Juarez on the sandy beach of Florida, and many others whose names are written in the Book of Life, rival the martyrs of the golden age of the Christian institute. The zeal of the Cardinal and the activity of the youthful Primate may induce them to examine the blood-stained pages of the Church's history and invite the early attention of the Holy See to the glorious record.

The landmarks of the Faith claimed possession of the entire Continent; Cabot reared the Cross on Northern shores of New England, Ojéda on the Isthmus of Darien, Ponce de Leon in Florida. The explorers of the country were, like its discoverer, all Catholics. Rivers and lakes and cities all bear the names of our saints and teach our mysteries. Their voice cannot be silenced nor the truth of their teaching gainsaid. They are monuments which time cannot crumble, revolution shake, nor war destroy; like the cross held over the heads of a city by the long, stern arm of the Cathedral spire, they vindicate the truth, preach the doctrines of revelation, refute error, and convert souls. There is nothing in science, in art, in learning, in nature, which is not a missionary to the world to speak God's truth and mercy to men, and tell the hidden wonders of His kingdom on earth—the *one holy Catholic* Church into which whoever enters not, *neither shall he enter into the kingdom of heaven.*

While the flags of Spain and France floated o'er the land, the missions increased, civilization smiled on the face of the desert, peace and security were enjoyed by the white man and the red. The cession of the territories to England was a death-blow which swept as with a besom of destruction the fruit of the labors of a century. Every step of the Puritans was marked with carnage, spoliation, and sacrilege. In the territories colonized by the English every living thing, every trace of Catholicity perished; the Continent from the St. Lawrence to the Gulf of Mexico resembled Central Europe after it had been overrun by the Vandal, Hun, and Goth. Like the tornado that desolated Savannah before the deaths of Bishop Barran and Gartland, the English hordes swooped over the land, and with fire and sword reduced to smoking ruins towns, villages, settlements, monasteries, and churches, murdered priests in the sanctuary, and Indian braves, not on the war-path, but in the prosperous fields of industry. Nothing, says Bancroft, escaped their vengeance; they burned the women, and flung the Indian babes into the flames. The tribes civilized by the French and Spaniards subsist to this day, when not brought in contact with the English and their descendants; they have vanished and perished without conversion in the territories colonized by the latter, and scarcely a trace of their former existence remains, except their names, sadly murmured by the waters, pressed by the light canoe of missionary or chief four hundred years ago. The blackness of ashes and a field of the dead now confronted the Church. Like the vision of the prophet, she stood—

> "Gazing o'er a boundless vale.
> Far as the eye could reach 'twas spread
> With the remnants of the dead.
> Morn arose and twilight fell,
> Still the bones lay bleached and bare;
> Midnight brought the panther's yell,
> Bounding o'er the human lair;
> Death sat on his loneliest throne,
> In that wilderness of bone."

What obstacle had Roman empire opposed to the preaching of the Gospel that the British Government has not arrayed against Catholicity? None whatever; the tortures were as varied and exquisite, the appliances as inhuman, the slaughter as world-wide, the persecutions as searching and as long. The enactments of her penal code would fill a volume; they disgrace the annals of the human race, and would be rescinded by the Senate of a Nero for their barbarity. In future times this will be considered the strangest phase in the history of the human race. The historian of the later Emperors tells us that in their times virtue was a state offence, and the wide world did not afford a shelter where a good man could hide and escape the vengeance of the law. It was precisely so in this country during a century and a half before the American Revolution. After having robbed and murdered millions in the Old World, they pursued with Satanic rage the fugitives to the New, and confronted them in the lone paths of the desert. The tomahawk of the Iroquois was less cruel than her legalized atrocity. Those who fled for safety to the hiding-places of poverty were branded with a mark of disgrace, more infamous than murder. The Catholics wandered like Cain, or herded with the obscure. Among the various tongues spoken by the early immigrants, no word could be found to express the infamy implied by Papist.

The altar before which a Charlemagne, an Alfred, and a St. Louis knelt, was designated in the statute-books as the *Idolatry of the Mass*. The brazen statue of the Babylonish monarch set up in the plains of Abraham would not have excited more dismay. Hundreds of thousands crowded on the now inhospitable shores of Columbus, Ponce de Leon, and La Salle. Without priest, or school, or church, or other ecclesiastical organization, their children forgot the Faith, or were ashamed to confess it. In the Carolinas and Georgia the existence of Catholicity was known by the penalties on the statute-books, as the miners in England to-day are said to have acquired the knowledge of the Supreme Being from the blasphemies which profane His adorable name. Like the perpetual fire of the sanctuary in the water-font of the

Prophet of Sorrows, the light of Faith lingered feebly in the land of Calvert, and under the ashes of the chieftain's desert chapel. In the city founded by the wise laws of the Earl of Limerick, there were a few Catholics, who made a periodical pilgrimage, for the reception of the Sacraments, to the only church with open doors in all the country; it was in Philadelphia.

At the commencement of the Revolution, the Catholic population became the bone and sinew of the army of Washington. The darkest hour precedes the dawn; the sons of the desert threw off their hateful bondage. After a long and bitter struggle of seven years, the young Republic sprang into existence. She had but one sole enemy to furnish traitors to the cause of freedom and resist her progress, by an invincible navy and. well-disciplined troops who were famed for prowess on the battle fields of Europe. Who was the hateful foe? History answers, PROTESTANTISM. Without the co-operation of Catholics, our independence never could have been accomplished; the effort would have been as abortive and futile as the Fenian raid on Canada. On the side of freedom stood Catholicity; on that of slavery and oppression Protestantism. She held the manacles ready to replace the sword, as it dropped from the grasp of the warrior, more hateful than the chains that rankled in the feet of the African from Benin and Loango, whom she brought as slaves to our shores, and bequeathed them, like her hereditary prejudices, as a sad inheritance, to be washed away in libations of blood. Catholics were a leading part in the great whole who gained our independence. All the Catholic countries of Europe furnished soldiers to fill the depleted ranks of the American army; their bones are scattered over every battle-field from Boston to New Orleans.

They supplied sailors to build and man a navy that defeated; on its own undisputed battle-field, the fleet that trod under foot every turbulent wave in the universe. The names of Barry and Carrol, Moylan, Lafayette, De Grasse, Rochambeau, Pulaski, and Kosciusko, will shine forever in the firmament of our country's glory, and tell future generations their nativity, their heroism, and their faith, as distinctly as historian's pen, or tongue of orator. The Catholics of Pennsylvania and New York supplied the army and the navy with the needed stores, the sinews of war. Spain was our earliest and best friend; her stores, her ports, her treasures were at the disposal of the leaders of the impoverished and bleeding army. Ireland, Poland, and the Catholic Indians were side by side with the native born in the rugged edge of battle. France furnished ten thousand men independently of her volunteers, three millions of dollars, and her fleet. A world-wide influence was created; the oppressor withdrew in impotence and defeat. The United States was baptized in the font of Catholic blood, protected in the stormy days of youth by Catholic armies, and raised to her proud eminence by the Catholics of Europe.

The Constitution of the United States is a Catholic instrument. It embodies the *Magna Charta* wrested by Archbishop Langton from the tyrant John on the plains of Runnymead, the right of representation to justify taxation, impressed on Europe centuries ago by Pope Zachary, and the principle of civil and religious liberty inculcated by Lord Baltimore in Maryland, and taught long before a Puritan destroyed the emblem of redemption, that marked the lone Catholic grave on the *Promontory of the Cross*. This palladium of our liberties is jealously guarded. Like the tablets of the Hebrew Legislator, it is treasured carefully in the Ark, on whose coverlid rests the golden crown of the benediction of God's Church. The Constitution, our Government, its preservation and prosperity, are in great measure the production of Catholicity. She once more recovered her ancient rights. National prosperity, civil and religious liberty, and the continuation of a republican form of government, all depend on the preservation of these rights. The *blessings* left behind by Protestant England were slavery, a corrupt Bible, savages on the war-path, and hatred of Catholicity. They are gradually disappearing, but enough of the tares remain for the exercise of the unrelaxed care and labor of the husbandman. Religious liberty, no less than civil, is the reward of unslackened vigilance. The saint prays, and watches, and trembles for his perserverance, while a single spark of human nature lingers in his breast.

After the din of war had died away, the country began to resume the industries of peace, and build the temple of liberty. Catholicity, the foundation of all just liberty, had no existence in the land as an organized body. The effort to build up society without religion is as vain as to attempt to *make bricks without straw*. The Ark of God tottered: the United States was an ornament to grace the title of the Vicar Apostolic of London, but too insignificant to cost him a thought. At the close of the war the Catholic population was estimated at 25,000. There were in the vast domain unworthy ministers, a disgrace to the Christian name; but there were also found many well-tried and true, especially the sons of St. Ignatius, who gathered up the scattered stones of the sanctuary and laid the foundations of the Church. The Sovereign Pontiff, yielding to the petition of the clergy, created Father Carroll first Bishop in 1790, and subsequently Archbishop. The United States of America was his diocese; he gathered up the dispersed; *the children of the slain became as arrows in the hands of the mighty*. Venerated as another Washington in society, and the rival of his wisdom, his patriotism, and his moderation, he died in 1815, after having shed the fragrance of episcopal unction on four dioceses, now archiepiscopal sees. The good never die; like a St. John Chrysostom in the East, he was the Patriarch of the West. One hundred zealous priests, five religious orders, and two hundred thousand Catholics lamented him as a common father.

The revolutions in Ireland and France increased the tide of immigration; many thousands of the faithful, with several good and holy French ecclesiastics, landed daily on our shores, swelled the number of Catholics, built the asylums of charity, the schools for education, studded the land with colleges and monasteries, and erected in the populous cities cathedrals, surpassing in magnificence several shrines of mediæval construction in the Old World. The Church kept pace with the growth of the republic, acquired a national character, and reclaimed her lost territory, sending out, as in the early days of Ponce de Leon and De Soto, a mitre and a cross to consecrate each newly-acquired territory another province of the Faith.

Men eminent in the walks of social life, in virtue, and science, and literature, an Ives and a Brownson, a Hecker and a Hewitt, a Bayley and a Wood, and others equally worthy entered into her fold. Her Provincial and National Councils, bearing the impress of the mighty minds of an England, a Kenrick, a Hughes, and a Spalding, imparted union, life, and vigor to the ever-increasing body. She acquired irresistible force from simplicity and uniformity of action. After every few years, the combined wisdom and experience of the hierarchy of both orders assembled in council, like the camping-plains of the Church in the desert, discussed plans and instituted means to meet the ever-increasing demands of the faithful, enforced the ancient and salutary discipline of canon law, corrected abuses, encouraged virtue and truth, created new sees, and like one man, breathed the living soul of Catholicity into the face of the entire Continent. Nothing escaped the vigilance of the fathers; schools, religious institutions, education, mixed marriages, the foundation of churches; Indian missions, the negroes of Liberia—every measure tending towards the advantage of religion—received due consideration. The wisdom and learning of the Council of Trent presided over their deliberation, and they sanctified the renowned activity of the American, by yoking it to the vehicle that bore the Ark of God.

The Church of the United States spoke in a manner becoming her position and dignity. By placing herself under the patronage of the blue mantle of the Immaculate Virgin, she accelerated the definition of the dogma. She comforted the weary heart of the Pontiff, when an outcast from the shrine of his predecessors and a fugitive on the face of alienated Europe, by inviting him to accept an asylum in the land of Washington, and govern the Church of God from the sanctuary of Carroll. At his feet she lavished the treasures of her wealth, and sent her pilgrims to console him in his sorrows. The highest honors of the Holy See were the acknowledgment of her fidelity and devotion, and nowhere are they more meekly borne than in New York and Baltimore.

The Church in the United States had not acquired this eminence without toil and combat; not born to greatness in this country, she created it. Her every step of progress was obstructed by difficulty; persecution accompanied her journey. During the period of her national existence is found the counterpart of the history of the Faith since, preceded by the Cross, it left the inner chamber on the day of Pentecost and began the march of time. It must be so until the last infant will have been baptized, the last penitent absolved, and the last prayer offered on earth. On all sides were religions without charity; the envy of Cain preyed on the vitals of their ministers, and drank dry the fountains of human sympathy. The meek followers of Christ were hated; the children whose treasures of blood and wealth established the government and built up the country, like their forefathers, were now treated as aliens on the soil which they had saved. Satan let loose the ministers of his rage, and an effort was made to wrench the world from God and nail His Spouse to the Cross with her Founder. Vain attempt! The arch-enemy had whistled for his troops; the purlieus of cities, the nightly conventicles of oath-bound conspiracies, miscalled societies, and the cities of Europe responded. Freemasons, nativists, odd-fellows, Orangemen, communists, infidels, atheists, apostates, and the victims of every crime forbidden by God and His Church, like a swarm of locusts sweeping over the impious realm of Pharaoh, blackened the air. From the shores of the Pacific to the Atlantic, from the icy coasts of the North to the sunny fields of the South, there was no resting-place for the Church.

The clergy were hunted like wild beasts, and compelled to shun the light of day. The religious, after having been vilified by the most corrupt literature that ever disgraced or perverted a people, were cast out at night in the midst of flames, among infuriated mobs. The Bishops escaped by miracle, churches and libraries were reduced to ashes, the graves of the dead rifled, and the ADORABLE HOST profaned. In the ranks of the faithful clergy and laity were many willing to lay down their lives for the Faith; they were neither cowards nor laggards; they were determined to die with arms in their hands, and make every city from Boston to Louisville another Moscow. In the councils of heaven, the time for Antichrist had not yet come. God, who sets limits to the waves of the ocean, bade the angry waters cease. Popular fury turned against itself, and terminated in the civil war. The battle-fields of Virginia were the outlet for the impious and disorderly masses; the body politic thus purged recovered itself: peace was once more restored. The Church of God gained by the strife; the work of her priests and religious in the camp and battle-field, the non-interference of the clergy with the ostensible cause of dispute: her wisdom, her charity, her sympathy with common suffering, endeared her again to the heart of the nation, and she sat like a queen, calm and unmoved in the midst of universal turmoil, desolation, and strife. House had been divided against house, brother against brother, States rent from their moorings, and the sects torn and dismembered. "*The nation that hated the Church was in ruins, the weapons raised against her had perished.*" She saw the last of Protestantism as a religious system. She suffered no loss, underwent no change; bright and fair and beautiful as when first planted in Kent by St. Augustine, in Ireland by St. Patrick, on the shores of Carolina by Bishop England, and by the side of the banner of the republic by the Patriarch of the American Church.

She is reproached with having suffered in her numbers by the defection of faithless children;—there should be more Catholics in the United States. True; all should be Catholic; so should England, and Germany, and the East, and all the world. If within half a century one has fallen away from the Faith and a soul has been lost, he must ascribe his misfortune, not to the fault of the Church, but to his own perversity. Every man in America can save his own soul.

What necessity can there be for going to seek a home in the backwoods, and placing oneself beyond the reach of the Sacraments, the holy influence of the Sunday Mass, and the religious education of children? The Church is not a mere human society, an oath-bound or benevolent confraternity, nor a heresy. She and she only is CHRISTIANITY. Whatever obstructs Christianity or truth, must be equally opposed to her; every sin of thought, word, and deed is a sin against the Catholic Church. As long as men abuse freewill, reject the grace of God, and violate the ten commandments, there must be defections; the reproach is, merely, the reassertion of the small number of the saved. The general defection at the end is the last crime to call down the long-delayed anger of God and bring the universe in universal death. "*Think you the Son of Man will find faith on earth when he cometh?*"

She has piped all day in the market-place. At the Vatican Council, her bishops and theologians were unsurpassed in dignity and learning by the prelates of any country. In theology, in controversy, in architecture, in literature, in every department of science, art, and enterprise, she has kept pace with the most advanced nations, and her learning beams over the universe. The Orders of the Church, from St. Benedict to the Paulists, flourish within her bosom. The student, the contemplative, the confessor, the virgin, the anchorite, banished from society in Europe, bloom in the sanctuary of the American Church. She has bishops as detached as St. Thomas of Canterbury, priests as holy as the Cure D'Ars, and missonaries as zealous as those sent to China and Oceanica by Jesuits or Sulpitians; monks as observant as the disciples of St. Bruno in the forest; nuns as angelic as the daughters of St. Clare or the companions of St. Teresa; hermits as austere as the disciples of St. Anthony or Macarius; Sisters of Charity and of Mercy glowing with the spirit of a St. Vincent de Paul; and a Catholic laity generous, devoted, and well-educated. Emancipated from the slavery of secular power, untrammelled by the favor or frowns of kings or princes, and indifferent to both, she is superior to the world, illustrates the blessing of civil independence, and opens to the admiring gaze of mankind the brightest pages in the history of the Catholic Church in the nineteenth century.

She has built the foundations of human liberty deep in society, proved that man is never better than when he is free, and has given an impulse to republican government that has awakened the attention of Europe and caused tyrants to relax the laws that crushed the poor, perverted education, corrupted the people, and enslaved the sanctuary. The prosperity of America keeps pace with the progress of Catholicity; they are indissolubly connected; and every blow aimed against the latter will more fatally affect the former. During the pontificate of Pius IX. two hundred and thirteen new sees have been formed, and over two hundred without concordats. It is a matter of special interest to know that of this number nearly fifty have been created in the United States within that short space of time, and are still yearly increasing. In the formation of her sixty sees and eight vicarates there was no concert of action with the civil authority. The advantage of this system became manifest, and a new era of prosperity commenced in all those lands to which mankind are looking as the advance guard of the human army in its onward march towards the occupation of the whole world. For the first time the world witnessed the glories of a free Church in free States, and republican government received an impulse and support never before accorded to it.

Immigration has sensibly ceased in late years, but the Church is increasing by means of Catholics born in the country and frequent conversions from all classes of citizens. "It will extend," said the illustrious Archbishop Hughes, "not by miraculous means, but by its own natural progress. Religion will not lapse and fall away into indifference and much less into infidelity." Slavery and the absence of immigration combined continued the Colonial *status* of the Church in the Southern States. Rescued by emancipation and the civil war, fearful remedies, from the prison in which she was confined for a century, she now holds the same position in the United States as at the consecration of Archbishop

Carroll, in 1790. Her progress, if not so rapid, will, henceforward, be brilliant and conspicuous.

The reader who accompanies the writer to *the City by the Sea*, to the highlands of Georgia and the Carolinas, and along the streams sweetly named by Cherokee and Seminole, will travel over many a rugged path and through tangled forests while tracing the humble tributary struggling on its way to swell the grandeur of the Church in the United States. The journey, though painful, will not be void of interest to all who love to trace the rise and progress of the Faith, whether on the banks of the Tiber or the Nile, the Susquehanna or the Savannah.

The following is the *ecclesiastical summary* of the United States, A. D. 1877: His Eminence Archbishop John McCloskey, D.D., Cardinal; His Grace Most Rev. Archbishop James Gibbons, D.D., Primate; Archbishops, 11; Bishops, 56; Priests, 5,074; Churches, 5,046; Chapels and Stations, 1,482; Theological Seminaries, 33; Theological Students, 1,273; Colleges, 63; Academies and Select Schools, 557; Priests' schools, 1,645; Asylums, 214; Hospitals, 96; Religious orders of men, 27; Religious orders of women, 44; Publishing Houses, 25; Periodicals, 40; baptized Catholics, eight millions (approximation).

"The marvellous impulse which the tide of immigration gave to Catholicity in the North and West was wanting at the South. Slavery existed. Labor was cheap. The immigrants found but few inducements in this state of things; and, comparatively speaking, the number was small that bent their steps toward this portion of our country. Hence, we must not expect this rapid advance of the faith which we we have witnessed in higher latitudes."—*Jno. O'Kane Murray's Popular History Catholic Church in the United States.*

CHAPTER I.

BISHOP ENGLAND.

Birth—Education—Ordination—Missions in Ireland—Condition of Ireland in the Eighteenth Century—Cork "Commercial Advertiser"—A Power in the Land—Consecration—Arrival in Charleston—Alone in the vast wilderness of the Church—Difficulties—Prejudices—Unworthy Priests—Society—Slavery—The Press—Poverty—Climate—Strangers' fever—No immigration—Personal Appearance—Eloquence—Ability as a Lecturer—Power over men—Caricatures on Catholicity—Purchase of Building lot—Cathedral of St. Finbar—Seminary of St. John the Baptist—Publishes his letters as advertisements—Appearance in the streets—The "United States Catholic Miscellany"—Declines an Irish See—Churches—Priests—Their character—The Sisters of Mercy—The Ursuline Convent—Popularity of the classical school—The negro his first care—Apostolic Delegate—Rt. Rev. William Clancy, Bishop of Oriel—Coadjutor—Labors—Character—Transferred to Demarara—His death—Female Colleges in America—Bishop England's labors—Missionary work—Begging adroitness—Not Gallicanism—Saves Stage Passengers—A storm in store—Etc., etc.

THE new diocese of Charleston was founded in 1820, and comprised the three States of North and South Carolina and Georgia. It embraced an area of 127,500 square miles, and contained a white and slave population of more than 1,063,000; of these about 1,000 were Catholics. The Methodists, Baptists, English Protestants, Presbyterians, were the controlling sects. The Huguenots also had many members.

It is a great mercy when God raises up in his Church a master mind capable of understanding the present, foreseeing the future, and providing for the necessities of the age. When clothed with Divine Authority, he is sent to announce the glad tidings of salvation to a distant country, whose inhabitants, notwithstanding the freedom of their institutions, and the excellence of their civilization, are seated in the darkness of unbelief and in the shadow of death, he is endowed from on high with all the graces necessary for the success of his mission. Such a man was the *Rt. Rev. John England, D.D., the first Bishop of Charleston.**

He was in his day the most distinguished bishop in the Catholic Church, and one of the foremost men in the world. He belongs to history, and though his labors were limited to an obscure diocese, his virtue, his writings, and his fame are the property of the world, the ornament of the Church, and the glory of the hierarchy.

Cork, Ireland, distinguished for having been the birthplace of Edmund Burke, the greatest statesman and philosopher of his age, Father O'Leary, the great controversialist, and Father Matthew, the orginator of the temperance movement in modern times, was also the birthplace of John England. He was born September 23d, 1786 ; made his classical studies in his native city ; studied law during two years under a distinguished barrister, and made his ecclesiastical course in the College of Carlow. His family were conspicuous for piety, patriotism, and social rank, and were of the race who suffered most during the terrible period of the penal laws, when every effort was made by the English Government to stamp out the life of the nation, and degrade the human mind by enforcing ignorance and making education a crime. His grandfather was incarcerated among felons, and left to pine in prison, for having taught a few problems in Euclid. His youth was spent under the shade of social disabilities, civil oppression, and religious persecution, unsurpassed in ferocity and cruelty by any former resistance to Christianity since the days of Nero.

The chain of slavery bound the Irish Church which, while it adorned the altar like the pontifical robe of an Apostle, still fettered the truth and sorely festered on the limbs of the nation, prostrating it as a lifeless thing at the foot of the oppressor, without social life, without ambition, without hope. Unlike all other nations, his country's history was writ-

---

*Authorities: Personal recollection ; reminiscences among the people ; Bishop England's Works ; Memoir by Wm. George Reid ; "Lives of Deceased Bishops," etc., by Richard H. Clark, LL.D.; Murray's History, etc.

ten in ruins. The castles of chiefs of mediæval sway, shrines where holy monks knelt and adored, monastic piles where apostles were prepared for missions in foreign countries, and the nobility of Europe educated for centuries, were laid waste. The cell of St. Brendan, who first discovered America, and the sheen of whose robes, like the lighted pillar of the Israelites, illumined the path across the ocean for future enterprise; the Cathedrals of St. Finbar and Coleman, whose massiveness defied the action of time, but was no match for heresy; the monuments of the dead, the educational institutions of an entire people, the heaven-born liberty of conscience, were all in ruins; and weeping Erin had nothing to console her but the purity of her daughters, the missionary spirit of her priesthood, and the slumbering might of her peasant's arm.

The dark gibbets permanently fixed and high as Haman's, the bleaching bones of dead patriots, frowning prisons and the convict ship freighted with its burden of young men and innocent females, banished to Tasmania or the remotest colonies, on some paltry pretence, were the familar objects to the view of the future apostle. Not the bells of Shandon, but the bells of Bandon, that flung their funeral knells o'er his infant slumbers.

Ireland has acquired a cosmopolitan character: her children, denied an outlet at home—indeed, they have no home but the world—seek the broad domain of the world as the theatre of their labors; they have left their foot-prints on every shore, their marks in every enterprise, their bones on every battle-field. The young Papist, as he was contemptuously called among his schoolmates, heard the whisperings of the Holy Ghost, like the youthful prophet, calling him to a higher vocation in the dark hours of his country's sorrows and his boyhood's tears. He was chosen to be the apostle of the new Continent and transferred from the banks of the River Lee, a Catholic Ilium, to the distant shores of Carolina, with a new St. Finbar's, whose free and merry bells would sound happier and sweeter on the placid streams of the Ashley and Cooper. Bold and dauntless in the struggles of early life, it required all the vigor of manhood to bear unmoved the announcement that he was called to be the founder of a new See, and the father of a long line of prelates, whose personal virtues and learning must derive an additional lustre from the brilliancy of the first golden link in the chain of succession. God, who is the author of nature and of grace, and who delights in the harmony of His works, disposes all things wisely and strongly for His purposes. Trained in the school of adversity, the future Bishop was well prepared to encounter the labors, the difficulties, and the trials inseparable from his mission. High vocations have corresponding pains, and rare dignities uncommon sorrows. The mitre is not always a crown of roses, and few brows that ever wore it befittingly have escaped the pain inflicted by its thorns.

Mr. England delivered a course of lectures during Lent at the request of the Bishop, while still in college; he also founded an asylum for unprotected females and established a school for the education of the youth. He was ordained in 1808 by Bishop Moylan, and by dispensation before his twenty-fifth year. He was rapidly advanced to the most important position in the diocese of Cork. As the President of the diocesan seminary of St. Mary's, chaplain of the prisons, parish priest of Bandon, in all situations we always find him admirably fitted for the duties of his varied occupations, eminent for all priestly virtues, an ornament to the sanctuary, and a blessing to his native city. Indignant at oppression and intolerant of persecution, he, second only to O'Connell, but more than any other man in Ireland, educated the minds of the people, taught them to hope, and struck off the manacles from their hands, eventually emancipated the Church after centuries of oppression, and gained freedom of conscience for every man in the British Empire.

Placed at the helm in stormy times, what to other men would be disaster and defeat was to him but inspiration and the prophecy of victory. His aim was high, his will unbending, and his purpose a quenchless flame. Editor and proprietor of the *Cork Advertiser*, a popular paper, he exposed the corruptions of the Government, the deceit and cunning of the administration, the impiety and festering immorality of the great, the public robberies of landlords, the extortions of the tithe-ministers, the crimes perpetrated under the insulted name of religion, the legalized oppression of the poor, the flagrant wickedness of the highest dignitaries,— his country's wrongs, they were all his own as well, and well he wrote them with pen dipped in blood. Europe heard the appalling facts for the first time, the calumnies and false representations of centuries were exposed; nations now listened to the tale of Erin's wrongs, and pitied her bleeding, dying condition. The majority of the English people were ignorant of the shameful injustice inflicted on the sister isle by Low Church, absent proprietors, and a titled aristocracy, wallowing in luxury and vice: if they did not swell, they did not endeavor to stifle the universal condemnation. None held a higher estimation for the individual English character than he: it was the Government that he combatted:—a government that had robbed the subjects of their religion, Ireland of her property; and having failed in perverting, enslaved or murdered the defenceless inhabitants. It was his privilege, in after days, to refute the calumnies disseminated on foreign shores, like the eloquent Dominican, and fling back on its source the universal falsehood.

He became a power in the land, or rather in the world; vice and iniquity in high places were rebuked, virtue lifted her crushed head from the earth, and tyrants crouched and trembled at the voice of this single priest. He had ambition, but it was worthy of his power. He never wrote or spoke trifles, as a priest in Ireland or a bishop in America.

He spoke on all occasions and uttered great truths with irresistible force and eloquence; the most enlightened audience, the most learned faculties, Legislatures of States, the National Congress, and all the world listened to him, disabused of their errors, and spell-bound by his matchless eloquence and gigantic powers of mind. Possessed of invincible powers, he brought them all into the struggle, and they were necessary for the accomplishment of his mission. "If," said O'Connell, "I had Bishop England at my back I would not fear the entire world before me." If you deprive him of his liberty you destroy half the man; among the very prelates a timidity wearing the aspect of prudence prevailed, unworthy of their station, but pardonable in a country where the steps of the episcopal throne were for centuries the road to the scaffold, where the cathedrals were thatched shanties, the churches mud-walled cabins, and the mountain hedge the shelter and hiding-place of the school and the academy; the appearance of a preacher would cause the dispersion of the pupils in all directions to escape arrest. Father England was recommended for a foreign mission to the Holy Father, and by a dispensation of Providence was nominated in 1820 for the new diocese of Charleston.

He was consecrated by Bishop Murphy, assisted by Bishops Moran, of Ossory, and Kelly, of Richmond, Va., in St. Finbar's Cathedral, on the 21st September, 1820, after having been twelve years a priest. Having resolved never to wear a mitre under the British flag, he refused to take the oath of allegiance administered to Bishops at their consecration, remarking,—"As soon as I reach my see, my first step will be to renounce this allegiance; therefore the form is now idle and useless." Taking shipping at Belfast, he arrived in Charleston December 30th, 1820. He was accompanied by Father Corkery, the first priest he ordained, two or three students, and his sister, Johanna Monica England. His diocese, as wide as the British Isles, was an ample field for his zeal, his learning, and apostolic labors. The prospect would discourage any man living who founded his hopes of success on human motives.

In 1821 there were but a few hundred Catholics scattered over that entire ecclesiastical district, and none of high social standing. There were but one or two apologies for churches, with congregations torn by scandals and dissensions, and only one or two priests, who immediately left the field; the death of Father Corkery soon after left him alone. He had scarcely a roof to shelter his head, and his advent was regarded as an invasion on religious opinions universally professed, endeared by family associations, and which their undisputed sway and peaceful possession endowed with the color of truth. The population was composed of but two classes, the whites and the slaves; the former were a bloated, proud, and wealthy people, forming an aristocracy as intolerant and inaccessible as those whom he had left behind; and the slaves, their property, as closely guarded against all interference as a miser keeps his hoard from the nightly burglar. Ignorance of the truths of the Church, religious bigotry, national prejudice, and education made that people as hostile to Catholicity as Rome or Antioch on the arrival of their first Bishop. Emigration had opened the way and established the Church in other sections, independently of all labors; the people only needed the services of a priest, whom they handsomely supported, and at whose bidding they contributed to the erection of churches with a generosity unsurpassed by any other people.

Before the gaze of the young Bishop, now in his thirty-fifth year, a scene of universal desolation was spread, without church, priests, congregation, or any other element promising success. A mission among the Chinamen, or in the most uncivilized islands in the Pacific, would have presented better prospects and brighter hopes; apart from the allurements of the martyr's crown, which he would have seized more readily than the mitre, for all his life was a long martyrdom, conversions would have been easier and more general, and a civilized people would hail him as their apostle. A false civilization and a high state of human learning and knowledge were his greatest difficulty and the chief obstacles in his way, as in the case of the first Christian missionaries. Whatever barriers the world then offered to the introduction of the Christian doctrine was here arrayed against Catholicity. In Rome and Athens, in Antioch and Alexandria, the schools of philosophy were in the meridian of their glory: science had unveiled all her splendors and irradiated the discovered globe from pole to pole; eloquence had exhausted all the resources of language. The ignorance of God and of all the truths which it behooved man to know grew in proportion: from the far-off India in the east to the Pillars of Hercules in the west, darkness and the shadow of death brooded over the face of the earth. Society was in the condition of the wretched traveller who lay the bleeding victim of cruelty, more dead than alive; in the road between Jerusalem and Jericho. From the crown of the head to the sole of the foot, there was no soundness in it; wounds and bruises and swelling sores, they were not bound up nor fomented with oil. The condition of the people entrusted from on high to the Bishop's care, was morally and intellectually the same; the deeply-rooted errors of the so-called Reformation, the broken and illogical fragments of Christianity, maintained by the various sects, and their concentrated hatred of Catholicity rendered them more incurable; their very knowledge was ignorance, and the lights of the eye darkness. How great must the darkness have been! In reality they never were cured, they died in their darkness and in their errors.

Immigration in the Colonial times was not accompanied, as at present, with the missionary embraced at the door of the church, and conducted to the communion-table, with the kiss of welcome from the mother's lip. Nearly all had abandoned or lost the Faith, many of them were ashamed of it, and Catholic names borne by men in the chains of error, in the seats of pestilence, in legislative halls, and in the high places of the land, were its sad memorials, like the ruins of churches scattered over his native soil.

Nor could the Gospel be preached to the slave, who followed in the steps of his master, embraced his religion, if he had any, durst go nowhere, connect himself with no church, nor marry without his owner's consent; they had no social position; their testimony would not be received in any court of justice; and, believed generally to be without souls, they were regarded as chattels; their preservation and propagation were regulated accordingly. As a necessary result, their moral condition may be imagined, but never can be described. Too deeply rooted, emancipation has not sensibly effected its cure. To tamper with a man's negroes was as perilous as to trifle with the honor of females.

There were scarcely any Catholic negroes but those owned by Catholic families. It was worse than idle to attempt to preach Catholic truths and piety to those unfortunate people, whose offspring were orphans with parents, and whose married people knew no life-partner beyond the fancy companion of the year. The tie did not always continue so long: the alliance if not agreeable was short-lived; the easy remedy was to go to the master and get another wife. The moral sentiment of the race has been so utterly corrupted, that even now after fifteen years of emancipation they cannot realize the requirements of the sixth commandment, and the efforts of our foreign missionary priests, as well as our own endeavors, fail in making them Catholics. I repeat this fact, merely for the purpose of giving my readers an idea of some of the difficulties that attended Bishop England's mission, and which St. Peter Clavier could not have removed; for the efforts of the saint were sustained by the faith of the slave-owners.

We must superadd to the difficulties that prevailed all over America against the Church, heresy and error were rampant every where; the vilest slanders the most cruel and unfounded calumnies, bold falsehoods, were teeming from the press, announced from the pulpit, and taught by the school-books, until the very name of Catholic was a disgrace. The lives of the professors of the faith of Jesus Christ were menaced, the infant institutions were marked for the flames, the profession of the truth disqualified from the holding of any place of honor or trust under several State Constitutions which had endorsed and embodied the old spirit of intolerance and hatred of the Colonial times, thus inaugurating the attempt to replace the manacles on the limbs of the heroes who broke the English yoke and made them free. A Jew, an Atheist, or a Catholic would not be believed on oath, nor trusted with the office of beadle or constable. There were but two churches between Baltimore and New Orleans. There were half a dozen Bishops in the North and West, holy missionaries and saints, filling the sanctuary with the fragrance of piety and the incense of prayer.

But they had not received from God the sublime calling to build up the Church with sword in one hand and torch in the other, fill the temple with glory, be warriors at the gates of Sion, and fight the battles of the Lord. It was Bishop England who overthrew all error in the land, refuted calumnies, rebuked falsehood, disarmed prejudice, broke down opposition, established sees, built the Church, conquered enemies, founded religion, and won respect for both classes of the hierarchy, not only in the diocese of Charleston, but all over the United States, and the sheen of his sword will flash its light on the Continent while a Christian treads its soil.

Another desperate evil, confined to no locality but prevalent all over the country, and one which inflicted the greatest injury on religion, was the number of unworthy priests who had been suspended from all priestly functions in Europe and flocked hither; apostates, heretics, infidels, freemasons calling themselves Catholic, came in large numbers to this free country, and set all ecclesiastical law at defiance. Apostles of Satan, they published pestilential books, denounced the spotless Church of our blessed Lord, and labored to corrupt the mind and heart of American society, and arrayed it against the Kingdom of God. This evil was not so prevalent in the diocese of Charleston as elsewhere in America, for the very obvious reasons that foreigners were not wanted, and the people were too proud to tolerate mountebank preachers in their pulpits. The absence of emigration was another great difficulty, and from all appearances must be permanent; the few who had courage to settle in the seaport towns, everywhere on the Southern coasts, were periodically swept away by the insidious attacks of yellow fever. Others returned to milder latitudes after having experienced the debilitating nature of the climate, which is exceedingly severe on Europeans for the first years, until the constitutions have undergone a radical change and they have become acclimatized. The process is painful. The surface of the skin becomes raw and irritable, frequently wearing the appearance of broiled flesh; heat-blisters cover the entire surface of the skin, and the victim tortured with a smarting sensation, banishing sleep and rest. The choral melody of millions of mosquitoes stinging or rather biting the exposed part of the body, both night and day, increases pain and induces a nervous irritability of long duration; the bite of a mosquito and ant are equally poignant; the former possesses more virus, and after the pain ceases, leaves a white blister behind. The beds are protected at night by a gauze netting, called mosquito-bars, without which it is impossible to sleep or rest. I have frequently worn gloves and knotted a handkerchief over the face at night when otherwise unprotected, which the excessive heat of 90 degrees rendered intolerable, and breaking them loose I preferred insomnolence and a promenade, after a day's hard labor.

Barely to exist, and make no effort of mind or body, is sufficient labor for many constitutions during the summer months, in our seaports. This condition does not prevail to the same extent at a distance from the coast; the climate in the interior is pleasant and healthy; nervous prostration is a common complaint in consequence of a long residence in our Southern latitudes, and induces a desire for the use of opiates and other sedatives, a temptation to which public men are more exposed than others. The glory of victory is commensurate to the labors and hardships encountered in its achievement. Any one of the difficulties that lay in the Bishop's path was alone sufficient to intimidate men of ordinary piety and firmness, paralyze their efforts, and lead them into retirement to mourn over evils which only God could remove. Their combination left him without a foothold. Judged by the laws of human prudence, the attempt to struggle against them seemed foolhardy in the extreme and made the introduction of Catholicity in Charleston as arduous as the task of the Patriarch to obtain a birthplace for the Son of God; He was as unwelcome here as in Bethlehem of old. In both instances there was extreme poverty, the Redeemer was born in a stable; driven from the only church in the episcopal city by schismatical trustees, the Holy Sacrifice was wont to be offered under an old wooden shed; subsequently the printing-office of the *Catholic Miscellany*. Poverty was the chief episcopal ornament and the first element of his success; the crozier may have passed for St. Patrick's pastoral staff, if history had not recorded that it was burned by the executioner on the public square in Dublin, during the reign of Elizabeth; often had the sacristan in after times to fasten the crook to the staff with nails. Once during an ordination the fastening gave way and the top dropped on the head of the kneeling candidate; the accident was mistaken by strangers as a *striking* part of the ceremony. Hurried to the helm in stormy times, what to other men would be defeat was to him inspiration and the prophecy of success.

His strength was a giant's, his will unbending, and his zeal unquenchable. He brought into the struggle immense powers, an abiding confidence in his Divine Master which no difficulty could shake, a faith superior to the powers of earth, and which danger and resistance served but to strengthen and increase. No man living had stronger faith; it was his life and soul; it was the unfailing power that animated all his labors, inspired his thoughts, planned his undertakings; he planted it on the Southern soil, mid difficulty and danger, with the heroism of the martyr and the unbending fortitude of the apostle.

Unlike most men, he led but one life, the public one; he threw all his energy of body and mind in this single channel, and the singleness of his aim made him irresistible. Like the ocean rock, he breasted opposition while the waves of bigotry and persecution broke in idle foam at his feet. Little men cowered before him, and vented their impotent spleen in the sectarian press. Every sorrow that afflicted the American Church he made personal; he consoled her and fortified her in all her trials; destroyed every combination, broke every weapon raised against the Spouse of our Lord, and awed the turbulent into silence. Born to rule men, it was said of him that he had missed his vocation; and that as a military commander Wellington or Napoleon would not have shone higher than he. But his was a more noble warfare, and the laurels won in the cause of religion and humanity will hang around his name and character, fresh and green as the palmetto under whose shade he planted the Cross, when bloody conflicts will have perished from human records.

He became speedily the Bossuet of the American Church; her counsels, her literature, and her character will always wear the impress of his talents, his learning, and his piety. In the worldwide domain of Catholicity there was no prelate who accomplished more good with less means and in the face of greater difficulties. God communicates Himself to man both by nature and grace; He manifests His wisdom rather in the magnificence of detail, and in the adaptation of means to the end, than in impossible extremes of higher excellence; hence St. Augustine says that He is not greater in the angel and less in the worm; He is equally God in every atom of His creation. It is impossible that He should not set a value on His works; He does not waste His gifts in the natural order; He is equally parsimonious and still more economical in the high order of grace which is the direct communication of His Divine nature. Although He fed the Capharnainites abundantly by the miraculous multiplication of the loaves and fishes, the fragments were commanded to be carefully gathered, to prevent waste. He bestows on each the graces necessary for the work to be done; He gives largely but not wastefully, wisely but not indiscriminately; He conferred on Dr. England all episcopal and apostolic graces in an eminent degree, all that was necessary for the accomplishment of the labors set before him.

Few men have enjoyed a higher or more universal reputation for eloquence; his lips seemed to have been purified with a coal of fire from the altar on high, and his tongue a flame of the Holy Ghost, running down from the day of Pentecost through an unbroken line of saints and pontiffs, illuminating nations in its path; abiding for the moment in this golden link, and then to pass with increased light to the end of time. Nor was ornament wanting to give it efficacy. Like theology queening it over all science, eloquence rules the minds of men. A mere acquaintance with the laws of rhetoric will not form an accomplished public speaker; he needs a thorough understanding of the subject matter in all its bearings; in its relation to other truths, in its connection with important philosophical and natural facts, on the influence which it has exercised over the destiny of the human race. If such were possible, he must be a general scholar; at least he must be familiar with the customs and the habits of the people whom he addresses, their prejudices and sympathies, their history, and the laws of their country; he must thoroughly understand the latent fountains of feeling and the secrets of the human heart. No man in modern times, and few in the world, enjoyed these elements of oratory in a higher degree. Superadd to these the inspiration of a heavenly mission, the truths of eternity, the destiny of the human soul; revealed religion taking its beginning in the far-off Paradise of God, walking with the patriarch before the Flood; on the plains of Mesopotamia, by the Nile, in the desert, by the headlong waters of proud Babylon, in Jerusalem the strong and faithless;—on the Cross, in the Church, through the march of ages, and ending with the last throb of the pulse of time;—all were marshalled by Bishop England with the skill of an experienced general; he led them on to the attack, battered down with irresistible force the high places of pride and prejudice, led captive the human mind, and made bigotry hide his face in shame and defeat. Of medium size, regular and manly features, strong, well-modulated voice, chiselled lip, high and retreating brow, strong-set jaw, an eye blazing and flashing like crushed diamonds, he stood the fearless tribune of a nation; clad in robes pontifical, Rome's jewelled signet glittering on his hand, and the pectoral cross, the gift of England's Cardinal, resting on his fearless breast, he appeared like the high priest of one world and the prophet of the next. Like the angel at the pool of Bethesda, he stirred from their lowest depths all the fountains of human feeling, and afforded healing to the multitude.

To rule over the minds of men is the greatest power on earth: the Southern people copied, though they could not equal Dr. England; they caught the inspiration of his lips; statesmen, jurists, and teachers cultivated the human side of the fascinating power, to the neglect of the divine, and became a nation of orators. Heresy itself, while it rejected the Cross, arrayed herself in its ornaments, and error was presented from the pulpits in a more fascinating dress.

In the court-houses, meeting-houses, town-halls, before societies literary and benevolent, in every town and hamlet, and in the cabins of the poor all over his vast diocese, he spoke incessantly. In the Senate chambers, in the halls of Congress, all over the United States, in the fashionable cities of Western Europe, he preached, when the honor of God, the salvation of souls, and the good of society could be promoted. The English-speaking world was his audience, and he was pronounced, by universal assent, the greatest pulpit orator of the nineteenth century.

This eminence was necessary in the Providence of God, to conciliate the favor of society, obtain a footing for religion, toleration for the Faith, and security for the life of the humble and despised children of the Church intrusted to his care. Nor was this influence limited to the diocese of Charleston; it was felt everywhere throughout the length and breadth of the young republic, and revolutionized the public mind. The funeral robe hung before the Holy of Holies, by the craft and cruelty of English heresy, and still remaining after the Revolution, as the last relic of tyranny and injustice, must be flung aside. The high honor was reserved for a foreign-born prelate, to rend the cursed veil and bare to the astonished view of a nation the hidden glories of the sanctuary. The country was amazed; many fell down and adored, others hesitated and faltered; the light pained the eyes of numbers, who became frantic as the enraged Pythoness at the shrine of Delphi, muttered threats in broken sentences from press and tribune, and wreaked their vengeance by brutal assaults on children and defenceless females, on the temples of God;—which only redounded to the good of religion and their own shame and confusion. Protestantism received its fatal stab from Bishop England. Its efforts in Boston and during the Know-nothing excitement were but the expiring throes of final dissolution. England found it necessary to suppress the publication of Catholic books; she muzzled the press, burned or confiscated the churches, banished or hung the priests, and made education a felony, lest there should be any outlet for the truth. When the safeguards of error are flung away and trampled to the dust, like implements of torture, by a free people, it is impossible for falsehood to prevail in the land. America henceforward must be either Catholic or infidel.

Bishop England never rejected an argument for an ornament; he always addressed the reason and understanding of men, whom he viewed as rational beings, and spurned all meretricious tinsel; his language was clear, strong, and distinct: he never was turgid or inflated. His simplicity was grand, he adapted his discourses to the learned and the illiterate. He laid down his position, defined it clearly and distinctly, the truth was next clothed in a proposition, the terms were discussed in all their relations, confirmed by correlative facts, corroborated by parallel reasoning; history, natural sciences, whenever they served his purpose, were made tributary to illustrate the argument with a phalanx of facts judiciously chosen.

After the refutation of plausible objections, he drew the irresistible conclusion, leading in a way in which fools could not err. His discourse swept on like a torrent, gathering strength in its course and irresistibly bearing away every opposition. Men listened, thousands wept, the heart was enlarged, the mind enlightened; the turbulent and stiff-necked were stilled to awe and veneration. as if spell-bound by the strains of heavenly music, and the chords of the human heart were swept by an angel hand. Horace or Ovid could scarcely have excelled him in the powers of the ridiculous; the *reductio ad absurdum*, was so complete as to cause the victim often to laugh at his folly and enjoy his own defeat. Though improved, no doubt, by cultivation, like the poet, he was indebted to nature for this rare gift. The ridiculous side of a question, its folly or extravagance were the most prominent features that presented themselves to his mind; to reach this point in controversy, and from which there is no escape, was the aim or burden of his discourses, oral or written. Familiar with his autography, while looking over one of his school-books, a Virgil, I read in his boyish hand, for even here the boy is the father of the man, a line legibly written on the margin, a memento of some nursery commotion, in which he seemed to have achieved a victory. "*John England is a bad boy, because he won't learn to dance.*" Were Plutarch the biographer, he might have selected this to unlock the springs of his native character, and at a glance reveal to posterity the secret of his irresistible power.

His printed lectures and addresses are by no means faithful copies of the originals. They want the spirit and all the other surroundings which gave life and vigor to the productions. They are the dead letter, the framework of thought and matter, and were written only after they were spoken, at the request of parties soliciting a copy of the address for publication; he always spoke without the aid of a manuscript. We must not suppose that he acquired this facility without much toil and labor; on the contrary, it was the result of close application and hard study in the early years of his public life. He encouraged a timid young clergyman to prepare himself for the pulpit by the assurance that he himself had written and memorized all his sermons during the first seven years of his ministry before he attempted to speak extempore in public. This lesson he assiduously impressed on the students whom he trained for the priesthood; he cautioned them against oratorical extravagances, or the servile appropriation of other men's sermons. Such persons, he said, would never excel, and he recommended the reading of a chapter from a pious author as more edifying and respectable.

He was no less conspicuous as a writer. As a controversialist, he was superior to any man of the age; rejecting the method of oral disputation, as of very questionable advantage, when momentary impulses or personal feeling are substituted for reason, he seized on the public press and converted the engine of heresy and error into the missionary of truth.

Conversant with the laws of rhetoric, familiar with the

various departments of science and literature, and armed with truth, his pen was a two-edged sword cutting keen and trenchant like a Damascus blade, and returned not to its scabbard until the adversary and his cause were left prostrate and powerless. In his native land, he had overthrown the most powerful enemies of his creed and country, and men durst not oppose him; in the land of his missionary labors, he encountered adversaries no less formidable, and organized combinations, with like result. The sectarian and secular press both were the formidable strongholds of error, teeming daily with flagrant falsehoods and misrepresentations, which were safe beyond the sound of his voice, and which the pen only could reach. Increasing and made bold by security, fortified by the sanction of great names, and tinged with a religious coloring, error had taken deep root in the soil, covering as by a network the entire country, from Labrador to the Rio Grande.

Unless at the risk of popularity and pecuniary loss, no editor could open his pages to a manly defence of the Faith. The publication of some spirit-crushed, deprecatory communication, more like a petition than a defence, and breathing only subjection and inferiority, was generally prefaced by an apologetical editorial for its appearance in a decent newspaper, stamping it at once with condemnation and contempt. The effort to change Dr. England in this manner was futile; it was like an attempt to bind the Numidian lion in the hempen toils of the hunter's gin. Like Sampson he tore down the pillars of the temple of Dagon and buried the idol in its ruins. His letters were refused publication. The book-stores, the window-shops in the principal streets, the tables of fashionable drawing rooms, were reeking with obscene literature and unseemly prints, and caricatures of all that was sacred and deemed holy by the civilization of eighteen centuries; even the pulpit declamations were unfit for the ear of modesty. The unchristian scurrility was embodied by reputable ministers, under the sanction of their Bishop, in the Catechism, to be committed to memory by children, and repeated every

Sunday in fashionable churches, under the strains of Handel's and Mozart's music. Heathenism had deified vice; by a law of inevitable necessity, heresy must develop all its deformities before it works its way back to the truths which it denies, and by which denial alone it subsists.

An extensive lot at the upper end of Broad street, then on the outskirts, but now in the heart of the city, was purchased; a temporary wooden structure was constructed for the celebration of the Divine Mysteries, and an humble cottage erected for the episcopal mansion. But how can he venture from his prison into the light of day and look into the face of honest people in the public streets with the independence of a freeman and the self-respect of a bishop? Pius IX., whose happy translation to bliss I have this moment learned, with Napoleon and Victor Emmanuel as his jailers, was not more closely imprisoned than Bishop England, by the misrepresentation of his faith.

The fate of an exile is hard under the most favorable circumstances; and the soil of the stranger is impatient under his footsteps: he is like an unwelcome guest at a banquet, whose bare presence mars hilarity. The Bishop only wore his staff in the sanctuary; with hands clasped behind his back, buckled shoes, the traditional knee-short clothes, frock coat with military collar, broad-brimmed Quaker hat, purple Roman collar, close-buttoned vest; without cigar or snuff-box, for he detested Virginia's weed, he walked down Broad street with the independence of a king. This soil and people were given him by divine appointment, to rule, and govern, and feed with heavenly bread and doctrine and lead into pleasant pastures. Like the Patriarch in Egypt, he stood erect in the midst of the people, he knew his throne was firmly fixed and ordained from the days of eternity, to be for all future time a faithful witness before the face of the Most High.

God had anointed him with His holy oil, whose unction flowed to the hem of his garment, and He had sworn in His holy place that He would shield him with His might and strengthen him with His arm of omnipotence. What had he to dread? He identified himself with that people as far as he might; he excused their frailties while he condemned their errors; and to his latest breath yearned over them with a father's love, and died in their midst, leaving them the inheritance of salvation and the treasure of his tomb.

He entered the office of the *Courier* or *Mercury*, deemed oracles of wisdom and learning, journals of national circulation and of high repute, around which clustered the learning, influence, and wealth of the proud State of South Carolina. He came to ask no favor; it was a right that he demanded—that of *publishing his letters as advertisements, the payment to be regulated by the same uniform rates of charge*. Amazement seized on the community; the right could not be denied. The stronghold of error was at last attacked and triumphantly carried by repeated assaults, each with renewed energy; every new resistance only provoked additional energy, until the fortress fell to the ground to rise no more. The hearth-stone, the book-stores, the window-shops, the pulpits were purged of their uncleanness like an Augean stable. On meeting Dr. England at a subsequent national council, the sainted Bishop Rosati, embracing him, said, "Let me kiss the hand that has written so many great things."

The influence of his pen had reached farther than the sound of his golden tongue. There was no household so remote as to escape the brightness of the light. The people were amazed as one who awakes from a dream in the night; their minds were enlightened, their morals improved, and they were convinced, if they were not converted. Wealthy planters expressed a desire that Catholic clergymen should be sent to instruct their slaves, to the exclusion of all other preachers. Catholics, hitherto despised, now raised their heads and stood erect like men, bearing the image of God. The Church was established and became a domestic institution in the three States. North Carolina shortly after effaced from her constitution the disgraceful article, dishabilitating Catholics for the exercise of civil rights. Churches sprung up. Priests were educated to minister at the altar, a sisterhood established to attend to the sick, and institutions of learning for the better education of the people. The Cross, transplanted from Erin, was now erected on Carolina's shore, whose warm sun will shine on its outspread arms until he ceases to run his course and sinks in the Western Ocean to rise no more. How sublime a mission, and how faithfully accomplished!

Nor were its labors or its blessing confined in the limits of the diocese: they were universal; the press was everywhere emancipated; the muzzle that bound it and made it the meanest engine of prejudice, superstition and vice, was thrown away, to be trampled under foot. But this triumph was not sudden and instantaneous; the foundations were laid; they were the result of labor, sufferings, and sorrow, and cost many a valuable life;—well spent, because consumed in the service of God.

Dependence on the favor or good-will of a secular press was too precarious; the Bishop was too shrewd to confide in its stability. All the acts of his administration were like the steps of a giant, leaping over mountains; he established a Catholic newspaper in the year 1822, the very first in the United States, called *The United States Catholic Miscellany;* during forty years it stood like a beacon-light on the watch-towers of the Church, dissipating error, refuting calumny, and inculcating the Faith.

It was conducted at all times with great ability by eminent and learned ecclesiastics, who passed the torch from generation to generation until its glorious mission was accomplished, and it was absorbed by the universal light of Catholicity shining on the Continent, from sea to sea. It lived until the year 1861, after the inception of the civil war,—when nearly all things perished in the South, except the labors of her first Bishop, which national disasters served but to develop and extend. Miss England aided her brother, for a long time, in conducting the *Miscellany;* her contributions frequently graced its pages, and her gentleness frequently toned down the stern logic of his articles.

The United States Catholic Miscellany claims for the

Bishop the high honor of being the founder of Catholic journalism in the United States. Few of the numbers have escaped the ravages of fire, time, and war. The Library edition perished by the disastrous conflagration in Charleston in 1861. The only copy extant is in the possession of the Bishop's family in Cork. It gives the early history of the diocese, and is invaluable as a rare collection of religious articles, science, and literature; it is a library in itself.

His works were prepared for the press by Dr. Corcoran and Father Hewet, and were published in 1859 by Bishop Reynolds in five large octavo volumes, of five hundred pages each, closely printed, in double column. They treat principally of controversial and historical matters, and contain several addresses; the most prominent are those on the "Pleasures of Scholars," "Duelling," "On the Character of Washington," "On Classical Education." His works adorn the most respectable libraries of the country, and have been very extensively rifled, to furnish materials for subordinate treatises; the selections running through them like silver threads of reason and thought, and giving life and vigor to more feeble productions. Many stole his arrows, but none could bend his bow. Few have acknowledged the favor or thanked the source of their inspiration; like the traveller who slakes his thirst and thanklessly passes on without blessing the limpid stream. Whatever he touched he adorned; his very adversaries became distinguished among men from the simple contact with his genius. In this manner Drs. Bachman and Fuller, Governor Forsythe, of Georgia, and others, acquired distinction and notoriety. In latter times many courted his notice, and labored to provoke a discussion; failing in the attempt, both they and their journals disappeared from sight forever.

Not only individuals, but the State was honored through him, and Charleston was raised from the obscurity of a Southern slave-mart to an eminence among the cities of the world, because indissolubly linked to his name by Pontifical appointment. Not by Calhoun, Hayne, or McDuffie, but by Bishop England, was THE CITY BY THE SEA exalted, even as the sword of the conqueror raised up cities in the desert.

The learned and exhaustive sermons of the late Bishop McGill could be faultlessly printed, as they dropped from his silver tongue, without the necessary change of a syllable. During his day he was the most polished and graceful preacher in the Catholic Church of America. Dr. England was familiar with many of the arts of life, and a printer of no small skill and alertness; when the weekly issue of the *Miscellany* was jeopardized by the temporary disorganization of the craft or the inability to employ sufficient labor, he had often gone into the office and printed many of his ablest letters as he composed them, giving immediate expression to the noble conceptions of his mind, not in voice nor ink, but in *type!* In his written discussions he invaribly, and at the outset, made a clear, plain statement of the doctrine, in accordance with the strict definitions of General Councils— divesting the subject of all ornamental or foreign matter; he begged nothing, conceded nothing, beyond the rigid demands of faith. He made no side issues, prescinded all rhetorical ornament, and rejected whatever was to divert thought from the austere line of reason; which like the decree of fate was gradually and relentlessly forcing its way step by step to the climax. Having reached the logical end, beyond which there remains but the paradise of fools, he relaxed and condescended to rest and sport awhile in their midst, amused them with bright sparkling of his wit; when all joined hands and gazed in silent wonder at the tall, white column of truth, firmly based on the soil of Carolina, and abiding as the pillar of Trajan on the soil of eternal Rome. Carolinians possess much of the generosity and fervor of the Irish nation; they clustered round and shed tears of sorrow over the bier of him whom no man could subdue while he lived and who succumbed only to the inevitable stroke of death. They mourned for him when the weapons of war had perished; but their brightness will rest on the Church which he founded, and enlighten her path to the end of time.

From the hour he received his appointment from Pius

VII. until the day of his death all the resources of his great mind and his marvellous activity, which caused the Cardinals to style him the "Steam Bishop," were spent in behalf of his diocese. In recognition of his eminent service and labors, he was offered the see of Ossory in his native land; but no earthly consideration could tempt him to resign his first diocese or change it for another. Like the prophet's mission, he must destroy and build up; the most self-sacrificing servants of God have dreaded the episcopal office and declined to enter on its duties, in the oldest dioceses, where the dignity alone is the greatest burden, and the administration requires only a head, and neither hand nor foot, and a detail from the imperial body-guard keeps alternate watch at the gilded entrance of the episcopal palace. Without scrip or purse, with a treasury rich only in poverty, but endowed with administrative faculties unsurpassed by the founder of any dynasty, for he was a king every inch of him, he began to organize immediately. He drew up his plans, stretched the lines far and wide, and laid the foundation deep and strong. His strength lay in his poverty. A rich man is the most useless thing in existence. Earthly aids are but clogs to the simple action of the Almighty, who prefers being alone in the performance of His most marvellous works, in order to show whatever is not Himself is nothing. It was not in the palace of Herod, in the gardens of Sallust, nor in the banqueting-halls of Lucullus, that the Gospel was preached, but from the Cross, in the dungeons of the empire, in the crypts of the catacombs, and among the refuse of the people. Having been furnished with funds for his journey to India by St. Ignatius, St. Francis Xavier, fearing lest his confidence in the Divine aid would be diminished proportionably, while on his way from the hospital in Lisbon to the ship which must transport him to Goa, distributed to the last cent his passage-money among the street beggars; poor, friendless, and alone, he converted millions, and became the Apostle of nearly one-half the globe.

The founder of that great missionary order bequeathed persecution and suffering as a priceless inheritance to his children. The founder of the diocese of Charleston transmitted to his successors in both orders of the hierarchy in a great measure the same, and a double portion of holy poverty, which they have up to this moment indisputably inherited, as the world bears witness : for who will contest their right of being poor, of possessing nothing but the old fishing-net of the Apostles, capturing the souls of men, and landing them safe at the feet of the Divine Master on the shores of eternity ?

Under its free and disengaged action, churches, religious institutions, and the asylums of charity arose ; missions were established, and the three States linked fast to the rock of Peter. From the Chattahoochee to the Roanoke, and from the French Broad to the Santee, within the space of a dozen years, churches were built wherever a knot of two or three families existed, and by their bare elevation preached the Faith and renewed the face of society. They were the landmarks of the pioneer, dedicating the rich and favored soil to Him who conquered sin and death, inspiring confidence for the present, and hopes for the future. To be sure, they were poor in architecture and frail in construction, and the materials not of setim wood; but the faith they inculcate is more durable than the ark or tabernacle.

Each was a great work in its day. If the erection of but one edifice in the midst of wealth and opulence entitled the founder to live in marble, or slumber on insculptured pontifical robe, defiant of change and superior to decay, what meed of encomium will match the indomitable energy which, in the space of a few years and pinched with poverty, erected two convents, an orphan asylum, a cathedral, a diocesan seminary, eighteen churches, and created a learned and zealous priesthood !

Perhaps St. Finbar's was relatively the most frail. It was a plain, unadorned frame building ; a gallery running around three sides, for the accommodation of his poor slaves, which might be reached by the hand from the floor beneath, gave it an humble appearance. It had a seating capacity for the accommodation of near seven hundred. The sombre shade flung over the adoring multitude, a capacious and handsome sanctuary, and the solemn music of an excellent organ, whose notes were responsive to the virgin touch of cloistered hand, the great Bishop officiating, and surrounded by a ring of missionary priests clad in vestments, each formed by his training, and in the words of Bishop Persico, every man worthy to wear a mitre,—all combined to throw a scene of solemnity on the place, rivalling the splendors of mediæval Cathedrals, where kings, soldiers, and nobles sank down in adoration, and a thousand bells rang out over the whole land the joyous tidings of the renewal of the Mystery of the Incarnation. The daughters of St. Ursula are in the choir, the priests and levites in the sanctuary, the Sisters of Mercy and their orphans, and representatives of every congregation in the diocese are in front; the laity and much of the refinement and intelligence of the city are on all sides; the successor of the apostles clad in the robes of holiness sits like a monarch on his throne. He reminded one of Onias, the high priest, wearing Aaron's breastplate, with crescent mitre that had not yet culminated in the double tongues of flame, knowledge and truth; encircled by his brethren, and the glories of Horeb and Sinai gleaming on his holy head. No wonder the selfish infidel exclaimed, that if he were King of France, none else should perform the sacrificial act. The glory of that house was surpassed in the interior by that of the new. It lasted thirty years, and when removed the entire community mourned its disappearance. When the fiery tongue of flame consumed the new Cathedral, a gem of architectural beauty, by a strange coincidence, the stained window over the sanctuary still remained intact, bearing the likeness of St. Finbar, sadly gazing on the ruins beneath, and keeping guard over the sepulchre of his co-laborer and admirer.

The Bishop's residence, an humble frame house with but four rooms and one the library, stood close by the Cathedral; and lying near, the still more frail building that constituted the Seminary of John the Baptist. It was formally established in 1824, and its first student was Andrew Byrne, the first Bishop of Little Rock. The Bishop's first effort was to form a domestic priesthood, animated with his own spirit, attached to the diocese and to each other by the ties of long-time friendship, common training, and equal share in labor and sufferings.

He formed wise laws, sharply ascetic, for the government of the students, gave an extensive and comprehensive system of education for their mental culture, appointed eminent men and venerable priests for their teachers, and presided in person over their studies. Many zealous and well educated young men, with strong faith and pure vocations, clustered around him and formed a priesthood the most self-sacrificing and devoted in the Church. They harbored no thought but religion, no aspiration but missionary toil, no love but God, His holy Mother, His angels and saints. They planted the Cross everywhere, preached the Faith, offered daily the holy sacrifice in church or cabin on their respective missions. They received many into the Church, extended and continued the labors of their illustrious master, and have gone to receive with him their reward immensely great. About fifty priests were educated and ordained in the diocese; as a body they are excelled by no diocesan clergy in learning, piety, and zeal; some left after many years' service for other fields of missionary labor, adorned colleges, and filled the Professor's chair with distinction and honor; four of the number wore mitres; the present incumbent of the diocese of Charleston is the élève and successor of its founder. Having obtained two places in the College of the Propaganda, he sent thither the native Catholic youth who aspired to the ministry, but the consolation of being aided by their priestly administration was reserved for his successor. He personally instructed the students in elocution, and many of their number rivalled the fame of their master; he conducted the class in theology, and his every lecture not only systematized, but embraced all the essential teaching of an entire tract. He also conducted the retreats of both priests and students, and was in every sense, during his episcopacy, the example of every good and perfect work and the light whose unfaded splendor was diffused on every side.

Like a faithful steward, he provided for all the wants of his Master's household, redressed every evil, met every demand. There are several departments of human suffering, which priestly ministrations are unable to redress or can reach. The periodical visitation of yellow fever devastated the homes of the Irish immigrant, filled the Potter's field yearly with a vast number of fresh graves, tenanted by strangers and the unknown dead, whose friendless condition gave a name to the destroyer, "*the Stranger's Fever.*"

A large number of helpless orphans of both sexes and of the most tender ages were left as waifs on the city, which humanely enough made ample provision for their preservation and temporal existence by the erection of a large orphan asylum, but left it under the control of sectarian management, thereby destroying the faith of the helpless inmates; chiefly the children of Catholic parents, stamped with the seal of their origin, anointed with the holy unction of Baptism, and called by a name which they never knew to remember. After arriving at the most dangerous period of human life, they were turned loose on the world without scarcely any religion, and left to be the sport of chance or the victim of design.

The large heart of the Bishop yearned with pity and he provided for the unfortunate innocents, by the establishment of the order of the *Sisters of Our Lady of Mercy.*

They are a diocesan institution, not connected with the sisterhood of that name, and were orally sanctioned by the Pope. In 1829 he introduced pious ladies from his native city and other parts of the ever-faithful Isle of Saints. Aided by the material co-operation of a pious lady, a native of St. Domingo, Miss Julia Datty, he formed them into an independent community, gave them the rules of the Presentation Order for their government; other well disposed females were also received, among whom were the Misses Mary and Honora O'Gorman, and their niece, Miss Teresa Barry, of Baltimore.

THE SISTERS OF OUR LADY OF MERCY.

The first vows were taken by the members on December 8th, 1830. Under his fostering care they grew to be a large, influential Sisterhood, capable of meeting all the necessary requirements of their institution, and fulfilling the end of their establishment as an order of charity. The sick were nursed, the poor relieved, and the orphan found an excellent, and often a better mother, than the scarcely remembered one, long in the grave. They consoled the dying, instructed the ignorant, visited the hospitals under their special care, all the most wretched and abandoned of the human race to whom the world had scarcely anything better to offer than the hospitality of a poor-house and the refuge of a grave. At first sheltered in a small house in Baufain Street, their increased numbers, their influence, the sphere of usefulness, and the popular voice demanded larger and more suitable accommodations.

A new and spacious convent was erected, at the upper end of Queen Street, by public subscription, and the proceeds of fairs, the usual method of obtaining funds for such purposes. It was completed about the year 1839, and the Sisterhood with the boarders took possession of their new house, where they still continue, and which has become the parent of many branches.

This work was the crowning glory of Bishop England's administration. Entirely exempted from human pride, free from all pretensions, claiming no privileges beyond their just merits, the Sisters became the faithful allies of the clergy, the ornament and auxiliaries of the Church, won their way into public favor, gained the respect and confidence of all classes, and their ministrations were accompanied with the blessings of the people, whether on the battle-fields of Virginia, in the hospitals of plague-stricken cities, in the prisons of the condemned, by the couch of the dying, or the cradle of the orphan. The field of their labors has been enlarged, additional houses, with a male orphan asylum have been opened in other parts of the city. Branches were thrown out, to Savannah, Wilmington, Sumter, and the order spread now nearly over the three dioceses originally forming but one.

Sisters Aloysius, Teresa, Mary Paul, Mary Peter, and Isidore were the successive Superioresses, all ladies of uncommon strength of character and superior excellence in the several departments of their noble vocation. The highest branches of female education were taught in their academies, whose popularity prevails throughout the Southern States. While wiping away the tear of sorrow from the face of suffering, they have swept away prejudice from hearts and darkness from minds which neither the eloquence, discourses, nor writings of their founder could disperse. It was the charity of the faithful that in the very days of the Apostles produced the first favorable impressions in the minds of the unbelievers in the Christian name, and the same manifestations of heavenly love produce like results, after nineteen centuries, in the Southern States.

The interest felt by the Bishop in the success of this order was so deep that he contemplated to induce his sister, who was the Superioress of the North Presentation Convent in Cork, to withdraw from her home and her distinguished position, in order to preside over the novitiate and train the new postulants in the spirit of their sublime institution. He desisted from the project at the refusal of Bishop Murphy to give his assent, in consequence of the advanced age of Mother Mary Charles England. Both my sisters, Mary Baptist and Mary Antonia, are members of the order, which I consider one of the greatest blessings of my family.

Constituted as society is, it could not be reasonably expected that the higher families and opulent class could consent that their daughters would intermix in the study-room, at recreation, and in all other domestic relations, with the children of the poor and with orphans. Before the heart of the people who composed the bone and sinew of society could be brought under the holy influence of the Faith, it was justly deemed necessary to reach it by means of the higher grade of education. The vast resources of his mind were adequate to every demand of society and every want of his Church; soon in his administration, and almost simultaneous with the establishment of the Sisters in the year 1834, he provided a large and commodious residence close to the Cathedral and divided from it by a wall and furnished with ample grounds for recreation. A convent sprung up within a short time, for the training and education of the daughters of the wealthy planters of the diocese, and all the advantages of refinement and culture possessed by the most favored cities and the first ladies in the world were brought to their doors and placed within their reach; some few households were provided with private tutoresses of foreign birth and at great effort and expense.

Female colleges are nuisances in America; they are rude and not unfrequently vulgar schools, often conducted by preachers and tutors of questionable fitness; where girls are shorn of the delicacy and refinement of manners that constitute their principal ornament and return home, spoiled in temper and disposition, graduates in the masculine deparments of collegiate instruction, ignorant of much it behooves them to know and cultivate; bold and forward women, developing into lawyers, physicians, surgeons, politicians, and statesmen, rebellious against their natural subjection and impatient of the restraints by which the Almighty shelters their virtue and protects their innocence.

It was when woman left the safeguard of her husband's dominion that she fell by the wiles of Satan, and introduced sin and death into the world; an experience which similar projects will confirm to the end of time. We know, and the history of our female colleges proves, that such places have frequently degenerated into seminaries of dissipation and idleness, necessitating their discontinuance. At times we have witnessed parents and brothers rushing distractedly to these putative places of learning and hurrying away the inmates. If one of the well-authenticated facts that transpire in some of those establishments had occurred in any Catholic female institute, the torch would avenge it and a pile of blackened ruins would mark the seat like the Sea of Sodom. We blush to think and the page refuses to recall any of those specifications, alas! too rife over the entire country, from the normal school to the boarding-house dormitory.

And how have they been characterized? By the summoning of a board of inquiry for the purpose of glozing over the *indiscretion* with some flimsy excuse, which tended to authenticate the events, without saving either the reputation of the individual or establishment, and contributing rather to defame all the inmates indiscriminately. Some female institutions are honorable exceptions; but on reflection, it will be conceded that persons of their own sex, and not men, are the proper persons to train and educate young women.

The United States have discovered, after mature reflection and sad experience, that the walls of our convents save the virtue of their daughters, as the impediments of our marriage sacrament prolong it during life and shield the happiness of woman from the aggressions of passion.

Bishop England in 1834 procured a colony from the Ursuline Convent at Blackrock near Cork, composed of religious ladies of the highest intellectual attainments, of unsurpassed refinements, and womanly accomplishments. They were connected with the leading families of society by close relationship, and eminent, even in the monastic life, for fervor and holiness in all ascetic observances. The community consisted of the Superioress, Mother Mary Charles Molony, Sister Mary Borgia McCarthy, Sister Mary Antonia Hughes, Sister Mary Joseph, and Sister Angela Delany. He planted them in the youthful diocese, now ranking among the churches of the oldest formation, and linked to the see of Peter, like Cork, Paris, or Vienna. They were intended to water the soil around its roots with tears of compunction, shed the lustre of their learning and virtue on her daughters, and plant in the new paradise the lily of purity, to diffuse its fragrance and scatter its sweetness on the moral waste.

But in this instance he was doomed to meet bitter disappointment, for the increase of his merits. His measures, and the high order of Catholic civilization introduced, were in advance of the backward state of society; the fears of sectarianism were aroused afresh, hostility was arrayed against the convent, its meek inmates were denounced and depreci-

ated. The Catholic body was too poor and feeble to sustain
them by their patronage, and after they had lingered on for
a period of twenty years they were transferred by Bishop
Reynolds to the arch-diocese of Cincinnati. The older members of the community returned to the parent home; those
of American profession were restored after a dozen years' pilgrimage by Bishop Lynch, and permanently located at Valle
Crucis near the State capital, where they renewed their
labors under more favorable auspices, extending their influence over the entire country, and counting among their
pupils and in their ranks the children of the first families
in the State of South Carolina. All Bishop England's works
were imperishable and went to their end, sometimes devi-
ously, but always unerringly; he left the impression of his
mind and hand on everything he attempted, and the seal is
indelible, marking the features of his Church and the progress of Catholicity everywhere. Bishop Lynch deserves a
due meed of praise for continuing the labor and realizing the
well-matured plans of his illustrious predecessor. Where
failure seemed most certain, success has triumphed. The
people admired the wisdom and zeal, that, mid trials and obstacles prophesying but disaster and defeat, planted this
now revered and cherished community in the State, which is
blessed by the acclamations of society and by the prayers of
his guardian spirit, now watching from his throne in heaven
the diocese founded by his labors, and consecrated alike by
his tomb and his churches; they alone have survived the
ravages of time, the desolation of civil war, the torch of the
incendiary, and the persecution of enemies. What else
remains?

The activity of his mind was restless and untiring. He
now turned his attention to the education of the masses, to
the diffusion of classical and scientific knowledge in his city
and State. He loved virtue, honor, and truth, and detested
vice, ignorance, and bigotry, with all the powers of his expanded intellect and devoted heart. He established a commercial and mathematical school in the city, appointed the
disengaged clergymen and the ecclesiastical students tutors

or professors, and also introduced other accomplished teachers from Europe for the same purpose. It rapidly grew into popularity, and was universally patronized by all the leading people. The halls and class-rooms were crowded with the youth of the city and State, who partook of the same waters of learning, without the slightest alloy of sectarianism, and refreshing all in its limpid course, without any discrimination of Catholic, Jew, or Protestant. It was the first unsectarian literary institute established in South Carolina. It flourished in full vigor for about seven years, extending to and after the year 1830. Professional men of all grades, even the clergy of the various denominations, generals of armies, statesmen, judges, senators, and governors of States, literary amateurs, all were here taught and fitted for their occupations, and the useful and ornamental avocations of life; to this day, they gratefully acknowledge their indebtedness to the Bishop's school for all they know.

He educated an entire people, raised Carolina to a pre-eminence in the Continent, for science, learning, and eloquence, which she still maintains, and always will, despite of adversity. In the words of Chancellor Kent, "He restored learning and classical education in the South." The State was educated by Bishop England, and became his pupil. She copied him throughout, imitated his eloquence, acquired his form and style of writing, erected schools, built colleges, founded humane institutions, and imbibed his spirit and learning; all except the priceless pearl of his Faith, which they cast away. But several have already picked it up, regarding all else as dross in comparison, and in some instances their sons now minister before the same altars, consecrate the precious blood in the same chalices used by him, and inherit the mantle of his mission. He enlightened, educated, and framed the people to the love of honor, truth, and self-government; and they knew it not, even as Egypt knew not Joseph. All was now fixed on a solid basis; religion was seated on her throne, diffusing around the beams of virtue, learning, and science; the press, the seminary, the orphan asylum, the Sisters of Mercy, the convent, the collegiate institute, numerous churches, holy

and eloquent clergymen, everywhere, from Columbus to
Fayetteville, fervent and endeared congregations and an enlightened and admiring people, all combined to raise up the
diocese to a high rank among her sisters, and she queened it
in the land.

Missionaries from outside were not necessary to remind
him of his duty to the slave. They were his first care, and
their condition won not only his sympathy, but the tenderest
solicitude of his administration; none since has accomplished
so much for the salvation and the amelioration of their condition. Ho began to teach them and founded schools, one
under a priest for the males, and the other for girls, under
the care of the Sisters of Mercy. He was shortly compelled
to desist and his efforts in this direction were blocked by
legislation forbidding to teach negroes to read and write,
under severe penalties, apart from social ostracism. He
arranged a separate service for the slaves, said Mass for
them himself Sunday mornings at seven o'clock, and
preached in the afternoons. In relation to similar duties he
regarded them of primary importance, and gave them the
preference before all others.

Any one henceforward who attempted to transgress the
legislation passed for the protection of property and to
prevent its deterioration, was regarded as a public enemy
and jeopardized his life. Compelled to desist, he saved all
he could, continued the schools, but limited their action
to the instruction of mulattoes and emancipated blacks.
Oral catechetical instructions were imparted to all who
chose to attend or were licensed by their masters. The
dusky child of Ham was dear to his fatherly heart.
They mourned at his death with unfeigned sorrow, and
they knew his solicitude for their welfare culminated in the
greatest difficulty of his life. His letters on slavery, in vindi-
cating a divine sanction for their condition, seemed to rivet
their bonds more closely and increase their hardship. But
they were never finished; he contemplated an addendum,
showing the duties of the master and the rights of the slave,
according to natural, divine, and ecclesiastical law; he died

before the accomplishment of his design, and God himself shortly after struck off their chains, when the Southern people insulted the human race by inculcating from the pulpit and the press the abominable doctrine, that a negro, or the entire African race of people, had no souls and were only a higher type of the brute creation, the connecting link between a monkey and a man. This degradation of the image of God invoked the speedy interference of the Father of Mercies in their behalf, who avenged the wrong. It is only under Catholic governments, where the Church can regulate the relative duties between the servant and the master, that slavery can exist as a Christian institution, and the human being protected against the injustices and passions of the owner, like every other member of society.

Since their separation from the mother country and the abolition of canon law, Catholic discipline is said to have relaxed in the West Indies. The Church has been laboring for years to restore sound morals and the strict observance of her precepts among the inhabitants ; an arduous undertaking, when the government, the most influential people, and frequently unworthy members of the clergy are opposed to the needed moral reformation. Clothed with authority by the Supreme Pontiff, Gregory XVII., the Bishop was sent as Apostolic Delegate to the republic of St. Domingo to restore Catholic discipline, revive the decaying spirit of religion, and enforce the observance of the laws of the Church in the land. He was courteously received, and entertained in a manner befitting the representative of the Pope, by President Boyer and the other lay and clerical dignitaries of the country.

He retained the mission for some time; shrewd, and wise, and prudent, he accomplished all that could be done in behalf of religion, and ordained a colored and well-educated native of the island. He made his reports to the Holy See, documents of deep interest, and preserved in the archives of the Church. He was assistant at the pontifical throne, and consulted in all matters of moment in relation to the American Catholic Church. But all his accumulated honors did not for a moment relax his vigilance or sympathy, which were directed to the wants and feelings of his own people, whose prejudices could not overawe, nor their passions deter him from the course of duty. He loved all intensely; their salvation was entrusted to his care by divine appointment; he wept for their frailties, condoned their ignorance, and prayed for their conversion. His advent was the introduction of Christianity into the country. In after years, an aged person living in the heart of the interior used to relate "that she remembered very well, while in her girlhood, when Christmas first came to this country; the shooting of crackers and all the merry-making was like the Fourth of July."

In the year 1835 and during the time of the mission to Hayti, in order to watch over the interests of religion during his absence, RT. REV. WILLIAM CLANCY, D.D., was appointed Coadjutor Bishop.* He labored under the disadvantages of a subordinate position under so great a man as Bishop England. Even when dead, first-class ecclesiastics declined the honor of being the immediate successor, and his crozier was grasped with fear and trembling. He was born in Cork, Ireland, studied in the College of Carlow, and was instructed in theology by Bishop England. With the exception of some missionary duties performed in the diocese of Cork, he spent the greater part of his time in college as curate or professor in theology, enjoying the esteem of Bishop Doyle and other illustrious prelates. He was noted for his charity, learning, and ability. Appointed Coadjutor to the Bishop, he was consecrated in the Cathedral of Carlow, February 1st, 1835, by Bishop Nolan, assisted by Bishops Slattery and Kinsella. He was visited by a severe illness, which impeded his preparations; and on his recovery he secured students for the diocese. He arrived in Charleston, November 21st, 1835, and was warmly received by Bishop England and the clergy. For two years he effectually aided in the administration of the diocese, made visitation, taught in the Seminary, was Superior of the female institutions, confirmed

---

* Authorities: *United States Catholic Miscellany;* original sources; reminiscences among the faithful; Dr. Clark's "Lives," etc.

and ordained. He assisted at the Provincial Council of Baltimore in 1837. He was a learned and eloquent preacher. In 1838 he was promoted Vicar Apostolic of Guiana by Pope Gregory XVII. After ten years he resigned that vicariate in favor of Rt. Rev. Dr. Hynes, in consequence of failing health. He died in 1847, in Cork, his native city, lamented by all classes, and lies buried among the great and good men who ruled that portion of the Church of God in the most stormy times—the Moylans, the McCartys and the Murphys, illustrious names among the hierarchy. Two eagles cannot live in the same sky; Dr. England's abilities in every respect rendered him naturally superior, *facile princeps;* all lesser lights faded before the effulgence of his beams; he must be alone, and none can be companion of his journey: this is one of the hard destinies of human greatness.

The Bishop was the greatest laborer of the Church in his day; no man in any sphere of life could have worked harder. For the twenty-one or two years of his episcopate he never knew a day's rest. Like a shifting pain, his only relief was in the passing from one labor or difficulty to another. During his perplexing controversies he was obliged daily to write over quires of paper, which he did without making a single erasure, having no time for ornament of style or even revision. This is why he limited to the closest definition of faith, his own particular belief to the contrary notwithstanding, the infallibility of the Pope, then an open question, and other leading points of controversy, to save time for other pressing duties, and give less scope to his adversaries. Under this view, all men acquainted with the nature of our warfare, will admire his shrewdness and vindicate him from the slightest shade of Gallicanism. Had he attempted to wade through all the objections advanced against the infallibility of the Pope, which the assembled wisdom and learning of the Church, under the guidance of the Holy Ghost, at a General Council, spent months in explaining and refuting, he had defeated his cause and given a triumph to the opponent. We know that several of the most distinguished prelates received the dogma only after Jesus Christ had spoken by the mouth of Peter. If this broad and truthful view had been taken, the splendid edition of Bishop England's works, gorgeously bound and presented to the Pope by Dr. Reynolds, would not have miscarried. In his position nice theological distinctions, reverence for opinion, literary ornament and finesse, very desirable in a college concursus and the result of a year's study, would have clogged his way, impaired the force of a popular argument, and marred its effect. If gentlemen could obtain their insertion in a daily newspaper at the advertising rates, paid out of a poor-box at the door of a poor frame church in danger of being burned by a mob, I am convinced their definitions would be equally short and logical: his were all pinched by poverty. It is easy to talk, is a trite but forcible saying. A literary offering more worthy of acceptance could not have been made to the Holy See within the century, under the circumstances.

Free from the nervous restlessness bordering on imbecility, and the infirmity of weak minds, his activity, founded on well-matured plans, was marvellous; it was eulogized by a Pope. He was everywhere and all times, when it was possible, on his mission. In every city and town and hamlet, in the valley and on the mountains, in the cots of the poor, in the mansions of the wealthy, in the woods by night, at the cross-roads, in the meeting-houses, in Masonic halls, everywhere you will find him, everywhere I and other priests traced his footprints; preaching, teaching, exhorting, administering the Sacraments, hearing confessions, writing his letters, preparing scientific and historical lectures, if he had a moment's respite; by the deathbed of the plague-stricken, in the streets of Charleston, his feet almost shoeless, blistering on the burning pavements, his tongue parched with thirst, his brow fevered, body and soul exhausted, and the whole man consumed by the labors of his ministry and the fire of his zeal, which *had eaten him up.* He was most companionable among his missionary priests, shared their humble shelter, cooked the scanty meal in common, and bore the hardships of their desolate lot. The visitation of the diocese was then quite a different labor, not facilitated by any of our modern improvements; the journeys were made by private conveyance, on foot, on horseback, in old jingles or sulkies, outside of the stage lines, often compelled to beg for a night's lodging in the humblest abodes, no protection from the night air, its heats and mosquitoes in summer, nor its cold and frost in winter, was often precarious and uncertain, and when granted, the poverty and slovenliness of the inmates made the hospitality often less endurable than the woods under the sighing of the night winds. He was often compelled to sit by the driver, exposed to the burning sun by day and the cold of the nights, on a journey of one or two hundred miles, in consequence of the excess of inside passengers in the stage. Once when disabled by fatigue and overpowered by sleep the lines fell from the hands of the driver, and the passengers inside, unconscious of the danger, were left to the caprice of the team, the Bishop caught up the lines, delivered the mail at the postoffice, and conducted all safely to the end of their journey, as the morning sun arose over the eastern hills and ushered in the day.

This remarkable man was equally competent to run a stage, and could with equal firmness grasp the reins of an empire as the lines of a coach-driver. He had visited all the chief towns and cities of the Union in the interest of his diocese and of religion at large, crossed the ocean four times when navigation was slow and perilous. He travelled over Europe repeatedly for the same object, sought aid from the society of Vienna, from the Holy Father, begged in Ireland, in England, in France, in Italy, wherever he could obtain a penny, a vestment, a book, or a breviary ; inducing well-disposed youths aspiring to the priesthood, and virtuous women who had a vocation for the cloister, to share his labors and his future rewards. The establishment of the diocese was a worldwide labor, and consumed all the days of his life. The details will be amplified in the following pages. Some men from their position and genius are so closely identified with public affairs that their lives form the history of the nation in which they live, or of the whole world, during their age, like O'Connell in Ireland, and Pius IX. at the head of the

Church. The diocese now, and for all future time, is so closely identified with the name of Bishop England, that by no convulsion can they be separated. His successors and all now engaged in the ministry and in the offices of religion in the three dioceses are developing his plans, perpetuating his labors, enlarging his mission. They owe their security in the service of God, and their position in the Church and in society, to the influence of his character, his learning, and his virtues. The generous heart of the Catholic Church in the United States, overstepping the dividing lines and making the voluntary concession of universal indebtedness, claim with his immediate flock a share in the glory of his ministry, and justly hail him as the light of the American hierarchy.

Suffering is the condition of our being and a law of the incarnation; the sign of God's favor and the earthly recompense of virtue. Experience, the establishment of the Faith everywhere, the history of the world, forbid us to imagine that the Bishop enjoyed the sunshine of peace and prosperity, while he broke the first ground. On the contrary, he partook of more than the usual share of trials allotted to prelates, whose severity is the antidote against the intoxication of elevation, and steadies man in the sober path of duty. He drank the cup of sorrows to the very dregs, and the bitterness of its water was never sweetened, save by the wood of the Cross. Besides the constant care of fostering the rising institutions which he had planted, the heavy burden of his vast diocese, the unremitting demands of the public for fresh publications of his mind, the strain on the brain and nerves of great men to maintain unimpaired their well-conceived honors, and the harassing drag of hard poverty, he was assailed by scurrilous attacks in the press on his manners and habits of life; even a mob threatened to destroy his labors in the city, and disperse or destroy his institutions. The former he treated with silent contempt, giving full publicity in his writings to the base allegations as his only defence; the testimony of the living witnesses of his private life and public conversation, were the irrefragable defence of his self-restraint and sobriety. In the present condition of society no man living could have passed through his life of labor and championship of the Faith, unassailed by calumny. Tried like gold in the furnace, he passed unscathed through every ordeal, while the arrows of malice, envy, and petty jealousy fell harmless to the ground.

Human motives, worldly praise, nor any earthly incentive, could have inspired his efforts and sustained him in his uninterrupted labors to the end. Only the grace of God from above and the spirit of prayer could have sufficed, by which alone the spiritual life makes its ingress into the soul. External duties, such as preaching and teaching others, yet more the administration of the Sacraments, will save no man, unless accompanied by prayer. They become causes of mental distraction, dry up the fountain of piety, and have caused numbers to perish while saving others, an evil which menaced the very Apostle of the Gentiles. Although deprived by his multitudinous duties and cares of leisure for long undisturbed meditations, often have I seen him, in the sombre shades of the Cathedral, only partially relieved by the gleam of the sanctuary lamp, absorbed in humble prayer and in union with his Maker. The fervor of his words, assiduity in reading the divine offices, the frequent reception of the holy Sacrament of Penance, the recital of his beads, his fervor and compunction, show that he lived a life of prayer, that it cemented all his works, consoled him in his difficulties, and was the mainspring of all his actions.

He was distinguished for three devotions always characteristic of the lives of men eminent for sanctity and holiness. He was extremely devout to the Blessed Virgin, and had the confidence of a child in her protection, which he invoked in all difficulties and dangers. He was eminently devout to our dear Lord in the Blessed Sacrament, and from this source drew all his strength and support. His letters to Dr. Bachman in defence of this ineffable mystery are unsurpassed in the English language. His charity towards the faithful souls was unbounded. The office for the dead and the High Mass, at which all the clergy and religious were expected to assist, were celebrated invariably on the death of any of the priests, of the members of the religous communities, or a benefactor of the Church. On these occasions his devotion threw a spirit of mourning and sadness over the entire diocese; it was like a family sad and inconsolable for the loss of one of its children. Not content to have built the Church, he adorned it with his virtues, filled it with his piety, and he died without leaving a stain on her fair name or blot on the escutcheon of his fame. Without this safeguard of prayer, profane ambition for preferments or worldly applause will steal into the sanctuary, paralyzing with anarchy, inefficiency, or stimulating to the erection of gorgeous churches, often monuments of the decaying temple of the Holy Ghost in a soul. It is doubtful if Solomon saved his soul by the building of his temple.

CHAPTER II.

BISHOP ENGLAND, CONTINUED—VERY REV. RICHARD SWINTON BAKER, ADMINISTRATOR.

A Slumbering Volcano—A Collapse—South Carolina saved from Disgrace by Bishop England—Last Visit to Europe—Dangerous Voyage—Sermons in Philadelphia and Baltimore—Last Sickness and Death—Universal Mourning—Lying in State—Obsequies by Rt. Rev. Francis Patrick Kenrick, D.D.—Miss Johanna M. England—Silly Imputations—No Privacy for Public Men—Eulogy by Bishop Kenrick—Very Rev. R. S. Baker, Administrator—His Early Life—Missions—President of the Seminary—Retired Habits—Personal Appearance—Administratorships—Holy Orders—Pastor of St. Mary's—Happy Death—Resolutions of St. Patrick's Benevolent Society, etc.

HERESY, like all error, is bigoted and intolerant; when planted by the sword and maintained by violence, it cleaves for protection to the secular arm, and endeavors to destroy the truth which it is unable to refute. *Let us kill Jesus and Lazarus also, lest the Romans come and take our country,* has been its maxim for nineteen centuries. This has been its war-cry in France, in England, in America, everywhere. When the sword of persecution has been sheathed it perishes or pines away into insignificance and contempt, for human passions are always mean and transient.

In the most favorable times, and when no cloud darkened the horizon, the Bishop of Charleston was standing on the thin crust of a volcano, which at any moment was ready to break into a raging fire and destroy every trace of his labor. If the Faith everywhere, like the spiritual life itself, had not been planted by the Cross, it would have lost much of its outward glory. The old spirit of intolerance only slumbered; it was rebuked and mortified, and awoke to avenge defeat and repair all losses.

A strong Union man, Dr. England always cherished the Constitution, but never entered into the arena of politics.

Having been appointed Apostolic Delegate to the Republic of Hayti, the ordination of a colored educated man, and the establishment of a school for the colored people of Charleston, —all were a subterfuge for raising the old party shibboleth, and unfolding again the standard of the Prophet. The community were excited by the insidious circulation of false reports. "This man," it was said, "is an enemy to the State; he is now even concocting in our midst a servile insurrection, the most brutal and bloody of all revolutions; he is planning our destruction; our lives and the lives and honor of our families are imperilled. Come, let us root him out, and let his name be no longer called amongst us." In public harangues, in the family circle, and from the pulpit, the same means were resorted to as in Boston, and for a similar purpose.

The pupils fell away rapidly from the literary institutes, and the lay teachers were dismissed in consequence. Consternation seized on the public mind similar to that which is said to have fallen on the Egyptians, when the idols fell to the ground at the advent of the Holy Family, in their flight from the miserable Herod. The streets were alternately desolate or else teeming with excited multitudes, warmly discussing the critical condition of civil affairs.

The season of discussion had passed, and the time for action was at hand, *Tempus agendi Domine.* Violence was now offered, and it become necessary to meet it with its own weapons, or perish like men and martyrs in the effort. The Irish volunteers, the brave and true men of the city, were called on. They organized, took the convent and ecclesiastical institutions under their protection, turned out with gleaming arms in their hands,—an array by no means contemptible. They offered no insult, manifested no bravado, but *showed fight;* the organization remained firm. It became evident that any attempt at violence would have buried the proud city in its ruins, and inaugurated the reign of terror and assassination which they affected to dread. The mayor and city officers, who had hitherto connived at the gathering storm, became suddenly active in the interest of peace: negotiations were begun, a truce established, the lives and property of the Catholic ladies were placed under the protection of the civil authorities, who gladly undertook the charge ; the citizens became their ready auxiliaries ; the volunteers were disbanded, and the State of South Carolina saved from the shame and disgrace that will forever brand with infamy the bigoted State of Massachusetts. The Carolinians never forgot the lesson. When passion had subsided, the people felt grateful for the interference, because they were prevented from disgracing their city and country before all the nations of the world and for all future time.

Massachusetts and South Carolina are much alike in the temper and disposition of their inhabitants ; the heroism of the Bishop prevented the similarity from becoming still more marked and decided. For this act the State owes him a debt of gratitude which she can never fully repay to his memory. Now that the institution of slavery, which brooded like an incubus on the land, has been swept away by universal acclamation, the light has been removed from under the bushel, and will beam brighter than ever, reflecting its beams far and wide over the country. A people yet unborn will bid his noble features live in marble by the side of the statue of John C. Calhoun, who was not a greater benefactor of the country and generation than Bishop England. Mr. Calhoun saved his State only for a time from Northern aggression, but inaugurated a fatal and mistaken policy. The Bishop resisted that aggression far more effectually, saved the State even from the violence of her own sons, and inculcated not only human wisdom and freedom, but the wisdom and knowledge of God which surpasses all understanding. The Church has now been too firmly planted to be torn up by mob violence, its roots run deeper into the soil than the majestic oak, whose branches are spread far and wide. It will never yield to the fury of the gale. The stability promised by our Divine Master to apostolic labors, indelibly marks the works of Bishop England ; they remain to this day like the Faith, and are renewing all their youthful life and vigor. The Collegiate Institute was renewed under Bishop Reynolds, and after having been suspended, is now re-established on a firmer basis, and the Brothers of the Sacred Heart, all competent teachers and self-sacrificing men, count three hundred of the youth of Charleston in their schools, a larger patronage than it ever enjoyed at any time from the beginning.

After the Easter of 1841 the Bishop visited Europe for the last time in the interest of religion in his diocese; after having paid his respects to the common Father of the faithful, he returned the following autumn, accompanied by the Rev. A. Doyle, the aged Superioress of the Ursuline Convent, Madame Borgia, and his niece, Miss Honora England, as a postulant for the veil in that distinguished order.

He bid a final adieu to his sister, the Superioress of the Presentation Convent, his brother, Rev. Thos. England, the parish priest of Passage, and a large circle of distinguished friends and admirers, whom he was never more destined to behold on earth. The voyage was long and boisterous; after fifty-two days, when it was feared the vessel had foundered, he landed in Philadelphia, broken in health and needing rest; for he too had been attacked by the malady—a malignant dysentery, which broke out on shipboard and raged with great severity among the passengers.

The Bishop waited on them in person; from his watchfulness and anxiety he was prostrated himself with the disease. Yielding to a pressing invitation, and while the guest of Bishop Kenrick, he delivered a course of lectures and preached seventeen nights successively, with all the power and vigor that were displayed in his best days. He also preached five nights in Baltimore. He held an annual convention and retreat for the clergy unflinchingly from the beginning in Charleston; they had assembled, the exercises were conducted by Father Barry, and they retired every one to his post, disappointed at not having seen the Bishop, who made the appointment while yet in Europe. The delay on the passage prevented his keeping the engagement.

When in Rome or elsewhere, he would make an appointment to administer confirmation and discharge some other episcopal duty on a certain day, and failed not to be present at the moment. He was never known to have broken an engagement; he kept his faithfully, despite of danger or difficulty, and he impressed this obligation on all his clergy, as an indispensable condition for success. The first sound of the bell was the voice of God summoning to any duty; the Mass, the confessional, Church devotion, must be attended with corresponding punctuality. The hand of death was on him now, and he knew it not. He had fought the good fight, he had kept the Faith, rest from all his labors was at hand, and the unfading crown was now within reach of his faithful hand.

Having returned to his episcopal city in December, he preached once or twice during Advent, and took part in the Christmas offices of the Church. He had a particular devotion to Church ceremonies all his lifetime, observed them minutely, always presided when it was possible; the offices of Holy Week and the solemnities of all festivals were conducted as gorgeously in the humble Cathedral as in the oldest churches in Europe. The students from their entrance into the Seminary were required by rule to recite the divine office of every Sunday in choir and in the sanctuary, and presided over by a priest, which not only instructed them thoroughly in reciting the breviary, but also gave additional solemnity to the other ceremonies. On Sunday mornings the Bishop always presided at the Little Hours introductory to the High Mass. Soon after Christmas, and on the commencement of 1842, he took to his bed, never more to rise from it. He lay sick three months under daily attention from Dr. John Bellinger, a distinguished physician, and one of his converts. No skill, no care, no prayers, could arrest the inevitable decree. His work was done, his mission fulfilled, and heaven waited for him.

Attended incessantly by his father confessor, the Rev. Father O'Neale, of Charleston, and fortified by the Holy Communion at intervals of a few days during the three months of his sickness, he prepared himself by prayer, acts of love and resignation, and of all virtues, to meet his Father and his God. He arranged all his temporal matters and the affairs of the diocese, appointed Very Rev. R. S. Baker, V.G., his Administrator, accompanied with a request that he be appointed his successor also in the episcopacy; made the profession of faith, and recommended his diocese and its institutions to the protection of our Blessed Lady, St. John the Baptist, St. Finbar, and his patron saints. Still vigilant even in his dying hours, he refused admittance to some Protestant ministers who called out of courtesy to visit him in his last sickness,—one of them, once an opponent, but drawn by his eloquence and matchless reasoning into the same circle of friendship with the children of the Faith. They were courteously dismissed; he was too wise to be ignorant that an interview would become a subterfuge for a statement that in his last moments he was converted and died a Protestant.

A solemn High Mass was offered in the Cathedral in his behalf April 10th, 1842, after which the clergy were summoned to his side. Prayers were offered up in the Synagogue for his recovery; he was a friend to the Israelites, and they cherished his memory with affectionate regard. Clad in the episcopal robes, he prepared himself to receive the Sacrament of Extreme Unction with great composure. When he received the crucifix into his hands he kissed it, saying "Sweet Jesus, who didst deign to die for me, in this ignominious manner, regard with compassion the condition of Thy servant, and be with him in the succeeding hour of trial." He addressed the kneeling clergy for about a half an hour in words of tenderness, counsel, and fervent piety.

In the afternoon the seminarians were also summoned to his bedside. We knelt down, and he blessed us with great tenderness and affection. He lay like a sick lion; all his strength was gone. The once manly frame was now a grand ruin from the ravages of sickness; nothing remained of his manly, noble form, admired by the gaze of millions, and never seen but in the gap of danger or in the van of battle, nothing remained but the quenchless lustre of the eye, through which the wonderfully gifted soul still blazed forth in all the splendor of its native brightness. I saw him next, and for the last time, the following morning, April 11th, 1842, at five o'clock, the hour when he arose to say his Mass during his life unfailingly The agony of death was on him; he had already received the Holy Unction; his episcopal robe and stole were on his neck, the ring gleamed from his white hand, outspread on the coverlid as if in act to bless. The venerable Father O'Neale, of Savannah, the faithful companion of his journeys, all the seminarians and priests of the city, were clustered round, fervently reciting the prayers for the dying in response to the senior. The Bishop deeply moaned in his familiar accents of voice; the sound became steadier every second, then there ensued a gurgling noise in the throat, like a broken effort at breathing; the physician held his clasped hand; an audible distinct word was spoken; it was the last on earth of many, MERCY! a whiteness suddenly diffused over the face, which now shone like the untrodden snow. After the priest had said, *Depart, Christian soul, out of the world, in the name of God the Father, who created thee, in the name of God the Son, who redeemed thee, in the name of the Holy Ghost, who sanctified thee*, he added, "*Let us pray for the soul of the departed. Bishop England is dead!*"

"*Consider, O Israel, for them that are dead, wounded on thy high places. The illustrious of Israel are slain upon thy mountains. How are the valiant fallen and the weapons of war perished! There was cast away the shield of the valiant as though he had not been anointed with oil. I grieve for thee: as the mother loveth her only son, did I love thee.*" II Kings, ii. chap. 20 v., etc. Such was the wail of the widowed diocese of Charleston for her loss.

Robed in pontificals, the remains lay in state in the Cathedral, and were visited by thousands of all classes with evident marks of heartfelt sorrow and regret. The city was in mourning, the shipping in the harbor and the public buildings lowered their flags to half-mast. Business was suspended, the bells in all the Protestant churches were tolled, the entire community were desolate and mourned as for a common father; the tears of the widow and the orphan, of strong men and of once powerful adversaries, fell fast and heavy on his bier. The lips that never spoke without striking at the heart of a big thought, awakening new ideas in all

who listened, were now silent in death. Like a conqueror
taking his rest, around him lay the fruits of his labors and
the trophies of his victory.

The Rt. Rev. Bishop Kenrick came from Philadelphia,
presided at the office, celebrated in pontificals the Requiem
Mass, and meetly pronounced his eulogy. He admonished
the people to be mindful of his teachings and imitate the
example of his virtues. "He it was," he said, "who had organized the Provincial Councils, framed their decrees, established the discipline of the Catholic Church in America, and
was venerated as its father." Most of the clergy of the diocese were in the sanctuary, and Masses were celebrated during the three days preceeding the sepulture ; prayers and
incense, mingled with the sighs of the religious and the
lamentation of a devoted people ascending on high before the
altar of God, made entreaty for the eternal repose of the departed spirit. Not only as a Bishop, but in all the relations of
life, he was a man honest and just and true—open and candid
as the broad day, without guile or deceit, the impersonation of
truth ;—the model of prelates, the very heart of Catholicity,
and adorned with all its virtues. His square and massive
firmness, simplicity and purity of character, stand monumental in the annals of the Church. He had founded the diocese of Charleston under difficulties and hardship ; her cradle
was rocked by adversity and poverty ; he watched over her
infancy, taught and nurtured and ruled her for twenty-one
years, and when she had attained her maturity, he committed her to his successors without a spot on her brow,
matchless in splendor and incomparable in vigor, the pride
of the Church in the New World, and its admiration in the
Old. His remains were interred under the episcopal chair at
the Gospel side of the altar; those of his sister, Miss Johanna
Monica England, which had rested in an humble grave at St.
Mary's Church since 1827, were exhumed and now buried
in the same tomb with her brother. Forsaking her father's
house, her kindred, and her country, she journeyed with
him across the perilous ocean, and was the companion of his
solitude, the solace of his sufferings, and the only comfort of

his life. Embellished with all the refinements of high Catholic cultivation and piety, she shone as a star in Southern society, her memory a spiritual thing of sweetness and a joy forever. The malaria soon snapped asunder the only chord that bound his affections to earth and still reminded him of his far distant home, and left him alone with his God. Like St. Benedict and St. Scholastica, they are united once more in the safe keeping of the tomb on Carolina's sunny shore, whose souls were already united in the many-mansioned home of the Almighty Father. As the beginning, so was the ending. Like the sun he rose in the East and set in the West, and illumined half the world in his passage. At his death he left in the diocese sixteen churches, twenty-one priests, two religious institutes of women, the Seminary, and a Catholic population of about 12,000.

At the hour of death St. Gregory Thaumaturgus, whose wonders rivalled the miracles of Moses and the Prophets, inquired of the attendants how many unbelievers were in the city of Neo-Cæsarea in Pontus, of which he was first Bishop; they answered seventeen. Raising his eyes to heaven, the man of strong faith exclaimed: "I thank my God, that was precisely the number of Catholics here when I began my episcopate;" and immediately after expired. Scattered over the three States comprising the diocese, Bishop England on his arrival in 1820 could have found scarcely a thousand Catholics; they increased to at least ten thousand before his death, about the number of white people in Charleston when he undertook the charge of the diocese; an immense gain, especially when we remember that immigration was repelled by the institution of slavery. Several from the humble walks of society were received into the Church, and some, but not many, influential people had also obeyed the Faith; that consolation was reserved for future administrations. The soil was broken and prepared, the seed sown broadcast over the land, bringing forth an abundant harvest after the sower was laid under its surface. It was not merely to those of their own time that the Apostles had been sent, but to the world and to all future time: their labors were commensurate with the extent and duration of the human race; a privilege shared by all who continued and perpetuated the ministry. No man lives to himself exclusively; the extension of thought by word or action of the most obscure individual creates an influence for good or evil which may abide until the last day, which alone can determine the measure of a man's merit or demerit. There are reasons adduced by saints for a general judgment long after the doom of each will have been irrevocably fixed.

The publicity which elevation gives to the actions and lives of the great is one of their many trials; nothing is hid; it is folly to imagine that the public mind, naturally jealous of elevation, will not watch the whole tenor of their lives, scrutinize their motives of action, pry into the deepest secrets, note and set down in a book the most hidden faults of public men, and drag them triumphantly into the light of day. *There is nothing hidden that shall not be revealed*, is a truth frequently verified on earth. All Israel was scandalized by the crimes of the erring King, when in his criminal efforts at concealment, he murdered Urias, confiding his secret only to the tomb. God is a witness of all things, and He frequently manifests our most hidden transgressions, to intimidate the sinner and restrain vice.

There were but three acts of the Bishop's life of whose propriety there was question—only among Catholics. Those outside the pale of the Church entertained no other feelings but admiration and esteem for his character and his life; it was his faith only that gave them offence. These were, (1.) The constitution of the diocese; (2.) Ordering the students to go into mourning for the death of Bishop Bowen, an Episcopalian; (3.) The calling-in a Protestant minister to visit a dying member of his congregation. In answer to the first, its object was evidently to keep the vestrymen within the limits of moderation, restrain aggression on the rights and immunities of the Church, check disorder, and prevent both schism and scandal; all which were accomplished. At Easter in 1809 there were only three communicants in Charleston. Trusteeism was at the bottom of the scandals, and

St. Mary's was schismatical for many years. The constitution eventually healed the disorder.

Socially he was agreeable, mild and attractive in manner and habits. All indiscriminately sought him in their difficulties, asked his counsel, received his advice with veneration, and shared his commiseration when their cares were beyond human redress. When duty or principle were not compromised, he made all concessions to the feelings of others, without sacrificing an iota of truth. His big heart embraced all the sorrows of his people, and had a responsive throb for each individual suffering.

At a public execution, when the victim of the law, an unfortunate Spaniard, owing to the bungling mismanagement of the scaffold, was being slowly strangled, frequently touching the ground with his feet after the drop fell, filling the assembled multitude with horror by his screams for the *coup de grace*, Bishop England rushed in, flung his entire weight on the knees of the wretched victim of this cruel mode of death when badly managed, and thus mercifully shortened the struggle for death, which was begged as a boon: he died without further struggle, and almost instantly. Aiding in the the execution of a criminal is forbidden by canon law to clergymen; it is a censure incapacitating for the reception of orders, and forbidding their exercise by one already ordained, without dispensation. Is there any man of common sense who will blame the Bishop for his humane act on this occasion? None save one who impiously supposes that the legislation of the Church is based on caprice, extravagance, and nonsense. You may as reasonably assert that a man in a shipwreck had sinned, because he ate a morsel of meat on Friday to keep from starving. The reader will permit me to ask in this connection, why does not the United States, like France and other countries, adopt a more humane method of executing her criminals, who are but the unfortunate children of the nation, if she will not have experienced executioners who make the art a study, and hang people decently, as they do in Ireland?

Father England was the chaplain of the Cork prisons,

when Jack Canty was hangman for the county and domiciled in the jail; that man used only silken ropes, took the measure of the neck, and weighed the condemned several days before the execution, and was wont to go through the process personally, in a modified form, for the sake of experiment. He accompanied the judge on his circuit, and could hang a man dead in a minute, if he liked him or was bribed for the purpose. He could make the process as painless as the operation of dentistry at the present time.

While on his visitation, and after having lectured in a court-house at night, in the interior of Georgia, the Bishop retired to rest, being much fatigued, and was shortly sound asleep. The host awoke him after some time with a loud knocking, and gaining admittance, asked if he could receive a visitor. Being answered affirmatively, a young man now demurely approached the bedside, sat on a cane-bottom, straight-back chair, crossed his legs, and acquainted the Bishop that he was a student and an aspirant to the Methodist ministry, and would be ordained the following day; that having heard his sermon, he admired the doctrine, and begged he would teach him theology! The Bishop received him with marked kindness, taught him the five principal mysteries of religion, and counselled him to cultivate and preach charity to all men. Having acquired pre-eminence among his followers, this harmless man during the remainder of his life boasted that he had learned his theology at the feet of the renowned Bishop England.

The gentleman who owned the City Hotel at Columbus, Georgia, speaking of the Bishop's frankness and independence of character, related the following anecdote to me twenty years after it occurred. The citizens were notified that the Bishop would be in Columbus a certain day, remain a couple of weeks and lecture every night in the town-hall during his stay. There being no Catholic here at the time who could afford him accommodation, and receiving no invitation from any of the townspeople, he engaged rooms at the hotel for two, and preparations were made for his accommodation. On the appointed day a knot of lawyers, gentlemen at large, and lookers-on lounged round, under the porch, and through the house, anxiously waiting to see him. There being no railroad then between Savannah and here, a journey of three hundred miles had to be made by stage or private conveyance. On account of its crowded condition, the heat and confinement were past endurance in warm weather, and the latter mode of travelling was adopted. Towards evening of a long summer day, an old jingle, drawn by two jaded horses, drove up to the door, two sunburnt travellers alighted, covered with sandy dust, and much road-ridden. None knew them; of striking personal appearance, apparently of the same age, and of marked individuality, they commanded the attention and excited the curiosity of the crowd. The shorter-sized gentleman of the two alighted first, entered the office, stripped off his coat, hat, and vest; washed his face and hands, demanded if there was any good wine to be had; when presented he partook of a portion mingled with water. After having brushed the dust from his garments, he readjusted them, took a ring from his pocket,—it was large and lustrous,—and approaching the desk, wrote on the travellers' register with his jewelled hand "✠ John Bishop of Charleston." "I never before saw such a preacher, so fearless, so sincere; *they* always take their drink behind the door. The men were all amazed, they were excited, and I can't tell what prevented them from giving three cheers, except the impropriety of hollering in church." The companion was old Father O'Neale, of Savannah. It is evident that the criterions by which we judge of men in general will not apply to this case; it is exceptional.

He interpreted and applied the law in its spirit, and not by the letter which killeth; by his wisdom and innate sense of right and propriety, and not running counter to the feeling and prejudices of his erring people, he disarmed their hostility; and if he did not succeed in gaining them all to God in his day, he reconciled them to the existence of the Church, and left her to do her work of conversion in God's own good time.

To call on a minister to assist a dying man was a humane

act in every sense; it was too late to attempt to convert the blameless ignorance of the dying man, and to disturb his good faith at the time would be an act of questionable propriety or mistaken charity; attempting to do so, under similar circumstances, I was very speedily dismissed. The presence of the minister was a human consolation, who with his hymns and prayers may have served to raise the parting soul to God and elicit an act of perfect contrition. Cardinal Manning insists that he has with great satisfaction observed much of the workings of the Holy Ghost among the fragmentary forms of Christianity.

Like the former, the badge of mourning worn around the hats of the students was an act of civility and respect to the memory of a good man, who, though erring in his religious opinions, had befriended the Bishop in his hour of adversity, and indirectly aided his efforts. There was nothing of the religious aspect connected with it, and it is far less reprehensible than assisting at the funerals and weddings of non-Catholics, attending public assemblies opened by prayer, or partaking of food seasoned by a preacher's long benison. How unexceptionably grand must a public life have been, when a scrutiny of sixty years fails to discover anything more deserving of reprehension?

Always preoccupied by care, and bending under a load of difficulties, he had no time to waste in cultivating all the amenities of leisurely life, which explains his imputed asperity of manner towards his domestics and subordinates.

I found him gentle and mild when more rigid reproof would be excusable. His voice, accustomed to other melody, was not skilled in the measured numbers of harmonious sounds; he was not a good singer, and this was its only defect. It was rich and sonorous, of vast power and compass, capable of filling any ordinary place of public speaking; but every attempt to strike a higher note was only a deeper inflation and louder intonation.

A young Seminarian on a certain solemn occasion, when the Bishop had celebrated the High Mass and laid his robes aside, donned the outer regalia in private in the sacristy; with crozier in hand and mitre covering a downy cheek, he looked a winged cherub. He faced round, intoned the *Benedicat vos* in a tone which any one accustomed to it would have mistaken for the Bishop's. Fascinated by his assumed grandeur, he renewed the blessing, and to his utter dismay he found the Bishop the recipient of the favor. To censure any one while wearing a mitre is rather serious; at the moment it would have been cruel, and would have struck the thoughtless youth to the ground. The usurper shunned the face of the rightful occupant during several days, until they confronted one another in the course of events. "Did you sir, put on my vestments out of contempt *or curiosity*," was the temperate reproof, with a gap left open for escape. " Yes, sir," was the vague answer. " If you succeed in being a worthy priest, without any higher aspiration, you will do well." Going to the principal of the Seminary he said, "Dr. Baker, I wish you would keep your boys from *making game of me.*"

There is nothing farther from the mind of the writer than to institute an invidious comparison, depreciatory of the merits and labors of the illustrious prelates who were Bishop England's cotemporaries, and who ruled and governed the Church of God with power and wisdom in their day. The emulation of the early Christians for their teachers, one saying *I am of Paul, and another I am of Apollo,* was severely reprehended by the Holy Ghost. It is the human spirit, and betrays an ignorance of the discrimination and economy with which God imparts his grace for building up of the mystical body of Jesus Christ, giving each *prout vult* "as he judges meet," the measure necessary for the performance of the work for which he was sent, and chosen before the foundations of the world were laid. Simon de Montfort was the bravest of the brave, but he did not receive the gift of tongues nor the grace of ecstasy; such would be a waste of gifts. The talent must not be hidden nor buried in a napkin, or under the chair of a bishop, under the severest penalty. Ecclesiastical dignities, or the office of the priesthood, are not meant for the exclusive benefit of the individual; they belong to the Church, and we all share in the graces, not in the dignities. One family, closely cemented by the blood of Christ, a bond stronger than death and commensurate with eternity; one body and one soul, the bone of His bone, and the flesh of His flesh, we are united also among ourselves, and as the Apostle expresses it, *Are members one of the other*. The graces of one are a general good, his honors and his sorrows affect all, like an aching limb in the body material.

Divest our Blessed Lady of the splendor of the Immaculate Conception, or the last infant who has gone to heaven after baptism of but one ray of their glory, and the brightness of every seat of bliss in Sion may be proportionably diminished; it would be the withdrawing into its eternal home, the bosom of the Blessed Trinity, of so much glory, perhaps never more to be outwardly manifested. As the spirit of fortitude abides in the individual soul after the imposition of the hands of the Bishop, and promptly meets every emergency, like a sentinel at the gates of a city, so God raises up great men, whom he replenishes with His spirit, to meet every emergency of time, or government, or country, like Pius IX. in Rome, Bishop England, Archbishops Hughes, Kenrick, and Purcell in America, each performing his own share of the predestined work, and all contributing according to his grace to the building of the Church of God, the perpetuation of the mystery of redemption, and the filling up of the number of the blessed. We all share in the glory and partake of the fruit of their labors, for to us were they sent.

If there be a strife, let us emulate their virtues, and ambition, the most perfect gifts. The religious institutes, the asylums of charity, the sanctuary are still open, perennial fountains of covenanted grace; so are the missions in Africa and China, leaving ample room for more virgins, confessors, and martyrs in the Church; her courts are wide, and the hand of God not yet shortened, who can raise up children to Abraham from the stones of the street, more worthy of His kingdom than we. Ireland having planted the Faith on our shores,

God sent hither also and chose from her sons the first great Bishops of the Church, to systematize, maintain, and consolidate it, whose zeal should animate, whose virtues should adorn, whose learning should enlighten and gain it respect and veneration among the nations of the earth. Worthy successors of all nationalities have entered into their labors, continued their work, and inherit their honors, scattering around the sanctuary the odor of their virtues. Generations yet unborn, and *The children from afar to whom is the promise made*, will arise and claim for Bishop England among the American hierarchy the pre-eminence of St. Augustine among the doctors of the golden age of Christianity, and style him with the Primate who never spoke words of flattery or exaggeration, THE LIGHT OF THE AMERICAN CHURCH, THE AUTHOR OF OUR PROVINCIAL COUNCILS.

After the demise of Bishop England, and by his appointment, VERY REV. RICHARD SWINTON BAKER, V. G., became Administrator, and governed the diocese during the interregnum of two years. He was born in Kilkenny, Ireland, of Protestant parents, June 24th, 1806. His father, who was an officer in the English army, died young and left the only child an orphan. After the lapse of a few years he and his mother were received into the Church. His aspirations were directed to the altar by his sainted mother, and he longed for a mission in a foreign land.

Furnished with a special recommendation to Bishop England, by Dr. Doyle, he arrived in Charleston in 1827, studied in the Seminary of St. John the Baptist, and was ordained priest in 1829. He was sent on the North Carolina missions, and after a year returned to Charleston and was placed over the Seminary as Superior and Professor of Philosophy and Theology.

Dr. Baker related to the writer, that having united a couple in marriage while in North Carolina, he got no fee, which the condition of the parties led him to expect, and was sadly needed to repair the inroads made by time and wear on his thin wardrobe. Being ignorant of the State laws demanding a civil license for the legitimate performance of the marriage ceremony, which was rather singular in one of his studious habits and caution, he married them without a license. Some short time afterwards a person genteelly clad called and handed him a folded paper, which he eagerly seized, not doubting but that it contained the expected *honorarium*, and an apology for the delay. On opening it he found that it was a warrant attaching his person, and placing him under arrest for a violation of the laws of North Carolina! It was his first marriage fee. When relating it many years after, none enjoyed the farcical disappointment with greater merriment than he.

Fathers O'Neale and Andrew Byrne were on this mission previously. They were stationed at different points, but occasionally met for the purpose of conference. Ascertaining that an Irish family lived at a long distance, and in a sequestered part cf the wilderness, they made up their minds to visit them, believing that they were Catholics. They accordingly set out at an early hour the next day, and reached their journey's end late in the evening. There was no human abode in the vicinity; on entering "the cabin fast by the wild wood" they were informed in all the harsh inhospitality of the North of Ireland accent, that the guid man of the house being absent, there was no room and they had better move on farther. By no persuasion or entreaty could they obtain food or shelter for man or beast; they were reproachfully refused admittance. Resolved to remain under all circumstances, and expecting more hospitality from the master of the family, on his return, they began to recite the divine office, walking to and fro on the front plot. Father O'Neale was an excellent singer and musician, and had conducted the choir at the Cathedral in Killarney, when a layman. After the office was finished, uncovering his flute, which he often carried on his mission, the solace of many a lonely hour and hearth, ere long a soul-subduing strain, one of the sweetest of his native land, softly, sadly stole on the air, filling it with matchless melody; the dumb animals, everything seemed touched and responsive to the irresistible charms of the music; it had soothed not the savage breast, but stirred up all the depths of feeling in the heart of a noble, though humble, Protestant Irish woman, steeled against impostors by the frequent abuse of her hospitality. Abundant tears, accompanied with fervent protestations of unintentional harshness, now press the acceptance of open-handed entertainment; a cordial reconciliation followed, the music was soon changed into more heavenly notes, and its influence more abiding.

Bishop England made it a rule to observe the law of primogeniture, and considered seniority in the priesthood the first claim for advancement to ecclesiastical preferment; he accordingly appointed the oldest priests respectively to the chief places of honor and responsibility, whenever they were not unfitted by circumstances. The first place was the right of the oldest priest, all things considered. The grapes that clustered around the rod of Aaron should have yielded wine for the chalice at the Last Supper, and the crescent of the high priest culminated in the mitre of the Prince of the Apostles, if, like Esau, the older priesthood had not sold their birthright and inherited malediction of the dying patriarch.

Mr. Baker's fitness caused his rapid promotion to the Presidency of the Diocesan Seminary, Superior of the Sisters of Mercy, Chaplain at the Convent, and pastor of the Cathedral. The necessity of supplying the outside missions with priests made it necessary that one man should fulfil so many duties at a time, and among the priesthood of the diocese none was found more competent than he. The dignity of Vicar-General was also superadded, an unmistakable proof of the high appreciation of his superior for the fidelity and zeal manifested in the discharge of his multiplied duties. He was a man of retired habits, never intermingled with the world, and led the life of a hermit in the midst of society. He never stepped outside the walls of the Seminary, except on duty. He observed this course all his lifetime.

As President of the Seminary, he was most assiduous in his attendance to duty, enforced the strict observance of the rules, and never tolerated the slightest relaxation. There was not nor could there be any institute in America more monastic, or conducted on stricter principles of moral training. The hours allotted for study, the frequentation of the Sacraments, the recital of the divine office, public and private exercises, were enforced with unrelenting severity. The time spent in studying and preparing for the priestly state in the Seminary surpassed in devotion and austerity the novitiate of many orders in the Church.

Not a few broke down, and the chosen who reached the goal were as thin as eremites, mortified as Trappists, and had the appearance of men come from the wilderness, when they stood before the people. The Rev. T. J. Sullivan, the ecclesiastical superior, and whose duty it was to conduct in person the religious exercises, enforce the observance of the rules, and preside immediately over the family, was as austere as Saint Seraphim, and the model of strictest observance. Rev. Dr. Lynch was the only officer on the premises who seemed to possess any kindliness of disposition; fresh from the Propaganda, and not quite divested of the student, thin, pale, and sallow-faced, he would occasionally mingle in our conversations, and entertain us with an anecdote. It was a hard regime, and was once relieved by the consoling assurance that our condition was now a paradise, compared to what was in store after we had got out into the world. A rumor prevailed on one occasion in the city that the students were extremely disorderly and of lax morals. After having traced the calumny to one respectable source, the Bishop enclosed the rules, written in his own handwriting, and covering a quire of foolscap, to the individual, accompanied with the request that if, after having read these rules, which were all punctually observed, he deemed any further observance necessary to suppress the animal, to please intimate the same and it would receive due consideration. Silence was the only answer. From 1840, when I entered the Seminary, until 1844, when Dr. Reynolds arrived to take charge of the diocese, a period of four years, Father Baker never missed attendance on class but on account of sickness.

All the clergy ordained in Charleston during fifteen years were taught by him, were trained under this austere discipline, were witnesses of every act of his life, and bear the same honorable testimony. He was a great man, and a priest of blameless life, pure as the snowflake, self-sacrificing and devoted to his calling. This testimony was confirmed by Bishop England on his dying bed. When about to appear before his Maker, he appointed Dr. Baker the Administrator of the diocese, and recommended him as the most competent and best calculated priest to continue his own labors; coming from so respectable a source, and under such circumstances, a higher recommendation for worth and merit no man living could receive. Whether the result of sedentary habits or close application I cannot determine, but his health was never robust.

Besides all his other labors, which gradually shifted from the Bishop's shoulders to his, rendering him the chief executive power for the diocese, and intended as a preparation for the full dignity, he was editor of the *United States Catholic Miscellany* for many years, leaving him without a moment's leisure, and depriving him of all needful bodily exercise and relaxation. In short, the man was overworked. The Bishop understood not how few could bear his own labors without sinking under the burden.

Under his control the *Miscellany* maintained its old popularity: his judicious selections, lucid doctrinal explanations, and courteous editorials adorned its pages. Above the middle height, of full, commanding personal appearance, but unincumbered by obesity, he was the type of ecclesiastical dignity. As a preacher he was unsurpassed. Always confined to the management of domestic affairs, the sphere of his labors was limited to the city of Charleston, and he was scarcely known beyond. His retirement, so close as to make his appearance in secular apparel a novelty to the beholders, increased his obscurity. Charleston alone was the admiring theatre of his famous oratory.

Slavery was a wall of separation, and it had so effectually concealed the progress of religion, the work and labors of the clergy, from the world abroad, that the diocese of Charleston was ignored and scarcely mentioned in the Catholic histories of the country, or hastily passed over as though it rested under the ban of an interdict, or *was situated in partibus*, and useful only to give an ornamental title to a Coadjutor Bishop. I provided myself with treatises, and searched in vain for any item of importance which would prove of interest to my readers. Clarke's "Lives of Deceased Bishops," and Murray's "History of the Catholic Church in the United States," recent and valuable publications, moderately enlightened the universal gloom.

Educated by Bishop England from his early manhood, and impressed with his views and thoughts, it was natural that the young Levite should form his style of oratory after that of his renowned preceptor; the similarity was so close that critics were at a loss to know where to draw the line of separation. The Bishop himself, in the warmth of admiration, would generously award him the palm of superiority. With equal strength and precision of language, but less gorgeous, fact and logic were closely combined; in a short time, he covered the whole field of the mighty question with like power and ability. Though silent in his grave, the Bishop still spoke through his lips, and Dr. Baker was henceforward the echo of his voice. Indifferent to the opinions or applause of the world, he consigned to the flames the manuscripts of his sermons shortly before his death, and none of them, not even an oration, was ever printed.

Archbishop Eccleston confirmed the appointment of Dr. Baker as Administrator, and he discharged the duties of the office during two years, with his accustomed ability, and gave no just cause of complaint to any one, and nothing more commendable can be predicated of any one who fills that office. The vacancy of a see, especially in its infancy, like the interregnum of a kingdom, is a season of great difficulty, and often fraught with danger; it should not be unnecessarily prolonged; caution and prudence are primary qualifications for the incumbent, together with firmness to maintain the preexistent condition of affairs, supposed to be good, without loss or detriment, and hand over the delicate trust to the successor, unaltered and unimpaired. Innovations or radical changes must be checked in order to create no embarrassments; it is mostly a *laissez-faire* system of government. Activity must be displayed in maintaining discipline among the clergy, upholding morals among the people, and religious observances in the diocesan institutes under his immediate control. Any higher display of zeal renders one liable to the suspicion of groping for purple shoes among the graves of the dead. A priest may be a very efficient bishop and an incompetent administrator, not only because it is more difficult to govern the affairs of a diocese in the latter capacity than in the former, but for the reason that the sacramental graces necessary for the performance of the duties are wanting. True, a cleric may, by Papal appointment, be clothed with episcopal jurisdiction for the purpose of government, and where the conferring of a Sacrament is not in question. Laymen have exercised this dangerous prerogative in Ireland before St. Lawrence O'Toole, and elsewhere, to the injury of religion and the scandal of the faithful; to do the work of a bishop adequately, the plenitude of the Sacramental grace is necessary in the providence of God.

The Sacrament of Holy Orders continues the work of man's redemption, makes the Incarnation ubiquitous, commensurate with all time, embraces all graces necessary for the conversion of the world, the salvation of souls, and the government of the Church of God. Like the rivers flowing through the midst of paradise, it is the source of all the other Sacraments, those copious torrents of divine grace that inundate the entire world. When torn from its protection, other Sacraments perish or become sacrilegious. It goes strongly and forcibly to its direct end, like Baptism, with a power that the inactivity or the imbecility of years can scarcely resist. In the older dioceses it is generally the maturity of years, rather than the activity of vigorous manhood, that the Church selects for the subject of this omnipotent Sacrament. The baptismal waters had no sooner touched the brow of the conjuror, than St. Cyprian sprang from his knees a glorious martyr of the Faith; the holy unction poured on the heads of men produces effects no less miraculous, transforming timid men into successors of the Apostles, enabling them to preach the Gospel, found churches, rule and govern them to the end of time, and be the shepherds of the entire flock, priests and laity.

To the difficulties of Dr. Baker's administration were superadded the extent of the diocese, embracing the Carolinas and the Empire State of Georgia, a dilapidated treasury, and institutions without adequate means of support, dependent on the patronage of the poor Catholic population, and the Sunday collection of the Cathedral for their subsistence. He obtained places for about one-half the ecclesiastical students in the Propaganda, and in other Catholic institutions; but even after this depletion, the remainder had a precarious support and often stood in need of the necessaries of life. He handed over to Dr. Reynolds the diocese in the same unaltered condition in which he had received it from the hands of Bishop England. He was a faithful administrator, met all the demands of his heavy stewardship with consummate skill and efficiency, and resigned the reins of government with more unfeigned pleasure than will be experienced by any one who will ever resume them.

Soon after his release he spent a few months in Europe for the restoration of his impaired health, and after his return was appointed to St. Mary's Church. He held this mission during the remaining twenty-six years of his long and eventful life. If it should be asked why he was not appointed Bishop, the answer is easy. The Church does not pretend to raise all her holy, learned, and competent priests to the dignity of the episcopacy. In the early ages of the Christian institute, nearly all worthy priests were decorated with the plenitude of the order. St. Patrick ordained with his own hands three hundred and sixty-five bishops in Ireland, independently of the numbers consecrated by others. So many bishops residing in monasteries and without pastoral charge gave rise to many inconveniences which were remedied by the altered discipline of the Church, prohibiting any man to be consecrated a bishop without a separate see, and so rigidly observed that to the present day, a Coadjutor who is necessarily subordinate to his superior must be titular bishop of some see where the succession has failed by the loss of the Catholic population, the growth of heresy, or the persecution of infidel rulers. *To sit at my right hand or my left is not mine to give; it belongs to those for whom it is prepared by my Father who is in heaven*, was our Lord's reply to the ambitious mother of the sons of Zebedee. The Holy Ghost assures us that the refusal does not imply unworthiness or inferiority of merit. St. Matthias was chosen by lot to fill up the number of the chosen twelve, broken by the apostasy of Judas, without any recommendation for superior claims to the rejected candidate, who seemed to have the better right from eminent sanctity, for he is surnamed the Just by God Himself.

Very Rev. R. S. Baker died January 30th, 1870. He was forty-one years a priest, during the greater part of which he governed the diocese of Charleston, either as Vicar-General or Administrator. He was pastor for many years of St. Mary's Church, where he lies buried. The gratitude of the faithful, the veneration and affectionate regard of his immediate flock, and the admiration of the city for his intelligence and moral worth accompanied him to the grave. Thus died at a mature age, a great and good man, a faithful priest in the Church of God, whose learning and virtue adorned the diocese of Charleston, and whose name will be imperishably connected with that of its founder and his father in God,—Bishop England. The diocese owed $35,000 when he undertook the administration; he paid $15,000 of the indebtedness.

The Rev. C. B. Northrop, ordained in 1867, succeeded as pastor of St. Mary's; his assistant is Rev. J. O. Schacte, a native of the city, who studied in Europe for the priesthood.

CHAPTER III.

RT. REV. I. A. REYNOLDS, D.D., AND RT. REV. P. N. LYNCH, D.D.

Rt. Rev. I. A. Reynolds, D.D., Second Bishop of Charleston—His Birth, Ordination, Consecration—A Congregation of Freemasons—Bishoprics declined—Arrives in Charleston—Personal Appearance—Simplicity of Dress and Manners—Ordinations—Students transferred to other Colleges—Sphere of the Sisters' Usefulness Enlarged—Catholic Collegiate Institute Restored—Active Orders Popular in America—The Bishop's Labors, Zeal, Activity, Piety, and Eloquence—Division of the Diocese—Ten Places for Priests—Cathedral Completed in Four Years—Consecrated Free of Debt—Archbishop Hughes' Sermon—Worn by Labors—Preacher Thornton's Conversion and Subscription—Character—Indomitable Will, Devotion, etc.—His Holy Death—Lamented by all Classes—Vindications—Failure of the Brisbane Immigration Scheme—Miraculous Escape of the Irish Volunteers—The First Railroad South—Wooden Wheels—Huguenots—Bartholomew's Day an Exaggeration and Slander against the Church—St. Lawrence's Cemetery—Gratitude of the Faithful—Rt. Rev. Patrick N. Lynch D. D., Third Bishop of Charleston—Parentage—Education—Ordination—Offices—Duties—Consecrated Bishop in 1858—Difficulties during his Administration—An Eccentric Fire—Loss of the Cathedral of SS. John and Finbar—Uninsured—Loss of the Library—The Episcopal Residence—Sad Prospects for Religion in the Diocese—Desolation by Fire and Sword—Rt. Rev. John Moore, Bishop of St. Augustine—Restoration—Reconstruction—Number of Priests Increased—At the Vatican Council—As a Writer and Preacher—Articles—Sermons—Payment of Debts—Non-residence Excused—Able to Speak for Himself—Still on the Journey, etc., etc.

THE Rt. Rev. Ignatius Aloysius Reynolds, D. D., was the second Bishop of Charleston.* He was a native of the State of Kentucky, and was born of pious Catholic parents, August 2d, 1798. Having made his primary studies in the Seminary of Bardstown with marked abilities, he completed his ecclesiastical course at St. Mary's, Baltimore, and was promoted to the dignity of the priesthood by Archbishop Marechal, October 24th, 1823, in the twenty-third year of his age. Full of zeal and fervor, he was appointed to many of the active missions of the diocese and discharged his duties with a fidelity that met the commendation of his Superior. St. Joseph's

---
* Personal recollections chiefly; original sources; Dr. Spalding's "Sketches of Kentucky;" Dr Clarke's "Lives of Deceased Bishops;" Catholic almanacs; Catholic Journals.

College in the city having been much disorganized, and heavily in debt, he was chosen President, and in a few years the debt was liquidated, order re-established, and the institution restored to prosperity. A first-class financier, methodical in his arrangements, and of untiring perseverance, he impressed his own character on the college, and it stood the monument to his name, his learning, and his virtues. He succeeded Bishop Kenrick, after his nomination to the see of Philadelphia, as Professor of Theology at St. Joseph's Seminary. A suitable subject for the highest honors in the gift of the Church, which she keeps in store for the deserving, he became the Vicar-General of the diocese, and efficiently aided the Bishop—the aged Bishop—in its government; endearing himself to the clergy by his prudence and moderation. The diocese of Louisville has given to the Church many worthy priests and distinguished prelates; Archbishops Kenrick and Spalding, Bishops McGill and McClosky, with others, are names that will be always deeply venerated by the Catholic Church in the United States.

The piety, ability, and eloquence of Rt. Rev. I. A. Reynolds attracted the notice of the hierarchy, and he was chosen to succeed Dr. England in the diocese of Charleston. The position was regarded as one of peculiar difficulty, because of the poverty of the diocese, the intolerance of the natives, the institution of slavery, and the eminence of the first Bishop, whose exceptional greatness the entire community would naturally expect to find in his successor. It was understood that the position was offered to Dr. O'Conner, the first Bishop of Pittsburgh, and that in his humility he declined the honor and the labor. Clergymen worthy to fulfil the office were unwilling to accept. For these and other considerations, the see remained vacant for two long years, and the machinery of administration was at a stand still, until it seemed doubtful whether the succession would be continued. Truly, those were difficult and trying times on the clergy of the long-widowed see. There were among the local clergy men capable of discharging the duties and maintaining the dignity of the episcopate, and who were subsequently decorated with the honor; but they were scarcely known outside the limits of the three States.

Unless necessitated by a grave reason, the appointment of Bishops to remote sees is of questionable expediency—is not the plan commonly adopted by the Church. Neither the governor nor the subjects know each other; they are ignorant of each other's characters, except by hearsay, which is mostly an incorrect channel of information; the appointment is a burden to both, and their relation is reserved and guarded, until better acquaintance, sometimes formed after many years, and perhaps grave mistakes. Unsupported by the moral prestige of former labors or eminent services in the cause of religion, unsustained by lifelong friends in the sanctuary, uncheered by social encouragement, the Bishop must begin his life anew, dating not from his first ordination but from his consecration.

To be sure, the commandments of God and of His Church are clear and plain, and it is the duty of the faithful to obey their prelates. However, the many cases presented daily for solution to the Holy See, the progressive course of moral theology, rendering a new treatise very desirable within every few years, evinces that local circumstances have modifying influence on ecclesiastical laws, and that the Church gives grave consideration to the customs, and even prejudices of communities, when they are not at direct issue with essential enactments or discipline. A Provincial Council is assembled for many causes, but especially to check excesses and abuses, maintain discipline, and resist serious tendency to relaxation, granting full liberty when it can be indulged with safety. There are at this moment many priests in the three dioceses originally comprising the see of Charleston; from this respectable body could be chosen worthy men to fill all the sees in the United States, as they become vacant, and the appointments would be unexceptionably good; but the measure would be unwise, detrimental to all concerned, and to the best interests of religion in general.

While engaged on a *questing* tour in the city of New York in 1856, the writer formed the acquaintance of the late Bishop McFarland at the residence of Vicar-General Quinn; both being partakers of the refined and open-handed hospitality of that respectable ecclesiastic. Dr. McFarland had just received his appointment as Vicar-Apostolic of Florida and was in doubt whether to acquiesce. I entreated him to accept the dignity, but to no avail. The press was then more guarded in the publication of advertisements than at present. As a conclusive evidence, to his mind, of the dangerous relaxation of morals in Southern society, he pointed to a medical advertisement in a Charleston newspaper. I adduced the traditional piety and Catholic spirit of the descendants of the persecuted Catholics of St. Augustine, as another motive; this argument was speedily quieted. A clergyman then in the city, it was advanced, spending a winter in the mild climate of Florida for the restoration of his health, was present at Mass on a Sunday in the Church of St. Augustine; his attention was awakened at seeing a blue ribbon dangling from the breasts of the men. Seeing there were no Irish in the congregation, and that this was only an ordinary Sunday, curiosity led him to inquire the cause. He asked if the day was not a suppressed national holiday among the Spaniards. "Oh, no!" was the answer "it is the Masonic badge for Sunday; the Catholics are Masons nearly to a man!" If this be the case, the present Bishop, Dr. Moore, must have a hard set to deal with, unless his zealous prejudices had plucked the ribbons from the buttonholes of his *Masonic children*. Bishop McFarland, for these and probably other causes, declined, and became afterward the saintly and venerated Bishop of Hartford.

Under these impressions he acted wisely; none could appreciate all these considerations more fully than Dr. Reynolds, and he often gave them expression. In reality I only repeat his sentiments. Despite of all the difficulties, he generously accepted the nomination, with every prospect of a mitre in his native State beckoning him to decline. He offered himself as a sacrifice to religion, and the people were grateful in consequence; no Bishop could be received with greater joy and acclamation both by priests and laity than he; even the non-

Catholic community were glad when he arrived. He was consecrated in the Cathedral of Cincinnati, by Archbishop Purcell, assisted by Bishops Miles and Michael O'Connor, on the feast of St. Joseph, March 19th, 1844, and took possession of his see the following April.

While Mass was being celebrated by the Rev. T. J. Sullivan, at 7 o'clock A.M., and after the consecration, a plainly-dressed gentleman walked into the sanctuary, apparently about forty-five or six years of age, wrapped in a dark brown cloak, above the middle size, but not looking tall on account of genteel fulness, but not ungainly or unbecoming. His nose was slightly aquiline, his features somewhat Napoleonic, his hair short and silvered. He knelt down heavily, uttering an audible sigh, whether the experience of fatigue or disappointment it was impossible to decide, and heard the remainder of the Mass with clasped hands crossed before his breast. After Mass he drew out a plain old silver watch, looked all around the wooden building, now his Cathedral; he withdrew without saying a word; this was the new Bishop. He was unquestionably a hard-working man, a priest in every sense of the word, and an excellent Bishop. There was ample field for his labors.

His first official act was to administer Confirmation and Holy Orders; after a thorough examination he ordained on the feast of Pentecost, the 26th of May, the following three priests —students of the Seminary: Rev. John F. Kirby, Rev. J. J. O'Connell, and Rev. P. J. Coffey. The Very Rev. R. S. Baker preached on the occasion, and the Bishop wept with piety and emotion after he had conferred the Sacrament. In the course of six years, at different periods, the following clergymen, also educated in the Seminary, were ordained: Rev. Messrs C. J. Croghan, J. F. Shannahan, J. F. O'Neil, Jr., Thos. Quigly, L. P. O'Connell, and Father Hewit, the Paulist. About the year 1851 the Seminary of St. John the Baptist, after having furnished sixty priests for the diocese, was discontinued, and the candidates for the sacred ministry sent to other colleges, either in Europe or America, for their education. The course of studies no doubt was more comprehensive, and the change more conducive to the health and tastes of the postulants, but it is impossible that it could produce a more efficient and devoted body of priests than the first missionaries who were formed in the old Seminary of St. John the Baptist.

The Ursuline Convent was thought unnecessary for a time, and one of the first steps taken by the Bishop was to induce the inmates to withdraw, but provision was made for their protection. The first foundress returned to Ireland, the younger members entered a house of the order in the archdiocese of Cincinnati, and Madame Augustine England, the Bishop's niece, was received into the Ursuline Convent at New Orleans, under Bishop Blanc. The convent and seminary having been established by Bishop England with great labor and expense, and endeared to the community by many and sacred associations, their removal was unpopular, and the measure regretted by all the faithful, especially as the former ill-will against the convent had subsided in the city, and the inmates had grown into favor with the Charlestonians. His motives were good, doubtless; none questioned the purity of his intentions, while the course was regarded injudicious, and the policy at fault. The erection of a grand Cathedral was the absorbing idea of the administration, and all things else must yield to this, or rank as secondary considerations. The old Seminary, the Bishop's house, and in time the old Cathedral, disappeared, and their site was chosen for the new church. In reality they possessed no architectural merit, and the thoughts of moving them had already occupied the mind of Bishop England before his death; he measured the ground and formed a plan for the building both of a church and the other adjuncts of a seminary and episcopal residence. Had God prolonged his life, this would have undoubtedly been the next, and probably the last undertaking; such had been his oft-expressed intention.

The ecclesiastical establishment was now transferred to the vacant convent building, the old seminary was remodelled and fitted up for a day-school for boys, which was sadly needed. The institute was well patronized, and flourished for a time, with Rev. Dr. Lynch as Principal, the Rev. Dr. Corcoran and other competent clergymen and seminarians as tutors. After three or four years, in 1850, it was discontinued; the class-rooms were deserted, only a few Catholic pupils remaining, scarcely sufficient to engage the time and attention of one teacher. When dependent on the patronage of non-Catholics for their maintenance, our literary institutions are doomed to a short existence, despite the ability and learning of the professors, and the flattering encouragement they receive at their first opening: Certainly the Catholic population of the city at this time, numbering about five thousand souls, was large enough to maintain at least one good school. Disguise it as we may, wealthy people dislike their offspring to mingle with the children of the poor in a class-room, or in any of the social realities of life; while the latter constantly complain of unjust discrimination in favor of the former.

The ranks of the clergy suffered no depletion during the administration of Bishop Reynolds. He discontinued the Seminary in 1851, and sent to Europe and to other colleges in this country promising young men, who, faithful to their vocation, returned after a few years thoroughly educated, and capable each of filling a professorship in any institution of learning in the land. Taking the positions assigned them, they became the faithful allies of the older clergy, worn out by toil and labor; in several instances they became pastors of churches, and conducted separate and important missions. In this manner we obtained as many clergymen as were needed, with supernumeraries; as many as fifteen young and active members were added to the number already in the diocese. This same course has been pursued ever since, and has proved to be a reliable means of maintaining the required number of clergymen.

During the first administration, Drs. Lynch and Corcoran were educated abroad; under Bishop Reynolds, Fathers Carr, McNeill, Patrick Kirby, and Flynn, with Drs. P. Ryan, J. P. O'Connell, and John Moore, now bishop. Dr. Reynolds became from the beginning a steady friend and patron of the Sisters of Mercy, preferring them to any other order of pious women in the Church. The Sisters sprang at once into a brighter existence, the sphere of their usefulness was enlarged, their capabilities of imparting instruction utilized, and their influence felt to the limits of the vast diocese. They fully met all the demands made on their charity, their intelligence, and their devotion to God and His Church. They were furnished with ample accommodation for all classes of pupils, inaugurated the day-schools, separated the orphan and boarding-school departments, with increased accomodations for their own growing numbers. Colonies from the mother house were sent to Savannah and to Columbia, the novitiate enlarged, and always a distinguished clergyman appointed chaplain. The veneration in which the order holds the memory of Bishop Reynolds is unbounded; they cherish him as their chief benefactor, after the founder. A leading feature in the American mind is to appreciate only what can be seen, and the people have adopted as national motto—"*Seeing is believing;*" hence their intensely outdoor character. Their passion for show and display, their religion, their education, and their pursuits lie in this direction; and at the first glance you see the best of any one. This is one reason why the active orders, the out-door religious who are seen in the streets, in the hospitals, in the schools, in the stores, are more popular and produce a better impression on the public mind in favor of Catholicity. Every man in the city becomes a protector and they can walk the streets at any decent hour, and receive every manifestation of respect, even from the bigoted and thoughtless.

Dr. Reynolds visited Europe in 1846, accompanied by Father Sullivan; he attended the National Council of this year, 1846, also of 1849 and 1852. He was a most faithful and vigilant bishop; his every thought, his energies, his whole soul were all absorbed by the interests of religion in his diocese. His episcopate was of short duration, and while in health he imitated his predecessor in toil and missionary labor. He visited the entire region, frequently administering Confirmation, reconciling difficulties, opening new missions, encouraging the clergy by word and example; for whose detachment, humility, and zeal he expressed the most unlimited admiration. He assured the writer that the pastor of any church in any Northern city was better provided with worldly goods than the Bishop and all the priests of the diocese of Charleston united. He preached well, and at all points, in season and out of season. His labors will be more amply detailed in their regular order in the following pages. He was an able, sincere, and eloquent speaker; his conversational powers were rarely surpassed. He studied the subject well and thoroughly, presented it in all its most striking aspects, and was exhaustive. He frequently preached controversial discourses, and I regarded his sermons on the "Real Presence," on "The Church," and on "Confession," unsurpassed by any one for close reasoning, fervid eloquence, and pathos. He was of a highly nervous temperament, increased by obesity, and the oppressive heat of a Carolina sun; he frequently preached for an hour or an hour and a half, with unceasing energy, never allowing the interest of his audience to relax, keeping it at high tension, and bearing away the admiration and sympathy of his hearers. It is doubtful if there was in America, during his prime and vigor, a greater pulpit orator.

Preparatory to the commencement of his long-cherished work, the Cathedral, and to secure more time and leisure for the undertaking, he obtained the consent of the fathers of the National Council for a division of the diocese in 1850. Georgia was erected, and very Rev. F. X. Gartland, V. G. of Philadelphia, was created the first Bishop. This act greatly advanced the cause of religion in the State. It was the most promising portion of the diocese, and under the succession of pious bishops, has far outstripped in growth the parent stock. Fathers Barry, Whelan, O'Neill, Sr. and Jr., Kirby, Duggan, E. O. Quigly, and James O'Neill, eight priests, become henceforward the subjects of the new Bishop.

Dr. Reynolds regretted having made the separation after some time; the number of places for clerical appointments were limited, and but few desirable missions left; which naturally engendered a spirit of discontent among his priests. Beyond the city of Charleston there were but three missions capable of giving a very slender support to a priest: these were Columbia, Wilmington, and Raleigh. At this period there could not have been over eight thousand Catholics in the diocese of Charleston, including both Carolinas, and about four thousand in Georgia. The civil war and slavery rendered the increase both slow and moderate; still, despite of these obstacles, they have advanced, and ere long the numbers will be reckoned by tens of thousands. The removal of the Seminary, of the Ursuline Convent, and the failure of the Literary Institute, and the separation of the State of Georgia from the diocese, limited the area of the Bishop's labors, and he commenced to build the Cathedral. J. M. Keilly was the architect. It was finished in about three years; the materials were cut red stone, imported by shipping from Vermont or Connecticut, at great expense, and hewn in Charleston; bricks would have been cheaper, and resisted the action of the subsequent fire better; the stone peeled off in slices and seemed as brittle as 'crusted sand; the style of architecture was Gothic or English ornamental, with a basement for the daily Masses. It cost about sixty or seventy thousand dollars, and was the handsomest church edifice in the Southern States; it was one hundred and fifty feet in length, seventy-two feet in breadth, and the spire two hundred and fifty feet high. It was begun in May, 1850, and consecrated April 6th, 1854. It was consecrated by Bishop Gartland, who sang the Mass; Bishop Reynolds, McGill, and Poitier, with all the clergy in the diocese, were in the sanctuary. Archbishop Hughes preached an able discourse on the authority of the Church, and eulogized the new structure in deserved terms. He had, he said, travelled far and near, and had admired many churches, both in the Old and New World, for magnificence of design, size, and space, but a more perfect specimen of architectural beauty, for its proportions, he had rarely seen. The fault found with it among the masses was, that it offered no accommodation for the poor people: the style forbade the use of galleries; a thousand people would fill it to its utmost capacity.

Few now living could have raised the sum necessary for its erection but Bishop Reynolds. He toiled late and early, begged all over America, in Europe, in Cuba, everywhere; and how he succeeded in obtaining the requisite sum is a wonder, yet the episcopal household suffered no detriment in the ordinary necessaries. The Secretary, Father Sullivan, assured me that when he wanted a dollar he knew where to find it.

I have not seen the accounts, but on a careful calculation, I have concluded that he expended about one hundred thousand dollars in the diocese within the short period of eleven years. Bishop England left a debt of $34,000, besides just annuities of $650. During the administration of Dr. Baker $20,000 were liquidated. Bishop Reynolds paid the remaining $14,000, with the annuities. The Cathedral may have cost about $70,000. The publication of the works of Bishop England entailed another weighty expense. The aid afforded the Orphan Asylum, poor missions, and the Seminary must have been considerable. Add to these, the amount paid for the new Cemetery of St. Lawrence, and the sum could scarcely be short of the amount indicated. There were scarcely any wealthy Catholics in the diocese; with the exception of $20.00 subscribed for the building of the Cathedral, his only resources were the pew rent and Sunday collection of his own church proper. He left no debts worth mentioning.

The Bishop's table was always abundantly supplied with healthy, substantial food. The students, clergy, Bishop, all sat at the same table, for he was like a father in the family, and delighted to be in their midst. After the reading, the conclusion of the meal was always graced by a scientific or other literary conversation,—chemistry frequently, a department in which the Bishop excelled; he often declared he would continue to use candles until people discovered how to burn water instead of gas, as St. Francis Xavier did in India. The Church was nearly free from debt; it was the burden of the administration: all thoughts, labors and movements were concentrated on this object. It was determined, and the accomplishment cost the Bishop his life. He had worn himself out, his nervousness increased, and he did not live long to enjoy the reward of his labors on earth. God mercifully spared him the pang of witnessing their destruction. Within a few short years, about six, that gorgeous pile, the pride of the city of Charleston, intended to remain always a monument of the zeal and energy of its founder, was burned to the ground, and scarcely a stone remained on another to mark the desolation. The flames in their fiendish fury shivered into fragments the very flags that covered the Bishop's tomb close by, and bared the interior again to the light of day. After all, it is only the good intention that has merit or value before God; it confers martyrdom without the sword, justifies the sinner in the Sacrament of Penance, and bestows heaven on one incapable of any bodily effort. It is the gold of human acts, and all besides is dross. That the Bishop now enjoys the reward thereof none who knew him doubts.

During the progress of the work on the Cathedral, four other churches were put up in the diocese, and the Bishop contributed somewhat to their erection; the church in Wilmington, built by Rev. Thomas Murphy, one in Charlotte, one in Chester, and another in Sumter by the writer. They still exist, like the humble and unknown in the daily walks of life, who are often spared when the shafts of death are sped with unerring certainty against the powerful and great in the high places of the world. Plain and humble churches are best suited for all the interests of religion in poor dioceses. The policy of Cardinal Manning is worthy of imitation, in refusing to inaugurate the inception of the monumental Cathedral in the city of London until ample provision would be made for the support of the orphans and the religious education of the children of the poor, who are in danger of losing their faith in the Godless schools of the huge metropolis. Time and the vicissitudes of human affairs have laid many a costly church edifice in ruins; even sees formed by the

Apostles have disappeared under the combined action of heresy and war, but the temple of one soul remains forever.

Of the many contributions, there was one which the Bishop prized beyond all others. A colored preacher by the name of Thornton, quite a clever fellow, was the servant in waiting around the premises. Busily occupied during the week, he prepared for his own sermons by attending and listening attentively to the Bishop's, impressed the leading points on his memory, and preached them over at his meeting-house in the Sunday afternoons. If a doubt or difficulty presented itself to his mind, he applied for explanation to the original. Controversy gradually arose and was maintained for a considerable time between himself and Preacher Reynolds, as he styled the Bishop. It terminated in his conversion, unlike many such discussions. He was baptized, instructed, and practised all the duties of religion fervently until the hour of his death, which was truly edifying. Thrifty and saving, he had carefully garnered all the earnings of a long life, which amounted to some few hundred dollars (probably five), and he bequeathed it to the last dime to the Bishop, for the building of the Cathedral. Preacher Thornton's gift was ever gratefully remembered.

Bishop Reynolds held the memory of his great predecessor in high esteem, which he testified by collecting his scattered writings and publishing them in five octavo volumes, with an able and suitable preface. They were compiled chiefly from the pages of the *Catholic Miscellany*, with great pains and diligence, by Dr. Lynch and Father Huet, a young priest recently ordained, who had made his preparatory studies in the Seminary, and was formerly a minister in the Episcopal Church. This publication cost a very large sum, and was a heavy drain on the diocesan fund; the subscription did not meet the full expense of publication. If the compilation had not thus been made at this time, most of the writings of Bishop England would have been lost, as the sources from which they were derived were destoyed by the subsequent conflagration.

The Bishop's health had been gradually declining for

nearly two years before his last sickness. He complained of an abiding pain in the chest, which his physicians called *congestion of the lungs.* His death was caused by overwork. During eleven years in the episcopacy, he allowed himself no rest; body, mind, and brain were constantly on the strain. Being of a highly nervous temperament, what to others would be trivial, was to him a burden and source of great pain; one thought often engrossing all his mental powers to the exclusion of all others. He never avoided an obligation; preached and performed all his functions like a martyr, and succumbed only to the stroke of death. He was a man of strong faith and tender piety, constant in prayer and meditation, in frequenting the holy tribunal of penance, choosing the humblest priest as his confessor. He was every morning at the altar as long as he could stand, and at an early hour; first in all the exercises of religion and devotion. He was a great bishop, a grand missionary priest, loved God and His Blessed Mother, advanced the interest of religion, wore himself out in the service of his Maker, and sacrificed his life for the diocese of Charleston.

He almost doubled the number of priests, created a new diocese, elevated the order of Sisters to a high standard of usefulness, built a splendid Cathedral, administered the offices of his diocese like a faithful steward, left other monuments of piety and zeal; accomplishing all in less than a dozen years. Confined a long time to his bed of sickness, he frequently received the Sacraments, was visited by Rev. Dr. Ryder, the distinguished Jesuit father, and received the Holy Unction with great devotion and resignation. The clergy, the Sisters of Mercy, and the Catholic laity were untiring in their ministrations, and he died mid the regrets of a grateful people. He calmly expired at the episcopal residence, on the 9th of March, 1855, in the fifty-seventh year of his age and the eleventh of his episcopacy. His obsequies were performed by Archbishop Kenrick, and a well-merited eulogy pronounced on the occasion by Rt. Rev. Dr. McGill, of Richmond.

He was buried by the side of Bishop England. He transmitted the see of Charleston to his successor without any debt, and without leaving a stain on her fair name or on the episcopal character. He made some mistakes in the commencement of his administration, but few who have worn a mitre have not done so. The most serious was the removal of the Ursuline Convent to another diocese. In his own mind he was justified by the consideration of their limited patronage, the fitness of the Sisters to educate every class of girls, and the necessity of a suitable residence for the clergy, when the building of the new Cathedral necessitated the removal of the old and weather-beaten shanties. No public man can hope to please every body; there is no bishop whose administration is in all respects blameless, and passes uncensured by priests and people. The Pope is as liable as others of his order to make mistakes in the administration of the diocese of Rome.

Bishop Reynolds was blamed for his participation in an immigration scheme. Out of gratitude to the memory of the prelate through whose ministry it pleased the good God to impart to me, unworthy, the ineffable grace of the priesthood, I feel justified in giving my readers the exculpating facts of the case. While doing so, I deprecate any intention of impugning the motives of the complainants. General A. H. Brisbane, a native of the State, was educated at West Point, an accomplished scholar, and a commander of first-class abilities. A company of Irishmen in Charleston volunteered for the Florida war, and were attached to his command. They were all Catholics but one; they prepared for the perilous Indian warfare amid the swamps by the reception of the Sacraments of Penance and Holy Communion, were blessed by Bishop England, and received, at the moment of their departure, each man a cross to be worn on his person. General Brisbane assisted at the ceremony, and was deeply impressed. The dashing boldness of the chief officer, and the hereditary bravery of the men, led them into the thick of the fray, and placed them always in the gap of danger. Several men of the other commands had lost their lives from the malaria of the country, camp diseases, and the arrow of the aborigines.

After the surrender of Osceola, and the war had ended, General Brisbane led back the volunteers in safety to the old Cathedral to make thanksgiving for their preservation, which was considered miraculous; only one man was lost—the non-Catholic Irishman. The garments of many were riddled with balls. The General and his lady, who was a Miss White, were conducted to the Faith, and professed it until death with unabating fervor. Having survived her husband, who died about the year 1851, she became an Ursuline nun under the name of Sister Borgia, and died at the convent, near Columbia, about the year 1872.

The General became proprietor of a vast tract of land in Baker, Dooly, and Early Counties, in Southern Georgia, probably a remuneration for his military services. He fostered the idea of making it a great Catholic colony, planted a tall cross in the center, and dedicated the territory to St. Ignatius about 1837. He introduced a number of Irish laborers, commenced and finished a railroad about forty miles long through the entire length of the domain, and terminating in Albany, on Flint River. He even had cars in running order constructed on block wheels. His idea was to bring the cotton trade of the Gulf States into Savannah by this route. The gigantic strides of railroad progress a few years later defeated his project and labors, and even isolated the locality more than ever. Remunerated only by the worthless railroad stock, the laborers suffered great privations, were in need of the necessaries of life, and many died from want and sickness. Rev. James Graham, the missionary priest, contracted the terrible Georgia chills in this manner, and soon after died at Macon under a renewed attack.

After the railroad project was abandoned the General turned his exclusive attention to the founding of a Catholic colony. Sincere and honest in his intentions, but warm and enthusiastic, he persuaded the Bishop to adopt his opinions, and add the sanction of his name and influence to the plan of colonization. The name of a bishop is a great power; it is, to a certain extent, the approbation of the Catholic Church in recommendation of a project, a treatise on religion, or a book of devotion. Without this *Imprimatur*, a prayer-book, a catechism, the simplest book treating on religion, should be cautiously eschewed by the laity.

Under this unquestionable guarantee, precluding the least suspicion of fraud or deceit, an immigration office was opened in Liverpool, under a Mr. Keilly. Relying on the truth of the statements contained in the printed circulars, quite a number of Catholics were induced to accept the terms, paid their passage, and embarked for this country. Like the Israelites, they sent a spy before them to examine the nature of the soil, the character of the climate, and all other questions of vital importance to the immigrant. The report was very unfavorable; the people felt disappointed; some were in Charleston, and others in the Northern Atlantic cities, but all said that they were deluded and deceived, that the Bishop's name and letters attached to the document were the cause, and they demanded restitution. He assisted them as far as he was able.

After having carefully preserved the circular, I found the statements made were all correct, with the exception of high coloring, the mark of a sanguine disposition and an earnest mind, convinced of the fundamental truth of the statement, and eager to impress the same ideas on others. Colonization schemes, like match-making, are rather a dangerous experiment, and at best a thankless undertaking. The prime mover will invariably be made the scapegoat for all future disappointments, for which he is not to blame, and which have their origin in the faults of the colonists. Bishop Byrne in Arkansas, and many other worthy ecclesiastics, made the experiment to their loss and inconvenience, and few have escaped blame. The colonists require maintenance, not only during the first year, but always, and frequently regard the disbursement of the purchase money a mere injustice; in short they are never satisfied. It is better that they themselves select their location; they will then appreciate any assistance, work more steadily, and if they fail, they have none to blame but themselves for the imprudence or neglect. Georgia and the section in question offer better advantages to immigrants than any of the Western States; the failure of the enterprise is to be regretted for many reasons. Not only success, but defeat, when the intention is good, have merit before God. The failure of the enterprise detracts no more from the reward of Bishop Reynolds than the loss of his Cathedral by fire, shortly after his death. I know one religious in this community who daily offers his life in defence of any of the prerogatives of our Blessed Lady. Who knows what crown he may receive in recompense? It is the proper intention that causes a mere vulgar assassination or execution to become a martyrdom.

The descendants of the Huguenots entertained a deep respect for Bishop Reynolds. It is a great mistake to call South Carolina a Huguenot settlement; they were the least in number of all the original colonists, as may be seen by the writings of the late Gilmore Simms. A small number of those people settled in the vicinity of Port Royal and soon spread over Edisto Island; their names and occupations are on record, and they were ordinary immigrants from France, and under no necessity of leaving their native country, save to better their condition, like all other European immigrants. Except in identity of sentiment and opinion, they have as little connection with the massacre of Bartholomew's Day, as Lafayette, Beauregard, or Stephen Girard, There is nothing in the annals of history more false than the attempt to implicate the Catholic Church in that crime; she had as little to do with it as with the roasting of Michael Servetus by Calvin, or the tin Walsingham boots in which Queen Elizabeth cooked with boiling oil the feet of Archbishop Healy and the other Irish Prelates before hanging them. It is evidently absurd to charge the Church with crimes which she condemns and abhors, no matter by whom perpetrated. Whether, as the best historians prove, only less than a hundred, instead of many thousands, as is falsely asserted, perished, it makes no difference; the principle is the same, the Catholic Church equally abhors the act, and had no participation in producing it.

The French descent of Bishop Reynolds on the maternal side endeared him considerably to that nationality, irrespective of party differences throughout the diocese. None of his sermons are published. His pastorals and letters on mixed marriages spread over the pages of the *Miscellany* are excellent specimens of composition, glowing with pathos and piety, and were universally admired. Slumbering side by side with his great predecessor in the episcopal city, may they be now seated in heaven, one at the right hand and the other at the left, of the Master whom they served so faithfully on earth!

Bury me not in Egypt, was the mandate of the dying Patriarch to his regal offspring. The Church at all times has manifested deep concern for the resting-place of the remains of her deceased children. In this spirit Bishop Reynolds provided a burying-ground for the Catholics of Charleston. There was no other work which endeared him more to the minds of the people; it stands a monument to his zeal and paternal solicitude for his flock, more durable than brass, marble, or our Cathedral pile. For generations the bodies of our dead were interred either at St. Mary's or St. Patrick's, sufficiently large to form only a few family grave-lots. They had become so crowded that the opening of fresh graves was an outrage both to the living and the dead. The city had provided the Magnolia, and though large enough for the accommodation of her dead for centuries, the Bishop could not purchase a section of it at a reasonable price for the Catholics. Like his predecessor, he never allowed his necessities to be made a means of extortion or unjust exaction. With his usual indomitable energy and confidence in God, he immediately purchased a large body of land, adjacent and nearer to the city, fenced it round save on the side close by the ocean's swell, erected the tall central Cross, consecrated it with great solemnity under the title of ST. LAWRENCE'S CEMETERY. Thus like the Good Shepherd he saved the souls of his people while living, and provided a resting-place for their bodies after death. Slumbering close by, the Atlantic will murmur a requiem over shepherd and flock, until that morning when ranging them in that radiant procession, they will be presented by him to their common

Father and God. The see of Charleston will always be proud of this golden link in the chain of her succession.

Rt. Rev. Patrick N. Lynch, D.D.,

Is the third Bishop and present incumbent of the see of Charleston, was raised in Cheraw, S. C., and born of edifying Catholic parents. The venerable Father O'Neill, of Savannah, discovering a vocation in the stripling, nurtured by pious parents, conducted him to the city and entered him as a student in the Seminary of St. John the Baptist in the early years of the administration of Bishop England; who after some brief period of time, sent him with Dr. Corcoran to Rome to be educated in the Propaganda. After having made the due course of studies, with distinguished ability, he graduated with great honor, and was decorated with the degree of Doctor of Divinity. Ordained priest in 1840, he repaired to Charleston and was stationed at the Cathedral, where he officiated until the death of the Bishop in 1842, and through the administration of Very Rev. R. S. Baker, until the nomination of Bishop Reynolds in 1844. He was editor of the *United States Catholic Miscellany* for some years, and had acquired favorable notoriety by his masterly and mild controversy with Rev. D. Thornwell, of the South Carolina College, and in which he defeated his antagonist in the estimation of men who could not mistake sophistry and asperity for argument. The new Bishop appointed him pastor of St. Mary's Church, principal of the Collegiate Institute, and also Vicar-General. All these offices he filled with ability and credit to himself. He also superintended, in a great measure, the work on the new Cathedral.

After the demise of Rt. Rev. Dr. Reynolds in 1855, the Vicar-General was confirmed as Administrator of the vacant see, which he was called to occupy in March, 1858, and was consecrated by Archbishop Kenrick in Charleston on the 14th day of March of the same year, assisted by Bishop Portier, of Mobile, Barry, of Savannah, and McGill, of Richmond, who delivered an admirable discourse on the occasion. The ap-

pointment of Bishop Lynch was received with acclamation
by clergy and laity. His administration fell on disastrous
times for the diocese of Charleston; the war of secession
was inaugurated in 1860; within a year a destructive fire commenced at the eastern section of the city, was driven by the
wind across its most populous portion, and finished its mad
course near the northwest terminus, leaving in its wake
a black streak through which General Sherman's army could
have marched, meeting few houses on which to practise
their favorite amusements. In its course it was the most eccentric conflagration ever witnessed. The new Cathedral,
the pride of the city, the residence of the Bishop and clergy,
the extensive diocesan library, and many a valued treasure
beside, were after a single night all things of the past. To
add still more to the calamity, the insurance policy on the
Cathedral building having expired, was not renewed after
expiration, through an oversight of the clergyman in charge
of this department of the domestic economy.

The city was deserted soon after by the inhabitants, during its bombardment by the Federal fleet. The State was reduced to beggary, and bordered on anarchy. There was
scarcely a good dollar to be found within its borders, and
the people were straitened for want of food or the com-
monest clothing. Misfortunes seldom come alone. Sherman led his army without remorse through the interior,
spreading ruin and desolation on all sides; and in the
conflagration of Columbia, destroyed St. Mary's College, the
Sisters' house, and the Ursuline Convent, established by the
Bishop at great labor and heavy cost, throwing the inmates
out into the flames.

Fire, famine, and the sword; not singly, but all at once,
plied their work of ruin, and left the diocese in a state of
poverty, wretchedness, and suffering unparalleled in any ecclesiastical district in the worldwide extent of the Catholic
Church. The Bishop, who had been on an honorable mission in France, in the interest of peace, returned, and immediately undertook to repair the losses as far as possible.
Under the most favorable auspices (as all who have tried it

will confess) begging is a most arduous and thankless task, and every dollar obtained is well earned. The human heart is a mine that reluctantly yields its golden treasures, and a man's purse is his weakest point.

The Bishop has been blamed for non-residence and prolonged absence, but facts will prove that it was in the interest of religion in his sorely-stricken diocese. The seaports of the North had been visited repeatedly, and many collections made, especially in New York. The Bishop's house in Broad Street, the Cathedral, the male orphan asylum, and new churches, must have cost a great deal of money and much labor. These, together with the increased number of clergy and religious, evince that, despite of all difficulties, the diocese of Charleston is now advancing, and is springing into life Phœnix-like from its ashes. In order to afford to the State of North Carolina all the benefits inseparably connected with the administration of a local bishop, he caused its erection into a vicariate in 1858, with the Rt. Rev. James Gibbons, D.D., as its Vicar-Apostolic.

He obtained the appointment to the see of St. Augustine as successor to Bishop Verot, of the Rt. Rev. Dr. Moore, whom he consecrated in Charleston in 1877.

Dr. Moore was born in Ireland, made his preparatory studies in the Seminary of St. John the Baptist, and was sent to the Propaganda by Bishop Reynolds, where he made the usual course of studies, and graduated as Doctor in Theology. After his ordination, he returned to the diocese about 1859, and was stationed at the Cathedral, where he faithfully discharged his duties until the death of Father P. O'Neile, the parish priest of St. Patrick's Church, whom he succeeded about the year 1863, and was appointed Vicar-General after the demise of Dr. Birmingham in 1872. He also had charge of the Boys' Orphan Asylum instituted by the Bishop, besides other offices of honor and trust. He is still a young man in the prime of life, and his election to the episcopacy was universally applauded. His zeal, learning, and spotless character render him a meet successor to the pious and devoted Bishop Verot. It is hoped that he will succeed in obtaining from the United States Government the Church property in St. Augustine, unjustly held.

Since his first return from Rome, Dr. Lynch attended all the National Councils held in Baltimore up to the time of his consecration, as theologian, and since then as Bishop, and was one of the Fathers of the late Council of the Vatican, leaving his mark on each for learning and dignity. He has written learned essays on a variety of interesting subjects, universally admired for literary research, clearness, and purity of language, and adaptation to modern advancement in science and learning. Though not as exhaustive as Bishop McGill, nor as gorgeous as Bishop England as a pulpit orator, Bishop Lynch is not surpassed by either in grand simplicity. A good personal appearance is a necessary qualification for a public speaker. With a tall, full, and senatorial mien, the hoary honors of many years in the priesthood circling his brow, and absolute self-possession, his first appearance raises the expectation of his listeners and conciliates their favor. His discourses are methodical and dry at the commencement, and his expressions quaint; as he advances, the lines extend, embracing the subject in its comprehensiveness, and exhibiting as in a panorama all its leading features, in strong language, unencumbered by useless ornament. Ready for great occasions and great subjects, he always utters great truths, and cannot be commmonplace. His letters on the Vatican Council, published in the *Catholic World*, are the most learned and ample description in English of that greatest event of the nineteenth century. The articles on our Lord's divine nature and on the standing miracle of the Church, the liquefaction of the blood of St. Januarius at Naples, are unsurpassed as essays; while his discourse on the occasion of the translation of the remains of the deceased Bishops of Boston breathes the air of the Catacombs, and will be admired long after he too, with mitre and pastoral staff, will be crumbled to dust. It is unnecessary to enlarge on the subject, for this generation; the Bishop is still strong and vigorous, and will most likely be able to speak for himself many years yet to come.

An additional cause of embarrassment was the payment of the money intrusted to his keeping by the Irish Catholic poor at the commmencment of the civil war. The subsequent worthlessness of the Confederate money, the loss of all resources throughout the entire South, and his diocese more especially, rendered this strictly a debt of honor; he has met many of the demands, and others too equally urgent and uncompromising. High destinies have corresponding pains; doubtless he has suffered much and has much to condone; being occasions of merit, all are blessings, and the grace of God can render a man equal to them. He will be met further on in these pages, as we pass through human life on our journey to the grave.

The author is indebted to an esteemed correspondent for the following notice of the Bishop's family, which possesses great interest and edification for the reader.

"Among the early Catholic settlers in South Carolina may be reckoned Mr. and Mrs. Conlaw Peter Lynch. When they landed in Georgetown, South Carolina, in 1819, there was but *one Catholic priest* in the State, and they had to carry their infant to Charleston to have it *baptized* by Rev. Dr. Gallagher.

"The town of Cheraw is situated at the head of navigation on the great Pedee River—was just mapped out and about to be incorporated by the Legislature. It suddenly became an important place, recommended to the planters on the river for its healthfulness, and became the best cotton market for the back country and North Carolina.

"Governor Wilson, of Georgetown, recommended this locality to Mr. Conlaw Peter Lynch, and gave him letters of introduction to General Harrington, of Marlborough. Mr. and Mrs. Lynch were very young, and had married contrary to the will of Mrs. Lynch's father, for which reason he disinherited her. This, with other painful circumstances, caused the young people to bid adieu to happy scenes of childhood and emigrate to America.

"In the spring of 1819 they took passage on the first steamboat that ascended the great Pedee River, but as the waters of the river were then low the boat ran aground near Marr's Bluff. The delay and exposure threw Mr. Lynch into a slow nervous fever, from which he should have died on the boat, had not Major and Mrs. Pouncey had him brought to their own mansion out in the Piney woods, and for six weeks bestowed upon him every necessary care and attention. Mr. and Mrs. Lynch never wearied of speaking with gratitude and affection of Major and Mrs. Pouncey and family, to whose great kindness they were so deeply indebted. Upon Mr. Lynch's recovery he sent Governor Wilson's letter to his brother-in-law, General Harrington, who sent a conveyance for them. Eventually Mr. and Mrs. L. reached General Harrington, but the delay and lateness of the season rendered business arrangements somewhat unsatisfactory. After extending the courtesies of his home to the travellers for a few days, the General secured a house for them in Cheraw, at Mr. Lynch's request. In those days there were few houses in the newly laid-out town, and those were built entirely of wood, something novel to Mr. and Mrs. L., accustomed to the stone-wall dwellings in Ireland. Mr. Lynch was fortunate in having secured from the beginning of his career the friendship of such gentlemen as Governor Wilson, General Harrington, and Major Pouncey.

"Now that our young people had selected a home for life in this remote place, they looked around to choose a site whereon to build; and Mr. L. immediately employed carpenters to do the work for him. In his delicate state of health after the fever, Mr. L. enjoyed the fresh pine, joined the workmen in their labors, and soon saw a handsome wooden house erected in the west end of town. From that time his health grew more stable, though never robust, and by the advice of his physician he continued to work in pine wood. This he did with success, always employing good workmen, and himself studying architecture and building. In 1820 the diocese of Charleston was established, and Rt. Rev. Dr. England brought out priests from Ireland and began the onerous labors of his diocese. But it was several years before he was able to send a priest to Cheraw. At length he sent one up into the country, and Mr. and Mrs. Lynch had *four children baptized* at one and the same time. There was not another Catholic for miles around, and had Mr. and Mrs. L. commanded less esteem it would be difficult to say what ideas would have been entertained respecting them as *Papists.* One man actually walked two miles after attending a camp-meeting, just to see a Papist, and whether he had the veritable "hoofs and horns." But after some conversation, during which Mr. L. noticed his scrutinizing glances, the man very pleasantly explained himself to Mr. L., who had quite won his heart.

"Happily Mr. L. was well versed in history and possessed a wonderful chronological memory, and could quote Scripture, chapter and verse, equal to any parson, and far more accurately than many; so that in controversy he was always ready for any argument, and by his quick Irish wit and pleasant manner could say much on doctrinal truth without ever offending. Indeed, he was never known to have an enemy.

"Mr. and Mrs. L. assembled their numerous little family regularly for prayer, and were most edifying and exact to instruct them in the truths of the Faith. On Sundays, in order to impress their children with respect for the Lord's Day, Mrs. L. was accustomed to dress them in their best clothes as if they were going out to church; then they were assembled for Mass-prayers; after which were read the Lives of the Saints. All spent the day very religiously at home, and with a quiet happiness, and in the afternoon Catechism class was held, and a prize given to the best in class and controversy.

"Thus were those children taught at a very early age to silently shun heresy, and at the same time to learn a reason for the Faith that was in them. When the priest came again to visit Cheraw he found the children well prepared for the *Sacrament of Penance*, and expressed the highest admiration for so well regulated and governed a household.

"The priest's visit of a week or ten days was always a happy epoch in this family—whether it was the Rev. Father

Stokes, or the Rev. Father O'Neill, or Rev. Father Birmingham, from Columbia, S. C., or Rev. Father McGuinness and Father Wheelan, from Fayetteville, N. C., or Rev. Father Murphy from Wilmington, N. C.,—all met a most cordial and respectful welcome—the children clustered around them to receive their blessing, and also words of encouragement and judicious praise, together with "bon-bons" and some pious souvenirs. How happy were they to merit such from the Rev. Fathers! Mr. L. could pour out his heart in sympathy to such a congenial friend and spiritual adviser—the best board was spread to refresh the fatigued missioner, who travelled in an open buggy from place to place, and was often tired, and hungry, and drenched with rain. Mrs. L. with motherly instincts renovated the scanty wardrobe of the saintly priest, and like the Sunamitess, represented his wants to her husband. They rightly esteemed the blessings beyond all price, which came to themselves and family with the priest's visits, and Mr. L. would have thought less than $10 a poor offering to a priest as a small token of gratitude, and only wished his means were commensurate with his desires.

"Not only the priest, but every one, was struck with admiration on seeing such a numerous family of healthy, intelligent children so united and loving among themselves, so devoted and obedient to their parents. What was it that gave such an uncommon tone to this family? *Religion.* Those children saw in their parents religion, fidelity, self-sacrifice, union, and all those beautiful domestic virtues which elevate the home circle and ennoble it. Hence, respect and obedience were easy and spontaneous.

"Mr. and Mrs. L. soon began to feel happy and proud in hearing the encomiums of the children from their schoolteachers, who pronounced them the most obedient and intelligent students under their charge, and they were often amused to find their eldest son mounted in his father's armchair, which he had wheeled around for a pulpit, holding forth to his delighted audience of little brothers and sisters. This was indeed an adumbration of the future. At length,

Rt. Rev. Bishop England made the visitation of his diocese, and on arriving at Cheraw was charmed to meet in this up-country a true Irish-toned family, so congenial, and his praises of their admirable domestic government were enthusiastic. The Bishop proposed that Mr. L. would send his oldest son Patrick to his own classic school in Charleston. Already there seemed to spring up between the illustrious Bishop and the youth those warm feelings which attract towards each other, persons of great disparity of age, and which are prompted by a profound respect and confidence on one side, and almost paternal affection on the other. The good Bishop already discerned in the youth a vocation to the priesthood.

"Mr. Conlaw Lynch's family are "the Lynchs of Galway," and the traditions of his family tell much of their sufferings in the cause of Faith and country, and many of them were self-exiled rather than endure the wrongs inflicted on their native and beloved Isle, and those remaining at home had founded Burses or Scholarships in the Irish College in Paris, that their sons might enjoy the advantages of education denied them at home. The great Liberator, Daniel O'Connell, had not effected Catholic emancipation when Mr. and Mrs. L. left Ireland. From time immemorial it was a pious custom in Mr. L.'s family, to consecrate the first-born to Almighty God, and while this was never mentioned to the child, the parents were only too happy if a vocation developed itself and verified to them that their offering was accepted by the Most High. Now Mr. and Mrs. L. were truly happy at the choice made by their first-born son—a choice wholly spontaneous and uninfluenced.

"Mrs. Eleanor McMahon Neillson Lynch was the daughter of Sue McMahon, cousin of Marshal McMahon, the present ruler of the French nation.

'In her youth she had often seen the indignation of her family aroused by the action of the Orange party, but the most appalling scene of her young life was to see struck down by the hand of an Orange hireling, her uncle, Hugh McMahon. It was but the work of a terrible moment. Scarcely had the fine, manly form of Mr. McMahon appeared on the platform, when the air was filled with cheers from the vast crowd which he was about to address ; he raised his hand in response to the salutation, when the assassin rushed upon him, plunged a dagger into his heart, turned, dashed into the crowd, and was lost to view. The orator of the day, the handsome and gifted Hugh McMahon, staggered, should have fallen, had not a dozen brave arms upheld him. All was confusion. This awe-inspiring scene never faded from the memory of his niece, though then but a little girl in the arms of a servant-man, who proudly held her up above the crowd. The bier of her uncle was draped in crimson, and Hugh McMahon laid in state.

"Although the church and family burial-ground were three miles distant, bands of pall-bearers, each wearing broad sashes of crimson on their arms instead of black crape, claimed the honor of bearing his remains, and would not allow either hearse or horse. This scene of violence, and others perpetrated by the Orange faction in Ireland, were narrated in a hush of reverence for martyrs of the Faith, and the children grew up firm, strong Catholics, although possessing neither Catholic schools nor Church privileges. As their children advanced to the age of receiving Holy Communion Mr. and Mrs. Lynch sent them off to some good Catholic institution, where they could be properly instructed and prepared for this most important act of their young life, and Divine Providence blessed them in an extraordinary manner.

"When their children became of a *marriageable* age, these prudent parents resolved to save them the sufferings to which they themselves had been subjected, and entering into their views, assisted them in every way as far as was right and proper. They possessed the entire confidence and affection of their children, who, on their part, would have been unwilling to take any important step without the consent and blessing of their beloved parents.

"While Mr. and Mrs. L. spared no pains to make home attractive and lovable to the young people, they were very exacting concerning all the proprieties of life, and never would tolerate levity or familiarity of any kind, and required a respectful courtesy and Christian dignity at all times, and that the "sweet small courtesies of life" should never be neglected. Few and far between as were the Catholic families of the diocese, Divine Providence heard the prayer of those good parents, and not a single mixed marriage occurred in that large family, though many a mile had to be traversed by the young people, to find a suitable match, and that, too, in days when there were no railroads intersecting the States as now. Before Mr. and Mrs. L.'s numerous family of grown-up sons and daughters had begun to settle off, the priest used to visit Cheraw once or twice a year. On these occasions Mass was said in the parlor, where the few Catholics in the neighborhood assembled, but Mr. L. now proposed to build a church, and accordingly donated a handsome lot nearly opposite to his own dwelling. He began making collections among his friends, who were remarkably generous, although none of them were Catholics; and soon the work was in operation under his own direction, and never did he use his drawing-board and "T" square with so much pleasure. When the church was completed and the deeds placed in the hands of Rt. Rev. Bishop England, it was a happy day for Mr. and Mrs. L. The illustrious Bishop, who had always been a warm personal friend, and now counted their oldest son among his priests, felt happy to send Rev. Dr. Lynch to spend a week at a time with his family, when crowds assembled in the little Catholic church —"Saint Peter's"—to hear his eloquent sermons, and to renew an acquaintance which had been interrupted by an absence of six years at the College Propaganda Fide, Rome, Italy.

"Happy and proud were Mr. and Mrs. L. of their twelve children, as they saw them entering on their various duties and callings of life, respected and esteemed by their fellow-citizens, and putting in practice the lessons given them from their infancy. Theirs was a spirit of faith and loving trust in the mercies of the Lord. One of the many striking instances of how this spirit was rewarded, occurred about this time. It was decided by Mrs. L.'s physicians that she should go to Dr. Sims' celebrated hospital in New York. While Mrs. L. was fulfilling so well the duties of a mother, she denied herself all travel, and even visited her friends comparatively little, yet she made their visits to her home so agreeable, that she may be said to have enjoyed society. Mr. and Mrs. L. started for New York, travelled slowly, taking Baltimore in their way that they might visit their Carmelite daughter, who was the first nun Mrs. L. had ever seen. Archbishop Kenrick readily gave permission that the invalid mother could enter her daughter's monastery and cell. She was delighted with all she saw, spent the day very happily with her daughter and community, rested on the little hard bed of the Carmelite nun, congratulated her daughter on her happy choice, and bade adieu again, for the last time. Having arrived in New York they sent their letters of introduction from their son, Dr. John Lynch, to Dr. Sims, under whose skilful care Mrs. L. remained some two months, by which time she was entirely cured. During this trying period, not only Dr. Sims, but also his wife and daughters, spared no pains to render her time agreeable. Mr. and Mrs. L. returned home by steamer to Charleston, and thence started by railroad for Cheraw. A heavy rain had washed away the bridge near Society Hill, and trees were blown across the track. The cars were going at a rapid speed, and in the dark of the evening Mr. and Mrs. L. were saying their Rosary, as was their pious custom, when suddenly the speed of the cars slackened—a plunge was heard—a jolt—and all stopped. The locomotive had been thrown to one side off the track by a tree lying crosswise. Surely it was a miraculous escape! Several of the passengers got out, a crowd soon surrounded the cars, but all efforts to move the locomotive proved ineffectual. God be praised! The night had become very dark, so finally it was determined to wait till morning for further efforts. Some of the passengers slept quite comfortably in the cars (there were no Pullman's sleeping-cars in those days), while others, Mr. and Mrs. L. among the number, were invited to share the hospitality of families living on and near the road.

"Next morning the mercies of the Lord were made manifest to them, for had the cars run fifty yards further, all would have been precipitated through the broken bridge! That Rosary was never forgotten, but often repeated in gratitude to our Blessed Lady. After enjoying the kind hospitality offered them, Mr. and Mrs. L. procured a carriage, and in a few hours reached home in safety, in Cheraw.

"Mr. Conlaw Peter Lynch lived to the advanced age of eighty-one years, having enjoyed fifty-six years of married life, fifty-four of which he spent in Cheraw, where he was beloved and respected by all who knew him. He was the father of fourteen children, twelve of whom he reared to maturity.

"His remains lie interred in the family burial-ground, surrounded by his children, several of whom preceded him to the tomb. Such was the respect in which he and they were held, that horses were not allowed to bear his remains to the church. He died as he had lived, and was sustained by the Sacraments of Holy Mother Church.

"Mrs. Lynch survived her husband seven years, but could not live where he was not, and in view of their once happy home. She spent much of her time at the Ursuline Convent, Valle Crucis, where her granddaughters were being educated, and her daughter and granddaughter are nuns. Also at her son's, in Columbia—Dr. John Lynch. It was while on a visit to her son and family that she received her summons to join the loved ones gone before, in singing the mercies of the Lord for all eternity! She was truly the valiant woman, whose husband trusted in her, whose children rose up and called her blessed. Her remains repose for a time in the Catholic graveyard in Columbia, but will be removed to the family resting-place in Cheraw, and placed beside him for whom she gave up home and country, and to whom she was ever a devoted wife."

CHAPTER IV.

MISSIONS IN THE CITY OF CHARLESTON.

Charleston—An Apology—Self—Ordination—Rev. P. J. Coffey—State of Religion—Charleston before the Arrival of Bishop England—Necessity of an unbroken Succession—The first Catholics—Early Priests—First Church—Liberty of Conscience—A Compromise—Fathers Gallagher, Cloriviere, Keating, Fenwick, and Wallace—A Schismatical Congregation—Formation of the Hibernian Society—Bishop England—Fathers McEncroe, Hayes, Byrne, Duff, McCool, Brown, Birmingham, McGrath, D. J. Quigley, Tuig, Rodman—Dr. Corcoran—Rev. P. O'Neile—Dr. Moore—Fathers J. Tuigg, H. P. Northrop—Fathers L. Fillion, Nelligan, J. M. Gore—Rev. Chas. Joseph Croghan—Rev. Thos. F. Quigley—Dr. Patrick Ryan—Fathers Hackett, Philip Gillick—Rev. Mr. Shadler—St. Peter's Church (colored)—Fathers Vigueront and Hurley—Cheraw—Father John Cullinane—Rev. J. Kedney—Father Healy—Number of Priests from the Commencement—Many leave for Just Causes—An Exeat—The Diocesan Oath—Difficulty of obtaining New Missions—Humiliation, etc., etc.

THE missionary labors of the clergy affording no leisure for literary pursuits, the records of the diocese were very limited, and the few that existed having perished by the ravages of time, fire, and war, I possess but scanty written materials for compiling these sketches. In their absence, I am necessitated to substitute *a good memory*, and perpetrate the solecism of *quoting myself*. The reliability of the statements will gain force from the fact that they are the recollections of a residence of nearly forty years spent on the scene of action, and a missionary life of thirty-six years, stretching over all sections of the diocese in the three States. I form the connecting link between the past and the present. What I have not witnessed, I have received on reliable authority; there are living witnesses of the facts placed on record. I can however safely assert that few public events have occurred, either in the diocese or the States which it embraces, that have escaped my recollection.

For our better acquaintance, I will inform the reader, who may accompany me to the end of the journey, that I was born in County Cork, Ireland, on the Feast of the Presentation of our Blessed Lady, November 21st, 1821. I attribute all the singular mercies of my long life in the priesthood to this coincidence. My vocation did not come by human suggestion. It was formed at any early day. I recollect nothing in my life beyond it. Conducted to the parish church, I know not whether led or carried, I saw the aged priest, Father Cornelius Buckley, saying Mass. I then determined to become what he was, and this is the first recollection of my existence. I made the primary studies principally in the city of Cork. Recommended to offer myself for the priesthood to the diocese of Charleston by Miss England, the Superioress of the North Presentation Convent, and Sister Teresa Murphy, a relative, who died about 1843, after having been a professed nun over fifty years, Father Delany, the present Bishop of Cork, examined me in the languages, and guaranteed that I was instructed sufficiently to enter on the higher studies of Philosophy and Theology. Bishop England sent for me. Accompanied by my sister Julia, a candidate for the Sisters' convent, I arrived in Charleston in November, 1840, entered the Seminary immediately, and after four years, study, was ordained Priest on the 24th of May, 1844, being Pentecost Sunday. Apart from preparation for class, I discharged, while a seminarian, the several duties of senior student, presiding at the divine office, over all the religious duties, and exercising a subordinate supervision in general. I was sacristan for the Cathedral, and catechist; I superadded the instruction of slaves in their religion; teaching catechism and prayers when I had a moment to spare, and prepared several adults for Baptism and the other Sacraments. I recollect no work of all my life that now affords me more consolation.

My class-mates were John Francis Kirby and P. J. Coffey. We were ordained simultaneously, and the first on whom Bishop Reynolds conferred the Sacrament of Holy Orders. We studied theology under Dr. Baker, and were taught the rubrics by Rev. Dr. Corcoran, who had returned from the Propaganda within the year. Rev. J. F. Kirby was sent to Augusta as assistant under Father Barry. I was sent to Savannah in a like capacity under Father O'Neile. Rev. Mr. Coffey was stationed at Newbern, on an independent mission, being the oldest. He was about twenty-six years old, the other gentleman and I were each only a few days over twenty-two years and six months. Our ordination was deferred until we attained the extreme limit which the dispensation could reach. Mr. Coffey after some time was transferred to Columbus, Ga., where he had a very trying time. He assisted the Rev. Thomas Malony in his last moments, and discharged all his duties faithfully, until again restored to the North Carolina missions. He labored several years in the diocese. He was some time under Bishop Kenrick, and also served on the mission in his native country. He died in St. Francis Hospital, in Jersey City, in 1876, fifty-eight years old. He was diminutive in size, and barely saved his distance from canonical impediment in this respect; his chasuble and alb were nearly of equal length. He received marked kindness at the hospital during his last sickness, was fortified with all the Sacraments, and died in peace with his Maker. He had always cherished a lively devotion to our Blessed Lady. Such, Saint Alphonsus assures us, is a sign of perserverance and of salvation. In the Cathedral he would have been as efficient as another, and an ornament to the sanctuary; but he was physically unfitted for the onerous duties of a rough mission. Before entering the Seminary he was associated with Mr. Denman in the business department of the *Truth-Teller* and also taught in Father Barry's orphan school at Augusta, where he contracted the Georgia fever, and never after fully recovered from its effects.

The Bishop is standard-bearer of the Cross, and the first missionary, by virtue of his office. After receiving his mission from the Pope, the history of the Church in every region begins with his appointment and labors. *Wherever there is a Bishop, there also is the Church*, says one of the doctors of the early ages, even without a temple, a priest, or a congregation; because it is the grace of his order to create. Anterior to the formation of the see, there is generally a state of disorganization and uncertainty, not unlike the twilight that invests the origin of nations when the poet's fancy becomes the most authentic record. The conversion of a people, and the perpetuity of the Faith, are indissolubly attached, by Divine Providence, to the episcopal order. It has been so from the beginning. Whenever the succession has been interrupted, the Faith has failed. Persecution and heresy understand this very well; the first blow was aimed at the Bishop. "*Strike the shepherd, and the flock will be dispersed,*" applies equally to all times. This is the reason why, in proportion to their number, there are more bishops martyrs than priests. If the prelates had been as steadfast in Germany and England, at the time of the so-called Reformation, as they were in Ireland, and subsequently in France, religion had never perished in the former countries; for the masses of the people were always Catholic in heart. In Spain, in Africa, and wherever the Apostles had planted the Church, we read that the custom was, invariably to ordain bishops and priests to continue their work. If St. Francis Xavier had been able to adopt this plan, his labors and his missions would perhaps have been perpetuated, and India at this day might be Catholic. In religion, as in all things else, an order and fitness has been established by divine economy; and to the observance God attaches the blessing of success. He wishes that we should not only do His will, but also, in the manner that He willeth.

In colonial times, the Carolinas were under the jurisdiction of the Vicar-Apostolic of the London district. The history of the Church, after the descent of the Holy Ghost, begins with the preaching of two Apostles, with stripes on their backs; it begins in Charleston with two Catholics, clad in garments equally ignominious, and scarcely less painful. *In the year* 1775, *two Catholic Irishmen were tarred and feathered*, charged with the doubtful crime of tampering with negroes. The above is the first item in the history of Catholicity in the Carolinas, and will serve as a text for succeeding

FIRST MASS CELEBRATED IN CHARLESTON. 141

chapters to the close of the civil war; the act was significant, and the prophecy of her future life. The first Catholics were some poor Irish immigrants or redemptionists, a name by which they were called, who were unable to pay for their passage; they were apprenticed on their arrival to the planters, who reimbursed the captain for the expense of their transportation. The Italians as a body have ceased to be a missionary nation. The first Mass was celebrated in Charleston in the year 1786, by an Italian priest, chaplain on board a ship bound to South America, which put into the port and remained for some time. At the solicitation of a few Irishmen, he landed, said Mass in an humble abode, at which twelve persons assisted, and departed, after having consecrated the soil to Catholicity by the act. Like the grain of mustard seed, it grew, and the number of the faithful was soon after increased by the advent of some Maryland Catholics and a few refugees after the massacre in St. Domingo. An Irish priest named Father O'Reilly, on his way to the West Indies, for the benefit of his health, arrived two years after, and exercised his ministry in their behalf. The first church in this region was erected at Newberne by the Gaston family in 1790.

Bishop Carroll was consecrated, and the United States placed under his jurisdiction, by the Holy See. About this period Rev. Mr. Keating came to Charleston, and they began the work of acquiring a church. Remote from episcopal supervision, and at a distance of six hundred miles from the nearest priest, some unworthy men exercised the holy ministry in Augusta and other places, to the detriment of religion and the scandal of the faithful; like some unworthy men of German nationality, who returned from their wanderings to their native country in order to obtain preferment under Prince Bismarck, whether as priests or bishops, married or single, it mattered not. An antiquated Methodist meeting-house was bought in Hazel Street, fitted up for the celebration of the divine mysteries, and called St. Mary's.

At the commencement the colonies never contemplated a

separation from the mother country, much less the establishment of a republic; the idea was suggested in the course of events; the measure was due to the wisdom and patriotism of Washington and his compatriots. The freedom of religious worship, now guaranteed under the Constitution, was a matter of necessity. All the popular denominations were represented by those who framed the instrument. Mutual jealousy and rivarly forbade the formation of a State Church; the preference of one necessitated the rejection of the other aspirants, who had an equal right, and they dreaded the consequence of a choice. The question was wisely dismissed and all the citizens were secured in the right of what is called religious liberty, the privilege of adopting every system of belief, true or false, or none at all, according to conviction, taste, or fancy.

But the odious discrimination against Catholics was continued by nearly all, and abolished only after many years; it still disgraces the escutcheon of New Hampshire. It was removed in South Carolina in 1790, and in North Carolina so late as 1835, by the influence and labors of Judge Gaston. St. Mary's Church was incorporated by an act of the Legislature in the former year. In 1793 Very Rev. Simon Felix Gallagher, a very learned and eloquent priest, a native of Dublin, Ireland, was appointed to the care of the nascent church by Bishop Carroll. Elected a professor in the Charleston College, his salary relieved the poor congregation of the burden of his support. His memory is very much revered in the city. With him the duties of his priesthood were a primary consideration; he discharged them faithfully, and with much credit to himself, and to the advantage of religion. His father was professor of mathematics in the College of Maynooth, where the young Levite received his education. His organized the Hibernian Society in Charleston, framed the rules for its government, and it still exists, a very strong organization. His portrait adorns the hall; he is painted as a middle-aged man, of sacerdotal appearance, holding a ritual folded in a stole used for sick calls. I found a very learned pamphlet written by him, in defence of the Sacrament of Penance and refuting calumnies against the confessional. Bishop Carrol intended presenting him to the Holy See for appointment as first Bishop of Charleston; but that choice was decreed for another.

He was the Vicar-General for a long time; he removed to Savannah in 1817, and after some years went to New Orleans. He died about the year 1830, at Vicksburg. He removed the old wooden structure in Charleston and replaced it by a substantial brick building, which lasted until burned down by the conflagration of the city about 1838; after which the present edifice was constructed. The Rev. Mr. Keating was in Charleston in 1790, and returned to his diocese of Baltimore. The Rev. Mr. Cloriviere was sent hither by the Archbishop in 1812. He was born in Brittany, of a noble family, in 1768, and was a schoolfellow of Chateaubriand. He was an officer in the army of Louis XVI., embraced the Vendean cause, became a major-general under Cadoual. His family name was Limoeslaw. Having been implicated in the conspiracy against the First Consul, he made his escape, after long concealment, to the United States, and entered the Seminary at Baltimore in 1808. He was ordained priest in 1812, and set out for Charleston immediately, in order to resist the usurpation of the laity; after much labor he succeeded in removing many abuses, and returned to Baltimore in 1820, when the see was erected. Appointed superior, he mainly contributed to the establishment of the Visitation Order. He died of apoplexy in 1826, and is venerated as a holy priest, and one of the founders of the Church in the United States. There were two other priests whose names are unknown to the writer before the Bishop arrived. There was also the Rev. Le Mercine for several years—1811.

Dissensions sprang up about this time in the congregation, between the English or Irish and French members. Both parties had built the church in common; and now, one wished to assume the control of its affairs, to the exclusion of the other. The controversy waxed more bitter, and continued several years, baffling the efforts of the clergy at reconciliation, and defying the authority of the Bishop. In this way it became schismatical, and caused a general scandal against Catholicity. One of the two parties spoke English, and the other spoke French, each insisting on having the sermon preached in its own language, to the exclusion of the other. Each party refused to remain in the church while a sermon was preached in the language used by the other. At the request of Archbishop Marechal, two Jesuits, Father Fenwick, afterwards Bishop of Boston, and James Wallace, arrived in 1817, and by their prudence and tact restored peace. Before resorting to harsh measures, Father Fenwick tried gentle means, and succeeded in a great measure. The Unitarians boast that they are the most orthodox denomination in the country. They suit all individuals by granting each the privilege to believe as much or as little as he chooses; provided he let other people alone in their opinions. Acting moderately, on this principle, the Jesuit suited both parties, and made them friends. He preached in both languages, alternately, the French and English, in rapid succession. He remained a year after the arrival of Bishop England. Father Wallace never returned; he became a professor in the South Carolina College, and died in 1851.

"By the prudent administration, the zealous discharge of every duty, and the edifying manners of these gentlemen, and by removing some of the causes of previous irritation, much good was effected, the people were reunited, harmony restored, and the Sacraments regularly approached by many who had been long absent." Such is the testimony of Bishop England in favor of these Fathers. However, enough of the leaven of the old spirit still remained to harass the early days of his administration; it forced him to abandon the idea of constituting St. Mary's his Cathedral, and caused him to erect another. Henceforward we may easily ascertain the history of the clergymen officiating in the city to the present time. Some have been already noticed, and others are reserved until we meet them on their respective missions, in conformity with the plan of the writer, to narrate the leading details of each separately. Among the first priests ordained for the diocese was Father McEncroe about the year 1824; he officiated some time in the city, and left for the East. He became Vicar-General of Calcutta, and also Administrator; he lived up to a very recent period, probably until 1860. He was a learned, pious, and zealous priest.

Rev. James Hayes died September 8th, 1835, in the twenty-fifth year of his age, and soon after his ordination. Rev. Martin Duff, a sub-deacon, died September 8th, 1828, in the twenty-fifth year of his age. Their remains are entombed near the old Cathedral. There was also for several years a Rev. John Birmingham stationed in the city, a good and zealous priest. The Rev. A. Byrne, afterwards Bishop, was ordained in 1827, and immediately entered on the mission. Dr. Baker succeeded at the Cathedral in 1830, for several years. Rev. T. J. Sullivan from 1838 to 1860, was first assistant. The Bishop or Administrator is the only Pastor in the dioceses of the United States. Applied to priests, the word has not its proper canonical meaning; it is a term of courtesy. Among the first priests, and anterior to 1830, we find the name of Rev. Jerome McCool, who was considered a good preacher, but did not live long; he died suddenly.

Rev. Dr. Brown, an Augustinian Father, who had been in Augusta in 1808 before the formation of the diocese, labored a long time on that mission, was sent to Rome in its interest; after his return, he was stationed at St. Mary's for some years until his death, about 1838. The Rev. P. J. Dunn was a native of Ireland, and made his studies in the College of Maynooth, where he received ordination early in the present century. After having served on the Irish mission some years, he immigrated to the United States, and was invited by Bishop Kenrick, of Philadelphia, to take charge of St. Michael's parish in that city; this duty he performed with signal zeal and efficiency. His learned lectures on the controverted articles of faith, and his conspicuous labors for the advancement of the interests of religion rendered him odious to its enemies, and marked him as an object for special vengeance of the Knownothings, a distinction which he shared in common with the celebrated Dr. Morierty, O.S.A. In May, 1844, the infatuated mob burned St. Michael's to the ground, and sought the life of the pastor. Having escaped haply from popular rage thirsting for his blood, he tendered his services to Bishop Reynolds, and was received among the diocesan clergy in 1840. He was placed in charge of the Seminarians, and officiated in the Cathedral parish and on other missions in and around the city for a time. He also served in Augusta with Father Barry, until transferred to the North Carolina department, making Fayetteville his headquarters. Here his labors were widespread, and his fidelity unsurpassed. He withdrew about 1853 to his former field of priestly ministration in Philadelphia, leaving behind him a name deeply respected for piety, learning, and the strict observance of ecclesiastical obligations. He was pastor of St. John's Church in Philadelphia during several years, and up to the period of his edifying and happy death, which occurred about 1870. He was about seventy-five years of age, fifty years of which were spent in the holy ministry. He was circumspect and guarded in manners, an enlightened and devoted priest, edifying in the whole tenor of his life, and was an eloquent public speaker. He was also connected with the Catholic press, and his writings were vigorous and lucid. He honored his profession by his life. Bent down by years and labors, he died the death of the pure and holy. The Rev. Michael McGrath was a native of Kilkenny, and ordained about the year 1837. He never accepted a mission, nor other pastoral charges. He was of rigid views, taught school, and said his Mass for about ten years, when he removed to Boston, and was assistant at a church in Charlestown. He returned to his first love in 1852, taught about one year at the St. Mary's College, and withdrew to Ireland.

He was on the mission in the diocese of Cork, where he is reported to have died about 1860. Very Rev. Dr. Birmingham succeeded in 1866, after the death of Father Sullivan, he having paid the common debt in 1875. Very Rev. D. J. Quigley, ordained May 3d, 1866, now occupies the position, assisted by Rev. Fathers Tuigg and Redman. One of the first efforts of Bishop England was to educate a native priesthood to minister at the altars of religion. Notwithstanding the catholicity of the Church, after the conversion of a country she relies on the native-born to fill the ranks of the clergy, take the place of the first missionaries, and continue their work. The facilities of travel and national intercourse are so great that immigration must cease to set in continuously at any given point, and is already diverted from the United States to other regions, equally inviting. In fact, every man in this age possesses a cosmopolitan character. The Church must look to the native Catholic youth for her future ministers, notwithstanding their reluctance to undertake the obligations of the priesthood.

The Rev. James Andrew Corcoran, D.D., was the first native-born Carolinian ever ordained. He was born in Charleston, March 30th, 1820, during the mission of Fathers Fenwick and Wallace, and was baptized by the latter. Having lost his parents by sickness at an early age, his boyhood was directed under the care of his maternal aunt, Miss O'Farrell, subsequently Sister Magdalene, who died in the odor of sanctity, in the Convent of the Sisters of Mercy, about the year 1860. Bishop England sent the youth to the Propaganda, the first gift of the new diocese, when but fourteen years of age. He made his studies with signal ability, and was distinguished among the learned and great men of his time in College, who since have ruled the Church of God and guided her destinies in the conversion of the world. After having graduated with the first honors, he was ordained priest December 21st, 1842. After the Bishop's death in 1843, he hastened back to his native diocese, and consoled her widowhood with his labors and the treasures of his vast erudition. Acquainted with all modern languages and almost a second Mezzofanti, perhaps there is not living a man who knows Latin better. Distinguished alike in the mathematical and other scientific departments of learning, his reputation is world-wide.

He was Secretary for the Baltimore Provincial Councils of 1855-'58, and the Plenary Council of 1866, and was at most of the National Councils held for nearly twenty years; preparing for the sessions, arranging the matter, framing the decrees, reducing all to order and system, beginning anterior to the meeting and continuing after. His learning, his theological lore, and his moderation were appreciated by the Fathers of the American Church. They expressed their esteem by choosing him with a few others theologian, and the representative Doctor of the Church of the United States, at the General Council of the Vatican, where he shone amid the assembled wisdom, learning, and holiness of Christendom. His name is almost as familiar in the Patriarchates of the East and in the sees of Europe and America as in his own native *City by the Sea*, which is proud of him, and whose inhabitants, Catholic and non-Catholic, revere and cherish his memory. It is very well known that the influence of her own native-born priest calmed the troubled waters in the excitement created by Knownothings, and by the turbulent apostate Leahy. In the odious sense of the term, Archbishop Hughes was not more opposed to nativism than he.

In the estimation of reflecting men, he is still more admirable in his humble labors as a missionary priest. In 1844 he was appointed Professor of Theology in the Diocesan Seminary by Bishop Reynolds, and educated an able body of priests for the missions, to whom he is endeared by the most tender recollections. During fifteen years, he imparted as editor, a new impulse to the *United States Catholic Miscellany*, which rendered it formidable to the enemies of our holy religion and a welcome visitor to all family circles. His catalogue and critical notes in the Diocesan Library were universally admired by the learned. During a quarter of a century his labors in the diocese were various; as superior of the Sisters of Mercy, pastor at Sullivan's Island, assistant in the Cathedral, at St. Mary's, as Vicar-General, as pastor of Wilmington, he was always faithful, always zealous, always blameless; while his mild demeanor and unpresuming manners endeared him everywhere. He is as unassuming as a child.

When the yellow fever prevailed in Wilmington with fearful violence and unprecedented fatality, in 1862, accompanied by the self-sacrificing Sisters, and regardless of life, at the call of duty, he hurried on to the relief of the dying. Taking the place of the plague-stricken pastor, Father Murphy, who never fully recovered from the effects of the malaria, Dr. Corcoran remained to the end, and departed only after the blessings of health were restored. Like the high priest of old, he stood between the living and the dying, and offered up his own life in their behalf, if it pleased God to accept the sacrifice. The sword of the Angel of Death was sheathed, and the destroyer desisted from his deadly work after a time. On the subsequent death of the pastor in 1863, he assumed his office, and held that position for some years, and until the nomination of Dr. Gibbons in 1868 as Vicar-Apostolic of North Carolina. After his return from the Council of the Vatican, at the invitation of the Archbishop of Philadelphia, Dr. Corcoran accepted the chair of Professor in Theology in the Seminary of St. Charles Borromeo; a position which he now holds, dispensing among the rising priesthood of the extensive archdiocese all the ecclesiastical science of the see of Peter, the head and fountain of faith and morals, aided by a long experience in the various duties of a missionary life. It is to be regretted that the diocese of Charleston, like Ireland, educates so many worthy clergymen only for the Church beyond her borders, and that she does not reap the full benefit of their labors. Superior to all occasions, equal to every emergency, great in every position in which he was ever placed, whether in a college, a general council, or baptized unto labor by the black vomit of a poor dying Catholic immigrant; whether in the pulpit, or at the head of the press, Dr. Corcoran imbibed more of the spirit of 'Bishop England than any other man living. Pennsylvania is a wider field for his labors and abilities than his native State. He also edits the *Quarterly Review*. The following letter is so characteristic and expressive of the unostentatious disposition of the man, that its perusal will afford a pleasure to the reader; its publicity cannot be deemed a violation of the privacy of personal correspondence:

"ST. CHARLES SEMINARY, Overbrook, April 12th.

"MY DEAR FATHER O'CONNELL,—I was born in Charleston, March 30th, 1820, and was baptized by the Rev. Dr. Wallace, whom you well knew. When nearly fourteen years of age I went to Rome with Bishop Lynch, and was ordained December 21st, 1842. Returned home in the end of 1843, and after Bishop Reynolds reorganized the Seminary, taught there till he broke it up in 1851. Was appointed assistant to Dr. Lynch at St. Mary's on the 1st of January, 1845, and came back to the Cathedral 1st February, 1846. I think I was chaplain to the Sisters from that time till I went back to St. Mary's (assistant to Dr. Baker), in the end of 1848. There I remained till January, 1855, when I came back to the Cathedral, and remained there till November, 1863. During that time I was also chaplain and confessor to the Sisters. In the autumn of 1862, when Beauregard sent four Charleston physicians to help the people of Wilmington, then suffering from the ravages of yellow fever, four Sisters and myself went with them. And that is the reason, I suppose, why after Father Murphy's death, the Bishop sent me to take his place in Wilmington. There I remained until September, 1868, when I went to Rome for the Council. I returned in the autumn of 1870, and here I am. I was secretary to the Baltimore Provincial Councils of 1855 and '58 and to the Plenary of 1866.

"Bishop England's sister died, I am pretty sure, in September (autumn certainly) of 1827. I was quite young, and sick (very sick, so that the Doctor felt my pulse once and pronounced me dead) at the time; but I remember well my mother and the rest of the family who had been at the funeral coming home and describing it, and telling amongst other things, how during the service, a little white bird (a canary or nonpareil, perhaps) flew into the church and perched upon the cornice, and remained there during the whole of the ceremonial. Please say nothing in my praise, as it does no good.

"I am glad that you are well, and in the enjoyment of

health, and I hope God will so continue to favor you in that and prosper you in all things.

"Yours truly, as of old,

"JAMES A. CORCORAN."

Rev. Patrick O'Neile was a native of Kilkenny, Ireland, and educated in the College of Carlow under Dr. Clancy, through whose influence he transferred his allegiance to the diocese of Charleston, completed his studies in the Seminary, and was made priest by the Coadjutor Bishop in 1836. The increased number of the faithful demanded the erection of a third church; the labor was cheerfully undertaken by the young priest two years after his ordination, and in a very limited time St. Patrick's arose on the outskirts of the city, called *the Neck*. The church is known from this circumstance as St. Patrick's on the Neck; the pastor was called Father O'Neile of the Neck, to distinguish him from Father O'Neill of Savannah. The physique of the worthy clergyman lent a sinister meaning to the title. Of fair complexion, above the medium height, with sandy-colored hair not quite red, and though once very slim and delicate, he in a short time grew to be a very large man, and was complimented by universal acclamation as the biggest man in the city, in short, *Father O'Neile of the Neck.*

He was one of the most tireless among the priesthood of the city, and to the time of his death never knew rest. The poorer class of Catholics, the Irish and German immigrants, and the most destitute were living in his parish, and he spent himself in their service. Whether from the accident of having broken down while preaching his first sermon, or the result of his situation, he paid little attention to eloquent preaching or literary studies, and devoted all his time, day, and not unfrequently the nights, in the service of the people and in the active duties of the ministry, visiting the sick in season and out of season, hearing confessions; he was the father confessor of the Bishops, religious, and seminarians. His life was spent in teaching in his large day-school, making pastoral calls, burying the dead, saying the early

Mass, and singing the High Mass every Sunday, preaching, officiating at Vespers, conducting all the services of the Church during Lent, Advent, and other seasons, and without an assistant. He performed more work in this way than any of the priests in the city, for a period of twenty-five years.

Throned in the hearts of the faithful, he was loved by every one, never made an enemy, venerated by all—Catholic, Israelite, Protestant, by the community indiscriminately. He rivalled Bishop England in this respect, and his influence was none the less, greater perhaps in his sphere, and greater than that of any other man in Charleston in his day. Father O'Neile was very dear to Bishop England as a friend and spiritual director. Always calm, patient, and charitable, governed by common sense throughout, and actuated by deep piety and devotion, he was the refuge of the sinner, the consoler of the afflicted, the orphan's friend, and a father of the faithful.. His charity was as universal as the light of day; all shared in its beams, and in want, sorrow, or suffering he was a refuge and speedy succor. So great was the reverence in which he was held that he could walk in the most crammed thoroughfares of the city in his soutane, with perfect impunity, and meet only manifestations of respect for the sanctity of his garment and his person. I encountered him in this costume one day, in King Street, and a Cardinal on the Corso could not receive greater tokens of deference. I know no other priest in the city who could attempt this with any degree of safety for the respect due to religion. As a matter of prudence it would not be commendable in general, nor was it frequently practised by him.

Spent by his labors in the vineyard of the Lord, he died at his post towards the close of the civil war, January 10th, 1865, after a few weeks' illness, in the fifty-eighth year of his age, of which he spent thirty years in the priesthood. Assisted in his last moments by the attention of the clergy and faithful, and aided by the Sacraments, the good and faithful servant went to receive the reward of his labors. With the exception of Bishop England, none ever died in the city more universally regretted; his death was deplored as a general calamity.

For a long time previous to his death he had been collecting money in his parish, to build a church, which was intended to replace the old frame structure. The funds were depreciated in value during the war, the investments failed, and his estate was bankrupt. Rev. John Moore, D.D., succeeded as pastor, and held the position until his appointment as Bishop of St. Augustine, in 1877. The Rev. H. P. Northrop now holds the position, who was ordained in 1865 in Rome.

Very Rev. Leon Fillion, V. G., was a native of Angiers, France, where, after having made his ecclesiastical studies with marked ability, he was raised to the dignity of the priesthood. Bishop Reynolds having visited the city of Angiers, Father Fillion, who was the chaplain to the House of the Good Shepherd, in his longing for a foreign mission, volunteered his services for the diocese of Charleston, and accompanied the Bishop on his return in the fall of 1849. Immediately after his arrival, he was installed as assistant at the Cathedral and tutor in the Seminary. Applying himself sedulously to the study of English, in a short time he acquired a sufficient knowledge of the language to render himself useful among the laity, and was promoted as first assistant at St. Mary's Church, under Dr. Baker. He was appointed chaplain at the Sisters', visited Sullivan's Island, and many of the stations in the neighborhood of the city.

The Bahamas having been attached by the Holy See to the diocese of Charleston, early in the episcopate of Rt. Rev. Dr. Lynch, were visited by Mr. Fillion, where he exercised all the offices of the ministry among a few Catholics, principally British soldiers. Rev. Father Nelligan, a convert, assumed the charge soon afterward as Vicar-General, and commenced the erection of a church on the soil so famed in history as the landing-place of Columbus and his adventurous crew. Father Fillion was created Vicar-General for the diocese by Bishop Lynch, and appointed pastor of St. Joseph's, which was purchased in 1859 from a Protestant denomination and prepared for Catholic service. Father F. expended much time and labor in making the necessary alterations, and invested all the means he possessed in payment of the expenses.

After a short time it assumed an imposing appearance, with suitable parsonage attached, and sprang up the fourth Catholic church in the city, in the center of a respectable parish, thickly settled with genuine Irish Catholics. In the missionary sense, no countries in Europe so strictly merit the title of *Apostolic* as France and Ireland. By the labors and suffering of their sons, the evils inflicted in the world by the sad apostasy of the sixteenth century are in a great measure repaired, impiety arrested, and the bleeding wounds of Christian people healed. Wherever the Cross has been erected for the last two hundred years, from China to Charleston, from the Pacific to the Indian Ocean, there stood an Irish or a French Catholic, at the right hand and the left. The pastor of St. Joseph's was very popular, and a universal favorite among all nationalities, especially among the children of St. Patrick. Low in size, every limb and feature beaming with intelligence, he was all life, all zeal, all piety, all activity. Nowhere in America can be found another body more free from sectional feeling or national prejudices, than the diocesan clergy; the odious distinction never existed inside the rails of the sanctuary; Father Fillion was as sincerely loved and cherished as if he had been raised from boyhood within the dingy room of the old Seminary of St. John the Baptist. His labors were increased by attendance on the sick, during the disastrous times of the civil war.

After a brief illness, and fortified with the holy Sacraments, he departed this life in the spring of 1865, and in the fifty-sixth year of his age. He was devotedly attached to his Bishops, and always cultivated feelings of sincere affection for his venerable brethren of the clergy. After having shared in their trials and privations for twenty-one years, he rests well in the field of his missionary labors. He sank down at the foot of the Cross, which, like the faithful soldier of Christ, he had borne manfully during life, and his grave is moistened by the affectionate tears of priests and laymen. Thus in a few years the shamrock, the lily, the rose, and the thistle are wreathed around the Cross planted by Bishop England on the sunny shores of Carolina. He was not the only one of his countrymen who contributed to build up religion in the Southern States; others, too, bore their share in the heat and burden of the day, who like him have gone to receive their wages from the Master of the vineyard. England also has her representative. The Rev. James F. M. Gore, who was ordained in that country, and devoted his life to the conversion and salvation of the emancipated slave, and was appointed to St. Peter's Church (colored), died after one year, November, 1876, in the thirtieth year of his age; his remains rest close by, after having obtained the crown of the missionary by one hour's labor. In the superabundant mercy of God, those who lose their lives in serving others, secure their own salvation, and shine like stars for all eternity. The communion of saints forbids the supposition that the interests which they advocated during life are terminated by death; they exist beyond the grave; are kindled by divine charity into more glowing fervor, and burn brighter before the throne of God. Their prayers, like their example, encourage us in the rugged path of duty, while their recompense streams like a beacon-light beyond the horizon of the tomb.

The Rev. Charles J. Croghan, the present pastor of St. Joseph's, was born in the County Galway, Ireland, in November, 1822, arrived in this country in the spring of 1841, and entered the Diocesan Seminary in October of the same year; the last student who was received into that institution during the lifetime of its founder. After six years' study under Doctors Baker and Corcoran, he was ordained priest by Bishop Reynolds, on the 11th of July, 1847 immediately after his elevation to the sacerdotal dignity, he was appointed pastor of Sullivan's Island, the usual course of preparing young clergymen for more extensive responsibilities. He was also appointed a teacher, in conjunction with other members of the clergy, in the Collegiate Institute, until it succumbed and fell through in 1850. The trials, privations, and labors of the missionary life all over the vast diocese differed little; they were shared by all, borne in his own measure equally by each one, and the life of one is the counterpart of the others, varied only by the coloring of individual character. On the occasion of the consecration of the new Cathedral, one of the bishops, at the customary dinner, proposed "*the health of the priests of the diocese of Charleston.*" Very Rev. R. S. Baker, the most eloquent of men, stood up as senior, paused for a minute or two, and merely replied, "*A difficult task for any one to undertake to speak of the priests of the diocese of Charleston.*" He then resumed his seat amid silence. He could say no more, for it would be equal to an attempt to eulogize all Apostolic labors and virtues.

During thirty-two years spent at the altar, and seven years as a student, Father Croghan has borne his own share and performed a man's labor. He was appointed to the Newbern mission, after the withdrawal of Father Dunn, which included nearly one-third of the State of North Carolina, Raleigh was soon added to the field of his labor, and continued to form a part of it for two years; he passed eleven years on the mission of the State. During that period, like his co-laborers, his life was Arabic; he had no fixed abode, and through poverty was unable to pay for his board. Though without scrip or purse, God never forsakes the missionary, and his mercy and protection abound in proportion as privation and sufferings increase. Wherever he went he was hospitably entertained. During his periodical sojourn in Newbern he was the guest of Judge Manly's family, of Judge Heath, of Edenton, of Mrs. Leroy, in Washington, in Halifax of Mr. Michael Farrel, in Scotland Neck of Mr. Thomas Farrel's family; all worthy and devoted Catholics, the co-operators of the clergy in planting the Faith, now mostly gone to their reward, but leaving inheritors of their religion and piety. In other towns and stations, he was harbored as chance and luck directed. Besides his ministry among the few scattered Catholics, the primary duty and the means by which Catholicity was preserved, he received many converts into the bosom of the church, prominent among whom was Judge Heath and family, of Edenton. The Judge died during the war, and was faithful to the end; he was prostrated by a severe attack of typhoid fever which had temporarily impaired his mental faculties; he never recovered. Father C. built a brick church at Edenton, and from the fact that four or five persons of culture and social influence beside the Heath family had embraced the Faith, he entertained the well-grounded hopes of building up a congregation of converts; but they were disappointed by the breaking out of the civil war.

In 1861 Father Croghan returned to Charleston, assumed charge of the German congregation at St. Peter's, obtained the country missions, and visited the soldiers in their camps along the line of the Savannah Railroad. In the spring of 1863, after the return of Father Lawrence O'Connell on account of camp sickness, Father Croghan was sent to replace him at the White Sulphur Springs, as army chaplain, where he officiated with great benefit to the sick and wounded, until the close of the war. He ranked in the army as Major Chaplain. With eight Sisters of Mercy, he was obliged to proceed to New York, in order to reach Charleston by water, in consequence of the destruction of all the Southern railroads by the opposing army. After arriving in Charleston, in July, 1865, he was appointed pastor of St. Joseph's Church, succeeding Father L. Fillion, who had died three months previously. The sacred edifice was almost in ruins from shells thrown from Morris Island. By labor and energy, it was again, in the course of a few months, fitted up for service. He was made heir to a heavy debt on church and pastoral residence. Always suited to the emergency, and fit for the occasion, the debt has been paid, and the ecclesiastical buildings restored and adorned with an elegance and taste creditable alike to Catholicity and the zeal and piety of the clergyman. In the diocese of Charleston proper, Father Croghan is the lone survivor of the band of older priests who succeeded to the first generation, inherited their spirit, perpetuated and extended their labors. In robust health, full of life, activity, and good nature, his labors are as assiduous as in early days amid the wilderness of North

Carolina, the camp fevers of the Savannah line, or the hospitals of the dark and bloody grounds of the civil war. He is a polished, forcible writer, a scholar of general information, and one of the most learned divines in moral theology in the United States. He is a sound, vigorous public speaker; always interesting, pregnant with matter, going directly to the point; his sermons are edifying and instructive, and unincumbered by verbiage or idle ornament. He has a happy manner of simplifying the truths which he wishes to inculcate, by illustrations derived from Holy Writ and the lives of the saints, which cover the entire subject, and indelibly impress it on the minds of the hearers. Of genteel, priestly appearance, tall and unbending like the Iron Duke, whom he resembles, he has his fault, but unlike that ungrateful son of Erin, he is not ashamed of it (his nativity). If this is not a fault, he has none; he is a man without blemish, and a remarkable priest, without reproach.

Rev. Thos. Quigley is cousin of the venerable Edward Quigley, who will be mentioned in the proper connection, but was a younger man and later in the field of labor. At the beginning of every religious foundation in these three dioceses, an Irish priest and layman are to be met with; this is generally the case wherever the English tongue is spoken. His Eminence the late Cardinal Barnabo remarked to the writer's brother that the places in the Propaganda, according to the intention of the founders, were meant to be filled by the native youths of all missionary countries; but that the Irish had at all times outnumbered all other nationalities combined; in fact, that it had become an Irish College, and instead of a native youth from Meliapore, Tasmania, or an Indian from the American coast of the Pacific, a young Irish lad would put in his appearance, fortified by the epistle of some Vicar-Apostolic. No higher testimony could be added in favor of the unflinching Catholicity of the Island of Saints, which old persecution and the blandishments of modern infidelity failed to destroy or moderate. Filling alike the high and low places of the hierarchy, sharing so abundantly in the honors, the labors, and suffering of

the Church Militant, we may without presumption expect
that their numbers are no less in the ranks of her higher
state.

Rev. Thos. Quigley was born in the County Tipperary,
Ireland, May 22d, 1826. After having studied a good course
of classics and mathematics in his native country, he joined
his cousin in Charleston and entered the Seminary in 1846;
having studied theology in Dr. Corcoran's class with L. P.
O'Connell and J. F. O'Neill, Jr., he with the same gentlemen was raised to the dignity of the priesthood by Bishop
Reynolds, March 23d, 1850. During his collegiate course,
he taught with his fellow-students in the day school. Always a close student and a ripe scholar, his knowledge of
divine and human science was profound and extensive. He
was assistant to Dr. Baker at St. Mary's until 1853, and became a zealous and efficient laborer in the vineyard. He discharged his duties with marked efficiency, prudence, and circumspection, features of character which distinguished him
through life, and carried him safely through subsequent dangers in his adopted diocese.

January, 1853, he was appointed to the mission at Hutchinson's Island, midway between Savannah and Charleston.
The congregation was composed of about 400 negro slaves;
every fifth Sunday he attended the church at Beaufort. He
remained on this mission until 1857, when he was again reappointed assistant at St. Mary's. In 1859 he was sent on the
missions of Raleigh and Fayetteville. In the spring of 1860
he bought the Baptist church, a brick building fronting the
State-house, and had it fitted up as a Catholic church. It
was dedicated on the following Sunday. Archbishop Hughes
preached on the occasion. He was in North Carolina during
the war, saw Sherman's army enter Fayetteville in March, 1865,
being the only minister who remained in town. Two days
after Sherman left he went out to attend the wounded soldiers,
after the fight at Averysboro. After the close of the war he
was removed to Newbern, attending Goldsboro and all that
extreme mission, saying Mass one Sunday monthly at
Raleigh. In 1867, at the invitation of Bishop Duggan, he

removed to the diocese of Chicago, and in September, 1868, was appointed by him Administrator of his Cathedral. In 1869 he visited his native country, was present at the opening of the Vatican Council, and made the tour of Europe, returning to Chicago in 1870. He was then sent to take charge of Danville, Ill., and remained at that point until 1876, when he was placed at Henry. On the division of the diocese it fell inside the limits of Peoria, where he now ministers with his usual ability and zeal.

He left many monuments of his zeal, and will be a long time gratfully remembered by the faithful over the missions of the central and eastern parts of the *good old North State*. He is of medium size, slender but wiry texture, mild features, overcast with a shade of asceticism; his carriage was grave and priestly. Although past the meridian of life, his declining years are as replete with labor as the early days on the banks of the Neuse and Cape Fear in the Carolinas.

Rev. Father Hackett after having made his studies in the Diocesan Seminary, was ordained about the year 1827, and served some years on the missions. He obtained his exeat and joined Dr. Portier, the Bishop of Mobile, where after laboring in the diocese for nearly twenty-eight years, he died in a good old age. He filled many appointments, and left several monuments to record his worth and efficiency as a devoted servant of the Lord. Prominent among his labors, stand the Church of St. Vincent and the pastoral residence. His piety and zeal endeared him to the good Bishop, to the faithful of his own Irish nationality, and all others, whether of native birth or European descent. Imbued with the spirit that burned in the breasts of the clergy among whom his early lot was cast, it accompanied him through life, and among his new co-laborers, an exemplary and honorable body of ecclesiastics, he was ever conspicuous for his activity, disinterested zeal, and scrupulous observance of pastoral and all priestly duties. He died shortly before 1860, about fifty-eight years old.

The Rev. Philip Gillick was ordained about the same time, served on the missions in North Carolina several years, and removed to New York. He was for some time assistant to Father Byrne, afterwards Bishop, at St. James' Church, and shortly after received separate and independent pastoral charges under Bishop Hughes. His services were very extensive on the Northern dioceses, and he made a fair record among the clergy and laity for piety and devotion to priestly functions. He died about 1860, in harness, his span of life measuring probably the two last figures of that date.

Rev. Patrick Ryan, D.D., was born in the County Tipperary, Ireland, in the year 1824; came to this country at an early age, and settled with his mother, a saintly woman, and other members of the family, at Locust Grove, Ga., where Very Rev. Father Whelan was pastor. His eldest brother was a physician of respectable standing, and removed subsequently to the State of Mississippi, where he was joined by a younger brother, Thomas, a M. D. also; and who was an ex-student of St. Mary's College, in Columbia, South Carolina, where he was favorably known for close application to study, the frequent reception of the Sacraments, and strong Catholic faith. He commenced his study of medicine in Columbia under the celebrated Dr. S. Fair, and graduated from the Medical College of New Orleans, where he died suddenly of heart disease, soon after he began the practice of his profession. The inheritor of the faith and name of St. Patrick was the first youth sent by Bishop Reynolds to the Propaganda, after his arrival in Charleston, and in 1845. He spent several years in Rome, and pursued his studies under celebrated divines, with remarkable proficiency. His piety kept pace with his learning, and he advanced in the one equally as in the other. In 1853 he was created Doctor of Divinity and ordained priest. On his return to the diocese, he officiated some time in the city. He was stationed in Columbia in 1854, visited its missions with advantage to religion and the salvation of souls; he also taught at the College. He was sent in 1855 to Raleigh, Fayetteville and Newbern, and other stations, an extensive ecclesiastical district, which he attended for nearly six years, sharing in all the privations and labors inseparable from the position. He was an object of special hatred to the Know-nothings, received many insults, and attempts were made to take away his life. He was of middle stature, thin, spare, with a steel constitution, and possessed of great power of endurance. Rigid in teaching and formal in manners, his ascetic habits were proof against the attrition of the tangled forests of the Tar State.

Being recalled to Charleston about 1860, he was sent as assistant to St. Mary's, and exercised his functions there and in several other stations in the vicinity, during the war. By the sick-bed, in the camps, among the soldiers, in the hospitals, his ministrations were assiduous, and his devotion self-sacrificing. After the war had ended he obtained leave of absence and revisited his Alma Mater in 1867, after having served about fourteen years on the mission of the diocese. In the Propaganda he left as a student an enviable reputation for piety; he again returned to replenish his soul with a fresh draught at the fountain-head of Catholicity. Invited by Archbishop Spalding, he chose the archdiocese of Baltimore as the field of his future labors, which have been spread over the city for the past eight years and up to the present time; at first with the venerable Father McManus, and since with Father McColgan, at St. Peter's. His renewed health affords reasonable ground for hoping that he will be spared many years longer in the service of the Church, and like the altar candle, burn brightly to the socket in laboring for the salvation of souls. In earlier times the Archbishop and he have both shared in the trials and privations of the vicariate; their recollections will tend to sweeten their present relation. May it be one of prolonged duration.

The Bishop purchased a church edifice of moderate size, which had been used formerly as a synagogue, adjusted it for Catholic service, dedicated it to St. Peter and bestowed it on the German Catholics as a *quasi* parochial church. Father Folchi, an Italian priest, a pious and zealous young man, after having been in charge for some time, resigned and accepted other missions over the diocese, off and on, for several years, till failing health induced him to retire to the Jesuit house in San Francisco, at the close of 1877. Father Lawrence P. O'Connell and other clergymen officiated at different intervals, with a mixed congregation of Germans and Irish. Towards the close of the war Rev. Father Shadler was installed regularly as pastor. He was about thirty-four years old, made his studies at Louvain. A practical man, of business habits, and devoted to his sacred calling, he accomplished much good in his own congregation, in the city at large, and the out-skirting missions. He remained in the diocese about seven years, and wishing to bind himself more closely to the sanctuary, he withdrew, it is said, with the intent of joining a religious order.

This course adopted by some of our clergy is justifiable by ecclesiastical law ; in countries where the endowments of the faithful, rich benefices, and parochial rights make the priesthood desirable, even in a temporal point of view, to the children of opulent and influential families, one's disengagement becomes greater and the regular state the more perfect. The heroism of the religious vows, rendering the practice of evangelical counsels the enduring habits of life, make it also safer and more perfect. But in a poor diocese, where the labor is great and the workmen few, the missionary life seems more meritorious ; otherwise the Gospel must be preached to the heathen, and the world converted, to the detriment of the apostle. Not by prayer alone, but by preaching and teaching, is the world converted. Without the safeguards of the regular clergy, and always in the gap of danger, the missionary priest is more in need of meditation, prayer, and all the other elements of the spiritual life, to secure the salvation of his own soul, maintain himself in his warfare to the end, against the world, sin, and *the rulers of darkness in high places*. The Apostles would have slumbered on gladly, in the consolations of the vision on Mount Tabor; but they were awakened and must descend to the common plain, do all the rough work set before them, until they gladly embraced the rough cross at the journey's end, by which only they can ascend to a higher glory.

Vigilant over the spiritual welfare of the emancipated slaves, the Bishop altered the character of the congregation at St. Peter's, and set it apart exclusively for the benefit of that race. They numbered several hundred, among whom are several converts, and monthly communicants. He supplied them with zealous and worthy priests, who devoted their lives to this portion of the faithful. One of them, Father Gore, fell at the post of duty. The good work is continued by the Rev. Fathers F. G. Vigneront and J. Hurley, imitators of the detachment and devotion of St. Peter Clavier. Their ministrations are consoled by increasing numbers, while the humility of their missions increases their honor in the sight of God and the Church. They belong to an order of clergymen established for the conversion of the negroes.

The Blessed Virgin primarily, St. Joseph, St. John the Baptist, the Prince of the Apostles, and St. Finbar are the principal patrons of the diocese. St. Peter is honored with four churches. Mr. Conlaw Lynch and family, of Cheraw, erected one in that town, situated in the southeastern part of the State, about thirty years ago, which was called by the name of the head fisherman. It is the centre of the surrounding missions, and embraces a moderate congregation, distinguished rather for piety and fervor than numbers. Having been periodically visited by Rev. Dr. Lynch and other priests, it was favored with the presence of a resident priest about the year 1856, when the Rev. John Cullinane was appointed pastor.

This venerable clergyman was born in County Clare, Ireland, about the year 1800, made his course of studies in the College of Maynooth, and after his ordination served some years in the missions in his native country. Preferring the labors of a foreign mission, he crossed the ocean, landed in British America, where he ministered for a time, and finally attached himself to the diocese of Charleston about the year 1850. He was stationed in North Carolina, afterwards at the Cathedral during the declining years of Bishop Reynolds, attended Sullivan's Island, the Frescati of the city, and several other points. He was transferred to Columbia by Dr. Lynch while Administrator, and visited in conjunction with the other clergy, many of the extensive missions connected with that church. After some years he was nominated for St. Peter's at Cheraw, a position he still holds, residing in Mr. Lynch's family. After a lifetime in the priesthood and twenty-eight years in the diocese, strong and hale, the time-honored veteran is still active and efficient in attendance on the duties of his sacred calling. Cheered with having devoted an unusually long life to the service of the sanctuary, this Melchisedech of the diocese keeps his eye firmly fixed on his ready reward.

The Rev. S. Kedney, a zealous young priest, after having served some time on the mission, died on the 29th of March, 1876.

Father Healy, an Augustinian religious, and a native of the city of Cork, died in the city at the Bishop's house, after a short illness, and soon after his arrival, about 1867. He is buried in the priests' lot at the Cemetery of St. Lawrence.

Out of some seventy or eighty clergymen who belonged to Charleston, about half left the diocese—some after a few years, and most after having spent their strength and the best years of a useful life in the trials and privations of their poverty-stricken mission. Some left to die in the charity hospitals of more favored cities, and like St. Cyprian the Martyr, sent their remains back to consecrate the soil which they trod while living with sore and weary feet, unknown, forgotten, and unappreciated. They were all justified, and some necessitated for want of adequate means of support, and more frequently still, for want of priestly employment.

A young diocese, it required corresponding qualities in its ministers, and there was no provision whatever made for sickness, old age, and the daily accidents that wait on human life. Faring worse than the disabled soldiers in the battle-field, they dropped down without the shelter of an hospital. In sickness they were an encumbrance on the floor of strangers and a trial to the charity of some poor parishioner. In old age they were in the way, like the venerable Father O'Neill, of Savannah. In their best days, they were like unbidden guests at a family table, who had worn their welcome threadbare. Some were compelled to become common schoolmasters, like Father McGinnis, in Charlotte, or cultivate bits of farms, like Father Quigley, Sr., at Locust Grove Station, in order to keep body and soul together.

Archbishop Spalding on the occasion of the installing of his present successor as Vicar-Apostolic of North Carolina, facetiously spoke to Bishop Gibbons in this manner: "I have educated you, raised you to the age of manhood, I have given you a ring, and now go root for yourself or die." This was quoted as Bishop Fenwick's parting words to Bishop Tyler, of Hartford, after his consecration. That great prelate had taken in, at a glance, the true state of our missions, even in their improved condition, and when the priests were wearing store clothes. I can conceive nothing more humiliating to a respectable priest, than to be compelled to ask a mission in another diocese, and where he is unknown. A cave in a mountain would be preferable; an asylum recommended as a boon by the learned Abbé Rouquette, of New Orleans, himself a hermit, to Loyson, after his apostasy. A man is frequently driven to inculpate others, and then the blame is thrown on the administration in defence of his own cause. Walking around the question, and viewing it in all its aspects, in the most favorable light, one must be contented to live and move and have his being in an atmosphere of chilling suspicion, harder to endure than the evils from which he is endeavoring to escape. Past services, many a well-fought battle, many a generous sacrifice, sorrows endured, trials and temptations subdued, with a heroism worthy of the greatest saints, disappear as elements of recommendation; nay, they frequently tend but to increase doubts; he must be compelled to live among the clergy of his new diocese as a *suspected priest*, the least desirable position in the whole world. I recollect none of those excellent men to have left laboring under a canonical disability or for any other than a justifiable cause—a truth confirmed by their future usefulness, their frequent promotion after some years to high places of honor and trust and the highest dignities in the American Church.

It would be wrong to refuse an exeat demanded for just theological reason. To receive a clergyman without it into another diocese would be also a grave irregularity. This care is indispensably necessary for the welfare and proper government of the Church. The contrary would reduce us again to the chaotic condition of the Catholic Church before the appointment of Archbishop Carroll, when the United States were under the jurisdiction of the Vicar-Apostolic of London. On a very slight pretence any priest could obtain faculties from the Bishop, and on landing exercise the offices of the holy ministry when he chose, as long as he chose, and remove himself indefinitely, as dictated by fancy or temporal interest. There were of course worthy men who were exceptions, but this does not remedy the wrong. The Church in framing her laws, leaves individuals out of the reckoning, and makes no calculations on the goodness of man. Our Lord did not trust himself to the Jews, *because he knew what was in man.* To this cause alone Bishop England attributed the greatest evils that afflicted the infancy of the Catholic Church in the United States.

This interpretation I do not intend to apply to the oath administered to her students by the Propaganda; its correctness cannot be questioned.

CHAPTER V.

BEAUFORT AND ITS MISSIONS.

Beaufort—Colleton—Walterboro—Barnwell—Pacataligo—Coosahatchie, a Fertile but Sickly Country—Inhospitality on the Rice Plantations—Confederate Revenge—Imbecility—A Splendid Place for Apostates—Michael O'Connor—The Fabian Policy of Making Converts—Mrs. Mary O'Connor—A Bad School for Converts—A False Religion thought better than none—A Pious Revenge—A Church built and donated to the Diocese—Miss Harriet Beal—Lawrence O'Connor—M. P. O'Connor, Esq.—Edward O'Connor—Father O'Neill, of Savannah, the first Priest—Father J. J. O'Connell first local Pastor—Two Catholic Families—Mrs. Aimar—A Preacher imposes Himself on a Dying Man as a Priest and receives his Confession—Grahamville—Sermon in the Free Church—James Malony—An Ursuline Nun—Col. John Ryan, of Barnwell—Drs. Duncan and Graham—Gillisonville—The Ryan Family—All Things live to God—God lives in Every Soul—Gardner's Corner—A Hospitable Dane—The Combahee Ferry—The Valley of the Achapoo—Overflowing of the Nile—War among the Fishes—A Mesopotamian Waste—Male and Female Alligators—Judge Burke—A New Youghal—A Loss to the Faith of 12,000 Inhabitants—Colleton—The Blue-House—St. James Church—The Magees, Mulloneys, and Old Settlers—Destroyed by Fire—Misses Susan, Harriet, and Sarah Bellinger—The Pinckneys—Church of St. Philip at Walterboro—Priests on this Mission—Fathers Hasson and J. P. O'Connell, D.D.—Patrick Nary, O. S. F.—Archbishop Hughes—Hutchison Island—Barnwell—Edmund Bellinger, Jr., and the Early Catholics—Judge Aldrich—Other Posts—Johnson—The McDonald and Caraduc Families—Sumterville—Ridgeville—The Purcell Family—Whippy Swamp—Sermon in Methodist Church, and at the Court House in Gillisonville—The Cotton beds of the South—The Barriers against Popery—An Opinion not a Prophecy—Bishop Andrew Byrne—A Successful Administration—Slavery Unprofitable—Slaves consumed all they made—Patrick O'Connell and Family—Four Priests and three Sisters of Mercy—A Good Father—Benefactor to the Church—A Munificent Endowment—Holy Life and Happy Death—The Writer's Difficulty in doing Justice to his Memory—Rev. Wm. Burke—A Brief and Useful Career—Pastor of St. Mary's—Death in Savannah—Remains interred near the Altar of the Blessed Virgin.

IN the fall of 1847 I was recalled from Georgia, where I had served on the mission since my ordination, and this extensive district placed in my charge. It embraced the southwestern section of the State, being the intermediate region lying between the South Carolina Railroad on the south, Edgefield and the Savannah River to the north, and Port Royal River to the west. Port Royal being the safest harbor on the Atlantic, and immensely superior to Charleston, invited navigation in very early colonial times, and was the first settlement of the Huguenots. The neighboring islands, celebrated for long staple cotton, the unsurpassed fertility of the country along the Edisto, the Coosahatchie, the Saltketcher, and other tidal rivers, and the alluvial nature of the soil in general, rendering the entire region exceedingly fertile, and the Egypt of South Carolina, corn, cotton, and rice are the principal agricultural products. One may travel an entire day over the broad outspread plains, a monotonous level, without meeting a habitable spot or white man's home, within reasonable distance. I have frequently travelled entire days without having met a human being; despite the extreme culture of the soil, it might have passed as uninhabited, were it not for the crowd of sweltering, half-clad, half-fed negroes, seen now and then in the distance, like Cossacks in the rear of the French army, and who in many instances did not know their master. It was the solitude created by wealth, guarding itself against the approach of man. There was not a more inhospitable country in the wide world; a cup of cold water from a spring was yielded to the demand of a stranger with the jealousy of the Samaritan; while a lone traveller, whose business led him from the highway, excited the curiosity and suspicions of the community.

In another day war found its way into their midst; the Confederate more than the Federal soldiers sought a cruel revenge for repulsive unsociability, by chopping their meat on pianos, kindling fires with libraries, and stabling horses in their halls. Without the least sympathy, they suffered more than any other people from the disasters of the war, and mostly perished out of existence. The palace of an Eastern monarch was more accessible than the mansions of these republican barons. It was regarded as certain death to live in the interior during the summer months. The wealthy class—there was but one class in the country—withdrew early in May to their fashionable residences or favorite retreats on the sea-shore, in the mountains of North Carolina, or to the popular watering-places of the North. In a worldly sense there never existed a happier people; unaccustomed to bodily exercise, and from inter-marrying, the race had deteriorated; they did not constitute either mentally or physically the bone and sinew of South Carolina. All that was necessary to crown their earthly bliss was found in some accommodating type of Protestantism, promising a heavenly reward to a life of inactivity, luxury, and ease, more befitting the last days of the Balylonish Empire than a Christian people. The Church of England was preferred, both because of the absence of the radical element and its aristocratic bearing. It laid no claim to be the Church of the poor. Catholicity was good enough, and to a limited extent among the slaves, provided it did not question the legitimacy of the marriages performed by overseers. To preach it to themselves was quite another affair, and the undertaking was bootless. If an apostate, who is always stung to the quick at the sight of any object capable of reminding him of his forfeited peace, wished to escape every remembrance of the Faith, no place could serve his purpose better than Beaufort. If one or two were to be met with, they were unnoticed in the crowd of unbelievers that made error popular. It was an old Roman maxim, that gold will find its way everywhere, even into the cell of the condemned. The same can be maintained of Catholicity; it works its way slowly, silently, irresistibly. After the first quarter of the present century, an Irishman by the name of Michael O'Connor landed from the City of the Violated Treaty, in Beaufort. An humble, virtuous man, and a respectable mechanic, he worked assiduously, plying his avocation with unslackened energy, and acquired a competency.

In 1830 he married a native-born lady, remarkable for intelligence, sound practical sense, and habits of industry. Her conversion was accomplished in an unusual manner, and without any direct persuasion on the part of her husband. He was wont to say his morning and night prayers by himself. On Sundays he retired to his chamber, shut the door, spent the forenoon in his private devotions, and allowed his better half to devote her time in visiting the Baptist church, to which she belonged, or in any other way agreeable to her religious taste; for she was always piously inclined. This regime went on for years. Convinced of the moral worth of her husband, his purity of life, strict honesty, temperance, and Christian faith, Mrs. Mary O'Connor was mortified in feeling; silently and without any complaint she endured the *laissez-faire* system to the end, unrelieved by the blessing of a single controversy. The family relations were unruffled by a harsh word, and though cherished tenderly, she grew to regard herself as one beyond the pale of religion in her own house. One of the first priests known to have visited Beaufort was Father O'Neill, Sr. The boat plying daily between Savannah and Charleston, commanded by Captain Budds, than whom a more prudent or safer seaman never trod the deck, touched at the O'Connor wharf when making the inland route, on certain days. Once in a while, if he could be spared from his duties, the tireless missionary would slip down to Beaufort and say Mass of a week-day, at Michael O'Connor's. This was the case since 1830. The union of the virtuous couple was blessed with offspring; the priest baptized the children soon after their birth, said Mass, administered Communion to *all* the congregation.

As the children grew in years, they were carefully taught the Catholic prayers, and the interdict of the mother assumed a more marked appearance. In a short time she became the most unhappy of mothers; all the children in the town, with Bibles and prayer-books in their hands, accompanied by their parents, on foot or in carriages, and to the clamorous music of merry bells, kept pouring along the streets in glee and gladness on their way to Sunday-school; while her boys, the smartest of any in class or play-ground, were confined to the house and were being brought up little infidels.

Worse still, the fashionable academy, and the only school where those boys could be taught, was ably conducted by an educated and unhappy man, who had abandoned the ranks of the priesthood, and was now preaching in the Episcopal Church. The conversion of the centurion is not the only example on record of the wonderful manner in which the grace of God avenges and consoles itself for the fall of an apostle. This was the only clerical defection from the Faith over which the diocese was ever called to weep.

The sectarian ministers and many fashionable ladies expostulated with the mother on the unhappy manner in which she was raising her children; without God or Christian belief, their frail bark to be launched on the ocean of human life without a star of hope to guide their perilous voyage.

She expostulated with her husband; he intimated that the children must be raised Catholics despite of the world, and at any cost; and that she might conduct their religious training, her education rendering her fully competent for the task. She was amazed at the open, unstudied proposal. She assented, for the simple reason that she believed a bad religion preferable to none at all, and might save them from sheer impiety in after life. He put in her hands Bishop England's large Catechism, the best book of the kind ever compiled in America; all the arguments of Divine revelation and of the establishment of the Church are comprised in a few chapters. The children got a chapter by heart every week. The class was increased by another accession. Miss Harriet Beal, a niece who resided with her aunt, was persuaded to get her chapter too; after some time, they all knew it from end to end, including the *serving of a priest at Mass*, and none better than the teacher. Mr. O'Donnell, who built the Sisters' house in Charleston, was employed about this period in erecting a new and handsome brick building for the family residence; he was well posted in controversy, and while staying in the family Catholic doctrines were often made the subject of discussion. The "End of Controversy," "Geraldine," and other good books were provided; firm, unhesitating conviction was the inevitable result. Mrs. Mary O'Connor visited Charleston, was received into the Church in 1843 by Very Rev. R. S. Baker. Her husband, it is related, knew nothing of the revolution that had been effected by the wonderful workings of the grace of God until he saw, to his utter amazement, his wife kneeling by his side and receiving the bread of life on the occasion of the next visit of the priest. It was the renewal of all the stored affections of a lifetime. God is the only true bond of union; the odious disparity of difference of worship that stood like a wall of separation crumbled to pieces, and they were now more closely united than ever. In the fervor of his gratitude to God, the husband exclaimed, "Why did you not tell me of this?" "Surely you never asked me," was the witty reply.

Mrs. O'Connor's domestic relations brought her into contact with many, and the family circle was extensive; all were brought under her influence. The spirit of Catholic piety breathed throughout; her residence was the home of Catholicity and the resting-place of the priest after many a long and weary journey. She never lost her first fervor; it burns bright and warm this day as at the first moment, while the reverses of fortune and the adversity of the times have served but to lend it a steadier flame. In 1846 the good master of the household unaided built a church, and bequeathed the edifice to the diocese. Five members composed the family proper, three sons and a niece—Miss Beal. The latter, a lady of rare excellence and piety, was united in wedlock to Dr. Graham, of Pittsburgh, Pa., and died in 1860, after some few years of a virtuous and happy married life. Miss Rosanna Kenedy from girlhood lived in the household; she was left an orphan at an early age, and was baptized in her infancy. Reared among non-Catholics, she knew nothing of the Faith in which she was baptized, until she acquired the saving knowledge under the influence of this truly Catholic family. She subsequently married Lieutenant Catherwood, of Savannah, and died fortified by the consolations of religion in 1852, leaving one child. Miss

Arden, Miss O'Brien, now Mrs. Maxwell, of Charlotte, were for a long time in the household circle, and received many of the graces by which it was favored from on high.

The boys were educated at Fordham during the presidency of Father Bayley, afterwards the Archbishop, and also under the administration of Father Thebeaud. Lawrence applied himself to the study of architecture; he married into a Catholic family in Baltimore. He superintended the work on the Cathedral in Charleston under Mr. Keilly during its erection. Michael P. studied law, and for many years heads his profession in the city of Charleston. Equally devoted to his faith and assiduous in its practice as the eminent jurist of his name in New York, he occupies a position of rival merit in his native State for legal lore, reasoning powers, and eloquence. Having married into the family of Captain Aveilhe, he is the happy father of a large and interesting flock of children, who are growing up in the knowledge and practice of the holy religion that adorned their ancestors on both sides, and made them great in their day. While a refugee during the war, in Columbia, I united Edward, the youngest son, to Miss Trumbo in the holy bands of matrimony. He is favorably known in mercantile circles for honesty, moderation, and business habits, as his brothers in their respective pursuits.

After a brief illness, Mr. O'Connor died in 1854, in the fifty-sixth year of his age, with all the consolations afforded by a well-spent life. True among thousands of the faithless, he never *entered into the counsels of the ungodly, nor walked in the way of sinners, nor sat on the chair of pestilence;* his remains rest under the shade of the orange grove in St. Peter's* Churchyard, awaiting the summons of his patron, the Prince of the Resurrection. Had he been an extortioner, he could by legal means have acquired most of the wealth of the community. By fair dealing, close industry, he arose to affluence from an humble beginning, won the esteem of the people, and left his children the knowledge of the Faith and the inheritance of the Kingdom of

---

* Called in the *Almanac* St. Michael's Church, by mistake.

Heaven—a boon surpassing all human understanding. May all his descendants cherish it in their generations, and prove themselves worthy children of an ancestor so firm, so honest, and so true. The family lost their property by the war, even the homestead, which was sold after the establishment of the treacherous peace, and when it was impossible for any of the family to be present to prevent its forfeiture. It is one of the many acts of injustice which fill up the dark record of the administration in South Carolina. In later years there were two or three other Catholic families. Mrs. Aimar, the respected mother of the Charleston family of that name, and of Mrs. Durband, who died in Columbia during the war. They were of French descent, worthy people, and proud of their religion. The other family was Scottish, and named Johnson; they were devoted and exemplary Catholics, but left the State and moved to Wisconsin.

The town was visited from Charleston by one or other of the clergy until my appointment. Rev. Dr. Lynch, on one of these periodical visits, preached a very learned sermon in the Baptist church on the Invocation of Saints, which produced a favorable impression, for the time, on the minds of his hearers. About this period, an Irish Catholic who had been employed on one of the plantations was attacked by the fatal country fever. Almost in the agony of death, he rushed to the town, hoping to find the priest. A letter was mailed for the nearest clergyman, but the sick man died before it reached its destination. Inconsolable at the idea of dying without the Sacraments, in his raving he was vociferating for the priest until the end. A minister represented himself as a priest and received his confession; he afterwards made no secret of it. But there was nothing serious to divulge. You will scarcely discover in the annals of civilized people another act to equal this in turpitude. Doubtless the iniquitous deceit practised on the dying man was a claim in the sight of the all-seeing eye for enlarged mercy and compassion. May that dear faithful soul rest in peace! None remembers his name; it is blotted out from earth, to be written in the Book of Life.

The parish was one hundred and twenty miles long, with a Catholic population of about one hundred persons, chiefly converts. There were four churches, about thirty miles apart, one from the other. Without intermediate communication by water or railroad, the priest was usually conveyed from place to place by the Catholic families; finding this mode too inconvenient to all parties, he provided a horse, and lived *all over*, without any fixed abode. A Sunday was devoted to each church, beginning at Beaufort and ending on the fourth Sunday at Barnwell, to return again *in circuito*. The fifth Sunday, being vacant when it occurred, was *ad libitum*. Grahamville is twenty miles north of Beaufort, and was reached by way of Boyd's Landing. There was here but one Catholic family—Eikeronkrotter, a Bohemian by birth, and married. He was devoted to his religion, and entertained the priest; the children were baptized: but the mother, an excellent women, was a Baptist, and persisted in her opinion. There were but two other Catholics in the village, which was a summer resort, and located in a pine country. These were Mr. Dubler, a German, and Miss Honora Griffin, a tutoress.

There was a *free church* in the village, where I frequently preached to large audiences. General Howard, the leading citizen, being a liberal-minded man, attended, and the others followed his example. James Malony resided at Pocataligo, farther in the interior, a Catholic, lived formerly at Coosahatchie, but removed to a healthier location. Mr. Malony was one of the first Catholic settlers, and was favorably known as an enterprising man throughout the country. His wife was a Bret, a Catholic family much respected and widely connected. Educated in first-class schools in Ireland, the females were cultivated, and surpassed the wealthier inhabitants in refinement of manners. They adorned religion by their piety and virtue. There were two children, both still living; the eldest, a daughter, is a professed religious at the Ursuline Convent, in the archdiocese of Cincinnati, to which place she accompanied the Ursulines in 1845. Patrick was educated by the Jesuits in the College of Fordham, and returned to his native State a ripe scholar and a good Catholic. Colonel John Ryan, of Barnwell Court-House, was a son of Mrs. Malony by a first marriage. He was in the mercantile business, firm in his religious belief and its practices, intelligent and well informed. He represented Barnwell many years in the State Legislature, and was the most popular man in that county. He had command of the militia, was an officer under the Confederate Government, and aided primarily in reconstructing the civil government under the administration of President Andrew Johnson, which was subsequently subverted by the appointment of Generals Canby and Sickles and others, irreproachable personally as officers, but made the engines by which the Radical party, headed by Stephens, Cameron, and Morton, accomplished the utter destruction of the Southern States. Colonel Ryan married Miss Duncan, a niece of Edmund Bellinger; he died about the year 1866, and left many children, who cultivate the religion and follow in the steps of their lamented father. They are connected with the Grahams, of Blackville, equally distinguished for education and piety. James Malony and his worthy consort have gone to rest, but they still live in the memory of their grateful offspring and of the remnant of the faithful who survived the terrible struggle.

Patrick Ryan, a native of the County Tipperary, Ireland, kept the hotel at Gillisonville; he married into a respectable family, and his wife, a superior woman, joined the Church, and died a devout Catholic in Savannah, whither they had moved for the purpose of educating their only child, a daughter, and bringing her up near the Church. She married a zealous Catholic and a worthy man. Both the parents died before the late war, and their remains rest with the faithful dead in that city.

Gardner's Corner is the site of a country store, whose history is buried far back in the fables of early times. Some two or three Catholics resided here and at Coosahatchie, a few miles distant, whose names are not remembered. The grave holds closely many a secret, which, with its numberless occupants, live only to God, before whom nothing is dead. Among the many marvellous lives which the Blessed Trinity lives simultaneously, that in each different soul of man, living or dead, is a theme of rapturous adoration. The consideration of the stupendous mystery will tax the power of human thought. On one day, He will spread before us the only true history of our race ever written; every son of Adam will have his own page, to be scanned by every human eye, and like the child's first prayer, never to be forgotten! In 1846 the store was conducted by a very worthy and energetic man, a Dane, of the name of Longballe. He was the only non-Catholic in this country who had extended to me an act of hospitality. I know nothing less changeable in man's habits than his early tastes; it is common to countries and individuals: the men who mowed the luxuriant hay on the Pontine meadows in the days of Horace were not an exception. Faint and weary, after a long journey over sandy roads, glistening like snow, in a burning sun, he would regale me with his favorite dish of pickled *Swedish herrings*, and furnish a bucketful of cool fresh water from his spring beneath the shade of the huge moss-festooned oak, under whose outspreading branches Chicora and Adusto, famed in Indian story, may have smoked in council the calumet of peace three hundred years ago.

After crossing the Combahee, one encounters the open rice-fields of the valley of the Ashapoo. At high tide the lands are almost on a level with the waters. At some distance apart, flood-gates are constructed, for the purpose of letting in the salt water through the deep-cut channels to inundate the rice plantations, which after the sowing of the seed are flooded with a sheet of water, like Egypt after an overflowing of the Nile. The reader can easily imagine that an agricultural scene of more varied beauty can nowhere be met with. In the spring, the abundance of shad, passing in shoals through the sluices, over the plains, is truly amazing. They have nauseated the appetite of hungry slaves, and were used for fertilizing purposes in former times. The run has not been so great in late years; whether warned by some mysterious secret of communication in pisciology of the fate of their *forerunners*, or the advance checked by the million sharks infesting the harbor, whose spawn, disentangled from the drooping willow branch or submerged sapling, are thrown on the beach by every wave. Like the Maremna in Southern Italy, white people cannot live in this country with any degree of comfort or safety during the summer and fall. For this cause, it will in all probability, for want of labor, unless the negroes cultivate it, become a tangled wilderness, like the once fertile plains of Babylon or the vineyards of Engeddi. Many of the owners of this country died of want after emancipation, and their lands were sold for a mere song. Like the rivers in Central Africa discovered by Livingston and Spencer in their search for the source of the Nile, perhaps still as hidden as the Ark, the alligator infests these waters and is the pest of the country. They are amphibious, and after devouring the fish in their aquatic abode, they will prowl about at night and traverse plantations in search of dogs and swine, while the female reclines all a summer's day by the side of a mouldering stump, with hundreds of her younglings sporting in a swarm round their wondrously-made parent, whose mail-clad heart God has filled with love and pity for her strange brood.

Elias Speith, himself a wealthy man, was the gentlemanly superintendent of many plantations in this country. He occupied a modest one-story residence, built and tenanted by Judge Burke, famed in anecdotes of the bench and bar, whose biography may be found among the reminiscences of the late Chief-Justice O'Neill. Cut on a pane of glass in a front window with a diamond, I traced in straggling letters *Ædamus Burke*. Both names prove at once the faith of this noted man, who was of Irish birth, and one of the early judges after the Revolution. Tradition says he was educated for the priesthood, was on his way to the West Indies, entered the port of Charleston, and here ended his wanderings. Having studied law, he soon acquired distinction in his profession, and was elevated to the bench. Without church, and scarcely priest or Catholic influence, he ceased to be known as a Catholic; but was extremely national. Like Agenor, the refugee from the sack of Troy, he called the divisions of his vast estate by the nomenclature of the localities in the South of Ireland famed for fairs or provincial amusements. The Lakes of Killarney, Youghal, Duhalla, and Mallow prove that he walked on a Cork leg. He was living in 1812.

Bishop England maintains that, calculating from the names of the people, no less than forty thousand had lost the Faith in the Carolinas and Georgia; leaving but twelve thousand Catholics in his diocese, when in its most prosperous condition, and towards the close of his administration. Collins Cross-roads, or the Blue House, in Colleton district, was about the first Catholic mission organized by Bishop England outside of Charleston. About forty miles from the city, and on the main road for travellers from the west, a large and commanding hotel was conducted by Dr. McGee, an enterprising Irish Catholic physician. The day-books recorded the names of many of the most distinguished men in the country during the first quarter of the present century. The house was painted a green color, which under the action of the weather changed to blue, and hence the name. The McGees, the Maloneys, the Purcels, the Foxes, the Bretts, the Ryans, and some others formed a respectable Catholic settlement. They acquired considerable wealth, were people of culture and character, and produced an abiding impression in favor of the Faith, gaining for it esteem and consideration among the wealthy planters. A church was built, a plain wooden edifice, and dedicated about the year 1826, under the title of St. James. By the year 1847 all the old Catholics had died but one, James Purcel, who died not long since. There remained one son of Dr. McGee's, he was an excellent young man, and a Catholic, who is said to have lost his life while in command of a company in Virginia. There was also an Italian, Joseph Pizazi, who practised the duties of religion, and died. I repaired the church, which had fallen into decay; said Mass and preached there on the second Sunday of each month. It was visited at this time by Bishop

Reynolds. A year or two after, it was burnt by a fire originating in the woods. I said the last Mass in that venerated shrine. Not a soul of those who flourished in its day was then living.

Miss Susan Bellinger joined the Church about 1830, and she led all her servants, for she had many, to embrace the Faith. She was pious, humble, and devoted to her religion, and led a life of unbroken self-denial and prayer. The first of her family who had found the priceless pearl of the Gospel, she lived for years isolated from her own kindred, who, with others, treated her wisdom as folly and madness. She was an humble instrument in the hand of God for the conversion of all that family, who listened to reason, accepted the grace of faith, and had the courage and fortitude to profess it openly, and glory in its practice. Dr. John Bellinger and family, the brothers Lucius and C. B. Northrop, and their sainted mother, all of the city of Charleston, were now fervent and humble worshippers before the altar of our Blessed Lady. Misses Harriet and Sarah Bellinger and their sister, Mrs. Pinckney, of Walterboro, with her husband, the descendant of the distinguished family whose name he bore, were baptized about 1844, and they formed a wealthy and influential body of Catholics; many of the slaves followed their example, and the children were all baptized. Miss Sarah Bellinger, at her own expense, erected a church at Walterboro, dedicated to St. Philip. Dr. Pinckney having died a year or two previously, Mrs. Pinckney, a Frenchman, Mr. Fryse, his wife and her sister, Miss Isabella Stephens, converts, were all the Catholics in the congregation. Subsequent to my transfer to Columbia, and up to this time, the station is dependent on the clergy of the Cathedral for spiritual ministrations.

During the cruel civil war Father Hasson, who was a chaplain in the army under command of General Canby, slain afterwards by the Modoc chief, built a church at Port Royal. It was upset by a tidal wave, and completely swept away, within a few years, and scarcely a trace remains. Father Hasson is a zealous priest in the archdiocese of New York, and also chaplain at Sing Sing. He left with the army on the cessation of hostilities. Rev. J. P. O'Connell, D. D., succeeded, while General Sickles was the military commander of the district and officiated on the island and in Beaufort. He withdrew for want of means of support and failing health about 1868, and now is the pastor of St. Michael's parish, Brooklyn.

Father Patrick Nary and another Franciscan father, an Italian, were placed in charge. They attended all the lower parts of the mission for a few years, and retired for a similar cause. A few negroes scattered over the entire section, at different points, the emancipated slaves of the Bellinger family, formed their congregation. For the past few years the country is visited mostly by priests from Charleston or Beaufort. Mrs. Marsh, a lady of Irish birth, of high culture, affluence, and piety, resided on Hutchinson's Island, which she had acquired by purchase, and cultivated by four hundred slaves, mostly baptized and regular in attendance on Catholic service. The island was attended by Rev. Thos. Quigley, and afterwards by Rev. F. J. Carr. After the consecration of the Cathedral in 1853, Archbishop Hughes was during some days a sharer of the hospitality of the Catholic proprietress. Being in advanced years, she returned to her family in New York City, before the breaking out of the war, and died as she had lived, faithful to God and esteemed in society. Barnwell Court-House is about forty miles' distance from Walterboro. Before 1847 it was visited from Augusta by Father Barry, who received Mr. Edmund Bellinger and his family into the Church, and who will be mentioned in another place. There was a church erected here, with a graveyard attached, and dedicated to St. Andrew the Apostle. The leading Catholics, with their families, were Edmund Bellinger, Jr., who moved to Columbia, and died about 1869; his widow and the children returned soon after; Dr. Duncan and Colonel Ryan, who married Mr. Bellinger's niece, Miss Duncan, Colonel Magher, who married the oldest daughter of that celebrated jurist; John Quinn, who also intermarried in this family; James and Mrs. Maloney, with some few single persons. Patrick Quinn, a teacher, who resided at Barker's settlement, and his family, were practical Catholics. Colonel Aldrich, the accomplished Speaker of the House of Representatives, and elected Judge after the restoration of home government, under Governor Hampton, with his family, was received into the Church and baptized by Rev. A. J. Ryan in Augusta, where he resided during the maladministration of the Radicals; self-banished, he prudently forsook his native soil, to avoid persecution, and mayhap a felon's cell in a Northern dungeon. When free from the heel of the oppressor, the State recalled her honored son and clad him with her judicial ermine; it never covered worthier shoulders. This station, and others over this mission, are visited from Charleston; also Aiken, where there is a church, erected by Dr. Persico about 1868; Blackville, the residence of the Graham family; Johnson's, the home of the worthy McDonald and Caroduc families; Ridgeville and Summerville, where there is a modest church erected by the zealous Purcel family, and some other few points, especially Georgetown, as may be seen in the *Catholic Almanac* of this year.

During the time which I served on the mission, after having ended the trip on the fourth Sunday of the month, I always returned to Beaufort by the way of Whippy Swamp, and preached in the Methodist church at that point. It was formerly the settlement of the Mulligan family—two brothers, one of whom was sheriff of Colleton district; they were Catholics, and the children after the death of their parents removed to Spartanburg, before the war, and unhappily lost the Faith. I also preached in the court-house at Gillisonville, to an audience composed chiefly of lawyers and county officers. This mission is very thin, and there are few Catholics west of Barnwell except the children of Mrs. Pinckney at Walterboro, and a few in Beaufort. It was at the beginning the most promising portion of the diocese, and like all other country missions, shrunk after the death of the first Catholics. It was not the consequence of neglect on the part of the bishops, or for want of priestly attendance. If such were possible, the care and attendance were excessive. It was produced by death, emigration, the unhealthiness of the country, the existence of, at the beginning, and the subsequent emancipation of slaves, the disasters of the civil war, the subsequent mis-government and the impoverished condition to which the country was reduced by so many adverse causes. In poverty, wretchedness, and social degradation, South Carolina was reduced to the condition of Ireland, after the wars of the Stuarts, under the brutal sway of Cromwell and Irvin. Religion has suffered immense loss; flourishing missions, planted with labor and expense, have been broken up all over the diocese. Moral and social evils frequently work out their own cure. The obstacles that blocked the way to final triumph have been removed. During forty years Catholicity moved on slowly but surely under slavery; she was still in the desert. The masters looked into her fair face and rejected her. In punishment then came the terrible civil or pro-slavery war, sweeping away with the unresistible violence of the whirlwind, the aristocracy, and wiping out forever the last vestiges of slavery. The country waded in blood, the flower and the youth, Catholic and non-Catholic alike, of the nation, were cut away, year after year, and the scythe of death reaped an abundant harvest. The arrogant pretensions and time-worn abuses of the past, all perished, and can never more be revived, for statesmen teach that revolutions never go back. Their war-cry is—onward! The surgeon who amputates a limb, although he performs but a humane and necessary duty, excites among men a certain feeling of aversion. The consequences of the war were repulsive, and we shrunk from it with dislike. But they have tended to purify the atmosphere of society, condemned and refuted a mistaken system of political economy, and broke down what the non-Catholic ministers always called *the barrier against popery, the cotton fields of the South*. That they were not mistaken the future will prove. The Church is now for the first time in her history in the South fairly started on her mission of enlightenment, civilization, and virtue. Before many years, what are now deserted missions will become Catholic parishes and episcopal sees. Among the many worthy priests who have labored well in this section are mentioned, the elder Father O'Neill, who received most of the Bellinger and Pinckney families into the Church, and Bishop Reynolds, who visited the several stations, preached eloquently, and administered Confirmation. He was an indefatigable missionary, and if he had not been impeded by his size and the heat of the climate, would have been as efficient as his predecessor.

Rt. Rev. Andrew Byrne, D.D., was one of the priests who visited these stations from the city about 1830, and was greatly revered among all classes.[1] Tall and portly, with auburn hair, and commanding aspect, he grew in after years into very large proportions, and at the time of his death was said to be the biggest man in Arkansas. The venerable and pious Mrs. Pinckney assured the writer that the main cause of the conversion to the true Faith, both of herself and her family, was Bishop England's Catechism, given her by Father Byrne, when she was a little girl, after he had performed a marriage at the church in Colleton. He was born in Navan, Ireland, December 5th, 1802, studied in the Diocesan Seminary, and when but a stripling, volunteered for the diocese of Charleston, and accompanied Bishop England to America in 1820. After having made his studies in the Seminary of St. John the Baptist, he was ordained priest April 11th, 1827. He immediately was sent out on this, and subsequently on the North Carolina missions, with his headquarters at Fayetteville—visiting all that vast region, where he endured the privations, sickness, and sufferings of his brother priests, until 1830, when he was recalled to Charleston. He was stationed as pastor at St. Mary's, created Vicar-General, and assisted Bishop England as theologian at the second Council of Baltimore.

He moved to New York City in 1836, and became assistant at the Cathedral. He was subsequently appointed pastor

---

[1] Authorities—Personal recollections chiefly; reminiscences among the faithful; Dr. Clark's "Lives of Deceased Bishops;" Catholic Almanacs.

of St. James' Church. In 1841 he visited his native country to obtain Christian Brothers to conduct schools in the city, by request of Bishop Hughes. After his return he was deputed to the charge of the Church of the Nativity. By his own efforts he purchased the City Hall, used formerly for civil celebrations, fitted it up for a church, and had it dedicated March 19th, 1841, to St. Andrew. The ceremony was performed by Bishop Hughes, assisted by a large number of the clergy, three of whom afterwards became Bishops—Messrs. Byrne, Quartier, and Bacon. He was appointed first Bishop of Little Rock, which comprised the State of Arkansas, the Cherokee and Choctaw Nations, and was consecrated by Archbishop Hughes at St. Patrick's Cathedral, March 10th, 1844, assisted by Bishops Fenwick of Boston, and Whelan of Richmond. His Eminence Cardinal McCloskey and Bishop Quartier were consecrated at the same time. Very Rev. Dr. Power preached on the occasion an eloquent discourse. Fitted by his long and faithful services in the Carolinas for his arduous labors in the new diocese equal in extent to half Europe, he immediately began the work of organization, accompanied by one priest from the North, the venerable Father Curry. He frequently travelled on his visitations from one point to another, seven hundred or one thousand miles. On November 1st, 1845, he ordained at the Post of Arkansas, Rev. Thos. McKenna, the first man raised to the priesthood in the State. He assisted at the sixth Provincial Council of Baltimore, at the first Council in New Orleans, held in 1856. He visited Ireland twice in the interest of religion in his diocese. Having obtained a colony from the Sisters of Mercy in Dublin, they established St. Mary's Academy, at Little Rock, an institution of superior educational advantages, and the parent house of many branches. His labors were active and wide-spread. Our Lord called him to receive his reward, still strong and vigorous ; he died in 1862.

During the eighteen years of his episcopacy he increased the number of churches from four to eighteen, with fifty stations, added twenty priests and six ecclesiastical students to the number of the clergy, which was but four at his arrival; he erected four religious institutions and twelve schools and seminaries, where there had been none; leaving behind a population of fifty thousand Catholics, numbering but five thousand when he began his administration. He had also projected many other noble works which his death prevented; first among these was the College of St. Andrew, at Fort Smith, for which he procured a tract of land a mile square, purchased by funds collected outside the diocese. He contemplated the establishment of a house of the Brothers of the Christian Schools at this point, and a diocesan house where the weary missionary could obtain rest and restore his health, when exhausted by labor and sickness in the duties of the mission. During his day he was considered one of the most laborious bishops in our hierarchy; he was a man of great zeal and prudence, and his administration was a signal success. His memory is cherished by all the faithful, and more than any by his worthy successor, the distinguished Bishop Fitzgerald.

The annual contributions for the maintenance of the clergymen over this entire region amounted to about one hundred and fifty dollars in cash. The horse and vehicle used in travelling were furnished by the Bishop, and the cost drawn from the diocesan funds. If converts surpass the Irish Catholics in the guarded and cautious observance of religious exercises, they are by no means, in general, usually as liberal in contributing to the support of the clergy or the building of places of worship, points which in their opinion should be governed by the strict rules of evangelical poverty. Besides, though these people were regarded opulent, like all others of the same class in the South, their wealth lay in slaves, which, in proportion to their increase, exhausted the produce of their labor, and frequently left their owners penniless. Old age, infancy, and sickness rendered the institution unprofitable as an investment; it would eventually, without any interference, have worn itself out: such has been its fate in all times. After twelve years of freedom, many, now, would gladly return to their former condition, while numbers offer to work without any other remuneration but food and raiment.

The fifth Sunday, whenever it occurred, I spent at my father's home in Savannah. Entertaining the highest admiration for the confessional and sick-call labors of the clergy of his native parish, I invited him to accompany me on one round to offer him an opportunity by personal observation and experience of instituting a comparison and forming a correct judgment. His conclusion was, "That he knew not what he asked when praying for a religious vocation for his children; and if there were high places in heaven they must belong to all priests who had perseveringly labored in this manner." At the end of the first day's journey from Walterboro to Barnwell, I invariably stopped over night in the same wayside house. The family were Baptist. I made it a rule of my life, first to ask permission, and then recite prayers in common for the household whenever I stopped. I was never refused; all joined, and the custom was productive of good. My aged parent, then in his sixtieth year, by his conversation and admonitions after my retirement, manifested much interest in the future welfare of the attentive family. A man of sound common sense, general information, and intellectual powers of a high order, he was a most enlightened Catholic layman, and he made a deeper impression, in this instance, than he was aware of. The people were in admiration of his teachings; they were ready to embrace his doctrine, provided he made it *Protestant, and became their minister.* He was invited through me, accompanied with a request to add persuasion, to remain behind, *accept ordination, assume pastoral charge, settle down, and become the local preacher of the settlement!* He had never before so palpably realized the fact that blameless ignorance may be found beyond the pale of the Church. He inherited St. Polycarp's hatred of heresy; a reproach against religion was a personal affront, the true Faith the only science he prized, and he knew it well. The practice of its duties was the paramount buisness of his long life, to which all other considerations were subordinate.

He always conducted himself as a stranger on earth; the cabin of the needy and the palace of the king, the beggar's rags, and the jewelled garments of the nobleman, had the same value in his mind. His conversation was in heaven, his most familiar companions, our Blessed Lady, St. Joseph, the saints and angels of God. His prayer was uninterrupted; all his occupation, his labors, his industry, even his indifferent acts ministered thereto, and were sanctified by its influence. His favorite devotions were assisting at the Holy Sacrifice of the Mass, praying for the dead, relieving the wants of the poor, and the recital of the Rosary of the Blessed Virgin. The beads were never out of his hands, except to be exchanged for an offering for the needy, or an implement of industry. Beyond the medium height, he was thin, spare, mortified in aspect, with a face bright and shining, especially when absorbed in prayer before the Blessed Sacrament. During a long life of seventy-five years, he never lost Mass wilfully, and never tasted flesh meat during the season of Lent. He never forfeited by word or act the esteem or respect of his fellow-man. This high position he maintained in his own family to the hour of his death; and amid his sons, now past the age of manhood, educated in the first seminaries of human learning, and several years in the care of souls, in the science of the saints, and in the spiritual life, he was still the master. Whatever of the spirit of religious vocation, of detachment, and of self-sacrifice they possess, this was its origin and source.

He was born in the parish of Donoughmore, County Cork, Ireland, on St. Patrick's Day, March 17th, 1783. After having reached manhood, by industry and close application to business, for his religious life was so well regulated that the time of prayer never interfered with his duties in society, he acquired an independent position, and though without landed estate, was the wealthiest man in his native parish. He married Ann, an only daughter of an English family from Cornwall, named Wray. Her father was received into the Church before his death by Rev. Dr. O'Callahan, known through the contest between Dr. England and Sir Nicholas Colthurst, with whom the Wray family resided, at Ardrum. She became the meet helpmate in his industry, the sharer and encourager of his devotions. The mildest and most pious of mothers, her influence shed a halo of gentleness and peace over the family circle, which was nothing short of a religious community, in the midst of the world. There were seven children on the hearthstone; one—Ann—died in youthful innocence in her twelfth year, and her remains, alone of her faimly, rest with those of her ancestors for a thousand years beneath the moss-covered, gray, desecrated walls of the ruined church at Matheha. Without any persuasion on the part of their parents, three sons and a grandson entered the priesthood, while two daughters and a granddaughter joined the Order of the Sisters of Mercy. The diocese of Charleston was chosen as the field of their religious labors. Sister Mary Baptist died in Charleston, after having been in the order twenty-four years; Sister Mary Antonio still survives.

His grandson, Dr. D. J. O'Connell, ministers at the Cathedral in Richmond, and is at this time secretary of his Excellency Mgr. Conroy, Bishop of Ardagh, and Apostolic Delegate to the United States. His sister, Mary Jerome, has been fifteen years a Sister of Mercy. After having given his children to the service of the Church of God, the now lone parents, bereft of all, from Benjamin to Reuben, repaired to this second Egypt in 1846. Having purchased an extensive property next to the Cathedral in Savannah, they settled down in that city, that their children might close their eyes in death; nor were they disappointed. Within four years, April 26th, 1850, my mother died, after having received the Sacraments with her usual fervor, and surrounded by both her daughters and others of the good Sisters of Mercy. After having rested some time in the family vault of Mr. John Cass, I subsequently translated the remains to St. Peter's Cemetery, in Columbia, where they now rest.

The surviving parent mourned her death for fifteen years. He was always liberal of his means for promoting the external objects of Catholicity. He paid for the education of each of his children in the colleges and schools where they made their studies, and they were no incumbrance on the diocese. The portion allotted to each one was given to the institution which he or she entered. The oldest son having received more than a *pro rata*, and which was afterwards increased by additional property in Columbia, there remained the property in Savannah, which, after having made a fair division, my parents conscientiously believed to be their proportion, and free from every just claim on the part of their children. The Sisterhood of Savannah being, at the commencement, straitened for the means of support, my father, by a deed properly executed, and of his own free will, without any undue influence, donated the property in question to that community forever, under the condition of one Mass weekly, in perpetuity, and a small annuity during his lifetime. The Bishop of Savannah for the time being is constituted the adminstrator of this property, for the end and purposes specified, the trust passing on to each succeeding bishop, after the removal of his predecessor by death or other cause. There are letters in the possession of the family from former prelates, gratefully acknowledging the favor, and its advantages to religion in the diocese of Savannah. The property is not only beneficial to the Sisters, but also an accommodation to the Bishop and clergy, on account of its situation and proximity to the church. It facilitated the establishment of the Male Orphan Asylum under Bishop Gartland, and perpetuated by his successor, one or more of the houses having been set apart for the purpose. After the death of Dr. Gartland, Bishop Barry and his clergy, both before and after his consecration, for several years occupied the other house, paying the usual rent to the Sisters. In proportion as Savannah progresses in prosperity, this property, located in the heart of the city, is destined to increase in value, and will become of incalculable benefit to the cause for which it was fairly, honestly, and deliberately devoted. The property was purchased from Messrs. Kelly and O'Conner, respectable men, and good Catholics in their generation. My father retired to Columbia, and lived in the St. Mary's College with the family, a favorite with the teachers, clergy, and students. The first to awake, he was first at the altar, having all in readiness for the Mass, which was his delight to serve. He edified the entire congregation ; his example led many to assist at the daily Masses, brought several to their confession who had not practised their duties for many years. He counselled the doubtful, encouraged the weary, instructed the ignorant, admonished the sinner, and by his example confirmed the good in the paths of virtue and peace.

Having endured a trying and painful illness during two years, nothing less than a prolonged death agony, which he bore as became him, and fortified frequently by the holy Sacraments, consoled also by the celebration of the divine mysteries in his chamber by special permission, he died on the Feast of St. Aloysius, May 21st, 1868. He was prepared for death by the Very Rev. Dr. Lynch, now Bishop, who performed the obsequies and preached the funeral sermom. Patrick O'Connell died in the seventy-fifth year of his age, and is interred in the family burying-ground in Columbia, with his deceased consort, Ann Wray O'Connell, and next to the grave of Sister Mary Baptist. A suitable monument has been erected over his remains. His oldest son, Trial Justice O'Connell, and some of his children are buried close by. He was the impersonation of Catholicity, as a layman the greatest benefactor of the Church in the Carolinas and Georgia. He illustrated her sublime teachings in the tenor of his life, walked blamelessly in the midst of a perverse and unbelieving generation, and lighted the way for others in the narrow path of God's commandments. In gratitude for his noble generosity and charity, the early Bishops of Savannah honored the anniversary of his death by a solemn Requiem Mass, at which the Sisters and their orphans partook of the bread of life.

The reader will easily understand how painful must have been the inditing of this section of the narrative, on account of its personal character. I would fain have omitted it, but a sense of justice required that every man should receive his due, despite of any personal feelings. It is more meet to do so at this time, while there are many living witnesses of the facts detailed, who will shortly slumber in the dust and common forgetfulness of the tomb. The professed object of the writer being to preserve the recollection of the benefactors of religion both among clergy and laymen, as far as can be ascertained, who were instrumental in its establishment, a wilful and serious omission would be unjust alike to the living and the dead.

Many have given much for religion; like the young man in the history of the Passion, divesting himself of the linen garment. Patrick O'Connell gave all, as easily as the beads drop from the wearied hand of a man at prayer overcome by sleep. His children, his family, his life, after a voluntary exile, and the garnered industry of many years, were lavishly bestowed; he counted them as dross, in comparison to the knowledge and super-eminent love of our Lord Jesus Christ. His gratitude for the gift of Catholic faith was so overwhelming that he would be willing to make any sacrifice as an act of thanksgiving. His case is not exceptional; many of his countrymen have done in like manner, and have given the Faith to the English-speaking portion of the human race.

In the spring of 1845 Beaufort, Coosahatchie, and other points of this ecclesiastical district, were visited by the Rev. Wm. Burke, while assistant priest at Savannah. He was born in the County Tipperary, Ireland. After having studied his classics in his native land, he entered the Seminary in Charleston about the year 1834, where he successfully studied the due course under Bishops England, Clancy, and Dr. Baker, and was ordained priest in 1837, being then only in his twenty-third year. He was immediately sent as assistant to the aged Father Brown at St. Mary's, who died shortly after, and Father Burke succeeded in the office, though young in years and but recently ordained. He held the position eight years, discharged its duties with singular ability; he won the love and esteem of his congregation. Polished in manners, tall, comely, and of superior personal appearance, with fine address, and popular as a public speaker, he was calculated to accomplish a great amount of good in the holy ministry, if his life had been prolonged. His once robust health gradually succumbed, and on the arrival of Bishop Reynolds he was relieved for the time being. He visited his native land in search of health and relaxation amid the hills and valleys of the Isle of Saints, the ruins of Holy Cross, and the wilderness of the fallen splendors of the Church of SS. Malachi and Columbkill. He returned buoyant with the hopes of re-established health; but they were evanescent as the bloom of the morning flower which withers under the noonday sun and fades before the rising of the evening star. He was assistant in the labors of the Savannah mission with the venerable Father O'Neill, to whom he was endeared by the holiest ties of priestly regard and spiritual affection. A great part of the time alone, compelled to say two Masses on Sundays, the last always sung, preaching, teaching, visiting the sick, all the weighty duties of that laborious parish proving too heavy a burden for his enfeebled health, especially in the heats of midsummer, he relapsed and died in the second year. Although ailing for months previous, and under the care of eminent physicians, his departure was somewhat sudden. Though moving about some days and discharging light duties, he grew faint one afternoon, and after having received the holy absolution, expired suddenly in the arms of his spiritual father and friend.

His death was regretted by all the citizens of Savannah. His remains, after lying in state for a time in the church where he had so faithfully ministered, were conveyed to Charleston, accompanied by his brothers and other mourning relations and friends, and placed in St. Mary's Church. Bishop Reynolds celebrated the Pontifical Requiem Mass, and performed the obsequies. A suitable discourse was pronounced by Very Rev. P. N. Lynch, D.D., before a large congregation and all the assembled clergy of the city. The body was interred hard by the altar of the Blessed Virgin Mary, whom he loved and served during his life, and who had provided a resting-place for him after death. He was a noble-hearted man, generous, affectionate, and confiding; many friends mourned over his grave: he never made an enemy. He departed this life in the year 1846, in the thirty-third year of his age, and the tenth of his ministry.

CHAPTER VI.

COLUMBIA, S. C.

St. Peter's Church—First Catholics—Laborers on the Canal—Opposition of South Carolina to Irish Catholic Immigrants—Refused Permission to Land in Charleston—The Church Founded in 1824—Corner-stone Laid by Freemasons—The Old Catholics Poor but Faithful—Names of Many—Distinguished Members of the Congregation—General Blanchard, Mrs. Semmes, James Claffey, J. W. Bradley, etc.—Refugees—M. P. O'Conner—Mrs. Durban—Ursuline Convent—Sherman—Vestrymen or Trustees—An Old Heresy in a New Mask—First Check in the Diocese—The Constitution Framed to Limit and Cure Abuses and Encroachments—Thos. Lenard and the Burning of the Charleston Convent—Speedy Punishment of Sacrilege—Stone-cutters in Columbia—Rev. Thomas A. Flynn—Piety and Early Death—Rev. James Wallace, his Learning, Faith, and Happy Death—The South Carolina College, its Character—Professor Lieber and the Iconoclasts—Controversy between Dr. Lynch and Professor Thornwell—A Sectarian College Maintained by Universal Taxation—The Library, an Unscientific Collection—The College Hospital—Fired on while visiting Sick Federal Soldiers—Colonel Corcoran, Lieutenants Dempsey, Connolly, and other Prisoners of the 69th Irish Regiment—The Prison Mass, a Picture—Etc., etc.

COLUMBIA, the capital of the State of South Carolina, is situated in Richmond County, on the eastern bank of the Congaree River, on an elevated plain, in a picturesque country, healthy and exempt from yellow fever and all malarial distempers. The Legislature, Lunatic Asylum, Penitentiary, and other State institutions are located here, besides denominational establishments, rendering this the centre of legislation, religion, and learning. Though there were one or two Catholic families in advance, we trace the earliest vestiges of a congregation to a body of Irish laborers, who were employed and introduced from the North, about 1821, to build the canal. At that time this was considered an arduous and expensive work; it runs along the rapids of the river, a distance of nearly five miles, from the upper bridge to Granby, where navigation ceases, and which at one time it was contemplated to make the capital of South Carolina. For many years past the canal has been superseded by the railroads, and it is now entirely useless for the purposes for which it was originally intended. Many of the workingmen died within a year or two after their arrival, from exposure to excessive heat in the day, and the miasma inseparable from the character and location of their occupation. Their remains were interred either in the old Potter's Field at the right of the depot of the South Carolina Railroad, or in the embankments of the canal; it made no difference to them where, as there was neither priest nor Catholic churchyard in the place.

Columbia was then but a village, not as old or respectable as Camden and other towns nearly forgotten. Most of those who survived, after the work was finished, returned to the Free States, except very few, who settled down, opened small stores, and formed the nucleus of a congregation. The State was always opposed to immigration, and what was called *white labor*, as endangering the institution of slavery. At a recent period, immigrants were denied permission to land in Charleston, and were forced to return by the same vessels that wafted them to shores more inhospitable than the quicksands of Byrsa. This mistaken policy militated against the best interests of the country up to and during the war; although all the foreign-born citizens living South fought nobly for her independence, yet they were outnumbered and overpowered by Europeans. Even when the General Government contemplated erecting a navy-yard at Port Royal, the people objected, on account of the possible danger to their cherished institutions. The citizens were intensely averse to harbor any one born beyond the boundaries of the slave territory. Our bishops and clergy were branded as foreigners, notwithstanding their naturalization oath; the Church of the most blessed God was denounced as alien and hostile to all the vital interests of society. A renegade Catholic or an Irish Protestant were exceptions; a Frenchman or a German, who were not sensitive about religious questions, were tolerated; but there was positive hatred against an Irish Catholic, or perhaps a Northern man. After many years of residence and intermarriage, the asperity of unkindliness would thaw into forbearance. This hostility did not prevail to the same extent in any of the other Slave States, nor perhaps in America, with the exception of Massachusetts.

The opposition of races, or of those who first saw the light of day in a different clime, against each other, is a feeling common to mankind, more or less intensified by a variety of causes, and the enduring consequence of original sin, palpable as death itself. A strange soil is never steady under the sore foot of an exile, whether on the shores of the Nile or the Edisto. All the innumerable multitude of men who now dwell on the earth, who have lived, or will yet live, were created to be as one family, and one with God; but, having fallen away from their centre, they are so divided among themselves and charity is so rare, that two or three gathered in *His name* is so great a wonder, that He promised to give them whatever they ask; men spurn not only grace, but the use of their natural reason; they bury themselves deeper and deeper in flesh and blood, until, like the uncivilized tribes, they hate, deceive, betray, fear, and murder one another.

About 1821, I find that a lot was purchased from a Mr. Taylor, and a brick church of respectable dimensions commenced to be built. Bishop England being absent at the time, and there being no permanently-stationed priest, the corner-stone was laid by the Masonic craft. The emblems were subsequently extracted by Rev. Dr. Birmingham, sent to Charleston, and were to be seen in the library of the Seminary of St. John the Baptist. It would seem from this fact that there were fallen Catholics among the fraternity, and indeed there is a tradition that a non-English-speaking priest in Charleston, before the arrival of Bishop England, was a Freemason. He was detected one morning bearing on his person the unmistakable marks of his nocturnal occupation, which, in his hurry, he had forgotten to lay aside. In God's Providence a church never can succeed nor prosper without a bishop; if a good man, eloquence is only a subordinate consideration.

In a new country like the United States, the closer the Apostolic custom is followed of erecting or multiplying sees, the better for the interests of religion. I have divided the faithful into three classes—the first settlers, those who settled down permanently about 1850, and those who sojourned temporarily during the war, either as refugees or in connection with the army. I have learned by tradition or oral history, for all the records of this church were burnt by Sherman's army, that the first Catholics were of good social standing. Emanuel Antonio left a large family, chiefly daughters, and but one son. Two of the children, Mrs. Watts, of Macon, Ga., and Mrs. Champy, of Orangeburg, retained the Faith and imparted the priceless gift to their offspring. Bishop England was often the guest of Mr. Antonio during his visits and on the occasions when he delivered his grand lectures before the Legislature, which, if they did not convert, convinced the hearers of their error. He had during his day less success by his sermons at the capitol than St. Paul at Athens. Those boasted seats of learning, in ancient or modern times, have never proved fruitful fields of missionary labor for an apostle or his successor.

Terence O'Hanlan and his wife retained the Faith to the last, and died at an advanced age about 1854, having received the Sacraments. All their children, men of good social position, unhappily fell away and died outside of the pale of the Church. They were all baptized and received the Sacraments in their early life. The three brothers, John P., Luke, and James Crayon, or Crane, always openly professed their religion, and never denied it from fear or favor. The two former owned what was known as Clarke's Hotel, and lately the Ursuline Convent, until destroyed by Sherman's army in 1865. During their time, the priest had a comfortable home; Mass was said on Sundays in the hall, and there was every prospect of a favorable opening for the Church, which was still in an inchoate state; but the time had not come; the family withdrew to more promising fields of enterprise and labor. During a quarter of a century, and until 1852, the congregation was composed of the few Irish Catholics who remained after the canal was finished, their children, a French woman, Madame Sibpt, a German family named Pape, who lost the Faith, and a few others, amounting to about one hundred souls at the utmost. James Crayon lived from the first a few miles outside of town, owned an extensive farm on Bear Creek, well-stocked with slaves and all agricultural requirements.

His wife was a good, devout woman, and raised her children in the fear of God. She died some time before her husband, who departed this life about 1858; both are buried in St. Peter's Cemetery, with some of their children. Mary, the eldest, married a Mr. Brennan, and left two children— Thomas and Martha, who was educated by the Sisters of Mercy, and married Dr. Sikes. Another daughter, Louisa, espoused P. H. Flannagan, who died about 1872, leaving many children, whom their zealous mother has endeavored to raise Catholics.

The other brother removed to Montgomery, Ala., where I have lost sight of him. The Duncan family are their descendants, to which Father Duncan, of the Society of Jesus, adds a lustre by his religious profession, his learning and zeal. Luke left two daughters, Susan and Catherine; the former married Colonel John Basket, an eminent lawyer; and the other General James Jones, both natives of Edgefield District.

Both the sisters were accomplished, and intensely devoted to their religion, for which they gained consideration among their associates, on account of their piety. Mrs. Jones' house was the asylum of the orphan, and the refuge of the friendless. The General, who was a kind-hearted man, and the true type of the Southern gentleman, afforded his wife full scope in the exercise of her works of charity; though childless, she was a mother to the needy, who will rise up and call her blessed. About the year 1854, when chosen by the Legislature Commissioner for the erection of the new State-House, General Jones removed his family to Columbia; his brother-in-law, Colonel Basket, transferred his establishment thither also. Mrs. Jones died the death of the just about 1862, and was mourned by the entire community.

After the war, the General returned to Edgefield, and resided at Vaucluse Factory, with which he had a business relation, where he died shortly after, and rather suddenly. After the first shock of paralysis he became insensible, and on the well-grounded presumption of virtual assent, he received Baptism from Miss Margaret Porter, an Irish Catholic lady, who lived a long time in the family as tutoress of the orphans, and was the inseparable companion of Mrs. Jones in her works of piety. The residence of the good and zealous Father Birmingham for years in the family, when he had no other shelter, all the surroundings and antecedents of the case, leave no room to doubt but that he had the intention of embracing the Faith; his fault was procrastination, often the infirmity of even the just. It is to be hoped that behind the dark veil that hung between the departing spirit and his surrounding friends, all was bright and cheerful from the light of God's merciful countenance. He was scarcely fifty-six years of age.

The code of honor, as it was erroneously called, prevailed in South Carolina up to his day. At least, it erases Christian forbearance from the roll of virtue, and robs man of the crown promised to the pardon of injuries, and which was always the grand distinguishing mark between heathen and Christian ethics. Masonry and itself are both arrayed against the charity of the Father and the Lord Jesus Christ, which has been infused into our hearts by the Holy Ghost. He was president of the board chosen to determine and administer the rules governing this relic of barbaric chivalry. Constituted as society is, the office was one of great honor. It is related that no case was presented at any time before this council that ended in a hostile meeting; it was a peacemaker. Both sides presented their difficulties; mistakes were corrected, explanations made, facts divested of false appearances, and the truth established. The party in fault made ample apology; if not, he was dismissed as unworthy of further notice, and beyond the pale of respectability. Reconciliation generally followed, lost friendships were restored and peace established. Although born and raised in *bloody Edgefield*, Adjutant-General of the State, President of the Code of Honor, and a man who never knew fear, General Jones was gentleness itself. He held a command in the commencement of the war, at the defences before Charleston, but resigned in consequence of a breach of military etiquette on the part of outranking officers; an intentional insult he would not brook; this was not a season for explanations or divided councils, and he withdrew. May we not say of him: *Blessed are the peace-makers, for they shall be called the children of God?*

Mrs. Basket survived her sister, and also her husband, and died about the year 1871. She raised four children. Thomas, the eldest, who was educated at Georgetown College, married in Florida and died rather young. John received his early education at St. Mary's College, Columbia, adopted his father's profession, and is now a respectable jurist: he married Helen, the oldest daughter of Major John R. Nearnsie, the architect of the new State-House, but now residing in Baltimore. Susan, the elder daughter, was educated by the Sisters of our Lady of Mercy in Charleston, and married David, son of Caleb Clarke, M. D., of Winnsboro. Her husband removed to Baltimore in 1866, where he lost his excellent wife. In her life there was nothing which was not pious and charitable; she has left a family of children to imitate their mother in faith and good works. The youngest daughter, Kate, no less distinguished than her mother and sister for zeal and piety, is married to Robert, son of Dr. John Lynch, and nephew of the Bishop; she resides in Columbia.

The father, Colonel John Basket, died about the year 1867. I received his profession of faith, baptized him unconditionally, and during his lingering illness administered to him the other Sacraments. He died with the utmost resignation, full of faith, hope, and charity; he fell asleep in our Lord, like a slumbering infant, without murmur or complaint. He died between the age of sixty-eight and seventy years. Reputed to be the best special pleader before the bar of South Carolina, persuasion hung on his lips. A niece, Caroline Wadlington, was also brought into the fold through the influence of her aunt and family, with whom she spent a large portion of her time during her girlhood. She was united in wedlock by Bishop Reynolds to Ellison Keitt, of Orangeburg, brother of Hon. Lawrence M. Keitt, a respectable statesman and an able public speaker. I received Mr. Keitt into the Church. After about ten years of a happy married life, spent in piety and in the discharge of her domestic duties, Mrs. Caroline Keitt died at her residence near Columbia, fortified by the holy Sacraments. She was an excellent lady; pious and devoted to all her religious duties; an affectionate mother, humane to her servants, and compassionate to the poor. She left several children; her oldest, a daughter, received her education at the Ursuline Convent at Valle Crucis. After the restoration of peace, Mr. Keitt removed his motherless children to his estate in Newberry. It is to be hoped that the children will cultivate the priceless inheritance of the true Faith left them by their parents, and in which they are baptized, and in their time bequeath the pearl of the Gospel to their own generations. *The promise is to you and to your children, who are from afar.*

Howard Haine Caldwell was born at Newberry, and was son of Chancellor Caldwell. After having completed the usual course of studies in the South Carolina College, where he graduated with great honor, he devoted his time to the cultivation of polite literature. He published a book of poems, much esteemed among the learned, for many exquisite poetical effusions and gems of rare thought. His elevation of sentiment, refined culture, and deep Christian feeling excited well-founded hopes of still greater eminence. Impressed strongly by ancestral and Scottish proclivities, he was much attached to Calvinistic teachings. After long and patient inquiry, he abandoned the tenets of John Knox for the mild maxims of our Lord, perpetuated in the Church. Having found the treasure of the Gospel, he loved the Catholic Church with all the devotion of his deeply affectionate nature. A master in the harmony of sound, he led the choir and dispensed the music in St. Peter's Church with devotion and thrilling effect. He married Agnes, the second daughter of Charles Montague, and their union was blessed by one child only, a daughter, who wore her father's features, though she cannot remember him. Never robust in health, death soon claimed for his own the gifted child of poetry and song. Fortified by the rites of the Church, he died about 1857, in the twenty-ninth year of his age, and his remains now slumber under the shadow of the temple in which he adored his Maker in spirit and in truth, and which he had so often filled with hymn and melody, during the celebration of the divine mysteries of our redemption.

The popularity of the Catholic schools—one the St. Mary's College, and the other the Academy of the Immaculate Conception, under the Sisters of Mercy, induced many respectable families to remove to Columbia for the purpose of educating their children; a Catholic church and school will benefit every locality, even in a worldly point of view. One of these was Charles Montague, a well-informed Irishman, and a practical Catholic. He resided many years at Fayetteville, N. C., the benefactor of the Church and clergy, who had struggled on for years, one after another, on that desolate mission, where they needed the necessaries of life. He transferred his family and property to this place in 1854. Mrs. Montague, who was a convert, and of French ancestry, died within a few years in a very edifying manner, and strengthened in the last conflict with the holy Sacraments, which she always frequented since her conversion. Six children survive. The eldest, Mary Catharine, espoused C. J. Bollin, and is now a widow. Agnes, the relict of Howard Caldwell, and the others, still live in different places; all adhering steadfastly to the Church. Mr. Montague after some time removed to Texas, and was for a period tutor in mathematics at St. Mary's College.

There were several Catholic ladies residing in the city for a number of years, who were held in merited esteem by the community, which they adorned by their accomplishments and edified by their virtues—shedding a lustre on our holy religion by their purity of life and tireless toil in well-doing. Margaret, the only daughter of Thomas Cullen, was to the manner born, and received her education at the Convent of the Sisters of Mercy in Charleston; she always faithfully practised the lessons of piety impressed on her tender mind by the devoted Sisters. For many years she conducted the choir with equal skill and piety, having succeeded the saintly Mrs. Comerford, who organized it in the earliest Catholic times. Miss Cullen is the last of her family; after the death of her parents she went to Augusta for the purpose of educating the children of her cousin, Hon. James Gardiner, where she still resides. The two brothers, James and Thomas, were worthy Catholic young men, and died in peace with their Maker, after having reached the years of manhood. Patrick, the eldest son, was a physician of notable respectability; he made his first medical studies under Dr. Simeon Fair, a brother of Solicitor Fair, and a leading man in his profession. He graduated at the Medical College in Charleston, practised many years in Sumter district, and finally in Savannah, Ga., where he died from the second attack of yellow fever in 1854. The malady was exceedingly fatal that year. Bishops Gartland, Barron, several priests and physicians were carried off. Dr. Cullen was the last who succumbed; he fell at the post of duty, after his associates had died by his side, and his memory will be always venerated by a grateful city. Miss Margaret Garnett was born in Dublin, of Protestant parentage, and raised in the best classes of metropolitan society. She received a first-class Continental education, possessed rare intellectual endowments, and was second to none in practical devotion. She joined the first pilgrimage from America to the Holy Father, and has remained in Europe since; a clause in her father's will renders her domicile there a condition for the inheritance of her patrimony.

She is of the family of Sir Garnet Wolsely, of Ashantee fame.

Under this recommendation I cannot omit the mention of Ellen McGinnis, second daughter of M. C. McGinnis ; Rosa, the niece of John W. Bradley, now a widow, and residing in Brooklyn ; the Misses Saunders and their parents ; Miss Mary Jelico, Miss M. Doyle, and her aunt of the same name; and many other good and worthy women, once worshipping in the congregation of Columbia; they will be known and praised when God will raise the just and render to every one according to his works.

Edmund Bellinger, Jr., stood at the head of his profession, having moved from Barnwell about 1854, where he built up an extensive and lucrative practice; he opened a law office in Columbia in co-partnership with his son-in-law, Colonel John Maher, a learned lawyer and an excellent Catholic. Mr. Bellinger also inaugurated a law school, which he conducted with eminent ability, and where he delivered lectures on subjects bearing on the profession, which were listened to with great profit by the young lawyers and those who had grown old in the temple of Justice. His legal lore, general information, and magnetic eloquence fascinated his hearers, and rendered his lectures literary treats of rare excellence. He was appointed by the Legislature to codify the laws of the State, and died while engaged in that duty, at the moderate age of fifty-six or seven. He received the holy Extreme Unction when dying; his remains were transferred to Barnwell, and interred in St. Andrew's Church. This occurred about 1860. He was during a number of years the chief support, or in other words the principal support, of religion on that mission, where there were so few Catholics: his hospitable mansion was the priest's home; he served the holy Mass daily whenever an opportunity presented itself. His name and influence gained consideration for the Catholics then at Barnwell Court-House. He was free from the weakness of some converts, who imagine they do Catholics a great favor when they embrace the truth and try to save their souls; they not unfrequently insinuate and even boast

that their parents or friends were heretics or unfortunate
Protestants. Now, this is all wrong ; the Church needs no
men, all need her. It is oneself and not another who is
favored by saving the soul from everlasting perdition, and he
is the debtor ; surely we should not glory in our errors, nor
those of our parents ; they are our shame, and what greater
crime than heresy or the believing of falsehoods about God
and contradicting the Holy Ghost ? Converts in this frame
of mind stand in great danger of apostasy. The soul that
will experience only miracles and consolations in the spiritual life will only with difficulty persevere; how much
greater is the danger for those who require not only divine
but also human consolations ? No persecution is necessary
to force them to renounce the truth ; they drop away like
diseased branches from the tree. Many, alas ! who served
God half a lifetime, and those again who have made heroic
sacrifices, have grown weary, looked behind them, and asked
back the vain trifles which in their early years they wisely
disregarded when weighed in the balance of eternity.
Many a bark that has outlived the storms of mid-ocean,
in the darkness of wintry nights, has been wrecked in port.
The defection of converts, like that of aged people, is something too terrible to be dwelt on. After Mr. B.'s demise all
his family returned to Barnwell ; he left two daughters, devout and pious ; and several sons, whom may God enable
to persevere in the Faith in which they were baptized, and
follow the example of their distinguished father.

Major J. R. Nearnsie was also in Columbia at this time.
An Austrian by birth, and a graduate of the Polytechnic
School of Vienna, he ranked high in his profession, and was
chosen architect of the new State-House. He professed the
Faith, and raised his children Catholics. Mrs. Nearnsie, her
mother, Miss Emma Clarke, and all the family were second
to no people in piety and fidelity to their religion and in
social position. The State-House was not completed at the
time of the sack of Columbia; it was injured and mutilated
in several parts, and the statue of Washington battered.
The work was discontinued under the unpropitious adminis-

tration of the Radicals, but enough remains to form an endearing monument of Catholic genius and enterprise. Mr. N. has lived in Baltimore since the close of the war. Now that fraud has ceased in the administration of State affairs, with the restoration of domestic government, it is to be hoped that he may be recalled to finish his noble conception, every stone of which has a tongue to proclaim his eminence in his exalted profession.

Dr. Lynch settled down in Columbia about 1855. He was born in Ireland, and married a daughter of Major McNamara, of Salisbury, N. C.; their union has been blessed with a large family of children, who all practise their religious duties. His father, Conlaw Lynch, of Cheraw, whither he was drifted by an accident, was one of the grand pioneers of the Faith in Carolina. He professed it openly when there were neither church nor bishop between Richmond and New Orleans. His piety and intelligence gained respect for the sign of the cross; like the Catholics of Japan, he would have raised his family in the Faith if they never saw tho face of a priest. I was reliably informed that five of the children, much grown, and like a young set of Baptists, were all christened at the first visit of a priest to that far distant section. God rewarded his fidelity; two of his daughters embraced the religious state; a third, Julia, won the crown of heaven at her parents' hearth. Many of the children after reaching the years of maturity died, all fortified with the Sacraments of salvation. After he saw his son consecrated third Bishop of Charleston, Mr. Lynch laid down his time-honored head to rest, at a patriarchal age, leaving a name dear to Catholicity and his numerous descendants.

The powder-mills were erected on the grounds now occupied by the State Prison, and conducted during the war by P. B. Garache, an enterprising and exemplary Catholic. He died after the surrender at St. Louis. He married a daughter of General McLane, the ex-Minister to England, and sister-in-law of General Joseph E. Johnston, of the Confederate army, justly styled the hero of the Seven Days' Fight before Richmond. She was truly devout, and never lost her first fervor. Two children remain to perpetuate the name and virtues of their parents. John Judge superintended a clothes factory for the army; he was an exemplary man, virtuous and honest; he was married to a lady of equal merit, and the only sister of Mrs. McGuire, of Wilmington, whose memory is dear to the faithful of that episcopal city and of the whole vicariate of North Carolina. The sisters Mary and Honora Murphy, the Cantwells, O'Briens, and many others, are deserving of special mention for piety and virtue. A large number of stone-cutters and other operatives were employed on the work of the State-House. They were nominally Catholic, but scarcely a half a dozen practised their religion or entered the church except on some semi-religious occasion, such as a wedding or a funeral. Of no advantage to the Church in any sense, they were, on the contrary, factious and censorious, and an exception to any body of Irish Catholics with whom I ever came into ministerial relations. One of their number got the lash for imputed interference with a slave on the subject of his emancipation, but to the extent only of indiscreet expressions, a circumstance which embittered the entire body exceedingly against the community. It was credibly reported that the aggrieved individual and many of his comrades joined Sherman's army, and returned to avenge this indignity. After the surrender, the broken and disheartened bands that passed through the smoking ruins, the forest of black, houseless chimneys, and the deserted streets, that marked Sherman's occupation of that once *proud City of Flowers*, exulted at the sight of her desolation and shouted aloud with a voice that sounded through the forsaken halls: *Hurrah for the Yankees! this is the city in which white men were whipped for talking to a negro.* These were native-born soldiers who fought to the bitter end for Southern rights, and were on their way to homes of poverty, faint and sick and bleeding. When the Roman legions thundered at the gates of Jerusalem, and the heavy tramp of marching troops, mingled with the loud cries of battle, resounded through the Holy of Holies, and a pagan band reduced to irreparable ruin temple and city, thousands mourned the fate of the faithless Queen of Nations; but few wept for Columbia, despite the cruelty of her destruction, an act unjustified by the usages of civilized warfare.

During the bombardment of the city of Charleston, and from the day when the first shell was sent on its mission of destruction from what was jeeringly styled the "*Swamp Angel*," the people lost all confidence in the safety of the city and fled to all parts of the interior of the State for shelter and the preservation of their lives. Their sufferings are inconceivable. They abandoned their homes and sacrificed their property by barter or by selling it for the illusory currency, which was not equivalent in value to common writing-paper, and they were informed so by Hon. Mr. Stephens, of Georgia, when he was urging a compromise, and the world knew we were defeated. The refugees were to be met at every locality, both in town and country, from the migratory Capital, from Georgia, Tennessee, Missouri, from every one of the Confederate States.

The increased number of strangers enhanced the value of articles of diet, which had become scarce, and of other goods also; boots averaged from $50 to $100 a pair, and all things else in proportion. They expected sympathy, and found none; they differed in manners, tastes, and sentiment from the native people, whom they called the peasantry, and became very unpopular. A spirit of antagonism bordering on hatred grew daily more intense, until they had become almost as odious as the Yankees. It illustrates how far self-interest can revolutionize the mind and warp the judgment of men; a little while longer, and we would be at the edge of the reign of terror; hence Sherman's march through the country was hailed with delight, until he began to leave ruin and destruction in his path. It will require many years before the prejudices imbibed during that period will have faded away from the minds of both people. A civil war, while it lasts, is the most merciless of warfares, and it snaps asunder the tenderest ties of human nature.

This estrangement of feeling did not exist among Catholics; they are held together by the band of religious union, which being divine, is the strongest of any, and will subsist under the pressure of the most trying severity; this is shown by the unity of the Church, which makes people of the remotest and dissimilar nations *one family*. The Catholic refugees were cordially received. They had the sympathy of their brethren for their sufferings, and were edifying members of our congregations. They found a priest everywhere, and felt at home wherever they could kneel before the altar of God. General Blanchard, who commanded the defences at Petersburg, and his family; M. P. O'Conner, of Charleston, and his saintly mother from Beaufort; Phil Fogartie, his mother and family; Mrs. Admiral Semmes, of Mobile; Mrs. Allemong, who lost her noblehearted son at the siege of Petersburg; the McCareys, Kennys, Trumbos, Ringolds, Poincignons. Durbecs, Figeraux, and many others endeared themselves to everybody by their moral bearing and genuine Catholic piety. We rejoiced when they were permitted to return and rebuild their deserted homes and ruined fortunes.

The Ursuline Convent had also received within its walls many of the daughters of the first families—Catholic and Protestant and Israelites—not alone for the sake of education, but also for protection; which goes to prove that, in fact, people do not credit any of the unseemly reports against our female religious institutions. It was never dreamt that a civilized country would deem it expedient in the hour of midnight to fling out into the flames of a burning city, abandoned to the pillage of a dissolute soldiery, inflamed with the worst passions of the human heart, a body of venerable and worthy ladies, with their band of little children, and all of the first and most respectable families, both Sisters and their pupils. I led that mournful procession from the desecrated Convent, through the lurid flames, to the graveyard of the church, where they remained until daylight, when the flames had spent their fury for want of food and human aid to prolong their progress, and until the sun shot his bloody rays over the smoking ruins of Columbia and a demoralized army.

Many of these here mentioned have gone to their rest. Mrs. Durban, of Beaufort, a daughter of the Aimar family, left us her precious remains, in the midst of the turmoil and the storm, while her meek spirit sought shelter in the bosom of the Almighty Father. Sustained by the Faith and its consolations, more Catholics survived the war than people of any other class, in proportion to their numbers; the loss of all their earthly goods, and of the most cherished members of the family, have not deranged a single individual amongst us, nor caused a suicide. Our holy religion alone will explain this exceptional preservation and vitality. We have been taught and we know that poverty, sufferings, and humiliations are not the greatest evils; there are many things worse than death. Viewed in the light of eternity, these were all blessings; death itself is the gate to immortal life.

For several years, at least between 1850 and '65, the Catholic congregation of Columbia ranked high for intelligence and respectability. The destruction of our religious and educational institutions at the latter date, threw the congregation back into its normal state, and retarded the progress of our holy Faith many years.

The permanent body, who formed the congregation proper, deserve a special notice. They were generally poor Irish people, and gained their support by conducting retail stores or services in the Asylum. As a body, the latter were our most edifying and respectable members. Numbering about one hundred persons—the women were virtuous without an exception; the men formed three divisions; some were good, others careless, and some disedifying in their lives, and all without social or intellectual standing. At one time, we had Mass in the jail on Sundays as regularly as in the church; many of our leading men were in prison, suffering the penalty for having violated the law prohibiting the selling of spirits to slaves. This was frequently the case, and women too shared in the disgrace. The clergy never enjoyed any peace among them; they were assiduously and intentionally harassed, and lived in the state of domestic warfare. Letters of complaint filled with futile or unjust charges, petitions for removal, and other odious documents of this nature, were being constantly, and for years, sent to each succeeding bishop, and against priests of irreproachable character. Personal violence was often threatened—the well-meaning were forbidden to contribute their miserable pittance to their maintenance, factions consisting of the very scum of the people were organized by some travelling merchant or barkeeper, in order to defeat the priest, and which were a scandal and disgrace all over the country to so great an extent that the clergy feared an appointment to a charge so odious and unchristian. Protestants had compassion for the priest, and not unfrequently interposed their cordial services to establish peace. All were the working of the Vestry innovation, that uncatholic institution, the very essence of heresy, which was universally introduced into the Church in the United States, and which had borne evil fruit and developed schism and scandal, its necessary results, in several cities. For the best ot purposes, and to check encroachments, it was systematized in the diocese. In the hands of unprincipled and bad men, it became the engine for the perpetration of these and many other outrages. If properly conducted, and composed of good men, lay-trustees may accomplish much good; but the vestry element is so undeniably heterodox in church government, that it can never he trusted. Bishop England compiled the "Constitution of the Diocese of Charleston," for the purpose of restraining abuses, and confining the action of vestrymen within the bounds of moderation; he himself suffered, and being forbidden the use of the only church in Charleston, was compelled to say Mass in a weatherboarded shed, known as the printing-office of the *U. S. Catholic Miscellany*. It not unfrequently happened that the least edifying members, sometimes notoriously immoral men, would secure their election on the board by intrigue and all other electioneering arts; we know that infields and Freemasons have been vestrymen In Columbia, as in Philadelphia and New Orleans, they resisted the efforts of the clergy for the promotion of religion and the salvation of souls. Their authority was absolute, and was exercised with terrible malice. On a certain occasion, when about fitting up a bench or two on a vacant gallery up-stairs, which was always a disorderly corner and occupied by people of questionable morality, for the accomodation of negro converts, and at an expense of only nine dollars, which was to be realized without making an appeal from the altar, it was strenuously opposed by that deluded body, and the leader, picking up a brick-bat, spoke thus to the young priest: "See here, sir, look at this brick-bat; you durst not meddle even with it without the consent of this board." Some people, Irish equally as others, after having accumulated, in the hardest manner, a few thousand dollars, become very arrogant and indocile; aiming at a false popularity, they will pander to the lowest passion of the people to reach some petty office; and in our thin congregations South, their great ambition was, to aspire to church government, and dictate both to bishop and priests.

You will scarcely meet one, who is improved in his spiritual life, by having served as a trustee, the temporalities of the Church become spiritual things, and their alienation visited with the penalty of excommunication. Despite the evils that have occurred from this system, and its inherent danger, pious and edifying men have served as trustees even in Columbia; but, as a class, the virtuous and well-disposed are too easily overpowered by the vicious: a bad man exercises greater power for evil, than a dozen honest men do for good. At the close of the Reign of Terror in France, it was ascertained that the moderate, the orderly, and the humane had been in the majority all over the country, even in Paris, Lyons, and Marseilles; but they were panic-struck and overpowered by the more audacious and unscrupulous minority. The discovery of their strength sounded the death-knell of Robespierre and the Jacobins or Freemasons.

Having endured a long time, like my predecessors, I determined, after having obtained the permission of Bishop

Reynolds, to end this persecution or resign my charge. Having prepared the people by public and private exhortations, I formally submitted the point to a vote of the congregation: *Shall there be vestry or not, henceforward?* The question was unanimously decided in the negative, and the vestry dissolved itself. The decision was ratified by the Bishop, and the body received its first check. But the difficulty was re-opened; the very men who had conformed and assented to their dismemberment repented and retracted; they declared their action *illegal and unconstitutional*, and refused to resign their trust into the hands of priest or bishop.

The controversy opened anew lasted a long time, and was conducted with much asperity. Sustained by the virtuous portion of the people, I persevered, convinced that nothing calculated to promote religion could be effected under such men. The church edifice was crumbling to ruins, and could not be put in repair; no clergyman could live in peace under their dominion. The annual stipend for the priest's support scarcely exceeded $150 all this time, and now there were two in the city and on its out missions. Finally, and after a desperate struggle, the opposition broke down, the former action was re-affirmed, and the pastor was left free to labor in the cause of religion, education, and the salvation of souls. This was an offshoot of the old schism in Charleston.

That a clergyman engaged in the duties of the mission, and encumbered at the same time with the erection of churches, school-houses, and other institutions, generally needs the counsel of experienced and prudent laymen, is very probable. The admonition of the Madianite priest to the Hebrew legislator was based on this prudent consideration, and in the hands of Providence was the means of introducing and establishing the Sanhedrim, which was composed of seventy-two judges, and became the infallible teaching authority of the elder dispensation. But the evils entailed by serious litigation and the misappropriation of funds, the incurring of debts more than the value of the property, outbalance the doubtful advantage of this purely uncatholic element of government that crept into the administration of the Church in the United States. This is the evil against which, in one form or another, the Church combated for centuries, and which, despite the triumph of St. Gregory VII., lingered on in England, and contributed to produce and perpetuate the so-called Reformation. Its introduction was blameless, and the result of the absence of responsible priests at the early formation of many of the congregations, and when even Freemasons have laid the foundations of churches. The Society of St. Vincent de Paul, besides the fulfilment of the duties of its organization, seems admirably suited to meet the requirements of the case. The selection of one or two good men by the pastor, who possess the confidence of priest and people, has been found by experience to be a satisfactory way of meeting it. They co-operate with the priest cheerfully and harmoniously, feel honored by the choice, and being good and worthy men, act with zeal and honesty.

I built the wall at the rear of the Cemetery in Columbia, and erected also the front wall, built in rock and brick masonry, with its magnificent iron gates and railing, which is an ornament to the city, with the aid of only one plain, well-disposed man, James Claffey. The St. Mary's College, the Sisters' Convent, and the church were remodelled, rebuilt, and enlarged without the advice or assistance of any one, save the hired mechanics.

Michael Comerford is the oldest Catholic now living in the congregation, plain, honest, and without guile; his life was uniform in virtue and piety. Having been twice married, his first wife, who was of French descent, was always first in every undertaking connected with the promotion of religion during the trying and difficult times of the early priests; she taught music and French in the most respectable families in the city, furnished to the church an organ of moderate power, was the first who built up a choir, which she conducted in the most edifying manner. Her maiden name was Dupuy; she died the death of the just, about 1858, leaving no issue. His second wife, Catherine Bogan, is a Catholic lady in the true acceptation of the word; a woman of uncommon generosity, piety, and charity. The other leading Catholics were the McElrone family, John Martin, Thos. Levy and family, the Jelicos, Thos. and Mrs. Leonard, all employed at the Lunatic Asylum, though in humble station, were worthy, pious people, and much esteemed. Mrs. Kehoe was the very oldest Catholic woman in the congregation. She left three children, who were married and who are also dead; Patrick, the only son, lost his life in battle, the second year of the war; Catherine, who was married to Alexander Civil, and left two sons; the third, Mary, was married to Wm. P. Lowther of Georgia, and is also dead; they were a virtuous and truly Catholic family; Edward and Patrick Scott and his wife, Adelaide, who is dead; Joshua Ford, Mrs. Roland Kernan, who brought her husband into the Church, Dennis McGinnis and family, the Saunders family, Thos., Patrick, and Richard Flanagan, John White, —these and some others constituted the standing congregation of St. Peter's Church for many years.

During the stormy times of the persecution of the priests, and when the vestry ruled supreme, John W. Bradley was the main stay and support of the clergy and the Church. He and James Claffey were the truest friends of religion in the city for many years. A great part of the time the pastor could not maintain his ground, from the pressure both within and outside, had it not been for the aid, the protection, and the sympathy of these good men in particular. The priest lived with Mr. Bradley; his house was his home in every sense of the word. He was born in County Derry, was a nephew of Hon. W. McKenna, of Lancaster, and by occupation a merchant, but not successful; it was said he was too honest to accumulate a fortune. He married Margaret, the pious and accomplished daughter of Mr. Thorington, of Montgomery, Ala., whom he was the means of bringing into the Church, and raised a large family. He removed from Columbia to Camden in 1851, in consequence of the depression of the times; and lost his excellent lady shortly after; of a delicate constitution, she soon succumbed under frequent ailment, and died young, probably about thirty-six years of age. Her remains are interred in the family lot in St. Peter's Church-yard. Mr. Bradley died in New York, in 1854, and received the last Sacraments from Vicar-General Quinn; his death was like his life, holy and edifying. His remains were conveyed to Columbia in a neat casket, and laid by the side of his deceased and beloved wife, in the presence of a large concourse of mourning friends. He was then only in his fifty-sixth year, but died full of merit and good works; virtue and not years constitute old age: hence, Saul, who filled the throne forty years, is said by the Holy Ghost to have reigned but two years in Israel.

The eldest born and only son, Edward, died soon after his father, before he had reached the age of manhood; he lived some time previous to his death with his uncle, who resided in Minnesota, and followed the profession of law. There were five daughters, who were placed under the care of the Sisters of Mercy in Charleston since their mother's death, and until removed and provided for by Mr. Daniel Devlin, of New York, a relative of the family. The two eldest, Sarah and Annie, married and died shortly after. The remaining three, Mary, Margaret, and Caroline, still live and are sharers in the affluence and affection of their relatives.

James Claffey, the noble and charitable man whose floor was never without the poor and orphan, died in 1873, in the fifty-second year of his age. His wife, Rose, who was in every way worthy of him, and whom none excelled in piety, died soon after her husband. Four children survive to inherit the name and virtues of their parents—Annie, the only surviving daughter, and her brothers, Robert, James, and Michael. Thomas Leonard was gardener at the Asylum, and died in 1853, about sixty-eight years of age. He was a well-informed man, and firm in faith and piety. He was employed at his occupation in the convent at Charlestown, and was actually on the premises the night of its destruction by the Beecher mob. He never tired of narrating events enacted on that terrible occasion, and one in particular, which was indelibly fixed on his memory, and which perhaps is not generally known; it goes to show how suddenly Divine justice avenges the crime of sacrilege. On the morning after that dreadful night, a well-dressed man appeared in a crowded office at one of the hotels, while the tragedy that had been enacted was being discussed; taking from his pocket a handful of consecrated Hosts, that had been emptied from the stolen ciborium, for whatever was of value was plundered, if it could be carried off, he filled his mouth with the particles, and in a jeering manner cried out, "*I can breakfast as well as the priest!*" Some of the sacred Hosts he replaced in his pockets. He withdrew, and in a short time was found seated in the water-closet, and cold in death; he was punished like Judas; the particles lay scattered on the floor in every direction, but were reverently picked up by a Catholic servant and carried to the church. The carcass of the unhappy wretch was exposed an entire day in a thoroughfare of the city, and not being recognized or claimed by any one, was buried somewhere out of sight. A similar scene of incendiarism, at least, would have occurred in Charleston and disgraced that proud city, if not prevented by the courage and determination of her great Bishop England, as related elsewhere in this volume.

The Flynn family were of the old stock of Catholic pioneers, pious and edifying. Mrs. Flynn having been twice married, had by her first husband two daughters, Mary and Elizabeth McKenna. The first, who married Mr. Mangum, died at an early age, leaving two children, a son and a daughter. Elizabeth, the second child, married Coleman Walker, and still lives to edify by her piety and good example. The widow subsequently married Patrick Flynn, a sincere Catholic; he died about 1871. Their union was blessed by the birth of three sons; Charles, the second boy, an exemplary and virtuous young man, fell at the battle of Chickamauga, while cheering on his men to victory. On visiting the scene of carnage, his bereaved father discovered the remains scantily covered with clay, where he had died on the battle-field, and transferred them to St. Peter's for interment. The youngest, John, died about 1869.

Thomas Augustine, the eldest son, was called to the holy ministry. He made his preparatory studies at St. Mary's College, Columbia, was sent to France by Bishop Reynolds, and after several years' study at the College of Cholet, where he was distinguished for his piety and ability, his strength gave way. Toward the close of his collegiate course his health had become so precarious, in consequence of the severity of the climate and the austere system of preparation by which candidates for the priesthood are prepared for the sublime duties in missionary France, that, after having received the Holy Order of Sub-deaconship, he was recommended to return to his native soil immediately, in the hope that the mild climate of the South might re-establish his enfeebled constitution. He was ordained deacon and priest by Archbishop Wood on his way home, and spent some months with his maternal relatives at Wilmington, Del. He passed the winter of 1867 under the paternal roof, and daily offered the Holy Sacrifice. Appointed assistant chaplain to the Sisters by Bishop Lynch the following summer, while acting in that capacity in Charleston, within a few weeks his pulmonary complaint made speedy inroads, and terminated, after a short struggle, his earthly existence for a life and crown in heaven. Tall in stature, mortified and meek in mien, he seemed a very angel at the altar. Enrolled in the shining ranks of the apostolic choir, he was translated before a breath of calumny had sullied his name or a sin stained his conscience. Who would deplore such a death? He was the first native-born Columbian ordained priest.

How different are the ways and graces of God towards men!—as much so as our individualities or features; no two are alike. Close by in the same graveyard lie the remains of Rev. James Wallace, a septuagenarian, who bore with fortitude the wintry blasts of a boisterous public life, assailed by jealousy and embittered by ingratitude. He was born in Kilkenny, Ireland, about 1783. He was one of the scholastics brought by Fathers Kohlman and Fenwick to found the New York Literary Institute, which reached a high eminence in its day as an educational establishment. Mr. Wallance had the reputation of being the ablest mathematician then in America; he compiled a learned treatise on astronomy and the use of the globes—one of the first contributions of the Society of Jesus to exact science in this country. After the college had been discontinued, Fathers Fenwick and Wallace, who was now ordained a priest, were sent on the mission to Charleston, where they officiated until the arrival of Bishop England. Father Fenwick, who afterward became Bishop of Boston, returned to Georgetown, but his co-laborer remained behind, and at the instance of Bishop England, accepted the chair of mathematics in the South Carolina College, to which he was elected by the trustees. He filled the position several years with distinguished ability, and elevated the character of the College for learning and science. The simple fact of his being a priest disarmed many prejudices against the Church among the rising youth of the country.

His term of office was the golden age of the College; but a spirit of opposition gathered strength daily, and culminating in a faction, deprived Drs. Knott, Wallace, and other learned men of their professorships, on the charge of infidelity, and to their places promoted men of inferior and mediocre attainments. In the Observatory could be seen for a long time, and perhaps up to this date, the telescope strewn about, a pile of ruins, like the disjointed bones of a mastodon, and since the ejection of Professor Wallace none of the teachers who succeeded was able to readjust it.

The institution finally became sectarian; the preachers of various denominations occupied professorships, and were the most perfect embodiment of anti-Catholic sentiment that found personality in any one body in the State. It lost its character as a literary institution, was the toy of the Legislature, and a nondescript place, where the sons of wealthy families formed mutual acquaintance, lived without restraint, and lavished health and means. The Hon. Wm. C. Preston, who was styled the Cicero of the United States Senate, and the most polished gentleman in the State, was removed from the presidency. It became the hot-bed of religious bigotry, nativism, and secession. A Catholic had no business there. A couple of youths who were enrolled among its students were perverted and lost the Faith. The struggling aspirations of talented young men, who possessed no means of education, were scarcely ever encouraged. Like the Episcopal Church in Columbia, she did not want the poor; other places were good enough for that class. The youth became utterly uncontrollable, and a nuisance to the city. Learning had become distasteful and unpopular.

It must be put on record, to the lasting discredit of the old College, that a scholar of national reputation, the compiler of our best encyclopædia for select historical matter, Professor Lieber, a German by birth, was expelled from her halls, his bust mutilated and ignominiously treated, in an outburst of ill-feeling against foreigners, if not against education. One who in after-times happens to read these pages will be at a loss to understand how formal opposition against the Christianity of sixteen centuries of the civilization of the world, and of nine-tenths of the present day, could have emanated from a reputed seat of learning in a State, and supported by a large and respectable body of citizens whose faith was assailed and misrepresented. Denominational education finds, in this instance, a strong argument in its favor, and the fallacy of claiming impartial and unbiassed education for Godless colleges is exposed.

It cannot be denied that many excellent and some distinguished men have made the collegiate course here. Domestic training, the village school, individual industry, and natural aptitude, have had a larger share in their intellectual formation than the Alma Mater. There have been more self-made men in colleges than the world is aware of; the great in all the walks of literature, science, and art attained their eminence by private study and labor. After the war the institution passed under the administration of the emancipated slaves and their co-equals, the carpet-baggers. It was contemplated to sell the building at one time. It is composed of straggling brick houses, scattered around three sides of a square, without order or architectural proportions. Since the classes were dismissed, and after hostilities began, it was converted into a hospital for sick and wounded soldiers. Father Lawrence O'Connell was appointed chaplain, to the horror of the civilians, who remonstrated on the ground that the Confederacy ought to have been satisfied with the lives of her unfortunate soldiers, and not ruin their souls everlastingly by so un-Christian an act. She must kill both body and soul! I visited some United States soldiers the evening before the sack of the city, and who, poor fellows, were ill in the College Hospital; the yellow flag was streaming from the roof, yet Sherman's shells flew around in all directions, and fell within a few feet of where I stood. Being in an exposed position, and in full view of the battery on the Lexington side, I am persuaded I was shot at, but escaped death under the providence of God.

What is called the Library is a miscellaneous collection of books unscientifically selected, some good, some bad, and the most part worthless and inadequate to enable a student to follow up the investigation of any department in the various kingdoms of literature and art in its details of modern progress; for science is still in its infancy. The formation of a library should be the first step in the march of advancement under the restoration of home rule. For its accomplishment the time and services of a learned librarian are needed; he must be no ordinary scholar, but a man of deep and general education. South Carolina can easily find such a one among her Catholic clergymen, for her constitution is not sectarian; all are her children, without distinction of creed, and are equally entitled to a share in civil offices, as they are obligated to bear the burden of her legislation. At this time the State can boast of the most fitting man in America for the purpose, a Carolinian by birth and one raised amid the tomes of the Propaganda Library, where many of the literary treasures of the universe are gathered,

Rev. Dr. Corcoran, of Charleston, now of St. Charles Borromeo's Seminary, Philadelphia.

After his connection with the college had ceased, Dr. Wallace moved to Lexington District, within a few miles of the city, and devoted his declining years to meditation and prayer. He led the life of a hermit, avoided all intercourse with the world, and scarcely saw any one but his confessor. I cannot ascertain that he took charge of the congregation at any period, but he said Mass, and exercised, when necessary, the other duties of the ministry. He was relieved from his obligations to the Society of Jesus. After a long course of preparation, and fortified by the Sacraments, he met his death with great confidence in God, and resignation to His will. Moderate in his mode of living, and thrifty in habits, a considerable amount of property had accumulated on his hands, consisting of three houses in Columbia, an island in Congaree River, called after his name, a strip of land along the canal, the site of the powder-works during the war, and now of the State Prison. Some slaves also appertained to the estate, but the most valuable escaped to the Free States after his death. All which, including the homestead in Lexington, he bequeathed to Bishop Reynolds and his successors in office, in trust, for the establishment of a Male Orphan Asylum in Charleston. The island, the farm in Lexington, and the penitentiary site came under the administration of Bishop Lynch. C. B. Northrop and J. J. O'Connell were the executors of his last will.

He died on the 15th day of January, 1851. Life and death both establish the truth of God's word; man could never devise so impartial a leveller as the latter; the vaunted equality and fraternity of communism are not a shadow in the comparison. It fills up all the valleys and brings down every hill of social distinction, leaving the human race in the same condition in which it enters into the gate of life. God's chastisements in time are all favors. In our fallen condition, it is both a mercy and a necessity; it is the end of sin and sorrow, the end of scandal, the correction of our errors, and the removal of social and moral evils. The evolution never ceases, but is accelerated by the aid of war, famine, and pestilence, as though the ordinary process was inadequate to meet the ever-increasing necessity. It erects the tomb of the young priest, whose hands are still fragrant with the sweet odor of sacerdotal unction, by the side of the time-worn minister who has grown hoary in the shades of the sanctuary; makes Adam and his last descendant cotemporaries; and gathers the entire race of mankind into a period of time, which a prophet and an evangelist both call *to-day*.

Colonel Corcoran, afterwards General, and a portion of the Sixty-ninth Regiment, captured at the first battle of Manasses, were transferred from Richmond to Columbia, and imprisoned in the common jail during the second year of the war. One of the vessels of our tiny navy having been captured, the United States threatened to punish the commander and his comrades as pirates; if carried into effect, the Confederacy was determined to retaliate by inflicting a similar death at the rope's end on the hero of Manasses and his soldiers, man for man, and preparatory thereto removed them to Castle Pinckney, in the harbor of Charleston. The Irish troops were the only soldiers who fought with credit, and made even a respectable resistance on the side of the North at that memorable battle, and where the South was defeated by her victory. Her already overweening pride was more inflated still, the imputed cowardice of her foes confirmed in general opinion, and none believed there would be another engagement; on the contrary, that all difficulties were at rest and decided by the sword. The country began the framing of laws, settled down into the pursuit of the arts of peace, made no provision for the coming struggle, and permitted her volunteer troops to linger in tedious inaction around the camp fires. Their first ardor had grown cold; tired of military life, they clamored to be disbanded, or permitted to return to their homes; many died of various diseases, and all were more or less demoralized. During this same period, the Northern people were marshalling their men and making all preparations necessary to meet the gigantic proportion which the conflict assumed.

Tall and slender, with fair complexion, and gentle as a maiden, General Corcoran appeared to be no older than thirty-five years. He and his shattered command were sincere Catholics, and deeply attached to the cause which they espoused, and for which they volunteered to serve in a body. They became an interesting portion of the congregation, and easily won the kindest regard and sympathy of the faithful generally, and especially of the Irish element. Attempting to visit them, immediately after their arrival, I was given to understand that a license from the Governor was necessary to secure an entrance. I made application to Governor Pickens through Colonel John Basket; as both were Edgefield men, I was persuaded the request would be more readily granted by this course. A refusal was apprehended, because of the deep animosity entertained against all Northern people, and especially against prisoners of war, open sympathy for whom would expose oneself to suspicion and serious trouble. Inquiring whether I was a true Southern man, and being answered affirmatively, I was sent a written pass, and had henceforward easy access to the prison. The General, Lieutenants Connolly, Dempsey, all the other officers and men were rejoiced to see the priest, and the pleasure was mutual. I visited them regularly, said Mass whenever I had an opportunity, and had material aid extended whenever the act did not imperil personal safety. I was frequently affected with sadness on beholding the weary and thought-sick looks of disappointment that greeted my visits, when there was no news of the exchange of prisoners to be communicated. This refusal was the greatest act of cruelty and injustice perpetrated during the remorseless conflict. Thousands perished in the stockades from exposure and want of all necessaries of life, hunger, sickness, and nakedness; and without blame: for our own men suffered in like manner, and from the same causes.

After having offered the Holy Sacrifice on a certain Sunday or festival, probably on Epiphany, 1862, and while addressing words of consolation to these brave men whose features bore the prison look, and into whose souls the rust of the felon's cell was rapidly eating its way, the door leading to the temporary chapel was suddenly thrown wide open, the turnkey abruptly entered, and in my presence, while in my priestly vestments, and at the altar, interrupted the service, spoke abruptly, slowly counted the heads with pointed finger, and twice over. I believe that the commandant had no sympathy with this act of his subordinate, for Colonel Shiver was a humane man and a benevolent gentleman, who had ameliorated the condition of those under his charge, and the survivors cherish with gratitude the remembrance of his many acts of kindness.

Those who had just received the Holy Communion were still kneeling at the altar. The General, having served Mass, was leaning against the wall near by. All the fountains of feeling, to their inmost depths, were stirred in every bosom, and the strongest contending emotion rapidly swept over every face in the group, like stormy clouds in the heavens. In proportion as man's liberty is limited and his rights curtailed, will his nature resent the attempt to infringe on the few that survive the ruin of his former state. Nothing is held more sacred in the social order than the rights of the wretched. This is the reason why the world condemns Sir Hudson Lowe's treatment of the fallen conqueror of Europe while chained to the rock of St. Helena.

These men then in a dungeon were ennobled by their chains, and had rights guaranteed even to the felon—liberty of conscience; the whisper of an early and ignominious death that sounded in their ears continually made these rights more sacred, and before the eye of the entire civilized world they were martyrs for the cause of their country. The leader of the chained band, by his constrained attitude of composure, endeavored to disguise his contempt for the cruel dishonor. A soldier who had made his communion was kneeling by the window; a cold sunbeam crept through the bar like God's mercy, finding its way everywhere, and played on his livid face; his shoulders were bent, and he wore an aspect of inconsolable sadness, like a community shocked by some recent sacrilege, and refusing to be comforted. Another looked dismayed as one who gazes on some deed of unnatural cruelty; all were horror-struck; their outraged feelings soon settled into the subdued sorrow of imprisonment; looking on the sign of redemption, they knelt, and with drooping heads received the last blessing. This was the last Mass said in this jail; it was not expected, nor could I expose the divine mysteries to further irreverence and insult; it was the first place burnt by Sherman's army, and after having been exchanged, the remembrance of that prison Mass may have nerved an arm to deal harder blows in the din of battle. Before my departure, the General said: "So this is the treatment you receive at the hands of a people you seem to like so well, and serve so faithfully. Among us no priest would be insulted in this manner in the performance of his sacred duties; nor, in fact, any other clergyman. Society would not tolerate it." I regretted the exhibiting of mortified feelings when I replied: "It were better if on both sides we stood aloof from the fray, and let those people fight their own battles."

The surviving members of the Sixty-ninth Regiment or of the Irish Brigade could erect no more suitable monument to the memory of their comrades than by transferring to canvas the *Mass scene in the jail of Columbia*, and let its facts disclose to future generations the sufferings, the patriotism, and the faith of Irish Catholics in the defence equally as in the formation of the Union. It would be acceptable to every section of the country; within a few years the statue of Lee will be as dear to America as that of Grant. Civil wars while they last are the most cruel of any, partaking of the asperity of family feuds. After peace is restored the sufferings and noble deeds of each party become the property of both, and contribute alike to the common fund of national glory, live in brass or marble, are perpetuated by song and story, and enrich the literature of the country. France is proud of the valor and indomitable perseverance of the

Vendeans; England, though she weeps, cherishes the remembrance of the hard-fought battles between the rival houses of York and Lancaster; the United States already mourns alike over the graves of Southern and Northern soldiers.

CHAPTER VII.

COLUMBIA, S. C. (*continued*).

Fathers Corkery, Stokes, McGinnis, Barry, O'Neill—Dr. Birmingham—Character, Labor, Missions, Life, Death—Church at Edgefield dedicated by Bishop Lynch—A Mitre lost by an Able Discourse—Comparison—Rev. Edward Quigley—Rev. J. J. O'Connell appointed in 1848—Extent of Mission—The Establishment of the Sisters of Mercy—Rev. L. P. O'Connell—Catholic Church the Patron of Learning—Prohibited in Ireland by Penal Enactments—Godless Teaching and its Sad Consequences—St. Mary's College—Professors—Popularity—Violent Opposition—Priests Stoned—Non-Catholic Patronage Unreliable—The College a Commissary Store—Opposition to the Church in Columbia—Mixed Marriages: their Consequences—A Reign of Terror—Organization for Self-defence—A Mandatory Petition—Firmness of Bishop Lynch—Rufus M. Johnston, Esq.—Vindication of the Priest—Marriage Fee—Etc., etc.

FATHER CORKERY, a native of Cork, Ireland, is said to have been the first parish priest stationed permanently in Columbia. He had the reputation of being an excellent public speaker, and, what is of greater importance, a worthy man. Moral excellence, zeal for the salvation of souls, and labor in the Lord's vineyard, more than eloquent sermons or profound learning, though desirable, leave an enduring impression on the minds of men, which influences in behalf of religion after human life is o'er. Mr. Corkery was such a man; he resided at the hotel with the Crayon family, said Mass in a suitable apartment on week-days, and in the public hall on Sundays. About the year 1824 he was changed to Augusta, where he labored assiduously for about two years, when, in attending the plague-stricken, and while administering the Sacraments, he contracted the prevailing disease, and died at the post of duty and honor. He was buried in the city cemetery, where his grave is still pointed out. He is remembered as a self-sacrificing and devoted clergyman, who laid down his life freely for his flock, and in the morning of his days received the crown won by others only after a long and varied life of suffering and care. After the transfer of Father Corkery, the Rev. Joseph Stokes ministered in the rising parish, without any fixed residence and as a regionary missionary, until about the year 1826. He was succeeded by Rev. John McGinnis, who remained until he was sent to Charlotte, about 1828, where he conducted a school and supported himself in this way until he left for the diocese of New York.

Father Barry, afterwards Bishop, succeeded and ministered to the spiritual wants of the people for about one year, when Rev. J. F. O'Neill, who had been on the mission in Fayetteville and Eastern North Carolina since his ordination, relieved him, and remained on the mission three or four years. He labored faithfully here, as on his other missions, and was popular with all denominations. It was during the time of Nullification, a political doctrine which he held in common with many leading and distinguished men, a circumstance which endeared him still more to that class. The church building, during the past eight years, was only roofed in from the weather, and in a very unfinished state, for lack of means for its completion. Father O'Neill was sent to Savannah, and Rev. T. Birmingham followed, about 1832. His pastorship comes down to 1844. He was a native of County Tipperary, Ireland, studied at Montreal until 1829, and at the Seminary in Charleston, where he was ordained about the year 1832. He was shortly afterwards stationed at the capital by Bishop England, a high tribute to his learning and efficiency. He occupied this position twelve years. During all his time in Columbia, he scarcely enjoyed one day's peace, but was bitterly opposed by faction after faction. Petitions were dispatched to the ecclesiastical superior, whether priest or bishop, praying an investigation or his removal, and for no weightier reason than the imputed want of a pleasing address; of medium stature, attenuated frame, sharp face, thin hair, and an uncommonly long nose, he looked the impersonation of mortification and ill health. His irreproachable life, joined to austerity of manners and habitual prayer, rendered him an efficient missionary priest, and the most successful questor in America or anywhere, in his time, in behalf of religion. He was well-informed, perfectly self-possessed in every circle, inside or outside of the sanctuary, interesting in conversation, and a respectable preacher. While saying Mass at St. Peter's on a certain occasion, when he doubtless prolonged his fervor to an unusual extent, the attendant grew tired, and betaking himself to other duties in the vicinity, such as sweeping segments of the floor, he returned at intervals, to notice the progress and minister if need be. The sacred office over, he then cast a look of manifest displeasure at the impassible fleshless American missionary, and said in a subdued voice: "*Pius IX. is a saint, and he says Mass in a half an hour.*" It is not expected that more than a half an hour should be spent in saying a Low Mass, unless the priest celebrates in private, and for his own devotion. The people get tired, grow weary and distracted, and will fall away from the daily Masses, if they are kept too long; except some pious few, who are found in every congregation, have little or no care, and happily, spend their time before the Tabernacle; but these exceptional souls are no rule by which to estimate the piety of the generality of the faithful.

Father Birmingham was popular among Protestants, and he induced a good many to embrace the Faith. He planted the oak-trees around the cemetery that grew to gigantic proportions, and made improvements on the church, which was situated between a theatre on one side and a circus on the other, without an intervening building or wall of separation. If the situation was not the most fashionable in town, it was by no means the dullest, especially in Advent and during the session of the Legislature. It not unfrequently happened that service was held simultaneously in all the buildings, and a distinguished priest, Dr. Baker, who was delivering a course of lectures, was forced to discontinue them, compelled to combat the wild beasts, like St. Paul at Ephesus.

He was cherished and esteemed by Bishop England, whom he, on his part, regarded as the greatest living prelate in the Church, and venerated as a saint. He was translated by Bishop Reynolds to Columbus, Ga., in 1844, where he labored with his characteristic zeal. In 1846 he received leave of absence for the restoration of his health, which had become very precarious; he visited several countries of the continent of Europe, and spent the winter in Rome. He returned in the fall of 1847, and continued to exercise his duties until the appointment of Dr. Gartland to Savannah in 1850, when he again returned to the old diocese, and was stationed on the Edgefield mission. He visited the various stations as far as Barnwell, and fixed his headquarters at the Cathedral, until he purchased a valuable piece of property in the village, including several acres of land and a genteel residence. He commenced building a church at Edgefield, when there were scarcely two dozen Catholics within the district, and up to this time they have not increased in number. The object in building so costly an edifice was to make this the site of a female religious institution, in which he was encouraged by the Bishop; but the intention was defeated by the location of the Ursuline Nuns at Columbia. The church is a massive, handsome building of granite rock, and destined to last for ages, with a capacity to accommodate more worshippers than are likely to fill it for many years. It would be an ornament to any city in America, and is more suited to a fashionable seaport than a country village in the interior of the State. When I visited this mission in 1860 there were not more than a dozen Catholics in the congregation, which a modest frame or brick building would suit better than a Gothic structure of mediæval grandeur, with bell-tower and organ, and none to occupy the vacant places in the silent aisles. These were Dr. Burt, Jr., a convert, with his wife and children, who have since moved to another State; the other brother, Dr. Burt, the elder, a convert also, an educated man, and the most fluent speaker in the district: he died during the war, leaving two daughters; the eldest, Sallie Roper, who was educated by the Sisters in Columbia, married Mr. Strother, retains her faith and practises it with fervor; the next daughter, Emily, married a Mr. Matthews, a convert also: these and an Irish family were the only Catholics I met at that time in the village and within the vicinity.

The number was still thinned by death and migration, and at this period there are scarcely more than at the inception of the work, a quarter of a century ago. The Church impresses the idea of her own durability in all her works; she knows she is commensurate with time; all generations are hers, whether in obedience or revolt. The priest looked to the future, if disappointed in his original intentions. He did not abandon the undertaking; he knew that even in Edgefield there was greater likelihood of the church being filled with true worshippers, in time to come, than there existed at the period of their erection that the wonderful structures of faith now in ruins or decay all over the British isles would be without ministers or a solitary Catholic to worship where millions thronged for several generations. It is not labor in vain, to the eye of faith, to make one spot on earth all that heaven can be (for its highest bliss is that God is manifested there), giving the wayfarer the privilege of the blessed—that of approaching in familiar intercourse the throne where the Incarnate God leads His marvellous Eucharistic life. He collected money for this purpose in all the Atlantic cities, from Canada to Louisiana. Engaged in the like occupation, for the rebuilding of the Sisters' house and church in Columbia, we entered into a copartnership, and collected conjointly, through Alabama and in New Orleans. We were hospitably entertained by Bishop Portier and Archbishop Blanc, but were not allowed to make an appeal from the pulpit; limited to what any man has a right to do,—ask privately for aid, if he needs it, for himself or for others, or for an object of public or private benefit. Unless undertaken under false pretenses, or otherwise reprehensible, no man living ought, in justice, to interfere with the common rights of both parties,—of one to ask and receive, of the other to give or refuse, whichever he thinks proper. We divided off the streets into separate walks, quested singly, and made an equal division of the proceeds at the winding-up. We were paid in specie, which, being chiefly silver, was both heavy and bulky, and most inconvenient for transportation. The porters suspected we carried treasures, because of the enormous weight of our trunks, and we were in constant danger of being robbed. It was only on our return to Mobile that we succeeded, by way of compliment, in procuring a bill of exchange on New York for the amount; we could not obtain paper currency for it anywhere. Truly, those were *hard cash times*. Father Birmingham paid court to the wealthier class, while I, taking the sections *stradatim*, extended my industry to all the Irish Catholics whom I met; it was useless to ask any others. I succeeded better in the end, and we arrived at the certain conclusion that begging is entirely *a foot work*.

The church was finished after some years of unremitting toil and hardship, and without the personal aid of priest or layman, save the plan which the architect of the State-House, Major Nearnsie, furnished gratis. It was dedicated in 1859 by Bishop Lynch, who sang High Mass, assisted by Rev. Thos. Murphy, of Wilmington, as deacon, and Rev. J. J. O'Connell, of Columbia, as sub-deacon, Rev. F. J. Carr, of the Cathedral, master of ceremonies. The Bishop preached an able discourse in the morning on the establishment of the Church and the sufferings of the early Christians. I preached in the afternoon, on the Real Presence. At the beginning of the war between the Northern and Southern States, Father Birmingham returned to Europe, where he remained until the restoration of peace in 1865; he collected all over the Continent, and realized a handsome sum for the advancement of religion; all which was faithfully applied to its legitimate object, under the direction or at the disposal of the Bishop. He was generously assisted and hospitably entertained by the Catholic nobility of England. The Emperor and Empress of Austria, the Cardinal Archbishop of Vienna, and the nobility of the court received him in the kindest manner, and extended material assistance, asking in return the blessings of the time-worn American missionary. He *failed signally only in one instance* throughout his lifelong missions—in the Court of Napoleon III., at the Tuileries. Having sought and obtained an audience, he explained the object of his visit to the saturnine Emperor, and detailed the sympathy he had received from crowned heads in other courts. The wily man, afterwards defeated by his own cunning, fixed his rayless eyes on vacuity, his face looked as unimpressed as if he heard him not, and he made *no reply*. An uncivil answer even would have been more respectful to the venerable missionary than a contemptuous and disdainful silence.

Father B. was warmly received by the Pope, the generous heart of the Catholic world, and by the dignitaries of the holy city. He was decorated with the title of Doctor of Divinity, an ornament becoming his enlightened piety, unswerving faith, and missionary labors. He subsequently made a pilgrimage to Jerusalem, kissed our Blessed Lord's footprints in the land of prophecy and promises ; knelt in sorrow at the Mount of Atonement, whose sacrifice he had a thousand times repeated in the Cathedrals, of the Old World, and oftener still in the wilderness of the New. After taking leave of the Holy Sepulchre, of the birthplace of Mary, and the cradle of the Church, he again turned his face to the Far West, and passing through the Appian Way of Irish and European immigration across the stormy ocean, landed safe in Bishop England's favored City by the Sea. The small number of Catholics in the diocese, and their poverty as a class, rendered constant appeals to other localities absolutely necessary to obtain pecuniary aid to erect churches and other religious institutions. The faithful in the three States that composed the diocese could not erect the single Cathedral destroyed by fire in the city of Charleston by such contributions as are considered elsewhere only reasonable ; hence she always, and from her creation, stood before the Catholic world in the garb of Lazarus. How long she is destined to endure this unenviable position, will depend on immigration, and on the increased prosperity of her children. "*The poor you shall always have among you,*" was the oft-repeated answer of

Dr. Birmingham in reply to those who murmured at the frequency of his demands on their charity.

After his arrival he was promoted to the office of Vicar-General, pastor of the Cathedral, and Superior of the Sisters of Mercy; these duties he fulfilled with his wonted zeal and fidelity, to the time of his death. Though now quite aged and feeble from frequent ailments, he could not desist from engaging in new enterprises for the good of religion. The old frame building that had been used as a church many years, on Sullivan's Island in the harbor, and always thronged during the summer months by Catholics from the city, had perished. He applied to the Government, solicited the *débris* of Fort Sumter, which was left in ruins after the bombardment by the Federal fleet, and began the erection of a solid brick building, which was completed and dedicated to *Mary, Star of the Sea.*

Rt. Rev. Dr. Persico, ex-Vicar-Apostolic of Agra, in British India, succeeded to the charge in 1867, and built a church at Aiken. He continued to work faithfully as an humble missionary priest, until transferred to the see of Savannah in 1870. He attended the Vatican Council, and voted affirmatively on the infallibility of the Pope at the first blush of the case, a question scarcely ever doubted by a sound Catholic before Jansenism and Protestantism. So universal was the faith of the world on the point, that it was not thought necessary to define it at any of the enlightened Councils of the Church. It became necessary at this time, in the providence of God, in preparing for future contingencies in His Church. Who can venture to say how many or how few other Councils will be held? If in his capacity as teacher of the doctrines of Christ, the Pope was and is infallible, and believed to be so always, the declaration of the fact was as opportune as the declaration of any other article of faith. A hesitation to affirm her belief would be unbecoming the mother of the millions who told the truth, and testified what they knew as such at the sacrifice of their lives. Bishop Persico resigned his see after nearly two years' occupancy, in consequence of ill-health, the cause of his leaving India, to which he was attached. Having returned to his native country, he was created coadjutor Bishop, in an Italian see, in 1878: He was a Franciscan monk before his elevation to the episcopacy. He was of a distinguished family, was born about the year 1822, and consecrated in early life. A pious man, and an eloquent English preacher, he was much esteemed. The resources of his personal property enabled him to become a benefactor to the Church. He left a rich endowment to the vicariate of Agra, where he is held in great veneration, and bequeathed a magnificent altar and other ornaments to the Cathedral at Savannah.

Dr. Birmingham attended the first Plenary Council at Baltimore as theologian. Many attempts were made from abroad, to improve the spiritual condition of the negro since his emancipation. It was contemplated by the prelates to elect a regionary bishop, to preside over this class of our people, and arrange for the instruction of those who were ignorant of the Faith. But the bishop of each diocese is the one appointed by Divine Providence to attend to the wants of all committed to his care, of whatever race, color, or condition, and he must render an account for them to the Bishop of our souls. A jurisdiction running over so many sees seems complicated, and may interfere with the local authority, or may cause a collision therewith, except in case of the regular clergy, who have their houses, furnish their own priests, and whose administrations are regulated by the canonical enactments of centuries. Dr. B. having been selected to discuss the measure before the fathers of the Council, pointed out its difficulties so manifestly as to have defeated it. The Rt. Rev. Dr. McGill, the learned Bishop of Richmond, complimented his success so highly, as to assure him that it had lost him a mitre; if the plan were adopted, he would be the bishop.

He visited New York in 1872 to seek medical aid, and within a few days after his arrival expired at the hospital under the care of the Sisters. His remains were sent to Charleston, and are buried by the side of his friend and venerated father in God, Bishop England, in what had been the sanctuary of the old Cathedral of St. Finbar. He was sixty-eight years old, and forty years a priest.

The Very Rev. Timothy Birmingham, D.D., in manners and disposition resembled Dr. Gallitzin; the latter possessed broader features of character. Both were intensely pious. Both labored during a long life to found churches and build up missions. Dr. B., with but nominal congregations, and without domestic resources, solicited the aid of the world abroad, and accomplished his works, unfriended and companionless. Each passed unscathed, through the fiery ordeal of persecution from false brethern, which served but to purify and strengthen in life's battle. Both fought the good fight, died at an advanced age, leaving their memory, their labors, and their priestly ministrations, a rich inheritance to the growing Church of the United States. If either had a fault, it was the intensity of zeal.

Rev. Edward Quigley took Dr. Birmingham's place in Columbia in 1854, when the latter was transferred to Columbus, Ga. Mr. Quigley's earliest mission was in Sumter District, his congregation consisting of but a half-dozen households. During his pastorship he lived in the family of Mr. Bradley. He improved the face of Church matters considerably: attended all the outside missions; held a fair, which was handsomely patronized; renewed and completed the church, which was unfurnished; and purchased an excellent organ, which is still in good condition after some repairs. He left in the fall of 1848, at his own request, much regretted by the people.

In the autumn of 1848 I was transferred from the Beaufort mission to Columbia, and discharged the duties of pastor for twenty-three years. Father Quigley was my immediate predecessor. I resided in the edifying family of John W. Bradley during two years, and until their removal to Camden. The mission covered more than one-half the State. I was alone, without assistant, until 1850, when Rev. L. P. O'Connell was sent to my relief. The territory was then doubled. We attended conjointly to the spiritual wants of all the Catholics scattered over the vast region of country stretching from Orangeburg on the west to Sumter, Camden, Lancaster, Charlotte, and Salisbury to the south and east; thence to Morganton, McDowell, and Asheville and the Warm Springs towards the north; thence as far as Raburn Gap in Georgia, and all intermediate points, especially Greenville, Anderson, Abbeville, Lawrence, Newberry, Union, and many other places—Columbia being the base of operations. The number of Catholics was very small, not four hundred permanently located in all, and very poor in worldly goods. The Hon. William McKenna, of Lancaster, was the only man of wealth. He died at an advanced age in 1859, bequeathing his property for the establishment of a male Orphan Asylum in Charleston. He was a true Catholic, an honor to his native and adopted country, a friend to the needy, and a benefactor to his Church.

The priest was contented if he received his travelling expenses, which did not always happen; he often returned threadbare, sick, and in debt, after his six weeks' incessant labor. During fifteen years all these stations were attended from Columbia. I remember but one person who died without the Sacraments, and his death was sudden; there were but two marriages unblessed, which were subsequently cured, and there existed not a solitary instance of the death of an unbaptized infant. We built four churches within this time, purchased a commodious building at the capital, and established a branch of the order of the Sisters of Mercy, and nearly rebuilt the church twice. The cost was heavy; about ten thousand dollars for all, and but a small share of it furnished by the local inhabitants. We begged the most of it in the principal cities between New Orleans and New York, and chiefly among the laboring Irish Catholics. It was labor lost to apply to any other nationality. Very few of the wealthy Catholics contributed; they had their local demands, and were forbidden in numerous instances to answer external appeals. Beggars rarely interfere with domestic charities; the class to whom they apply are mostly

ST. MARY'S COLLEGE FOUNDED.

a floating population, who only on occasions of this character give anything for the Church. Questing in this country has become unprofitable of late years, from its frequency and the universality of the occupation. Thomas Stanley, a generous layman, contributed two thousand dollars to the purchase of the Sisters' house, bearing the obligation of a monthly Mass in perpetuity.

In 1851 we erected the St. Mary's College, a chartered institution in which our youth received a first-class education. It flourished many years, and until destroyed by Sherman's army at the sack of Columbia, in 1865, together with its valuable library. The Sisters' house and Convent were burned at the same time, and their inmates cast out among the flames. Vicar-General L. P. O'Connell co-operated with me in these labors, until appointed post chaplain of the Confederate army in Western Virginia, and Superior of the devoted Sisters who had charge of the hospital for sick and wounded soldiers. I must have preached or made public addresses a thousand times over this extent of country, and lectured *repeatedly* at the most important points, being the first priest who had had that honor. I received many, probably three hundred persons into the Church, slaves and free people. I do not make these statements from a spirit of vainglory; others have done as much and labored as ceaselessly. Fathers Barry, Birmingham, and Quigley have gone over the same ground. Bishop England visited his vast diocese by private conveyance or stage, and preached wherever he found a Catholic. My object is to give an idea of the labors, privations, and self-sacrifice of the priests and bishops who built up our earliest missions, and of which people accustomed to modern facilities of travel can have no adequate conception.

Sermons preached in court-houses, and all places of civic gatherings, are generally well attended by all classes. Their demeanor is always attentive and respectful. Despite their prejudices, which are honest in most instances, Southern people exhibit outward respect for the Christian religion, no matter by whom professed. Indifferentism is rampant, and steadily progressing since the close of the war. The old bitter hatred or sneering contempt for the Church is giving way before her heaven-born teachings. Thousands of soldiers died in the Faith at the posts where we had our chaplains or the good Sisters, and many who were spared have continued in the fold since their return. That the war was mainly caused by the combined efforts of all the Protestant sects against the *peculiar institution* is an undeniable fact; while it is equally notorious that Catholicity stood aloof from every unholy alliance. The kindly feelings of our people, whether of native or foreign birth, to the actual government, and the sympathy of the Holy Father for the distracted and bleeding condition of the country, and other moral causes, have entirely revolutionized the public mind in our favor, notwithstanding the fact that many ecclesiastics in other sections exerted an unenviable zeal in recruiting for the Federal army. It is remarkable that when churches have been erected, the seats thrown open for all, and the public invited by the press, but few attend, except on rare occasions, and even then only the more enlightened or good-natured. It may be attributed to a reluctance to assist formally at our service. We can scarcely imagine how much men of the world fear public opinion; human respect is their God; even it was only *after dark* that Nicodemus called on Christ. Ladies, too, are unwilling to mix with the poor, who are always in the majority, for, as in the days of the Apostles, "*we have not many nobles among us: but the poor we always have.*" These objections do not exist against public and civil assemblies; they are divested of the religious aspect.

That our blessed Lord manifests His freedom of choice amongst His creatures is illustrated in the preference of Jacob and Aaron to others apparently as fit for the offices. The altar is His throne on earth; unworthy people ascend earthly thrones, in order to show, according to St. Augustine, that He is sole King, and that worldly honors are not the reward of virtue. He has shown Himself most jealous of His regal priesthood, and forbids any one to approach, unless when called from above. To minister to God as priest of the New Law, and offer the Sacrifice thereof, is the highest dignity and honor possible on earth, ennobling not only the individual, but also distinguishing his immediate kindred. Some families are particularly blessed in this respect, constituting almost a sacerdotal race. There were five such families in the diocese: the O'Neills, the Quigleys, the Kirbys, the Northrops, the brothers Carr and McNeal, and the O'Connells. Three brothers and a nephew bearing the latter name minister at this time before the altars of religion in our country. Very Rev. Laurence Patrick O'Connell, V. G., was ordained priest in the old Cathedral in Charleston by Bishop Reynolds, March 23d, 1850, and appointed my assistant in Columbia the same year. He was born in the parish of Donaghmore, County Cork, Ireland, September 26th,. 1826; having acquired an extensive knowledge of mathematics and the necessary languages, he entered St John's College, Fordham, under the presidency of Father Thébaud, where he studied an extensive course of philosophy. Bishop McQuade, Fathers Madden, McCarthy, of the Church of the Holy Cross, in New York. and other worthy clergymen were his cotemporaries in 1846. His parents and part of the family having settled permanently in the South, he considered it his home, and having offered his allegiance to the diocese of Charleston under Bishop Reynolds, he entered the Seminary and finished his studies under Dr. James A. Corcoran, Rev Messrs. Thos. Quigley, J. F. O'Neill, Jr., Patrick Kirby, and J. Gibbons were either his classmates or cotemporaries; excellent priests, now dead or on other missions, leaving him the sole survivor in the diocese. Immediately after his ordination, he was stationed in Columbia and its missions, where he discharged his duties with fidelity and zeal until 1861, when, after having been pastor of the German Church in Charleston, he was appointed army chaplain, and with the Sisters of Mercy under his care, took charge of the hospital at the White Sulphur Springs, Greenbrier County, Va. His health failing, he was returned to the post at Columbia in 1865. He ranked as Major in the Confederate army.

In 1863 he took charge of the desolate missions in Western North Carolina, with Charlotte as his headquarters; a position which he still retains. He was created Vicar-General by Bishop Gibbons in 1868.

With the slow and expensive mode of travel then prevailing, the visitation of the several outlying stations was both difficult and laborious, and scarcely performed in less than six or eight weeks. A week was not unfrequently spent in attending a sick call. Often, on his arrival, the patient was found not only convalescent, but immensely better in health than the penniless, wayworn missionary.

Modern improvements in travelling serve God's purpose, and are advantageous to religion. With the present facilities, a single priest can attend to all the duties of a mission with less inconvenience than a dozen could a quarter of a century ago. The railroad is, in this sense, the modern missionary; Mr. Morse's invention subserved a purpose which he never contemplated, and promoted an interest to which he was as averse as any man of his day.

The Church is the patron of learning; she has propagated and perpetuated it in the world. Science and truth are a unit; the virtues are a concatenation, and even the Divine perfections are simply one and the same. Revealed truth and science, being each an emanation of the Deity, cannot possibly be antagonistic or contradictory one of the other. Reason is a flash of divine light; if, under its uncertain ray, men assert that there exists a contradiction between them, it is because they draw their conclusions too hastily, and imagine that reason testifies where it does not. All science, mental and physical, is auxiliary to religion, and being rays of divine truth, they array themselves directly by the side of Revelation, and theology queens it over them. As all light is gathered into the sun, so is all truth into the Church. Separated from the centre of unity, all revealed truths become inharmonious, and natural truths are perverted to subserve the cause of error. Infidels and their milder companions, heretics, have always combated Christianity by corrupting the fountains of education, falsifying historical and perverting natural truths. Education is simply a knowledge of facts; it is not exclusively confined to schools or books. He who knows most facts is the best educated man: error or falsehood subsists only by the truth they deny; they are not facts, and the most extensive acquaintance with deceit and fallacies do not form an educated man—no more than the cultivation of vice can form a virtuous man.

To promote the best interest of religion and society, secure a Catholic education, for our youth and preserve their faith, a plan was formed to establish a Catholic college at the capital, in addition to all other priestly labors. Having purchased suitable buildings towards the northern end of Main Street in Columbia, in the year 1857, we opened a boarding and day school. The building is one hundred and twenty feet long, of solid masonry, with ample hall and class-rooms, dormitory, and all other suitable appendages, affording ample accommodation for at least one hundred students. The patronage was respectable, for the first year or two, and a charter was obtained from the Legislature. The name and title of the institution, as created by act of the Assembly, was *The St. Mary's College, Columbia, S. C.*, with powers to confer all collegiate degrees, and hold in a corporate capacity untaxed property to the amount of fifty thousand dollars. The charter met with great and prolonged opposition in the committee-room, through sectarian bigotry, hostile to liberal education, and was wrung from the opposition by the efforts of E. Bellinger, Jr., and other liberal-minded gentlemen in both houses, at the last moment of the session, and became a law.

The staff of professors was select and competent, under Rev. J. J. O'Connell as President, and Rev. L P O'Connell, Vice-President, Julius Posi, Thos. Cleary, Michael Walshe, Richard O'Brien, Chas. Montague, Professors; Rev. J. P. O'Connell, D.D., Rev. P. Ryan, D.D., for a time also. The library was the most select private collection of books in the State, after that of the Seminary in Charleston, containing valuable works, paintings, archæological curiosities, and cabinets of priceless value. Respectable youths were free to enter, irrespective of creed; a supervision of their morals, conformity with the public duties of religion, and compliance with rules, were the only reservations, being necessary for the maintenance of order and discipline. After the calling of the roll, studies were opened and closed for the day with a suitable prayer, in which all joined. The first class for Catholic boys was invariably the catechism daily, while ample time was appropriated for more special instruction in the duties and mysteries of religion, and in proper time for the worthy reception of the Sacraments of Penance and the Holy Communion. The system worked harmoniously, and gave general satisfaction. The non-Catholic youths were free to assist at their peculiar service on Sundays, under proper guardians, and the Israelites spent their Sabbaths at the synagogue. The boarding department was filled with boys of all ages, and some students beyond the years of manhood; they were of all denominations, from nearly all parts of the South, and even from Cuba, while the day-school embraced nearly all the respectable children of the city, all meeting in their appropriate classes.

St. Mary's was a republic of letters, the most respectable educational institution in the South, and the only unsectarian one in the State, a blessing appreciated by Catholic and Israelite patrons in a very especial manner. The College course consisted of three departments—the Preparatory, which embraced all the branches of a thorough English education and the rudiments of higher studies intended to be pursued; the Commercial, comprising mathematics, algebra, and the other departments implied by the term; the Philosophical, which, besides *Belles-lettres* and both ancient and modern languages, comprised the natural sciences, metaphysics, ethics, etc. The curriculum was comprehensive, well sustained, and merited the commendation of the learned. General John S. Preston made an endowment of a gold medal annually, for excellence in elocution, and Governor James H. Adams of two others as premiums in the mathematical department. The annual exhibitions were civic festivities, lasting during two days, and obtained the privilege of holidays over the entire city; very large sums of money were expended in the stores by parents, guardians, and other visitors, in preparing the pupils in a manner becoming the occasion. Not only the intellectual and moral interests of the community were promoted, but also their mercantile prosperity. Gentlemen of the first position for culture and learning were chosen to preside over the awards and distributions of premiums at the public exhibitions. Governor Wade Hampton, Administrator Lynch, D. D., Edmund Bellinger, Jr., and others of equal note graced the occasions in this capacity.

After a half a dozen years, the tide of prosperity was brought to an ebb. South Carolina grew jealous of the Catholic College, the slumbering bigotry of sectarianism in its every ramification awoke with desperate rage. The aid of the pulpit and the press, of wealth and social influence, and all other available appliances, were assiduously invoked to crush the monster; threats of incendiarism, midnight assault, and violence were frequently made.

The fiendish spirit of Knownothingism blew the flames of hatred and bigotry into open violence. Confidential messages were sent by reliable men to be prepared for an assault at any moment. The day-scholars dropped off by numbers daily and in gangs, stoned the clergy and their former teachers in the public streets, and insulted them on all sides. An armed band made their way in midday into the hall where the students were assembled for roll-call, and publicly insulted the professors. I was the only one of the clergy present; the young men, armed with their slates, and other weapons of defence furnished by chance, rose to their feet and prepared to resist the assault at the peril of their lives; subdued by this formidable display, rather than by my forbearance, they retired, contented with their triumphs. A mild and gentle correction of a refractory pupil was made a subterfuge for exciting popular indignation; maliciously causing his nose to bleed, he reached home, and besmeared with gore over face, hands, and shirt-bosom, was led back by his father, displayed in this unseemly manner through the public streets. During the nights it was deemed necessary by the teachers and other friends of the institution to sit up, keeping armed guard and watch over the safety of the youths, while asleep, lest they might be consumed before morning by the mob of Columbia, as was threatened, in the ruins of St. Mary's, like the holocaust that were burned to death in the theatre of Brooklyn. There were several orphans in the institution, who were gratuitously fed, clad, and taught. The great body of the pupils were of tender age, the children of wealthy and respectable parents, residing in distant States and localities; surely they never dreamed of the danger that menaced the life and safety of their children, when, confiding in the honor of the State, they were intrusted to her care and sent to her capital to receive the advantage of her education in her law-established literary institute. But they were shortly removed, or rather driven away, Protestant and Catholic equally; bigotry gained the day. The students were reduced to a few orphans in the boarding department and a small number in the day-school. The generous mother of virtue and science, that had fostered and educated several hundred youths, an entire generation, fitting them for all the honorable and useful situations in life, for the altars of religion and the legislative halls, for the plough and the battle-field, was destroyed, stripped of her honors, and condemned to a precarious existence, after the first blush of youth and usefulness. Still she struggled on to the opening of the civil war, and during its prevalence. It was hoped that, with the return of peace, gentler feelings and milder counsels would prevail; that the fires of fanaticism would be abated by common suffering; that it must be remembered that her classes had been thinned to fill the ranks of battle; that a better state of society would be inaugurated, and that she would start into a fresh life, renew her youth and vigor, her former usefulness and position. But these expectations were never realized; she had not seen the worst, and was doomed to be utterly swept out of existence. A faithful type of the Confederacy, her youth was fair and promising, her life short and bitter, and she perished in disaster and ruin, the same hand levelling both at one stroke. All the first-class male schools established in the diocese were overthrown in this manner, through hostility to Catholic training and culture, but not with equal violence. It is useless to attempt the creation of Catholic literary institutions in the South, if dependent for maintenance on any other than Catholic patronage, unless they enjoy a competent endowment. Non-Catholic patronage is fluctuating, always variable and unreliable, and will give way under public excitement, jealousy, and prejudice. It has been already related that in connection with the diocesan Seminary, Bishop England formed a classical school. It was the pride of the the city of Charleston, and merited the high commendation of the celebrated Chancellor Kent, who affirmed that it *revived classical literature in Charleston, South Carolina.* Bishop Reynolds, about the year 1849, restored and conducted the Institute on the same plan, aided by ripe scholars and men who had won the prize of excellence in the first colleges in Europe and in the world. The present Bishop was Principal, with the learned Dr. Corcoran and other clergymen, equally competent, as tutors. The same old spirit was revived, rival institutions were established at great expense, general patronage withdrawn, and Catholic education placed under ban. Tested repeatedly, inaugurated by the great prelates of the day, and conducted by the best scholars of the country, our colleges have not succeeded permanently. A future effort to revive them on any other basis beside Catholic patronage will prove equally abortive. The safest plan is to make them *eminently Catholic;* the growth will be slow, but sure and reliable. It becomes more necessary at this time, when the normal schools, with their un-Christian tendencies, are growing rapidly into public favor and are supplanting all denominational education. Our female religious schools, having been conducted more in accordance with the principle of *modified exclusiveness,* are deeply rooted in the several communities where they exist, —have gradually conciliated public favor, and given better advantages of instruction to the children of the female sex, than our boys possess.

The country sadly needs the introduction of the educational orders of religious men, like the Jesuits, the Franciscans, or Christian Brothers, and many others equally efficient. If by industry and the endowments of the faithful, they acquire an independent support, it is more desirable; the members will be better contented when possessed of a competency for the infirmities of age, and their convents will become permanent establishments for religion and learning in each diocese in the American Church. Our efforts in behalf of learning are not fruitless of good results; we have taught hundreds of influential men, of great moral worth, who bless the clear fountain of their early education, and impress on their descendants the firm conviction of its superiority over all other systems; they will hail with gladness its renewal in more propitious times and under better auspices.

Catering, doubtless, to public feeling, a Confederate officer inflicted the irreparable indignity on the St. Mary's College of impressing it into the service, and converting the lower departments and hall into a commissary store, and at a time when the clergy were domiciled therein, and also many of the children of refugees in attendance both in the boarding and in the day-school departments. It was a subterfuge to escape from field service for reluctant conscripts. The men on duty kept guard, continually interrupting the regulations and violating the rights of domestic life, adding insult to injustice, and thus outraging every feeling of humanity. A similar act of unprecedented cruelty was contemplated against the Ursuline Convent and its inmates, and was arrested only by the most strenuous efforts. My expostulation was vain, and the project was abandoned only by the interference of some men of influence, whose sense of right and decency revolted and was shocked at the attempt. In this particular case, there was little of value, scarcely anything save some trace-chains and old harness, packed in cumbrous pine boxes under the name of government stores, to render the act plausible. The cases were much worn by friction, as though frequently transferred from one post to another, for the discreditable subterfuge already mentioned. It is a well-known fact, that abundant supplies were at many of the commissary posts, hoarded with a miser's grasp for this purpose, while the war-worn veterans were dying in the trenches, from scarcity of food and clothing.

The disclosure amazed the Federal troops. When marching through the Carolinas, they replenished their stores from the public commissariat, but long since regarded rather as private property. That the bad management of this most essential department has defeated many a good cause is abundantly proved by the history of warfare; there are not a few who regarded it a chief cause of the fall of the Confederacy; every endeavor to find a remedy for local grievances by an appeal to Richmond would be rewarded only by loss of labor. We had ceased to possess a civil government for a long time. We were ruled by the caprice of a captain, or other equally irresponsible functionary, at many of the posts. General Hampton, by his personal and almost unaided efforts, of which I was an eye-witness, saved Columbia, and handed it over unsinged and safe to the tender care of Sherman: he had scarcely a corporal's guard of citizen soldiers to support him, who were heroes only at the polls.

In the winter of 1864, while occupied in the duties of the confessional on a Saturday evening at the church, I was called to the vestibule by a young woman of genteel appearance and lady-like address, whom I never saw before this interview, to my knowledge or recollection. She informed me that she was engaged to be married to a non-Catholic young man, whose name she mentioned, but whom I did not know. She spoke of her relations, who resided in Charleston, and whom I knew to be respectable people, and intermarried with some of the leading Catholic families in the city, inquiring what arrangements were necessary to be made for the intended marriage. I explained them, and directed the intended bridegroom to call that evening, to make preliminaries for the publication of the bans then required. She withdrew, and I gave the topic no further consideration. The next evening (Sunday, between seven and eight o'clock) she was announced at the St. Mary's College, where the clergy resided, and made her appearance, accompanied by a tall, portly young man of military appearance, and whom I judged to be about twenty-two years of age. A widow lady and both her boys, virtuous persons, though in humble circumstances, came also with them. The young man assured me that he had served in the army during the past year, that his family resided in Darlington, that his father and he were painters by trade; that the young woman was employed in the family; that they came for the purpose of being married by the priest, she being a Catholic, and that they intended leaving for home, at a long distance, early the following morning by the railroad. The representation was plausible. I concluded that the refusal of my ministry would be dangerous to the virtue and character of the female, and for her sake shuddered at the consequences that might follow. I enjoyed the privilege of dispensing in a limited number of mixed marriages, to be renewed on application; and the publication of the bans was known to have partially fallen into desuetude during the disturbed times of the war. I had already united several Catholics in matrimony all over the mission, without this serious qualification, their place of domicile rendering it useless and impracticable. I determined to save the girl from ruin, and firmly believed the course would be sustained by sound theology, and ratified by the approbation of all unbiassed minds—an opinion which I still hold. My brother, Rev. Joseph P. O'Connell, D. D., who had recently returned from the Propaganda, from which he had graduated in a class of which the illustrious Bishop Becker, of Wilmington, Del., Drs. McMullen and Butler, of Chicago, and other priests, equally distinguished for virtue and learning, were members, was in the house, and I consulted him. He confirmed my views, and recommended me to marry them. The ceremony was performed in the public parlor, and was witnessed by the aforementioned people and by Mr. John McGuire, a respectable Catholic man, who was on a visit, and in conversation with me in my apartment when the party were announced. A man-child, born in due time, was the fruit of the marriage.

Suspecting no dishonesty or fraud, I sent the marriage notice for publication to the *Carolinian*, a city paper at this time published under the editorial management of Dr. Gibbs, Sr. The announcement unearthed the facts of the case, and created a storm of popular rage and excitement unsurpassed by the arrival of Sherman's army. The young man was the son of respectable parents living in the city, who were not consulted, and were in entire ignorance of the unnatural conduct of their son; the young woman was a waiting-maid in the family. The disparity of condition was not so wide; of the two she was the greater sufferer. Marriages not only more disproportionate, but radically defective in contract, and annulled by dirimental impediments, were performed by ministers then in the city, and who were loudest in their denunciations of the priest. An atmosphere of falsehood and misstatements filled the air, misled the public mind, and clouded the simple facts of the case on my side to so great an extent that it was difficult to reach the bottom truths. The bridegroom was represented as a boy only fourteen years of age, the bride a worthless servant in my family, who by my agency and by means of my confederates had seduced the innocent boy, drugged him with opiates, and led him in a state of resistless insensibility, a victim of the darkest plot of Satanic iniquity, to perform a part in a sham marriage. I wrote a calm statement to the parents and for the press; but they would not receive it. I made ample and conclusive explanations, to influential men, and they were dismissed as the machinations of an astute and corrupt mind. The storm was confined chiefly to the better class of people, and gathering additional strength, both in the number of dupes and the multiplication of false statements, went abroad and swept over the country. I stood disgraced on the battle-fields of Virginia, and while passing through the streets men would point the finger of scorn at the man who had only saved an unprotected female from the machinations of a plot. Her participation is unjustifiable, but is mitigated by the natural desire of making an advantageous match, and the influence that men often gain over the female heart. I have no doubt but she loved him, and to her irreparable cost. The community, both men and women, gloated on the reports with a relish and pruriency discreditable to their delicacy of thought, demoralizing to the youth, and the emanation of minds familiar with the indecencies of Maria Monk, the lubricity of Smith, and the corrupt anti-popery literature of Hogan and the Harpers. The occasion was greedily seized as a favorable opportunity for pouring out the vials of sectarian hatred and wrath against the Church, in the person of her unoffending minister. The movement was headed, first and most bitterly, by the non-Catholic Irish. An Irish Episcopalian, a leading member of that denomination, and the most cherished members of whose family were Catholics, ladies of unexceptionable culture and piety, denounced the marriage in public as the consequence of the abominable doctrine of the celibacy of the clergy,—a discipline advocated by the most respectable members among the Protestant clergy. Next were the several preachers, then the Mayor and city officers, and lastly the leading men in town. Unwilling to perpetuate an odium on any family, I intentionally suppress the names of those engaged in the nefarious combination; but I feel myself at liberty to mention with every mark of honor the few who stood aloof or afforded tacit sympathy and support,—the Hampton and Preston families, the physicians, the Superintendents of the Asylum and State Arsenal, and some very few others. The bank officers and the prominent lawyers took a leading part in the solid persecution; a stronger opposition was seldom arrayed against a single man, alone and defenceless, for what could a few Catholics avail against the population of an entire city? I offered up my life freely to my own good Lord, and determined to die at the post of duty. I received anonymous communications from pretended friends, recommending speedy flight. Menaces of violence and of untold cruelty were everywhere rife, assaults of nameless barbarity suggestive of the Reign of Terror were profusely discussed, and in order to prepare the public mind for the enactment of some frightful crime, the press was teeming with harrowing descriptions of mob violence, outrage, and incendiarism. Burning, maiming, and the promiscuous slaughter of the family were among the items of the merciless programme. Human ingenuity was stretched to devise some new and unheard-of torture, that would be an astonishment to all nations from its refined cruelty. The lower order of people had some sympathy for the woman, because of her rank, and could not be persuaded to undertake the perpetration of the contemplated outrages.

Failing in the city among the roughs, their next effort was to bribe the volunteers with a promise of barrels of whiskey; for this purpose the regiment from Pickens was approached, where they lay encamped preparatory to their departure for the scene of action, and were very warmly urged to acquiesce. The proposal was dismissed with contempt, and treated as an insult to the honor of the organization. Many of the men, being from the up-country missions, were my personal acquaintances. A Florentine named Francisco, but called Sanco, became spokesman; he with his father and brother lived on Tunnel Hill. "We," said he, in good English, "are come to fight the battles of the country; it would ill become us to resolve ourselves into a city mob, for the perpetration of arson and murder, patronizing a civil broil of the nature of which we are ignorant. From our knowledge of Dr. O'Connell, we are inclined to believe him the aggrieved party, and incapable of committing the crimes you allege against him. It ill becomes you to make the proposition, disgraceful both to yourselves and to your city. We will not be your confederates for all the whiskey in Columbia." Sanco lost his life in that campaign. Every effort was tried to collect a mob; but without success. God is stronger than man, and can easily defeat his machinations. He laughs at our plots. After some weeks the question shifted slightly from the individual to the Catholic body, and they manfully prepared themselves to meet the issue.

For a long time a deep-rooted feeling of opposition had been at work against the increase of Catholicity and its institutions, and at last obtained expression in this way. Philip Fogartie, of Charleston, James Claffey, John McGuire, Thomas Leavy, Tim. T. Whelan, Messrs. Shannahan and McNulty, with others equally determined, organized a strong body of fearless men, that kept guard in alternate bands over the priest's residence, which was expected to be attacked every night, and its inmates massacred. It was contemplated to renew the scenes of blood that were enacted at the Philadelphia riots, and wipe out with a besom of destruction every vestige of Catholicity from the capital. If the torch were once applied to the St. Mary's College, the Church, or Convent, the city would have been reduced to ashes by a conflagration more imposing than that of Sherman's army. A house would scarcely be left standing. The men of the congregation, feeling the pressure of the approaching struggle, were pledged to defend their rights to the last extremity, sell their lives as dearly as possible, and if necessary perish to a man. Residing in every part of the city, a system was planned, a firm resolution taken, and promises mutually pledged to set fire, every man to his own house, simultaneously, on the first assault, and reduce the city to a pile of ruins. A massacre would be the inevitable consequence, and an imprudent act would have brought on the crisis. Some bales of cotton at the Greenville depot were fired after dark one night, and this was understood to be the signal of the assailants for the attack. There was a general rush to the place of rendezvous. The leaders on both sides were strongly represented. After the flames were extinguished, the crowd quietly dispersed for the night, without manifesting any disposition to begin the riot. It is most likely that an inkling of the intent of the defensive body crept out and intimidated the others. Be this as it may, they changed their tactics soon after, and inaugurated another course.

Father Laurence O'Connell returned from the army in

Western Virginia about this period of the difficulty, dismissed the household guard, and professed himself capable of repelling from within any assault from a mob, by firing on them should they attempt an invasion of the premises. If their intent of violent assault was further manifested, he determined invoking the military protection of the post commander. I attribute the momentary lull and the change of plan to a higher interference. I opened a novena to our Blessed Lady in the Church, which was perfectly and unanimously attended, accompanied by the retreat of the congregation, and closed by the communion of the faithful. I most firmly believe that our preservation was obtained by the Mother of God, whose protection I have experienced, not only in this instance, but in all the perils of a long missionary life. She arrests the danger, and none ever asks her aid in vain. She knows what her Son suffered from the rabble in the streets of Jerusalem, and she sends her angels to rescue her clients from the hands of merciless men. When plotting iniquity the sinner leaves God out of his reckoning, and his arm is too short to reach his end. The Father of mercies will interfere to mar his plots and foil his calculations, defeating by the very measures that promised success. Haman was hanged from the gibbet which he had prepared for Mordecai.

I carried my life for months in my hands, and was ready at any moment to resign it. When called by duty, I always took the most direct streets leading to the points, and in the thoroughfare, and at all hours of the day and the night, and not a hair of my head was injured. The martyr's crown is not for every one; it would be presumption to ask for it. Our holy mother the Church bids us pray that the time may be peaceable and the fear of enemies be taken away. The will of God meekly embraced, and the common wear and tear of perseverance in our ordinary duties, is the plain road to salvation. A truce between belligerents is the harbinger of peace; in the course of popular excitement, and in difficulties of this nature, a day gained is an advantage to the assailed, and gives time for reflection.

At this crisis in the history of the struggle the immediate family, the most interested, would fain desist; but the question had already gone beyond their control and assumed its proper aspect. They possessed the means of correct information. The young woman was living in the family up to the hour of her marriage, and could not have been my servant. They also knew the age of the young man, that he spent the day of the marriage at home as usual, in his ordinary frame of mind, and laboring under no artificial or stupifying influence, neither drunk nor drugged. They could not help crediting the truth of my written statement, from their personal knowledge of the facts, and they openly reproached the son with having deceived me and denied his parentage. After the explanation had been made and the first few moments of excitement passed, the family became passive. Another event transpired which threw additional light on the subject. Rufus Johnston, Esq., President of the Exchange Bank, and brother of Colonel Wm. Johnston, of Charlotte, a gentleman of irreproachable name, great moral worth, and social influence, while undergoing the tonsorial operations of the knight of the shears, and concealed by the familiar disguise of the process from ready recognition, unavoidably listened to an excited conversation between some young men who had entered the shop and were waiting for their turn on the chair of state. The bridegroom was the centre of the party; he was bantered on the success of his intrigue, reproached for his cowardice in denying the act and afterwards attempting to shift its odium on the priest. The tone of conversation, the thorough acquaintance of all with the primary proceedings, and other unmistakable indications of a concocted plot, filled Mr. Johnston's mind not only with misgiving, but also dismay, while the stalwart boy of fourteen was conclusive evidence of untruthful statements. Without having troubled himself with a personal inquiry, and seduced by general report, he was betrayed into the combination, and had become an innocent abettor of the injustice. To err is human, but to persevere therein is diabolical, is an axiom of a saint. Mr. Johnston instantly separated from the party, and indignantly erased his name from among many signatures attached to a paper containing false statements corroborating the unfounded and iniquitous charges already in circulation, and denouncing the man O'Connell in the strongest terms of hatred and contempt. It had been hawked about the city for many days previous, not in shape of a petition for my removal, but as a mandate to that effect, of a compulsory character, addressed to the Rt. Rev. Bishop Lynch, and leaving him no alternative, not even the right to investigate the truth of the charges, but demanding his assent to facts that seemed so clearly established by an imposing array of names, as to leave no room for reasonable doubt of my criminality. Any attempt to examine the back facts of the case appeared not only superfluous, but implied disrespect to the intelligence, respectability, and Christian feeling of men who were interested in the preservation of sound morals, and who, as a community, were sorely aggrieved by the perpetration of so serious a misdemeanor in their midst. No man, it was stated, having a family felt safe, and each in his turn might have to lament a similar misfortune.

It is amazing how plausible human ingenuity and cunning can render a bad cause, and cast a veil of deceit and sophistry over errors and crimes which deceive the well-meaning and often gain the sympathy of multitudes. This was the means by which he who is styled the Apostle of Misfortune made immorality popular, and the philosopher of Ferney introduced infidelity into France, and attempted to sap the foundation of Christianity everywhere. The form of the signatures on the face of this precious document, framed and patronized by first-class lawyers, was suggestive of a funeral urn or sepulchral vase, containing the ashes of the heathen dead, as they are dug from the ruins of Pompeii and the buried tombs of the Appian Way. Theology, law, intelligence, and wealth were even arrayed in separate columns or classifications. The names of the several preachers came first, and separated by an intervening blank, over those of the lawyers; the banks formed the stem, and the city authorities and leading citizens formed the base; the erased but still legible name of Rufus M. Johnston was prominent, and had no small weight in breaking the entire vase, and seemed prophetic of its disaster. Like the Congressional committee that seated Mr. Hayes, it repelled any investigation of bottom facts. Failing in their efforts at personal outrage, and defeated in the execution of their plots, they labored to accomplish another revenge by forcing the Bishop to dismiss me through intimidation. But they mistook their man. There is not among the American hierarchy a bishop who holds the crozier with firmer hand than Dr. Lynch. The present is begotten by the past of a necessity, and it is the only way that leads to the future. The contest has resulted in the good of religion; the patient and unbending course pursued by the Bishop was worthy of his great predecessor, and has convinced the State of South Carolina that the secular power is not an element in the government of the diocese of Charleston, and that no combination of laymen, either within or outside of the Church, can interfere with the judicial prerogative of the chief pastor, defeat his decrees, or annul his appointments. Successor of the Apostles and heir to their firmness, the Bishop of Charleston and his co-laborers, the clergy, can suffer contempt, slander, persecution, and even death itself, in its worst shape, and at the hands of a mob, but they never desert the post of duty. The very females, the nuns and sisters, cannot be intimidated; we are not cowards, neither clergy nor laity; a lesson taught more than once to the people of South Carolina, and which they cannot easily forget.

After receiving the document, he immediately answered, assuring the party "that he would examine the case diligently at an early day, and make known the result of the investigation; that Rev. Mr. O'Connell was entitled to a fair trial, and if found in fault must suffer the ecclesiastical penalty of his transgression. Meanwhile, the examination of witnesses must be the first step in the process; that he would visit Columbia, and required the young man to be produced, as the leading and most indispensable witness for learning the truth." This announcement fell like a bombshell in the camp; the party was discomfited, chagrined, and mortified; the new course was regretted and condemned by the more violent, and a return to former measures advocated. The case had outlived this state; a renewal of the old attempts was judged impolitic; there were only threats of private assassination made. The Bishop, true to his engagement, appeared on the scene, sought the witnesses; these on my side were readily produced; they were closely sifted, and examined with the utmost scrutiny; all were unanimous, and confirmed my statements. The facts were so plain and simple that it was difficult to build an argument on them; no elucidation could be more favorable than the plain, simple statement. The other party refused to produce their witness; he was sequestered and not allowed to appear at all; no rebutting testimony could be produced; no jurist could have managed this case with greater skill, patience, and impartiality than the Bishop. Prescinding all public rumors and malicious or idle reports, he divested the facts of all exaggeration or excrescence, presented them in their natural attitude, and after a formal and judicial *résumé* of the case, refuted all the false charges. He drew the inevitable conclusion that *I was innocent, and had violated no law*, and finished by congratulating the gentlemen on the vindication of the character of a worthy but maligned clergyman.

But a long and elaborate correspondence had been maintained before the conclusion was reached and the judgment rendered. The party did not easily abandon the controversy; their case and its most trivial adjuncts were urged in the most forcible and formal manner, and to use a common expression, *they died hard.* For close reasoning, arrangement of argument, logical acumen, and acquaintance with civil and canon law, Bishop Lynch's letters were a masterpiece of forensic composition. I had taken copies; but the collection was destroyed together with my library by the fire of Sherman's army, which, like death, levelled at one stroke the evidences of the accusers and the accused. The combination lost spirit, and its members gradually fell away, as they have since passed, one by one, out of human life, and few now survive who then took active part in that exciting scene of passion and prejudice. Yet they struggled on, impotent for harm, until the fall of Stonewall Jackson some months later, and yielding to a superior abstraction, finally dissolved.

CHAPTER VIII.

COLUMBIA, S. C. (*continued.*)

Academy of the Immaculate Conception now established—A Monthly Mass in Perpetuity for Brother John of the Cross—Thos. Shanley—Funds collected abroad for the Repairs of the Sisters' House and twice for the Church—Small Offerings of the Congregation for Religious Purposes—Withdrawal of the Sisters Regretted—The Members of the Community—Sisters Mary Baptist and Antonia O'Connell—Life, Labors, Suffering, and Happy Death of the Former—Rev. J. P. O'Connell, D. D.—Destruction of Columbia by the Federal Army—Soldiers Perish in the Flames—Unburied Remains—A Scene of Horror—General Sherman halts his Troops in Front of St. Mary's College—Merry Bells and Sorry Songs—The Ursuline Community conducted to the Church in the midst of the Flames—Spend the Night in the Church—Conveyed to the Methodist College—The Order brought from Ireland by Bishop England—First Religious—Sister Augustine England, Sister Borgia—Other Religious—Mother Mary Baptist Lynch—General Sherman Protects the Honor of Women and the Lives of Citizens—Met by Dr. J. J. O'Connell on his entering Columbia—An Evil Genius—Fire not communicated by Burning Cotton—A Scene of Desolation—Attempts made to burn the Convent by the Mob of Columbia—Saved by its Location—Peace restored—A National Disgrace—End of St. Mary's College: after Fifteen Years' Struggle, shares the fate of the Confederacy—The valuable Library, Paintings, Cabinet of Arts Destroyed—Vestments, Sacred Vessels, Relics of Saints, etc., robbed from Safes, broken open—Scene of Violence and Sacrilege—Chaplain Major L. P. O'Connell made Prisoner—The City in Ruins—Peace of Death—Camp-followers in Columbia—Demoralization—Statue of Washington Mutilated—Isolated Protestant Churches burned—A Protestant Church Saved by the Cross—An Empty Bottle well corked—Lost by Fire, the Transport General Lyons—Stonewall Jackson's Scout—His Tragical End—Resurrection—A National Disgrace—Chaplain Major Very Rev. L. P. O'Connell—Sheriff Dent—Governor Pickens—General Hampton—Doctor Kennedy—Reparation of Church—Protection of Cemetery—Departure of Priests.

THE Academy of the Immaculate Conception, under the care of the Sisters of Mercy, was established in 1852, and was well patronized and in a self-sustaining condition until 1858, when it was occupied by the Ursulines, after their return to the diocese. The dwelling, alterations, and its furniture cost over four thousand dollars, which was procured in part from the sale of the priest's house, yielding about eight hundred dollars. Thomas Shanley contributed two thousand dollars. The remaining portion was collected among the people, by the means of fairs and appeals made to the congregation, the chief contributors being the clergy, my father, Patrick O'Connell, and James Gallon; others were extremely moderate in their offerings. It was deemed necessary to remove a menacing wall and commence extensive repairs, which were nearly equivalent to building the house anew, and which rendered necessary additional expenditure of about one thousand dollars. The church had also fallen into decay. The enlargement and restoration thereof at this crisis increased the embarrassment. All entailed an indebtedness of about four thousand dollars. It was idle to expect that even a tithe of the necessary sum could be collected at home; I went abroad, and after a year's labor collected the greater part of the amount throughout the country, generally in the seaport towns, commencing with New York and ending in New Orleans.

After having spent four or five years in Columbia, the Sisters returned to Charleston, having accomplished a great amount of good in the cause of religion and humanity; their departure was regretted by all the community. The Superioress was Mother Veronica Cogney, who died about the year 1876, in the eightieth year of her age. Mother Mary Paul Harris succeeded her in the administration of the house, who in her time was followed by Mother Xavier Dunn. The members of the community were the Misses Curtin, Sisters Mary Charles and Gonzague, Sister Mary Patrick Doud, Sister Ignatius Clark, one of the first members of the community, Sister Aloysius Daily Sister Agatha McNamara, Sister Gertrude, Sisters Mary Baptist and Antonia O'Connell. The former accompanied me from Ireland in 1840, and entered on her novitiate under the superintendence of Mother Aloysius McKenna. On the formation of the new colony in Savannah, she and a younger sister who had taken the vows in 1846 were chosen to build up the new community. In the prime of life, endowed with great strength of mind, a fund of good health, and inexhaustible zeal, she applied herself with self-sacrificing devotion to her mission of charity and education, and contributed in a decided measure to the permanent establishment of the Sisterhood in that city. Mother of the orphans, and ever at the bedside of the sick and the dying, she spent herself in the service of the homeless, the suffering, and the poor. Having been stricken by the yellow fever, which devastated Savannah in 1854, although she temporarily recovered, she nevermore recovered her strength, and her health gradually succumbed. Called upon in the providence of God to endure the heaviest crosses of the religious life, after fifteen years, she with her sister returned to the parent house, under the administration of the incomparable religious, Mother Mary Teresa Barry, and in a short time became a confirmed invalid. Reduced to a languishing condition, she was for years fastened on a bed of excruciating pain, until it pleased our merciful Lord to release her. Having said the community Mass in the Convent Chapel in Charleston, and while administering to her the Holy Communion and yet in the sacred vestments, after she received the bread of life, with unutterable fervor, she lifted herself up unaided, and eagerly seizing my arms in both hands, she exultingly called on the name of Mary, fell back on the pillow, and was dead. She cast a last look—it remains to this day in my heart; for nothing burns, nothing melts so profoundly, as the last look of some loved one in death. Though hourly expected for months, the announcement to the community, on my return to the chapel to finish the Mass, fell on them like a new revelation from God. She went to her heavenly recompense on Sunday, the Feast of St. Basil the Great, May 14th, 1873. The Rev. Dr. Moore, the present Bishop of St. Augustine, performed the obsequies, and I transported the remains to Columbia, and buried them by the side of both her parents, in the Cemetery of St. Peter's Church. She was in her forty-fourth year, twenty-four of which she spent in the religious state. To have lived and died a Sister of Mercy, is the greatest eulogy that can be pronounced on any woman of the age; a single word would be superfluous; it may with modesty be added that among the saints her piety was conspicuous. Sister Mary Antonia still lives, to pray, during her life-long retreat, for the living and the dead.

The Rev. Joseph Patrick O'Connell, D.D., was born and baptized on Christmas night, 1832, and was called after the Patriarch and ruler of the Holy Family. In 1846 he entered St. John's College, Fordham, and made the regular collegiate course. To prepare more directly for the holy ministry, he entered the diocesan Seminary at Montgazon (Maine et Loire), France, in 1850, where he pursued his studies until 1853, when he was sent to the Propaganda. Having finished the regular course, he graduated as Doctor of Divinity, and was ordained by Archbishop Bedini in 1858.

He suffered severely and nearly lost his life in the accident at the Convent of St. Agnes, when the Pope and a large number of students and ecclesiastics narrowly escaped death from the falling of the floor. He is one of four who suffered most severely, and possesses a medal commemorative of the fact. In 1858, after his return to America, he was stationed in Columbia. Henceforth and during the term of fourteen years he endured the labors and sufferings of that mission in common with the other clergymen. During the interval he was Chaplain at the Convent, Professor in the College, and had exclusive charge of the Western North Carolina missions during the war. His labors were ceaseless among the prisons and sick soldiers, all over the country from Salisbury to Port Royal. As an humble missionary priest his conversation among men was blameless. After the war he was transferred to Port Royal, and had charge of the Beaufort and Colleton mission. There were scarcely one hundred Catholics—all very poor people—over the entire district; the priest could not obtain his support, and after two years withdrew to North Carolina. Two Franciscan Fathers left the region for the same cause.

After having labored sixteen years in the least inviting and most barren missionary regions of the diocese, and broken in health, Dr. J. P. O'Connell transferred his allegiance to the illustrious Bishop Loughlin in 1874. He is at this time pastor of St. Michael's Church, which, together with its imposing parsonage, he himself erected. His contributions to our Catholic literature are much admired, especially "The Beauties of the Sanctuary," and the "Devotions for the Children of Mary," translations from the French. He has prepared for publication a "History of the Church," which it is hoped will shortly appear. His priestly labors are spread over many pages of this volume. He is an eloquent and popular public speaker and a pointed and ready writer.

Thomas Shanley, who made the donation for the Sisters' house, was born in the County Leitrim, Ireland, and was a man of uncommon fervor and piety, as his acts testify. For several years he superintended the extensive plantation of Colonel Wade Hampton, the father of the present Governor. Having entire control of a large number of slaves, he manifested unprecedented skill and humanity in their management, and was in the full sense of the word *a faithful steward*. Zealous only for the better gifts, he returned to Ireland in 1851 and was received into the Monastery of St. Joseph at Clondalkin, near Dublin, and after having made the novitiate, was professed by the name of *Brother John of the Cross*. He led an austere life of monastic observance, distinguished among the brotherhood for profound humility, detachment, and fervor. He compassionated the slaves for the want of religious instruction. If Catholics, he believed their condition would be happy; they only needed the Faith. He died about the year 1870, in the midst of his brethren and in the fervor of his heroic engagements. His remains mingled with the dust of the holy and just of ages, who have won for their country the enviable title of the Isle of Saints. A monthly Mass in perpetuity was the only condition of the bequest of two thousand dollars made to the Sisters' house. Bishop Reynolds formally assumed the obligation on the part of the diocese. The obligation was transferred by Bishop Lynch to the Ursulines, when they succeeded the Sisters in their house and academy, as may be ascertained by reference to the diocesan records. During part of the year before the surrender, Columbia was the most Catholic city in the Southern States. The non-combatants flocked thither as to a sanctuary, a last resort before the vanguard of the Federal armies, and brought their treasures. The streets were thronged by the most distinguished in learning, wealth, and influence; the church at the Sunday Masses was filled with fervent worshippers, the flower of Catholicity in all our Southern congregations; and the convent halls were thronged with maidens of all denominations, for the sake of protection as well as education. Every family weeping for its dead or the defeat of the cause, in which all was staked and lost, cast universal dismay over the public mind, and all other considerations were forgotten in the common calamity.

The Church was at last popular; the only evidence of ill-will was the occupation of the halls of St. Mary's College by the Confederate Government and their conversion into a commissary department. Still there were students in the institution, all the out-lying missions were faithfully attended, and friendly feelings prevailed on all sides. The Church was the mainstay and the comfort of the afflicted people. But her outward glory was short-lived and evanescent as the bloom of the morning flower which vanishes at eve; it perished with the Confederacy. A period of universal prosperity and peace is not unfrequently the harbinger of corresponding adversity. This was illustrated even in the condition of the city. A gentler people, a milder climate, and a more thorough domestic peace never existed in Columbia at any former period. It was like the last song on which the minstrel bird breaks its heart and dies. The United States army, having crossed the Savannah River, was daily advancing on the city, and its doom was at hand.

Columbia was sacked, pillaged, and two-thirds of it burned by the Federal army, on the night of the 17th of February,

1865. Many of the details have passed into history; the greater part will never be known. Whether the act was committed at the connivance or by the express orders of the commander, makes no difference. The denial implies what is detrimental to the character of the General as a military disciplinarian, and at variance therewith. His concurrence has been persistently denied. I do not undertake to decide the question; I limit myself to the narration of facts of which, in common with many thousands still living, I was the eye-witness.

It was erroneously reported outside the Confederacy, and before the truth could be made known, that the fire was communicated by some bales of cotton burned by the Confederacy. The statement found its way into the life of Bishop England, so ably written by Richard H. Clarke, L L. D., in his "Lives of the Deceased Bishops of the United States." The mistake was doubtless unintentional on the part of the accomplished author.

Since the above was written, I have been honored by the following card, which is conclusive, and fully meets all the requirements of the case. I insert it in the interests of truth and justice, and also because it portrays the candor and sincerity of that Christian gentleman, whose writings adorn our literature:

"NEW YORK, July 5th, 1878.

"REV. DEAR SIR,—I have heard with sincere regret that a passage in 'The Lives of the Deceased Bishops of the Catholic Church in the United States,' title 'Bishop England,' had been quoted adversely to the good Ursulines, as an authority against the claim in Congress for damages caused by the burning of their convent at Columbia, S. C., by the United States army under Sherman. Upon turning to the passage alluded to, I find it expressed in the following terms:

"'Their buildings were unfortunately destroyed by fire, during the late civil war, and Congress declined indemnifying them for their losses, on the ground that the conflagration was supposed to have been occasioned, not by the acts of the Federal soldiers, but by fire accidentally communicated to them from the cotton which the Confederates had burned.' It was not my intention to assert that the firing of the convent was not done by the Federal troops, but was caused by the burning of cotton by the Confederates, and the above language does not bear such a construction. I think I have been misquoted. I simply state that Congress rejected their claim, and then I give the motive that actuated Congress in so doing, the supposition on their part, that the convent was destroyed, not by the Federal army, but by the accidental communication of fire from the cotton which the Confederates had fired. Congress may have been mistaken in their view of the facts, but it was this impression that caused the defeat of the bill for the Sisters' relief.

"So far as my inquiries have enabled me to judge, I am convinced that the supposition or report on which Congress acted was an erroneous one. I am reliably informed by an eye-witness, who led the inmates of the convent through the flames, that it was Sherman's army, and not the Confedate cotton, that fired Columbia, and that no cotton was burning when the army entered the city.

"The property for the burning of which the Ursulines now claim indemnity, was the home of defenceless ladies, whose lives and property were all devoted to the purposes of religion and education. The plea that might be made in favor of burning any property in time of war does not apply to this. It was property consecrated to religion, and its inmates were non-combatants, rendered so doubly, first by their sex and refinement of education, and secondly by the sacred calling which they had adopted and so faithfully followed. 'Tis a grief to me that any word of mine should have been quoted against so just a claim. It would be a happiness to know that I had on the contrary assisted in supporting it.

"Respectfully yours,

"RICHARD H. CLARKE.

"To REV. J. J. O'CONNELL."

The statement has been so often contradicted that further discussion seems idle. In their march through the city, the writer accompanied the advance-guard in the forenoon, and the main body, under the personal command of General Sherman, in the evening of the same day as they took possession, and at either period there was no fire on the streets or in the environs of the peacefully and quickly surrendered city. One fact can never be disproved: *it was only when in possession of the United States army that the fire originated, and that Columbia was destroyed.* How far the commander is to be inculpated, I leave the world to judge.

It has been asserted that the Fifteenth Army Corps, which he led into the city in person, consisted chiefly of desperate characters, who always performed their work thoroughly, and were kept in check or in the rear on the march, when it was meant to protect private property. Their being ordered to the front when South Carolina was reached, gave a significance to the movement well understood throughout the entire command. At signals simultaneously shot up from different points, and in the shape of sky-rockets, the work of incendiarism and pillage was inaugurated throughout. By midnight not a house nor store remained on Main Street, in all its length, from the State-House to Cottontown, inclusively. The depots of the three railroads converging in the city, and the surrounding houses, all the stores, the old State-House, and many other buildings, several churches, the St. Mary's College, the Ursuline Convent, the Sisters' former house, the hotels,—were an undistinguished mass of smoking ruins. The residences of the wealthier class, located near the headquarters of the general officers, were spared on account of their fortunate proximity; and very humanely, the houses in the neighborhood of the Lunatic Asylum; if by chance, it was a remarkable interference of God.

The dwellings that escaped the flames were plundered by successive bands of soldiers of every article of value, who swarmed everywhere, like relays of ants in an ant-hill, and loaded similarly with bundled treasures. ·The search for buried treasures was universal and minutely industrious. The fresh graves were probed and sounded with steel rods prepared for the purpose. The first passions were revenge and lust of plunder; but they gave way speedily to intoxication, and the city became flooded with evidences of great good-nature; it was fortunate. The soldiers discovered in the stores an abundance of spirits and indulged too freely. They became suddenly generous and sympathizing, bestowed with one hand what they had taken with the other, frequently aiding the women, the sick, the aged, and the children in their efforts to escape to the City Park, or to the fields for shelter. All the men were not equally desperate and abandoned; there were many humane and religious men among them; a fact which refutes the charge of universal depravity, frequently urged against this corps. It is alleged that the body of respectable Western troops forming the Second Division, and commanded by General Blair, were kept aloof, and not permitted to cross the Congaree until the next day, after the work of ruin was accomplished. It was thought they would have interfered, if not from a motive of sympathy, to save the honor of the army.

The conflagration baffles all description; imagination cannot paint its dreadful realities. Towards midnight the city was one sheet of white and red flames, everywhere triumphant, and spread industriously by combustible appliances prepared for the purpose and carried in pots with brushes and matches. The night in God's mercy was perfectly calm; the Angel Guardian of the city chained the winds, and not a single breath escaped his hand.

After licking up, like the fiery tongues of serpents, all combustible matter, splintering granite, and smelting iron, the flames raised their satanic forms on high, pierced the clouds of night by thousands, and wreathed, twisted, and coiled, like the poet's fiends in combat. The lurid glare lighted up the heavens beyond the high lands of Santee to the east, and the distant hills of Chester to the north. In measure as the fire was gaining on the doomed city, and advancing into its heart like the serpents of Laocoon, the inhabitants were retreating in dismay; sick people on litters, or leaning on the young; children in their parents' arms, or clinging on in a trotting walk; every form of human misery and distress, painful and ludicrous, could be witnessed in advance of the merciless monster. They forced their way through dense masses of disorderly and desperate men, blocking up the ways, swearing, robbing, swaggering, and victimizing the colored people in a manner which this page refuses to record, reeking with all the crimes which degrade men in their most abandoned state. A Western man, looking thoughtfully on, called it a second Moscow. It resembled rather the lower regions, with all the imps unchained and celebrating the Saturnalia of sin.

None of the citizens lost his life by the flames or otherwise, while many of the soldiers, whose caution was overcome by liquor or thirst of booty, perished. Their charred bones were subsequently dug from cellars in numbers, on the rebuilding of the houses. This, it was said, caused the issue of the order at daybreak, to desist from further destruction. Many tired and sin-worn soldiers, lying on the sidewalks and in the burning dwellings, were kindly rescued by the unoffending citizens and removed to a place of safety.

They could have been assassinated with impunity, but not one, I am persuaded, lost his life in this manner. The Rev. Dr. Dennis J. O'Connell distinguished himself by an act of heroic charity in rescuing from the flames one of the gang who set his father's house on fire. After the departure of the army some remains were found unburned. I rescued some from brutes, and caused them to be cared for.

I said Mass the same day and consumed the Hosts (blessed be God) to prevent sacrilege. The city was shelled during all the previous day from the Lexington side, and the people were in great consternation. There were no civic guards of any reliability, and the poor class of whites and negroes became disorderly; the commissary stores were abandoned, and they became wealthy for a day, like gamblers. The citizens became very much alarmed for their personal safety, and anxiously awaited the occupancy by General Sherman, for their protection. I approached him at the head of his troops, and he courteously halted the column. Robed in soutanne, and with my breviary in hand, which I was reciting at the time, I meant my presence to be suggestive of mild and humane measures, should a contrary course be intended. Suspecting no general calamity, I solicited protection for the religious institutions. He hesitated, paused, referred me to the Provost Marshal and at the suggestion of an officer, who rode at his left, seemed relieved and moved on. *That officer, whoever he may have been, was General Sherman's evil genius;* seeing his hesitation, his embarrassment, and the unusual courtesy of a halt of an entire army division, he checked the plea for moderation working at the heart of the commander, and the fate of the city was sealed. To him chiefly I have always ascribed the loss of Columbia, and the numberless evils and crimes which followed in its wake.

The Marshal, an Englishman, too candid to add mockery to wrong, had the candor to refuse me a guard, intimating its uselessness. In many instances they first began the work of plunder after the given signal. A correspondent of the New York *Herald* advised me to prepare for the night, and conceal, if possible, the consecrated vessels of the altar.

I was the innocent cause of detaining in Columbia many families who were fleeing before the Federal army since it first touched South Carolina, and were disposed to retire still farther into the interior. I assured them there was no just cause for alarm, that the men were under the stern command of the inflexible Sherman, that man of iron will, a gentleman of first-class military education, second to none during the long strife for skill and bravery, of elegant social connections, and under true Christian influences. He, I maintained would not stain the sword that cut the Gordian knot, keener than any; or sully the laurels won in many a well-fought field, by any act discountenanced by the usages of civilized warfare.

I was not entirely disappointed in my estimate of his character. He certainly protected the lives of the citizens and the honor of white women; the opposite crimes, notwithstanding an unworthy boast to the contrary, were certainly not perpetrated. All were out doors, and no crime of violence could be hidden; compared to them all other acts were of minor importance. It is a redeeming feature, which I record with unfeigned satisfaction; it harmonizes with the well-known character of the General for military discipline; when his will could awe into moderation the Bashi Bazouks of the army, maddened with the worst passions of human nature, and unchained at midnight, in a burning city. It was reported that the penalty of death was attached to the violation of this order: otherwise, the fate of Columbia might have been a blotted page in the history of our country as dark as the massacre of Thessalonica, or the outrages of the Turks in Bulgaria.

Great allowance must also be made for the excitement of the times. Indignation was everywhere entertained against South Carolina, and especially against her capital, where secession had been inaugurated. Public sentiment seemed to demand some signal vengeance. The ruin of the city was celebrated throughout the North by the firing of cannon and a general jubilee. But these cities have since suffered more extensively, if not by the sword, by the flames; and are, perhaps, destined to suffer still more. The disbanded troops were ripe scholars, and are not likely to forget the lessons taught them in the Southern campaign. The system of incendiarism has been propagated; Communists have picked up the brand to redress real or imaginary injuries inflicted on the laboring class by society, and the developments are becoming daily more alarming. The disbanded soldiers could not be expected to labor or suffer from want, while witnessing the wealth and prosperity of the country which they bled to save. They cherish in their hearts the sentiment expressed by Field-Marshal Blucher when passing through London with his brilliant staff, after the final defeat of the Emperor: "Mine Got, what a fine zity for to zack!" These truths have been sadly illustrated since the close of the war. The bells that rung merrily at the conflagration of Southern cities have since learned other notes and sung sadder rhymes.

Deluded by the common hope of protection, the Ursulines requested their Chaplain not to remove the Blessed Sacrament from the chapel. Towards dusk, and at the early outburst of the conflagration, I removed the ciborium to the Church, and reposed the Most Holy in the tabernacle; I was accompanied by Mr. Poincignon, of Charleston, now dead. The church was safely guarded to the last. It seemed as though our dear Lord would be with us in that hour of trial and danger; I am persuaded that His Eucharistic Presence wrought our safety, in the same manner as He had protected the Sisters from outrage in India during the Sepoy insurrection, when the women were insulted, and afterwards nailed to trees and walls or fences.

I returned to the Convent, round which were collected dense masses of people. It was the hour of midnight. While passing through the crowd my watch was robbed from my person. Headed by the crucifix, in the trembling hands of the Superioress, a mournful procession was formed. Mid smoke and fast-approaching flames, accompanied with the crackling noise of falling houses, and the din of the immense rabble, appearing like fiends in the lurid glare, I conducted the Sisters and their children to the church and graveyard, where we remained in fright and terror until daybreak. When the order was issued to desist from the work of incendiarism, as was currently reported, I was amazed at the rapidity with which it was executed; streets but a few moments previous almost impassable, and through which it was necessary to pick one's steps among the numbers buried in sleep and drunkenness, were shortly as silent as the hour when Christ, *like the thief in the night*, will come through the gates of the morning to judge this sin whose name is legion.

The venerable Sisters and their children, all the first ladies in the country by birth and education, after having spent that dreadful night among the graves of the dead, without a change of wearing apparel or food, were conducted to the vacant Methodist Female College, where they remained, persecuted by petty annoyances, until transferred to their present home at Valle Crucis.

The residence of Hon. John S. Preston, called the Hampton House, was occupied by some army officers as their headquarters. When about vacating it, to resume their march, it was ordered to be burned. Their retreat being in the vicinity, the religious ladies interfered and prevented the splendid mansion from sharing the fate of the houses of the poor people on Main Street. It must be put on record, that the poor, and those who had no share in the struggle, were the chief sufferers.

Bishop England, early in his administration, and by his personal influence, procured a colony of ladies from the Ursuline Convent at Black Rock, near Cork, Ireland. They volunteered to venture on the perilous voyage across the boisterous main and erect a convent by the side of the Cross, on the shores of Carolina, and bring within the reach of the daughters of the South the advantages of an education which only the princes and nobility of Europe could afford their children.

Miss Maloney, a lady of rare piety and accomplishments, was the first Superioress. She died in 1838, revered in religion and honored in society. Madam Borgia succeeded her, and after governing the community several years, she returned to the parent house in Ireland; she died in 1853, full of years and merit. She was a lady of noble descent; her family was that of the Earl of Desmond. Her writings adorn the literature of the order. Mother Antonia Hughes was sister of Rt. Rev. Dr. Hughes, Bishop of Gibraltar; she was a lady of varied and extensive accomplishments; she died in 1854. Mother Angela was sister of the illustrious Dr. Delany, the present Bishop of Cork. Madam Augustine, who was one of the sufferers by the fire, is daughter of Edward England, a respectable merchant in Cork, and niece of the lamented Bishop England. After the lapse of a quarter of century spent in religion, she returned to the convent of her native city, in consequence of the loss of her health. Mother Ursula is an English lady, and the Superioress of the Ursuline Convent at Tuscaloosa, Ala. Madam Borgia was the relict of the late General A. H. Brisbane, who graduated from West Point Military Institute. He was a convert, and acquired fame in the Seminole War in Florida. His lady was also a convert, and of the White family of South Carolina. Being childless, she took the veil after the death of her husband, and died at Valle Crucis. Mother Mary Baptist, the present Superioress, is daughter of the late Conlaw Lynch, Esq., of Cheraw, S. C., and sister of the distinguished Bishop Lynch, of Charleston. There are several other ladies equally worthy; this is the class of persons thrown out of house and home into the flames, amid a disordered mob of ribald soldiers, and their property wantonly destroyed. They will most likely be indemnified for its loss, but not for the sufferings endured on that terrible night and subsequently.

On the accession of Dr. Reynolds to the see of Charleston in 1844, the older members of the community returned to the parent house, and the others withdrew to the archdiocese of Cincinnati, where they sojourned until the appointment of Bishop Lynch, at whose solicitation they returned and resumed their former position of usefulness in the diocese. They occupied for some time the house used by the Sisters of Mercy, until transferred to the City Hotel, a palatial building purchased for a convent, and admirably suited for the purpose. Their academy soon rose into favor, and obtained a handsome patronage from respectable citizens of all denominations.

The convent occupied a prominent position in the centre of the city, having been formerly used as a hotel. The alteration, it was thought, militated against the mercantile interests of the neighboring stores, and a system of persecution was inaugurated by one of the store-keepers, a man of foreign birth. The slumbering prejudice of the community against our female institutions was utilized; a violent and protracted opposition began for the object of compelling the inmates to abandon their newly-acquired possessions, and return to their former residence. Efforts were made to raise a mob either to destroy the convent or disperse its unoffending inmates. On national holidays, the most depraved characters in town, unruly white boys and negroes, might be seen collected on the street in front of the convent, burning tar-barrels, firing pistols, Roman candles, and torpedoes; indulging in all manner of ribaldry, provocative of mob violence. Mr. Mooney, an ex-Mexican soldier, kept guard over the premises for some time. The city authorities were admonished, and their protection invoked, to no purpose; some of the body were interested in the scheme. There was no man in the capital who had sufficient courage to raise an arm in defence of these persecuted ladies.

It was frequently dangerous for vehicles or men on horseback to pass by the convent. Trusting to a generous steed, I once rode indignantly through the band of ruffians in the midst of their disorders, and was about to return, but yielded to the remonstrance of a spectator. I was personally acquainted with the ringleaders; they were cowards, as such people generally are. They slunk away, God only knows their intent, on that memorable Christmas day. He uses the weakest means for carrying out His wise purposes; I may have been the instrument to prevent untold misfortunes in this instance. Its situation saved the convent; if it had been isolated the infamy of Charlestown would now rest on Columbia, and the disgrace of its subsequent destruction would not tarnish the laurels of the United States army. The mode of its accomplishment was too much of a good thing, and there is a possibility of overdoing a thing. The torch was not directly applied to the convent, the Sisters' house, or the St. Mary's College; they perished in the general conflagration. There were several men in the army who sincerely regretted their loss.

It is the desire of the country that the Government should indemnify the Sisters of the Ursuline Order for the loss of their property. A claim has been presented in their behalf by Senator Robertson, for the moderate sum of $100,000. The future historian who picks up his pen will gratefully record the ready concession. The Catholics were the greatest sufferers by the conflagration of Columbia, not only in personal property, but by the loss of their institutions, which was a general detriment to religion all over the diocese. The library of St. Mary's College was a most select collection, containing rare works of priceless value, which cannot be replaced. The books were the property of three brothers, priests, the collections of a life-time, selected without reference to expense, from the bookstores of Europe and America. The text-books of ancient and modern languages, of theology, history, philosophy, and of the arts and sciences, were the productions of the best masters. The literary treasures were unsurpassed by any private library in the State.

The College, not inaptly called a rural palace, was an object of special attraction for the incendiaries. Immediately after the given signal, the rooms and the entire premises became so thickly crammed that it was next to impossible to move until the flames rendered the place untenantable. A scene of plunder, disorder, and sacrilege was inaugurated, which baffles description. The iron safes, deemed fire-proof, yielded to the repeated blows of the sledge in the hands of the marauders, and their sacred contents were scattered on all sides. The rabble scrambled and scuffled to grab whatever objects came next to hand, or escaped being trodden under-foot. The priest who begged for the holy oil stocks was cursed and insulted. They drank whiskey from the chalices, passed them round as drinking cups, and exulted in the sacrilege. Every article of value was borne off and deposited in the booty wagons for future partition. By a just retaliation, they never left the waters of Carolina, and are now among the hidden treasures of the angry ocean.

The fire at the College was fierce and rapid in its spread, and roaring like a furnace, the smoke from the burning and falling walls and timbers rolled in grand, massive clouds, spangled with millions of sparkles of flying fire, and at intervals flashed with tongues of flame; the appalling grandeur of the scene gave it a fascination. There was not a change of clothing, nor a breviary saved from the establishment. The family were all forced out of doors. Dr. Joseph O'Connell was at Salisbury or Charlotte, in attendance on the sick at the stockade. Rev. L. P. O'Connell, who lay sick in the house, after his long services in Virginia hospitals, was dragged out in the night-air, and kept as a prisoner under guard until morning.

Indignant at being withheld from a participation in the riot of their companions, the guard resembled in temper the men who led St. Ignatius from Antioch to Rome to be devoured by the wild beasts for the amusement of the cultivated citizens of that refined metropolis. History repeats itself; and with few modifications men are always and everywhere the same, whether in Rome under Nero, in Paris under Robespierre, or in Columbia.

Camp-followers are as old as warfare, and peculiar to no country, but common to all. They follow in the tracks of all armies, finishing in the way of spoil and plunder what was left by the soldiers, until universal desolation marks their march. After the departure of Sherman's army, a motley crowd crept from their hiding-places, like the rabble at Moscow, and digging up the ruins of the College, sedulously examined every particle of the debris until scarcely a pinch of the ashes remained unrifled. Men whose antecedents promised a higher degree of decency, mingled in these disgraceful acts. When warned to desist, they reluctantly withdrew, only to return in a fresh gang by stealth, or under the cover of night. Crime is contagious. One sin, like the original transgression, becomes the parent of another, and its baneful effects contaminate not only the present but unborn generations.

It would be beyond the purpose of this narrative to detail all the acts of vandalism perpetrated in the unfortunate city on this occasion. Many of them have already passed into history, and may be found in the lucid article from the pen of Rev. L. P. O'Connell, which appeared in the *Pacificator*, or in the history of the burning of Columbia, by the late

Gilmore Simms. I will merely add, that nothing of a religious or national character was deemed sacred. The statue of Washington erected in the new State-House was mutilated. The bronze Palmetto monument, recording the names of the Carolina soldiers slain in the Mexican War, was badly injured, several names removed, and an attempt made to destroy it thoroughly. The old State-House was utterly destroyed, whose halls had so frequently resounded with the eloquence of Hayne and McDuffie, and thrilled with the gorgeous language and irrefragable arguments of Bishop England, the light and glory of the American Church. Four or five Protestant churches were intentionally destroyed. The Episcopal church was saved by the Cross. Affecting to be more Catholic than the true Church, the congregation erected several crosses on the parapets of the walls, with a profusion bordering on the ludicrous. Under the impression that the building was superlatively Catholic, a Western soldier of Catholic parentage successfully resisted a gang of desperadoes, who approached with combustible fluid, the usual manner of destroying detached buildings. By remonstrance and resistance he saved it from the common fate, remarking at the same time: "I have wrought much evil during this campaign, but I have done one good act, I have saved a Catholic church from being burned, and the intelligence will gladden the heart of my father." The sign of redemption often works wonders, even when used only for ornament and display.

The fact recalls the remembrance of an event recorded in the writings of the fathers of the desert. A Jewish peddler, overtaken by night, at a remote distance from a human habitation, found shelter in an old, abandoned pagan temple. Having composed himself for a night's rest, he was alarmed at finding himself in a Pandemonium, where fiends held council, and were relating to their prince the several attempts made at creating mischief, and planned future projects of evil for the next day. The Jew instantly made the sign of the Cross, or blessed himself, as the early Christains did, in moments of danger. A page imp was deputed to examine the intruder. Approaching, he gazed into his face with manifest amazement, and returning reported to his Satanic majesty that the intruder was *an empty bottle, well corked.*

Claiming to be an impartial narrator of events, and without prejudice against either section of the Union, I close this chapter with the following event, to give my readers an idea of the difficulties which the Church encountered in the diocese, both under the United States and the Confederate rule. In this respect I can trace but small difference. Catholicity suffered under each. A law was enacted in Carolina ordering the clergy into the ranks. At my entreaty it was modified by his Excellency Governor McGrath, who wrote out individual exemptions, detailing the venerable priesthood for hospital and other post duties.

In the church-yard of Columbia is a grave tenanted by as brave a man as ever lived; yet neither side will claim any honor from the life of him who fills it; his history contradicts the war-cry of our secession orators: "We will welcome them with bloody hands to hospitable graves." It has been shown that South Carolina denied the hospitality of her shores to outsiders and Catholics; the hospitality of her prisons, and even the much-vaunted hospitality of her graves, by denying a refuge to the unfortunate dead, and by the formal act of her chief magistrate violated the tomb, the asylum and shelter of the most wretched of our race; and, after exhuming the mouldering remains of the human body, exposed them to the light of day and the gaze of men, even when in an advanced state of decay.

A young man, scarcely out of his teens, a native of Richmond, Va., who served in the responsible capacity of scout in Stonewall Jackson's brigade, composed of Irish and native-born soldiers, arrived in Columbia in 1864, about a year before the close of the war; his mother was a widow; in belief he was a Protestant. As a reward for gallant and daring acts, untarnished fidelity, and distinguished service among the bravest of our troops, he obtained a furlough, and fate impelled him to seek relaxation among the chivalrous youth of the gallant Palmetto State. He made a sad commencement in Columbia, which brought him, and perhaps justly, to a tragical end. God brings good out of evil, and his misfortune was the means of his sincere conversion, and happy, though ignominious, death. He associated with the wild young men of the city. In a drunken frolic, and while maddened by the headlong passions of thoughtless youth, they visited at night a disreputable house over which a notorious character had presided for many years, pandering to the most degrading passions of lawless and immoral men. She was a Jewess, a rare exception to the women of her creed and race, who, like the Irish females, are proverbial for their chastity. Not for booty's sake, but in order to obtain the means of indulging in a prolonged debauch, these reckless young men agreed to rifle the premises of its ill-got treasures. To accomplish this with greater impunity, it was proposed to reduce the mistress to a state of insensibility by administering chloroform. The perpetration of this nefarious act fell to the scout by lot, and he administered the fatal drug without the remotest intention of destroying life. Abandoned by all her heartless accomplices, and more from neglect than by an overdose, the unfortunate creature gradually sunk, and, after some day or two, died from exhaustion, weary if not sated with sin. The young man fled to Montgomery, Ala., was pursued by the police, arrested, and brought back in irons to Columbia.

Shortly afterwards he was put on trial, convicted of murder in the first degree, and condemned to death. Alone and friendless, he must expiate the guilt of all his associates, who escaped unmolested. He gained the sympathy of the virtuous people of the community on account of his youth, of past usefulness, and the unintentional nature of the act; this was his dying declaration, and the thought consoled his last moments. It was reported that the women petitioned his Excellency Governor Pickens for a pardon or commutation of sentence; the men presented a counter petition, which outweighed the first, and left no hope for the child of death. It is flattery to assert that the weaker sex possess more influence than the other; not even as much in most cases of importance or weight. The condemned man turned his thoughts to God immediately, and prepared to meet like a Christian the death which now faced him, but fled from him in all the battle-fields of Virginia. I visited him; he begged to be instructed in the Faith, an obligation which Rev. A. J. McNeale undertook and zealously discharged. He committed the catechism to memory, was baptized, and received the Sacraments repeatedly before his death. His conversion was another unpardonable sin in the estimation of many. While being led to execution, he affirmed that he had no desire for executive pardon and preferred death to life, that he might never more offend God. Few men ever meet death under similiar circumstances with less fear or greater resignation, flowing not from vain ostentation or insensibility, but the result of humble repentance and confidence in the Divine mercy. He was also comforted by the reflection that his widowed parent would be ignorant of his tragical end until it was consummated. Having been handed a glass of water at 'the moment when about to step on the scaffold, he passed it to me adding with a smile: "Under no circumstances should a man forget his good manners or his religion."

After a few suitable remarks addressed to the Sheriff, he knelt, kissed the crucifix, received absolution, and without a struggle passed into the unveiled presence of the Supreme Arbiter of life and death. After the requisite time, the body was examined and life pronounced extinct by Dr. Kennedy, an able physician, deputed by the proper authority to authenticate the fact. It was entrusted to me for burial. I conveyed it forthwith to the church, where it remained the entire afternoon, the following night, and until 10 o'clock the next day (Saturday). Many hundreds in separate gangs, comprising people of every rank, visited the dead body; some made floral offerings, while quite a large number accompanied the remains to the grave, the first spot hailed by the rising sun, and the last to which he bids his evening farewell, in that "crowded acre of the Lord." Sheriff Dent, some members of his family, and people of the first respectability, assisted to manifest their appreciation and esteem for the Christian and edifying manner in which he died.

During this time a storm was gathering which no stranger could foresee, and which culminated shortly after the interment. It was rumored that, either by natural means or supernatural agency, I had raised the dead to life and conveyed him to a place of concealment and safety. It was demanded that I must produce him, at the peril of my life; the same rude scaffold and fatal rope were already prepared for another execution. If I had resuscitated the man from a comatose state, such would have been an act of humanity entitling me to the gratitude of mankind, and to the applause of scientists for the new and valuable discovery. If by the power of heaven I had restored to life one dead as long as Lazarus, and in his condition, I deserved the veneration due to a saint; the multitudes should flock around and embrace the Faith whose truth was reasserted by so conspicuous an attestation of its divinity. The crowd never reasons; the streaks of insanity which a French philosopher declares runs through the brains of every man, show their edges, if not waking, either sleeping, or in a mob.

During the entire Sunday, an oppressive silence brooded over the city, as if ominous of some dreadful fate or deed of unnatural cruelty. Fear seemed to have taken possession of men's minds, and they conversed in a subdued voice. The physician who attended the execution and examined the lifeless body, the Sheriff who accompanied it to the grave, people who remained until the last shovelful of earth was packed on the mound, approached the Governor and established the facts beyond doubt or cavil. In the face of these irrefragable proofs, instead of treating the idle or malicious rumor with merited contempt, he issued an order for the exhuming of the body. In a cemetery situated in the heart of the city, which had been consecrated by Bishop England, where many distinguished people had been interred for nearly seventy years, surrounding the church on three sides, and during service at 4 o'clock Sunday evening, at the moment when I held the sacred humanity and divinity of our Lord in His Eucharistic life uplifted in benediction over the faithful bowed in prostrate adoration before the present Deity, at such a moment, in such a place, and at such a time, the grave sprinkled with holy water and blessed with prayer and incense, was dug open, and the poor, festering corpse, over which the requiem had been pronounced, and which was formally intrusted to the keeping of the parent dust, until the angel came to break the long slumber, and after a short and stormy life, full of every ingredient of human grief, was again exposed to the light of day.

An arrogant, intolerant, and bigoted people are capable of perpetrating any cruelty whatsoever. The dark mysteries of decomposition had made fearful progress, accelerated by the excessive heat of the season; the effacing fingers of decay had blotted out the lines of the features beyond easy recognition. There were present besides the grave-diggers and sight-seers, Dr. Kennedy, Sheriff Jesse Dent, a humane gentleman, General Wade Hampton, and Chaplain Major Lawrence O'Connell, both from the Army of Virginia. The habiliments of the dead, a wreath of flowers which had been placed on the breast of the body, and other details, indirectly established its identity. The witnesses paused. The hesitancy was cut short and rebuked by the chaplain, a man of priestly appearance, soldiery and commanding mien, who fearlessly threw himself in the gap of danger, as he stared indignant at the act itself, and the timidity of the blameless officials, by asking sternly, "*if this be not the body of the scout, whose is it then?*" The grave was hurriedly closed a second time; the dead at last was left to slumber on, and all withdrew. We know how dangerous is the attempt to crush or interfere with man's passions; here, more than in opposition to purely dogmatical questions of belief, lay the secret of the world's resistance to the saints and martyrs of all ages; heresy is the offspring of passion. General Wade Hampton's presence was, I am convinced, in the interest of law and right. He and his kindred were ever on the side of justice and moderation. *Honor and truth* are his motto. The odium of this act falls on the community, rather than on the Governor, who was a humane man, but too easily influenced by popular prejudice.

The injury inflicted on the weak is always cowardly, and intensified in proportion to the inability of the sufferer to vindicate or protect himself. Even incivility to females, the aged, and people in sorrow or suffering, is condemned by the humane. The erring who feel the lash of conscience, find pity instead of reproach, while an injustice to any of this class is abhorred by all the human race. Only savage tribes torture their victims. Tiberius never granted to the victim of his tyranny, according to his historian, the mercy of death; on the contrary, he asserted that it cheated him of his revenge. But he never dreamt to violate any of the thousand tombs strewn along the Appian Way; they were all as sacred, in the mind of the tyrant, as the mausoleums of Scipio and Agrippa.

England, by exhuming the remains of Cromwell and the regecides, and hanging them in chains at Tyburn, after the Restoration; France, in the intoxication of her mistaken liberty, violating the vaults of St. Denis and flinging to the beasts the remains of her kings, her Richelieus, and her Turennes, whose back her enemies never saw; both merited the execration of the human race. Such acts of barbaric revenge disgrace a nation, outrage the better feelings of our nature, and serve but to win commiseration for the dead, especially if their lives have been unfortunate. Death is in a measure a reparation for all the transgressions of a life; we shudder to draw human frailties from their dread abode. Let the dead rest, is the voice of the world and of Christianity. We, in our turn, will need the same indulgence.

When the angry passions of the hour had subsided, and reason resumed her sway, the young scout, brave in death as in the battle-field, was pitied, and the sorrow of the community was like the night wind sighing through his perilous paths in the dark forests of Powhattan. But such was not the hospitality of South Carolina in the days of yore, when the Sumters, the Calhouns, the Englands won for her a proud eminence in the galaxy of States, and her shores and homes were the reputed refuge of the oppressed of all nations.

The foregoing and similar instances are related for the purpose of conveying to the reader a correct idea of the deep-rooted prejudices existing against Catholicity, the persecutions she suffered, and the obstacles that obstructed her path from the very beginning in Carolina. For nearly half a century she was regarded as a social evil, imperilling the prosperity and morals of the community, and blighting their intellects with ignorance and superstition.

The church was twice renovated during the pastorate of the brothers O'Connell; first in 1857, when it was greatly enlarged and remodelled. It was dedicated anew by Bishop Lynch, after his consecration in 1858. It continued in good condition during another decade, when the original sections crumbled from a fault in the architecture, and a general reconstruction became necessary. A wooden railing in front and at the rear was constantly in disrepair, and the cemetery was trodden and frequently pastured by the city cattle. There was no remedy for this dilapidated condition; for the people were suffering for want of the absolute necessaries of life.

In 1867 Fathers Lawrence and Joseph O'Connell both repaired to the more fortunate cities of New York and Brooklyn, and with much toil and labor, collected among their friends sufficient funds for the performance of the work. The church was again renewed, both inside and outside, and a brick wall of solid masonry built on the rear to protect the graves from exposure.

A handsome pair of iron gates, and a railing set on brick masonry, with granite coping, arose in front and running the entire length of the sidewalk. All the premises were substantially protected, and assumed an ecclsiastical appearance. The present condition of the church is the result of that effort.

The congregation contributed but little at any time to the establishment and maintenance of the church and other religious institutions. They owed their existence to the liberality of Irish Catholics in all the seaports lying on the Atlantic coast of the United States. There were but one or two wealthy men in the Church, who were by no means the most liberal.

This work having been accomplished, the two priests withdrew to other missions in the war-worn diocese. Between 1865 and '70 the congregation shrunk to its original size, and there was scarcely sufficient employment to occupy the time of one priest. Luxuriant grass waved in the principal streets, and the cattle pastured in the once thronged and fashionable thoroughfare. The rapidity with which vegetation springs up in a ruined city is positively amazing; it is as rapid as the growth of vice in some fallen soul. A very few years would suffice to make New York as much a wilderness as Thebes or Luxor.

In 1871, in consequence of impaired health, I removed to the missions in Western North Carolina, where I was instrumental in the introduction of the Benedictine Order, whose habit I wear.

The Ursulines transferred their institution to Valle Crucis, within two miles of the city, and are well patronized. They also conduct a day-school in Columbia. Father Fullerton is the present pastor, a zealous and efficient priest; the Church is gradually acquiring her former prosperous condition.

CHAPTER IX.

COLUMBIA AND ITS MISSIONS.

A Fair in 1849 for the Erection of a Priest's House—House sold for the Establishment of the Sisters' Convent—Peculation at Fairs—Fairfield, etc.—The Clark Family—An Ursuline Nun—Extent of Missions in 1848—Orangeburg—Col. Lewis and Family—James Jones—Mrs. Frederick—Lancaster—Hon. William McKenna—The Celebrated Will—Bequests often Defeated and cause Scandals—Rev. D. J. Quigley—His Mother and Sisters—Ordained in Rome—Stationed in Charleston—Sarah Mittag—Other Catholics—C. B. Northrop—First Missionaries—Converts—An Execution—The Northrop Family—Edifying Life—Reflection—Sumter in 1848—Created a Parish in 1837—Fathers Birmingham, Quigley, and Guilford—Sumter and Spann Families—Judge Rice—Lectures in Town Hall—Hon. T. J Coglan and Lady—Small number of Catholics, and Scattered—John O'Connor—Brian Cavanaugh and other Catholics—Cavanaugh's Ditch—William G. Kennedy and Sister—William Logue—The Sisters save Sumterville—Their Introduction and Establishment—Father McNeal—Mrs. Fulton—A Brilliant Christening—Hon. T. J. Moses—A new Church—Lectures in Manning Court-House—Rev. T. J. Sullivan—His Life, Labors, Character, and Death—Buried in St. Laurence's Church—Inducement for Immigration to Sumter County.

DURING the session of the Legislature in 1849, I conducted a fair in Columbia for the purpose of erecting a house or presbytery for the priest. This mode of realizing funds for religious objects, being then novel in the city, was well patronized by all classes, and the sum needed was netted—about eight hundred dollars. It was about half the amount contributed by the public. Articles were purchased at the stores, and sold on commission; peculation crept in; charges were made for time and services. The tables most gorgeously furnished and extensively patronized, rendered the least returns. After a week we closed with the forementioned proceeds, and two or three family quarrels on hand, the general result of such undertakings. No article should, under any circumstances, be offered for sale at fairs, unless gratuitously furnished, and the price applied to the charity proposed. A contrary course is an injustice to the community who pay their money for the object for which it is solicited, and care not for the articles; it also defeats the end to be obtained, and opens the door to fraud, injustice, and peculation. The prelates have already turned their attention to the evils connected with this mode of raising money by picnics, excursions, balls, theatrical representations, etc. They were reluctantly tolerated in cases of great emergency, are now forbidden in some dioceses, and will be prohibited ere long throughout the extent of the Church in the United States.

A commodious house was purchased at the right hand entrance of the church, and immediately adjacent. The entire square, with its theatre and various buildings, could have been bought at the time for fifteen hundred dollars, except the hotel at the southwest corner of the lot. I occupied the house for some time until the clergy withdrew to St. Mary's College. The title was invested in the Bishop of the diocese, in trust for the congregation, and remained so for nearly eighteen months, until the house and lot were sold by the consent of Bishop Reynolds, and the proceeds invested in the Convent of the Sisters of Mercy, which was occupied by them about five years, subsequently by the Ursuline Nuns, and finally burned by Sherman's army.

The transfer was made at the request of the congregation, who also petitioned the Ordinary, believing that the establishment of a branch of the Sisters of Mercy would promote the interests of Catholicity exceedingly in the city, and outweigh the advantages of the parsonage then unoccupied. Nor were they mistaken; during their sojourn, the pious and self-sacrificing ladies won the esteem of the people, defeated and disarmed prejudice, and reconciled the public mind to the claims of the Church in a wonderful manner. The priest's house was purchased by a Catholic; it is exceedingly convenient to the church, admirably adapted to the object for which it was secured, and may eventually revert to it. Every step taken for the establishment of religion in the diocese was attended by an amount of labor and pain incredible to the faithful of more favored regions, and calculated to excite the admiration of those yet to come.

In Winnsboro, Fairfield district, resided Dr. Caleb Clarke and his brother William, natives of Maryland, who professed the Faith of Lord Calvert with a pride befitting their descent from the cradle of civil and religious liberty in the United States. The second brother died childless, in middle age, after having received the last Sacraments with ample and edifying preparation. The elder brother, who still survives, married a sister of the Hon. Joseph A. Woodward, who represented his district in Congress several years. She embraced the Faith, and never lost her first fervor to the hour of her death, which occurred about 1861. She raised all her children in the true Faith. They received all the advantages of education afforded by our leading Catholic institutions. The youngest daughter took the habit of religion at the Ursuline Convent at Valle Crucis, of which she is an edifying member, under the name of Sister Agnes. Mrs. Clarke was visited by God with a long and painful illness, before her death, which she endured with the patience and resignation of a saint.

Mrs. Rickenbacher, *née* O'Connell, resided at Orangeburg. She was extremely old. She recollected having witnessed the execution of Foster and his wife, who kept the Four-Mile House, near Charleston, and were convicted of the murder of many of their guests, whose hidden remains were discovered on the premises in every possible state of decomposition. It is surmised that they were connected with the Murril gang. They were above the common class, and had entertained the first people in the country frequently. Their crimes and punishment caused a great commotion in the community at the time. The female was a woman of graceful manners and fascinating appearance. She expected a pardon, to the very last moment, from the Governor, who was present at the execution. She cast an imploring look at him, but he frowned a denial of clemency. A little pile of dried grey bones, lying in a corner at the museum attached to the Charleston Medical College, was pointed out to me in after years as those of Foster and his wife. Traditions of crimes of this nature are frequent all over America on the lines of public travel, before the introduction of railroads, which are the means of saving numberless lives, despite the many and distressing accidents which mark their history. The facility of travel and comparative security of life which they afford amply repay society for expense or local disadvantages, apart from all other considerations.

Mr. Jones, an Englishman, and his entire family, pious Catholics and respectable citizens, resided at Orangeburg; also Mr. Champy, a Frenchman, two of whose children I baptized. At the invitation of Colonel Ellis, I lectured in the Court-House, and the citizens, who generally attended, expressed their admiration for the beauty and harmony of Catholic truth. At a later period, Mrs. Lewis, the wife of Colonel Lewis, of Virginia, converts, and connected by the ties of kindred with the Floyd family and the first people in the country, resided with her daughter, Mrs. Frederick, a few miles from the town. The high social position of the family, their piety and firm devotion to the Church, together with the considerations of affluence and a superior education, won respect at least for the Faith in the community. By the civil war they lost an ample fortune,—in short, everything but their religion,—and returned poor to the White Sulphur Springs, in Greenbrier County, of which they were proprietors. Mrs. Lewis was a woman of rare intellectual endowments, and conversational powers of the first order; but the gifts of grace were more abundant still, were cultivated with greater care and unremitting perseverance. In South Carolina, as in Virginia, they were the benefactors of the Church, and endeavored to show their gratitude to God for bringing them out of darkness to the knowledge of the truth. How dreadful must be the guilt of those who wilfully abandon it! Strangers shall come and take their places in heaven, while the children of the kingdom will be cast forth into outer darkness.

The number of conversions taking place daily in the

Church, and by which the ranks thinned by the defection of some few of her faithless children, is an illustration of this divine visitation and just retribution. Satan and his rebellious hosts were the first heretics; all who have opposed the authority of God's Church, from Cain to Antichrist, are their descendants and disciples, according to the declaration of St. Jude. But God will not be defeated in his ends by the malice of his creatures, and the lost thrones become the prize of others, yet unborn, but found more worthy of the forfeited inheritance.

Camden, situated about thirty-five miles south of Columbia, was one of the most barren spots in the entire mission. A church edifice was begun during the pastorship of Mr. Quigley, and sold for debt before its completion. There were scarcely any Catholics of means in that place who felt the slightest interest in religious matters. Bishop Reynolds declined assuming the debt on his accession to the see of Charleston. The amount could not have been very large, for the building was wooden, of moderate size, and situated in a dilapidated country town. There was some complication, which terminated in the sale of the church at public auction. It was bought by a Frenchman, who converted it into a dwelling-house.

In earlier times this place was repeatedly visited by Bishop England. He lectured on those occasions to the *elite* and wealthy people who possessed the surrounding fertile country, and owned fancy residences in the town, which boasts of the DeKalb monument and preserves his remains. I subsequently preached in the Town Hall; such discourses effect permanent good in the community at the time, by bringing the few Catholics to confession, and confirming the wavering faith of some others. Nowhere in America have greater efforts been made by the Church to keep her own than in the diocese of Charleston, by the untiring labor and zeal of her bishops, priests, and religious. Nowhere in the civilized portion of the globe could there exist an ecclesiastical district so strictly a missionary ground. It seemed to be labor lost, if the fruit be estimated by the number of converts. During the period of sixty-eight years, and since the formation of the diocese, about fifty influential families have joined the Church in the three States. This is a great victory, when we consider the value of a soul, the influence they may exert in favor of the truth, and the fact that an Apostle, the first of the Apostolic College who suffered martyrdom—St. James, the patron of Spain, is said to have brought but five adults into the Church. Many individuals, poor people and negroes, have been converted, children baptized before death, and the Faith preserved among the adults or immigrants generally ; all forbid us to conclude that the labor of so many ecclesiastics of all ranks is fruitless.

One family resided in the town who always adhered to the Faith,—the Campbells. The father had not yet joined the Church ; the mother, raised in Charleston, was a most excellent and pious woman, who taught her children their religion and their obligations to God and man. After travelling a distance of about forty miles by stage, over a sandy road, running through a dreary, thinly-settled country, in an easterly direction, one catches a glimpse of the Court-House in Lancaster, the principal building in the paintless town. This county is one of the oldest settlements in the State, and is bordering on the old county of Mecklenburg, N. C., where Andrew Jackson was born. The natives are thrifty and industrious, partaking of the character and disposition of the inhabitants of the neighboring State of North Carolina. Father Birmingham regularly visited Lancaster, Camden, etc., between 1832 and 1844, and it formed portion of the mission of Rev. T. J. Cronin, between 1838 and up to the time of his death in 1842. He received Mrs. McKenna and other converts into the Church. He converted, and assisted at his last moments, a criminal who was executed about 1841, and made the first impression in the county in favor of Catholicity. Father Guifford succeeded, and made visits until 1846. The place was thenceforward visited by the Columbia priests and Father McNeal, until the close of the war, when the faithful had mostly died or moved to other places.

The faith and piety of one family who resided in the village rendered it an agreeable station where the missionary, wearied with his journeys and toils, could rest a few days and recruit his strength for fresh labors ; it was like an oasis in the wilderness. Early in the present century, Hon. William McKenna settled here, opened a store, and conducted an extensive mercantile business for many years. He was a native of County Derry, Ireland ; shrewd, thrifty, and enterprising, he prospered, and in the course of time accumulated a fortune. He married Miss Annie Cousart, a native of the county, wealthy, and well connected, who joined the Church and died fortified by the Sacraments. Mr. McKenna survived many years, retired from mercantile pursuits, and devoted his attention to his farming interests and the care of his slaves, who were numerous, and for whose temporal and spiritual welfare he provided by all possible means. The negro children were all baptized, many of the adults had become Catholics ; all were taught the catechism and their prayers on Sundays, and they retained the Faith while under Catholic influence, and until emancipated. The humane master was much esteemed by the community in which he lived, and represented the district in the State Senate with great ability. He caused the creation of a professorship of the French language in the South Carolina College, and warmly advocated all measures of public interest to the country.

He left no issue by this marriage, and died March 11th, 1857, in an edifying manner, fortified by all the rites and consolations of the Church, which he always venerated and cherished more than life. He bequeathed the greater part of his property in trust to the Bishop of Charleston and his successors in office, for the establishment of a male orphan asylum in that city. Rev. J. J. O'Connell, J. W Bradley, C. B. Northrop, and Thomas M. Belk were appointed the executors of his will. It was contested, on the unjust grounds of mental incapacity, and undue influence on the part of the clergy. After much litigation, great unpleasantness, and loss to the estate, the parties made a compromise by which about a third of the proceeds of the property came into the possession of Bishop Lynch. The war which followed immediately after the arbitration, the emancipation of the slaves, the bankruptcy of the country, the valueless currency, and the insolvency of the debtors, rendered the estate nothing worth, defeated the laudable object of the testator, and left him but the merit of good intentions. The property benefitted no person connected with its administration, or interested in the bequests, except to the extent of the value of a few negroes bought by the Bishop for the sake of preserving their Faith, and subsequently sold to a Catholic family. A portion of the real estate is now lying waste, in consequence of the inability of the court to decide who are the legatees. With the exception of the forementioned item, the McKenna estate will sarcely benefit any one concerned.

Nor is this an exceptional case; numerous instances of this character are rife over the length and breadth of the country, and the litigation has given occasion to the spread of many scandals. Religious bequests, as a general fact, are sure to give rise to ceaseless and vexatious suits at law, and the sympathy of society and the courts favor the contestants, especially when the *will* was made in behalf of Catholic charities. This, in several instances, seems to be a just retribution in punishment of the parsimony of withholding from God, during our lifetime, what will be of no further earthly use to us when dead; gifts made to religion during one's life are rarely litigated; on the contrary, men laud the charity of the donor, and his generosity is admired and commended by the voice of the world. Without entailing the privation of the means necessary for the maintenance of our condition in life, this course affords the benefactor the consolation of witnessing the just and faithful application of his charities to the contemplated purposes, and of being followed to his grave by the prayers of the orphan and the blessings of the faithful. It is the duty of the Christian to endeavor that the temporal favors enjoyed through life should not be made an occasion for offending God after his death, dwindles away and fades into insignificance. Every man should attend to his own personal affairs while he enjoys life and strength; that others will do so when he is no longer on earth, with the same zeal and industry, is more than we may rationally expect. All wealthy people are in peril of having their clearest intentions, most distinctly stated in their last will and testament, defeated; the danger increases if made in favor of Catholic objects, and the responsibility of applying the grants should if possible be borne by the individual; otherwise he may justify the words of the prophet: "*He heaps up riches, and knoweth not who shall gather them.*" These remarks are not meant to apply simply to the Hon. William McKenna; the views were amply grasped by his astute and cautious mind; but he was unable to put them in practice, because of his declining years and the peculiar circumstances of his situation. He died in the seventy-eighth year of his age, still vigorous in mind and intellect. His remains were carried to Columbia and interred in the Catholic cemetery, in the family lot by the side of his sister, Rose, the mother of John W. Bradley.

His household was composed of his niece, Mrs. Quigley, *née* Barre, an elderly and pious lady, who died March 10th, 1866, and her four grown children, Ellen, Catharine, Mary Ann, and Daniel Joseph, the youngest son, who was born in Scotland, and was trained for the holy ministry. He made his preparatory studies at St. Mary's, Emmettsburg, read an extensive course of theology at St. Mary's, Columbia, S.C., and repairing to Rome, finished his ecclesiastical education in the American College under the presidency of Dr. McClosky, in 1866. Immediately after his return to South Carolina he was stationed at the pro-Cathedral, where he has been discharging the onerous duty of pastor up to this time, with zeal, efficiency, and prudence; he is also Vicar-General, the assiduous instructor of the youth in Christian Faith and practice, and the establishment of respectable Catholic schools engrossing much of his time and labors.

Sarah, the eldest child of J. F. G. Mittag, Esq., was a most amiable and edifying Catholic. She was educated partly at Georgetown, and illustrated in her life and actions all the virtues that adorn her sex. She died in 1851, after having reached the age of womanhood, and was fortified with the holy Sacraments, which she frequently approached during her lifetime. God called her to an early reward, and before her peace was impaired by the cares and annoyances of human life. The Misses Cruise, two sisters who taught a respectable female school, Patrick McKenna, and Mrs. McLaron, were exemplary and pious Catholics, and are now dead. The latter died in 1866, and left two children, Catharine and Felix, who still survive and adhere to the Faith inherited from their sainted mother. I frequently lectured in the Court-House, on the principal doctrines of the Church, and generally obtained good audiences. I was the second, and Father Cronin the first, who preached the Gospel in this place. The Catholics were few in number, but edifying and respectable members of the community. It is sad to reflect that none have succeeded in the place of those who have passed away or died, and that the faithful have dwindled down to one or two in Lancaster, so favorably and extensively known in days gone by all over the diocese. The war and death played sad havoc here among all classes, and at this time it may be justly named "The Deserted Village." The seed scattered in toil and labor still exists in the bosom of the people, and may fructify in God's own season.

C. B. Northrop, Esq., removed his family thither about the opening of the civil war, and made his permanent home at Lancasterville. If his life had been spared, doubtless he would have perpetuated Catholicity in the country. Born in Charleston, of a respectable family, he was educated in the State College, and followed the profession of law in his native city. A man of general information, rectitude of life, and magnificent conversational powers, he in a short time stood at the head of his profession. He represented the city in the Legislature at a time when the appointment was a recognition of merit and a mark of public esteem. Reared by a most excellent mother, a strict member of the Episcopal Church, he adhered to that creed until middle life, when thought and reading disabused him of his errors, and he renounced them unhesitatingly, heedless of consequences, and rather desirous that sacrifices might be the reward as well as the test of his generosity. To live a lie would be abhorrent to his nature.

Shortly after the death of Bishop England, and during the administration of Very Rev. Dr. Baker, he was received into the Church, and he had his children baptized. His mother, the elder Mrs. Northrop, had already embraced the Faith. She was a woman of rare excellence and strength of mind, and a pattern of all the virtues of the Christian matron. Doubtless her prayers won for him and her other children the grace of conversion. Her daughter, Mrs. Bellinger, was already a fervent, devout Catholic; and another son, a graduate of West Point Military Academy, and Commissary-General of the Confederate States, Dr. L. Northrop, who was brought under obedience to the Faith at a later period. Lawyer Northrop became identified with all the interests of Catholicity in the diocese for nearly a quarter of a century. Enlightened in the science of salvation, and in the knowledge of God, religion became the leading principle of his every thought and action; the frequent approach to the Sacraments the consolation of his life; and the observance of the Divine Law the joy of his heart. Full of merit rather than years, he was summoned to receive his reward suddenly, but not unprepared, because he always lived in the friendship of his Maker.

After having reached Winnsboro, Sherman led his army by a lower route through Camden and Lancaster, by the identical road traversed by the English under Tarleton a century before. His horses' hoofs left their prints on the battle-ground which drunk the blood of the brave DeKalb and his heroic few. The march to the sea was everywhere marked by smoking ruins, the destruction of property, and wide-spread desolation.

Arriving at Lancasterville, the houses were visited by several gangs of soldiers in quest of treasures or booty,— one succeeding another incessantly while the most trifling article of value remained. Several prominent citizens fled and hid themselves in swamps and such recesses as seemed inaccessible to the brigands, or "bummers," as they were styled in the army. It was of no avail, because the slaves knew all the secret places, and either pointed them out, or conducted the marauders in person.

During this occupation, Mr. Northrop died of apoplexy, according to the general opinion. He raised several children. John fought in the Southern army, was wounded, and became blind for life ; the eldest, Lucius, having adopted his father's profession, was educated to the bar, and, fulfilling its duties with marked ability, was raised to the bench, and discharged the office of Judge with credit to himself and profit to the State. He was appointed District-Attorney for South Carolina by President Hayes in 1877. The two other sons, Henry P. and Claudian B. Northrop, faithful to the religious influence of their early training, cultivated a vocation for the holy priesthood, and now minister at the altars of religion.

Sumter was visited by Father Birmingham and other priests occasionally, until created a parish in 1837, with Father Quigley first pastor. In 1842 he was removed to North Carolina. On his appointment to Columbia in 1844, Mr. Quigley again revisited his old friends, and continued to do so until my appointment in 1848.

The earliest and leading Catholic families were the Sumters and Spanns. Mrs. Sumter was the relict of the distinguished Revolutionary general of that name, and after whom the district is named. She sprang from the first families in France before the Reign of Terror, and retained her Faith, which she practised with fervor and zeal. She left three sons. The two oldest died during the civil war, but did not receive the Sacraments at their death, nor for some time previous. The third still lives, and is not numbered among us, having renounced the Faith and traditions of an illustrious name and family. There were two daughters: Mrs. Bender, who lives in Europe with her husband, who filled an Italian mission under one of our past administra-

tions; the other, Mrs. Brownfield. They are the worthy
children of a great and good Catholic mother. Mrs. Brownfield led her husband to embrace the true Faith. He died
in Charleston after the war, fortified with the rites of salvation. They raised a large family of children in the knowledge and practice of the obligations of the Church. One, at
least, of the daughters has joined the self-sacrificing Order
of the Sisters of Mercy. The Spanns were also influential
and zealous. The widow of Charles Spann was a Catholic
lady of refined culture and extensive education; she spent a
great part of her fortune in the raising and cultivation of
the silk-worm, and was enthusiastic for the introduction of
this department of industry into the Southern States. Her
attempt, however, proved a failure, for want of experience
or skilful operators. She left one or two sons, and as many
daughters. The eldest daughter married Judge Rice, of
Charleston, a convert, but since dead. The second, Mary,
married into the Manly family, of Raleigh, and is still
living and blessed with children. The others removed
to Galveston, Texas. The mother died at a venerable
age. In the winter of 1848 I visited Sumter District,
such being the name by which the divisions of the State
were called until altered into that of county by the Convention of 1868; the lower sections were called parishes.
I spent a few days at the Sumter place, then occupied by
John Brownfield, who had married into the family. The
only Catholics in the vicinity were Mrs. Poole and her family, an excellent and devout lady, who brought her husband into the Church soon afterwards. Her daughter Sarah
was an accomplished girl, edifying and devout, and conducted the choir at Sumterville until her health failed.
Mrs. Poole and her sister, Mrs. Hulbert, were great benefactors of the rising congregation of Sumter, first in every
enterprise undertaken to advance religion, and by their edifying life made an abiding impression on the community in
favor of the truth.

About 1838 a church was erected in the vicinity of these
families at a place called Providence, a few miles north of

the town of Sumterville, attended by only a few struggling Irish Catholics, the congregation not numbering over thirty souls in all. I said the last Mass offered in the church, on a Sunday, with none to assist save the attendant at the altar. There was no congregation, in our most modest acceptation of the term, and the church was entirely abandoned in the solitude of the wilderness, and liable to be destroyed by fires.

It was sold the year following by the consent of the Bishop, and the proceeds invested in the future church of the county town, to which I repaired on this occasion, and became the guest of Hon. T. J. Coglan, who was the intendant, a man of independent character, and held in esteem by the people. His lady, though not a member of the true fold, aided with untiring zeal and industry to establish the Church in Sumter. Her house was, during many years, the home of our Bishop and priests, where they met with a generous welcome and a refined hospitality. To the co-operation of this family especially, with the exertions of the priests, is the town of Sumter indebted for her church, her increased population, and all the blessings, not only spiritual, but temporal also, which follow her establishment. Sumter would have shared the fate of Columbia, when occupied by Federal troops, and was spared only by the entreaties of the Sisters, who had a house and institute in the town.

Hon. T. J. Coglan was baptized in Charleston, by Rev. Dr. Gallagher, and his recollections extended considerably beyond the advent of Bishop England. It was his fate to live isolated from a priest or church, but he preserved the Faith, and aided to propogate and localize it in the heart of the State, more than any other layman. A man of sound practical judgment, he opposed secession, stood aloof from the excitement and madness of the hour, was a lone man in the community, and remained unmolested to the last. He was summoned to assist in framing the new constitution, was elected State Senator, and afterwards Sheriff of the county. He filled these offices with integrity and ability, and was one of the few honorable men who composed the radical mis-Government of down-trodden States. Always faithful among the faithless, he withdrew and plied his customary occupation when he found that the administration was only a legalized system of fraud and robbery. He sought to retrieve the ruined fortunes of his native soil; failing in this, he was the last to become an accomplice in the crime of her oppression.

During the following year, 1849, I visited the station repeatedly. There being no connection by railroad, I journeyed by way of Clarendon Depot, on the Camden road, and thence to Sumter by stage, which was the usual route for many years. I said Mass in an humble apartment owned by the baker, and which was attended by a dozen Catholics who were scattered over the entire section, in the humblest employments, unknown, unfelt, and depreciated; but they were all dear to God, and known to His saints and angels. These were the widow O'Brien and two children, her sister, also a widow, with two small children. Both married after some years and raised many children, who are now grown, and some of them married to persons of their own religion, all devoted and sincere Catholics. Mrs. Harney and Mrs. Johanna Bogan still live, and give promise of many more years of usefulness and edification. They were of the Kenny family, who had settled near Providence, worthy and virtuous people, now all dead and at rest in our Lord. The parents were genuine Irish Catholics, and are fondly remembered by their offspring. Patrick O'Sullivan was an intelligent man, intensely Irish and Catholic; sufficiently eccentric to give him individuality, he will be long and favorably recollected in the district. He died during the war at the hospital in Greenbrier Co., Va., which was under the care of the Sisters, and in which he served as steward; he was about fifty-six years old. James Barret, an ardent Catholic and a well-informed man, with his brother, John Hennigan, deserve honorable mention, as the first pioneers of the Faith in this country. After the erection of the church they married and raised children, who perpetuate their parents' piety and devotion. Thomas Feeny, Mr. Harney, and Brian Cavanaugh, were worthy people, and inferior to none in zeal and the observance of all religious duties. The two latter left worthy and truly Catholic families.

Mr. Cavanaugh never allowed any body to insult his religion in his presence with impunity. Having served in the Seminole War, under General Brisbane, the distinguished convert, he retained through life the independent spirit of the soldier. While engaged in the humble occupation of ditching, the employer who came to examine the work after many days, wantonly uttered one of the stale calumnies against the Church. Possessed of more than ordinary intelligence and information, Cavanaugh made a correct and well-merited answer. After a moment's pause, and hesitating whether he might not administer a wholesome reproof in the way of castigation, he adopted a more prudent but no less significant course. He levelled to the surface the ditch in all its length, the work which had cost him days, nay weeks of labor, silently withdrew, and never more returned. He erected a monument to his memory, more durable than brass or marble. The locality has been since called and marked in charts, maps, and deeds of conveyance as *Cavanaugh's Ditch*. According to reliable tradition, the first Mass offered in Sumterville was said in a small room attached to John O'Conner's bakery, and by the writer. He had three brothers employed in different places over the State—Edward, Thomas, and James, who all died within a short space of time. Having married Miss Ellen Bogen, their union was blessed by the birth of three children. The first died in childhood, the second, Frank, alone survives, and the third, Kate, who married Mr. Heweston, whom she led to profess the Faith, died in the year 1876. Mrs. O'Conner departed this life about the year 1869, and her husband about ten years later, after having married Miss Harriet O'Reilly, who became the devoted mother of the orphans. Mrs. Ellen O'Conner was a superior woman, humane, devout, and charitable. Having prospered, they acquired a competent share of worldly goods; their liberality to the Church, relief of the needy, and general benevolence, increased in proportion.

Their house was during many years the home of the clergy, and religion had no better friends or worthier disciples in that country.

Mrs. O'Conner had two other sisters and a brother, William Bogan, who still live, have many children, and are prosperous in this life, without forfeiting the well-grounded hopes of the future. Identified with the origin and growth of Catholicity in that place, they have shed around the odor of piety and good works. Margaret was married to Thomas Monahan, who died soon after the close of the war. Blameless in life, unimpeachable in manners, prudent and industrious, he was the true type of a Catholic gentleman. Catharine, the other sister, married Michael Comerford, of Columbia, and her devout life is an ornament to the congregation. Their cousins, the Misses Margaret and Mary Ann Doyle, are equally deserving of eulogy and commendation. It is a remarkable fact that vice is hereditary in many families, and is commonly called *a bad drop in the blood*, and virtue in others. Without stopping to explain the causes, which are very obvious, excluding *necessity*, and leaving freedom of action unimpaired, the latter priceless inheritance can be asserted in behalf of the Bogan family; may it be propagated, and descend to their future generations.

During the first year and at different intervals I preached either in the Court-House or the Town-Hall, and my discourses were well attended. I explained the principal controverted points of Faith, and lectured for a week each successive night, on the establishment and marks of the true Church. The arguments were cogent and conclusive to the minds of the better educated people, and many expressed their conviction of the truth of Catholic doctrine. They even urged the building of a house of worship, and promised material aid. We purchased from the Methodists their meeting-house and lot, situated in the most elevated part of the town, and admirably adapted to our purpose. On examination the edifice was found to be safe and substantial; the oldest Protestant church in that country, it was endeared to the community by long associations. It was remodelled, and after some labor and expense, became a very fair Catholic church, surmounted by a cross, and ornamented with a genteel sanctuary and altar. Hon. T. J. Coglan was the head mechanic and principal agent in the transaction. The lot contains an entire square. It was immediately protected by a handsome paling, and was converted into a cemetery, which was sadly needed. The remains of those who died heretofore were buried in woods, or removed to Charleston. Catholics will never permanently locate where there is no church nor graveyard. Irish people cannot be reconciled to the idea of being buried outside of consecrated ground. They abhor it as much as did the Patriarchs in Mesopotamia and Egypt. Hon. F. J. Moses, afterwards Chief-Justice, and all the Israelites were foremost in extending aid and sympathy; also Colonel Mayrant; so were Doctors Richardson, Witherspoon, and the people generally. After a period of thirty years, that generation has mostly passed away. Would they had corresponded to the graces they had received, and to the light of that Faith which they had so generously contributed to establish and diffuse. It is certain they rendered it accessible to their descendants, by planting the Church in their midst.

In the summer of 1849 the church was dedicated to St. Lawrence, Martyr (not to St. John, as reported in the *Catholic Almanac*), by Bishop Reynolds, in the presence of a large audience, to whom he preached an admirable and convincing sermon on confession and the absolving power. It was one of the greatest efforts of his life, and was long remembered by the inhabitants. I offered the Holy Sacrifice of the Mass on the occasion, and the Bishop administered Confirmation to the candidates, among whom were William G. Kennedy and his sister, Mrs. McKain, both converts, and whose ancestor, but a few years before, occupied the pulpit of that church as its pastor. While a student in the South Carolina College, Mr. Kennedy, then a young man, read with deep interest the controversy conducted at the time between Rev. Dr. Lynch and Prof. Thornwell. Too well-informed to mistake assertion for proof, he concluded that the Catholic arguments remained unanswered, and the correctness of his judgment was confirmed by Hon. W. C. Preston, whom he consulted. He made the acquaintance of a young man of Irish birth, William Logue, Esq., who immigrated to Edgefield at an early age, and had barely a tradition of the Faith. Both entered on a thorough examination of the teachings of the Church, which resulted in the conversion of William Kennedy and his accomplished sister, who shortly afterwards was united in wedlock to Dr. McKain, of Camden. The young convert was soon left a widow with two children, whom she studiously raised in the Gospel treasure so mercifully revealed to her. William Logue studied law and practised his profession both in Savannah, Ga., and South Carolina. He married in Edgefield, brought his wife into the Church, and died about 1856, leaving one child. Colonel Kennedy was also admitted to the bar. He cultivated literature very extensively, and composed some admirable poems on religious subjects, which are destined to live. He married in the family of Dr. White, a wealthy and distinguished physician. His wife is a lady of rare accomplishments and true piety, and on whom I poured the sacred waters of regeneration. The family now reside in the town, and are bringing up their children in the fear and service of their Maker, and in the true Faith, a boon esteemed infinitly more than the opulence swept away by the civil war.

When the church was finished, many worthy accessions were gradually made to the worshippers, conspicuous among whom were Messrs. Moran, Reardon, Twony, Morrisey, Eberhart, Miss Owens, and their pious families. The number increased during the war, although most of them returned to Charleston. The congregation is now permanent, and sufficiently large to occupy the services and time of a stationary priest. Among the refugees was Mrs. Fulton, of Wilmington, a convert to the Faith, and a most estimable and devout lady. Left a widow at an early age, by the request of a dying parent, who was not a Catholic, the only child, a daughter, was placed under the care of the Sisters of Mercy, a step which brought both into the Church. Miss Kate married Mr. Wright, of Wilmington. Her first child was baptized by Primate Spalding, on the occasion of the installation of Bishop Gibbons as Vicar-Apostolic of North Carolina, in the year 1868. There were present, beside the mitred prelates, Very Rev. Dr. Birmingham, Rev. Messrs. L. P. O'Connell, J. B. McManus, H. P. Northrop, M. Gross, and J. J. O'Connell, who were recipients of the hospitality of the venerable hostess. Mrs. Price, a convert also, and a sister-in-law to Mrs. Fulton, was in Sumter with her child during this time. Her husband, the accomplished editor of the Wilmington *Journal*, embraced the Faith, and two daughters entered into the self-sacrificing order of the Sisters when established in the vicariate of the zealous and faithful Bishop. Many of the leading families from the Cathedral parish sought refuge here in those disastrous times. Messrs. Budds, of the *Courier*, Bernard and J. F. O'Neill, John McKeegan, Martin Duggin, Mr. Maloney, with their households, Miss Mary Harvey and her two sisters, with several others, were prominent among the refugees for great moral worth and respectability. Lieutenant Pamphero, a gallant young Catholic officer, and a native of New Orleans, was slain at the fight at Dingle's Mill, three miles from town, April 9th, 1865.

The Sisters purchased a house and lot in 1862, and transferred some of their community and the boarders thither. After the war they made additional improvements, purchased a more extensive piece of property in a central position, erected a large and commodious convent building, where they conduct a boarding and day school, and are handsomely patronized by all denominations. They were accompanied by the Superior, Rev. T. J. Sullivan, who shared in their labors, and ministered to the spiritual wants of the religious and the congregation, until his death in 1865; his remains are buried in a vault under the church. In 1865 Rev. A. J. McNeal was deputed to the charge of the Sisters and the mission, and has officiated, during the last thirteen years, with zeal and ability in this promising field of missionary labors. Funds were collected in 1875 to build a new church and remove the old one. It will be a handsome and substantial structure, and is now in process of erection. Thus, after nearly seventeen years of assiduous care and exertion, was Catholicity established in the town of Sumter. Aided by Fathers L. P. and J. P. O'Connell, I gave the people an opportunity of hearing Mass one Sunday in each month, and frequently on two. They were never once disappointed, no infant died unbaptized, and no sick call was neglected. I was the first priest who preached the true Faith in the town. Bishop England had done so once before. I also preached in the Court-House in Manning shortly after it was built, and when the county was formed by cutting off a section of the Southeastern part of Sumter. This occurred in 1859.

There was but one Catholic residing in the new county, in whose humble residence I offered up the Adorable Sacrifice of the Mass. The Rev. Edward Quigley was the first priest stationed in the district, and at Providence. The facilities of travel, salubrious climate, great fertility of soil in the produce of cotton, vegetables, and cereals, and the religious institutions, offer paramount inducements to immigrants to settle in this county. Before many years Sumter will probably possess the largest congregation of any inland city in South Carolina.

Early in the present century the Rev. Timothy Joseph Sullivan was born in the County Cork, Ireland. His early piety attracted the notice of Father Matthew, who received him under his tutelage, encouraged his aspirations, and cultivated his vocation for the holy ministry. Having acquired a fair English education and respectable knowledge of the language of the Church, about middle life, and after a youth spent in virtue and devotion, he was received into the diocese on the most favorable recommendations by Dr. England, made his ecclesiastical studies in the Seminary of St. John the Baptist, under the Rev. Dr. Baker, and was raised to the dignity of the priesthood about 1838. He was appointed assistant in the Cathedral and Superior of the Seminary immediately after his ordination, and some time later, Ecclesiastical Superior of the Sisters of Mercy, and Diocesan Secretary. The duties entailed by any one of the offices were sufficient to occupy the time of any ordinary man; the amount of labor which they imposed on him was incredible. Strictly abstemious in his habits, a man of prayer, and a devoted servant of God, he curtailed his hours of sleep, removed all intercourse with the world beyond his ministerial offices, worked day and night, and spent himself in the divine service for a quarter of a century. Untiring in attendance on the sick, assiduous in the confessional, and vigilant over the candidates for the sanctuary, whom he formed by word and example, he gave himself no rest, nor do I remember him to have taken five minutes' recreation at a time during four years spent under his guidance as director of the Seminary. Dark-featured, of the medium size, slightly stooped, and of a nervous temperament, his constitution was robust but not cumbrous. He was not a polished preacher, but always well prepared in subject matters, and his mind was stored with facts. The grand truths of redemption startled and impressed his hearers from the plainness and simplicity of their unadorned utterance. The people liked to hear him preach, Protestants no less than Catholics, and in preference to the most admired pulpit orators in the land; verifying the saying, "that the life of the preacher is more than one-half the sermon." He added austerities to his labors. Notwithstanding his early rising, he denied himself the indulgence of fire in winter, when the weather is moist and bitter cold in Carolina, cutting more sharply, according to the experience of travellers, than northern winds on ice-ribbed coasts. Doubtless his labors were lessened under the administrations of Bishops Reynolds and Lynch, or he must have succumbed earlier in life. In company with the former, he visited Europe in the summer of 1846, when the complaint of which he died, the asthma, commenced its attacks. A great benefactor to the good Sisters, he used all his exertions to build up the institution, and render it not only efficient in the two-fold works of charity and education, but a religious house in the strictest sense of the word, where the spirit of God alone breathes and animates every heart, and the members love one another, and give their life for the love of their neighbor.

When the city of Charleston was being shelled by the Federal fleet, a portion of the community withdrew to Sumter for protection for the children. He also accompanied them, now in impaired and feeble health. The iron constitution had yielded to the wear of care and time, and the once strong man was now tottering on the brink of the grave: the laborer will be shortly summoned to receive his wages from the Master of the vineyard. He died in the third year after his arrival in Sumter, June 28th, 1865, after having suffered intensely for a long time from the asthma, which, with its searching cough, deprived him of rest, especially when in a recumbent position. Towards the dawn of day he might slumber brokenly, but it was not indulged. He would drag his enfeebled form to the church, pale, spent, and weary, to offer up the Holy Sacrifice, which he never omitted while he could stand at the altar. The Holy Unction, which he had, at the peril of his life, so frequently administered to others at the hour of death, was in God's mysterious Providence denied him at his departure from the battle-field of life. Eminently distinguished for devotion to the Immaculate Mother and St. Joseph, they doubtless assisted him in that hour of danger. Owing to the unceasing embarrassment of the times, travel by railroad was interrupted, save for Government purposes. After an effort it was found impossible to obtain transportation for the remains to Charleston.

He was interred in a durable vault, close by the altar, in the church of St. Lawrence, where it is hoped his blessed remains will rest until the martyr hails him in the morning of the resurrection. Unaffected and self-possessed, his manners were easy and simple. His piety bordered on the rigid type, possessing more shade than sunshine, and his character was above suspicion. He was about sixty years old. The companion of bishops, the model of priests, the director of religious, the father of the orphan, and the friend of the needy, he rests with the great prelates and missionaries who established the Church in the Diocese of Charleston; his virtues, his labors, and his name, like theirs, will be held in long and sweet remembrance.

The doctrine of exclusive salvation is a popular objection in this country, and is frequently urged against the faithful as conclusive evidence of their bigotry and uncharitableness. "We believe none but Roman Catholics can be saved, and consign to everlasting torments the world besides." In its common acceptation, or as generally understood, this is purely a Protestant point of belief, and a calumny against us in its extent and meaning. It is formally taught in some, and implicitly by most denominations, by the fact of their separation from the Church originally, and from each other mutually. The separation actually proves that they believe future happiness unattainable, or in peril, beyond the narrow limits of their own petty sect. They unanimously agree in denying salvation to the heathen, or to whoever does not know and believe in Christ, whether by his misfortune or his fault. Like the truth, of which she is the depository, the Church must of necessity be unyielding, and equally intolerant of all and every contradiction to her Divine teachings. Error and doubt can afford to be accommodating, but the conflict between truth and falsehood must be eternal and irreconcilable. She hates no one. She loves all, and endeavors to instruct and lead them to God. She must perpetuate and render ubiquitous all the blessings of the Incarnation, until the end of time; like preservation, which continues the first creative act so interruptedly as to admit of a difference between them only in thought or imagination, but none whatever in reality. As it is true to say of anything, while it lasts, that it is being created, it is equally true, in like manner, to say that God always lives in His Church, and teaches therein all truth. She must necessarily assert herself, condemn error, and be co-existent with the human race. *Erient oculi tui videntes preceptorem tuum* is the assurance of the prophet. She will reign in heaven for all eternity, after having gathered into her bosom the saved of all nations, tribes, and tongues.

The great difficulty in making converts is to impress on their minds a correct idea of the Church; immediately they either obey her, or become heretical when this is accomplished.

It was the course pursued by the Apostles and the first missionaries. The converts were kept in ignorance of the most sublime mysteries until after they had been baptized, during the time when the "Discipline of the secret" prevailed. When presented, the doctrines were unhesitatingly accepted, on the principle that they were taught by the divine authority of the Church, which could not lead them astray. The individual articles of belief, though possessing each its own specific proofs of credibility, were not examined. It is out of the question that nations can be converted on any other basis; implicit faith embraces all details. *Lord what wilt thou have me to do?* was the most comprehensive profession of Faith the Apostle could make.

That none can be saved outside of the true Church, simply means, that none can be saved but by the merits of Christ's most precious blood, of which the Catholic Church is the channel, being Christ's mystical body. Otherwise, its establishment had been superfluous, the labor of missionaries, the suffering of martyrs vain, the Sacraments unnecessary, and the profession of the Faith rather an inconvenience and disadvantage than a blessing or favor.

It is not, however, an article of our creed, that all who die beyond her visible pale and outward communion, must perish; this is the certain penalty of obstinate and wilful resistance to the truth when known, or sufficiently promulgated; or of an ignorance, equally criminal, in refusing to solve doubts or investigate truths, when duly presented. The baptized children of all denominations, until they come to the use of reason, and are capable of rejecting the Faith by an act of the will, are Catholic; people who live in invincible ignorance, and who are willing and disposed to embrace the doctrines of salvation when known, belong also to the Church; our Lord enlightens every man who cometh into the world, and furnishes him with sufficient grace to save his soul. The Jew, the Mohammedan, or the Pagan, may obtain salvation, or any other person outside the visible pale of the Catholic Church, on this principle of faultless ignorance, if they observe the requirements of the natural

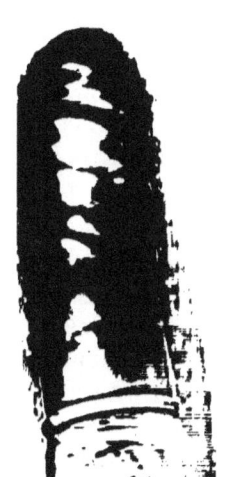

tutelage of their parents and guardians, rude and ignorant people, and those to whom the Gospel was never preached?
 The multitude who never think independently, but follow in the beaten track of the world, is incredible. Numbers have no better arguments for perseverance in their religious opinions, than that they inherited them from their parents. I fear the number of honest and virtuous dissenters is very limited among the better-informed classes of society; they will not even listen to the claims of the Church, but reject it at the first blush, for the same reason which led the Jews to deny their Messiah, the very object of their religion, —unpopularity. The once vigorous and irresistible Reformation, in its many forms, is now effete; it has reached its logical and inevitable end, infidelity or indifference; its followers now are at best, Christian only in the name, absolutely regardless of all revealed truths, and of the future welfare of the everlasting spirit. The ardent and sincere inquirer after the truth will, in God's mercy, eventually be led into the portals of the Church, like Cornelius the Centurian. Being the ordinary way of salvation—the path trodden by all the martyrs and saints, if any one has reached the gates of heaven by any other way, it is more than we know, and God has reserved to himself the profound secret. Certain it is, as the annals of the world show, that a saint was never made, a nation converted, nor a miracle wrought, but in the Catholic Church, and they are unerring attestations of its heaven-born mission.
 If people prayed to be led into the truth, the Father of Mercies would enlighten them, and their prayers would not remain long unanswered. We should thank God daily for the inestimable gift of Faith, and not expose it to the danger of temptation, by reading bad books, or frequenting the conventicles of error. If not cherished and cultivated by performing the duties it inculcates, like any other virtue, it can be lost or become dead, and its recovery is unquestionably more difficult. Our separated brethren have no proper conception of the Catholic doctrine regarding the Church. Their ideas are borrowed from other religious bodies simi-

larly called; they regard it as a purely human association, established, perhaps, by Our Lord in some indefinite form, maintained by man's agency, accomplishing much good and evil, and teaching doctrines, some true, and others erroneous. That the organ or channel through which Christ conveys to us His revealed truths and mysteries is itself equally Divine, they do not realize. It is remarkable that learned infidels have obtained to a full conception of this article of our Faith, but with as little profit to their salvation as the others. *He who believeth not shall be condemned.* What must he believe? *All that I have taught.* By what means can we attain to certain knowledge? By the Church, *the pillar and ground of truth*, and guided by the Holy Ghost. *Whosoever hears her not must be considered as the heathen and publican.*

CHAPTER X.

COLUMBIA AND ITS MISSIONS—CHESTER, YORKVILLE, SPARTANBURG, ANDERSON, LAURENS, NEWBERRY, PENDLETON, WALHALLA, TUNNEL HILL, ETC., ETC.

Chester—Father O'Neill Interrupted while Preaching—Rev. John McGinnis—Origin of the Bloody Shirt—Our Lady of Mount Carmel—Church bought from the Presbyterians—Catholics—Father Alfred Young—Refugees—Fathers J. P. O'Connell and Folchi—Trial-Justice O'Connell and Family—Rev. D. J. O'Connell, D.D.—Newberry—Catholics—South Carolina Missionary Ground—Unionville—Philip Dunn—Spartanburg—Rev. E. McGowan—Fields—A Lone Catholic—Lawrenceville—Sermons in the Court-house—The Seventh United States Infantry; Lieut. Spears and Lady—Joe Crews—Sad Missionary Prospect—Abbeville—John Enright; Death of his Nephew in France—The Bishop and the Bible—Power of the Sign of the Cross—Anderson—The First Priest—A Large Audience—Capt. McGrath—M. Kennedy—Refugees—Fidelity of a Negro—Rifled Vestments and an Invisible Chalice—Pendleton—Preach from a Protestant Bible—Hon. J. C. Calhoun—Walhalla—Settled by German Immigrants—Hon. D. Bieman an Honest Democrat—Col. James O'Connell—First Sermon in the German Lutheran Church—Rev. T. C. McMahon—James McCairey—The Blue R.R.—Tunnel Hill—A Fancy House—Indian Burying-Ground—Five Hundred Catholics—St. Patrick's Church—Sweet Auburn—A Grand Celebration—Umbrellas Introduced by Railroads—Meat on Friday—Governor Perry—A Riot and Loss of Life—Three Innocent Men unjustly condemned to Death—Exertions to obtain a Reprieve—Pardoned by Governor Alston—Faction Fights cause sad Consequences in England and France, everywhere—A Tribute to the Irish Race—Work Abandoned—The Deserted Village—Magnificent Scenery—An Elevated Cemetery—Montalembert's Tomb—O'Learey's Settlement—A Rheumatic Audience—Reflection—Kerry Irish among Natives—A Pair of Boots more attractive than a Sermon—A Wrong Diagnosis, etc., etc.

CHESTER, lying about sixty miles northeast of Columbia, is the principal town of the county of the same name, and situated on an abrupt hill, rugged on all sides, lending it an unique appearance, which gave rise to the popular tradition that the town was planned and laid out on a national holiday, probably on the 12th of July.

The early settlers were non-Catholic, or, as they prefer being called, Scotch-Irish, immigrants from the strongholds of Orangemen in that party-ridden country. Isolated from the seaboard for many years, and when wagoning was the ordinary mode of travel and intercourse, their hereditary prejudices became localized and intensified. Bishop England was the first to assault their rock-ribbed fortresses. On a subsequent occasion Rev. J. F. O'Neill, Sr., continued the work, and while preaching controversy, his favorite theme, he was rudely interrupted and forbidden to proceed farther in his discourse by one of the celebrants of the Battle of the Boyne. Accustomed to such manifestations of bigotry, and of a character truly national and expansive before opposition, he retained his self-possession until the rage of his adversary was spent; and then, after an interval of silence, retorted with great force, continued his discourse, enlarged on a number of cognate topics, and became master of the situation. His sermons were voluminous and their duration often measured by hours. This occurred about 1830. Rev. John McGinnis preached some time after, and in the court-house also, before a large number of the non-Catholic *Macs*. It was in summer, and the weather oppressively hot; he begged permission to take off his heavy coat and work in his shirt-sleeves. An air of amusement reigned throughout, and no voice was heard either in assent or disapproval. *Silence gives consent*, he added, while removing the garment from his shoulders to the bench, and then continued his lecture. The audience were in admiration; they declared it was the greatest discourse ever delivered in Chester; he was warmly invited to return, with the assurance that they would be always glad to hear him. The secret of his success is interesting—it was the *shirt he wore;* the material was rough linen, unbleached, and commonly called *bandle cloth*, generally worn by the poor in the linen districts of old Ireland, whence these people had sprung, and still in use among them. A bandle-cloth shirt will serve for a lifetime, and is equally durable as the garments of the Israelites,

that survived the wear of the desert for forty years. When
new they can stand erect on the floor, and the more tender-
skinned found it necessary to run them under the mill-
hopper before use. As stubborn as the hair-shirt of St.
Thomas of Canterbury, they become pliant and endurable
only after years of wearing. It was by his shirt rather than
his eloquence that Father McGinnis gained his triumph; to
him, and not to Senator Morton, must be accredited the
introduction of this species of argument into modern oratory, and the bloody shirt was subsequently very popular
in Congress.

In 1851 I began my visits to this place, which were
generally monthly, continued for a period of fifteen years
with slight interruption, and aided by Fathers L. P. J. P.
O'Connell and A. J. McNeill. I lectured often in the
court-house on top of the hill, encouraged by the townspeople, who had lost many of their old prejudices, and had
become modernized in feelings and manners. I looked
around to inaugurate a church. There was in Chester at
this time a watchmaker, a man of piety and influence,
named George Bowers, who had a large and growing
family. On the Charlotte and Columbia Railroad were
several employees, men of strong faith and blameless
poverty, prominent among whom as section masters were
the brothers Patrick and Peter Ryan with their families;
the first was slain in battle, and the second lost a leg and
died shortly after in consequence. Nearly all men in
public works were forced into the army. There were also
the Carrols, the Duffys, the Brophies, the Highlands, the
McCormacs, and some few others. The aggregate property
of these people was not worth one thousand dollars.

I purchased the old Presbyterian church, a brick structure with a large lot adjoining, in a central location, and
increasing in value with the growing prosperity of the
town. The cost, with the necessary alterations for Catholic worship, scarcely exceeded $500. The citizens con-
tributed freely, and the Presbyterians in a body made a
handsome subscription. By the generous co-operation

and active services of Mr. Bowers the church was ready for dedication in 1853. The Bishop being unwell, I performed the ceremony before a large assemblage, and preached an argumentative discourse on the holy sacrifice of the Mass, the sole object and purpose of church, priest, altar, and Christian worship. The church was dedicated to Our Lady of Mount Carmel. My only assistant in the ceremony was Mr. Alfred Young, a convert, a native of the Northern States, and an accomplished musician, who was on a visit to his brother-in-law, Mr. Dougald, a merchant doing business in Columbia. After his return home he joined the Paulists under the administration of Father Hecker, was ordained priest, and still lives, an edifying and zealous member of that missionary order which has done an incalculable amount of good to religion by missions and Catholic publications. Wm. Hunter, Esq., and his family subsequently settled in Chester, and he died here. There were several refugees during the war both in Chester and at Yorkville, situated in the neighboring county, and connected by a railroad twenty miles long. The Bakers, the Chazals, the Swiggins, and other leading Catholics of Charleston resided on these missions until the restoration of peace, and promoted the interest of religion by their piety and edifying example.

At Yorkville there was for many years but one Catholic man, Hugh McGinnis, who was advanced in years, and, though married, left no children; he was a pious man, and died during the war. Jeremiah O'Leary, who married into the O'Hare family, was a good man, and died about 1850. He left many children, whom I instructed in the faith with great pains, and was fully encouraged by their mother, who was not a Catholic. I fear they have fallen away. They were all baptized. Thomas O'Farrell married a sister of Mrs. O'Leary, but he ceased to practise his religion, and neither he nor his numerous offspring are known as Catholics, which is to be regretted, because they are a respectable and industrious family of children. Father Joseph O'Connell attended this mission during the war; the faithful having died or removed to other places, but few remained, and it was scarcely attended at all for a long time until the appointment of Father Folchi, who remained some years and withdrew to the Jesuit house in California toward the close of 1877.

At this date Fort Mill is the principal station in York County. The family of my oldest brother reside here, and constitute a small congregation among themselves, under the care of a widowed mother, distinguished for piety and strength of character. Trial-Justice Michael O'Connell, the eldest of the family, was born in Donoughmore, County Cork, Ireland, in 1816. He emigrated to Columbia in 1852, where he dwelt, and had his children educated at the St. Mary's College, until his house was burnt by Sherman's army in 1865. He then withdrew to Fort Mill with his family, and settled on a valuable and extensive farm. He was the father of twelve children, eight of whom survive. The oldest, Patrick Joseph, received a European education, and returning home after the war was elected to the Legislature for several years; he married Frances, the eldest daughter of the Bradshaw family, by whom he left one child, and died at his residence in Gaston County, in 1875, fortified with the holy sacraments. He was about thirty years old. The next son, Michael, graduated as doctor of medicine from the University of Pennsylvania, and practises his profession in the city of Philadelphia. The third son, Dennis Joseph, studied for the holy ministry, and after a preparatory course in Baltimore was sent by Archbishop Gibbons to the Propaganda for the diocese of Richmond. He was in the American College, under the presidency of Rt. Rev. Dr. Chatard, and was raised to the dignity of the priesthood in 1877, after having graduated with the first honors of his class. He is now stationed at the cathedral in Richmond. As Procurator he was delegated to receive the Pallium from His Holiness Pius IX., in 1878, for Archbishop Gibbons, a duty which he ably discharged. At this time he accompanies the papal delegate, Mons. Conroy, as his private secretary in his visits to the various sections of the Church in the United States and Canada.

Sister Jerome, the eldest daughter (Annie O'Connell), became a Sister of Mercy and has been fifteen years in the order. A temporary retirement was recommended for restoration of impaired health. The other children still live with their mother at the homestead. Trial-Justice O'Connell died in 1874, and received the last sacraments at the hands of his brother, Dr. Joseph; his remains were conveyed to Columbia, and now rest in the family burying-ground. He was a man of strong faith, practical piety, devoted to frequent prayer, and brought up his children in the fear and knowledge of God; he was impartial and fair as a justice of the peace, and his decisions were always approved by popular commendation and the higher commendation of the bench.

Newberry is forty miles north of Columbia. There were seldom more than half a dozen Catholics in the entire county. I visited the place on horseback before the opening of the Greenville Railroad. I preached in the courthouse in 1849 to a moderate audience, prominent among whom were a few lawyers. The Baptists and Methodists were the leading denominations, and more than commonly prejudiced against everything external, whether in religion or nationality. Mr. Craft and his family were the sole Catholics; he was a German by birth and a truly religious man. He moved to Arkansas, to Bishop Byrnes's colony, a few years afterwards, for the purpose of being near a church and educating his children in the faith. Patrick Scott, of Columbia, succeeded—a worthy man, who, with his only child, Adelaide, educated at the convent, were the only representatives of the Church for many years. George Boland settled here also, and had his children baptized; their mother not being of the household of faith, and without an opportunity of catechetical instruction, they stand in imminent danger of falling away. Ellison Keitt and his family also resided in this district.

At Helena, the company workshops of the Greenville

Railroad, two or three Catholic families lived temporarily; the most prominent was Edward Saunders, a respectable man in advanced age, and who died about 1858. There is scarcely a civilized country in the universe where there are so few Catholics and where the faith is less known than in the upper region of South Carolina; all the State is strictly missionary ground, and it is only after long years of arduous toil that the faith has obtained a footing. The occasional visits of the priest or a sermon serve to keep the solitary Catholic in the practice of his religious duties; in God's providence the seed sown in toil and labor may produce its fruit in due time. With but few exceptions it was individually and by families, chiefly among the poorest classes, and not by multitudes, that the world was converted outside of Jerusalem.

Unionville is still farther north of Newberry; while many of the leading people are called by Catholic names, there are but two Irish families in their midst who are Catholic in belief—Messrs. Dunn and McNally. Alone and without sympathy, they kept the torch of truth burning brightly in the midst of universal darkness, and yet the people believe they are enlightened while groping in the shadow of death. Mrs. Grant, the sister-in-law of Philip Dunn, is a Catholic and married to a Scotchman, who belongs to the Church. They are good men, have sent their children to the convent to receive a religious education, and they, it is hoped, will become a nucleus for the diffusion of the knowledge of salvation to that benighted race.

At Spartanburg, which is about twenty-five miles to the north of Union, there is but one family partly Catholic —the Mulligans, who removed here from Beaufort District. The mother and grandmother, whom I prepared for death, were pious and devout ladies of Northern birth and converts; they retained the true faith with unswerving fidelity and practised its precepts, but, unhappily, the children, both male and female, became Methodists. Their father, who was an Irishman by birth, was at one time sheriff of Beaufort County, secured for his children the services of a Catholic tutor in the person of Mr. McGowan, of whom I prefer making mention in this place. He was adopted into the seminary, made his theological studies under Very Rev. Dr. Baker, and was raised to the priesthood by Bishop England about 1837; he ministered on the missions of North Carolina in Fayetteville, Newbern, and Raleigh during eight years. On the elevation of Bishop Reynolds to the see he was recalled to Charleston and officiated in the cathedral and on Sullivan's Island, and was mainly instrumental in the erection of the first church on the island, which was wooden and of modest dimensions; it lasted eighteen years, escaped the war hail of shells that rained around during the bombardment of Fort Sumter, and was finally displaced by a huge tidal-wave that nearly reclaimed the island shortly before the close of the war.

About 1847 Father McGowan transferred his allegiance to the Diocese of Little Rock, was stationed at Fort Smith several years, and is now preparing to receive the reward of his life-long labors and perseverance in the trials of a missionary priest.

Spartanburg is the site of the Wooford Methodist College, and as Methodistical as a town can well be. The soil is·stony and rugged and not well adapted to agricultural products save on the borders of the streams, but abounds in iron ore and many mineral springs. In point of healthiness it is unprecedented. There were some few Catholic refugees who sought shelter here during the bombardment of Charleston. Foremost was Alexander Cunningham, for many years a respectable builder in the city, and who, by his industry and honorable enterprise, accumulated a competency of earthly goods. During half a century he and his pious lady were prominent in every enterprise undertaken for all charitable and Catholic objects, in the Cathedral parish especially. Three children, whom they raised in the love and peace of God, were the burden of their care, and they still survive to continue in their lives the example of their virtuous parents: two daughters and a son. The elder, Mary, is still single; her sister, Elizabeth, I united in marriage to Captain Hall, of Charleston, a worthy man and well connected. Mrs. Cunningham died some time before the war. The father, now grown old and feeble, was taken sick at Spartanburg. I administered to him all the rights of religion. Blessed by its consolations, and his last days cheered by the affectionate care of loving children, he died the death of the just.

There is but one Catholic family in the town, as far as I can remember—Mr. Twitty, a respectable merchant and a convert, who married a Catholic lady, who led him to the knowledge of the truth. A family by the name of Fields live in the vicinity of the Rolling Mills, whom I visited and was the first priest whom the grown-up children remember to have seen. In infancy they were carried by wagon a distance of nearly two hundred miles to be baptized. They learned their prayers, had a fair knowledge of the mysteries of faith, and loved the Catholic Church. Their parents were unlettered, but they knew God and his commandments. I admitted them to the Sacraments. Many instances of this kind are to be met with, which are startling revelations of the ways of God, and condemn those who, with better advantages, lose the knowledge of the faith and the way of salvation.

In 1866 I began to visit Laurens Court-house, which lies in the same region and is connected by railroad with Newberry. Two or three companies of the Seventh United States Infantry were stationed here. They were chiefly Catholics, and several of them, especially those who had families, were good and pious. Lieutenant Spear, a native of Boston, and his lady were here, he being an officer in that command. He had been a Baptist minister in New England. I received both himself and lady into the Church and baptized them under condition. They were zealous and persevered in the faith. I said Mass in the court-house frequently during my visits, and also preached in the evenings for the faithful and on Sundays for the community at large. On those occasions I vindicated at least, at considerable length, the most objectionable of our doctrines to the Protestants—the Absolving power and the Real Presence. The officers at the post and the male portion of the community attended generally, but the ladies refused to mix with the soldiers at public service. The companies were shortly afterwards recalled to Columbia, and were subsequently sent to the plains to fight the poor Indians, who had the barbarity to refuse to be robbed and swindled by the agents of the Government or to receive missionaries who were in search of Indian wives.

During my visits I was the guest of Mr. Joseph Crews, and found in his family a liberal hospitality and refined courtesy. At the time he was unpopular in the State on account of his politics; if justly so he dearly paid for it by his sudden and violent death. Doubtless he bore a great part of the odium of the evil doings of others. At his home I found him a courteous host, a kind father to his children, and loved in his family. Let him sleep on and none reproach him now in his untimely and gory grave. Mrs. Farrow, née Mary Ann Brady, was the only Catholic residing permanently in the town. I married her some years previously, and she was now a widow with one male child, having lost her husband in the war. She was born in Columbia, where her sister resides and is married to Charles Carrol, an enterprising and worthy citizen. There were three or four Irishmen working on a farm in the vicinity on shares, very much dissatisfied and anxious to get away. They were receiving a third of the crop for their services in its culture, and furnished their own bread besides; it was not remunerative. Negroes, who contrive to exist on next to nothing, will accept the terms readily, but white laborers do not find them sufficient for their maintenance. A more equitable system must be adopted to encourage immigration and beckon it into the State.

There is no visible improvement in the condition of Catholicity in this vast section of country up to this time;

on the contrary, it has rather retrograded during the Radical maladministration, which was as unpropitious as slavery itself. In the absence of immigration it will take ages to bring the inhabitants to the knowledge of the truth. Heresy has so hopelessly debauched the minds of its followers in regard to revealed religion that it has become an abstract sentiment or a guess, and they are incapable of appreciating a logical system of divine facts. Heathen lands and barbarous tribes to whom the Gospel was never preached are a more encouraging field for missionary labor. The observation will apply with equal justice to the vast tract of country within the limits of the diocese of Charleston. The disheartening prospects serve but to increase the merit of those who spend their lives on its barren fields.

Abbeville lies northwest of Columbia at a distance of over one hundred miles; it claims to have been partly settled by French Protestants. The country is fertile, well adapted to the cultivation of the staple produce, corn, vegetables, and the grasses. As a class, the townspeople are cultivated, had been wealthy and always intensely un-Catholic, with a strong infusion of the North of Ireland spirit. There resided in the village three or four Catholic families, edifying in life and well informed; prominent among whom stood John Enright, a native of Limerick. He was held in high esteem by all the community. He married a native-born lady, who joined the Church and died about the year 1859, leaving three children. The eldest, a daughter, was educated at the convent, and after having arrived at the years of discretion she joined the community, made her religious vows, and is now a devoted nun; two brothers also survive and give promise of persevering fidelity to their parents' faith. A nephew, Timothy, was sent to France to study for the sacred ministry, and died about 1871, before the completion of his studies; he lies buried in the land of St. Louis, God having crowned with early recompense his good-will and heroic intentions.

Mr. Enright married a second time, and chose for his companion Mary, the widow of Michael McElrowe, of Columbia; he died about the year 1873, about fifty-six years of age, and was buried by the side of his brother Jeremiah in the city cemetery, who departed this life some time before, and whose children he adopted. John E., a very uncommon man, owned an extensive cotton-gin factory, and travelled extensively for the sale of his goods. He lived many years in Central Georgia; while staying at Covington and boarding at the hotel the town was visited by the Methodist Bishop. The pseudo Bishop, on Sunday delivered one of the disgraceful tirades against the Church, which were then very popular; amongst many other false statements, he asserted that *Romanists were forbidden by the priest to read the Bible.* Stopping at the same hotel, Mr. Enright, who heard his sermon, came to the dinner-table armed with his Douay Bible, and placing it by the side of his plate, sat next to the great and pompous dignitary radiant with apostolic airs. Towards the close of the dinner Mr. E. stood on his feet, and in a clear, firm, audible voice, reprimanded the Bishop for his uncharitable and ungentlemanly discourse, false and slanderous, as far as it pretended to be a statement of Catholic faith; in proof of which he held up the Bible, *Ecce signum.* He offered to pass it around the table; it was not necessary; he completely confounded and overthrew the assailant, who withdrew in defeat and dismay as though he had swallowed a poker which he found too hard to digest.

Mr. E. won the sympathy of all present, and become the hero of the hour. The other left the following day, smarting under the humiliation of his ignominious defeat, felt the more keenly for having had a reputation for honor and truth. It is sad to think how much prejudice will blind the understanding and lead captive the judgment of men otherwise candid and impartial. Truth is so powerful that, even when oppressed, it will defeat error in its most pompous form, like the pebble from the sling of the shepherd boy. This is no solitary case; many such instances will occur to the mind of the reader. I have known the bare sign of the cross to disconcert the most formidable adversary, and strike his lips with babbling nonsense.

During the pastoral visits, which were regular and continuous, Mr. Enright's house was the clergyman's home, the chapel for divine service, and the centre of reunion for the faithful. This place was visited by Dr. Birmingham, from Edgefield, up to 1860, when it was again joined to my mission.

In 1866 I preached in the court-house on confession and the system of repentance inculcated by the Church for the reconciliation of the sinner. The doctrine excited the admiration of the hearers, but without any further result except to compliment the preacher. There lived here at this time two brothers—the Roaches—who were good men, brought their wives into the Church, and were bringing up their children in the faith; B. O'Conner and wife, a daughter of Alpheus Baker, of Lumpkin County, Georgia, and the excellent family of the same name; Charles Cox, of Gaston County, North Carolina, a carriage-maker by trade, and some few others who were single and only transitory. The religious status of this station remains unchanged up to this date; it has been visited of late by Father Folchi. Among the citizens at large may be mentioned with commendation General McGowan, of Irish descent and fame, in our army during the late civil war; also Judge Wardlaw, than whom a purer or more impartial man never graced the bench in the State of South Carolina.

Andersonville lies to the north of Abbeville. It is a town of considerable importance, and the county runs into the mountainous range of the State. It is delightfully situated on an eminence, contains many imposing residences, and is surrounded by a healthy and productive country. It was visited periodically for fifteen years, and the first Catholics were introduced as operatives on the Blue Ridge Railroad, commenced shortly after 1850. I was gazetted as the first priest who preached in the town or who ever visited it. The inhabitants gave me a large audience, and manifested a respectable amount of liberality and good-will, which increased with years, in consequence of my having entertained and sheltered their volunteer company in Columbia when preparing for the campaign in Virginia. It was called the Anderson Guards, and was commanded by Capt. Whitner, a son of Judge Whitner. I was elected an honorary member of the company—a body of men who served faithfully from the beginning of the war, and were nearly annihilated. The Captain, Lieut. Benton, and some few disabled men are still living. The Catholics were Timothy Whelan and his brothers-in-law, William and James Shannahan; the two former perished in the transport steamer *General Lyon*, on the voyage from Wilmington to New York in 1865, as already mentioned. The widow and the children now reside in Wytheville, Western Virginia; their house was always the home of the priest during his visits. Captain John McGrath commanded a company during the war, and distinguished himself for his honorable conduct and bravery; he is married and has a promising family of Catholic children; he is much respected by the community, and a sincere Christian. Michael Kennedy has a large family of children, now grown, well instructed in their religion, and complying with its obligations.

Both those gentlemen abandoned their occupations, and visited Columbia, Charleston, Savannah, and other cities, to collect funds for the purpose of purchasing a lot and building a church, which has not been commenced so far, owing to some untoward circumstances. Mr. Burke, William Kidney, now dead, and family, at Slabtown, and some few others, were the stationary and resident members of the faith.

Anderson was honored by the sojourn of some families who sought shelter here during the last years of the war, when the frequent shells showered on the city from the blockading fleet in the harbor made Charleston untenantable. Captain Romulat and his household were of French origin, edifying in manner of life, and attached to the faith of their ancestors. Captain Matheisson's family were equally conspicuous for the possession of all the virtues that adorn the Christian. The Holy Sacrifice was said in their house at stated intervals, when the faithful all assembled around the altar, decorated with a taste and gorgeousness worthy of the sanctuary of cathedral churches. Julia, the oldest daughter, married Mr. Milner at this time. These worthy people, at their departure, bore with them the esteem of the citizens of Anderson, and left an impression behind favorable alike to their city, their name, and their creed. A leading dry-goods merchant Captain Matheisson was for many years, and in early times draper to the ecclesiastical bodies of the city, and lays claim to the promise attached to one of the works of mercy.

The following incident will be interesting, as exhibiting the peculiar nature of the trying times of the civil war and the fidelity of the negro race: I owned a body-servant, young, active, and smart, who accompanied me on this mission after the surrender in 1865. Although not a Catholic, he was expert at preparing a hall for lecture, seating an audience, and preserving order. He styled himself Joseph P. O'Connell, in compliment to my brother, and among genteel colored society would vaunt the D.D.

A month after the surrender, while visiting this mission, and there being no possibility of obtaining a conveyance, I travelled on foot from Belton to Anderson, a distance of about fourteen miles, accompanied by Captain Gant, of Charleston, and my man Joe. He bore in a valise the altar furniture and vestments. He refused his freedom after emancipation, and, like others, left the homestead weeping like Hagar and Ismael.

The day was hot and sultry; at intervals we encountered fragmentary bands of Wheeler's disbanded cavalry, scouting on all sides in search of booty, but confining their depredations chiefly to horses and mules, which they frequently untackled from the plough and led to Kentucky and Tennessee. Free from all military restraint, they filled the country with terror and consternation; they differed little from Sherman's army in their march to the sea, except that the track of the latter was marked with smoking ruins, blackened walls, and the remains of animals wantonly slaughtered by the road. The desolation on all sides resembled that spread over India by Hyder Ali.

On approaching the town in the decline of the day, we sat down to rest, tired and weary, under the shade of an oak. Presently a straggler drove up, reined in his horse, and demanded in terms of reproach and profanity what I carried in the valise. I answered him plainly and truly; it did not satisfy him. He took me for a bank officer bearing treasures, and with further imprecations ordered the valise to be torn open and the contents exhibited. His face was a map of original sin, unrelieved by a solitary ray of grace or goodness. The first object that met his leaden look was the crucifix, a beautiful work of art, and vividly portraying the last dying agonies of our Divine Redeemer. It occurred to me that having been nursed at the breast of a Christian mother, some reminiscence of religion might still linger in the moral wastes of his strong heart. I pointed to the cross in attestation of the truth of my statement, reluctant to expose to profane handling the holy robes of the Sanctuary. I gently expostulated on the uselessness of further examination. His curiosity seemed excited and his anger provoked. With revolver in hand, and uttering curses deeper still, he hurried the search to the last article. While unfolding the alb, to my utter dismay, the chalice, which lay wrapped in its folds, dropped out and rolled along with a tinkling sound on the gravel. It is marvellous how rapidly thought accumulates under certain contingencies. I reflected how the labors of the past month were lost, how often I had imperilled my life in vain among roaming bands of demoralized troops, returning to ruined homes after disaster and defeat, and responsible to God alone for their deeds, and for whom they cared but

little. Now at the very portals I had failed; the anxious
people who had not seen a priest for a long time could not
have Mass offered for them, nor approach the sacred
mysteries, and may not be visited again for another year.
This and more besides I thought; it was all prayer, and
with the speed of lightning reached the heart of Mary, and
was answered with like rapidity. The disappointed ma-
rauder did not see the chalice; he slowly rode off murmur-
ing profanity. Capt. Gant, an educated and conscientious
non-Catholic, stood amazed at the prodigy; he affirmed
that *the communion cup was invisible to the highwayman
while plainly seen by all the group.* The faithful negro
servant Joe stood aside, closely watching, with ready
though concealed weapon, the slightest movement of the
brigand; any attempt at violence would have cost him his
life and laid him a corpse at his horse's feet, for Joe was
an unerring marksman. Fortified by commendatory letters, he afterwards gained employment as an officer's servant at the garrison in Charleston. After a while he was
led to commit some trivial faults, unbecoming, however, in
a gentleman bearing his title; acting on the admonition
of Alexander to the timid soldier who bore his own name,
"Either change thy name or thy conduct," he chose the former, dropped the D. D., and was known afterwards as plain
Joe.

Pendleton for a number of years, and from an early
period, was the county town of Pickens district until a
division was made and the seat of justice removed to Pickens Court-house. Shorn of its honors, the deserted town
faded gradually away, and in later times became a very insignificant village. My first visit was during 1853, when it
received a new impulse from the opening of the Blue
Ridge Railroad. I preached in the Court-house, to a very
slim audience, who had collected out of curiosity to see and
hear the first priest who had ever put in appearance in
that far-distant section of the country. The most startling event of the occasion was that I used the Protestant
Bible, brought personally by the hotel-keeper, and *preached*

from it, to use the common expression. I had done so repeatedly, and always with a good effect in the minds of the hearers; the fact was a practical refutation of many a slander. Often had they been assured at their Bible meetings that if a Catholic clergyman of any grade, from the lowest to the Pope, could procure a Protestant Bible, he could no longer continue a Papist. I found only a few Catholic laborers in the vicinity, but none in the town.

The residence of John C. Calhoun was in the outskirts. After his death the library was sold, not by the volume, *but by the shelf,* and at a nominal price. At the sale there were few present who would risk fifty dollars for the entire collection. He and the other leading statesmen of his day are reproached for having manifested no Christian sentiment at the hour of death; they died like philosophers, and not like Christians. Catholics they would not, and Protestants they could not, be. One was unpopular, and the other unreasonable; like broken glass, there was no connection, no system bearing a divine impress, or which could stand the test of a logical mind. The humility of the cross was too heavy a burden, or its wisdom too profound for the pride of reason and intellect, and they dismissed the subject of religion entirely from their thoughts. Mr. Calhoun, originally spelt Callaghan, was of near Irish descent. A pure statesman and a strictly moral man, of a logical turn of mind, his writings are as arid as formulas, and his arguments connected like inventories. His speeches were regulated like the movements of machinery, and the superior and close reasoning, wanting the fulness of Webster or the exuberance of Clay, will never be read by the masses of the people. His policy was fatal to the country, by condemning manufactures, and confining the industry of his countrymen exclusively to agricultural pursuits; it was based on the institution of slavery, and fell with it. He inaugurated secession by the doctrine of nullification; during his lifetime he kept the headlong tendency towards separate State government in check, but when death relaxed the hold of his strong hand on the helm, shipwreck and disaster followed.

While Vice-President, Hon. Wm. McKenna, of Lancaster, called on him, and during the interview Mrs. Calhoun, who had been recently confined, was receiving in an adjoining apartment the felicitations of a fashionable lady on the happy event. With the curiosity attributed to the sex, the visitor enquired the name of the child; it was Patrick. "My good Lord, you have spoiled the child by such a name," was the exclamation of the fashionable connoisseur of nomenclature. The Vice-President became slightly nervous, moved into the lady's boudoir, and courteously remarked, "If this child lives and becomes as worthy a man as he after whom he has been called, his name will be no disgrace to him." During their day Bishop England and Mr. Calhoun divided the admiration of the State between them; if the light of faith had been shed on the gigantic intellect of the latter, his fame would be as world-wide as that of O'Connell or Montalembert.

The town of Walhalla is north of Pendleton some dozen miles, and situated on a level plain at the base of the mountains, with Tunnel Hill looming proudly in the distance, the blue clouds resting on its broad shoulders. It was settled between 1840 and 1850 by German immigrants, mostly Lutherans. They are thrifty and industrious, and the old folks mostly contented with a frugal competency, the reward of honest labor. Some became discontented and left for other localities. In 1850 there were about fifteen families permanently settled; some employed in merchandise, and others at farming. A mineral and grain country, and the inhabitants mostly poor, there were no sources for the rapid growth of wealth. The proximity of the railroad, and the large number of men employed on the tunnel, checked the growing discontent and promised brighter prospects. The town grew up rapidly; all able-*bodied* men found remunerative employment, and business flourished for a period of eight or nine years, until the work was discontinued by the refusal of any further aid from the State. In 1852 I found two Catholic families among the Germans: Dauch and Crawfort, who left after some time; the former was a Prussian, and both loved their faith. There was one English-speaking Catholic family, the O'Connells. Col. James O'Connell was an intelligent and enterprising young Irishman, and had the contract for rock-work over the culverts and bridges. He married Miss Anne Gunn, who, with her sister, were natives of Virginia, and received their education with the Sisters in Richmond during the administration of the worthy and patriarchal Bishop Whelan.

At the commencement of the war the volunteers poured down from the mountains like a torrent, and a company was organized, who chose O'Connell for captain. The sons of the wilderness were a dashing set of fellows, coalesced into a regiment, and ultimately formed a brigade. They fought out to the bitter end; their ranks melted away like snow-flakes from camp diseases and showers of grape-shot. The captain soon rose to the command of the regiment, and while gallantly leading his men in one of the battles before Richmond, during the Seven Days' fight, he was seriously wounded and borne by his companions from the field, blood-stained but victorious. War-worn and disabled for life, he returned and lingered on in a disabled condition; after a partial recovery he limped his way to Staunton, Virginia, the native place of his wife's family, where he met those who could sympathize with him in his sufferings.

Captain Bieman kept hotel at Walhalla. He was a liberal-minded and popular man; elected to the State Senate by the county, he was one of the few if not the only Democrat in that odious body, whose dishonesty in the South has rendered the party a by-word, a synonyme for dishonesty throughout the country; it is to be regretted, for there are many worthy men in the body, and it has proved itself to be the poor-man's government. The Hon. Mr. Bieman maintained his seat during that fatal administration, and with unsullied name and character.

During the good times before the war the Germans built a very neat church in the town. Towards its completion, a misunderstanding springing up between the congregation and their minister, he left for another appointment; sojourning at the same period in the place, I was courteously invited to open the church and preach. I acquiesced readily, and was the first who held service and preached in the Lutheran Church at Walhalla. I had preached repeatedly at other places in the town. During fifteen years, this and all other stations connected with Columbia were regularly attended and service held frequently every month. A good many natives embraced the faith and persevered. After the war the town relapsed into its former state, and as it stood before the opening of the tunnel. The Catholics moved away, and but few now remain in the county; they will be the seed to grow and increase until the Church becomes once more a power in the country as it was in days gone by.

James McCairy and his family reside at the Falls, within a few miles of Walhalla. Having purchased an extensive and valuable tract of land in a delightful situation, he removed thither from Charleston, and is now permanently settled in the county. Messrs. Black and McAlister, with their extensive households, and other Catholics, all relatives, are settled around and form a moderate congregation among themselves. Having tendered a valuable farm as a homestead for a stationary priest, according to report, the premises, with moderate aid from the outside, will be an ample support, and the permanent residence of the clergyman will be the means of establishing the faith and perpetuating it in this promising locality. This is the only country place in the State in which the Church seems to have a fair opening, and it will be made available in God's providence for the interests of religion and the salvation of souls.

The Rev. T. C. McMahon having transferred his allegiance from the diocese of Kingston to Charleston during the episcopate of Rt. Rev. Dr. Horan, about the year

1868, and having ministered some time over the entire region, now resides in this place and performs priestly duties for the faithful in Walhalla.

Open communication by railroad between Charleston and the Western States was many years in contemplation. A number of capitalists organized and formed a company. A charter was obtained from the legislature under the name of the Blue Ridge Railroad Company, with an appropriation, and the work began by connecting with the Greenville Railroad at the Anderson terminus; this occurred about 1850. It was a gigantic undertaking at the time, but it has since fallen through from a variety of causes. The Spartanburg and Western N. C. Extension are more feasible, less expensive, and already in running order to Asheville and the Valley of the Frenchbroad. The principal obstructions that lay in the path of the first road was Stumphouse Mountain, about three miles wide, and which it became necessary to tunnel, and hence called Tunnel Hill.

The original name was no less appropriate; early in the century a daring huntsman of the range, as a protection against the nightly approach of the bear, the wolf, and the savages, the most numerous inhabitants, constructed a log cabin on the outstretched branches of a giant oak, the monarch of the forest, and sheltered on three sides around from the wintry winds that came howling down from Northern wastes. He lived, like St. Simon the Stylite, a number of years sole monarch of all he surveyed, happy and unmolested, and at last fell under the inevitable stroke of time, which spares neither high nor low. I beheld the tall stump shortly before it fell to the ground, crushed by the weight of years. At some distance may be seen, to this day, the ruins of the Necropolis of the Cherokee, whose early history no man knoweth; unlettered slabs of granite rock, frequently scattered on all sides, mark the resting place of the unknown dead. But Assyrian kings and Egyptian potentates are no better remembered, though they sleep under mausoleums on whose brow forty centuries have made no impression. It may be written, without danger of contradiction, of this race of Nature's noblemen, so ruthlessly swept away by the white man, that the neighboring hills oft echoed with the exhilarating shout of the chase as they pursued the deer or buffalo up the sunless ravines; and the stillness of the nights was often broken by the orgies of the war-dance and the piercing battle-cry.

That the graves were rifled on the southern slope of the mountain, in quest of the traditional treasures entombed with the remains of chiefs, is evident from the disordered situation of the mortuary slabs, scarcely two of them lying in the same direction. This being a gold region, the cupidity of adventurers may have enticed them hither in the earliest days of our colonies. Mr. Simms intimates that this may have been an Eldorado of the adventurous Spaniard, no less than the realms of Montezuma.

The mineral wealth of the country has never been unstored. Some feeble attempts were made, the effort not exceeding what miners call prospecting. It has been truthfully asserted by one who has experience in both that if the same appliances were used as in the gold-fields of California the recompense would be as favorable in this region.

Messrs. Humbird & Hitchcock, having contracted with the company to open the tunnel, brought from Pennsylvania and New York a number of Irish laborers, chiefly Catholics, to perform the work. This was about 1854. An attempt was already made to open the work, but too feeble to afford reasonable hope of early success. The present body comprised about five hundred people of all ages. Many of the operators had families, and kept boarding-shanties for the unmarried men. Having lived on public works for years, where all the disorders of the camp prevailed without any of its restraints, the people stood sadly in want of the unremitting care of a resident priest. Having become numerically the most important point on the entire mission, I immediately set about organizing for the permanent residence of a priest, and made this the headquarters of all the up-country missions, beginning with Anderson. I constructed a frame church large enough to accommodate the people, and an adjoining priest's house. It was dedicated to St. Patrick. I was efficiently aided by my brother, Father Lawrence, and towards the end by Father Joseph, who was ordained in 1858, and spent his month alternately with us on the hill. I established a school, which was conducted by James Caisy (now at the company's shops in North Carolina) and by Cornelius Gorman, where the children of both sexes were instructed and thoroughly imbued with Catholic principles. Some of the men were addicted to the use of ardent spirits, whenever they found means and opportunity to indulge their favorite passion, from which as a necessary consequence followed many other vices, besides squalor, neglect of all religious duties, and an untold amount of bodily discomfort and suffering. I organized a temperance society, held weekly meetings, and maintained it regularly to the last. This was the only means of succeeding among the people. Before a year the most abandoned were reclaimed from their evil habits and were changed to pious and exemplary Christians. Its influence gathered strength daily; the sober no less than the intemperate became members; all belonged to the society and kept their pledge with great fidelity. I obtained a promise from the contractors to dismiss from the work any one who violated his pledge or encouraged a faction fight —a measure productive of great good. In a short time the face of things was entirely changed. The people were well-clad; the church was always full on Sundays and at the night services during Advent and Lent; the sacraments were frequented; discord, violence, family broils ceased; and they who had never saved a dollar before now possessed a neat "pile" (the railroad term for money), which was laid up in the only bank that had not failed during the war or after. The priest's bank refunded all its deposits in coin at the beginning of the trouble. There was nowhere a more orderly, sober, and edifying congregation; many of the natives embraced the faith, and the wilderness blossomed like the rose.

The 19th of August, 1858, was a great day. A rumor went out that the State intended to withhold any further appropriation, and the company invited all the country to meet for a celebration in order to bring popular sentiment to bear on the threatened action of the legislature. The flocks that had ranged the mountains free were made tributary, and yielded their flesh to regale the appetites of the many thousands who had assembled for this object alone, like the Capharnaimites. The flags of many nations were streaming from several points, and the stands were graced by many eminent public men and accomplished orators, prominent among whom stood ex-Governor Perry, of Greenville. The St. Patrick's Temperance Society passed two by two in procession through an audience of wondering natives, headed by a marshal mounted on horseback. The rear was brought up by two priests and the German military company, in uniform, and commanded by Captain D. Bieman.

This was a generous act on the part of the Germans; a rumor was in circulation for some time that the Irish would be mobbed on that occasion by the jealous natives and a general riot inaugurated. Both parties were well armed with concealed weapons; any attempt at violence would be followed unquestionably by a general massacre. To intimidate as well as to aid, if necessary, the well-ordered military company volunteered their services in defence of their fellow-citizens of foreign birth. But there occurred not the slightest interference. This body of well-dressed, sober, and orderly men, by their appearance no less than their numbers, would have cut their way through the most formidable resistance and spiked the guns of a brass-battery at the siege of Richmond. They were treated discourteously by the committee of arrangements, although the efficient operatives whose stalwart arm had already broken the heart of the mountain, and decidedly the most respectable people at the celebration. Their pastor, who was no less a benefactor, was not invited to open the proceedings with prayer, as is the usual custom on such occasions. Their treatment bore the trade-mark of bigotry and jealousy in every instance. Friday was the day appointed for the feast, for the simple reason that Catholics would not eat meat on that day. But they were avenged by the farcical termination. The native masses, fascinated by the odor of the barbecued meats, broke loose, assailed the tables, devoured all they could, and purloined the balance, making a clean sweep. Now the Irish and Germans received the undivided attention of the orators, and were made important by their isolation.

Governor Perry is an accomplished gentleman and a graceful public speaker; Colonel Allen, of Barnwell Courthouse, produced the most abiding impression by asserting that the use of umbrellas mainly depended on the progress of railroad enterprises. He remembered the time when no man could wear an umbrella without running the risk of being "chunked" from behind a fence and losing his life. After much labor and expense they succeeded in obtaining a railroad in the low country, and what was the result? Every man could carry an umbrella with impunity, an advantage which they would possess in common with their more fortunate fellow-citizens when this road would be completed, and without which the world must soon come to an untimely end.

The speaker was a man of good sense, and he playfully adapted his discourse to the capacity of his listeners, a rare quality in public speakers. While all else was forgotten the pleasantry of Colonel Allen still provoked a smile. All was in vain; the stockholders got no aid from the State, and the work stopped. If completed it would have been of incalculable advantage to the Confederacy. Four shafts were sunk to the level of the grade and worked to meet in two or three directions. Comparatively little now remains unfinished; but from appearances it is as impassable as the little between Agrippa and Christianity.

Uninterrupted peace is seldom of long duration for individuals or communities; it is not man's condition on earth, and the time should be employed in preparing for the coming adversity which it prophesies. Ill-will and jealousy had been growing for some time among the local inhabitants toward the foreign laborers, who were believed to have usurped all the remunerative labor to the detriment of those who, from their habitation, seemed to possess a better claim. Their inability to perform this description of labor was never considered; after a fair showing they had proven absolutely incompetent for lack of strength and perseverance. The introduction of Irish labor was a necessity; the capacity of the others was found to be limited to the offices of wood-choppers and teamsters. The pent-up feelings soon broke out into open violence and aggression. On a certain Sunday afternoon, while Rev. L. P. O'Connell was officiating in the church and the disengaged were quietly enjoying their needful rest, on all sides a gang of natives who had come from a distance, some even from Georgia, assailed the church with kicks and blows and other demonstrations loud and menacing; they had been lying in ambush previously to assassinate the priest. Without any provocation whatever they shot into the crowd of unoffending men, and instantly awoke the slumbering lion, who, unarmed, returned the assault, picking up whatever weapon came next to hand. Being so few in numbers, the assailants fled, but were hotly pursued and overtaken at Shaft No. 2, where Smith, the leader and instigator of the riot, was slain immediately, while the others effected their escape. The two who committed the justifiable but unnecessary homicide fled to Tennessee. The deed was not approved by the pursuants, who only had determined to administer a wholesome chastisement. It served as a warning, and may have prevented more serious acts of violence in the future; all ideas of provoking a conflict were henceforward abandoned.

A day or two after three men were arrested who had no

share in the act of killing ; one was at home with his family at the time, and the others at most loiterers or lookers-on. As far as a participation was concerned the arrest of the priest would be as justifiable. The prisoners were soon placed on trial, were defended by law counsel employed for the purpose by a general subscription among their aggrieved fellow-laborers. They were tried at Pickens Court-house ; under the instruction of the judge, the jury, without any hesitation and in very indecent haste, returned a verdict of wilful murder in the first degree, and the judge passed sentence accordingly, based on the most flimsy testimony, not only false but contradictory, and despite of adequate rebutting evidence. The alibi of the married man of the party on trial was irrefragibly established, but it did not avail to save him from the ignominious sentence of death by the gallows. The annals of the courts in South Carolina furnish no parallel for this case in illegality, injustice, and cruelty.

The sentence was pronounced with a degree of barbarity scarcely equalled by the infamous Norbury, who laughed at his helpless victims, while this judge sneered at his, slandered their religion, and insulted their piety. He preached a sermon to the men whose condemnation he had secured and plotted, recommended them to cast away their prayer-books, to take up the Bible for the short time left them on earth, to put their trust in God and not in the priest who had deluded them, for he or no one else could arrest their just doom.

I visited the condemned men in prison, said Mass in the jail, and administered to them the Holy Sacraments. The sheriff, Colonel Hagood, extended a refined courtesy. He not only expressed his sympathies for the prisoners and conviction of their innocence, but gave me the use of his parlor and left me with the men free and unconfined by bolts or bars.

The time being short, I immediately commenced to labor for the protection of their lives, and I knew that the best, and perhaps the only, successful course was to create a public opinion by exposing the iniquity of the proceedings. In this I received available assistance from Rev. Dr. Corcoran, the fearless editor of the *Catholic Miscellany*, who exposed the transaction and stamped it as nefarious. I next approached many of the leading jurists of the State, personal friends of the judge, and brought them to interfere, if not for the sake of the unjustly condemned, at least in behalf of the judge, to save him from the guilt and infamy of judicial murder. I sought and obtained an interview with his Excellency Governor Alston, who was civil, but assured me he deemed it necessary to make an example for the protection of good morals and the interests of society; that passing by one day, a Sunday, he found the men very rude and violent. I know he formed his opinion from having witnessed a few boys and young men engaged in playing at ball for recreation on Sunday evening after the services of the church were closed for the day.

I was dismissed, however, with the promise of giving due consideration to my representations, and coupled with an invitation to return in the course of a day or two. Governor Alston was a courteous and humane gentleman. He was a long time President of the State Senate, and his administration as Chief Executive wise and honorable and free from partisan spirit.

I had scarcely left the vestibule of the Executive Department when I encountered the judge, who spoke to me with apparent embarrassment, and who informed me that he was on his way to ask the Governor in person to interfere in behalf of the men under sentence of death at Pickens Court-house. He seemed to be more in earnest about it, if possible, than I. The sentence was rescinded without any delay and transmuted to a mere nominal penalty of confinement for some few weeks. The document was placed in the hands of the sheriff by Senator Sharp a very short time before the day set apart for the inhuman execution of the men who came to build up the wealth and prosperity of the State. In this manner was averted from the State of South Carolina a disgrace which must have sullied her name before the civilized world, and rendered the character of her judiciary odious to all who are emulous for justice and the preservation of the lives and liberty of the human race.

The great disgrace attached to the character of Irish laborers in this country is a sectional spirit which has frequently developed into faction fights, culminating in acts of violence and loss of life. This can be traced to many causes, running several centuries back in the history of the nation, originating in questions long since defunct, but perpetuated by the ruling Government for political purposes and the maintenance of their usurped powers. In the history of the human race we find it to be a universal failing from which no nation or people is free.

The recent cruel war, and the sectional prejudices underlying society; the War of the Roses in England; the provincial animosity, developing into open riot and rebellion, and restrained only by the superior force of the Government; the Norman and Saxon conflicts; the disorders under the Heptarchy, prove that faction fights are not indigenous to the Irish race alone; they crop out among all people. If we cross the Channel, the fact is still more sadly illustrated by the bloody orgies of every dominant party. In every country on the globe, civilized and barbarous, the sad truth is everywhere written in letters of blood, even in families. It is the consequence of original transgression, aggravated by every additional crime. Union with God is charity and peace. When separated from him we are disordered, and are even separated from our very selves. The spirit of Cain benumbs the sentiment of fraternal charity and love, and induces universal alienation, rendering men natural enemies one toward the other. This has become the normal frame of the human mind. People will combine, from motives of self-interest, for mutual protection, and to resist an external pressure. The conquerors return in triumph and consolidate a power, which ere long crumbles under the renewed action of domestic strife, is dismembered, and its separated fragments become the easy prey of the domestic tyrant or neighboring enemy.

Charity is so rare on earth that the strongest human ties, not even the marriage bond, can always secure its possession. First born of the Gospel, cradled in humility, and strengthened by self-denial, it is accompanied by every virtue, theological and moral, without a missing link in the golden chain; often makes man invulnerable by fire, or sword, or torture; transplants him to his native skies, and raises him to the honors of the very altars of God. Allied to faith, with its loss among the nations, it seems to be taking its flight from earth, leaving behind the universal night of error that will precede the second advent. *Think you the Son of Man will find faith on earth when he cometh?* The Irish people are not exempt from the common faults and infirmities of the human race, and, without claiming for them a superior excellence above other countries, or glossing over the faction fights of railroaders and miners, I unhesitatingly assert that, as a nation, they are the most humane, kind, and Christian people now living—an eminence undeniably established by the universal assent of all nations. The purity of Erin's daughters is proverbial; and to praise her sons at home or abroad is to eulogize honor, valor, honesty, and truth.

Some attempts were made by a few tramps, who came for the purpose, like wolves in sheep's clothing, to provoke party strife; but sobriety, peace, and good-will were too firmly established to be easily interrupted. The clergy adopted a mild and prudent course, were sustained by the virtuous, the industrious, and well-meaning, and the disorderly were compelled to fly away in contempt and defeat. This provincialism was at all times a sentiment unknown to the Irish Catholics in the diocese; it never for a moment obtained footing inside the rails of the sanctuary; the laity heeded not what section of the parent country first bore them, nor enquired, except for the purpose of gracing the unmeaning formality of conversation. The contrary feeling is universally wrong, and unbecoming the children of the saints, who are united by a common nativity, a common faith, a common persecution, and the common hatred, or at least dislike, of the balance of mankind. But, thank God! it is because they are Catholics, hold the faith of St. Patrick, and refuse to call themselves Scotch-Irish at the bidding of the regicides and the pseudo-reformers.

The State in 1859 refused any further aid for the prosecution of the work, probably with a view of hoarding its wealth for future and proximate contingencies. As in the quarries of Egypt four thousand years ago, the men threw the drill and hammer on the shelves of the rocks, plunged into the light of day, and dispersed themselves all over the continent, from Brazil to California and Canada; how easily might that valuable body of hard-working men, sons of toil, have been induced to abide in the State, and enrich her by their labors, their industry, and their blood! Common civility and the encouragement of employment would have sufficed. They would have formed an abiding nucleus for future immigration. The altered and more judicious policy now inaugurated will labor in vain for many years to induce that class of immigrants to seek homes on her uncultivated fields and inhospitable shore. Some few remained behind: Michael Boyle, John Burns, and Patrick Duggan are the only tenants of the Hill—now literally the Deserted Village. It became a rendezvous for conscripts during the war, who domiciled in the church, burnt the flooring and the weather-boarding for firewood, and abandoned it in a state of irreparable ruin. I visited the station for the last time in 1871, and said Mass in a portion of the building till then in a good state of preservation. During the past year—1877—that also, after having endured a quarter of a century, yielded to the wear of time and the fierce night winds that, ice-loaded, come howling from the snow-capped mountains of Georgia and the bald faces of the Blue Ridge peaks, spreading wintry desolation around, and indignantly effacing every trace of human improvement from the red man's home.

I found it expedient to open a burying-ground during the work, to prevent the survivors from transporting the remains of the dead the entire distance to Columbia for interment in a Catholic cemetery. At the expense of much labor, inconvenience, and cost, three or four bodies were already conveyed thither, a week being generally spent in the performance of the sad duty. Four or five persons lost their lives in the work, and several died from natural causes.

There is not on the continent another resting-place for the dead that can rival this one in all its surroundings. Greenwood Cemetery, or Chateaubriand's Tomb on the coast of Brittany, fade into insignificance in the comparison. Far up on the summit of the mountain, the last resting-place of Heaven's light, and at an elevation of several thousand feet above water level, the southern slope of the country, as far as the eye of an artist's glass can ken, undulates at its base like a blue sea; every trace of agricultural break is hid from view, and the remotest town seems in the distance like the white wing of a lonely sail on the horizon of the ocean. Nature adorns the graves of the humble dead with a gorgeous pageantry unrivalled by Eastern kings, and the solitude is broken only by the splash of silvery waters rushing down the rugged sides of the superb mausoleum. Baptized children and aged innocence could find no such place of sepulture outside the hoary stillness of the Catacombs. Catholicity can be maintained and spread all over this favored location by zealous care and assiduous cultivation. Besides those already mentioned, some of the natives were baptized, and still adhere to the faith. John White and family; Mrs. Slater, who lost her husband in the war, is a pious Catholic, and raises her children in the faith; Capt. Goings and his household; and, in short, several others, scattered around within an area of thirty miles, will afford ample occupation for the missionary, and loudly cry for spiritual care and nurture, like Erin's children in the vision of her Apostle, who with tears and outstretched arms invoked his speedy advent. In the days of reckoning it is labors and the nurture of the seed that will wear the crown rather than high places, which may too often, as in days of yore, be their own reward. Father Folchi labored faithfully and with great zeal and profit on this mission until he retired, at the close of 1877. His place is now happily filled by another clergyman, Father Smitz.

The continued maintenance of the succession of missionary priests is ample evidence that the foregoing considerations have due weight on the mind of the ordinary and give promise that the mission will be permanently upheld.

There is no clergyman on a mission who has not saved souls by the sacraments, at least by baptism, and who has not only taken away sins but prevented many—a consideration that cannot fail to console and encourage him on the most arduous missions. The bare sight of a priest in this country does people good. It was the prevention of a sin, or its speedy punishment, that confirmed a perpetual high-priesthood in one line of the Levitical tribe.

Pickens was divided and a new county created in its northern section by the Republican legislature towards the close of their rule in the State; it was almost the only popular act passed, and was duly appreciated by the mountaineers. It is named Oconee; the Air-line Railroad passes through, which is of invaluable benefit. Without it the people would be entirely separated from communication with the outside world; there was scarcely any money in circulation, and the produce of the soil was the general medium of exchange. The character of the country is hilly and mountainous, with valleys of great fertility; the lands were cheap, seldom over a dollar per acre for unreclaimed tracts magnificently timbered, and the soil adapted to the raising of corn, tobacco, grain, vegetables, and every variety of mountain fruit. Horses and mules are scarce, and the farm-work is performed with the aid of oxen. A buggy, or even an umbrella, would be a rare sight. Horned cattle constitute the chief source of wealth in the county; the most opulent own several, and all in one vicinity; gathering into a common herd, extensive but less numerous than those of Texas, they range the mountains with the freedom of buffaloes and roam for many miles unmolested, meeting abundant pasture in summer on the uplands and in winter in the coves and sheltered valleys that nestle between the rugged mountains. Early in the fall the drovers arrive from the low countries, and, making extensive purchases, drive the herds to the markets of Charleston or Augusta. The cattle average about ten dollars each.

The streams abound with fish and the forests with game, especially the red deer. A fatal distemper almost destroyed the entire race a few years since. During one entire summer they came down in companies from the mountain's coverts into the plains by the water-courses, fearless of man, and died after slaking their thirst. On examining the body the tongue was invariably found to be black and in a state of decay. The inhabitants are improvident, inclined to indolence, and consequently in need of the necessaries of life in many instances; the possession of a rifle, a peck of meal, and a dog for the chase seems to limit their ambition.

Sadly deficient in morals, the Civil Rights Bill was for them a superfluous legislation, and the divorce law a post-factum attempt at legalizing a pre-existing condition commonly prevailing, and popular by general observance. Woe to him who attempted to become an informer! A speedy departure for quarters unknown was his only safety. Some preachers claim two calls, one for the pulpit, and the next to save some particular congregation for which the particular individual is alone fitted; to this benighted region none received the second call.

A family, cut loose from the workmen of Tunnel Hill about 1857, purchased a farm for one hundred dollars, and permanently settled in the heart of this country, at a place twenty miles distant, and bordering on the North Carolina line; it was the mercy of God, for they were the first who introduced religion and morals into the region. Their name is Leary. There are two brothers, John and

Timothy, with their mother, a nonogenarian; the former is married and has three children, and the latter is a single man; both are advanced in years.

Having acquired a competency by labor and industry, they are independent, and the most respectable family in the vicinity. Though to the manor born, the children speak the Irish language, which is the vernacular tongue of the household, with a raciness and elegance that would win the applause of Father Tom Burke and excite the admiration of Archbishop McHale for the pure Kerry dialect. It is rich to hear how fluently they recite the Rosary and the Catechism in that tongue that was never the vehicle of heresy, and whose accents refuse to be inflected into the utterance of falsehood against Divine truths. Because of its numerous synonymes and words of double meaning, English is the language of error and heresy, and Irish that of unflinching, unequivocal truth. If it is impossible to curse in Japanese, it is almost equally so to lie in Irish; at least, it must be a square lie, divested of all evasive subtleties.

During my last visit, in 1870, I was delighted to have found one Catholic among the natives, a convert of the name of Nichols, who was baptized by Father Lawrence O'Connell at the Sisters' hospital in Greenbrier County, Virginia, during the war; and hearing there was a priest in the neighborhood, he came to make himself known. I preached on a Sunday in September, on the sloping side of a hill, after having given a week's notice. There were a good number present, considering the sparseness of the population. I explained the necessity and the fact of a Divine revelation, and the principal mysteries of religion. If but imperfectly understood, it was not for lack of simplicity of expression, or the obscurity accruing from brevity. I used the plainest words afforded in English to convey my ideas, and spoke from breakfast time till noon. There happened to be in the audience a centre of great attraction, a young man who wore a pair of new boots. He was insensible to any other object, and, by stretching and all imaginable twistings, riveted the attention of the invidious mountaineers, who were chiefly shod in Adam's leather.

Noticing with no small degree of curiosity that about a third of the audience leant on crutches, or limped on walking-canes, I enquired the cause and found it to be rheumatism. It is the prevailing complaint, confining some to bed for years, and keeping numbers on the rack during the decline of life. The causes are very obvious; their houses are extremely primitive, with rickety doors or stoppages, constructed of rough logs, loosely covered overhead with boards, and searched by every passing gale. The enormous pile of wood burning and crackling on the unlimited hearth, while it scorches the front, leaves the shoulders and rear to shiver in the surrounding snow and rain.

CHAPTER XI.

COLUMBIA AND ITS MISSIONS—GREENVILLE, CHICK SPRINGS, MERRITTSVILLE, WILLIAMSTON, ETC., ETC.

Greenville—President Johnson—Soil and Mineral Waters—But two Families, and poor—Father O'Gora of Illinois—James Gallon, his character; returns to Ireland; betrayed by his bankers; at the Hospital of the Little Sisters of the Poor—James McPherson, a stanch friend to Religion; his house the only church; non-Catholic—Bigotry in Greenville—Not permitted to preach in the Court-house—Catholicity not as respectable as Jugglery—A Yankee priest in Greenville; great excitement—Service at Swandale's Hotel, attended by Strangers—McBee's Hall stoned by white boys—Narrow Escape of Mrs. Mitchel—Injury—Miss Susan McElheny—The Semmes Family—Major Fitzgerald, his death; buried in Greenville—Mrs. Fitzgerald—Mrs. Senator Semmes—Mrs. Ives—Commodore Raphael Semmes, his career, happy death; a tribute—Hon. Thomas J. Semmes's Wisdom and Ability as a Statesman—Governor Perry's kindness—Ornamented family Burying-place—A Reflection—Chick Springs—Properties of the Waters seldom fairly tested—A general Resort—Lectures—Rival Sermons—Biblical Orthodoxy—Shipwreck—Destroyed by Fire—Loneliness—Site for a School—Mr. Talbird—Immigration has passed into the Interior—New Sees—Catholics—Excitement during the War in Greenville—A Philosophical Schoolmaster—Spoiling for a Fight—A pleasant Journey; a narrow Escape—A glorious sunset—Excellent ice-water—Mountaineers—Cæsar Head in 1851—A Niagara of the Desert—Casket of the Medal of the Immaculate Conception—Natural Scenery depreciated by the Carolineans—Apostrophe of Travellers—Reflection—Williamston—Lecture at the Springs—B. Reilly and Family—Pedlars' disreputable Modes of selling their Goods—Samuel Lover—Remarks of Bishop Reynolds—Reflection—A Baptist Settlement—Father Folchi, his life, labors, and missions—The new Church; Liberality of the Citizens—Dedication—Sermon by Father Clark, S.J.—Ex-Governor Perry—Immense change in the People of Greenville.

GREENVILLE, at the terminus of the railroad of the same name, is a flourishing town, situated on a level plain, and in the centre of a fertile agricultural district, connected with Columbia and Charleston by railroad, and at a distance of two hundred miles from the former place, in a northerly direction. It has been for many years a fashionable resort during the summer months for the opulent and pleasure-seekers. The unsurpassed healthiness of the country, the beauty of scenery, rivalling in grandeur the most favored regions, and its mineral springs, celebrated for sanitary purposes, all combine to render this the most favorite section in the State.

With a population of five thousand people, five or six churches, the work-shops of the Greenville Railroad, the court-house, Baptist College, Female Institute, and two or three hotels, besides any number of private boarding-houses, it is a town of considerable importance, and destined to become a centre of commerce and education. In its early days, and when but a mere village, it was the scene of the humble labors of President Johnson; and when in his strictly sedentary handicraft he fitted rough homespun for the brawny shoulders of the Greenville beaus, he commenced toiling upwards in the strife of life. He went from here to Greenville, Tennessee, where he located for life, and was among the many self-made men that the United States can boast of. He was Vice-President under Lincoln's second administration, and succeeded to the Presidential chair by the tragical end of the President. Father Barry was the first priest who visited Greenville, about the year 1850, and Rev. L. P. O'Connell the next, who came in the following year, both in the pursuit of health and the performance of the priestly duties. I organized the mission in 1852, and made arrangements for a regular attendance at appointed times, yearly, until 1869. In the place I found only two families who were Catholic, and very poor; the brothers John and Peter King, the latter unmarried, were both exemplary and pious, but their straitened circumstances limited the sphere of their influence in a fashionable and wealthy community. They both died, the former leaving a widow and three children, now grown to manhood and trained to religion and piety by a saintly mother.

John Keenan, the eldest son of Terome Keenan, of Ashville, married a Scotch lady and settled here. His wife, an excellent woman, joined the Church; their union was blessed by a large family of children, who were carefully instructed in their religion, and were brought up in the fear and love of their Maker. By perseverance and piety the descendants of both the families would be able, within a few years, to leaven the surrounding mass of incredulity. John O'Gora, called Love, being the English rendering of the name, resided a few miles outside the town, whose wife and sister-in-law I baptized, and also two or three children. He was a brother of Father Thos. O'Gora, who died in 1877, at St. Joseph's Hospital, Chicago, after having been the worthy pastor of St. Rose's, Wilmington, Ill., for many years. At my solicitation the eldest boy was adopted by his uncle, who prepared the promising youth for future usefulness.

James Gallon, correctly Galligan, was for many years the head acting man and chief steward of the Mansion House, the leading hotel, conducted by Swandale and Irwin. He was born in the County Monaghan, Ireland, about the year 1800, and immigrated to this country in early life. Low in stature and used to labor from childhood, his activity was incredible and his industry tireless. He was the impersonation of Catholicity in his sphere in life; irreproachable in morals, his fidelity, integrity, and honor were above suspicion; his faith, piety, and devotion abiding; humble in thought, word, and action. The people relate to this day, as an illustration of honesty, that he went all the distance from Greenville to Ireland to pay, in person, a debt contracted by his father, and which poverty prevented him from liquidating before his death. Mr. Gallon did not experience a corresponding honor from those whom he trusted. Of a confiding disposition, and judging men from his own standpoint, he frequently confided his earnings to others either in trust or as an accommodation, and his confidence was often most inhumanly betrayed, and where he least expected. Mr. Swandale, subsequently the sole proprietor of the Mansion House, an Israelite, was an honorable exception.

Mr. Gallon's services were invaluable to his employers, and more especially from the unmeasured manner in which he identified himself with their interests. Always inconsolable from the loss of the Sunday Mass, and the other spiritual disadvantages accruing from the absence of a local clergyman and church, he sighed for those blessings; God fulfilled his wishes.

After a score of years spent in this manner, he resigned his office at the Mansion House, removed to Columbia, and lived in our family for twenty years. In the St. Mary's College, as économe, about the church, the sisters' house, and all things else connected with religion, and where the services of a layman could avail, he was untiring. Always reliable, and first in every good and laudable work, leaving wherever he lived a bright and shining example of religious bearing and conversation, he was a pattern of virtue.

Having moved with the family to Gaston County, N. C., in 1871, his health became extremely infirm. Afflicted, during thirty years, with an inflamed and ulcerated leg, from which he suffered a daily martyrdom, he sought and obtained entrance into the hospital in Richmond established by the indefatigable Bishop Gibbons, and conducted by the Little Sisters of the Poor, where he met all the care and attention becoming his condition, and which can be dispensed only in a religious institution. I visited Richmond in September, 1877, at the instance of the bishop, said Mass in the convent, at which he assisted in improved health. He departed this life the following spring, fortified with the sacraments and in peace with God and man. Few, if any, in his sphere in life produced a more favorable impression on the public mind in behalf of Catholicity. He fills an honored grave.

The house of Mr. James McPherson from the commencement was always the home and shelter of the priest, where there was a room appropriated for his especial use; the holy sacrifice of the Mass was said in the front room, neatly furnished and sufficiently spacious to accommodate all the

Catholics on week days and Sundays; besides all others who desired to assist at Catholic worship. Here the children were taught the catechism, Mr. McPherson being the leading catechist, confessions heard, and faith expounded for many years and during the erection of the new church in 1877. Born in the Highlands of Scotland, hale and sturdy, blameless in manners and irreproachable in character, and in high repute in the town, it is to be regretted that he, the strongest friend of religion, always its advocate and promoter, is not himself a Catholic but is a deacon in the Presbyterian Church. His wife, Mrs. McPherson, is of Irish nationality and a pious and devoted Catholic lady; they are childless, are a long time married and in the evening of life. Their residence was the cradle of Catholicity in this town, and may God in his mercy bring this noble-hearted man into the true fold! It would be a source of sorrow that one who all his life-time had been in a sense an apostle of the truth and the champion of the clergy should die without its consolations and, like the unhappy prophet, admire it from afar: *How beautiful are thy tents, O Jacob, and thy tabernacles, O Israel!*

The Carolinians, in proportion to their wealth and intelligence, were opposed to Catholicity; the leading and influential people treated its claims with supreme indifference and as unworthy of serious consideration, and the lower class followed their example. The inhabitants of Greenville were no exception to this rule. In several instances the advertisement of a Catholic discourse or sermon served rather as a warning to keep aloof, as if the slightest contact was dangerous to religion and respectability. When whispered abroad that there would be a Catholic discourse at a private residence, some people would probably steal in at night; but they mutually feared each other to attend in public, unless the movement was patronized by a colonel or some leading citizens. The people of this town were so bigoted formerly that I was refused the court-house for a *course of lectures*, though it had been used but a day previous by a mesmerizer or necromancer; all similar characters were welcome to use it whenever court was not in session.

During the summer of 1868 Father Waldron, an aged and venerable priest and a convert, stationed in Maryland, visited this country for the benefit of his health; while at the hotel he saw many persons collecting after dark into a place of public assemblage to attend a lecture; he also went out of curiosity, and shortly ascertained that it was a Bible meeting, at which most of the *élite* of the town, men and women, assisted. After the usual programme an orator, aspiring to a foreign mission and glowing with indignation at the abuses of popery, denounced the withholding of the Scriptures from the laity as its greatest abomination. At the conclusion Father Waldron mounted the stage, asked leave to speak, and was reluctantly permitted. In a few words he gave his history: a Northern man and a Protestant, who had entertained the same erroneous views just expressed, became acquainted with the true state of the question, which he wished to explain. He was now a Catholic priest! The excitement which followed can be better imagined than described. The women left immediately; the indignation of the audience was expressed in all the ways common to disorderly assemblies. They threatened to assail him; the rumor of the assault on their camp spread far and wide, and is still fresh in the minds of the people. It was the first ball shot *directly* into the stronghold, and, worse still, by a Yankee priest!

Mr. Swandale, the gentlemanly proprietor of the hotel, who died during the war, a German by birth and a liberal man, lent me the use of the ball-room, which I used for a chapel when needed, and where I lectured before a select audience collected principally from the guests of the hotel. At a subsequent period, and when it was impossible to be accommodated, I obtained the use of McBee's Hall from the proprietor, Verdry McBee, Esq., a wealthy and courteous man, raised in North Carolina, who was in extreme old age and would accept no recompense. I preached a course of lectures in that place, afterwards destroyed by fire, which were attended mostly by the refugees from Charleston. This occurred in the summer of 1863. The ill-feelings of the citizens were immediately aroused at beholding this first inroad made on their long-cherished prejudices and opinions; a crowd of white boys were encouraged to assemble in front of the hall by night, and often in the day-time, for the purpose of interrupting the divine service by boisterous ribaldry and street noise, and divesting the assemblage of the appearance of respectability lest the community may be tempted to assist. They went so far in their hostility as to stone me through the windows while at the altar. Among the Charleston refugees then stopping in Greenville were the Mitchell family, inferior to none in the State for respectability, moral worth, and social elegance, and all edifying and practical Catholics. The mother and two of her children occupied the front bench, next to the altar, and while engaged in fervent recollection one of the stones, violently cast by the gang in the street, struck the floor close by her person. It was an outrage on common decency and religion, disgraceful alike to the civilization and hospitality of the Greenville people, who owed the prosperity of their town to this class of people. I expostulated, but none fathered the promising youths, and, as a matter of course, the interruption and outrage were the wild freak of some mischievous boys who were nobody's children. I continued my ministrations during the prescribed time, but it was not deemed prudent for ladies to attend the lectures in future. The hall was accidentally destroyed by fire within a short time, and never since rebuilt; on the site is now a store-house.

I received into the Church about this time Miss Susan McElheny, an accomplished young lady and respectably connected in the city. She was presented for baptism by Mrs. Semmes, herself a convert, and the wife of Senator Thomas Semmes of Louisiana. That distinguished and holy Christian family were in Greenville at this time, and stopping at the hotel. Always Catholic, and descended from a race of people who never bartered their religion for the sake of filthy lucre, during the civil war they rose to unrivalled distinction, and the annals of the Confederacy contain no name more tenderly cherished by the country. Marylanders and the Irish beyond all others are both equally proud of their holy faith, and the Semmeses claim it as their highest honor.

That Catholicity is the mother and fruitful nurse of heroes none can deny who admit the heroism of martyrdom. To sacrifice life for the sake of virtue and truth, when unpopular and oppressed, is the duty of every Christian. In the absence of either, life is dishonorable and not worth having. All the genius of Catholic faith and the fulness of its martyrs' spirit they brought into the struggle, and clung to it to the last when others had abandoned the cause. Single-handed, and with but a few gallant hearts, Admiral Semmes won and maintained the mastery of the seas for years, like another Nelson. He swept commerce from the waters, defied a whole navy which had more than once discomfited and defeated Britannia on her own favorite battle-fields, inflicted a stunning blow on the commerce of the opponents of the South from which it has not yet fully recovered, sustained the failing fortunes of his country to the bitter end, established its dominions on the deep, and carried its battle-flag undipped and unsullied to the remotest shores.

The Confederacy sank with the *Alabama* in the waters of republican France. Free from the slightest imputation of cruelty or unnecessary harshness towards his captures, he was the very Bayard of chivalry in his irresponsible path through the solitude which his unaided arm created on the ocean. It is a well-known fact that, if other general officers were as faithful and self-sacrificing as he, the tale of submission had never been told; and, if properly sustained, Lee and Semmes had been an overmatch for any single opposing power. Yielding to the common weakness of disparaging what we are incompetent to subdue or incapable of obtaining, a common effort was simultaneously made to brand with the odious name of pirate the undaunted Christian commander, duly commissioned by a recognized belligerent power, who by his skill and bravery, more than England's great admiral, became the Neptune of the seas, and whose name will be the war-cry of the united nation in future conflicts on the unsteady battle-fields of the deep. Fiction and song will weave many a golden web around his exploits, and his name will live while virtue, honor, and courage are cherished by the warrior and the patriot. Fortified by the sacraments, he departed this life in Mobile, Alabama, in 1877. The last scene was tranquil and calm, gorgeous too, by the consolations of the faith, as golden sunsets on the western waves sobbing sadly by his final resting-place.

Let his monument be erected, not in a city, but on some Southern promontory, in the land he loved so well, and surmounted by a cross, emblem to the mariner at night of salvation, rest, and peace. No less for him than for Constantine it was the sign that sustained and led him in triumph into the harbor of peace. Raphael Semmes was born in Charles County, Maryland, and died in Mobile, Alabama, August 18, 1877. He was son of Thompson Semmes and Kate, his wife, daughter of Arthur Middleton, of Virginia.

William Symmes, of Poundisford Hall, Somersetshire, England, came to America with Lord Baltimore in 1633, having been driven from his native land by religious persecution. He is the ancestor of Admiral Semmes, and of the well-known Catholic family of that name scattered throughout the Southern States. From the mother he is descended from "the Douglass" of Scotland, who, with so many of the nobility and gentry, sought an asylum in Virginia during the Protectorate of Cromwell. Raphael Semmes married Anna Spencer, daughter of Oliver Spencer, of Cincinnati. His cousin, the Hon. Thomas Semmes, was elected Senator for the State of Louisiana in the time when only men of ability, decision, and firmness of character were summoned to the councils of the nation. Called to the most important committees, both in Montgomery and Richmond, his prudence and wisdom were equal to every emergency or danger. The Senate was the arena for the leading minds of the country, and in the contests of these giants of intellectual power Mr. Semmes was conspicuous for close reasoning, lucid statements, and purity of language. If the measures proposed and advocated by him had been adopted, many of the disasters which befell the cause would have been averted. He married Miss Knox, daughter of a wealthy and influential citizen of Montgomery, Alabama, but of patronymic heterodoxy. The union was God's mercy, being the means of bringing her and others of the family into the true Church, which she adorns by her zeal, her piety, and her charity. It is blessed by an interesting flock of children.

Mrs. Ives is a sister of the senator, married to a gentleman of this name and a Catholic, who, with her interesting children, shone like a gem in the gifted family, and was the soul of piety and fervor.

The elder sister was married to Major Fitzgerald, a native of the city of Norfolk, Virginia, and a lieutenant in the United States Navy at the breaking out of the war. Like many other gallant men, he resigned his commission and refused to unsheath his sword against his countrymen. In middle life, full in features, and comely in appearance, he seemed born to command men, though gentle in disposition, unoffensive as a child, which lent additional grace to his cultivated deportment. His heart was an unfailing fountain of affection and piety, combining singularly in his person the two elements, courage and gentleness. While preparing for the most perilous command in the gift of the Government, he retired to Greenville to spend a short time with the wife of his bosom and her family.

In the midst of life we are in death, and he delights to speed his arrow at a shining mark. Within a few weeks he was attacked with paralysis, and, after a brief illness, was struck down like an eagle plucked from his eyrie in the neighboring cliff by the hunter. He died August 9, 1802. The family despatched immediately to Columbia for a clergyman, but before he had time to arrive the soul had fled to the bosom of his Father and God, and in peace, for, independently of a well-spent life, unshaken faith, abiding hope, and abundant charity, he had received only a few days previous the holy sacraments of penance and the Blessed Eucharist through my ministry. His Excellency Hon. Benjamin F. Perry urged the acceptance of a grave in his ornate family burying-plot in the cemetery of Greenville, which was gratefully accepted. In a subsequent visit I offered the holy sacrifice of the Mass for the repose of the departed soul, and made a pilgrimage of affection to the grave that held the remains of the soldier of the seas. Some gentle hand had strewn flowers over it. It lay close by a marble cross handsomely sculptured, and adorned with surrounding emblems of nautical life and erected to a member of the Perry family, who had also shared in the perils of the deep and was gathered to rest in early life. Our entrance into the world and our departure therefrom are the two most important events in human life, and those of which we are most ignorant; we are not consulted about either. Our Lord wills that we fall directly into his own hands, lest the ignorance of our understanding and blindness of our will interfere with his eternal plans of mercy and love in our regard, and thus deprive us of the glory and bliss for which we are created. We die when it is best for us, and the circumstances of time, place, and manner are ordained for the accomplishment of these objects.

Captain Fitzgerald now sleeps far away from the din of strife, of deadly conflict, and the noise of battle. Many of the faithful will breathe a fervent prayer for his eternal repose, and the night winds will whisper a strain as sweet and plaintive over his mound of earth in the distant valley as the requiem of the blue wave of eastern waters.

William Bushby Fitzgerald was born in Norfolk, Virginia, March 12, 1822; died at Greenville, South Carolina,

August 9, 1862. .He was son of Edward Fitzgerald and Mary, his wife, daughter of William Bushby, of Virginia. He was of the old Geraldine stock of Ireland, so famous in the annals of that country, and a descendant of Colonel John Fitzgerald, aid-de-camp to General Washington, and, through the mother, of the Lees of Virginia. William B. Fitzgerald, until the breaking out of the civil war, was a lieutenant in the United States Navy, and was brevetted by Congress for gallant services during the war with Mexico. At the time of his death he commanded a regiment of artillery in the Confederate army. He married a Miss Semmes, a cousin of the great Admiral's. His remains still rest in the cemetery at Greenville, South Carolina, the grave having been blessed by a priest of the Church.

Mrs. Fitzgerald is all that high culture, piety, and education, joined to rare intellectual powers, can make a woman. Among the first band of devoted pilgrims from our shores she represented the faith and devotion of her sex in the youthful Church of America, and offered these like incense at the feet of the Holy Father, at Lourdes, and before many famous shrines hallowed by the veneration of millions during the ages of piety.

Her sister-in-law, Mrs. Senator Semmes, was the worthy companion of her devotions. A heart empty of self and the world will be ever filled to its utmost capacity with the consolations of the Father of Mercies, who delights to communicate the largest measure of his heavenly gifts to all who seek him only, and for his own sake rather than for his gifts, which will be abundantly added, for he never comes empty into the soul that craves him.

Five miles to the east of Greenville are two mineral springs, one sulphur and the other chalybeate. The action of the waters is mild but permanent, effecting a radical cure in several cases of a chronic type, and beneficial to all who use them for a reasonable time. They were the property of two brothers, Reuben and Pettis Chick, natives of Newberry, and called by their name. Like all watering-places, they were patronized by the gay and youthful in quest of pleasure or matrimonial alliances. Many returned home at the end of the season debilitated from constant excitement, and emphatically denying the sanitary properties of the waters and denouncing similar haunts of pleasure and amusement in general. The invalids were the smallest number among the guests. Some of these, after having sipped the cold and sparkling liquid bubbling up in silvery sparkles from the generous heart of the rock, would leave too soon for other resorts, unbenefited, and asserting that the ball-room was the greatest attraction. Dyspeptics and people suffering from a variety of stomach complaints and nervous prostration were always benefited after two weeks, and gathered sufficient strength for the labors of another year, after which period they returned to be again rejuvenated by the elixir of life.

Being on my mission, I visited the Chick Springs every summer and spent several days at a time; there were always some, and not unfrequently several, Catholics at the place, besides many wealthy and intelligent people from all sections of the country who had never made the acquaintance of a Catholic priest. I said Mass in a private apartment for the faithful, and got the use of the parlor for sermons on Sundays. The Chicks were courteous and liberal-minded men and well fitted for their occupation. A feeling of general good-nature and liberality prevailed throughout, induced either by personal acquaintance or the thawing of sectarian asperity under the humanizing influences of social intercourse, or both. Be this as it may, the guests invited me to preach, and attended in force with great decorum, refusing to assist at non-Catholic service elsewhere. During the summer of 1807 I found at the hotel a good array of Catholics and honest enquirers of the truth. Among the latter were Colonel Province of Florida, Messrs. Hardy of Columbia, S. Brown of Charleston, and others. Among the Catholics were E. S. Keitt, Esq., and his pious lady, who were brought up with those people, some Irish pedlars; poor fellows! they always and everywhere gather around the Church as their only home in their wanderings. Prominent among the faithful was Richard Hogan, of Charleston, his pious and excellent lady, and their only son and child, Thomas, who was educated at St. Mary's College, and soon after served in the Western army under General Bragg, and returned home safe with an honorable record.

Richard Hogan was an active, enterprising man in easy circumstances, and the most zealous Catholic in St. Patrick's Church during the pastorship of Rev. P. O'Neill. I lectured during two hours one Sunday on the holy sacrifice of the Mass. I opened with suitable prayers, and Mrs. Mayben, the sister-in-law of Hon. William Mayben, the Mayor of Columbia, with a select band, volunteered sacred music for the occasion. The discourse was favorably received and produced an excellent impression, which could scarcely be otherwise, for I was well prepared and posted in all the leading theological arguments on that inexhaustible subject, the living soul of Catholicity, embracing all latreutic and relative worship and adoration, fixing the earth as the veritable seat of the adequate worship of Almighty God amid all his creation. The audience was select and intelligent, among whom was a Baptist clergyman from Charleston, who was also engaged to preach in the afternoon. A spirit of emulation crept out and seized on all the Sunday-sobered guests, who had limited the circle of their engagement to the free use of the waters. Each side had its patrons, who warmly claimed superiority for their favorite in Biblical doctrine. The controversy waxed warmer, and forfeits were pledged that the priest would not nor could not attend the sermon of his rival. The stakes, of course, were forfeited. The preacher was a fairly-educated man and a good orator of the Furman, or Baptist, University in the neighborhood.

He selected a grand theme, the Marriage Feast, which he painted eloquently and correctly in its historical features, and applied the parable strictly to the duty of fraternal charity. I grieved to think how little that grand illustration of the Gospel was understood by the speaker or his hearers. After a while he dwelt on the uncertainty of human life, illustrated by the recent loss of an ocean steamer, which was described in a graphic and forcible manner; he concluded an hour's discourse by condemning in no measured terms the general ornaments of the hotel people, and especially the immorality of dancing. He affirmed that all at the place were irretrievably lost; he absolutely wept tears, copious tears, of sorrow, at the loss of so many poor, miserable, sinful creatures. But they fell in vain, for he had none to sympathize with him and return his sighs. After the explosion of the steamboat his hearers dropped away rapidly, leaving Mr. Hogan, the priest, and a few people his sole listeners. Perhaps the defection was the true cause of his tears. It was unhesitatingly decided, without a dissenting voice, that the Catholic priest was incomparably more orthodox, that his doctrine was strictly Scriptural, and, yet more, preached from the Protestant Bible, which graced the centre-table of the reception room, and which he knew by heart, from cover to cover.

This favorite summer resort was partly abandoned during the war. It exchanged proprietors, and passed into the possession of Mr. Butterfield, the popular hotel-keeper of Charleston. Miss Eugenie Passalaigue and her sister, Mrs. McGrath, were the only Catholics whom I found here towards the close of that disastrous epoch in the history of the South, and there were but few guests besides. Soon afterwards it was burnt down, whether by design or accident is a question; it is now only a pile of skeleton ruins, without a trace of what it once had been, forlorn and deserted, the spring still emitting unceasing streams of limpid waters, gushing rapidly by, and none to taste their sweetness or imbibe their invigorating influences. In their heedless ripple they seem to murmur a sad refrain to the thousands who, in the flush of life, affluence, and beauty, loitered around in days gone by, but now slumbering under the turf in the sleep which knows no waking.

After all, by a strange disposition of Providence, the

situation and all the surrounding possessions passed into the possession of a Catholic family, and may, in the near future, become the seat of a Catholic institution. For a convent, with a boarding-school for young ladies, its advantages are unrivalled, and a movement in that direction was formerly made on the part of the owners. Mr. Talbird, a native of Beaufort, purchased the property towards the close of the civil war, and made it the permanent family residence. He was a man of enlightened mind and liberal in sentiment. Having married an accomplished and devoted Catholic lady, who was educated at the Convent of the Sacred Heart, under the auspices of Archbishop Hughes, he faithfully fulfilled the conditions of his marriage, and, far from interfering with the religious rights of his wife, encouraged her in the observance of all her spiritual duties, and in the education of their children in the faith of the mother. He placed his eldest son, Thomas, at St. Mary's College, and, residing in the town for some time, conducted his child regularly every Sunday to Catechism, and assisted at the Holy Sacrifice with every outward mark of piety and respect. He shortly after embraced the faith and returned to Beaufort. The suggestion of purchasing the fashionable resort for a religious and educational institution came from this source, and it was hoped that it could be realized.

The unhealthiness of our seaports and the frequency of yellow fever unfit them for centres of education. The cheapness of provisions, the healthiness of the climate, and the facilities of communication render the interior far more desirable, and they must, in the nature of things, henceforward receive the preference. Immigration has already passed from the border cities to the interior of the States. It is better for religion; the Church will take deeper root in the soil, become more national, and lose much of the European aspect. The head or centre of railroad communication is as suitable now for the creation of a new see as was the head of navigation a century back; unless immigration ceases the dioceses will multiply as rapidly in the

South as they have done in the Northern and Western States. It is the immigrant and not the convert who has built up the Church in the United States.

Messrs. Tighe, Fahey, and Moore, the bishop's brother, resided in Greenville during the war; also Thomas Miles, his mother and sisters, an edifying family from St. Patrick's parish in the city of Charleston. Mr. Miles had been a student in the Ecclesiastical Seminary; but, fearing the obligations of the priesthood, wisely concluded in time to work out his salvation in another sphere of usefulness. Patrick Brady, a teacher, resided at Merrittsville, on the southern slope of the Saluda. He married into the Hightower family and brought his wife into the Church. I visited his house and said Mass there in January, 1861, and narrowly escaped being lynched as the recompense for my missionary labor.

After the ordinance of secession had been passed by the convention, the act was applauded in Greenville and received with an ovation everywhere. The people were in a state of the highest excitement, and longed for the day when they would be brought face to face with the enemy. The galloping of troopers, the sharp cracks of the pistol, and the howling of the canine race, breaking on the silence of the night, gave the town a very formidable and warlike appearance. But the day was coming when they were offered ample opportunities to display their valor. Their record as soldiers was honorable; they were not wanting in the hour of trial, and there were no laggards among them. There were no braver men in the Confederate Army than Col. Hoke, Capt. Cauble, and others, many of whom lie under the blood-stained soil of old Virginia. The Rev. Mr. Arthur, to whom Greenville owes her handsomest church edifice, was one of the most efficient Protestant chaplains in the army.

Returning from my visit to the mountains, as already stated, and accompanied by the demure and Solon-like teacher, at his recommendation we left the stage-road, which the severity of the weather had rendered nearly impassable, and, in preference, took another leading to the left from Merrittsville, circuitous and deemed better. Our experience more fully confirmed the truth of the wayfarer's maxim, *Never to leave a highroad for a byroad*. The new route was not only longer but, if possible, in a worse condition than the one rejected, leading through a sparsely settled country commonly called *an out-of-the-way place*, and travelling over red hills cut into deep gullies, with a clay-bottom, as a foundation, of the consistency of mortar, and embedding the wheels of the spring-wagon hub-deep. We were ten miles distance from the town, the day was declining, and the winds from the snowy hill-tops piercing cold: misfortunes seldom come singly.

The red-colored horse was one of the most inveterate balkers in the country. We entered into a compromise and lightened the burden, when he refused to yield to the persuasion of the lash, already spent to the stump of the whip. The learned compromiser leaped from the wagon and led the way. Ilderim slowly followed in his tracks, as if in a brown study, and again balked for further parley. We were forced to accede to his unconditional terms, and agreed to make the remainder of the journey in common on foot, if he would be so good as to carry the empty vehicle. He reluctantly consented and walked on, dull and slow, until we reached a creek intersecting the road in a hollow; the water was muddy and foxy as the Tiber, and unfordable for foot-passengers. Compelled by necessity, we re-entered the wagon at the very borders of that unpoetical lagoon. His good nature gaining the ascendant, the winded steed bore us across—no, as far as the middle of the pond, as if measured by mathematical accuracy, and stood in the current as immovable as an iron horse. The imperturbable master intimated that probably it would be necessary to procure a pine-torch and blaze him out. It became evident that I must rely on my personal efforts to obtain shelter and protection for the night. I stepped from the vexatious conveyance, and, with the aid of logs and fence-rails, reached the opposite shore, drenched and not in the most amiable frame of mind. Like the blind-eyed doe in the fable, danger comes from quarters least expected, verifying in a measure the French maxim that it is the improbable that mostly happens; in which there is much truth, from the fact that the thoughts and ways of God are as remote from ours as the heavens are elevated above the earth, and also because the opinions and judgments of no two men are exactly alike on all subjects.

Having reached a weather-bleached frame-house, to hire or crave assistance—for the people of this country expect payment for the slightest service they may render, or for any article of the least value—my appearance excited suspicion. Town-people are known at the first glance, and I heard a voice in an adjoining apartment whispering that "*the man had on store clothes*," a very noticeable singularity, when only homespun is the material of fashionable costume, and frequently dyed an art color. Failing in my application, and suspecting no danger of a personal assault so far, I reached another house, further on the way, and detailed the history of my disaster with all the circumstances becoming one in my situation.

I besought shelter for the night and immediate assistance for the detached part of my company, yonder freezing in mud and water. The mansion was entirely exposed to the weather on one side, and partly sheltered by upright boards and some sheaves of fodder; it was owned by a house-carpenter, which explains its dilapidated condition, for mechanics are like physicians—they seldom take their own medicines. The proprietor was absent; his place was occupied by a midde-aged man of slight build, a mechanic also, and of Northern birth, who, on listening to my statements, manifested no readiness to comply with my petition but a great deal of incredulity in the truth of my statements. An over-zeal for the crimination of another for the purpose of shifting suspicion from one's self is an infirmity of our fallen nature.

The artisan withdrew, and soon after returned with the master-builder, who was, in reality, an honest fellow, but his suspicions were awakened. With greedy ears he drank in the fresh recital of the oft-told tale, and, accompanied with the junior members of his family and his subordinate, moved towards the direction of the branch, apparently rather with the intent of verifying the truth than affording relief, for his tardy gait betrayed a great amount of misgiving. I followed after, for I already understood that, if not absolutely under arrest as a spy and dangerous to the peace of the community, I was under strict surveillance, and it was regarded unsafe to leave me behind, lest I might attempt to escape. Soon after another man joined in the procession, which, after a brief parley and some furtive glances cast behind, crawled on; then came another, and another, and so on, until it swelled into alarming proportions and wore the aspect of a determined body on a lynching excursion. They split into separate knots, eagerly discussing the merits or demerits of the case; after a while would unite as if for the purpose of general consultation, and, arriving at some unanimous course of action, they simultaneously halted on the borders of an oak-grove and in the dusk of evening. I saw my danger and prepared myself to meet it with becoming fortitude. I believed my hour had come at last, and that I was doomed to swing. The simple pleasure of existence is so intense that we all part with life, even when unhappy, only with great reluctance and sorrow. It is God's first great gift, and even our Blessed Lord held death in abhorrence, as alien to his nature and the work of sin.

The sun was sinking behind the western hills, and, though often seen and admired in the gorgeous splendors of his retirement, when, flinging his glorious mantle on the attendant clouds, he sank to rest after his daily labor, never before had he appeared half so beautiful. He looked like the naked eye of God blazing on the universe and searching all the hiding-places of human guilt and sorrow. Inspired by the scene, I raised my soul in communion with its Author, and in an agony of entreaty besought the protection of her who appeared to the evangelist clothed with the sun, and begged also the immediate defence of my angel.

I approached fearlessly, repeated that I was the Rev. Dr. O'Connell, the priest of Columbia, and on my missionary labors in this neighborhood; that my companion and his connections could not be unknown to them, neither could others of my flock in Greenville; that the Hon. Benjamin F. Perry and the leading men of the town were my personal acquaintances and several of them my friends. I claimed the right of being conducted to their presence, and cautioned any man against maltreating me at his own peril. There was a moment of suspense; some broke loose and departed; one aged man approached good-naturedly, called me by name familiarly, said he had formed my acquaintance some time ago and heard me preach at Chick Springs. I was saved, and this was not the first time that I had experienced the miraculous interference of Providence for my protection during a life of a quarter of a century unremittingly engaged on all the most perilous missions of the diocese, conversant with dangers and unrelieved by a single ray of human hope. *De omnibus his eripuit me Dominus.*

The teacher and his steed were extracted from the mire and led to our rendezvous for the night, which was intensely cold and searched by every passing gale. I retired, not without well-grounded alarms of an assault before morning, which I anxiously awaited. My sleep was broken and disturbed, and my heart was gladdened when the day-star unbolted the gates of the morning and ushered in the monarch of the day. Mine host had given me an assurance that there would be no further dangers, and finished by stating that, having once travelled as far as Florida, he had met many incivilities on the way, but he had always managed to escape them and was at last returned safe to his family, and was glad when he found himself once more in a quiet and orderly community. I employed him to drive me to the town, and paid him handsomely for his services. I was conveyed to my friend, Mr.

McPherson, to whom my conductor and the entire party were very well known, and amongst whom I could not have been a stranger. Mr. Brady returned home by another way, and believed himself well recompensed for his participation in the perils of the former day's journey by an array of learned words gathered from my conversation and carefully noted in his pocketbook for future use in his academy. "Hypothesis" was a treasure in itself.

Though yielding to none in fidelity to the laws of the country, and second to none in maintaining the contested rights, I have become convinced by my experience that the state of society in the South under the institution of slavery was not in harmony with the civilization of the nineteenth century. Emancipation was a blessing, however deplorable the process. In God's providence it has exercised a healthy influence on the manners of the people, and future generations will reap the fruit of the labor and sufferings of all who perished in the struggle.

The greatest natural curiosity in *this land of the clouds*, and that which all travellers are expected to visit, is Cæsar's Head, a mountain about a score of miles northwest of Greenville, and in Pickens County, not far from the line. At its base are valleys of great fertility and beauty, interspersed with limpid streams of water, cold in summer and in winter sheeted with ice, clear as the purest crystal. If the excellence of the water be the best recommendation for ice, no market in the world can afford an article superior to or equal to this, from the abundance and variety of mineral springs uniting and commingling in one common flow. Sheltered by mountains on three sides, and exposed to the warmth and the bland gales of the south, the atmosphere is mild and pleasant in the heart of winter, when he holds his sceptre of frost and snow only a short distance overhead. As if pursued by a prairie fire, the birds of the air, herds, and flocks, and all the animals, gather into these sheltered homes and spend a pleasant winter in the dangerous proximity of man. The mountaineer and his rifle are as inseparable as the Arab and his steed, and subserving the same purposes—protection, subsistence, and amusement. Both inhabitants of a wilderness, they share the tastes and pleasures peculiar to their situation.

The arms of the law and of war are long, when those irresponsible men who roam at will, seeking security amid inaccessible barriers, are unable to escape the vigilance of the one or the iron grasp of the other, and answer the first summons of the sheriff or the recruiting-sergeant; like a man's evil deed, they will be sure to find him. From neglect, the ascent by the eastern road was extremely difficult, and after the war impossible; under the most favorable circumstances, and in its best condition, the road was always rugged, steep, and dangerous. In the summer of 1857 I walked over it, and arrived at the summit by sundown. There was accommodation for travellers in small detached cabins, very old, and lending to the plateau the appearance of an Indian village. The property belongs to Col. Hagood, a sexagenarian, a plain country gentleman of large proportions, simple in manners, and primitive in his tastes. Generous and large-hearted, he presided over the hospitality of the peak with princely munificence.

Enquiring when I could visit the point of attraction, he smiled and answered: "You are on it, and can see it in the morning." The broad daylight revealed only the rugged, broken scenery common to all mountain regions, varied at intervals with detached strips of rough husbandry scattered around, and forming sorry specimens of farming. While loitering in search of a guide, I suddenly reached a level space, and fell back instantly, like one who has seen the ocean for the first time or the created beatific vision of God! I was standing in the clouds, at an elevation of two thousand feet perpendicular, and beneath yawned an abyss, square cut, and filling the soul with wonder and awe. The beholder is bewildered at the dizzy height, and men of the strongest nerve shrink from a near approach; some have confessed to the strange temptation to precipitate themselves headlong into the distant world beneath, and refused to encounter a second view. The human mind can scarcely grasp the sublimity of this Niagara of the desert, whose smoothed edges suggest that for unnumbered ages some unknown Mississippi had thundered over its rugged side and buried itself in the ocean that once broke in idle foam at its base.

Other mountains are higher, and seem to have risen more deliberately at the divine mandate, leisurely strengthening their position by unassailable breastworks of immense barriers, whose stability promises security to their everlasting reign against the unrelenting assaults of time and the accidental inroads of human art. This is an exception and the peculiarity forms its defiant grandeur. Bursting into existence like an archangel, it stood erect, though bearing on its unbending shoulders an entire continent, and fell into ecstasy before the throne, gazing steadfastly beyond the heads of Teneriffe and Etna, as if awaiting expectantly the second coming through the golden portals of the East.

Its elevation would have been more merciful than the pinnacle of the temple to the son of Zebedee, who witnessed the transfiguration of his humble master, in company with the meek son of Amram and the dread seer of Israel, when Thabor was radiant with the glory which he inhabited before the world was. Was this the mountain of temptation from whose summit Satan pointed out to the Redeemer all the kingdoms of the earth and their glory, or stood it isolated in the Deluge, the last resting-place of heaven's light, and where the last hopes of a drowning world had perished? Science has not yet read the lettered pages of its history, and it stands a wonder and a mystery, secret as the hiding-place of the hoary Thesbite and the patriarch, who in the morning of creation walked with God and was translated, when sin and iniquity had effaced the lingering glories of Eden from an alienated world.

Before my departure I entrusted to its keeping a gift, the only offering ever made worthy of its acceptance, and a prophecy, mayhap, of more abundant favors. The doctrine of the Immaculate Conception had been recently defined, and I reverently dropped into a side-rent a medal commemorative of the dogma, and blessed by the hand of the world's Pontiff. That the sacred deposit will be inviolably kept none doubts. Like the rock on which the Church is built by our Divine Lord, which time cannot crumble, persecution shake, nor error destroy, the day may not be far distant when Catholic piety will erect here also a shrine of holy pilgrimage, when the Lord of hosts will dwell among men on the throne of the universe, and the morning sun, that now idly gilds the purple face of Mount Malachy, will hail the chalice of salvation and extend still wider the horizon of the prophet's vision. *My name is great among the Gentiles, and in every place, from the rising to the setting of the sun, a clean oblation shall be offered to my name, saith the Lord God of hosts.*

The strongest temptations against faith have their origin in the goodness of God; the immensity of his favors is oppressive, and their profusion renders them familiar and commonplace, like day and night or the sight of a cross. It is only to the man of prayer that the Creator becomes visible in his works and nature displays her charms; the clean of heart only can see God. The people of South Carolina, at great expense and labor, will wander over remote and ungenial regions in search of health or amusements, when they possess those advantages abundantly within their own borders, unsought and unknown, and which, in after-times, will attract strangers from afar, who with one acclaim will affirm that nowhere can be found sweeter waters, a healthier climate, bolder mountains, or lovelier valleys. It is only in the light of faith that all her beauties can be seen, appreciated, and enjoyed.

The Rev. F. A. Smitz has been appointed the local pastor, residing at Greenville, and ministering to the faithful over the entire mission, embracing Anderson and the intermediate stations as far as Tunnel Hill and the Leary Settlement in Oconee County. A man of learning and piety, he has an ample field for the exercise of his zeal, and his nationality will render him acceptable and efficient to the

German element of the population. This gives confidence that the Church will become a permanent establishment in a region so highly favored by God, and that the work inaugurated by so many trials and continued for nearly a quarter of a century will not languish, but be perfected by a succession of devoted missionaries, who, within the space of a few years, will plant the cross in all the towns throughout the land.

Williamston lies about twenty miles south of Greenville, on the railroad running to Columbia. It was a village of considerable importance, possessing a hotel, one or two churches, and several cottages occupied as summer residences by invalids and aged people who were attracted from the low countries by its healthiness and the healing qualities of a copious mineral spring strongly imbued with sulphur. The retirement and calm quiet of the place endeared it to this class beyond the more populous resorts of the country. The master of the hotel was an excellent man and a courteous gentleman. At his invitation I lectured in the dining-room on a Sunday afternoon to all his guests and several of the villagers, in 1856. The apartment was spacious, well filled, and tastefully adorned with festoons of evergreens and fragrant flowers, which dissipated the odor of the repast, savory to the hungry but disagreeable to the sated appetite—a true picture of all earthly enjoyments, and unlike heavenly nourishment, which, while it satiates, increases the desire and excites the craving for more.

I offered the Holy Sacrifice at the residence of Mr. Bernard Reilly, who had removed his family hither from Columbia to spend the summer. One of the first Catholic settlers, he resided in the city for nearly forty years, and identified himself in a great measure with the interests of Catholicity. He married Miss N. Means, who was led to embrace the faith, and who adorned it by a long life spent in the practice of piety and all good works. Entirely free from the devotional eccentricities of some converts, her life was uniform and conformable to the practices of religion, as if she had been born in the faith. She raised a numerous flock of children, and impressed on the mind of each the primary obligations of fidelity in the science of God. The greater part of them died, some in infancy and others after reaching the years of maturity. One son, William, still survives. Her eldest daughter, Catharine, married James N. Stein, whom I received into the Church, and who died about the year 1850. His brother occupied a hotel in Greenville, was a respectable merchant, and, though a non-Catholic, was always liberal in sentiment and courteous to the ministers of our creed. Mrs. Stein married secondly, and died at Jacksonville, Florida.

The next daughter, Cecilia, resides in the same place, and married Mr. McCants. Cornelia was united in marriage to Robert Lynch, the bishop's brother, who died after some years. His widow afterwards married C. T. Callan, a Catholic also. Alice, a sweet and gentle girl, died young, and appeared before the judgment-seat radiant with the piety and innocence of her unsullied youth. Mrs. Reilly died about 1875, advanced in years but still vigorous in mind. Her remains rest in the same vault with her children who had gone before, and who, it is to be hoped, received her soul into the tabernacles of the just, to which she had conducted them by teaching and example.

She survived her husband in her pious widowhood many years; he departed this life in or about 1864, about sixty-eight years of age. He had accumulated a considerable amount of property by industry and close application to business, and always bore the reputation of a fair, honest man; minded his own business without interfering with others—a wise way, which carried him safely through life. Afflicted for many years with a lingering, incurable disease which confined him to his room, he bore his affliction with patience and resignation, and was fortified with the last sacraments in the hour of his death. Having suffered during life, he was mercifully spared the additional infliction of outliving the loss of his property, and died before Sherman's army, like a destroying angel, swept away every vestige of the accumulated industry of a lifetime.

From the early settlement of the country Irish pedlars have traversed it persistently, no dwelling, be it ever so humble or hidden 'mid rocks and mountains, escaping their searching industry. This has been the case all through the South. The occupation was as perilous as laborious; few localities are unstained by the blood of one of the friendless and unfortunate, while all retain the traditions of dark deeds of violence and midnight assassination. None ever earned money harder than the packmen. Their mode of disposing of their wares is of questionable morality, and can be reconciled in many cases to the principle of justice only by the fact that everybody is convinced they will cheat if they can; it is a species of gambling. It is claimed, very justly, that the loss of time, labor, and the risk of life entitle them to a fair recompense, and they obtain no more; also that they actually sell their goods cheaper than the city merchants. This they can afford to do, having no rent to pay and being exempt from tax and many other expenses connected with town life.

The affected greenness and child-like simplicity, bordering on idiocy, that disguises the cunning of the Irish Yankee are of the past. None but the unsophisticated negro will now mistake their tinsel for gold; neither will the guttural brogue, resembling very much the sound of brute animals, or the pretended ignorance of any civilized tongue induce the people to believe that they have just landed from the shores of the Green Isle, and their table-cloths genuine Belfast linen. Sometimes they are related to have renounced the use of both speech and reason, and suddenly, as if by miracle, everything an assailant of their creed or country says is answered with a power of argument and fluency of English that would be no discredit to the first Bishop of Charleston.

They never were known to have denied their religion; the attempt would be useless. They always clustered around a priest when met in their wanderings, contributed very freely to his support or to the building of a church, and went to confession. They certainly have created a very unfavorable impression on Southern society against their native country and the Catholic Church by false pretences, untruthfulness, and low cunning. It is a blessing that the business is disrupted and the evil diminished.

Railroads are great civilizers; the number of country stores at cross-roads and the heavy county taxation have rendered the employment unprofitable and abolished it, except in remote localities beyond the reach of modern improvements. *Othello's occupation is gone!* I have known exceptions to the general class—men who were honorable, pious, and truthful; besides deserving the protection of God and gaining respect for their religion and their country, they fared better and accumulated more money, illustrating the proverb that "honesty is the best policy." Bishop Reynolds declined an invitation to an entertainment of Sam Lover on Irish eccentricities, which were but caricatures of the natural characters, adding: "I can entertain no respect for one who attempts to raise money by exposing his own countrymen to the ridicule of strangers and exciting laughter at their expense, be his representations true or false." The travelling merchants repeatedly forced the sale of their wares by intimidation, when they could do so with impunity; or, if it suited their purpose better, became mute as dumb beasts, gnawed with their teeth plank palings, tore down fences like raving maniacs, perpetrated many antics inconceivably ridiculous and almost incredible to those who had not witnessed them. In towns and among communities who had witnessed no other specimens of my countrymen I was gazed at with extreme curiosity, and candidly asked if ditchers, pedlars, and railroad hands did not constitute the Irish race exclusively. After I had spoken at a public meeting in Columbus, Ga., an Episcopal minister complimented me by remarking in his speech that "*it was his opinion* that an Irishman was as capable of receiving an education as the natives of any other country!" The masses of our countrymen are poor, to be sure; it is not their fault, and blameless poverty is no disgrace. But we detest any attempt to retrieve our condition by means both dishonest and unworthy of our ancestors, our country, and our religion. If our forefathers had had the baseness to betray their country and their God, their children had not pined under the reproach of poverty and ignorance.

Among the masses of non-Catholics in this country few attach themselves to one church in preference to another from a conviction of the truth of its doctrines or their superior claim to credibility; the comparison is rarely made, and at most the contrast is confined to one or two points. The motives of adherence are the same which influence the Turk in adhering to the Koran, and would justify the heathen in persisting in his idolatry—the accidental circumstances of birth or locality. The latter is the principal motive-cause in the South. Every settlement has its own favorite denomination. Each new-comer is expected to conform under the penalty of exclusion from cordial relations, or the odium of heterodoxy, or the starting of a *new religion*. There are Methodist settlements, which are the most liberal, and Presbyterians, and Baptists. The latter is the prevailing sect in all this region, for no reason that I could ascertain beyond the abundance of its waters. By personal experience I have found them to be the most prejudiced against Catholicity; in this respect they are all "Hardshells" and no "Softshells." By a startling device of the arch-enemy, they exclude from the kingdom of heaven the innocents—those to whom it belongs by a special right under the covenant, and who have not forfeited it by personal transgressions. *Suffer little children to come unto me and forbid them not*, is a divine mandate. They corrupt the Scriptures and refer the generic pronoun to adults only. *Tis* in Greek and *Quis* in Latin mean man, woman, or child, and is fairly rendered in English by "any man, a man, or any one"; they are all equivalent. Their acceptation would exclude women equally as children. In like manner they limit the meaning of baptize to one mode only—that of immersion, without any foundation in the etymology of the word; for it implies any application of water to the body which can be deemed a cleansing or washing. King James's Bible, a corrupt translation made by pseudo reformers to sustain their novelties, for which there was no authority in written or unwritten teachings, is justly condemned, not for its many errors, but for not having translated the word $\beta\alpha\pi\tau\iota\xi\epsilon\iota\nu$ to "immerse," and a new translation demanded in the interest of this error and for the purpose of condemning the other forms of baptism—by aspersion or infusion—thus attempting to force the Word of God into an advocacy of error and pervert it to their own condemnation. Each form was practised; all the Church demands is that the water should be sufficiently copious to constitute the matter of the sacrament. The corruption of the Scriptures to accommodate them to errors was an old plan, and practised by heretics from the beginning. Even in the early ages St. Jerome affirms that the Rabbis had perverted the Bible so far as to have destroyed the strongest prophecies proving the divinity of our Lord. At the present day, when our friends the Jews are reading the Hebrew Bible in their synagogues on the Sabbath, they fondly believe it is pure and free from error, when the fact is it is as false and corrupt as the version of King James or any other modern falsification of the Scriptures. Luther condemned his own, and maintained there was not a correct translation of the Bible in all Christendom.

The Baptists adhere to the baptism of John, whom they claim as their founder, using the poetic license of Virgil in describing Æneas as the contemporary of Dido, or the Freemasons in electing Hiram grand master. John's was not Christian baptism, and his disciples were baptized by the apostles, which would be a sacrilege if it had been the Christian rite. What became of the body or when did it exist? Where were the Baptists during fifteen centuries after the announcement of the Gospel? John of Leyden, a tailor, in the year 1524 founded the Baptist Church in Münster, Westphalia. The antiquity of the sect is not proven by the fact that their mode of baptizing was occasionally used in the beginning; to maintain that similarity in one or more points constitutes an identity destroys all individuality, induces the most ludicrous conclusions, effaces every line of distinction in physical and intellectual existence, and leads to pantheism. The history of the world, that has noted all human events and transmitted to us every change in religion and government, has not been able to discover it before this date. Like those streams which bury themselves in the bowels of the mountains and run amid the chambers of the earth, some lost for ever from human sight and others breaking out again into the light of day, whose history, like a confessional secret, no man knoweth, the Baptists' waters were hidden, denying a drop to all Christians for that long period of time, and now grudgingly refreshing only a few aged, world-weary sinners.

The tenets evidently overthrow the entire Christian system and entirely deny the necessity of baptism in every form; for if our Lord established an ordinance for universal observance under the severest penalty and made its observance impracticable under given circumstances, he would damn without a cause and reprobate without a crime. How can the aged, the sick, the dying, the prisoner, and many others be baptized? Either it is not necessary at all, or God has rejected those unfortunates and all others for centuries who were not validly baptized according to their opinion, giving a command which it was impossible to observe, overthrowing the object of his Son's mission, and denying his declaration "*that he willeth the salvation of all men, and none should perish.*" They assert practically the tenets of election and reprobation more forcibly than the Calvinists, depriving the Father of Mercies of all his love and justice, and rendering man's condition as desperate as Satan's—renewing the mythology of the ancients by placing the human race in the position of Tantalus, up to the chin in limpid waters which sportingly escape the burning lip, as if its angel were a mocking fiend.

The baptized children of all other denominations go to heaven, while they ignorantly condemn their millions of innocents, banish them from the light of God's face, which is called darkness or the privation of the beatific vision, a loss which we cannot appreciate, though, with St. Thomas, the Church believes they are free from the pains of sense and enjoy God by reflection or in the abstract. I have met a great deal of sincerity and honesty of opinion among these people.

Although there are educated men among their ministers, they are not the most popular in rural districts, where illiterate men are preferred as preachers, through whom the spirit is supposed to speak directly, whereas the former only dispense their learning. While on a mission in Georgia, near Covington, in 1845, I remained one night with a Baptist minister, a very kind and simple man, who treated me courteously and asked me to offer family prayer. In relating the history of his life he said his father was a poor man, had seven sons, of which he was the youngest, and, being uneducated, he was compelled to preach the Gospel to obtain a support. They are expected to read the first chapter that presents itself on opening the Bible, and elucidate it without the least preparation. These sermons are rare specimens of exegesis, and are often standing pleasantries over the settlement. It is related of one whose orthography was much at fault that, having chosen this· for his text, "You strain at a gnat and swallow a camel," he read it thus: "*You strain at a gate and swallow a saw-mill.*"

Father Folchi spent some time on this mission. After having labored ten years on the several missions of the diocese with unsurpassed zeal and fidelity, in consequence of ill-health he retired to the Jesuit College at Santa Clara, California, regretted by both clergy and laity.

The following extracts, furnished by a letter of this distinguished missionary to the writer, will interest the reader not only from the information which they convey but in showing how much the public mind has changed in favor of Catholicity since the close of the civil war. Like Governor Wise in Virginia and Hon. A. H. Stephens in Georgia, in years past, his Excellency Ex-Governor Benjamin F. Perry now defends the rights of his Catholic fellow-citizens in South Carolina. By such statesmen only can our government be preserved and its blessings perpetuated.

Rev. A. M. Folchi was born in Rome, Italy, in the year 1834, made his studies in the Roman College, where he took the three degrees, and at an early age joined the Society of Jesus. He was sent to Maryland in 1853, and after three years was recalled to Europe and was appointed Professor of Theology at the University of Innspruck, Tyrol. He was ordained priest in the Cathedral of Vienna in 1864. In consequence of feeble health, he was dispensed for a time from the community life, and in 1867 accepted a mission from Bishop Lynch in Charleston. He was entrusted with the care of the colored people, and organized the church and congregation amid many difficulties. He also had charge of the Italians, which, unhappily, he found a difficult and unproductive mission, on account of secret societies which opposed all his labors.

After several years of untiring service in the city, he was attacked by the yellow fever and was reduced to the last extremity. On his convalescence he was sent to take charge of all the out-missions in the up-country as far as Greenville, embracing Newberry, York, Chester, Fairfield, Edgefield, Barnwell, Beaufort—in short, two-thirds of the State and a section of North Carolina, now forming three or four separate missions. He had as many as thirty different stations, preached and administered the sacraments, and made several converts, prominent among whom was a distinguished German physician residing at Williston, Edgefield County, who expired shortly after his baptism. The devoted father continues:

"Seeing the necessity of building a few churches, when we

could gather a certain number of Catholics, I began with Greenville Court-house, when, the few and very poor Catholics not being able to stand the expense, the Protestants offered their assistance with much alacrity and generosity. I was almost importuned, I may say, by their entreaties to have a church ; of course, they wanted immigration in their thrifty and charming town. I engaged two Protestant gentlemen of respectability to go around for the subscriptions; in a couple of days they took in about $2,000, from $20 down to $5 ; even two ministers put in their names.

"While the Greenvillers were highly commending and encouraging this action of the citizens, a Baptist preacher from the surrounding country came out in the *Enterprise* furiously against it and the Catholic Church, and warning loudly his brethren against the danger of fostering such projects, and, *horribile dictu*, that some, besides, of the Protestant religion should contribute towards the erection of it, etc. Ex-Governor Perry took up the gauntlet in our favor, and on my next visit to Greenville I found that the public attention had been taken up with a warm discussion on the subject of the Catholic Church, till then little spoken of or known at all in that locality, and that Governor Perry had treated the subject very ably as far as could be expected from a non-Catholic, exploding the bigoted and narrow-minded objections brought forward, and showing how advantageous it would prove to their community to have a Catholic place of worship. The preacher left the field well cured, and of course this helped to do a great deal of good in our favor. One of the gentlemen that collected the subscriptions, Mr. V. E. McBee, gave me one acre lot for the church, in a fine locality. Meanwhile, service was held at the unoccupied mansion of Mr. Choice, one of the most distinguished non-Catholic gentlemen of the place, whilst he denied the use of it for the same purpose to a Protestant minister.

"I made the plans in concert with an architect in Charleston, and with the approbation and blessing of the Bishop I set to work. The church is 67 by 35 in the clear ; can seat 230 persons. The contract with Captain Cable was about $2,630. He was to furnish blinds, sashes, and doors, hardware and altar; pews extra. The whole cost about $3,500. It was dedicated to Our Lady of the Sacred Heart of Jesus by Bishop Lynch on the 15th October, 1876, being started and completed entirely in four months. Rev. W. A. Clarke, S.J., from Baltimore, delivered one of his masterpieces of eloquence for the occasion. There were, besides, from Charleston, several clergymen, a batch of the cathedral altar-boys, and Mrs. Barbot, of St. Mary's, with a very select choir, all volunteers. It was a grand day for Greenville; they had never had such a treat.

"I forgot to mention that in the month of May we had a *fête champetre*, or garden feast, on McBee's lawn, which was a grand success. Although the move came from us, still the non-Catholics took it up with a wonderful alacrity, and with a few exceptions the active members, as well as contributors, were almost all non-Catholics. Nay, I heard some Protestant ladies had already proposed among themselves to get up something of the kind to help us. I went collecting also in Charleston, in the spring of last year, to pay off the debt left. I wish to mention that I was very kindly received and helped by Captain Ryan and his crew, of the ill-fated U. S. steamer *Huron*, then lying in Charleston. The Bishop also, notwithstanding his many pressing wants, contributed generously towards finishing the payment.

"I thought the next in turn to have a church should be Anderson Court-house. That congregation had lately increased considerably by a number of Polish families come fresh from their unfortunate country to work in that county. The poor people were famishing for a church. Some funds were already put up for the purpose, but would not be sufficient. I tried to console them by showing them, at one of my visits, a plan for their church, which indeed was my wish and desire to build for them, but was not able at the present. The thing remained so when I left that dear mission. It was a laborious one, of course, considering my feeble health, the extent of territory and the rough nature of it, the few poor and thinly-scattered members. But still how great is the consolation of the missionary in attending those poor but good and fervent Catholics, who would wish to be able to show their gratitude for what you do for them—for coming to visit them, and offer the holy sacrifice, and bring the comforts of religion into their most lonely and poor abodes!

"I had the good fortune also of being the feeble instrument of the conversion of two malefactors, whom I attended at the scaffold, one of them at Chester Court-house, a light-colored man, a desperate character, guilty of several crimes. He had been visited with no effect by the different Protestant ministers of the town. Almost given to despair, he gave his assent to the suggestion of Judge Mackay's accomplished wife, a Catholic, to send for the priest. I went immediately; there was no time to lose, only two days before the execution. In brief, God granted him the grace of conversion to himself and to the true religion. I baptized him the evening previous to the execution, and went with him to the scaffold, when the last use he made of his hands before being tied was to bless himself before the immense multitude of people from the surrounding country and counties. It astonished every one to see such a change as he manifested, as well in his devotional actions before dying as in the very sensible speech he made to the dark crowd.

"And, before concluding, I shall mention also that I paid a couple of very satisfactory visits to the Catawba Indians, York County, who had never heard even anything of the Catholic religion. The last time I preached to them, and explained the first notions of our duties to God and of our religion, they paid considerably close attention. I got them to sing afterwards, and then they got me to do the same. They eagerly accepted some pictures and catechisms, which they proposed to read or have read to them, and study the religion. I enclose a letter sent me afterwards by the old chief before leaving South Carolina.

I made several attempts to get to their place, and was only a few miles from it; but the cold weather, the rising of the river, and failing to get a horse after walking as far as the river, prevented me from visiting them again. As I informed the bishop of their good intentions, I expect he provided for them.

LETTER FROM THE OLD CATAWBA INDIAN CHIEF IN SOUTH CAROLINA.

"YORK COUNTY, S. C., October 6, 1877.

"REV. A. M. FOLCHI:

"DEAR SIR: I embrace the present opportunity of writing an answer to your very kind and welcome letter. This leaves me and all the people in moderate health, hoping it may find you enjoying the like blessing.

"We would have liked to have had another visit from you on your return. All we can say is, God's will be done. As far as I can learn, they all expressed a great desire to hear you again. All that I have spoken to about your denomination and faith appeared very well satisfied. We want you to return, or else write to your most worthy bishop to send some other priest of the Catholic Church to our poor nation. Although we are poor, yet we would like to be remembered by the Church. Please excuse my not writing to you sooner; I could not get any one to write the letter for me, and therefore you must excuse me. Please write as soon as you can, and let us all know what is the result. I will say we want you to return to us.

I will come to a close by asking you to remember us all in Christ.

"I am, your most obedient servant,

"WILLIAM GEORGE, *Chief*.

"Please direct to Rock Hill, South Carolina."*

The diocese of Charleston possesses at this date (1878)

---

* The author attends this mission at present.

fifteen priests and as many churches; seven or eight academies and schools, conducted by the Ursulines and the Sisters of Mercy; a number of day-schools for boys, conducted by the Brothers of Mary; three female religious institutions, and a devoted Catholic population of about ten thousand souls. Having rebuilt her churches, and repaid many of her losses, and gathered several into the fold with the above numbers, and under the kindly feelings and growing liberality of the Carolinians, who at last have come to recognize her as their own domestic institution, her progress will be rapid; she will scatter her blessings everywhere, from the mountains to the seaboard, and the names of England and other bishops and clergymen will be as revered in the history of the State as those of Calhoun, Hampton, and Perry.

CHAPTER XII.

VICARIATE OF NORTH CAROLINA—WILMINGTON, NEW BERNE, RALEIGH, FAYETTEVILLE, ETC., ETC.

Vicariate of North Carolina : Wilmington—New Berne—Raleigh—Fayetteville, etc., etc.—His Grace Most Rev. James Gibbons, D.D., the first Vicar-Apostolic, afterwards Bishop of Richmond, Archbishop of Baltimore, and Primate—His Missions, Labors, Converts, Churches, Writings, etc., etc.—Establishes the Sisters of Mercy—Regrets for his Transfer to Richmond—Very Rev. Thomas Murphy, V.F.—Life, Labors, and Death—Very Rev. James A. Corcoran, D.D.—Resident Catholics—Fathers Gross and Moore—Missions—Congregations of Converts—New Berne—Fayetteville—Raleigh—Early History—First Priests—Catholics—Rev. Peter Whelan says the First Mass in Raleigh—Rev. Dr. Ryan—Know-Nothingism—Mr. and Mrs. Murray—A Martyr to Intolerance—E. D. Griffin, his Character—Rev. Thos. Quigley—Purchases the Baptist Church—Its History, Subscribers, Dedication—Archbishop Hughes—Bishops Lynch and McNeirny—Vicar-General L. P. O'Connell—Fathers Gross, H. P. Northrop, J. J. Reilly, J. B. White, Fr. O'Keefe—An Unpleasantness—A Hope Still—Ex-Governor W. W. Holden—Distinguished Converts and Catholics in North Carolina—Dr. Ives—Judge Gaston—Biography—Chief-Justice M. E. Manly—Judges Heath and Moore—Catholicity finds its Way more Recently into Western North Carolina—Five Churches—The Benedictines—But few Catholic Negroes—Causes—Their Character—Habits—Efforts for their Conversion.

NORTH CAROLINA was the first part of America settled by an English-speaking colony, and as early as 1585. It embraces nearly every variety of soil and climate peculiar to the United States, and abounds with ores and mineral springs. It is nearly as large as the State of New York, containing an area of forty-five thousand square miles and a population of one million inhabitants, a thrifty, intelligent, and law-abiding people.

The Methodists, Baptists, and Presbyterians are the leading denominations. Catholics are in the minority, scarcely numbering two thousand. The State formed part of the original diocese of Charleston until created a vicariate by his Holiness Pius IX., by a Bull dated March 3, 1868. The Rt. Rev. James Gibbons, D.D., Bishop of Adrymatum *in partibus*, was the first vicar-apostolic.

He was born in Baltimore July 13, 1834, and was baptized in the cathedral. He was educated in Ireland, and graduated (1857) at St. Charles's College, Maryland, completing his theological course at St. Mary's Seminary, in 1861. He was ordained at St. Mary's Chapel the same year by the late Archbishop Francis Patrick Kenrick, D.D. He was assistant to the late Father Dolan at St. Patrick's, Baltimore, and subsequently appointed pastor of St. Bridget's, Canton. He was also secretary of Archbishop Spalding, by whom he was also consecrated in the cathedral of his native city, at the same time with Rt. Rev. Dr. Becker, Bishop of Wilmington, Delaware, August 16, 1868. He was translated to the see of Richmond July 30, 1872. He administered the vicariate until October 3, 1877, when he was translated to the archdiocese of Baltimore. Very Rev. F. Jansen is now the administrator.

In North Carolina the Catholics are more distinguished for their piety and social standing than for their numbers. In these respects they rival the faithful in the sister States. With so many enlightened Catholics in the first ranks of society, little prejudice can exist. A desire to learn the truth and embrace it is very common, and at this time a more encouraging field for missionary labor nowhere exists in the Republic. *The harvest is ripe, but the laborers are few.*

A zealous and active bishop, to continue the labors of Archbishop Gibbons, would reap an abundant harvest of souls.

It is no disparagement to the eminent men who preceded him, and whose lives adorn our annals, to say that he advanced the cause of Catholicity in the State during his brief administration in the most eminent degree. The residence of a bishop in his see is unquestionably of prime necessity for the interests of religion. The evils of absenteeism, in this case, are no less detrimental to the cause of the faith than of the landlords to the prosperity of Ireland. The progress of Catholicity will be retarded in a region remote from the episcopal chair and ruled as an outlying province. This was the cause of many of the evils of the first missions, remedied only after a thorough organization and the increase of new sees.

The transfer of Bishop Gibbons was universally regretted. His zeal, his eloquence, and his writings met all the demands of public sentiment and expectation. The amiability of his disposition and his unaffected manners endeared him to all classes, conciliated the feelings of the people, and won him friends and admirers. The Carolinians, from the mountains to the seaboard, were proud of their own bishop, the Catholic Bishop of North Corolina. Many flocked from all sides to listen to his eloquent sermons. In the providence of God he was elevated to a higher dignity, and for the interests of the Church at large; yet a more honorable position than the one vacated could nowhere be found in the American Church.

He is a man of the medium height, with a fair complexion, lightly built, and slender—the youngest bishop, and now the youngest archbishop. In the prime and vigor of life, and blessed with a sound constitution, he gives promise of many years of usefulness in the sublime dignity to which he has been called. Great candor, solid piety, extensive learning, tireless activity, and kindness of heart are leading features in the character of this distinguished prelate. Under his guidance religion will flourish in the Republic. In the wider sphere of action in which he moves his renewed efforts in her behalf will exercise a greater influence.

After having succeeded the lamented Bishop McGill at Richmond, his jurisdiction stretched from the Potomac to distant Georgia, and his influence among both orders of the hierarchy was proportionate to its extent. A prelate of unquestionable moderation and reliability, of eminent administrative powers and a recognized champion of the faith, who refuted error without wounding charity or interrupting the amenities of social intercourse, he was a meet successor to a Carroll, a Kenrick, and a Spalding. The bishops of the province, with singular unanimity, chose him the coadjutor of the distinguished Archbishop Bayley, whose health was rapidly declining; the appointment was readily ratified by the Holy See on the demise of the former prelate. Dr. Gibbons succeeded with universal acclamation. Having been born in the city, baptized, ordained, and consecrated in the Cathedral, he certainly has a right to know his people and they also to know him.

He received the Sacrament of Confirmation from his Grace Archbishop MacHale, at an unusually early age and in the first blush of boyhood. The child accompanied his pious parents on a visit to their native land. After some time he, with many others, were being prepared for the sacrament before the advent of the archbishop. To his great disappointment, James Gibbons was rejected for the sole cause of deficiency of age. Without human counsel, the sprightly boy mingled with the favored group, and, being presented by the presiding priest, received with them the seven-fold gifts. The act was prophetic, as though the Holy Ghost had marked him for the plenitude of his graces at an age that excited the admiration of the Fathers of the Vatican Council.

When he was consecrated for the vicariate in 1868 he found only two or three priests, about the same number of humble churches, and a thousand Catholics, scattered at different points all over North Carolina. He had no arm to lean on but God; he was all-sufficient. His difficulties can never be portrayed. The amount of labor he was capable of accomplishing is incredible. He travelled night and day, and by all modes of conveyance, new and obsolete. His visitations were incessant. He knew all the adult Catholics in North Carolina personally and called them by name. He administered the sacraments in garrets and in the basements of houses, preached and lectured throughout, always ready and prepared for every emergency. In the meantime he opened a school and taught therein, conducted a written controversy, wrote elegant pastorals and the most practical and least offensive doctrinal treatise that appeared within the century. He received many converts into the Church and entire congregations, established the Benedictine Order in North Carolina, the Sisters of Mercy in Wilmington, ordained some dozen zealous priests, erected a half-dozen new churches, and opened several schools.

It is evident that this vast amount of labor, signally blessed by God and performed within so short a time, could have been accomplished only by a man of prayer and a devoted servant of our Lord.

Under the altered aspect of controversy, "The Faith of our Fathers" meets the wants of society, and is adapted to public taste. It contains a clear exposition of all the doctrines of the Church misrepresented or denied by non-Catholics. The several points are explained, and their truth indicated in a concise manner; the leading arguments are drawn from reason, the Holy Scriptures, and the writings of the Fathers of the golden age of Christianity; they are conclusive and unanswerable. Free from the repulsiveness of dry disputation, the book is strongly argumentative, while its occult power solves all difficulties and refutes the popular objections against the faith. A few copies annually distributed among the members of the legislature and the jurists at the sittings of the supreme court would, ere long, enlighten the entire State. A small sum for the propagation of the faith could not be invested more profitably than in this manner.

As a pulpit orator the archbishop has few equals in the country. His delivery is graceful and pleasing, his manner polished, and his voice clear as the sound of a silver bell. His sermons are pregnant with deep thought, and glowing with his own fervor and sincerity. None tire of listening to him; clearness of utterance, distinctness of statement, and close reasoning are the leading traits of all his discourses. He assisted at the Council of the Vatican;

he was the youngest bishop in the august assembly, but old in virtue and experience. Activity is a dominant feature in the character of this eminent prelate; he is the enemy of procrastination, and will accomplish noiselessly the most important enterprises in a shorter time than would be required by another to think about them.

In 1869, having purchased a suitable house and all other necessary adjuncts, he procured a colony from the Order of the Sisters of Mercy, of Charleston, and established them in Wilmington. This was an incalculable blessing to the citizens and a lasting monument to the zeal of the archbishop, and will ever make his memory dear to the inhabitants. He also opened in the same year a day-school for boys in the basement of the church, in which he taught, and which met merited patronage; his labors were coextensive with the State.

The Rev. Mark Gross, a native of Baltimore, and brother of the distinguished Bishop of Savannah, was the partner of the bishop's labors from the beginning, and is at this time the pastor of Wilmington, assisted by the Rev. Patrick Moore, a young, zealous priest ordained about three years ago.

The Church of the Good Shepherd, at Mount Olives, was erected by Father Gross, and dedicated in November, 1876; the congregation consists chiefly of converts baptized by the zealous pastor. Laurinburgh, Tillington, Smithville, Green's Station, and Newton Grove are all visited by Fathers Gross and Moore. In the latter place a new church, St. Mark's, was recently dedicated; the congregation are all converts, and number over a hundred people.

It now becomes necessary to turn back a few years, connect the past with the present, and give the early history of the establishment of the church and missions of Wilmington. Very Rev. Thomas Murphy, V.F., was the first pastor. He was a native of County Carlow, Ireland, studied some time in the celebrated college of his native place. After the nomination of Dr. Clancy to the coadjutorship, under Dr. England, the youthful aspirant to the priestly dignity transferred his allegiance to the diocese of Charleston, completed his studies in the seminary with marked ability, and was ordained in or about 1836.

After having exercised the functions of the priesthood in the Colleton district, he was stationed in eastern North Carolina in 1838. Fayetteville was his headquarters, and he resided a great portion of his time in the family of the late John Kelly. New Berne, Raleigh, Washington, and all eastern and middle North Carolina formed his parish for many years. At one time he was the only priest within the limits of the entire State. He built churches, made several converts, and kept the thinly-scattered members of the flock in the faith. Whatever of labor, privation, and suffering fell to the lot of any priest in the diocese may with justice be claimed for Father Murphy. At one time or another he domiciled in every Catholic family on his missions, called each one by name, shared in their sorrows, rejoiced in their prosperity, was loved and esteemed as none ever was and few can expect to be. His name was a household word, and his memory one of the sweetest reminiscences in the early history of Catholicity in the Carolinas and Georgia.

Though small in numbers, the Catholics were an influential body in the State and respected for their intelligence and moral worth. He was the peer of the best. He was created Vicar-Forane by Bishop England. In 1844 he was transferred to Georgia to heal an unpleasantness.

His great common-sense, peculiar tact, and gentleness rendered him a general peacemaker, and whenever the occasion arose his services were invoked for this purpose by his superiors. The dove was sent out on the angry waters, and always returned with the olive-branch of peace. When pronouncing a funeral sermon over his cold remains, Bishop Lynch, after expatiating on the amiability of his disposition, compressed his social qualities in a single sentence: "In his breast he possessed a woman's heart."

Having accomplished his mission in Georgia, he was restored, after a year's absence, to his devoted flock in North Carolina. About 1846· he·was stationed in Wilmington, and forthwith began the erection of a church; hitherto there was none. This had been from the commencement the least important station in the State, containing but a very few poor Irish immigrants; the town was sickly besides. But no Catholic family, however poor or humble, was neglected; these were periodically visited, together with the soldiers at the garrison at Smithville.

After a few years the Church of St. Thomas was finished, with a commodious parsonage and residence attached to the rear of the church. The situation is elevated and the lot the most eligible in the city. The church is a neat and solid brick building, sufficiently large to accommodate the faithful. The edifice, lot, organ, and all the other accompaniments cost a large amount, collected principally outside the diocese. New York, New Orleans, and all the intermediate cities were canvassed; the pavements of many a long and weary street were worn by the weary step of the self-sacrificing priest. His labors were crowned with success. The church was dedicated about 1849 by Very Rev. P. N. Lynch, D.D., assisted by the venerable Father O'Neill, of Savannah.

Wilmington, like all southern seaports, is periodically devastated by the yellow fever. In 1862 the plague ravaged the city with unprecedented severity, and hurried multitudes to an early grave. Many fled; gloom and sadness hung like the funeral-robe of death over the doomed city. Worn out by the incessant visitation of the sick and dying, the priest was attacked and his recovery despaired of. In utter abandonment to the will of God, Very Rev. Dr. Corcoran and three Sisters of Mercy hurried to the aid of the stricken pastor and afflicted flock.

Father Murphy slowly recovered and rallied for a time, but he never more regained his former strength, and, after lingering in a state of semi-convalescence for a year, he died, July 12, 1863. I was summoned to his bedside, but he had expired before my arrival. He had been visited a few days previously by Rev. T. I. Sullivan, on his way to the army hospital in Virginia. He was fifty-five years old, and twenty-seven years a missionary priest.

He was buried in the basement of the church on the feast of St. Bonaventure, July 14. The Requiem Mass was offered by Dr. Moore, the present Bishop of St. Augustine, who was connected by marriage relationship with the illustrious dead. Bishop Lynch delivered the funeral discourse. The church was filled with mourning members of the congregation, numerous citizens, and sympathizing ministers of other denominations. His death was lamented by the faithful all over the diocese. He was laid to rest and his honored grave hallowed by incense and prayer. The tears of the old and the young mingled with the white sand of his loved Carolina as it dropped lightly from anointed hand on the coffin-lid of the toil-worn missionary and beloved priest.

He was a man of comely appearance, with regular, handsome features, hair originally black but now frosted, and above the medium height. His face was candid and open as the broad day; his dress was neat, grave, and clerical, and his manners polished; his acquaintance was courted by the most distinguished people. Religion was the basis of his character and lent an additional charm to a disposition naturally gentle and conciliatory. Always at the altar, regular and edifying in the performance of his priestly obligations, he left behind him the memory of shining deeds and a venerable name. He was a ripe scholar, a graceful and fascinating public speaker.

My intercourse with him was intimate and interrupted only by death. He was always pious, always cheerful, and even playful. He was distinguished for two leading traits of character. The first was a singularly sweet and mild temper. Though severely tried, often wronged, and even harrassed, I never heard him utter a severe word against any human being. He found a ready excuse for the frailty of others in thoughtlessness or in some other palliating feature of human weakness. The other trait, though not of so high an order, is rarer still among men. This was a never-failing, genial manner—a cheerfulness welling up from the depths of his soul. The most sorrowful could quaff animation and life at its borders. He was grave when graveness was becoming, but never peevish. He dispelled gloom and languor whenever it approached him as if with a sudden burst of sunshine. He had an exhaustless stock of anecdotes, and he was inimitable in telling them.

The boisterous main, that sings loud refrains over the remains of many a gallant seafarer on the fatal shore of Carolina, will sob lowly as it touches the tomb of Father Thomas Murphy, the dove of the sanctuary. Sweet spirit, rest in Jesus!

In 1869 a bishop's throne graced the sanctuary of St. Thomas's Church; its occupant was destined by providence to fill the highest ecclesiastical position in America as Primate of the Church. He was inaugurated by Archbishop Spalding in the presence of many distinguished clergymen. I beheld the splendors of the American Church clustered in that humble temple. The golden cross of the first Bishop and Patriarch of the United States was shining on the breast of his distinguished successor; the mitre of North Carolina adorned the unwrinkled brow of her long-sought bridegroom; gorgeous vestments streamed from the shoulders of aged missionary priests; the altar, like the pillar in the desert, was a blaze of light; a devout people were prostrate in adoration before the Lord of Hosts, seated on his earthly throne in their midst. On witnessing the scene I thought how the soul of that first missionary whose remains were slumbering beneath must have exulted on his seat of bliss on high, and joined with kindred spirits in giving praise to God, who had so abundantly crowned his labors. "Thus shall every man be blessed who feareth the Lord. Glory and riches are in his house, and his memory shall be in perpetual benediction."

After the death of Father Murphy, Very Rev. Dr. Corcoran was appointed pastor, and held the position five years, until the arrival of the bishop in 1868.

The most prominent Catholics at this period were Mrs. Fulton, a convert, and her sister-in-law, Mrs. Price (her husband joined the Church and two of her daughters the community of the Sisters of Mercy), Mrs. Maguire and her sister, Mrs. Judge (names dear to the church), the Montagues, the Baxters, the Kings, and many others whose names are called in heaven.

Some Catholic immigrants settled on Pamlico Sound as early as 1737, and Bicknell says they had a priest. They disappeared at the Revolution without leaving any records; tradition is silent on the subject.

At the creation of the diocese of Charleston in 1820, and during many years after, all eastern North Carolina formed but one mission, was served successively by the same clergymen, and has the same history. Nearly every priest in the diocese, at one period of his life, was stationed here; their names and the time of their ministrations are found in all the records, and their history is already written in other connections.

The Catholics were few, but steadfast in their religion. In the entire region scarcely one lost the faith. The Church maintained her own, gained moderately by conversions, but without signal increase. The causes are already detailed, and they were equally operative in all the Cotton States. The first church in the diocese is said to have been built at New Berne by the Gaston family, and previous to the Revolution. I have ascertained by valuable information, furnished by the zealous missionary, Rev. J. J. Reilly, that Bishop England made his first appearance at New Berne May 24, 1821, six months after his arrival in Charleston. The bishop during his visits, from 1821 to 1824, performed the duties of missionary priest. The first priest in New Berne was Rev. Father Cleary, who came from Ireland to visit a kinsman in 1811. He died shortly after, and his remains are buried in the Episcopal churchyard.

Father Carney, from Baltimore, visited the mission in 1819. Rev. Francis O'Donohue was the first clergyman permanently stationed in North Carolina; this was in 1824. He retired in 1827, and was succeeded by Father Sennen (Dr. Cooper), a convert, who, from rigorous fasting during the Lent of that year, was attacked with brain fever. He was conducted to Charleston in a state of mental derangement, and recovered his faculties while on his journey. His recovery was miraculous. His austerities were frightful; his first fervor rendered him a meet companion for Sts. Paul or Macarius in Thebais. The bishop and Father O'Neill of Savannah, after having arrived at Wilmington, placed him on board the steamboat and withdrew for a short time. On their return they met him on the wharf perfectly restored, and anxiously enquiring about the past. While in the cabin, a lady passenger reproachingly remarked: "That's a crazy priest." Healing, like a flash of lightning, came with the reproach, and reason resumed her throne. An accomplished gentleman, he calmly approached and thanked the party for having been made the instrument of his instantaneous recovery by the tender compassion of our dear Lord. For further particulars I refer the reader to the chapter on Augusta, Georgia.

Rev. John Barry and Rev. A. Byrne were on this district between 1828 and 1830. John Kelly at this time conveyed three lots to Bishop England, and a church was built in the town of Fayetteville on said property.

Rev. R. S. Baker was the pastor in 1830 and again in 1834, Rev. Peter Whelan in 1832, Rev. Philip Gillick in 1836, Rev. Francis Farrel in 1837, Rev. Thos. Murphy and Rev. A. Doyle in 1838, for several years.

Bishop England, on a visit to New Berne in 1829, urged the building of a church. The congregation held a meeting and resolutions were passed sustaining the motion. The building was placed under contract, and finished the following year (1830). It is a plain but neat wooden structure, 60 by 40 feet in dimensions. With the furniture, organ, and paintings, it cost, including the building lot,

$6,500. The funds were provided by a legacy of Dr. Joseph H. Keys, of Warren County, who left a considerable sum to be equally divided between the Roman Catholic Church and the Episcopal Church in Eastern North Carolina. From this source the sum of $4,000 was received. The remainder was contributed chiefly by the following persons: Bishop England, William Gaston, John Devereux, Matthias E. Manly, Francis Lamotte, Peter Brayman, and Benjamin Goode.

The mission was attended by the following clergymen: Rev. Thomas Mullony, about two years, until 1840; he was born in County Limerick, studied at Chambly, Canada, was ordained in Charleston in 1838, and died at Columbus, Georgia, in 1844; he was about thirty-two years of age; the Rev. Edward Quigley, from 1840 to 1844; Rev. P. J. Coffey, from 1844 to 1849; Rev. P. J. Dunn, between 1849 and 1853; Rev. C. J. Croghan, eleven years, from 1850 to 1861; Rev. Patrick McGowan, four years, between 1830 and 1844; Rev. Dr. Ryan, between 1853 and 1859. The Rev. Thomas Quigley succeeded Father Croghan, and spent eight years on this mission.

New Berne was captured by the United States forces in 1862, and Father Quigley's ministrations were impeded until the close of the war. During the last two years of the struggle Father Brüke, a military chaplain, and Father Willet, S.J., officiated at New Berne. Two Redemptorists, Father J. Enright and Father Gleason, were sent thither by Archbishop Kenrick at the close of hostilities. They took the church and parochial residence in custody and saved them from being destroyed, like the other places of worship in the town.

The first Mass ever celebrated in the city of Raleigh was by the Rev. Father Peter Whelan, about the year 1832, in a boarding-house kept by Matthew Shaw, a Presbyterian. A church was built here in 1834, known as the first church. It cost $800, and was dedicated by Bishop England, who often said Mass and preached therein. It was subsequently sold, and is now attached to the Yarborough Hotel.

Messrs. John O'Rourke, Murray, Kane, McGowan, and some Irish mechanics employed on the State-House liberally contributed to the payment of the expenses.

The writer is indebted to the Rev. J. B. White, the present zealous pastor, for the following interesting early history of this church: "Although the public was fully aware that a missionary priest occasionally visited the city, and that some sort of services were being held by the Catholics, yet the fact that they were about to build a church rendered the priest himself liable to insults and Catholics generally to petty persecutions. What was still more shocking to the local prejudices of the people, the wife of James Murray, who before her marriage was a member of a very large, respectable, and influential family, about that time became a zealous convert to the faith. This first conversion in the city, however, had the effect to allay the intense feeling of bitterness among the people, whose curiosity was by this time fearfully aroused. Nature had lavished upon this good lady a double share of genial goodness, which, being combined with true faith, and supported by the blessed sacraments of the Church, rendered her for the time being a protectress to the little band of Catholics of the city of Raleigh. Aided by her faithful husband, she often shielded the priest, for the time being, by hospitality and kindness. By patient rebuke, rather than by argument, she could always silence the enemies of the Church, hence the bitterest of the bitter would invariably hesitate to attack the Church in her presence. This good lady died, in the year 1868, as she had lived, a zealous, practical Catholic, and an untiring friend to the priest and the poor.

This little church was under the watchful care of the great and good Bishop England, of Charleston, South Carolina, who, after dedicating the church, about the year 1835, gave several sermons and lectures, as occasion would offer, thus instructing the citizens, who prior to this time were totally uninformed in Catholic doctrine. When visiting the city the Bishop was almost invariably the guest of Mr.

John O'Rourke, who was always the recognized friend of both bishop and priest, and whose ample means afforded him an opportunity of showing his generosity. Although married to a Methodist lady, his house, heart, and purse were ever open both to the church and priest. Father Whelan was succeeded by Father McGowan about the year 1840, who for three or four years attended the spiritual wants of the faithful at Raleigh, who numbered at this time about one hundred and fifty souls. He spent the greater part of his time in Raleigh, and had good cause to congratulate himself for the kindness received from the *whole* people, who held him in very high esteem. He was a man of great tact and genius, which, combined with piety, rendered his administration in Raleigh useful and long to be remembered. The State capitol was by this time entirely finished, and a large number of mechanics, who had been employed from a distance, returned to their homes in the North, a few having remained in Raleigh, among whom we may mention the names of Michael A. Prendergast, wife, and sister; John Kane, Patrick McGowan, and a very few others, making in all seventy-five souls. Father Dunn attended to their spiritual wants for some time at this period.

Rev. Dr. P. Ryan was stationed here in 1854, when Know-Nothingism was rampant in the town. Even the priest himself did not escape the fury of these infatuated persecutors. On one occasion, while passing one of the most public streets of the city, he was violently approached by one of the members of a Know-Nothing lodge with the threat of "death to the priest," and escaped by taking refuge in a Catholic house near by—the house of Michael A. Prendergast. Many other insults did this good priest endure from time to time, not only in Raleigh but in other parts of his mission. He was driven to the necessity on one occasion, while in Pittsborough, Chatham County, of calling upon the proprietors of the hotel for protection, being threatened by the mob with a coat of tar and feathers. On another occasion, while on his way to Fayetteville, he was refused a night's lodging in a public-house on the highway, which caused him considerable trouble to obtain lodging elsewhere, it being late in the evening. This was during the years 1855 and 1856, when no Catholic in this community, let him or her be ever so obscure or humble, escaped the ostracizing influence of Know-Nothingism.

James Murray was an Irishman of unreproachable character, and the favorite of all parties. Well known in the city, and for thirty-five consecutive years holding public positions of trust under Federal, State, county, and city authorities, he was, by the deliberate and combined influence of Know-Nothingism, dispossessed of each and every one of these different positions, so long held with honor to himself, his country, and his religion. Not satisfied with this, he was pursued still further, and successfully opposed in his efforts to secure a more humble position whereby he could obtain a living for himself and family. This was the crowning act by which the fiendish plans of the Know-Nothing Order were carried out in Raleigh, and, strange to say, this very act was their death-warrant in this locality. The people of Raleigh had long since learned that there was nothing to fear from Catholicism if James Murray was a fair representative of that faith. While without a murmur this good old 'Irish Catholic patiently submitted to these things, the people were the more inclined to pity, and to enquire what it all meant. The abuse was not the worst, by far, that this faithful old man was called upon to endure. While an official on duty in the court-house, court being in session, he was repeatedly struck on the top of his head with a large stone in the hands of a notorious Know-Nothing (still living), from the effects of which he in after-years lost his mind, and died in the lunatic asylum. The only punishment the assassin received for this diabolical act was a slight fine and imprisonment just long enough to cool off.

Father Ryan was at this time assisted more or less by all the Catholics of Raleigh, who numbered, perhaps, about 100 souls; his main support, however, depended upon John O'Rourke and E. D. Griffin. The latter, formerly of New York, was a convert from Episcopalianism, highly educated, and a man of considerable wealth. This good and zealous Catholic remained in Raleigh only a few months, however, owing to his conscientious scruples on the subject of negro slavery. He insisted that the priest, when in Raleigh, should remain in his house and partake of his hospitalities, besides contributing one hundred dollars annually to his support. He was also of great assistance in organizing and instructing the few Catholic children in the Sunday-school, which had been previously much neglected. He was by marriage connected with one of the most respectable families of Raleigh (the Heywood family), all of whom were Protestants. In fact, his zeal knew no bounds; his faith was truly remarkable for this or any other age. He "lived by faith," and would deny himself every comfort in order to instruct the enquirer after truth. He was always unhappy when not engaged in the performance of some office of Catholic charity, which he invariably performed under the direction and guidance of his priest, Dr. Ryan. There are many still living who bear inexpressible gratitude to him for his kind instructions, which in one case worthy of mention was the direct means of converting an entire family, three of whom he had the happiness of seeing enter the Church. The father and mother of this family were formerly Methodists, and were subsequently admitted to the Church, by Baptism and Confirmation, with their children, all of whom still reside in Raleigh. After spending a few months in Raleigh, this good man returned with his family to New York, where, about the year 1865 or 1866, he died as he had lived, full of Catholic zeal and faith.

After four years Dr. Ryan was recalled to Charleston, and the Rev. Thomas Quigley appointed his successor in 1859.

There being no priest's house in Raleigh, the discomforts at times were almost insupportable. The priest was very much opposed to the plan of going from house to house for his meals and lodging, as his predecessors had done. Board and lodging at the hotel while in Raleigh would consume more than his income, judging from the prospects before him. Hence he at once concluded to engage board at the hotel, and call upon Bishop Lynch, of Charleston, for whatever additional amount of money would be required to pay the same, and lodge as best he could in the church. His room was a part of the church steeple, partitioned off for the purpose, and a portion of the time his bed was an old sofa, loaned to him by some lady of the congregation. Having little or no heating arrangements, his health was much impaired during the winter season from cold and exposure. This was manifest to everybody; still he could not be induced to change his mode of living, until driven by necessity after the breaking out of the war. From this time to the close of his labors in Raleigh he was the welcome guest of John O'Rourke, Patrick Ferrall, and others.

After entering regularly upon the duties of his mission, his first great effort was to dispose of the old and secure a new church in a more suitable part of the city. He learned that the Baptists of Raleigh would sell their church, being in the act of building a new one. It was offered at a reduced figure, which, however, the sale of the present Catholic church and lot could not meet. Mr. Quigley, by great exertion, and aided by the bishop, realized the necessary sum. He also bought an additional lot adjoining the east end of the first purchase, thus rendering the property compact and entire.

About this time John O'Rourke donated one and a quarter acres on the eastern side of the city for the purpose of a graveyard, the faithful having been hitherto interred in unconsecrated ground. The same gentleman and John Kane also gave thirteen panels of wrought-iron railing, which they erected at their own expense in front of the church. Patrick McGowan and Patrick Linehan built a brick wall, coped with granite, running the entire length of the church on the north side. It cost $500, and was their individual contribution.

In 1849 the Baptist church in front of the State-House was purchased by Rev. Thomas Quigley, and fitted for Catholic service. The original cost was $2,250. Bishop Lynch contributed $950, and the congregation $920.

I subjoin the subscription-list for the purpose of recording the names of the early Catholics of this mission, and others who were also benefactors to the Church:

John O'Rourke and William Grimes, each $200; John Kane and Michael Farrel, of Halifax, each $100; collection in Columbia, S. C., $105; and a collection in Wilmington, $123; Judge Manly, Patrick Farrel, P. McGowan, J. H. Murray, Thomas Callen, Henry Petit, Mrs. F. D. Miller, each $50; Patrick Linehan, M. A. Prendergast, James F. Taylor, Thomas Grier, each $20; James O'Farrel, $15; Rev. Thomas Murphy, F. Brennan, J. B. Barbee, C. Donohue, P. W. Keenan, John Hopkins, Mr. Sullivan, Cornelius Gorman, Mrs. Grimes, Hon. Daniel Barringen, Wm. A. Walsh, each $10; Governor W. W. Holden, James McElrone, Bernard O'Connor, Dennis Denehy, James Carney, and several others, each $5. The latter gentleman was subsequently lost on the transport *General Lyon* in 1865. Like Governor Wise in Virginia, Governor Holden defeated Know-Nothingism in North Carolina.

Patrick F. Nolan and E. B. Gilligan were the carpenters. The sum of three thousand dollars, at least, was expended on the church. A great part was realized by collections made all over the three States by the zealous priests.

The church was dedicated, under the title and invocation of St. John the Baptist, June 3, 1860. The ceremony was performed by Bishop Lynch, assisted by several priests, among whom was Father McNeirny, the present Bishop of Albany, then accompanying Archbishop Hughes on his way to Chapel Hill, to deliver a lecture in the University of North Carolina, by invitation of the students.

Being in delicate health, the archbishop preached from his chair in the afternoon on "The Critical Situation of the Pope," and he predicted that God would again restore the temporal possessions of the Holy See, as he had formerly done on like occasions. The Rev. John Cullinane officiated at Fayetteville some time before 1860. Subsequently the Rev. H. P. Northrop and Rev. L. P. O'Connell were on these missions several years, and until the advent of Bishop Gibbons in 1868. The Rev. J. N. Townsend, an Englishman and a convert, was stationed at Fayetteville, and officiated during a period of seven years on these missions. He returned to England in 1877.

The Rev. J. B. White is now pastor at Raleigh. He is engaged in erecting a new building on the site of the former church, which was removed on account of a defect in the architecture rendering the edifice unsafe. Father White's energy and zeal will shortly complete a massive and imposing building, which will be an ornament to the faith and to the capital of the State. This zealous clergyman filled an office of high trust under the Federal Government. He retired from the world, and after having finished his studies, was ordained to the vicariate by Bishop Gibbons. He ministered in eastern North Carolina for some time, and also at Wilmington. In 1877 he was stationed on the missions of Raleigh and Fayetteville.

The Rev. J. J. Reilly is the pastor at this time of New Berne, and the several stations comprising that extensive and laborious district. He visits Kingston, Goldsboro, Enfield, Wilson, Halifax, Weldon, Washington, Greenville, Tarboro, Edenton, Plymouth, Elizabeth, and other points. He was ordained by Bishop Gibbons in 1873 on the Feast of St. Mark, and was stationed in the following year at Fayetteville. This able and self-sacrificing clergyman officiated in Raleigh between 1874 and 1877, when difficulties still fresh in the public mind rendered the position undesirable, and required great prudence on the part of the pastor for his own and the welfare of the Church in like manner. But he was equal to the emergency. The writer is indebted to Father Reilly for many of the historical events depicted in this chapter.

Very Rev. L. P. O'Connell, at the instance of the bishop, opened a subscription among the parishioners at Raleigh for the support of a resident priest. The annual contribution was deemed sufficient for the object, and the Rev. J. V. McNamara was installed pastor in 1869. After five years and much unpleasantness he was removed, and the vacancy filled for some months by Rev. Mark Gross, of Wilmington.

The piety, zeal, and charity of Father Gross won back the alienated esteem of the community for our holy religion, and many difficulties were shortly removed. He was returned to the Wilmington church, and Father J. J. Reilly, during the two following years, restored the piety and charity of the distracted and sorely-tried congregation, leaving little in this respect to harrass the mind of his venerable successor, Father White.

The difficulties in this instance have been made public, and the details, being of little interest to the reader, are omitted in the interests of charity; in calmer moments they will, with divine aid, let us hope, be repaired. Father McNamara is a talented man, and had done much good in his early years in the cause of religion; let us pray that he may be speedily restored to the unity and peace of his sorrowing mother the Church!

The Rev. Mr. O'Keefe visits Windsor and other stations in eastern North Carolina.

Public opinion in North Carolina is favorable to the Church, and this sentiment is general among the educated classes. The grace of enlightenment has been vouchsafed as a counter-mercy for the greater number of the faithful in more favored regions. The presence of numbers brings the Church daily face to face with the inhabitants, and scarcely leaves an excuse for ignorance. This movement was created by the learning and example of men who from time to time filled high offices of honor and trust in this commonwealth, refuting by their lives the calumnies ventilated against the faith. The movement gathered strength from the conversion from the ranks of Protestantism of persons eminent for virtue and intelligence. Prominent among the women were Mrs. Fulton, of Wilmington, the Misses Fisher, of Salisbury, and other ladies; among the men, Dr. Ives, Judges Manly, Heath, and Moore, Colonels Caldwell, Bradshaw, and other gentlemen no less influential.

Like the Oxford movement and the conversion of the Earl of Ripon in England, the return of Dr. Ives to the Church was the most stunning blow that Protestantism ever received in America. The manly step unsettled the faith of many, if they had any. The institution never recovered from the shock; it was the prophecy of its dissolution. When a man of Dr. Ives's social standing, conceded abilities, blameless life, and learning, the pride of the aristocratic Anglican Church and the foremost man among its hierarchy, laid down the insignia of a usurped office at the feet of the successor of St. Peter, a blow was dealt at the head of the decaying fabric that felled it to the ground like the idol in the temple of the Philistines. Since then controversy assumed another direction; our writers and lecturers amuse themselves in delivering funeral orations over the scattered limbs, and, like Bishop Spalding, of Peoria, discuss the causes that directly induced its overthrow.

Levi Silliman Ives, LL.D., resided at Salisbury a great part of his time while administering the affairs of the Episcopal Church of North Carolina. He was born at Meriden, Conn., September 16, 1797.* His early years were spent with his father on a farm at Turin, Lewis County, N. Y. He was sent to the academy at Lowville, but his studies were interrupted by his services under General Pike during the war with England. He entered Hamilton College in 1816, in order to study for the Presbyterian ministry. He withdrew to recruit failing health, induced by too close application to study, and in 1819 joined the Episcopal Church, studied under Bishop Hobart, was ordained deacon in 1822; he also married Miss Hobart. In 1823 he was created presbyter by Bishop

---

* Authorities: Original sources, traditions in the vicariate, Murray's "History," Catholic journals.

White, and officiated as such at Batavia, N. Y.; in Philadelphia, and at Lancaster, Pa. In 1831 he received Protestant consecration as Bishop of North Carolina, and filled the office for twenty-one years. In 1852 he visited Rome, embraced the faith, and with his robes threw off a burden which had crushed him for years, impaired his manhood, and made him a slave. He left the shrine of the apostles a free and happy man, and received from God the consolations of a conscience now at rest in recompense for whatever sacrifice he had made. None ever loses in exchanging the world for heaven, the praises of man for the friendship of God, and a troubled conscience for the peace of the Holy Ghost. The domestic war now ceased, and he ever more dwelt in peace.

His enemies awarded him tardy praise for fidelity to the dictates of conscience, and consoled themselves for his defection by attributing his heroism to mental infirmity. He was foolish according to the maxims of the world, whose wisdom is folly in the sight of God, and was denounced in the severest terms of condemnation. He lectured frequently on various subjects and composed learned treatises on religion. He established the Catholic Protectory, and was its first president. He bequeathed to it his valuable library, and left it, in both the male and female departments, in a flourishing condition at the time of his death. He departed this life October 13, 1867, fortified with the sacraments and strengthened by the blessings of the Church he loved so well:

At the commencement of every important undertaking it was his custom to approach the Holy Communion, in order to obtain grace and strength from the all-present Man-God. The virtues and greatness of the man threw a halo around him, which the prejudices and passions of the world could not disturb. Religion shed its hallowed rays along his pathway to the grave, illumined the shadows of death, and conducted him to the throne of God, for whom he had abandoned all things. His example will open the same path to many a weary and doubting mind, strengthen the faint of heart, and teach unborn generations the wisdom of serving and loving God. Even on earth he received the hundredfold—he gained the esteem of the world by despising it, and died in the friendship of his Maker.

The Hon. William Gaston was the greatest lay Catholic in America.* To him more than to any other layman is Catholicity indebted for the establishment of the Church in the Carolinas and Georgia. Contemporary with and nearly of the same age as Bishop England, their very politics had a similar complexion. In their day they stood conjointly before the country among the greatest representatives of the Catholic Church. Their influence was national; they were a mutual aid and support. At the time that Bishop England was addressing the legislature of South Carolina to obtain legal recognition for a female religious institution in Charleston Judge Gaston was delivering before the Convention of North Carolina, in 1835, the noblest defence made by a layman in the cause of Catholicity in the United States. By his efforts the clause in the Constitution discriminating against Catholics was expunged. His discourse was a masterpiece of Christian oratory; its fame survives the din of battle and the conflict of civil strife. "He was," in the language of Chief-Justice Ruffin, "a great man, a great judge, and the most illustrious jurist the State ever produced."

Hon. William Gaston, LL.D., was born at New Berne in 1778. His mother, Miss Sharpe, was an English lady of rare firmness of mind, unswerving piety, and endowed with all the accomplishments acquired in the first circles of European society. She formed the character of her son, and laid the foundation of his future eminence and usefulness. In his infancy he lost his father, an eminent physician and a true patriot. Of Irish birth, he became an object of peculiar dislike to the invaders. A party of the

---

* Authorities: Original sources, letters of Rev. J. J. Reilly and letter of Rev. J. B. White, Wheeler's "History of North Carolina," Dr. Clark's "Memoirs," Murray's "History," contemporaneous journals, traditions in the vicariate.

English ruthlessly shot him down, unarmed and before his own door, while engaged in transporting his family and little children to a place of security.

In 1791 he entered Georgetown College, its first student. After some time he was transferred to Princeton, to study the course necessary for his intended career in life. He graduated with first honors in 1796. He went on the eve to Philadelphia to receive the Holy Communion, that he might be fortified with the bread of the strong for the coming contest. He was admitted to the bar in his native State in 1798. His great abilities, high moral character, and learning soon raised him to the head of his profession. In 1800 he was elected State Senator, and in 1808 was chosen Elector of President and Vice-President of the United States. In 1811 Mr. Gaston died, universally regretted. In 1803 he was elected to Congress, and after two years was re-elected for a second term. His course was one of unsurpassed brilliancy; he was the peer of the greatest statesmen of that age. His lofty character, wisdom, and learning raised him to the highest eminence, commanded the respect of his political opponents and the admiration of all.

On retiring from Congress he resumed the practice of law, and was elected to the bench of the Supreme Court of North Carolina, a post which he continued to adorn to the hour of his death. The ermine was never worn with more unsullied purity or justice administered with a fairer hand. No influence, no power could turn justice from the even tenor of its way. Strict, stern, and inflexible, he taught the people to respect the majesty of the law, reformed their morals, and while he made them law-abiding, he made them Christians and Catholic unawares. Endowed with a firm and astute mind, versed in all legal lore and enlightened by religion, every question was closely sifted and all his decisions displayed unsurpassed ability. Catholicity framed his noble life and character; it was the source of all his greatness, made him the admired and loved of all his countrymen. The State is proud of her Catholic son; his name is a household word among the people;

towns and the county in which I write bear it. The Constitution was remodelled in compliment to his faith, his virtues, and his feelings.

In social life he was a model gentleman, one of the kindest and most considerate of men. He raised his children in the faith and bequeathed it to them as the most priceless inheritance; the world, its losses and advantages, weigh nothing in the balance. Before there was a priest at New Berne he gathered the faithful around him on Sundays and read the Mass prayers with humility and fervor.

He calmly expired in Raleigh January 7, 1844, in the sixty-sixth year of his age, and fortified with the holy sacraments. His life and conversation were so blameless that the clergyman who attended him in his last moments, Rev. Edward Quigley, declared it to be his opinion that he had never offended God by mortal sin. In his death the Church lost one of her most obedient children, North Carolina her most honored son, and the country one of her greatest ornaments.

The Hon. M. E. Manly resides at New Berne, advanced in years but still strong and vigorous. The venerable jurist is no less an ornament to his profession and the Christian name than his illustrious father-in-law, Judge Gaston. His lot fell on more unfavorable times.

The Supreme Court of North Carolina is composed of three judges, the chief-justice and two associates. Judge Manly was one of the associate justices from 1858 to 1865, when he was removed from his office by the military government. He was elected to the Senate of the United States for a term of six years, from 1867 to 1873, but was not permitted to take his seat, in consequence of his refusal to take what is known as *the iron-clad oath*. He did not immediately succeed Judge Gaston, but Judge Ruffin, who resigned, and whose unexpired term was filled by Judge Manly. He was presiding officer of the Senate of North Carolina in the winter of 1866-7, when he was elected United States Senator, as already stated.

Shamefully displaced by political revolution, he is

honored in the highest courts of the State. Eminent as a jurist, unsullied as a judge, sincere and fervent as a Catholic, Judge Manly's name will ever shine conspicuous in the annals of the Church in North Carolina.

The missions of western North Carolina are more recent; they began at the opening of the gold mines in Mecklenburg, in 1828-35, by Chevalier Riva de Finola. The first churches built west of Raleigh are St. Mary's and St. Joseph's, in Gaston, in 1843; St. Peter's, at Charlotte, in 1852; St. Lawrence's, at Ashville, in 1869, St. James's, at Concord, in 1870.

Until as late as the year 1850 these were stations, visited at intervals by the clergy from Columbia, South Carolina, or Augusta, Georgia. At this time we have a Benedictine house, with a church, priests, and several monks.

There are but few Catholic negroes in western North Carolina; I know but one, an old woman.

The salvation of the negro race, both before and after emancipation, in the Southern States has been a subject of deep solicitude to the Church. Special missions have been established for this object, churches were opened for them exclusively, but the harvest of souls thus far has not been as abundant as was expected. There are many causes for this on the part of the negroes, which will always be an obstacle to their conversion to Catholicity. They are naturally a sensual race of people, and their former condition of servitude aggravated the fatal propensity. Piety and the obligations of the married state they cannot realize, with rare exceptions.

They will learn the prayers, receive baptism, and attend the divine service with fervor for some time, but, impatient of moral restraint and the unity of the marriage bond, they cannot be permitted to approach the sacraments, and frequently fall away. If Catholicity were a system of singing, sensational preaching, and vociferous prayer, and limited to external observances, they would join the Church in thousands. Since their emancipation they are opposed to mingling with white people in religious worship. Though nominally attached to some sect, they know no religion, and have none, and are in some localities relapsing into fetichism. Their nocturnal assemblies are boisterous demonstrations or clandestine political gatherings. They were demoralized by political adventurers and tricksters, who made use of their votes for the purpose of plundering the impoverished country.

Thus deluded, their condition is in many instances worse than at any former period of their existence. They are indolent and improvident. If they can procure food they will make no further effort to improve their condition. The rising generation is still more indolent; they learn next to nothing in their schools, and they are rapidly dying for want of medical care and the necessaries of life. The race will gradually disappear unless confidence is restored between them and their former owners—their true and best friends.

In former times few of them were Catholic except those belonging to Catholic masters, who had their children baptized and led their parents to embrace the faith by teaching and example. Freed from restraint and their moral influence by the issue of the late war, many disappeared and are known no more as children of the faith. I have known exceptions to these general facts. We must never tire making the effort for their conversion. The baptism of but one dying infant would be an immense recompense for the labors and sacrifices of a long missionary life. It is related of St. Francis Xavier that, after having baptized an aged man, he declared it to be his opinion that such was one of the main objects for the accomplishment of which God had sent him to the Indies. This man had lived in accordance with the requirements of the natural law, and our Lord would not permit him to die outside of the pale of the Church.

The prejudices of the races are so strong that social equality can never exist between the white people and their former slaves. The children on both sides are unwilling to go to the same schools or mix at play and recreation. A white teacher, male or female, who conducts a school for colored children loses caste and will not be received in genteel society. These are barriers which render the chances of improving their religious condition by education very slender. They merit our deepest commiseration. Their sins and ignorance are a misfortune rather than a cause of condemnation, and the deep-rooted evils of the system from which they have emerged.

The Church is making all reasonable efforts to convert and improve them. It is an arduous undertaking, but time and patience will surmount all difficulties. It is chiefly by her ministry that the race will be preserved. As a class they are not addicted to the use of ardent spirits, which is an encouragement. Impelled by the violence of passion, several have grievously transgressed since their emancipation, and grievously have they paid for it.

CHAPTER XIII.

CHARLOTTE, SALISBURY, MORGANTOWN, SWANNANOA, ASHEVILLE, ETC., ETC.

St. Peter's Church in Charlotte—Laying of the Corner-stone—Small Number of Catholics—Difficulty of Travel—First Priests—Early Catholics—A Fair—Collections Abroad—Fathers Maginnis, Stokes, Guifford—Father Cronin, Founder of the Mission—Fathers Bermingham, Barry—Fathers J. J., L. P. and J. P. O'Connell—Father McNeil—Difficult Position for a Priest—Prayers for the Dead—Decorating Graves—The Whited Sepulchre—Reflections—Greensborough—St. Agnes's Church—Salisbury—Col. McNamara—The Rouche Family—The Misses Fisher—Cols. Caldwell, Bradshaw—Fertility, Health and Beauty of Country—Southerners: their Prejudice, Selfishness, Sufferings—Introduction of Catholicity—The Keenan Family—Col. Lee—Bishops Barry and Gibbons—Fathers O'Connell—Priests—Sermons—Other Catholics—Death of Terence Keenan—Perseverance of the Children in the Faith—Causes of Perversions—Mistaken Liberality—Popular Lectures—Sin of Unbelief—Apostate Nations never Reconverted, Individuals Rarely—Reasons Thereof—Reflections—Contrition and Remorse—Asylum Necessary for Disabled Priests—Open Confession of Faith—St. Lawrence's Church built by the Fathers O'Connell—Interior best Adapted for Diocesan Institutions—Adjoining Stations—Death of Father Carr—Mass on Mount Mitchell—Feast of St. Rose of Lima—Catholic and Protestant Names—Destiny of Asheville—First News of Secession—How Received—Cause of the Overthrow of the Confederacy—Feast of St. Dominic—Escape of Conscripts, etc., etc.—Fidelity of the Slaves—A Volcano—The Beads the True Test of a Priest—Archbishop Gibbons' Anecdote, etc., etc.

ON St. Patrick's day, 1851, I laid the corner-stone of the church in Charlotte, N. C. It is a rough gray granite block, without any memorials, civil or ecclesiastical, and visible at the northeast corner of the edifice. An audience of several hundred persons had assembled about three o'clock P.M., and were seated either on the building materials or on the greensward. The evening was mild and a stillness was in the air. Attired in suitable robes, I stood on the smooth side of the foundation-stone and preached two hours on the infallibility of the Church;

none left the assemblage. As the Southern sun was sinking in the west the corner-stone was lowered to its place. The simplicity of the ceremony impressed the people favorably, especially when two recent converts headed the procession —William Hunter and H. Maxwell, Esqs. They were leading Presbyterians; I baptized them a short time previously. They were faithful to the end, and now rest. The church was dedicated the following year, on the festival of S.S. Peter and Paul, and named in honor of the first Pope and Prince of the Apostles. The ceremony was performed by Bishop Reynolds, in presence of a large congregation, chiefly non-Catholics. He delivered an able discourse on the "Real Presence." I said the Mass, the first of many thousands offered in the church; it was served by the bishop. On the same occasion he administered confirmation to the above-mentioned persons, to Matthew Leper, Mrs. Hunter, and Misses Maxwell and Groner, converts. The bishop again preached in the afternoon, on "The Absolving Power." Joseph, the eldest son of Mrs. Hull, née Lonergan, was then baptized.

The church lot is located at this time almost in the heart of the city; then it lay at the extreme northern limits of the town. It comprises two acres. I was offered the entire vacant square, a bare old field, for the sum of five hundred dollars. It was impossible to realize it and build the edifice besides. I applied to the bishop, but he was unable to contribute any more than one hundred dollars. The Charleston cathedral was being built, an undertaking that left the bishop penniless. In this way property which in after times would be of immense value was blamelessly lost. This is not an isolated case. Hon. W. McKenna of Lancaster, the Foxes, Sadlers, Caldwells, Alexanders, Spurgs, Wilsons, and all the people of Charlotte liberally contributed. The enterprise cost about one thousand dollars.

At that time there were scarcely one hundred adult Catholics in Charlotte and the adjoining missions. They were poor people, but virtuous, and full of zeal for religion. They all contributed according to their ability. Aided by the non-Catholic citizens, the sum collected was sufficient to purchase the building materials and pay carpenter hire. Four mechanics in masonry, the early pioneers of the faith in this region, built each one wall over and above his subscription in money. These were Patrick Harty, Edward and James Lonergan, brothers, and their nephews conjointly, William and James, one wall. Fortified by the sacraments of the dying, they have all gone to their reward.

There is a break in the southern wall, caused by the explosion of war materials near the depot at the close of the war. The wall has been pronounced safe, and St. Peter's may last many years.

Our successors, whose lot will be cast on the brighter days now dawning on the South since the abolition of domestic slavery and the restoration of home rule, will, doubtless, feel an interest in the details of the planting of the faith in the several points of these missions. How much that would edify and please is already fading away from the memory of men!

I first visited Charlotte in the spring of 1850. It was then a straggling inland town, having no railroad communication with the world outside. The houses were strung along one or two streets, and were wooden, wilted and bald with age. There were only three brick houses; one was the old Episcopal church, in which I preached by invitation. It was complimentary to the growing convictions of Dr. Ives, who had occupied the pulpit the Sunday previous. He was very popular. The recruits from the various sects are generally distinguished for learning, and leading members of society. They are lauded to the skies until they indicate their manhood by abandoning their errors and seeking their salvation in the one true Church. Thenceforward they need expect no favors, not even rights, from their former admirers. "My friends and my neighbors have drawn near and stood against me; and they who praised me swore against me, and uttered vain things, and studied deceits all the day." This will apply to Dr. Ives.

The usual mode of travelling at that time was by stage, which was extremely wearisome, especially in midsummer, on account of the excessive heat and the crowded condition of the republican vehicle, lumbering under its living freight of panting humanity. It frequently took forty-eight hours to accomplish the journey from Columbia in mid-winter, when the roads were almost impassable and the weather bitter cold. The distance is one hundred and ten miles. It was the terminus of the nearest railroad.

Stationed in Columbia for nearly a quarter of a century, in conjunction with my brothers, it became necessary to make the journey by the way of Camden and Lancaster to afford a half-dozen families an opportunity of approaching the Holy Sacraments at regular intervals. By this route three days were spent in making the journey. Allen Cruise, of Charlotte, was the obliging mail agent. He was always kind and attentive. His excellent daughter, now Mrs. Butler, has since joined the Church.

The Rev. A. J. McNeil served on this mission about four years previous to 1860. He is a native of South Carolina. He was sent to the Propaganda during the administration of Very Rev. R. S. Baker, where he studied assiduously, and was ordained about the year 1854. He served on all these missions from Winnsborough, South Carolina, to Gaston and Salisbury and all intermediate points, between 1855 and 1860. An eloquent preacher and a devoted priest, he made several converts, and is held in high esteem by the faithful. He erected a priest's house to the rear of the church and made other desirable improvements. He also liquidated a debt, by collections abroad, still encumbering the church, and occasioned by the accidental loss of the account-book and subscription-list in the hands of a collector.

Father McNeil was stationed in Columbia, in 1860, as assistant and also chaplain of the Ursuline Convent. After the destruction of the convent by Sherman's army, in 1865, he was sent to Sumter, South Carolina, where he still faithfully labors in the service of God as pastor of that church and chaplain to the Sisters of Mercy. He conducted a fair recently, and is superintending the erection of a new church in the town.

The missions were attended between 1851 and 1356 by the writer and Rev. L. P. O'Connell, and from the latter date until 1860 by Father McNeil. He was succeeded by Rev. J. P. O'Connell, who ministered during the disastrous period of the civil war. Towards the close of the conflict the money-makers were transferred thither from Columbia for greater security. Their services were superfluous, for the spurious currency was better executed, of equal value, and as widely circulated as the genuine. There were many and truly edifying Catholics among them. This increase and the stockade at Salisbury, where many thousand unfortunate prisoners were confined and dying daily by hundreds, kept the missionary closely engaged.

Throughout this terrible time he labored with singular zeal, fidelity, and disinterestedness. After the sack of Columbia General Sherman led his army to the coast by a lower route, and in this way Charlotte escaped the fate of the former city. The country was conquered before he set foot on it. General Beauregard held his head-quarters in Charlotte shortly before the surrender. During his occupancy a strong effort was made to convert the church into a commissary store, like St. Mary's College in Columbia. The sacrilege was prevented by urgent expostulation and an earnest effort of combined influence.

While it lasted, and on several occasions, the Confederacy exhibited great ill-will to Catholicity, and at a time, too, when so many Catholics were bleeding in her cause.

The Very Rev. Lawrence Patrick O'Connell, V.G., has been pastor since 1865 in Charlotte, and over its extensive outside missions, as far as the Tennessee line, embracing Salisbury, Morgantown, Old Fort, Asheville, Henderson, and all other intermediate stations. Cabarrus and Greensborough were recently attached to the Benedictine Mission of St. Mary of Help.

He finished the church in Greensborough in 1876; it was dedicated by Archbishop Gibbons in the feast of the saint in whose honor it was named in the same year. He was assisted in the ceremony by Fathers Wolf, O.S.B., Gross, and White. There is a small but fervent congregation in the town, among whom Major McNamara, a Canadian, is eminent for fervor and attachment to the faith.

A very unpleasant affair; still fresh in the public mind, rendered the pastor's position difficult and disagreeable. By his forbearance, prudence, and piety he has succeeded in calming the troubled waters. He established peace among his people, whom he won back to God and their duties. As a body, we must have trials, no less than individually. To expect uninterrupted peace is to be ignorant of human frailty, of the experience of the past, and the warnings of the Holy Ghost. Of course, the Church has only men to work with; all true men are not externally Roman Catholics, nor are all Catholics true men. Made up of human materials, it is open to all the perilous infirmities of man. I am convinced by personal observation that cases of defection among the clergy often do a general good, notwithstanding the sin and scandal; we ourselves make most of the noise by attaching too much importance to them. I am assured that here lay Father Lawrence's greatest difficulty.

Catholics should understand that the sacraments and the grace of God do not destroy man's free-will nor the dangerous propensity of his nature. Were this the case, men nor angels, while in their probation, could not merit; for freedom is necessary for the love and service of God. A heaven of saints ready-made was not God's plan in creating us, nor could it be a source of voluntary allegiance and love.

In 1869 Fathers L. P. and J. P. O'Connell conducted a fair for the rebuilding of a new church. The result was in the highest degree creditable to the liberality of the people of Mecklenburg and a decided expression of their appreciation of the moral worth of both priests. They also conjointly visited the cities of New York and Brooklyn, where they collected, chiefly among their own friends and the laboring classes, funds for the erection of churches at other stations, and which will always remain as monuments of their self-sacrificing devotedness.

As far as I am able to ascertain, the Rev. Joseph Stokes was the first priest who regularly visited this country, about the year 1824. He labored faithfully on all the outside missions, and was stationed in Savannah about 1827, and ministered there until about 1832. He subsequently transferred his allegiance to the New England States, and died on the missions shortly before the late war. Having no written records, I am compelled to rely on memory or oral traditions for some dates, and in minor matters claim an approximation only to accuracy in some instances.

The Rev. John Maginnis succeeded, and about 1827 he made his studies at the seminary in Charleston and was ordained priest by Dr. England. He faithfully officiated in the districts of upper South Carolina and this section many years. He conducted a day-school in Charlotte for some time, which was well patronized, and by this means he obtained his support. He purchased a house and lot, and the former was temporarily used as a church. Father Maginnis accepted a pastoral charge in the city of New York shortly after 1830, and held St. James's Church several years. About 1850 he moved to San Francisco and served under Archbishop Alemany. He is mentioned in Gleeson's "History of the Catholic Church in California" in the following manner: "The oldest Catholic church in San Francisco is St. Patrick's, in which Mass was first celebrated in June, 1851. Father Maginnis was then the only priest in San Francisco who preached in the English language. He divided his services between St. Francis's Church, in Vallejo Street, and St. Patrick's." He died at the post of duty about 1860. He was a low-sized man, industrious, pious, and circumspect in manners. He left a favorable record wherever he discharged the functions of the holy ministry.

The mission embraced one-half of both the States of North and South Carolina. Father Bermingham came after Rev. John Maginnis and visited the entire region with indefatigable zeal, between 1832 and 1838, when the Rev. T. J. Cronin was appointed pastor. He was a native of Cork, and was raised under the tutelage of Father Mathew in a society of young men, who, under the patronage of St. Joseph, combined for mutual edification, and had for their special object the practice of that angelic virtue which eminently fitted the patriarch to be the spouse of the Immaculate Mother of God. The Rev. T. J. Sullivan, of the cathedral, belonged to the same pious confraternity. They made their studies at the Seminary of St. John the Baptist in Charleston, and were both ordained about 1838. Father Cronin, having approached death's doors from an attack of yellow fever, never afterward possessed robust health. He arrived by sulky from Charleston, after having made a journey of near three hundred miles in this manner, his only mode of travelling over his entire parish. This vehicle is now rarely seen in the country, and is chiefly confined to cities and race-courses. On an uneven road it is easily capsized, as I have learned by my own experience, having used it a long time on my missions in Georgia.

Father Cronin had no home; he lived four years in this way from house to house, not knowing frequently where he could stop during the night or get the next meal, visiting the scattered sheep and preaching the word of God whenever he could procure a suitable place. He was an agreeable and persuasive speaker, always glowing with unaffected fervor and genuine piety. He was universally respected by all denominations, and among the faithful revered as a saint. At Lancasterville, South Carolina, he visited in prison and converted a man named Sweat, under sentence of death for having slain another at a shad-fishing ground on the Catawba. The poor fellow was well prepared, and he met his death in a truly Catholic manner. A resignation so gentle and unostentatious was unexampled in public executions. The people never knew a criminal who expiated his transgression and paid the penalty of the law in so Christianlike a manner. They were moved; some joined the Church; the Catholics were consoled, and an impression made which abides to this day, although the event is forgotten among the rising generation.

We read of many conversions, but they are rarely, if ever, in our times the work of any single priest or bishop. They are the result of a long and many-linked chain of graces working silently, often for years, and, after much wrestling, God at last proclaiming his victory. They who to-day obey the faith have been either convinced or hesitating a long time before. In a certain community in South Carolina many respectable and influential persons became Catholics. Some were of Paul, and others of Cephas or Apollo. Thirty years previously Bishop Byrne, while a priest in that country, and assisting at a marriage, gave a Catechism to a genteel, sprightly little girl. It was read and cherished. I have traced the movement to that simple fact; the now venerable matron ascribes it to the same cause. I unhesitatingly believe that my opinion will be sustained by the experience of clergymen who have labored any time in the Lord's vineyard. Of the many on whom I have poured the waters of baptism, there is scarcely one adult whom I can claim as my convert in the closer acceptation of the term. The exceptions are confined chiefly to the apostolic labors of missionaries among the heathen.

The dead frequently preach more forcibly than the living. The humblest individual makes, by his life and acts, an impression on his fellow-man which will have an influence for good or evil long after his memory has faded from the world. This is pre-eminently true of Father Cronin and nearly all our priests who now sleep in Christ, and the honor may be justly claimed for many of the laity who practised their religion.

After having exhausted his strength in the service of the

Lord during four years, Father Cronin died in Salisbury, in the autumn of 1842, at the residence of Mons. Rouche, a faithful Frenchman, whose wife had embraced the faith, an inheritance now prized by their worthy descendants beyond all earthly goods. There was no clergyman with him to administer the sacraments provided by a merciful God for that critical hour, and by means of which he had consoled the dying moments of many others; he was comforted by the recital of the prayers for the departing by the pious family, and expired in the embrace of his crucifix. This has been the fate of nearly all the priests who died at the outside stations. I do not remember one who had an opportunity of receiving the last sacraments. Like St. Francis Xavier at Sancian, noble souls are permitted to die in circumstances resembling their Divine Master in the privation of human aid. At first he was buried apart and close to the public road, but in a retired spot. His remains were afterwards transferred to a plain, substantial tomb in the cemetery of the Church of SS. Mary and Joseph, which he had inaugurated, and for which he had secured a suitable piece of ground while living. It is a country place in Gaston County, and on the banks of the majestic Catawba, whose bright waters meander hard by. The graves of the faithful dead, all his contemporaries, lie scattered round. The laity, it is reported, did not remove the chalice from the hands of the dead before the interment; it was buried with him. On the completion of the church, and when the body was exhumed for removal to its final resting-place, the chalice could not be found; it was evidently stolen from the grave. The custom of burying articles of value with the dead serves but to expose their remains to desecration by exciting the cupidity of the impious, who, like the infuriated mob at Boston, scruple not to rob the very dead. This is a gold region, and the thirst is so insatiable that within the present year, and in this vicinity, a grave was violated and the teeth extracted for the sake of the trifle of gold with which they had been filled. What a painful illustration of human depravity!

Father Guifford was pastor for six years, and was succeeded by Father Barry in 1848. He made periodical visits from Augusta until 1851, when he withdrew and the writer was appointed to the mission. Between 1827 and 1833 the gold mines in Mecklenburg were extensively worked by a European named Chevalier Riva de Finola. His mansion afforded both hospitality and a chapel to Bishop England during his visitations. Several Catholics were employed, but after the suspension of the work in 1833 they left, and a few remained.

Patrick Harty and his wife, an excellent woman, permanently settled in the town previous to this period. They gave their children a Catholic education; some died in early life, and others later. The eldest daughter, Mary, and the youngest son, James, still live in Charlotte; but recently the youngest daughter, Anne Elizabeth, died at the age of womanhood. Educated by the Sisters, she was accomplished, pious, and devoted to the practices of her religion. She conducted the choir, taught the children in the Sunday-school, and shed around the odor of a virtuous life. Universally regretted, and after the ordeal of a long and painful sickness, she went to rest, and sleeps in our Lord. The parents died previous to the war, fortified with the Holy Sacraments.

Part of the family having died before a Catholic cemetery existed in the country, and from a reluctance to disturb their remains, all are interred in the old cemetery, called the Presbyterian from its proximity to that place of worship. The inscription on the tomb is the only Catholic memorial in that white monumental field of the dead. Catholicity is so consonant with reason that the denial of any one of its tenets often produces practically grotesque consequences. The rejection of the doctrine of purgatory and of the veneration due to the sign of the cross leaves no mark by which to distinguish between non-Catholic and pagan grave-yards. How dreary do those places appear when unrelieved by a single emblem of Christianity expressive of the trust and hope of the dead in future immortality and bliss. Emblems of the Masonic craft, of trade and occupation; weeping cherubs, willows, and widows; the empty sand-glass and remorseless scythe of Time, with the superfluous cross-bones, are chiselled on many a bald gray slab. Antiquated mottoes, trite aphorisms, quaint snatches of silly rhyme, and much more, equally inappropriate, constitute the sad, dull necrology of a modern Protestant grave-yard in this country, and illustrate their religious opinions—a mixture of truth and error. They are unworthy of the dead, although the tributes of sincere affection. Many of them were distinguished in their day, benefactors of our race, and honest, if mistaken, in their belief. Salvation is not denied to all who die outside the visible pale of the Church, but to the obstinate sinner and the deliberate impugner of the known truth who both sin against the Holy Ghost and die impenitent. Surely the cross or other impressive sign of man's redemption should mark the remains of those who professed the Christian name and meekly bore life's burden. People are at a loss to know how to dispose of the dead, just as were the citizens of Rome at the decline of the republic. Entire communities are exercised on this point and learned men harrassed. It seems decided that in future no interments can be made inside the walls of cities, and for good sanitary reasons. The cemeteries are ornamented and costly monuments, erected with a waste of wealth and display of splendor rivalling in magnificence the parent metropolis, thus in a sort reviving the ancient apotheosis of the dead. Love is stronger than death, and lives beyond the grave. To assist by our prayers and precious ministrations our departed friends is a dictate of our nature. It must express itself in some form; the heart yearns to show its love and remembrance. Those who are denied the lawful exercise of this conviction, the heavenward face of the soul, find an outlet by lavishing the rich treasures of the heart and millions of money in funeral pomp and mortuary ornamentation, while many thousands of the living perish from want of the bare necessaries of life in the streets of our fashionable cities. This custom divests death in a great measure of its native repulsiveness, and mars the stern lessons it is meant to impress on the living. A halo of poetry is thrown round it; it is now a fanciful dream. People unworthy of life and unfit to die, long, with Mirabeau, to go to sleep in flower-decked graves, under the popular, motto, "Peace to his ashes."

Cremation is growing rapidly in public favor; societies are organized for the horrible purpose of burning the bodies of the dead, and are erecting new Gehennas for that object. It is worthy of remark that since the introduction of this infidel and old heathen practice the loss of life by fire is greater than at any former time. Its patrons are free-thinkers. Few think of the immortal soul, or heed whether its abode be in peace or in sorrow. The reproach of St. Augustine to the great of his time, *who perished with a noise*, will apply with still greater force to this day and its irreligious tenants: "*Cruciantur ubi sunt, laudantur ubi non sunt.*"

When contrasted with this vain pomp and material idolatry, the obsequies of the Church are really sublime. The Requiem Mass is offered; the grave blessed; the living pray for the soul of the dead; the body is restored to the dust from which it was fashioned by its Maker—*dust to dust*—and until that day when Christ will restore all things.

The French Catholics of New Orleans decorate the graves of their dead on the second day of November, annually, with crosses and other pious devices. But their devotion does not rest here, nor is it confined to mere outward display or idle ceremony; it is only the most slender consequence and trifling adjunct of a higher sentiment and deeper conviction. "It is a holy and a wholesome thought to pray for the dead, that they may be loosed from their sins."

As many are omitted in particular services by their friends, either through ignorance or neglect, this is the day set apart by the Church for the commemoration of all the faithful departed, and in consequence styled All Souls' Day. In the forenoon the people assist at the Holy Sacrifice of the Mass, and offer up their prayers, in union with the universal suffrage, for all who died in the friendship of God, but who are not sufficiently cleansed from earthly stain to enter into the holy of holies, and still are in a state in which our prayers only and not our floral offerings will avail them.

The congregation in Charlotte numbers about one hundred and fifty souls. The following are the principal members: Mrs. Gross and family, John T. Butler, John Phelan, Patrick Phelan, Edward Madden, Mrs. Hand, Mrs. Hull, Cornelius Myers, Michael Healy, James Manning, M. Murphy, P. Gallagher, J. McGowan, D. Murphy, and their families, with many others equally worthy of mention.

Salisbury was an old station. The early Catholics were Major McNamara and his household. He had married into the Henderson family, of Revolutionary fame, and raised his children in the faith. The sons removed, one to Texas and the other, Robert, to Columbia, where he died about 1860, fortified with the Holy Sacraments. The eldest daughter married John Lynch, M.D., of Cheraw, South Carolina, and lives in Columbia, surrounded by a numerous offspring, well instructed in their religion and practical Catholics. The fourth and youngest child, a daughter, forsook the world and its fascinations in early life, devoted herself to the service of God in the order of the Sisters of Mercy, and at this time is superioress of the convent at Sumter as Mother Agatha.

The next family in the town conspicuous for piety and fidelity are the Messrs. Ronche. The father was French, and highly respected. The sainted missionary, Rev. T. J. Cronin, died at his residence in 1842. His wife, Mrs. Ronche, neé Smith, is a convert, who, after the death of her husband, raised her young children, a large circle, in the practice of their religious duties. Without priest or church, and surrounded by non-Catholic influence and the seductions of the world, she has succeeded in making them as Catholic as if reared under the shadows of Notre Dame. Grown to man's estate, they now appreciate the worth and devotion of their incomparable parent.

Salisbury, during the war, was a noted stockade for captured Federal soldiers. Many thousand Irish and German Catholics were among the prisoners. The scarcity of provisions, the growing numbers of captured soldiers after every engagement, and the refusal of the Federal Government to negotiate an exchange, all combined to make Salisbury a death-pen. The amount of suffering endured, the numbers who died from want, fever, and other camp complaints is incredible. The details would exhibit the worst features of the war, harrow human feeling, and do no good. The writer prefers to let oblivion rest on the scene, and let the unknown and forgotten dead sleep on in their undistinguished graves.

Major Mallet was the officer in command, and no blame can be attached to him. Rev. J. P. O'Connell, D.D., attended to the spiritual wants of the dying. He spent himself in their service, and his labors irretrievably impaired a constitution naturally elastic and robust. His earthly recompense was not in greenbacks, but in a plentiful currency of microscopic animalcules.

The Rev. A. J. McNeil for a time also shared in this distressing mission. To escape death by starvation, many of the prisoners renounced their allegiance to the Federal Government, joined the Southern army, and were faithful to the last. Had an exchange of prisoners been arranged on both sides, an Anderson, a Salisbury, and a Fort Delaware would not disgrace the records of the civil war.

Mr. Buise, a convert, and his family are also residents of Salisbury, and attached to the faith.

Miss Christine Fisher embraced the truth soon after the commencement of the civil war. She was an unmarried sister of Colonel Charles Fisher, who, after having raised a regiment of volunteers, bore the brunt of the fight at the first battle of Manassas, and died gallantly at the head of his command. He was universally respected in the State, and was president of the North Carolina Railroad. Accomplished, popular, and humane, he was the Bayard of the Southern army, and his blood was the first to enrich the battle-fields of Virginia, the mother of heroes and statesmen. He had married a daughter of Hon. David Caldwell, eminent as a just judge and a learned jurist. Three very young children survived both their parents, and were left orphans to the sole care of their aunt.

Educated in the first female institutions in the land and gifted with rare intellectual powers, Miss C. Fisher saw and felt the want of faith around her and its consequences. Guided by her own intellect and the grace of God, she became a humble and obedient child of the faith without human counsel or persuasion. She brought into the Church a cultivated mind and a pure heart, on which God silently kept watch from her infancy, and made it a sealed fountain of his own love. She tasted the joys of the world in their most refined form and amid the fascinations of an ample fortune; but nothing presented itself to her thoughtful mind so fair as the image of our dear Lord and his Mother, fully revealed in the true Church only. She loved him henceforward; she never knew another love; he took the place of the lost one in his gory grave: this was the secret of her strength.

Her brother's children were before her, reduced from affluence to comparative need by the disasters of the nation; she at once prepared herself for the work of their education. The most beautiful and intellectual of characters was devoted to their care. A woman of women, she gave them every element and feeling of her nature, lavished on them the treasures of her great heart, and, more than all, the treasures of the true faith.

She was brought up in the doctrines and practices of the Episcopal Church, to which her friends belonged. Her relation to her brother's children rendered her position one of peculiar hardship. The brilliant light of truth which had dawned on her soul dispelled all darkness, but the profession thereof and the noble step she had taken placed her tacitly under the ban and isolated her from her wealthy and influential relatives. It is not too much to say that none other entered the Church, in her day, in the face of so many difficulties, any one of which makes thousands cowards and sends them hypocrites to a hopeless grave after having lived an untruth half their lives. "The queen of the South will rise in judgment against this generation." The opposition that slumbered in the minds of many was formidable. It was hoped that her self-respect, her interest in the orphans, her love for her brother's name would deter her from impressing on their tender minds a creed professed only by a few low and ignorant foreigners.

There was no support from abroad—not even the presence of the minister of religion to impart consolation and speak words of encouragement. It is a better glory if our faith be nurtured far from the help of all external things, and left alone in the wordly barrenness with God and his angels. But few there are whose weakness will not fail in the isolation. Sorrow was her constant companion and her earthly portion and ceaselessly searched every recess of the heart, like a chilling night wind in a lone sanctuary.

Prudence directed all her steps. Her *élèves* received the best education the country could afford, and were left free to choose their own religion. The influence of that bright life could not leave them long undecided. The decisive step was taken in each case only after the years of maturity had been attained.

A contrary course would have been indecorous, imprudent, and detrimental to the general good of religion.

Frederick, the only son, was baptized by Dr. J. P. O'Connell, after he had graduated from the State University at Chapel Hill. Both the sisters, Frances C. and Annie B. Fisher, were baptized by Vicar-General L. P. O'Connell.

To join the Church in this community was a greater

sacrifice for these ladies than the embracing of the monastic state by others in more favored countries. At an early age, in the flower and bloom of youth, they renounced the world. Its blandishments, so dazzling to youthful imagination, had no power over them. Surrounded by an atmosphere of purity and devotion, they were enamored of the beauty of virtue. The faculties of their expanded minds were so absorbed by the glories of the house of God as to render them incapable of perishable interests and blunt them to the fleeting glories of a day.

Frances C. Fisher, under the *nom de plume* of Christian Reid, as a writer of fiction is one of the brightest names that adorns the literature of our country. She is the greatest of modern female writers in her chosen field, because the most chaste. She saw in the writings of the day circulated among her own sex the sad consequences of the want of true faith. She loved them with the fervor of a generous heart, and she has labored to elevate, purify, and refine them by the fascinations of golden fiction.

Her genius is surpassed only by her virtues. Purity is the principle which gives coloring to every feature of her mind. It shines forth with a radiance which illumines her whole character and brightens every page with a silvery light. Her works are read in every part of the English-speaking world—far away in Eastern lands and far away in the West, where the sun sets beyond the boisterous summits of her own loved Carolina.

We have each of us something more true, something more personal, than the common life fretted away and vexed by a thousand cares. The influence of our words and our virtues live after we are gone and are our second and better life.

The learned and eminent jurist, Richard Caldwell, Esq., Colonel John Bradshaw and his family, and others. emulous of the example of these devoted ladies, have entered into the ark of salvation. This example sheds its influence on all sides, condemning the timidity and cowardice of numbers, encouraging the faint-hearted, and will remain a sweet and holy remembrance in the vicariate for future ages. "Blessed are they who confess me before men. I will confess them before my Father who is in heaven."

Asheville, situated in western North Carolina, is built on a level plain, surrounded by hills and mountains of great beauty. Travellers claim for it the grandeur and magnificence of many of the most favored retreats on the Rhine or in the Tyrol. There is not a healthier place in the world. Besides the Warm Springs, there is an untold variety of mineral waters, which entice hither invalids from all sections. The soil of the surrounding country is exceedingly fertile and adapted to all kinds of farming and stock-raising purposes. The quantity of game in the forests and the variety of fish in the limpid brooks and marvellous rivers make this the hunter's paradise. God's presence is more intimately felt in some places than in others, and this is eminently true of the former. It seems impossible not to admire and love God here; it is difficult to decide which is the more inspiring, winter or summer, for each has a beauty peculiarly local, which can be rarely witnessed elsewhere. The surrounding chain of mountains, like an amphitheatre, isolates the whole section from the world outside, and few persons visited it except youthful adventurers and the opulent, who, having their own conveniences, could travel at leisure and with comfort. The distance to Greenville, by way of Hendersonville, Flat Rock, and across the Saluda Mountains, about sixty miles, was seldom accomplished in less than thirty hours, and when no accident occurred. The ascent of the stage was slow and tedious. I have spent many a weary hour in the crowded vehicle, both in summer and winter, when the only relief I could obtain for stiff limbs was to alight and walk whenever we reached a station. The scenery over the Saluda range and the water-falls on the streams interested us during the day, and at night the stage-horn, echoing through the distant hills, aroused fancy, reconciled us to each other, and to all other things for the time.

A great many planters and slave-owners from the rice plantations and all the sea-coast of South Carolina purchased many of the most desirable places in the country, and more especially in the vicinity of Flat Rock and Hendersonville—in short, as far as the Tennessee line near the Warm Springs. They cleared the lands and ornamented them, erected commodious residences, and transferred their gorgeous and fashionable establishments hither every spring and remained until frost in the fall. They contributed but little to the general improvement of the country. Their slaves supplied them labor, and store goods were furnished from abroad. The natives were kept at a great distance, and if they were employed at all, only for menial occupations at inadequate remuneration. A feeling of great bitterness sprung up between both classes, which was developed into open violence after the war broke out. They were the greatest sufferers and had the least sympathy of any. Compelled to fly from their lowland homes early in the struggle by the proximity of both armies, all their possessions were laid waste and wantonly destroyed, as far as possible. They found no better treatment in the interior; the mountaineers hated them as cordially as did the Yankees, and visited their places with like vengeance. Many of their residences were burnt down, the flocks and cattle destroyed, they themselves driven away by threats, violence, and assassination. It was a wheel within a wheel, and none pitied them, for they were mainly instrumental in putting the first in motion. Unaccustomed to labor, and raised in luxury and affluence, they were reduced to great wretchedness and poverty. Those who survived the conflict succumbed soon after. Nearly all that generation of people are now dead. They were elegant talkers, but not otherwise a highly educated people; they could sit down all day and converse over a fox-hunt without the introduction of any more elevated topic. Though certainly not cowardly, their soldiers were noisy, demonstrative, and incapable of enduring the labors of a prolonged contest; they soon melted away, and the ranks were so thinned that it was necessary to double or incorporate the brigades with other organizations. After the publication of Bishop England's works, there were scarcely a dozen copies sold in the State outside of the Catholic body, although he was the ablest champion of Southern rights, and they were justly proud of him. This may have resulted from prejudice or reluctance to heavy reading; in either case, it is not complimentary to their intelligence or liberality. We hope better things from their offspring, who have come out chastened from the ordeal of long and bitter sufferings.

Despite their intolerance, they were the unconscious medium through which the Church worked its way into these Alpine fastnesses. Miss Callahan, an excellent woman and an exemplary Catholic, who served in the capacity of stewardess in a worthy and exceptional family, introduced her married sister and the entire household, consisting of the father and several children, from Ireland, purchased a farm within two miles of the town from Col. Lee, and settled them on it permanently. This was the origin of the Keenan family and occurred some time about 1835. With all the energy of our early settlers, they soon built a house, cleared the primeval forest, and became independent. They were exemplary people, and though not affluent, they won the esteem of the entire community by their industry and virtue. Col. Lee, from the first, was a warm friend and patron; he conducted on the best and most enlightened principles of education, for many years, a first-class academy, where the sons of the most opulent families in the low country were educated. He still lives and continues the same honorable occupation. He generously gave the family employment and taught the ungrown children the rudiments of a sound English education, for which they were shortly in a capacity to make him ample recompense. Their parents' great anxiety was to obtain the ministrations of a priest, to enable themselves and the children to approach the Holy Sacraments. Augusta, Georgia, was the nearest point from which one

could be spared, and in due time they were consoled by
Father Barry. They were never entirely reconciled to the
country until then. For fifteen years they were visited regularly from Columbia, and since suffered no privation of
priestly services. Father Barry, remembered more as a
priest than a bishop, was the first who preached at Asheville, and in the Court-house. He was not a fluent
speaker, and though his utterance was embarrassed his
piety and sincerity always made a favorable impression.
In fact, he was the first priest that came here; he was a
man of intense humility; his chief aim was to reclaim the
wanderer from the faith, bringing the remiss to practise
their religious duties, correct the vicious, and instruct the
children. I lectured some time after in the Town Hall on
the Blessed Eucharist, and Bishop Gibbons also, in the
same place, delivered a learned discourse on "The Invocation of Saints."

The other Catholics scattered over the country were two
or three Irish servants, one a teacher by the name of
Brady, who married a Miss Hightower, residing on the
southern slope of the Saluda, whom I baptized. Count
de Choiseul lived near Flat Rock during the summer
months; he had been French Consul before the accession
of Napoleon III. After the death of the Countess, to
whom I administered the last Sacraments, some time in
1853, he sold his beautiful place and returned to France.
Both his daughters remained, but were scarcely known as
Catholics, and in this connection I have lost sight of them.
Mr. Durbec, of Charleston, rented the hotel at Flat Rock,
which was well conducted, and, during his occupancy, a
place of considerable resort. His wife, a sister of Capt.
Aveilhe, and all his family were truly Catholic, well instructed, and proud of their religion. The family returned to Charleston too soon for the good of the country,
which they would have edified and enlightened. I baptized a man named Barnet, who resides at Hendersonville,
where I preached in 1868, in the Court-house. He married
a respectable Catholic young woman, and their union is

blessed by many children, who are being raised in the Faith in the midst of error, and without a solitary Catholic within the range of their associates.

Fortified with the Holy Sacraments, and regretted by all his neighbors, Terence Keenan departed this life about the year 1870 at a patriarchal age. His widow still survives him. He left seven children, all married but one, who chose the better part. She forsook the world and joined the noble order of the Sisters of Mercy, in Charleston, of which she is a most efficient and edifying member. The others, whose lot is cast in the middle-class of society, are all worthy people, and each raising a large family of children in the knowledge and service of God, and in love of his holy faith. John, the oldest son, is married, and resides at Greenville, S. C.

Archbishop Gibbons relates that when the Rev. L. P. O'Connell first visited Asheville, in 1850, on presenting himself to the Keenan family, the venerable matron, supposing him to be an impostor, refused to receive him. He readily produced the vestments, as the most unquestionable credentials of the truth of his priesthood and mission. She became still more incredulous, and grew indignant, remarking, "You are not the first of your sort who has tried to impose on us by this same trick. These things may be easily procured, and the attempt has been made heretofore by other preachers for the iniquitous purpose of deception. Quit the house this minute." He did so, but loitered round until the return of Mr. Keenan, who was absent, believing he could more easily persuade him that he was a priest. To occupy the time more profitably, he commenced to recite the Rosary of the Blessed Virgin. While the beads were dropping through his fingers, the pious lady, who was a spectator from the inside of the house, drew near meekly and sorrowfully, besought his blessing and forgiveness, and received him as an angel from heaven. "I beg your Reverence's pardon," she said ; "I know now you are the Lord's holy priest. *I may be cheated by oth'r means, but never on them beads ;* the Mother of God would not allow it. Come into the house, Father Lawrence, you must be tired."

Hugh and Jane live in the ancestral homestead. Ellen, who was united in matrimony to Martin Doyle, resides in Savannah, and rejoices in the advantages of Catholic education for her growing offspring. Mary is married to A. L. Cordell, a native and a convert, and has grown up children. Catherine's husband, William Wright, has also embraced the doctrines of the Catholic Church. Margaret married Peter Cox, an exemplary Christian and a man much esteemed for industry and virtue. He now occupies Millgrove, in Cabarrus County, the former seat of the Harris family, and he is never more happy than when dispensing a refined hospitality to priest or bishop that may visit his section of the country. The secret of the perseverance of this numerous family of children was the good example of their parents, their habits of industry and sobriety, and their entire exemption from all sectarian influence in matters of religion. They were never inside a Protestant church. We must not refuse a due meed of praise to their indefatigable clergy, though some of the family were grown before they beheld a priest to know him.

If all our early immigrants had been equally emulous for the inheritance of the truth, how many that are now lost would have been saved! At least, by this time, one-half the population would belong to the Catholic Church, the civil government would be secure, and the entire country bloom like another paradise of God. Her valleys of romantic beauty would rejoice in the abundance of peace, and the mountains and hills be glad to re-echo the sound of the Mass-bell. Many a soul is lost by a false and mistaken liberality. It is not an act of kindness to our brother to give the sanction of our presence to his errors, which in their practical application are fatal to his eternal welfare.

It is always best to live and speak the truth openly, like the Church in defining the Infallibility of the Pope at the Vatican Council. Expediency, human prudence, or the fear of temporal inconvenience are no excuses for mutilating or glossing over the faith to make it palatable to unbelievers. It is certain the world never will relish the truth, excuse it as best we may. Unlike the law, the Gospel does not stutter, nor does the apostle stammer or lisp; he has the gift of tongues, and must speak the whole truth without fear or favor. The institutions and the mysteries of the Church are not ours, but belong to God, and we have no right nor power to modify them, much less can we explain them away.

Some people prefer moral to doctrinal sermons. It is difficult to fix any certain rule; but morals are not the exclusive property of the Church; they are common to all, both pagan and Christian, and form the basis of all order, law, and society; they are the most popular, being based on common and undebatable ground. Now, faith comes by hearing, or lawfully-commissioned preaching. If our faith be not explained and defended, how will you make converts? I have known controversial sermons addressed to congregations exclusively Catholic to do more good than moral exhortations; for by these the mind is enlightened, popular objections not unknown to our very children are solved; numbers who resisted ordinary appeals for years opened their hearts to the grace of God, and approached the holy tribunal of penance. It would be well to bear this fact in mind in a country where the faith of our youth is daily exposed to shipwreck by the sophistry, fallacies, or sneers and infidel tendency of the age. The faith must be preached to all nations before the day of doom. The accomplishment of this commission will be a sign of the coming of the Son of Man. How far the injunction has been already observed, and how extensively rejected, is known only to God.

Faith is God's best gift; even hope and charity follow only from it. When sufficiently proposed and the motives of its credibility shown to be conclusive, its denial or unbelief is the greatest sin man can commit. It is the immorality of the mind, which is immensely worse than that of the heart. It is one of the sins against the Holy Ghost, and implies that God may be deceived himself or could deceive us, or that the manifestation of his will was unnecessary. It is not permitted us to look over the doctrine of revelation and reject those which seem improbable or impossible—that is, to believe on the authority of our own understanding, which is not faith. Faith is believing on the authority of God, and on sufficient evidence, truths beyond our comprehension, the knowledge of which is necessary for the information of our minds and the direction of our acts. The distinction between essential and non-essential doctrines is entirely gratuitous and without any foundation; a mixture of truth and falsehood is not a system; it is only a speculation. God is equally offended by our refusing to believe one point as by our refusing to believe all, because each rests alike on the same motive of belief, and it is equally an opposition to God's truth and authority. No man can pretend to adore his Maker by the belief or profession of a falsehood, be it ever so plausible, any more than by the violation of a moral command. A nominal Catholic who believes all the Church teaches is nearer to God than a morally virtuous infidel; for, while neither can expect salvation in that state, the former already worships God in paying him the homage of his understanding, the noblest part of man's nature, and at any moment his faith may enkindle charity, which in an instant would destroy his sins, bring him to confession, and reconcile him to his Maker.

The severity of God's visitation on the sin of heresy and schism is manifest from the historical fact that no people who as a nation rejected the faith and threw off the yoke of Jesus Christ have been reconverted or reconciled to the Church. This will apply to every country overrun by heresy, from Arianism to the so-called Reformation inclusively. The same may be maintained of apostates; scarcely one out of a thousand is reconciled to the Church by penance. St. Paul says it is impossible or extremely difficult. Surely the cases are rare.

A weak instrument in the hand of the Almighty, I restored to peace, and in doing so reconciled to themselves, people who had offended nearly in all. They were the purchased of the Precious Blood. Before the world was made the Father of Mercies counted their sins over and over again; yet he loved and created them, and sent his Son to die for them. Doubtless some who fell off from the true faith have been reconciled, but such instances are very rare. Apostasy being the sin of the intellect, its malice is intense and of the nature of Satan's apostasy. Humility is the philosophy of our condition as creatures, and the Holy Ghost says that it exalts and ennobles us, while pride debases. Sinners are and will be proud, hence the world hates confession. Humility alone imparts that confidence which consoles us and encourages the effort to rise, because it comes from the grace of God. Nature is not grace and possesses no remedy for the maladies of the soul; all attempts to rise again based thereon are ineffectual and the assertion of a heresy. Apostates possess no strength of resolution, and are bereft of steadfastness of principle. Excessive grief wastes them away for a time, but it is not true sorrow; and if not despair, is the result of mortified pride or the shadow of the remorse of the reprobate.

These truths are made manifest in the case of Judas. He sorrowed even to death, confessed his sins to the priests of the temple, repaired the scandal before the public, and made entire and immediate restitution; but, like his prototype, Cain, perished by despair. He wanted confidence in God's mercy, which alone saved Peter, whose crime, no less heinous, was aggravated by perjury. Remorse and human sorrow avail nothing, whilst contrition elevates though it humbles, consoles while it afflicts, and restores the fallen to his former state of grace and friendship with God. Our penitents are the brightest jewels in the crown of the divine humanity, but there are few apostates among them. Priests and bishops apostatized, but never a pope. All the early heresies, those of later times, and the rejection of the mystery of the Incarnation in its many forms were nearly all the work of perverse ecclesiastics. No state or condition in life secures a person from falling into sin; the company of our Lord did not secure Judas. Even Ozius, who, as apostolic delegate, presided at the Council of Nice, fell into the error which the Church then condemned. In our own day converts returned to the errors they had abjured. Heresy seems to have exhausted its fecundity of innovations, and nothing more remains to be invented. Protestantism, because not the king's daughter, places all her excellence in external observances, and she manifests an unwillingness to receive into her ministry men of tarnished reputation and reprehensible morals. Such men do not last long; they perish from the intoxication of the passions to which they abandon themselves to find a refuge from thought.

There is no man living so helpless or more to be pitied than a priest who becomes unfortunate. His training unfits him for any of the useful and honorable occupations of society by which he may obtain his livelihood. The laity reject him, his superiors will repose no further confidence in him; he is flung like a weed on the world and can never look to any quarter for hope or help. A good name is as necessary for a clergyman's usefulness as for a woman's respectability; in this respect they are very much alike, and in its absence both are contemptible. In every age and in all denominations there have been and there still are men who disgrace their profession and the Christian name by the disorders of their lives, denying by acts what they believe in theory, who have not practised what they preached. One who commits a fault is not necessarily bad; it may have been an accident and wanting in the requisites constituting moral guilt — in fact, no sin at all, and yet possessing disqualifications for the exercise of the sacred functions of the ministry. No bishop can be expected to intrust the care of souls to a fallen man.

It is a tremendous privilege to step into the holy of holies and into the sanctuary of the human heart; they must render a strict account for all whom they permit to enter. If a bishop's judgment respecting the worthiness of those who are to receive and exercise spiritual jurisdiction is conclusive, he must not be blamed for the faithful discharge of a most solemn duty. The salvation of the clergy is committed to the charge of the bishop equally as as that of the laity, and more especially so. When a priest makes a mistake or falls, unfortunately his usefulness is impaired by his act, no matter what his criminality may be. Prudence, mildness, and the clearest proofs of guilt should direct the judgment of the ordinary before passing a sentence of condemnation or suspension, particularly in a country where the priests are unprotected by parochial rights or canon law, and are absolutely at the mercy of their superiors. No man is impeccable, and none but the pope infallible, nor even he in administering the affairs of the diocese of Rome as a bishop, but as the Vicegerent of Jesus Christ in teaching the truths of faith.

We must stand by episcopal judgment until, if erroneous, it is annulled by the Holy See, which has not unfrequently happened after an appeal. To both parties this is a trying mode of adjusting domestic difficulties, but often necessary.

I have observed that in cases of wrong suffered at the hands of a superior, and remaining unredressed after proper explanation, it is better to suffer patiently and wait for God's interference, which will inevitably come in due season, as the reward of not having given public scandal. The greatest need of the Church in the United States is a retreat for aged and otherwise disabled clergymen. In no country on the globe have the Catholic people so liberally erected all institutions necessary for the educational, religious, and bodily wants of the faithful than here. We have asylums for the orphans, hospitals for the infirm, and houses of refuge for abandoned women who have been reclaimed, but we have no shelter for the unfortunate of our clergy, who, as a body, are the best men on earth. The

ASYLUM NEEDED FOR DISABLED PRIESTS.

small number who fall are not bad in all cases. All they require is a place of retirement, where, sheltered from the world, they may do penance, confess, and amend their faults, prepare to meet their Maker, or take resolutions for a better future. If any of our prelates attempt this noble undertaking he will find himself munificently sustained by the liberal offerings of clergy and laity; he will be the means of saving many a good man, and of restoring several to usefulness in the Church; his memory will be blessed, and held in perpetual veneration. The adaptation of this region for such an institution suggested this train of thought to the writer.

During Bishop Gibbons' first visit to Asheville, in 1868, a vacant space, containing about seven and a half acres, in the centre of the town attracted his and the clergy's attention. A more suitable site for a church and other ecclesiastical buildings could not be found. It was purchased at a moderate sum from Colonel N. A. Woodfin, an eminent lawyer, now dead, who also contributed handsomely towards the contemplated object. The people were anxious for the establishment of a Catholic church. I waited on the principal citizens, and they responded very generously to my appeal for assistance, with but three or four exceptions. The interruption of the work on the Western North Carolina Railroad, on account of fraud and general mismanagement, which caused much litigation and excitement at the time, severely militated against our undertaking. Major Turner, an engineer, John Malone, and other contractors, with their large force of operatives, sold out and withdrew. It is conceded on all sides that these men are the most liberal in their offerings for the erection of our churches; here they were incapable of making the payments they promised, and the priests, Fathers L. P. and J. P. O'Connell, were driven to the alternative of collecting money abroad to pay for the site and build the church or desist from the undertaking. They succeeded, after much labor, in realizing the necessary funds, and the following year a commodious brick building was erected, and dedicated by Bishop Gibbons under the invocation of St. Lawrence.

Thus, after many years, Catholicity at last found a home in the mountains. On account of its healthiness, agriculture, mineral, and other resources, and when the railroads now in course of construction will be completed, Asheville cannot fail to become a populous and a fashionable city. She will possess many sanitary, religious, and educational institutions, and will not only vie but she is destined to become, ere long, one of the largest inland cities in the Southern States. I am convinced that the people are now living who will see the first Bishop of Asheville, and that a cathedral, and all the other institutions which cluster around it, will adorn the vacant grounds lying round the Church of St. Lawrence.

The interior of the country is better adapted for diocesan institutions than seaport towns; it is healthier, and the means of living cheaper.

The causes which directed concentration to the seaboard will cease in proportion as immigration forces its way inward, which is its natural destiny, and as facilities for travel and transportation increase. The progress in this respect is so gigantic as to have annihilated space and even difficulties. In future economy and health will mostly determine the location of our colleges and other institutions. None of our Southern cities along the Atlantic shore can ever become places of extensive education. Periodically they are devastated by yellow fever or other malarious distempers of the most malignant type. All who can, flee away to more favored regions in summer, or run the risk of early death. Even our bishops are often absent most of the summer and fall, and cannot return to their charge before frost. In every diocese there are regions as healthy as any on earth, like Asheville and many other cities, which, in the course of events, must become centres of episcopal administration.

A worthy family, consisting of three persons—the parents, who are advanced in years, and an only son—made their way in later times to Morganton; their name is Tute. This is the chief town of Burke County, and on the way to Asheville. The priests and bishop make it a stopping-place, remain a day or two during their visits, and preach in the Court-house. Vicar-General O'Connell has done so repeatedly, and Bishop Gibbons also, under the patronage and direction of Dr. Happoldt, an educated and liberal man, though not yet a Catholic. He is a native of South Carolina.

There is also a hermit among these mountains. A more suitable place can scarcely be found for the anchoretical state. An acre of ground, a spring of clear water, and a hut supply him with all he asks from this world. If contentment, solitude, security for life, food and raiment, scant but sufficient for his wants, can render a man happy here below, he is eminently so. On this continent there is not a more independent man. Having joined the first pilgrimage to Rome, he obtained, after his return, episcopal sanction for this mode of life, and he rivals in austerity and sanctity the fathers of the desert. As this will never reach him, I can say without incurring the danger of offending his humility that he *is* a man of God. He lived a long time in the most rigorous order of the Church, obtained a dispensation, and now, like another Antony, hallows by his praise and prayers the caves of those cloud-piercing mountains. Who can tell how many world-weary souls may follow his example, and seek here for peace and rest? A company had been formed, and an extensive purchase of land been made in Henderson County, and in the direction of Haywood, for the purpose of introducing and planting a Catholic colony. It fell through for the present. This location forms part of what was formerly known as Transylvania. It possesses advantages for this object unsurpassed by any section of the United States. Such an undertaking must succeed, and it confirms all my hopes of seeing Catholicity prevail over the entire region. Already the Benedictines are established in Gaston County, close by, attend the missions, and are preparing to receive pupils into their favored institution.

The Rev. Felix J. Carr died of consumption in Asheville, at the Keenan residence, in 1862. Born in Chester, South Carolina, of edifying and pious parents, and losing his father in his infancy, his mother moved to Charleston and raised him in the love and service of God. He was adopted by Bishop England into the diocesan seminary, where he studied some time until sent to the Propaganda. Ambitious in the pursuit of learning, endued with mental faculties of no mean order, and formed under the favorable system of education at the fountain-head of ecclesiastical training, he became a ripe scholar and acquired a large fund of varied information. Having cultivated an extensive knowledge of the leading departments of science, literature, and art, pious and devoted to his vocation, he became an efficient and agreeable public speaker. In consequence of the political troubles in Rome towards the close of the pontificate of Gregory XVI., he, with his class, received Holy Orders before the completion of the usual course of theology. When he arrived in Charleston he was appointed an assistant at the cathedral and tutor in the school then conducted by Bishop Reynolds. He attended Walterborough and other stations in the vicinity, and always discharged the holy duties of the priesthood with zeal and commendable fidelity. After nearly fourteen years of labor the insidious disease claimed for its victim a constitution always frail and delicate. The skill of medical science, the tenderness of friendship and family affection essayed in vain to arrest the daily inroads of the fatal but illusive malady. A change of climate was recommended, and he sought the mountains. It was too late; immediately after his arrival he gradually sunk. His last days were consoled by the ministrations and prayers of the good people around him. He breathed out his soul while calling on the name of his Maker. He was about thirty-six years of age. His remains were removed for interment to the city by his surviving brother, Rev. A. J. McNeil, and now lie by the ruins of the Cathedral of SS. John and Finbar. He was the second native of the State of South Carolina who was ordained priest; Rev. James A. Corcoran, D.D., now of Philadelphia, was the first.

Some time after the commencement of the civil war the slaves were removed from the scene of conflict as far as possible and sold. The worthless currency was invested in this manner; people were so infatuated as not to perceive that one was as precarious as the other. The number of slaveholders was increased. A compromise with Mr. Lincoln on the basis of remuneration could benefit only the new proprietors into whose hands the property had already passed. The wealthy had become poor and the speculators opulent. The people were willing to sacrifice the lives of their sons and of the honest, poor soldiers, whose families were straitened for want of the necessaries of existence at home, but they would not consent to part with their slaves or their imaginary money. A more mercenary people or inefficient Government could not be found; most of the time we had only a military despotism, which dwindled down into committees of public safety, often embracing men of questionable reputation. The country bordered on anarchy. Among the great masses of the Southern people, all the poor whites and others who owned no slaves, secession was very unpopular. After the first year the law of conscription was enforced at the point of the bayonet, and was generally avoided when possible. I have seen men manacled and dragged into the ranks by force, like malefactors. Many of the more influential who were conscripted escaped by exemption for detailed service in the commissary department, while others were engaged in hunting down deserters or recusants in the woods or mountain fastnesses, and using dogs for the purpose. When the Confederate money became as common as rags, the war for a time became more popular from the expectation that it would be valuable in the event of success. It was the mercenary spirit that overthrew the Government. Emancipation would have gained us world-wide sympathy, and would have disarmed our enemies, if we had had the patriotism to pass the ordinance and anticipate the Lincoln decree.

Flat Rock is above the level of the sea 2,100 feet, nearly 1,000 feet higher than Greenville; Asheville is 2,290; Cæsar's Head, 3,200; Cashier's Valley, 4,000; whilst Mount Mitchell, or the Black Mountain, rises to an altitude of 6,711 feet, and is the loftiest peak this side of the Rocky Mountains. A remarkable mass of serrated mountains surround it, leaving a gap to the south. If a photographer visit this region, he shall be amply rewarded by the inconceivably picturesque and bold mountain scenery such as this. There are two peaks, Clingman's, so called from the distinguished general of that name, whose measurement was unanimously accepted as correct, until Professor Mitchell, of the State University, claimed a greater elevation by some few feet for the point which now holds his remains. For some time the controversy between both claimants and their respective friends waxed warm, and culminated in much asperity of feeling. The question is still undecided. While engaged authenticating by additional proof the accuracy of his measurement, the professor lost his life in the effort, and by this fact succeeded in giving his name to the mountain. Being absent for several days, fears were entertained for his safety, increased by the return of his faithful dogs nearly famished. The people of Asheville and the intermediate country began a thorough search, and after much exertion discovered his lifeless body in Caney River and beneath a steep, rugged precipice. He evidently missed his way, and while groping in the dark slipped and was dashed to pieces among the rocks lying in the bed of the torrent.

Peat is very abundant near the extreme top; the tortuous road is deep and muddy at several places even in the middle of summer. An undergrowth of dwarf shrubs and the cedar, which is utterly worthless for any useful purpose, even for fuel, are the most numerous trees as you ascend higher. This mountain cedar is of a soft, sobby texture, and

may be chopped with but little effort. There is an open
space the size of a city square near Clingman's Peak ; it is
almost level, without trees of any description, and covered
with verdure, having no trace of cultivation, how caused,
tradition does not say. The area of the mountain is a
vast extent of country, embracing many thousand acres,
stretching north towards Yancey County. The soil is
a dark loam, unavailable for remunerative agriculture, and
valued at about ten or fifteen cents per acre. The south
side is warm in summer, but on nearing the top the tem-
perature is cold and chilly, the winds from the continental seas blowing strongly without interception. The road
leading from the residence of Judge Baily, at the foot of
the mountain, is winding, rough, and difficult of ascent.
Excursionists make the journey generally on foot, but the
weaker may ride safely on horseback a great part of the
way, computed to be five or six miles, being all up-hill.
The property belongs to the heirs of Mr. Patten, an excellent man, of Irish birth, hospitality, and enterprise, but
now dead. After heavy expense he succeeded in building
far on towards the summit, on a narrow table-land, a house
of entertainment for pleasure-seekers and excursionists,
known as the Mountain Hotel. Sand, timber, and all other
building materials were brought from the base of the mountain on the shoulders of slaves, the only available way.
During the war it was deserted, and became an inaccessible
shelter for deserters and renegades, conscripts and outlaws.
They burned for fuel the doors and outhouses, reducing
the premises to a condition of decay and ruin. I slept one
night here during the month of August, 1866, when it blew
almost a hurricane and the wind was very cold, although
there was no snow on the ground since July. Bears, foxes,
and other game still abound over the entire region, and the
streams are full of speckled trout. I know no more de-
lectable place on the face of the globe for innocent and
healthy amusement and recreation.

Accompanied by a half-dozen others, I visited the mountain that year. We travelled all day on the level road

running by all the sinuosities of the beautiful Swannanoa, a clear, bold stream, named after the daughter of an Indian chief. After having rested during the night at the late Judge Baily's, we were fresh enough to make the ascent in the morning. Having reached the deserted hotel in the afternoon, we found shelter inside its menacing walls for the night. Early the following morning, and as the sun shot his first rays in great splendor over the distant eastern hills, diffusing all around a flood of golden light far more brilliant than St. Peter's illuminated, I erected an altar and said Mass. It was the Feast of St. Rose of Lima, the first flower of the American Church, August 30. There could be no temple more sublime or more worthy of that Holy Sacrifice. The majestic mountains that stood around on all sides, like the ancients before the throne of the Lamb, seemed to bare their heads in tumultuous adoration before their Maker. I imagined they rejoiced after centuries of waiting in being able to pay their first act of jubilant homage to the Hand that raised them up, the unbending witnesses of his power, wisdom, and goodness. All present partook of the Bread of Life, one a sincere convert, A. L. Cardell, the son of a Protestant bishop, and his children, youths in their teens; Mrs. Anne Keenan, and a daughter of Terence Keenan, now an edifying Sister of Mercy, called in religion Sister Genevieve.

I trust that in time to come, when the number of the faithful will have increased, the remembrance of this solemn dedication of the entire region to our saint will be perpetuated by an enduring memorial, and that the name and invocation of St. Rose will bless a country so fertile and rivalling in beauty of scenery the most favored portion of God's earth. We noticed at a distance, in the cleft of a steep rock overlooking a valley of almost unearthly beauty, what looked like the outspread wings of a dove. On approaching it, we found it to be a marble cross, erected to the memory of a daughter of Mr. Patten, a sweet child, who died in her innocence, and lies buried in the city by the sea. Although not of the household of the faith, the father was evidently a man of elevated thought and Catholic instincts. We departed after having restored and fastened the cross in its niche, from which the hand of some vandal had torn it, and with effort, for it had been solidly imbedded in the rock. It may have been the act of a pious iconoclast or noted scientist. Human learning cannot impart the gift of faith, destroy prejudice, or subdue the passions; nay, it intensifies the evil propensities of the mind and heart, and, when emancipated from the grace of God, makes men—even philosophers—the slaves of error and monsters of vice. The history of the human race forbids this fact to be called in question.

This is unquestionably a volcanic region. A rumbling noise was heard and smoke was seen ascending from Bald Mountain in the autumn of 1877. The inhabitants were terrified, and many fled from the vicinity. On a subsequent examination a fissure near the summit was discovered a few yards wide. Several theories are advanced by scientists on its formation.

There is a great deal in a name, and a Christian one would give an additional charm to this country. We are forbidden to call our children in baptism vulgar or unchristian names. In no country of the civilized globe will you find so many people spoiled by their names as in the United States. The same fact may be predicated of places. The various departments of mechanism, agriculture, and occupation are the inexhaustible sources of nomenclature; pet abbreviations aggravate the odious custom, and now genteel names are daily becoming more scarce. The Indian names are preferable both in sound and meaning. A name was originally meant to be descriptive of the object to which it was attached. The only respectable names in America are Catholic. The cities were called after and in honor of some mystery of religion or some saint; and the new discoveries also received the title or were designated by the festival on which they were made.

God's names are his perfections, and form the most

comprehensive treatise extant on the divine nature for the entire human race; his name is his praise. The Church adores the mystery by a solemn festival and special service. The truth is clearly impressed on the minds of her children, who with unshod footstep approximate as closely as reverence may permit; and hence her grand nomenclature for dates, localities, and individuals. We know how many names were first given from heaven to be called on earth; the world and all that it contains is God's world, and not ours, and must return to him; as it already bears the image, it is meet that the inscription also should be expressive of the origin and destiny of all things.

At the close of the war I visited this section of my mission in a wagon, all public conveyances having been discontinued. Commencing at Morganton, I made the entire circuit of the county in this manner until I reached Greenville, South Carolina. I spent six weeks travelling. I had only the ordinary two-horse vehicle, with the usual canvas cover and the adjuncts of a kettle, frying-pan, and some bedding, besides a litter of straw. I knew I must camp out at night by reason of the reluctance of the people to receive strangers under their roofs during the unsettled state of the country. My companions were an ex-Confederate soldier and his little son. At the end of the first day we reached the Catawba by sunset. It was Saturday, the 3d of August, and an unusually warm day. At this ford the river is of moderate proportions in summer, and slow, as if resting after its struggling efforts to force a way through the rough gorges of the mountains. All the other streams rising north of the Blue Ridge, with this solitary exception, flow into the Mississippi. We camped by the riverside, and, having prepared our simple meal, well seasoned with Arcadian sauce, partook of it with a relish. By early dawn we forded the stream and hastened on, in order to reach by noon the house of a Catholic family where I intended saying Mass. The day was Sunday, and also the Feast of St. Dominic. Respect for the divine mysteries of our redemption forbade their celebration in any of the houses remotely scattered by the roadside, lest they might be exposed to ridicule or profane curiosity. We made so little progress during the morning hours, now spent, that all hope of reaching the desired locality within the canonical time was abandoned. The sun overtopped the eastern hills, man and beast grew faint and weary, for suffering, like danger, levels both. All lawful prayers are heard, some after a long time, others by the granting of a better gift, and some instantly. An ejaculation may defeat an army, avert a thunderbolt, or save a soul in the last moment. I fervently prayed that I might be led to a suitable place where I could offer the Holy Sacrifice. How easy it would be for him who provided his Immaculate Mother with a place for his birth to renew the favor for the mystic oblation. We halted by a stream of clear water gurgling by. I noticed that it was spanned by the trunk of a tree smoothed into the level of a foot-bridge. Led by curiosity, I crossed over, and within a few yards, in an angle sheltered from the road by tall trees, a neat, new, clean, untenanted house of moderate dimensions, suddenly burst on my view. It was a school-house. In a short time a genteel altar was constructed out of the pine boards profusely scattered around, and I said the Mass of the great Patriarch of the Order of Preachers. The surroundings were in keeping with the historic records of many of his sons. Every innocent object of sense—a word, a feast, or a name—will often quicken our devotion and kindle it into a flame. I have made thanksgivings for at least eleven thousand Masses since I was ordained, but never before nor since have I experienced the devotion and consolation vouchsafed on that occasion. Years afterwards I revisited the unknown chapel, and found it in the same good order and condition, still unoccupied and unmolested either by time or the hand of man, as though it was guarded and watched over by the angel of this wilderness.

How sad that many of these lone valleys, not unworthy of angels' visits, have been the scenes of crime and guilt, and each has its tale of horror to tell! The harmony of creation is marred by the iniquities of our race. Whatever is beautiful in nature, rational or inanimate, is the lurking-place of evil. The Mountain Meadows of Utah are a fairy-land, but they will ever record the most shocking massacre of modern times. Farther on, the road, once an Indian trail, passes through a sequestered opening of moderate size, and so abruptly hemmed in by frowning oak-clad hills as to seem without either ingress or outlet, forming a palace, an amphitheatre, or a prison, whichever imagination may choose to fancy. From time immemorial travellers and traders made it their favorite camp. Being sheltered on all sides round, vertical rays or rains chiefly visit it. The scenes of revelry and festive enjoyment, the deeds of daring and of death related by the glare of the night-fire, all the incidents that transpired within these majestic walls, if put on record, would fill many a volume.

During *the late unpleasantness* a detail of exempts, a class always detested, were conducting some conscripts or recaptured deserters to the next military post for trial and subsequent transfer to the dreaded battle-fields of Virginia. They passed by this way. The bitterness of party strife on the part of the captors yielding to more gentle thoughts, and humanity reasserting itself in the presence of the grandeur of natural scenery, they relaxed their vigilance. The captives, perceiving their advantage, instantly arose and mercilessly slew them. They fled like lightning, and were shortly as free as the deer on their native mountains. Now imagination hears a death-wailing in the night winds that moan in that blood-stained vale, and no lone man will camp there.

I was the first who brought to Asheville the intelligence that the Ordinance of Secession was passed by South Carolina, at her Convention in Columbia on the 20th of December, 1860. On my arrival by stage, at a late hour of the night, I found quite a number gathered round the fire at the Eagle Hotel, and impatiently waiting to learn the result of the assembled wisdom of the neighboring State. They were alarmed on hearing the fact ; it was entirely disapproved and denounced in the most emphatic terms, accompanied with fatal forebodings which were, alas! but too true, and were shared eagerly by the very men who so strongly condemned the proceedings. Shortly afterwards I was solicited to address the citizens in order to reconcile them to the general expediency of the measure, which I declined. The people had complaints to make, but they loved the Union and were led to a disruption by the persuasion of politicians, and subsequently by the stringency of penal laws enacted for the purpose.

The portion of Columbia sacked by Sherman chiefly belonged to the mercantile and poorer classes, who were as strongly attached to the Union as he, and who hailed with joy his occupation of the city. The war was no rebellion; no statesman will designate it by that unjust term; it was the legitimate assertion of constitutional rights, and this conviction brought into the field twice the number of men necessary to win independence if properly managed, but they melted away under injustice and neglect. They were badly handled and were paralyzed by the incompetency, jealousy, and treachery of some of the head officers. Tens of thousands died for want of food, clothing, shelter, or medical attendance. May the ornamentation of their graves when dead expiate the cruel injustice they endured. The poetry of the inception had fled under the terrible realities of the protracted struggle. The fashionable women who even promised to marry none but a soldier now despise the sight of an armless or crippled Confederate. I saw them begging food; they were refused even common sympathy. If the South had been true to herself she never would have been subdued. She became the victim of her faithlessness. The destiny of nations is in the hands of God. Slavery was an evil, and it would eventually have destroyed itself by territorial limitation.

The fidelity of the slaves during the war is without a parallel in the history of the world. Outnumbering the white population, whose protectors were absent in the army, and none but disabled men, women, and children left, an ordinary negro insurrection could easily have destroyed every living white person. Under these inducements, and the additional one of the knowledge of their emancipation, they remained faithful, cultivated the soil, raised provisions for the support of the army, defended the person and property of their owners from injury; even they were anxious to join in the fray and share their fortunes if intrusted with arms. The refusal was the most fatal mistake of the Southern people, whose policy was a chain of blunders. They can never repay the negro race the debt of gratitude which is so justly due them. It shall not be forgotten. Even the hostile interference of the adventurers who came after the war scarcely interrupted it. The former master is the black man's best friend, and both races will move henceforward in harmony, domestic governments having been restored to the South.

CHAPTER XIV.

BENEDICTINE PARISH—INSTITUTE OF ST. MARY OF HELP, GASTON AND CABARRUS COUNTIES.

A Narrow Escape from Drowning in the Catawba—Irish Faith—St. Mary's Parish—Soil, Climate, Productions—Early Settlers—The Lonergans and other Families—Valuable Property Lost to the Jesuits—Civilizers of the Modern World—A Prosperous Land—Old Irish Names—Converts—Privations of the Clergy—Fathers Guifford and Barry—Lawrence O'Connell—The O'Connell Property Conveyed to the Benedictines—An Institution and College Founded—The Benedictine Family—Right Rev. Abbot Wimmer—The Order—Field Sports, etc.—Irish and German Immigration—Persecutions—Nativism—Scotch-Irish—Cabarrus—The Barnhardt Family and other Converts—St. James's Church—The Priest's Oak—Attempt at Assassination—A Narrow Escape—An Age of Controversy—An Opposition Parson—Predestination—Protestant Rule of Faith, the Road to Infidelity—A Foe Conquered.

IN the autumn of 1852 I narrowly escaped drowning in Thompson's Ford. Having reached Charlotte late on Saturday evening, on my way to officiate at the Gaston church on Sunday, the brothers Patrick and Peter Cox met me, by appointment, with a conveyance to bring me to their residence, in the vicinity of the church, an arrangement which gave time to hear the confessions early, before Mass, in order not to keep the people waiting too long. It was the regular Sunday, and it was a standing rule in the diocese never to disappoint on the day or time for service, especially on the outside missions. This strictness is of vast advantage to the faithful; it saves them from losing Mass, or entering the church at an unreasonable time and interrupting the service. Punctual attendance to the first summons of the bell is a sure test of strict observance in all religious houses.

It had rained heavily during several days. Arriving at the ford by dark, and ascertaining that the water-marks were invisible, we should have known that the river was unfordable. I was then ignorant of this caution.

On being asked if we might venture, I unhesitatingly answered in the affirmative. Looking one at the other, and mutually enquiring if they had said their morning prayers, without further hesitation my companions boldly urged their steeds into the yellow flood, like Aminadab at the Red Sea, but with different results, for neither foot of horse nor chariot-wheel found resting-place. My guides were sober, sedate men, timidly cautious in all their undertakings, and raised in this vicinity. If there was any danger in making the attempt, I imagined they would not have consulted one utterly unacquainted with the crossing at any season. I believed they were expert swimmers, and was mistaken here also. They were brought up in a holy dread of water. Skill would have been of no avail ; even a Boyton could not prevail against the resistless force of that giant stream.

The night was densely dark ; we were floated down the current like a feather. One of the riders swam his horse towards me ; transferring my person from the buggy, I took the back seat. The generous steed, as if conscious of danger, nobly breasted the headlong tide. After having been drifted down a considerable distance, he reached the opposite bank in safety. Aided by the overhanging willows, I crept out and was saved.

Floundering and pawing, man and horse turned back and braved the danger anew, to discover, and aid if possible, our lost companion, for we were parted midway. In an agony of prayer I besought our preservation from the Mother of God, and who ever asked her in vain ?

> "For never yet was gentle word
> In honor of the Virgin spoken,
> That was in heaven's court unheard
> Or did not heaven's grace betoken."

The ford was several hundred yards wide ; nothing could be seen, and no sound heard except the dull, deep roar of the waters, combining the boisterous voices of many a mountain torrent from afar. After a death-like suspense horses and riders approached, spent and wearied. Before reaching the shoals, where death would have been inevitable, the traces and harness dropped from the horse, as if parted by an invisible hand. Peter Cox sprung on the animal's back and effected his escape. The vehicle and its precious contents were swept away.

Remonstrating on the rashness of the undertaking, to my astonishment I was answered "that they knew the dangers, that no one ever before was known to have crossed the Catawba with safety at this place, and, under the circumstances, that our preservation was a miraculous interposition ; but, taught to believe in the priest and obey him implicitly, they concluded that the feat must be accomplished, and never once doubted the result." The intercession of the Divine Mother and this Irish faith which planted the cross in the United States alone saved us from a watery grave. The inhabitants, when relating the fate of some and the narrow escape of others, in years past, along the course of this treacherous river, give due prominence to this adventure, which acquired publicity the following morning.

After the congregation had assembled, they, and many others in the vicinity, set out in search of the wreck. It was discovered at a considerable distance, high and dry, landed on the shoals at Tuckaseegee Ford, near Fite's Mill. Nothing, not even a strap of harness, was missing. Only a hearse was needed to make the day for ever memorable in Gaston. The only inconvenience was occasioned by the delay in drying the vestments ; they and the wilted Massbook bear to this day evidence of that night passed in the Catawba. The chalice did not fare as well. It was subsequently robbed from the safe, in St. Mary's College in Columbia, by Sherman's army when they sacked the city. It must have been lost in the transport *General Lyon*, burned off Hatteras, and freighted with the treasures of the unfortunate South.

Patrick Cox died in the spring of 1877, and is interred in the parochial cemetery among the remains of his pious parents and relatives. He leaves a widow and one child, a son. He was sixty-six years old, a man of strong faith and devoted to his religion. His sister Elizabeth lives on the old homestead; she is married to James Mulligan, an edifying, exemplary man, and raising an interesting family of Catholic children.

The following account of the foundation of the Benedictine Monastery of Our Lady of Help, Gaston County, North Carolina, originally appeared in the *Catholic Review*:

"Led by the hand of Providence, about half a dozen Catholic families, of Irish nationality, forced their way into the interior, purchased farms, and permanently settled in the eastern extremity of Gaston County, about the year 1830. For their future home they selected a fertile upland, situated within twelve miles of Charlotte, very productive in all the cereals, and also fruit and vegetables. The waters teem with fish and the woods with the wild turkey and other game. The muscadine folds its arms round the oaks untrained by the hand of the vintner, making the forest a prolific vineyard, and yielding not only choice fruit for the table but also a most delicious wine, known as the Scuppernong, which can be used for the Holy Sacrifice. The gathering and pressing of the grape is all the labor required to harvest this valuable crop. Gold mines are numerous and of inexhaustible richness. Brandy is extensively distilled from the apples and peaches, and is the source of considerable emolument. Beer made from the fruit of the persimmon and locust trees is a favorite beverage, and rivals lager in flavor and raciness. Cotton is planted extensively and is remunerative; the tree grows to a greater size than in South Carolina, but is not equally productive. The season here is shorter, the pods do not all mature before frost, and the third picking is stained and of an inferior quality, but the first and second pickings are unexceptionably good. The water power is immense, capable of working any amount of machinery, and the situations admirably adapted for the erection of factories. We already possess some in good paying condition and running well. When the country recovers from the disastrous consequences of the civil war and the subsequent misgovernment, they will spring up on all sides.

"There are ample facilities of skill and labor, but capital is wanting, not only in this department but for the development of all the other sources of prosperity. The climate is very mild and temperate, in no season reaching the excesses of the northern latitudes. A heat of ninety degrees in midsummer is a rare occurrence. The cold season lasts no longer than three months. Cattle and all the domestic animals find abundant pasture in the fields and by the watercourses, requiring neither food nor shelter, except between Christmas and April. The country cannot be surpassed for healthiness; elevated, and being the intermediate region between two rapid rivers which form a water-shed, all the dampness is drained off; there are no swamps nor pools, and consequently no malaria. Old age, accidents, and the ailments incidental to all habits or conditions of life are the chief ministers of death. Lands command a fair price and can be readily purchased, but are steadily increasing in value since the advent of the Benedictine Fathers and their community.

"The first Catholic inhabitants were a superior class of immigrants, thrifty, persevering, and industrious; some were distinguished for simplicity of manners and innocence of life; the women were virtuous and devout, and all were sincerely attached to their faith. They loved the Church as dearly as their own souls, and contributed to its establishment and maintenance, to their utmost abilities. The Lonergan family was the most numerous, consisting of four brothers, heads of so many households. They and all the early settlers are now dead, only one, Pierce Cahill, survived the war, who, with the Duffys, the Coxes, the Millers, and the Hawkinses, were all alike an honor to their country and to their faith. The Lepers, grandchildren of John Lonergan, practise their religion; the descendants of Mr. Cahill, the three widowed daughters of Edward Lonergan with their numerous children are favorably known to the Church. John Ryan, James Mulligan, the Gatens brothers, Matthew Armstrong, John Hand, Patrick Rafter and their families, and others equally worthy, are the edifying representatives of all those who have gone to their eternal reward.

"Dallas is the county seat, a town of considerable importance and the terminus of a railroad. There is only one Catholic family in the community, the children of Andrew O'Brien, who died previous to the war. A citizen of this county sent his sons, one or two, to the Jesuit College at Georgetown to receive their education. In payment of their fees, or in gratitude for the care bestowed on his children, tradition does not say which, he bequeathed the society an immense tract of land, now of incredible value. O'Brien was sent by the society to claim it in their behalf. But it was too late; the claim was not urged in time to prevent the squatters from acquiring legal possession by the statute of limitation, and the property is for ever lost to the order. Although he failed in accomplishing the object of his mission, Mr. O'Brien acquired some real estate, and married the widow of a Protestant minister, whom he was the means of converting. The children, now grown to maturity, and their aged parent steadfastly adhere to their religion. Edward Lonergan, Jr., the last surviving male descendant of the family who bore the name, having been a long time in ill-health, visited his native country that he might obtain relief; on his return he died at sea, and is buried in the Atlantic Ocean near the American coast. He was a just, generous, and enterprising man, and the entire community lamented his death. Having adopted the Leper children, he educated them in the faith, and they now inherit the old and hospitable homestead.

"The Collenders of York County, South Carolina, also belong to this ecclesiastical district, and are worthy of mention for their unflinching adherence to the truth though isolated and born among a people hostile to their creed and race. About 1840 two brothers, Lawrence and John, found their way to this far-distant part of the State, nearly at the base of the King's Mountain. Having purchased a tract of land, they maintained themselves by their unaided exertions during a period when white labor was depreciated, and none but a slave owner was deemed worthy of respect or consideration. White poor people were barely tolerated, and always regarded with suspicion; learning and talent fared little better when unaccompanied by the sole excellence. Lawrence, the elder brother, died in 1873, after having endured for a long time, and with the patience of the martyr, a most painful ailment. Being unmarried, Lawrence became a second father to the widow, an excellent woman, and her four orphans. He instructed them in their religious duties, and trained them alike to habits of industry and virtue, an education which enlightened and directed them in after-life, conducted them safely through the perils of the war, and the subsequent dangers connected with the disorganized state of that country, during the Ku-klux excitement, when the inhabitants were chased by the Federal troops with bloodhounds. Though least befriended and the most exposed, they were peculiarly favored by Providence, to whose merciful care they attributed their protection. None could have stronger temptations to fall away from the faith, and they will rise in judgment against all who have done so; they form a living proof of the fact that the faith can be preserved under the most adverse circumstances. The father of these children, when in middle life, in the depth of winter, would travel twenty miles on foot, wade swollen creeks and swim rivers nearly frozen over, to hear Mass on Sunday.

"On Sundays the church is frequently filled to its capacity, yet there were never one hundred Catholics in the parish at any time; the others are enquirers after the truth. Some join the Church occasionally, and though not numerous, the converts are all well informed and respectable, among whom may be mentioned Mrs. Florence O'Connell, *née* Bradshaw, widow of the late Colonel P. J. O'Connell, John Hand and family, with others equally worthy though of less note. It was in this manner and by a class similarly situated that the Gospel was disseminated over the world since the days of the apostles, that the beacon-lights of religion were kept burning when her altars were overthrown by the English and German heresies, and that the doctrine of Jesus Christ has been established in recent times wherever conquest or discovery has thrown open a new country to commerce or civilization.

"Suffering is the law of incarnation; in the order of Divine Providence difficulties and trials are not only beneficial but necessary for the salvation of many souls. What is true of individuals will apply with equal force to the Church at large. Several succumbed under the opposition of the world, but the faith, hope, and charity of those who braved the storm increased. It was the number of believers that suffered momentary decrease, but not the virtue of those who survived. The Blessed Virgin, standing at the foot of the cross, had more faith than all the world to the day of doom. The sword of the persecutors enriched the Church with the blood of millions of martyrs, peopled heaven with saints, and, after having propagated, perpetuated the teachings of our Lord. The true believers at all times naturally clustered round the centres of apostolic and episcopal authority; in their numbers they found a solace for the loss of all things and a mutual support against the hatred of the world. Like the apostles on Thabor, they would remain always at the feet of their Master, and the circle of their influence would be circumscribed by narrow limits.

"Having no church edifice in his extensive district, and only three in all in the State, a few acres of land was donated to Father Cronin by William Lonergan for ecclesiastical purposes. The situation is delightful, on the public road, within a mile of Thompson's Ford, and on the western bank of the Catawba. The distance to Charlotte

Dallas, and Lincoln is nearly equal. A railroad bearing the latter name now passes at no great distance. Before he had made much progress in the undertaking, Father Cronin, the founder of the mission, died, and was buried in the vacant lot; the isolation of his grave was a pressing appeal to the devotion of the Catholic community, and hastened the completion of the work. John Guifford succeeded to the mission in 1843, and immediately commenced the building, which is a plain frame structure, sufficiently capacious to accommodate not only the Catholics but the strangers, who attend in large numbers to hear good sermons. Money was collected over the diocese, wherever a dollar could be obtained, and within two years it was completed, free from debts, and dedicated by Bishop Reynolds, under the title of SS. Mary and Joseph. An extensive burying-ground is attached, protected by a substantial stone wall, where all the Catholics who die throughout the entire region are interred. John Prendergast, one of the Lonergan family, an accomplished mechanic, conducted the workmanship. It is a model cemetery in all its details, and extensively copied in this and the surrounding counties. The priest's grave is in the centre, surrounded by the dead of two generations, who patiently await the second coming.

"Rev. John Guifford was a native of Scotland, where he studied for the ministry, and was ordained priest about the year 1827 by Bishop Scott. After having served some time on the mission in his native country, he arrived in Charleston in 1838, tendered his allegiance to Bishop England, and was adopted into the diocese. His first appointment was to the church of Providence, in Sumter district, where he is said to have endured the privations common to all the other clergy on country missions. Perhaps his entire congregation did not exceed twenty-five souls, and but two families. After the demise of Father Cronin, he was transferred thither by Very Rev. R. S. Baker, the administrator during the vacancy of the see of Charleston, and until the nomination of Bishop Reynolds. Having completed the church in Gaston, about 1847 he removed to the diocese of Chicago, and served some time on the mission, until declining strength induced him to retire into a religious house, where he spent his closing years in preparing to meet the Bishop of our souls. He was an accomplished orator, having studied rhetoric under the tragedian of his name. Fascinating as a public speaker, he always attracted a large audience. He preached the grand doctrine of the Church in a most forcible manner. He did not adopt the pagan style of oratory, so unbecoming in a priest, and so degrading to the word of God. His sermons were Christian, the ornaments selected from Scripture: this was one of the secrets of the fame and success of his preaching. His sermons are not published.

"Very Rev. John Barry, from Augusta, Georgia, made pastoral visits to Gaston at regular intervals during those years while there was no priest permanently stationed anywhere on this entire circuit. At the close of 1850 it was attached to Columbia, and remained so for a period of fifteen years, with some interruptions, extending the limits of that parish to the magnitude of all Ireland. The small number of priests in the diocese, about twenty in three States, the want of parochial residences, and the inadequate means of support necessitated the regulation. The policy of Bishop Portier, of Mobile, was found to be the best for the interests of religion and of the priest; he never stationed a man where he could not be respectably supported, otherwise even Catholics will depreciate him; and constituted as society is, he will not accomplish as much good. Priests humble and simple in their habits will be frequently met with in opulent congregations; but their mode of life, being voluntary and not of necessity, gains them additional influence and respect. Having an excess on the one hand is more dangerous and more productive of evil than absolute want or than apostolic poverty. A dandy minister of any denomination is the most odious fop in society, and rarely possesses any moral weight. On the withdrawal of Father Barry, caused by the erection of the State of Georgia into an independent see, I visited alternately with my brother, Rev. L. P. O'Connell, the church, and held service there, at least once in six weeks, and oftener whenever it was possible. Father McNeil spent about two years on the mission, and was succeeded by the Rev. J. P. O'Connell, D.D., who served during the trying and disastrous times of the civil war. The jubilee published by the pope to obtain from Almighty God the blessings of peace was very quickly answered; the war, after four years of bloody strife, came to a close immediately.

"The services of Father Lawrence O'Connell as post chaplain at White Sulphur Springs, Greenbrier County, Virginia, having ended, he returned. He had ranked as major in the Confederate army. Gaston County was selected as the field of his future labors. Attending to the sick and wounded of both armies, his health suffered, and has never been fully restored. Under this disadvantage he has most faithfully discharged his duties as pastor for fourteen years to the faithful of his vast district. With Charlotte for his headquarters, he visits, at this time in which I write, Cabarrus County, Salisbury, Morganton, Asheville, Hendersonville, and all the intermediate stations. His health, though by no means as good as formerly, promises many more years of usefulness in the Lord's vineyard. He is a solid and able public speaker, a sincere, grave man, and an efficient priest. On his first visitation Bishop Gibbons created him Vicar-General, and he has filled the office with commendable meetness and efficiency. He has been living many years in the sacristy at the rear of the church in Charlotte, said to be in summer the hottest place in the town. When the present edifice will be replaced by the contemplated new one, a suitable residence will be built for the pastor, or, perhaps, for the bishop. Before then another generation will have passed away, and people yet unborn will reap the harvest sown in suffering and in tears.

"With the sole exception of legalized persecution, the

priests of the diocese resemble the clergy in England in their privations and labors during the period between the great apostasy and the emancipation.

"Having planted the faith, they watered it with their tears if not with their blood, kept it alive by the sacrifice of all that was dear to them in life, enduring obloquy and contempt while watching its slow growth, and after a weary life died at their lone posts, cheered by the solitary consolation of having performed their duty. A life of greater discomfort, more cheerless, or less esteemed by this world could scarcely be found among civilized people. If hatred and social ostracism, unappreciated labor, pinching want, and frequent hunger may supply the place of the scaffold at Tyburn or the faggot at Smithfield, these homeless men were martyrs. Slavery was so great a barrier between North and South that these men of unsurpassed detachment and unquestionable purity were unknown beyond its limits. Clergymen from outside, doubtless worthy men, were nominated for new sees or succeeded to old ones; unaccustomed to the insidious nature of the climate and strangers to the genius of Southern society, they never became thoroughly domesticated, and prematurely succumbed under the burden of their administrative labors.

"Toward the close of 1872 I purchased the Caldwell place, situated midway between Charlotte and Dallas, within one mile of the depot, on the Air-Line Railroad, and only half an hour's ride from Charlotte. The land is mostly level, eminently adapted to all farming purposes, and contains several hundred acres. About two hundred acres are cleared and the balance is in timber, consisting of oak, pine, hickory, and all other varieties common to this country. Springs of the purest water are abundant and the climate is unsurpassed for healthiness. King's Mountain, of historic fame, looms in the distance, and Spencer's, close by, stands like a sentinel thrown out by the Blue Ridge to keep guard over the entire valley, whilst the roar and dash of the water-falls on the South Fork may be heard day and night, especially at the approach of rain. There are several gold mines on the premises, and one in particular of immense wealth, and for which fifty thousand dollars was offered and refused. Nowhere on the continent could be found another place better suited for a religious and literary institution than this. Being but a short distance from the city, it possesses all the advantages without any of the drawbacks of a town as affecting the morals and training of youth, while its proximity to the railroad brings it in direct communication with the world outside. It is one of the oldest settlements in western North Carolina, dating back to very early colonial times, and afterwards became historical from the conspicuous part borne by its lordly occupant, Captain Samuel Caldwell, in the War of Independence.

"The only direct male descendant of the family now surviving within the limits of the State, Captain S. P. Caldwell, inherited the ancestral domain. Owing to the pressure of the times, it became encumbered and was sold for debt. In this manner I came in possession of it by purchase. When restored to order, for it lay a long time in a ruinous and neglected condition, I conveyed it to the Right Rev. Dr. Gibbons by a deed for the establishment of a religious and educational male institution. Promptness of action is a leading trait in the bishop's character. He will have a convent, a monastery, or a popular school established in the vicariate in a less space of time than another would require to think about them. He negotiated immediately with the Benedictines of St. Vincent's, Westmoreland County, Pa. The donation included the harvested and growing crops, provisions, implements of husbandry, beasts of burden, horned cattle, flocks of sheep, swine, household furniture, gold and all other minerals—in short, everything on the premises.

"Rev. Herman Wolfe, O.S.B., arrived in the spring of 1876, and having made a thorough examination, accepted the gift and acquiesced to the conditions. He returned to St. Vincent's; all he had done was presented to the chapter, was approved, and received the sanction of the venerable Abbot Wimmer, the distinguished founder of that celebrated institution. Early in the summer of the same year Father Wolfe returned with four Brothers. They took possession and entered on their duties. Little, however, was done the first year. In June of 1877 the abbot visited the institution, called it St. Mary of Help, directed the building of a commodious chapel, and furnished an excellent organ, service having been held previously in the principal apartment of the dwelling-house. The church is now finished, and the first Mass was said in it on the Feast of the Nativity of the Blessed Virgin Mary, September 8. Father Joseph Keller has labored as a mechanic on the work from early until late in his anxiety to provide as soon as possible a suitable repository for the Most Holy Sacrament. All the Catholics residing within a reasonable distance and many dissenters attend the nine o'clock Mass and sermon on Sundays, forming a very select congregation. The neighbors are already as familiar with the sound of the convent bells from four o'clock in the morning until eight o'clock at night as if they were raised under the walls of St. Vincent's. The advantages of St. Mary's to this community are obvious; the people will be educated in religion and human science, and even the temporal interests of the section will be promoted. Some grown persons are already receiving instructions under Father Keller. That many will be brought into the one true fold is beyond a doubt.

"On the occasion of his first visit the Right Rev. Abbot gave instructions to erect a college-building, to be joined to the pre-existent house, formerly used as a hotel, which will make an imposing edifice; it will be finished by November, and can accommodate as many of the Catholic youths as may apply. The following religious are now in the community and are the founders of the new house and mission:

"Very Rev. Herman Wolfe, O.S.B., prior, was an officer in the Confederate army. He was born in Kiel, Holstein;

he became a convert to the Church, and served on
the mission in Richmond and at other stations; he attends to the duties of this parish and also to Concord
in Cabarrus County. Rev. Joseph Keller, O.S.B., is
sub-prior and assistant on the missions. He arrived in
February of the present year accompanied by Fathers
Oswald and Maurice, of Hope's Island, near Savannah.
He is an active young man, a native of Bavaria, born in
the Palatine, on the left bank of the Rhine. He has worn
the habit six years. He made the novitiate and ecclesiastical studies at St. Vincent's, where he was ordained by
Bishop Dominec. He preaches admirably in English nearly
every Sunday.

"Brother Philip Cassidy, a grave, middle-aged man,
who was born in County Leitrim, Ireland, is the prefect
of studies. No one can understand his duties better or
perform them more faithfully. He is an able teacher and
a devoted monk; he advanced the cause of religion in
Pittsburgh, Chicago, and many other places. He has
adorned his profession by a monastic life of twenty-five
years in the practice of evangelical perfection.

"Brother Ulrich Baird is by birth a Belgian, and is still
in the prime of life, although he is professed seventeen
years. He served during the civil war in the Federal
army; he and his superior were on different sides, but they
are now at peace and engaged in the warfare of salvation.
He is a man of varied mechanical and industrial acquire-
ments and of invaluable benefit to the rising monastery.
He can do every thing, and a better monk does not exist
in America.

"Brother Bartholomew Freundel is thirty years in religion, and a native of Bavaria. Like the patriarchs on the
plains of Mesopotamia, he tends the flocks and they know
his voice. A lover of solitude, his conversation is with
God in unbroken communion and prayer. In this brotherhood of rival perfection, he is eminent for detachment and
simplicity of manners.

"Brother Alteman Alt is also a Bavarian, and professed

eighteen years. He is a venerable man of austere manners, but tempered with unearthly sweetness, and gentle as a child, one of the marks that distinguish good and virtuous people from wordlings. Like his progenitor, he eats his bread iu the sweat of his brow, tills the soil, and is harvest lord.

"Brother Draude is the Benjamin of the family; he is five years in the order, and a native of Hesse-Cassel, Prussia. Inheriting the name and profession of St. Placidus, his manhood beams with the prolonged innocence of youth. His duties are various—excitator, gardener, chorister, and, like Baronius, *coquus perpetuus*.

"The first students are two boys from Richmond, of German parentage—one named Antonio Laumann and the other Henry Gerhardt—candidates for the choir, both talented and promising youths. The next in succession are Frederick and Samuel Gross, sons of Captain Gross, of Charlotte, who, if God prolongs their days, give hopes of future usefulness.

"With all its advantages, St. Mary's bids fair to become, ere long, the most flourishing religious institution in the land. Vocations will be formed both for the sanctuary and the choir. The sacred influences of religion will be spread around until the wilderness will blossom like the rose, and the praises of God day and night fill the air, breathe in the valleys, and mingle with the voice of the waters.

"In the early part of the present century, the Benedictine monasteries of Bavaria having been suppressed and their property confiscated, King Louis restored the Monastery of St. Michael, Metten, also St. Stephen's, at Augsburg, and several others. When it was proposed to found a seminary for the German missions in the United States, the Society of Missions at Munich sent Father Boniface Wimmer to undertake the work. He arrived in 1846, accompanied by sixteen Brothers and four students in theology. The result was crowned with signal success, which the Holy See acknowledged by raising St. Vincent's to the dignity of an abbey in 1855, and appointing Father Boniface Wimmer the first mitred Abbot. His jurisdiction extends over ten States, having establishments and missions in as many dioceses. None wears his dignity with greater prudence and humility than this second patriarch of the monks of the West.

"The perfect organization of the order, the area of its labors and influence will extend until its widening circles embrace the entire country, instruct the ignorant, and bring back the wandering to God.

"After the dismembering of the Roman Empire, and when civilization was swept from the face of Europe by the Hun, the Vandal, and the Goth, religion, learning, and science found their last resting-place with the sons of St. Benedict. After the storm had spent its force the educated classes were either massacred or reduced to slavery. The fierce barbarians took possession of the soil, built huts in palaces, pastured their horses in cities and stabled them in churches. These holy men tamed the rude conquerors by their mildness, taught them agriculture, all the arts of industry, mechanism, and the pursuits of civilization and peace. They made them Christians and made them men.

"Inheritors of the virtues of St. Benedict, the zeal of St. Anselm, and the learning of St. Thomas, those annointed heralds of the cross have transferred their disinterested labors to the Carolinas and Georgia, renewing their former glories and making this wilderness of the American Church to blossom like the rose.

"In the strict sense of the term, there are no public amusements in country places all over the State. In their social relations the people are generous, cordial, and unaffected. The women have their quilting parties as in the good old times. Log rolling, house raising, threshing, and corn husking are occasions of general gathering, vulgarly called 'frolics.' They are accompanied with any amount of innocent hilarity, anecdote, and rural sport. In this way the burden of tedious and expensive labor is relieved by common and mutual participation, which also engenders kind feeling and generous friendship. They are rarely attended with drunkenness or other excesses, for the Carolinians are a sober people. The negroes are never excluded; they are a very important element in the gathering, and receive their full share of the work and entertainment. The second table, replenished with ample store, is the only distinction, an arrangement most agreeable to both parties. In the fall of 1851 I married Julia, the second daughter of John Lonergan, to Matthew Leper, a convert. The ceremony was performed at the residence of the bride's father, at the South Point, and was witnessed by all the neighborhood uninvited. Wedding-cards would create jealousy by making invidious distinctions, and give offence.

"The festivity lasted nearly three days. Party after party in regular relays did full justice to the proverbial hospitality of the family; the children received their due share of attention, while the rear was creditably brought up by the thoughtless and contented slaves. Music, dance, and song ruled the hour, according to the taste or caprice of the individual. The refreshments were regulated by the same law that governed the feast of the Assyrian monarch—*as much as each man would without persuasion.* During all the time nothing unbecoming had transpired; none gave, none received, offence, and there was no excess in either eating or drinking. Nothing occurred to mar the pleasing recollection of that wedding; the actors have now passed away, and their remains sleep under the sod in the valley. The succeeding generation walk in the footprints of their ancestors, and form a community equally honest, impartial, and true.

"The field sports are varied and exciting; each selects the department most agreeable to taste and fancy, or as determined by chance of companionship. A solitary angler will sit all day on a gray rock, surrounded by waters and interrupted in his bootless musings only by a nibble or a prize, while the more robust will sweep the shoals at night, gathering into their nets the cautious tribes that during the day lie hidden in their deep resorts, and venture out only in the dark for prey or play in the moonlit rapids.

"The wild turkey is extremely shy and cautious, as though aware of its value, and the captor must possess an equal amount of adroitness and cunning. Clad in russet homespun, and companionless, the fowler will burrow in the hollow of a rock or hide in a pile of brush-wood, and, mimicking with his whistle the chirp of the birds, entice them from their concealment, and at the crack of his rifle secure the prize. Occasionally they are decoyed into pens; having once entered, they cannot discover the mode of escape; like pride, they always bear their heads aloft and never once look to the ground.

"There are numerous flocks of partridges; the mode of capturing them by a gun and on horseback is at variance with the code of honor governing the sports. This bird is always on the alert at the approach of any living thing that may be dangerous, except a horse. Mounted, you may ride into the midst of the clutch, drive them before you into the net like tame ducks, and capture the entire brood.

"On a dark night in the fall, when the persimmons are ripe on the trees, the opossum hunter is in his glory. The shifting glare of the pine torch, the bay of the hounds ringing out in frequent peals, the hunter's horn echoing from the hills encroach on the silence and glooom of the night; now the woodman's axe resounds from the hollow oak where the prize has in vain sought a last refuge. His savory flesh will be the delicious repast of the sportsman as he returns at the first blush of the morning, thinking with glee of the night's adventure and hungry as Esau after the chase."

The Irish are pre-eminently the missionary people of the nineteenth century; being driven from their native country by persecutions, like the early Christians under the pagan emperors, they have become the instruments in the hands of God for the conversion of the world.

For the space of three hundred years all the powers

of the earth were arrayed against the Catholic Church, all at once, and up to this day at least singly. All godless nations and individuals, openly or indirectly, assail by a fatal necessity the tabernacle of divine truth. Ireland, in recent times, is the only country in the world where it seems to have taken shelter. The sword, the flames, the rack, the hungry beasts bounding in the amphitheatre, and all the torments that the merciless ingenuity of man could devise were invoked against the meek followers of our Lord. In order to render them the reproach of civilization, the fountains of education were corrupted, history falsified, and civil disabilities enacted. Branded as the enemies of God and man, they were driven from human habitations and hid themselves in caves and dens, in the remotest deserts, and in the bowels of the earth. Bishops, priests, and laity shared the same fate. There was no region traversed by a Roman road or visited by a galley in which they were not to be found, always and everywhere aliens and the offscourings of the human race, regarded as the enemies of God and man, whose extermination was deemed meritorious. They carried the faith whithersoever they went, built churches, established sees, and converted nations. No wonder, the propagation of the Gospel is an irrefragable proof of the divine origin of Christianity.

This same course, under some modification, is still in operation, and produces like results. The oppression of centuries has banished the Irish race from their native land, leaving them neither home nor country, and dispersed them over the face of the globe. They abandoned all for conscience' sake, and preferred exile and death before apostasy. Like the Israelites in the desert carrying the ark, they bore the faith wherever they wandered; they planted it in the towns and cities in the British Isles, whence it was banished; in America, in Australia, wherever the English tongue is spoken, they have built churches, founded institutions of piety and learning, furnished congregations to worship before the altar, priests to minister thereat, bishops to rule and govern the Church of God, monks to sing his praises, and religious orders to nurse the orphan and cheer the dead, damp gloom of the hospital.

"No man can love Catholicity and hate the Irish," said a distinguished convert; yet there are found not a few who are ashamed of their origin, as though it were a disgrace to be the children of the saints and the blood of martyrs was ignoble. The prejudices against this race, like those against the sons of St. Ignatius, are the inspiration of infidelity and irreligion. Immigrants, with some exceptions, are the poorest and least educated class of their native country. Their descendants and others are mistaken when they imagine them to be true types of society, when they were but the peasantry, though the best educated of any in Europe or the United States, despite the penal enactments of the British Government against their education. They could have been better instructed in human science if they had abandoned the knowledge of God for the teachings of Darwin and Huxley in the godless schools, preferred this world to the next, time to eternity, and the body to the soul. If they became Scotch-Irish, their degenerate sons would not be ashamed of them; the difference is in the religion, and this is what is the matter. In fact, the descendants of respectable Irish Catholics are proud of their ancestry; an opposite feeling is presumptive evidence of inferiority of birth.

But few Catholic German immigrants settle in the South; the majority are non-Catholic, and are connected with Socialistic and Masonic societies, both inimical to Christianity. Those who speak the same language and who are unacquainted with that of the country will naturally unite and form a class. As evil communications corrupt good manners, they become indoctrinated with the sentiments and opinions of the greater number, follow their example, and are swallowed up in Masonry, which effaces from the soul the unction of the Holy Ghost and substitutes the mask of anti-Christ for the sign of our redemption. Out of the many thus led astray few, if any, are converted; they die in their sins.

Europeans who do not speak English, in order to save their own and their children's souls, had better seek homes in rural districts where congregations and clergymen speaking their own language exist. In the Southern States, when living at a distance from the seaport towns, they are extremely isolated; after a few years they drop off, and are no longer numbered among the children of the faith. During the Know-Nothing excitement an effort was made to introduce its spirit into the sanctuary. The vigilance of our episcopacy arose, and rebuked the attempt at disintegration, so utterly foreign to the genius of Catholicity. It was nipped in the bud before it had time to produce its bitter fruits of anarchy and mistrust among the faithful. It is true that, since the days of the apostles, the Church relies on the native-born to fill up the ranks of the priesthood, and continue their labors. The United States are exceptional, being inhabited by a heterogeneous people. The great majority of the Catholics are of foreign birth, who, with their children, imbibing their teachings and sentiments, form our congregations almost everywhere. A priest or bishop born on the banks of the Shannon or the Rhine is as much at home before an American congregation as if he first saw the light on the shores of the Hudson or the Susquehanna.

This will continue until the Church acquires native, self-sustaining congregations whose youth are willing and able to undertake the duties and obligations of the sacred ministry. The hierarchy would be shorn of many of its brightest ornaments if deprived of the ecclesiastics of European birth. It was quite a curiosity to meet a native-born priest until recently. It is a singular mercy that the vocation is now more generally cultivated, and in a short time we may hope to find even native-born monks.

In 1876 Cabarrus County was attached to the Benedictine parish of St. Mary of Help, and has been attended by the Fathers. Concord is the shire-town, and is situated twenty miles east of Charlotte. When I first visited the country, in 1851, it was but a small village, falling into decay, and without a single Catholic within its limits. In the vicinity, and at a distance of two miles, is now a Catholic settlement, an important station, visited for a quarter of a century by each of the priests of Charlotte successively.

There was but one Catholic family in the community on my first visit—the Barnhardts, of German descent, and received into the Church by Father Guifford in 1844. The children were well instructed in the faith. The mother was a woman of rare excellence; she lived a saint, and died at an advanced age about 1866. It was through this family that Catholicity made its way into Cabarrus County. Joseph Barnhardt had been a Lutheran, was a man of superior intelligence, and held in deserved esteem by his countrymen for uprightness of character.

Having borrowed a book on controversy from the father of the Cox family, he studied it closely, and read also the discussion between Bishop England and Dr. Bachman on the Real Presence. Receiving the grace of God, he readily embraced the faith. He furnished his family with the most select authors on religious subjects. The books were borrowed by all the neighbors and sedulously perused.

They were regularly visited by the priests, who prepared the children for the reception of the sacraments, and made the acquaintance of the people, who concluded finally that Catholicity was as good as any other religion, if not better, and certainly the oldest. The children, when grown, intermarried, and led their companions into the Church. Messrs. Goodman, Blackman, Seaman, and several others joined the Church from time to time, under one or other of the visiting clergy. Colonel Coleman, a distinguished gentleman, and a convert also, removed from Raleigh, and now resides in Concord. Within the space of twenty-five years nearly all the settlement have embraced the faith.

This history illustrates the incalculable responsibility of each individual, and the influence of a single human life for good or evil, the merit or demerit daily accumulating, and the reward or punishment increasing in proportion, perhaps, to the end of time. Joseph Barnhardt died at a mature age about 1858 in the friendship of his Maker, but the memory of his virtues and his exemplary life are still fresh and know not death.

In the autumn of 1852 I preached in the settlement on a Sunday to an immense multitude, collected from the surrounding country, and whom no house could accommodate. Seated on the greensward and protected from the sun by the spreading branches of the forest trees, they listened attentively to a lengthy explanation and defence of the Sacrament of Penance. The Hon. Mr. Barringer and other distinguished men were in the audience; several expressed their admiration of the doctrine and intimated a desire to contribute to the building of a church.

Their wishes were realized twenty years after by Fathers Lawrence and Joseph O'Connell, who collected money abroad and put up a church, which was dedicated by Bishop Gibbons about 1872 under the title of St James's. George Goodman donated a spacious piece of ground for the purpose; under his zealous supervision all the congregation contributed more or less in the way of labor toward the erection of the rural temple. St. James's Church will be more durable than the Priest's Oak, so called for having canopied with outspread limbs, on the former occasion, the speaker's person and shielded him from the fervent rays of the Carolina sun. Having braved the wintry blasts of many years, it finally yielded to the storm and was laid low in the dust, like that generation of people who now rest from their labors and sleep under the sod of the valley. Only God and his Church live on for ever; time or death makes no change in either. "I am with you always, even to the end of the world."

If the open profession of the faith in the midst of an entire people ignorant of its teachings and hostile to its propagation by one raised in the bosom of the Church and to the manor born be a just cause of commendation, how much more so in the instance of one similarly situated and a convert! For years Mr. Barnhardt was alone and a stranger among his kindred, mistrusted by the people among whom he was raised from his infancy. During the Know-Nothing delirium he was treated as an enemy of his country and its laws. "Verily the sons of his mother fought against him." This will be illustrated by the following fact:

During one of my visits in 1854, after my retirement at night to the priest's apartment, which was a genteel shed-room, Mr. B. approached and directed me to make the fastening secure on the inside. He manifested equal industry in barring the entrance from the outside. On enquiring the cause of this unusual precaution, he assured me that my life was in danger, and that he expected a mob would attack the house some night and kill me; that I was deemed by the neighborhood an envoy or emissary of the pope, and had come for the sole purpose of upsetting the Government; that it was resolved I should not escape with my life. He also assured me that a certain man known to him lay in ambush in the woods, and kept snapping his hitherto unerring rifle at me until I was out of sight, and that it hung fire every time, a circumstance which never before occurred. It was subsequently believed that I bore a charmed life, and I was called the *Invulnerable*.

I disarmed his apprehensions by telling him that I could desire no greater happiness than to lose my life in the cause of religion, and that I did not believe that God deemed me fit for the martyr's crown; I afterwards slept calmly during the night. There are few missionaries who have not experienced a miraculous interference for their protection; this was not the only instance in which I found that my life was carried in the hand of God.

The faithful who reside in cities always feel a security and find protection in their numbers, and in the sympathy of the well-disposed and inoffensive citizens. They can form no adequate idea of the isolation and friendlessness of their brethren. Scattered over this vast extent of country in the years preceding the late war, and without priest or church, they were, to a certain extent, the apostles of religion, the nuclei of future congregations, and the centres from which the light of faith diffused its beams afar and enlightened those seated in darkness and in the shadow of death.

The following incident will remind missionary priests of similar hair-breadth escapes from death by flood and field, and confirm still more the fact of the watchful care of our Lord over all engaged in his work.

On one of my subsequent visits to this station I reached the farm-gate fronting the residence after dark. Two roads branched round a mound and led to the mansion, situated at the summit. One was new and in good travelling condition; the other, from neglect and heavy rains, was worn into gullies and impassable; any one acquainted with it would never attempt to pass over it with a vehicle. A subsequent examination revealed all its perils. The night was dark and damp. I drove a stubborn and balky horse, halting every now and then at the worst places, and, after much and forcible persuasion, starting into a gallop. No wonder *halting* was a legal impediment to the Aaronitic priesthood, and in its moral application incapacitating for the reception of holy orders.

Bodily and mental deformities are often allied, except among the virtuous, who subdue nature by grace. I was often doubtful if I could reach my journey's end that cold, rainy winter day, and I knew not where to stop for the night among the dreary Revolutionary houses along the road, each suggestive of the first blush of republican independence.

That it is the unexpected that often happens gained here a fresh proof. I had reached my destination, but here lurked the real danger. With malicious instinct the angry brute rushed up the deserted way, rock-strewn like the dried bed of a wintry torrent, and overhanging a rugged precipice. He halted suddenly at the very gap of danger, and commenced backing still nigher to the perilous edge of the rough ravine. Instinctively springing from the buggy-seat with the energy of one whose life depends on the speed of a jump, I landed at his head, grasped the end of the reins by the bit, and struggled to save him by tugging in an opposite direction. He seemed to understand the danger as well as his dethroned master. He reluctantly yielded, pulled forward a little, and, elevating his bald-faced head on high, dealt me an unmerciful blow with his chin over the forehead, which felled me to the ground. He looked as if he desired to paw me to death with his hoofs, or tear me to pieces, while I lay prostrate; for he seemed possessed of the ferocity of Sejanus, the imputed man-devouring steed of Tiberius, fed on spiced human blood hot from the veins, and the petted executioner of the emperor's court favorites.

Like unchristian men, he took revenge for imaginary wrongs when chance offered. Recovering myself, I was not aware of the extent of my injuries, and only felt a sensation of gentle warmth over breast, neck, and face, and an inclination to totter at the knees. It was the glare of a pine-torch that revealed a man weary, spent, and bleeding. I was consoled at the thought of having shed my blood on our Lord's mission. How many had longed for the favor! The effusion of the last drop in heart and veins would be gladly yielded in this cause, and it was often thirsted for on this and other missions. I have an instinctive horror of falling into the hands of my fellow-man, often the most merciless of God's creatures.

The cruelty of a mob is diabolical, more insensible to human suffering than flames, floods, and wild beasts. They often became all heart to pity and spare the martyrs. The conversion of the masses that flooded out from the purlieus of Jerusalem to jeer and mock at the dying agonies of the world's Redeemer is adduced by the Evangelist as proof of our Lord's omnipotent power over the human heart. "And all the multitude of them that were come together to that sight, and saw the things that were done, returned, striking their breasts " (Luke xxiii. 48). It was a miracle of grace.

A quarter of a century ago Protestantism was a power in the land, turbulent, boisterous, and intolerant of contradiction. When rebuked by controversy and incapable of maintaining itself by fair argument, it broke into open violence, and attempted to blot out by open violence the Church of God.

Immediately before the civil war it was rampant and aggressive throughout the South. On steamboats, in hotels, in the conventicles, in the daily press, in the family circle, in the novel, we were unceasingly assailed; the most infamous apostate was worth his weight in gold. The opposition had reached its climax and must be averted by a superior distraction or end in a general massacre.

I received into the Church in the year 1851 a respectable family who lived in Mecklenburgh County, and who had been Presbyterians, and one a ruling elder. This was an unpardonable offence, and caused a weighty scandal, to remove which a vigorous effort was deemed necessary. Within a year, and when making my missionary rounds, I visited the neophytes with the intent of spending the night, saying Mass and administering the Holy Communion the following morning. Previous notice of my intended visit had been given. On my arrival I was surprised to find the preacher installed in my place and very coolly playing the pastor.

I learned afterwards that he came under the subterfuge of an invitation which had been extended to him' by the family when some doubts still remained, and before they had joined the Church. He deferred his call until he could meet the priest, defeat him before his dupes, and lead back the parents in triumph to the original fold. The young man was in the vigor of life, a graduate of two universities, and respectably connected. He expected to be *facile princeps*. The event is related in consequence of the notoriety it obtained and the interest it created in the entire community.

Civilities were scarcely exchanged when, Bible in hand, he arose to his utmost proportions, buttoned his parson-coat closely to his person, proposed family services, and attempted to begin operations. There were many persons present; the pious family gazed in evident surprise, and referred the intruder to me for his answer. I calmly and firmly answered *No*, and assigned my reasons, which are known to all Catholics. I showed how piety, honor, principle, charity forbade participation in a service conscientiously believed erroneous and unwarranted by divine authority—yea, forbidden. His reply was characteristic of the times and of his creed, with which I was better acquainted than he: "Shall I, a native-born American, be denied the inalienable right to read my Bible on my native soil, watered by the blood of my ancestors, and by a foreigner?"

During thirty-five years in the ministry I never courted a controversy, and avoided it unless forced on me as a duty, as in this and similar instances. The faith and salvation of others were imperiled; life itself was nothing in comparison. He was by no means an illiterate man; he made the best defence possible for a Protestant, and quoted fluently from the Scriptures. Now, Christianity cannot be defended against the infidel on Protestant grounds. I have learned by experience that the simplest mode of upsetting such men is to demand their proofs for the authority of their book before you allow them to quote it.

Calvinism directly assails the divine nature in limiting the mercy, the justice, and the compassion of the Creator, and denying the universal application of the merits of Jesus Christ to the human race. It is impossible to reconcile with the true idea of God the unreasonable partiality claimed by a handful of people for themselves at the end of ages, and to the utter reprobation of the entire human race. No wonder such teachings have led to general infidelity. Burns, by "Holy Willie's Prayer," has laughed away Calvinism as thoroughly as Cervantes smiled knight-errantry out of Spain by his "Don Quixote."

Before God all time is one active, unsuccessive present. It is only in respect to eminence, and not to time, that God's decrees have precedence. Before he foresaw aught else, humanly speaking, he decreed to create angels and men, and predestined them to happiness. They were both created in the state of grace, and he chose no certain number so as to exclude others. When he foresaw the free rejection of his grace by some, and their free demerits and the free correspondence of others, that prevision did not predestine the loss or salvation of either, necessitate their action, nor deprive them of their liberty—the essential condition of their being, and limited only by truth in act or principle.

It was only after this prevision that there was any election or reprobation at all; it is man's own choice. His liberty was secured throughout. There is none of the lost who can attribute his ruin to any other cause but his own wilful opposition to God's grace. We are as free as air, and without our liberty we would not be men. We owe our liberty to our life, and that to God's predestination. How can that act impair our liberty without which we should not have existence?

Grace is founded on the permission of sin. Without this terrific mystery angels and men would not be free, and freedom is necessary for merit. A heaven of saints ready made from the beginning would not be a source of voluntary allegiance and love. All the difficulties about grace, predestination, and sin vanish under personal experience. We know, each of us, that we have not corresponded to a tithe of our graces; that our lives have been a series of miraculous interferences on the part of God; and that his infinite mercy alone has saved us many times from being eternally lost in the hopeless homes of those who die in mortal sin.

Human reason is nothing less than a ray of the divine mind imparted to man; but it is so slender that if not properly directed it bewilders and leads him astray. If emancipated from the safeguards of divine authority, it will inevitably lead him into the extremes of folly, superstition, and vice. Cicero confessed as much when he declared that many of the teachings of the philosophers were as silly as the ravings of maniacs. Protestantism furnishes the most sad illustration of this fact found in the annals of the human race. Spurning in the most vituperative manner the Church of God, after having converted the Gentile world, enlightened the nations, and saved millions of souls, the founder of every sect claimed for each one the authority denied the Church of all ages and nations, styling this rebellion the emancipation of the human mind from the darkness of superstition and the cunning fables of priestcraft.

The system is a flagrant contradiction of the plainest maxims of common sense, subversive of all law, order, and social authority. Its establishment cost the Thirty Years' War, and deluged Europe with blood.

What was the basis of this wonderful conspiracy against truth? Private interpretation as the rule of faith, never practised, and the inevitable road to infidelity and universal scepticism. Preaching, the baptism of infants, the erection of churches, all forms of worship, commentaries on the Bible, catechetical instructions, family devotions, religious education, all church polity and organization, and every form of religious worship is a denial of this delusive theory. If ever practised, it must have made as many churches as individuals. Its spirit is plainly illustrated by the thousand different sects into which Protestantism has been split, each teaching doctrines contradicted by the others, and in the concrete inculcating all the doctrines taught by the Church against which they had rebelled. There is no point of Catholic doctrine which has not been taught by some Protestant sect.

When two persons contradict each other they cannot both be speaking truth; it is precisely so in regard to two or more churches. They all quote the Bible as their authority. The Bible is the Word of God, and essentially true, hence it cannot teach contradictory doctrines; the contradiction arises from the manner of applying it. Like a case prejudged by a jury, each individual is impressed with opinions already formed, and he will give the text a meaning reconcilable with them. According to this rule, every man and woman each has the right and is obligated to frame a religion according to their understanding of Holy Writ, or none at all, and it will be equally true and correct however contradictory. On no other principle does Protestantism allow conviction. If he be consistent, a Protestant must be an infidel before he can become a Christian. For as conviction can be based only on individual enquiry, he must first come to the years of discretion, and then a long period must elapse while making the investigation before he can receive baptism, during which time he can have no religion at all; he cannot pick up even Mormonism for his comfort.

Before a Protestant can make an act of faith a long and complicated course of study is necessary, and for which no man living is competent. He must satisfy himself that the Bible is the Word of God, that it is inspired, that it contains the full revelation of God, that it holds all the books that have a right to enter into the collection, no more, no less. He must convince himself by an amount of learning which would tax a St. Jerome or St. Augustine that there exist no corruptions, no interpolations, no falsifications. We do not possess the originals of any of these books, and the readings in all the ancient copies are so diverse that the Protestant Archbishop Usher declares that no two are alike.

The books were written in remote times, and in different languages, all now dead and not in use. The leisurely enquirer must possess a knowledge of these obsolete languages, Hebrew, Chaldaic, Greek, and Syriac, sufficiently comprehensive to be convinced that the translations are all correct, when, in fact, of the many hundreds no two of them agree, and some Protestants are now attempting a new one, after condemning all the old as false and corrupt.

These are but a few of the difficulties attending the preliminary investigation of this wonderful speculation miscalled the *Bible alone as the rule of faith*. There are many others which no man living can solve. St. Augustine declares that "he would not believe the Bible at all except on the authority of the Catholic Church." It cannot be defended on any other ground. Deny the infallibility of the Church, and you must reject the Bible, like the infidel.

Supposing this preliminary examination satisfactorily made, how will the rule be applied when you can form no opinion which has not been rejected and condemned by thousands as learned and sincere as you? If all the commentaries and controversies regarding the meaning of Scripture were collected, they would form a library more extensive than the one burnt in Alexandrea by Amroo.

Archbishop Gibbons, in his admirable work, states that there are one hundred different interpretations of the four words of consecration, "This is my body."

Quite a number of persons were attentive listeners to the protracted debate, and were amazed at the easy defeat of their chosen champion of a now defunct cause. Sympathizing with him on the serious consequence to him of his imprudence, we shook hands, and, to use his own words, "parted in charity."

There are in the vicariate of North Carolina at this time:

Priests on the mission,	7	Boarding-school of St. Mary's Help,	1
Churches and chapels,	13	Parochial schools,	4
Female academy,	1	Stations,	21
Female religious institution,	1	Clerical students,	4
Benedictine house,	1	Catholic population (an approximation),	2,000

CHAPTER XV.

SAVANNAH AND OTHER MISSIONS.

Savannah, Georgia: Situation and Appearance of the City—The Church—Cemetery—A Necropolis—Yellow Fever the Ruin of Southern Cities—Probable Transfer of Sees—First Priest—Fathers Lecarron, Brown, Lemercure, Cooper, O'Gallagher, Cloriviere—Lay Extreme Unction—First Church—Rev. Messrs. Healy, Stokes, Barry, McGinnis, McEncroe—Rev. J. F. O'Neill, Sr.—Accomplishments—Early Piety—Bishop England's Missionary Companion—Character—Popularity—The Nestor of Savannah—People crave him for their Bishop—Habits and Order of Life—Old Hickory—An Able Writer and Controversialist—Extensive Mission—Seven Hundred Communicants in 1845—Temperance and Rosary Societies, Schools—The Church of St. John the Baptist—The Sisters' Convent and Orphan Asylum—No Money, no Church—Institutions mark the Progress of Religion—The Order of the Sisters of Our Lady of Mercy spread over Georgia—An Extensive Parish—Brunswick—St. Mary's—Rev. John and Andrew Doyle—The Dufour Family—Rev. Mr. Maine—Bishop Barron and Dr. Varella as Missionaries—A Saintly Priest—Father O'Neill sold his House and Gave all he had to Build the Sisters' Convent and Orphan Asylum—Early Catholics—The Blois Family—A Faithful People—A City fit for a Bishop—A Long Life and Happy Death—O'Connell and O'Neill—Samuel Lover a true Irishman—Father O'Neill at the Siege of Savannah—Bishop Tuigg at the Sack of Petersburg—A Rubrician in the Desert—Two Living Candlesticks—Right Rev. Francis Xavier Gartland, D.D., First Bishop of Savannah—Ordination—Priestly Dignities—Labors—Popularity in Philadelphia—Personal Appearance—Zealous for the Beauties of the Sanctuary—Coming Events—An Encouraging Prospect—A Submissive Clergy—Labors—The Cathedral of St. John the Baptist—Tears wept at the Thought of Death—An Earthly Paradise and the Last Day—Thabor and Calvary—"The Rage of their Arrows hath Drunk up my Spirit"—A Glorious Death—Bishop and Martyr—Right Rev. Edward Barron, D.D., Missionary in Africa—Labors in the Diocese of Savannah—Pen Picture—Character—Death from Yellow Fever—"Three Saints one Grave do fill, Patrick, Bridget, and Columbkillo"—Right Rev. John Barry, D.D.—An Œcumenical Priest—Rev. Edward Quigley—Missions, Labors, Zeal—The Companion of the Bishops, and alone during the Pestilence—The last Soldier in the Battle, and the last of Bishop England's Priests—Confessor and Pontiff—A Prince of Peace—The Good Samaritan—A Second Tobias—Father of the Orphan—Apostasy of Döllinger and Loyson—The Man of Prayer—St. Sebastian's Arrows—Consecrated Bishop—A Dance—St. Philip Neri—Père la Chaise—Brought Home.

GEORGIA embraces an area of fifty-eight thousand square miles, and, according to the last census, has a population of over one million. In 1850 the Catholic population could not exceed five thousand.

Savannah was my first mission; immediately after my ordination I was sent thither as assistant to Father O'Neill, in June, 1844. The great number of trees along its sidewalks, in its public squares, and its private lots gave it the appearance of a forest city. The broad streets were beds of white sand, so deep that the noise of travel or commerce never reached the ears of the sick or the sleeping. In this respect the life-weary inhabitants enjoyed a quiet death, accelerated for many in the midst of their days by the turgid waters of the loitering river, and the malarial rice-fields of South Carolina that skirted on the east, while the swamps on the west and north administered an equal dose of deadly poison. It was justly called Savannah, for the situation is merely a sand-bed surrounded by swamps.

The church was a plain brick building, lying on the outskirts at the southwest extremity, on the commons and in view of the cemetery, where the dead of many generations were gathered into hospitable graves, surrounded by a red brick wall, guarding many a secret of disappointed hopes and untimely ends. The western extremity was reserved for Catholics, whose graves were opened anew at the end of each decade to receive new tenants, until the entire surface became the débris of human remains. The old families possessed vaults where their deceased relations were protected from this inhuman but unavoidable invasion. The strangers who died friendless were interred in the Potter's Field, like malefactors, a disposition less repulsive than the crowding of them amid the still festering remains of the recent dead.

This nuisance has been remedied of late years by large and commodious cemeteries, both for Catholics and non-Catholics, separately, at a distance which the city cannot reach in many centuries, though accelerated by the rapid strides of modern progress.

The Catholic population of the city hardly reached one

thousand at this period, and four thousand would be the excess all over the State of Georgia. The immigrants generally gathered into the seaport towns. Unaccustomed to the severity of the climate, they were swept away at each periodical return of the common scourge of the Southern cities—yellow fever. Now that the causes which necessitated this concentration are removed by railroads, and other centres of education, commerce, and merchandise formed, the sees may be also transferred, and the Catholic Church spared the affliction of mourning over the untimely graves of bishops, priests, and thousands of her children who fell in the midst of life and usefulness. Back of those death-prisons and charnal-houses stretches a country vast in extent and unsurpassed for beauty, healthfulness, and fertility.

Remote from the chair of episcopal authority, and subject to all the evils incidental to that condition, Catholicity could have made but small progress before the arrival of Bishop England, and the connection of the State with the Carolinas, forming the single see of Charleston. If, as we are reliably informed, there were but three Easter communicants in that city in the year 1809, there were probably none at all in Savannah. The first Catholics were a few Irish and some refugees from San Domingo. They were all generally visited from Charleston by a chance priest, and had scarcely a resident pastor. It is related that in the first quarter of the present century a French priest had exercised his ministry in their behalf for some time, but was lost at sea on a voyage to the West Indies. From valuable information furnished by Right Rev. Dr. Lynch, I learn that Rev. Mr. Lecarron was here in 1812, and before or after him another, name unknown. Rev. Robert Brown officiated in Savannah, Augusta, and Charleston, 1809 to 1838; Rev. Mr. Lemercure, about 1812 for several years; Rev. Mr. Cooper, of Augusta, who afterward went to Europe, and Rev. Mr. Cloriviere about 1817. The Rev. Dr. O'Gallagher was removed thither in 1819, and remained for about three years.

While describing the spiritual destitution that prevailed in the diocese before his appointment, I heard Bishop England relate from the altar, with tears in his eyes, an affecting incident. On the occasion of his first visit to Savannah he was approached by an aged, grief-stricken man, who, in a voice interrupted by emotion, described the death of his oldest son. He was a young man, generous, noble-hearted, and kind. Raised in the knowledge of the faith by domestic training, whenever they were visited by a priest, which rarely occurred, the youth embraced the opportunity of approaching the sacraments. In more mature years he became remiss for a time, swayed by the thoughtlessness of his youth and influenced by the example of companions more unreflecting still. He was struck down by the relentless pestilence and marked for an early grave. In its first stage and before reason slumbered in the deep lethargy of this insidious destroyer, which, like death, knows no waking, the young man most piteously cried out for a priest, but in vain. It was as futile as the attempt to call one from the dead. The soul then thirsting for absolution must bear the burden of its faults and frailties to the feet of the Sovereign High Priest for remission. The weeping parent prayed incessantly by the couch of the dying, and the soul was bid to depart. The homeward-bound spirit refused, and still struggled for life. He needed confession, and he must make it before he can go in peace. Like a lay-pontiff, the father received his son's dying confession, with the injunction, if of any advantage, to impart the same to the first priest who may arrive. Then, taking a vial of holy-water, he applied a few drops to each of the organs of sense wont to be annointed with the holy oils, in the name of the Father and of the Son and of the Holy Ghost, placing on his breast the crucifix, the anchor of the Christian hope. The weary soul slumbered on until death, it may be hoped, laid it to rest on the bosom of God. With the number of zealous clergymen and the facilities of receiving the Holy Sacrament now in Savannah, the faithful at this day little dream of the spiritual privation of their predecessors.

A dwelling-house was purchased and altered for divine service and used as a church about the year 1820. The clergymen who henceforward served on this mission successively until in 1830 were Fathers Stokes, Healy, McGinnis, McEncroe, Barry, and others, of whom mention has been already made in connection with the mission in South Carolina.

The Rev. Jeremiah Francis O'Neill, Sr., was ordained by Bishop England in Charleston about 1826, after having made the usual course of studies in the seminary. He was stationed in Columbia, South Carolina, and on the several missions over both the Carolinas until about 1832, when he was sent as pastor to Savannah. He was born at Lixnaw, County Kerry, Ireland, A.D. 1792. Having applied himself at an early age to study, and endowed with mental faculties of a high order, he became an accomplished scholar in his native country, and connected himself with one of the educational orders in the city of Dublin. A man of rare intellectual attainments, he was a good mathematician, an accomplished musician, and a gentleman of polished manners. Devoted from his earliest years to the science of God, and well grounded in the religious life, he became a great accession to the diocese, and was fitted by a long course of preparatory training to become the companion and chief coadjutor of Bishop England in establishing Catholicity in the Carolinas and Georgia. Religion was the basis of his character; it was his life, his soul, and absorbed all his existence.

Others were equally pious, but his social qualities, literary attainments, and facility of writing and speaking rendered him more efficient among all classes. Whatever he possessed, whether acquired by study or by the grace of God, all were employed in the service of his Master and for the good of souls. Neat in apparel, refined in manners, ready in anecdote and wit, he was a welcome guest in every circle of Southern society. His presence graced every civic occasion of respectable pretensions, and he was venerated as the first man, whether as a gentleman, a priest, or a scholar. Men of all ranks, the governors of States, senators of the land, judges on the bench, scholars in the various departments of science and learning courted his acquaintance and honored his presence. So exalted was his moral influence that he could assail wrong and reprove vice not only among his own people but wherever it existed in the high places of the land; none ever resented the reproof. Non-Catholics frequently brought him their complaints, consulted him in their difficulties, and corrected the erring by the threat of his name.

After having buried two generations, the third grew up under him, and he was regarded as the Nestor, who was connected at one time or another in some endearing relation with every family, rich and poor, in the city. When by the appointment of a bishop he ceased to be priest of the only church, the Protestant community of Savannah, unsolicited and unaided, asked for permission to build a Catholic church for him subject to his pastoral administration. Restrained by his remonstrance, the community desisted from holding a public meeting to urge on the episcopacy his appointment as Bishop of Savannah. During the life-time of Bishop England, and when it was contemplated to erect the new see, he was the nominee of the clergy of the diocese to fill the office.

His habits were so strictly regulated by the voice of prudence, and the division of time so closely adjusted by the requirements of duty, that he found leisure for everything. Fifteeen years in Savannah without an assistant, he never missed an hour of his office, a sick call, a week-day Mass, a confession, a funeral, or a social appointment, unless by some uncontrollable cause. This order and system of regularity accompanied him during a life of nearly half a century in the priesthood. During all that period he never once gave occasion for scandal, and discharged all his duties with the fidelity and unrelenting perseverance of a Cistercian. There was scarcely a mission in the three

States on which he had not been stationed. The constant companion of Bishop England in his early visitations, he divided with him the trials and labors of his episcopacy, smoothed the rugged path by the cheerful participation of missionary duty, planted the faith conjointly with him, and in his own sphere shone with a lustre as brilliant as his master's. Always before the public, few men ever lived who could have passed through so long a life without detriment to the spirit of devotion or remissness in priestly functions. Not unlike General Jackson in physique, he favored him yet more in energy of action, unflinching purpose, and indomitable perseverance. Men were struck by the resemblance, and the priests often playfully called him Old Hickory.

His pen was a formidable weapon in controversy; whenever the occasion called it forth, the blows which it dealt were weighty and final. For pungency, satire, and close argument he was seldom surpassed as a controversial preacher. He riveted the attention of his hearers, and whether one hour or two, or mayhap three, he was always interesting. The details of his controversial rencontres, *bon mots*, and missionary excursions would fill a volume. His journeys in the pathless forests on horseback and in the old-fashioned sulky, by day and by night, when one-third of the State formed his parish, and his attendance on the sick and dying in seasons of yellow fever and pestilence in Savannah are still remembered with admiration, while the full measure of his labors are only known to God, who will keep rewarding them during the endless days of eternity.

Shortly after his appointment to Savannah he organized a congregation, animated with his own spirit and fervor, and second to no other in the diocese for practical piety, charity to the poor, frequent approach to Holy Communion, and liberality in contributions to the erecting of religious institutions. After a term of fifteen years, the writer recollects to have witnessed seven hundred persons receiving the Bread of Life where there had been but a few poor

Catholics a short time before, scattered amid the outskirts of the city. Sunday-schools, which he attended in person, day-schools for the children of both sexes, temperance societies, confraternities of the Most Holy Rosary were established; nothing calculated to promote the decency of divine worship, the good of religion, or the salvation of souls escaped his vigilance or was unaccomplished.

The old church was too small for the accommodation of the increased number of the faithful, and in a short time the Church of St. John the Baptist arose amid the sand. It was a plain, substantial brick building, with galleries and organ, and a capacity for seating nearly one thousand worshippers. On the day of its dedication the holy-water from the aspergill of the bishop blessed the largest church edifice in the diocese, as free from debt as the Temple of Solomon. *Pay as you go* was his maxim. A massive and imposing edifice with a proportionate debt, increased by accumulated interest, like an encumbered estate, is a poor legacy for a successor, dependent for liquidation upon the vacillating tide of Irish immigration. When the funds were expended the work was suspended, and the clink of the trowel was the merry sound that announced the glad tidings of a replenished treasury.

The number and assiduity of his labors left him no leisure for literary pursuits, and curtailed his hours of sleep. The establishment of an orphan asylum, an academy for the education of females, and a convent for the Sisters were works of pressing necessity and paramount importance; they were shortly inaugurated. He never failed in an undertaking; his reliance on divine aid and in the generosity of the people were unbounded. The congregation was poor, but the people were liberal, and the natives of Georgia, as a class, are far more so than their neighbors in Carolina. Lots situated close to the church were purchased, the work commenced, and within a reasonable time the Sisters' house sprung up, one of the most commodious and imposing public edifices in the city.

It is known as a fact that he never begged a dollar for

this institute beyond the city. By means of collections in the congregation, and among many non-Catholics, the price was obtained, a boon of unspeakable advantage to Savannah and the country at large ; such institutions are the landmarks that show the progress of the faith localizing religion, and adding new territories to the dominion of Catholicity. The institute readily fitted into the groove of its vocation, shed blessings among the couches of the dying and plague-stricken, and became popular as a boarding and day school. Appreciating its advantages, the Catholics dispersed over the entire State sent hither their daughters to reap the advantages of a religious and domestic education, without undergoing the inconveniences and expense of exile and banishment from their native home.

In 1845 a colony was obtained from the mother-house at Charleston, which consisted of five religious—the Superioress, Mother Vincent Mahoney, Sisters Agnes, Aloysius, Mary Patrick, and both the Misses O'Connell, Mary Baptist, and Antonio. They shortly formed a novitiate and threw out many branches. At this time they have flourishing establishments in Augusta, Atlanta, and White Bluff. Under the fostering care of the successive bishops, the entire diocese is the enlarged field of their labors, and all the faithful are partakers in the blessings of their vocation.

The growing years and increasing labors of the distinguished missionary demanded priestly aid. I was with him from spring until the winter of 1844. I was transferred to Macon, and the Rev. Wm. Burke, of Charleston, substituted in my place. After his death, in 1846, the Rev. J. F. Kirby was transferred from Macon, and held the position till the arrival of the first bishop, and after, but in another capacity. The relief served but to facilitate more frequent visits to the outlying stations. Tybee, Beaufort, Jeckel Island, and other points at the mouth of the Savannah River, McIntosh and Bulloch Counties, the South coast of Georgia, East Florida, Key West, Amelia, and other islands on the Atlantic coast were included in the parish.

At Brunswick there was but one Catholic, an aged seaman named Captain Aker, who was married to a fervent Irish Catholic woman. I said Mass at their residence in the fall of 1844, and they both approached the sacraments. At St. Mary's there resided a most excellent Catholic family—pious, devoted, and zealous for the faith—the Dufours. The once famous bank at St. Mary's having honorably retired, the building was purchased and converted into a safe and comfortable chapel. I preached in it, and used for the celebration of the divine mysteries a very ancient chalice, bearing on the pedestal the name of Rev. Father Maine, a priest who had officiated on the islands and in Florida in the close of the last century. He vanished from the memory of men, but left no disedifying recollections at his departure.

The Rev. Father Andrew Doyle was stationed here about 1840, and remained until 1844. There were two priests of this name, both natives of Leinster; they studied in Charleston, and were ordained by Bishop England in 1837. John returned to Ireland without having remained long in the missions of the diocese, in consequence of impaired health. Having regained his strength in the home of his childhood, he served long and faithfully in the priesthood in Ireland, and went to his rest revered, honored, and venerated.

Father Andrew was in Ireland during the last visit of Bishop England, and returned with him on the same passage. After the death of the bishop he received his exeat from Very Rev. Adm. Baker, and accepted an appointment in New York City. After his ordination he was placed on the mission in eastern North Carolina until transferred to St. Mary's, Georgia. He resided in the Dufour family; the parents were French, but their children native born and educated in the faith. Mr. Doyle ministered rather as a chaplain without a congregation, and this was the sole cause of his departure. He was a very tall, slim man; he died about 1850.

Bishop Barron and Dr. Varella, both in declining health,

and for the purpose of escaping the severity o
north, spent their winters in this mild climate ar
tended to the spiritual wants of the faithful ove
mission. The latter was a native of Cuba, pastor c
Church of the Transfiguration in New York, and
general of that diocese. He was distinguished as a
troversialist, a faithful and devoted priest. In Sava
and among those islands his memory is held in deep
ration by the faithful and all who made his acquaint
How he lived was a wonder to his friends, for he
everything he had to the poor—the clothing off his
the spoons from his table, all went when he had no n
to bestow. After nearly thirty years' labor in the minist
died at St. Augustine, whither he had returned for h
February 18, 1853, in the sixty-sixth year of his age. I
seldom been more agreeably disappointed in the per
appearance of a man than in this instance. After h
said Mass in the church in Savannah one day in 1845
while disrobing in the sacristy, a plain man, rather di
tive in size, walked in, slightly wet from rain, with th
and freedom of one who felt at home in the *adytum*, n
tirely warranted by his *personnel*. His dress was thi
seedy, his shoes heavy and not unlike small coffin
minding one of Napoleon's first appearance in mi
boots, his figure attenuated, face sharp and fleshless,
an olive complexion bordering on the Indian. A p
gold spectacles bridging a prominent nose riveted n
tention and seemed not in keeping with the *tout ense*
In a sweet, subdued voice he answered the silent en
of my glance: "I wish to say Mass. I am one Varel

The leading Catholic families in the city at this p
were all zealous, devout, and liberal, and animated
the spirit of their pastor, who had set before them a
lesson of detachment. Having acquired some per
property, on which he was residing, a genteel and
modious house in a town lot, improved by other si
buildings, which he meant to serve for the conting
of old age, he unhesitatingly sold all his propert

applied the proceeds to build the Sisters' house and orphan asylum. He became houseless, and lived, both he and his assistants, in the family of Mrs. Blois, a widow lady, who, with her aged mother, sister, and husband, had lost all their possessions in the insurrection of San Domingo. Mr. Blois, on returning to the island some time after the insurrection to make enquiries about his property, was cast away at sea and nothing more heard of him. His bereaved widow, with but small means of support, had, besides those already mentioned, a family of four children, whom she brought up in the fear and love of God and in the strictest observance of Catholic duties. This excellent and pious lady and all the family were endeared to the Catholics of Savannah and to all the early priests and bishops for kindness, hospitality, and unsurpassed piety; the older members have gone to receive their reward, but there still remain those who inherit the name, respectability, and Catholicity of their revered ancestors.

The O'Byrnes, Dillons, Prices, and Guilmartyns, Michael Prendergast, at whose residence both the bishops died, John Cass, Dr. John Riordan, the Legriels, the Dempseys, Captain McMahon, Pierce and Wm. Condon, Philip J. Punch, editor and proprietor of the *Georgian*, the Taylors, John Sherlock, and many more were well-deserving people, benefactors to religion, and co-operated with the great priest in all his works for the honor and glory of God and the good of religion. Nor should we pass unnoticed Mrs. O'Flynn Prendergast, a pious and devout woman, the mother of an only child, the present zealous and exemplary priest of Augusta, Father C. C. Prendergast. Nearly all this generation of kind and noble-hearted people now rest in the consecrated cemetery; but their piety, their liberality, and their faith were inherited by many of their descendants. They are venerated by a numerous and influential body of the faithful, who walk in the footsteps and enjoy the blessings of their fidelity despite of many difficulties and obstacles to perseverance.

The edifying deportment of the Catholic people as a

body; the large number of weekly and monthly communicants, exceeding that of any other church in the diocese; the many converts, the practical piety of the Catholic slaves, and the good reputation of the citizens for moderation and liberality induced the fathers of the Provincial Council, when creating new sees, to give Savannah the preference before Augusta, and in 1850 nominated Dr. Gartland as first bishop.

Seldom in America was a city so well prepared for the dignity as Savannah. She was adorned as a bride, and received the bridegroom with joy and acclamation. Father O'Neill resigned without regret the pastoral care of the church into the bishop's hands, without a scandal, without a debt, and without a blemish on his own fair reputation during a pastorate of twenty years. He bequeathed nothing worse than abundant work for a young bishop and clergy, and the prospect of a periodical return of yellow fever, to keep them steady in the path of duty by the prospect of a near reward, ready to drop from God's hands everywhere, but here especially.

The venerable man outlived not only this but three other administrations, and died under Bishop Persico, July 12, 1870, about eighty years old, and nearly fifty years a priest, forty of which were spent in Savannah. His missionary labors, his devotion to the priesthood, and his influence never waxed old. He was in a wonderful measure exempt from the infirmities of old age in his body, while his mind was absolutely free from the puerile senility of ancients. Some time before his holy and edifying death he suffered the fracture of a limb, which, though it healed, had confined him to his room, and served but to clothe his familiar slim and spare person with an aldermanic robe. On this topic he was wont to remark playfully, "If you wish to grow fat, break your leg." He was as a father to all the young priests on the mission, and often shared with them his wardrobe, his purse, and even his bed when necessary.

He is buried amid the faithful in a large field of the dead, whom he baptized in infancy, consoled in trials, and reconciled to heaven during life, fed with the Bread of Life, and sent before the tribunal of God marked with the sign of salvation, and anointed with the unction of the Holy Ghost. Envy does not smite the peace nor jealousy disturb the repose of the dead. The remains of many holy men, priests and bishops, who fell martyrs at the post of duty are scattered around, like the slain in battle, but none fell more revered, or who had done so much good for his faith and generation, or more lamented, than he. Though favored with a term of life rarely allotted to man in our generations, and borne to his grave laden with the honors of time, he carried with him the esteem and the love of all who prized virtue and worth. An entire people wept for him. The sands so often pressed by the hurried footsteps of duty rest lightly on his bosom; the night-winds sweeping from the Gulf over the orange-groves of his long and weary mission breathe their perfumes around his tomb, guarded by the sleepless sentinels of the dead, who, while living, surrounded him at the altar, and are now waiting to accompany him after the resurrection to the mercy-seat of God. "Blessed are the dead who die in the Lord; they now rest from their labors, and their works do follow them."

To be exempt from the storms and trials incidental to a career so long and public is more than our condition warrants. He had his own store of them, and they were heavier and more bitter than commonly fall to the lot of men. Practical common sense, sound judgment, and a cheerful disposition, joined with conscious worth and the perennial feast of a good conscience and a blameless life, sustained him to the end. Devotion to our Blessed Lady, frequent prayer, and a deep spirit of the religious life were the alembics that extracted the honey of God's grace from the lion-mouth of adversity, and riveted him more closely to his Maker. In the spiritual life, amid external duties or in trials, he was not unlike, in his measure, St. Joseph Calasanctius, the founder of the Christian schools in Italy. May the founder of the Church and missions of

Savannah, and the co-laborer of Bishop England in planting the cross in the diocese of Charleston, now rest in peace in the hands of his Master. Future ages will venerate his name, and the example of his life, virtues, and labors will encourage numerous priests yet unborn in the path of duty. "Well done, thou good and faithful servant!"

About 1840 he spent the winter in Florida and Cuba, to obtain relief from what was pronounced to be consumption, which had made fatal inroads on his constitution. He was painfully coughing for nearly two years. Unrelieved by those mild climates, he returned home to die, it was thought. Long experience and extensive reading rendered him skilful in medicine, yet he consulted the most eminent physicians. The usual remedies were applied, but to no advantage. Doctor John Bellinger, a zealous convert, instituted a thorough examination, and, to the surprise of medical men, ascertained that the cough was produced by an elongation of the palate extending to the throat. A single clip of the forceps removed the cause of the malady, and restored the patient to accustomed health.

He visited Ireland about 1835, and said Mass at the Convent in Killarney. The Liberator served his Mass, and while at breakfast afterwards enquired about his old friend, Bishop England. None got the advantage of Father O'Neill in the play of wit or argument; every lance raised against him was broken. Slavery became the topic of conversation. Mr. O'Connell's views on that subject were already widely known. Waxing warm, the missionary, fixing his keen gray eye on the broad face of Counsellor O'Connell, remarked: "As a statesman, your ostensible mission is to improve the condition of your countrymen. You went out of your way to cast a nettle on the grave of the father of my adopted country. If you succeed in rendering the condition of the Irish peasantry, in a temporal sense, as comfortable as the Southern slaves, you will accomplish much; you are now talking too soon."

In the winter of 1846, in Savannah, Samuel Lover invited the priest to attend his caricature of Irish character, called a *soirée* in the advertisement. He declined the invitation unhesitatingly. The two meeting on the streets the following day, the humorist enquired the reason. "In the farces compiled for the amusement of your own class of people you have insulted my cloth," was the ready response. "Ah! but do you not recollect how I brought the priest out towards the end?" "Of course I do. You are the ideal of all your jokes; like a true Irishman, *you kill before you cure.*"

Soon after his appointment to Savannah, and during the progress of the grading of the railroad to the interior, many hundreds of Irish laborers were employed on the work. The head contractors, who resided in the city, having delayed the monthly payment of the men for a considerable time, they suffered for the necessaries of life, and entertained well-grounded apprehensions of fraud. After some unavailable messages, they suspended the work, organized a strike, and, marshalled in a formidable, mob-like body, were making their way towards the city. Wild and exaggerated rumors went before them; they were bringing certain destruction; the assault was intended to be made at night, and their programme doomed the city to the flames and the inhabitants to destitution; those savage Irish were already within a day's journey from the gates. A panic seized on the inhabitants, the militia were called out, the military companies organized, and war materials provided. The city was almost placed in a state of siege. A council of war having assembled, it was unanimously decided to meet the foe in advance and mow them down with cannon-ball and musket-shot. Father O'Neill appeared on the scene of civil commotion, took in the situation at a glance, and, in chiding accents, denounced all this nonsense. He requested the mayor and other leading men to accompany him, remarking that even Indians made a parley before they fought. After having pledged his word and assumed the responsibility of the safety of life and property, his proposal was accepted, and the excitement ceased. This reasonable proposition and the calm, firm demeanor of that single good man (not unfrequently called *stamina*) calmed the troubled waters, and peace was instantly restored.

A few hours' ride brought the delegation face to face with those early strikers, who formed a disorganized body of unarmed men, indignant at the frauds and injustice of railroad contractors and speculators in refusing to pay their hard-earned wages, and were going with their hands in their pockets to ask redress for their grievances. The head of the embassy made a harangue in Irish, embracing both the dialects—the Kerry and Connaught. The worthlessness of this mode of seeking redress, its imprudence and imminent danger, averted by his own timely interference, were strongly impressed on the minds of the workingmen. They halted, and, adopting the plan of the Savannians, chose a half-dozen of their leaders to accompany the pacificators on their return to the city to arrange all difficulties and make peace, a consummation reached without difficulty or delay. If this mild and judicious course had been inaugurated more recently, at the inception of the railroad strikes in the Northern States, millions of money, many lives, and the reputation of the country would not have been so uselessly and universally sacrificed. After having wrought much evil, the rebellion was arrested only, after it had reached Pittsburg, by the manly and fearless interference of Dr. Tuigg, the illustrious bishop of that city.

Anecdote is the most faithful delineator of character, presenting before the mind the individual in his proper and personal attitude. On solemn occasions Father O'Neill was the chief ornament of the sanctuary, and a stickler for rubrics; if possible, he never neglected the least ceremony. When, on the outside missions, many of the natives were present at Mass to gratify mere curiosity, out of respect to the divine mysteries he invariably explained the ceremonies and the nature of this supreme act of divine worship at the commencement. The length of the vindication may be judged by the following incident: Before beginning Mass, and now in his vestments, on a Sunday, in the interior of Georgia, he made the customary explanation. Turning to the altar, erected under a bower in the open air, duly protected, and handsomely ornamented by the choicest products of the forest, he was surprised to notice that the candles lighted at the beginning were completely consumed, and, in his own words, "not a snuff was left in the candlesticks." A fresh candle could not be procured for love or money in all that section of country. Necessity is the mother of invention; it was the origin of many of the ceremonies now clustered around the altar; the enlightened Catholic can read in the sanctuary the summary of the history of the Church and of divine revelation from the beginning. How to say Mass without lights was the difficulty. It would be a sin to omit a leading rubric without a grave necessity, and did the justification exist under the present circumstances? Could not the State of Georgia afford a substitute for the candle of the Catacombs? He procured two pine torches, stationed two living candlesticks at each side of the altar, on bent knees, placed a lighted torch in the hands of each, and offered the Holy Sacrifice.

Many amusing incidents in the life of this incomparable man exist among the people, and their recital will interest the missionary for many years to come.

The seventh Council of Baltimore proposed to the Holy See the erection of several new sees, and amongst the number that of Savannah, embracing the entire State of Georgia and all Florida east of the Appalachicola River. The Right Rev. Francis Xavier Gartland, D.D., was nominated for first bishop.[*] He was a native of Ireland, and was born in the city of Dublin in the year 1805. He made his studies at Mount St. Mary's College, Emmittsburgh, was ordained priest by Bishop Conwell in 1832, was immediately appointed assistant at St. John's Church with Father

---

[*] Authorities: Reminiscences of the Author. Original sources—Rev. Edward Quigley, "Lives of Deceased Bishops," by Dr. Clark, Catholic almanacs, contemporaneous journals.

Hughes, and succeeded him as pastor after he was nominated for the coadjutorship of New York. Having discharged the obligations of his charge with great fidelity and zeal, Father Gartland won the confidence of Bishop Kenrick and the esteem and affectionate regard of the faithful of the city of Philadelphia. Raised to the office of vicar-general, he aided the bishop in his administrative duties, advanced the cause of religion, and endeared himself to the clergy. Firm, yet mild and conciliating, he passed unscathed through the turbulent times of the Know-Nothing riots, and was the most popular priest in the city among all classes. Besides his deep and fervent piety, these qualities admirably fitted him for the appointment of first Bishop of Savannah. He was consecrated by Archbishop Eccleston, assisted by Bishops Kenrick and O'Connor, at St. John's Church, September 10, 1850, having been eighteen years priest, and five years vicar-general of the diocese. I met him at the seminary in Charleston later in the fall, and accompanied him to his see.

He was a man of medium height, genteelly robust, with light-brown hair and fair complexion. His attire was grave, and the episcopal ring the only ornament of jewelry worn on his person. His voice was strong, clear, and of vast compass, and cultivated by practice only ; he assured me he did not know a note scientifically. In preaching he gave every syllable its full value of sound, and every note in church music was equally honored. While this gift prolonged the ceremonies, it was of great advantage in preaching, rendering what would have been otherwise very plain, gorgeous, solemn, and impressive. The quarter of an hour sermon of a Paulist would abundantly fill up his half-hour, the usual length of his Sunday discourses. The priestly robes, all the ceremonies of the Church, the decorations of the sanctuary, public affairs, and confraternities were leading objects of his devotion. In such matters there was no bishop in America more industrious. If a vestment was carelessly folded he could not rest until it was restored to its former creases, and he usually attended to it in person. His soul loved the beauty of God's house, and was zealous for all that concerned the decency of divine worship. This vigilance extended to surplices worn by the youths who served at the altar on Sundays.

Separated for life from the friends whom his worth and eminent services in behalf of religion united to him, now travelling on the southern waters far away, and beginning the episcopacy in a slave State of whose priests and people he knew nothing except by reports not always favorable, he became thoughtful and silent. I remarked that his prospects were encouraging, that he was a young bishop in the vigor of manhood, had a promising diocese, with four thousand Catholics, faithful and true, and a priesthood of blameless life devoted to the cause of religion, who were ready to welcome him with open arms. Perhaps his pensive mood was the shadow of future and unexpected events, for they are what generally happen. In the wide domain of the Church no priesthood could be met more obedient and deferential to a bishop than the clergy of the diocese of Charleston. A clique or faction was never sprung nor a schism created or opposition arrayed against the episcopal authority. An accidental discussion of the expediency of some administrative measure, from which the official acts of no public man can be exempt, was the utmost extent of dissatisfaction—a spirit which animates the clergy of the three dioceses to this day.

Bishop Gartland, like a good soldier of the cross, entered strenuously on the work before him. He visited all parts of his diocese repeatedly, ordained two priests, endeared himself to all classes, and enlarged the Cathedral of St. John the Baptist. It was rededicated June 26, 1853. Bishop Reynolds preached in the forenoon, and the writer in the evening. In the sanctuary were Bishop Barron; the present worthy bishop of San Antonio, Dr. Pellicer, and a goodly number of the clergy. The church on both occasions was filled to its utmost capacity. Few of the adults then present are now living; others fill their places, to be speedily removed in their time and make room for others. Thus, like waves of the sea, our generations rise and disappear in the ocean of time.

The year after his consecration the bishop travelled extensively in the Northern States, and visited his native country in the interests of religion. He graced by his presence and aided by his wisdom the deliberations of the eighth Council of Baltimore. At the division of a diocese the clergy may select either section for the field of their future labors. Dr. Gartland warmly urged me to return to Georgia. My engagements at Columbia prevented me from complying with the request.

I visited the city to perform a duty of filial affection towards a venerated parent, whose remains had been for a long time reposing in another's tomb. It was during August, 1854. The city basked evening and morning in the golden light of a southern sun. The trees were in full bloom, the gardens diffused the rich fragrance of their flowers on all sides. In the public squares and at the base of the Pulaski monument a great many children played in the happy innocence of childhood. All was life, gayety, and happiness, and the city seemed like a very paradise of God. But, like Herculaneum or Pompeii before the eruption of Mount Ætna, it was marked for speedy destruction.

It is remarkable in the history of nations and individuals that a seven years' plenty frequently goes before a famine, and a Thabor before a Calvary. A man eminent for piety always regarded a consolation as the precursor of great trials, and the warning of unusual spiritual desolation. The proverbial calm not only follows but as frequently goes before a storm. On the Sunday the bishop preached and published a Requiem Mass for the repose of the soul of the Rev. M. Sharidan, who had died at Columbus. In the course of conversation during the afternoon he promised to extend a like favor to me after my death. In the providence of God I have been spared to return the intended kindness at the altar during twenty-three years.

The good die soon, while we are spared to acquire more fervor or be better prepared.

I never saw the bishop after; he was then the picture of health, but he was ripe for heaven. Judging from some cases of sickness which I attended during my sojourn, I strongly suspected that even then the yellow fever was in the city. The Catholic body seemed marked in a special manner for death, like victims of expiation for others. A Southern hurricane swept over the city, unroofing the cathedral, the bishop's house, and many other residences. The clergy, few in number, were incapable of attending the great number of the sick. The bishop went bravely to work, during night and day traversing the now desolate streets, passing from house to house, administering the sacraments, blessing the dying, and consoling the living. It now became his turn, and the good shepherd was attacked. He was conveyed to the residence of his friend, Michael Prendergast, where he received all the attention that pious care and medical skill could afford. Harassed in mind and spent and worn in body by labor, his strength was exhausted; he sank slowly, and, fortified by the aids which he brought to others at the sacrifice of his life, he fell asleep calmly on the bosom of our Lord and Saviour. First in every good work, he illustrated in his life and actions the admonition of the apostle to his faithful disciple, St. Timothy. The good shepherd gave his life for his flock, and doing so found it. He will be ever gratefully remembered by all the people of his diocese, Catholic and non-Catholic; a strong and bright light in the hierarchy, he will live in the example he set, and be venerated in Savannah as her first martyr bishop.

He increased the number of the clergy during his brief episcopate of four years, erected three new churches, created as many missions, renewed the cathedral, and established many societies and confraternities, lasting monuments of zeal and piety. He purchased a large tract of land outside the city for a Catholic cemetery, so much needed, and he now rests under the soil which he had consecrated to God. His memory is sweeter and his tomb more honored than if it were built in the valley of the Susquehanna or bedewed by tears shed from the pinnacles of more gorgeous temples in more favored cities. Towards the end of his administration the Catholic population had become double, but it was thinned by the pestilence and calamities which befell the Church ; many years passed before it regained its lost numbers. He died September 20, 1854, in the forty-ninth year of his age, having been a priest eighteen years and four years bishop.

Right Rev. Edward Barron, D.D., bishop of both the Guineas, who was assisting in visiting the sick, died gloriously on the first of the same month, only a few days intervening between the deaths of both the bishops.[*] He was born in 1801, and was brother of Sir Henry Winton Barron, of Waterford, Ireland. He studied in the Propaganda, where he received his diploma as Doctor of Divinity. Having spent a number of years on the Irish missions in the United States, he united himself with the diocese of Philadelphia. He was appointed pastor of St. Mary's Church, president of the Theological Seminary, and vicar-general of the diocese. The Holy See expressed a desire that two priests, one from each of the dioceses of New York and Philadelphia, should be chosen to go to Liberia and labor for the conversion of the Africans. Dr. Barron and Rev. John Kelly, of New York, zealous and apostolic men, volunteered for that mission. They embarked, together with Dennis Pindar, a lay catechist, in December, 1841, for Cape Mescarado and thence proceeded to Cape Palmas.

They landed at their destination in February, 1842, and began the mission with great energy and were rewarded with considerable success. The next year Dr. Barron returned to the United States and went to Europe, in order to obtain more laborers and pecuniary aid from his ancestral estate for the missions. The Holy See raised this re-

---

[*] Authorities : Personal recollections, Shea's "History," Letter of Rev. Edward Quigley. Original sources—Dr. Clarke's " Lives of Deceased Bishops," Catholic almanacs, journals, etc.

gion of Africa to a vicariate in 1843, and Dr. Barron was created bishop. Seven priests and three lay brothers of the Society of the Sacred Heart of Jesus accompanied the bishop on his return, and the work of conversion was inaugurated with renewed energy. Within a year six of the noble band died from fever and the effects of the climate, after having established the mission. Bishop Barron, Father Kelly, and the Rev. John M. Maurice, of New York, were also prostrated; enfeebled by sickness, it was impossible for them to continue their labors amid such devastation. The Holy See transferred the mission to an order of priests trained for the conversion of the negroes. Bishop Barron and Father Kelly returned to the United States.

He was offered another diocese, but declined and worked in more humble duties on the missions in Philadelphia, St. Louis, Florida, and finally in Savannah, where his labors ended with a glorious death. He was in the North when the account reached him of the prevalence of the yellow fever, and he hurried on to unite his feeble strength and heroic zeal to those of Bishop Gartland. Enfeebled by long disease and exhausted by constant labor for two weeks, he was himself attacked by the pestilence. In the climax of his severest sufferings the violent storm spoken of tore the roof from the bishop's house, where he lay, and exposed him in this condition to the fury of the elements. Transported in haste to the residence of Mr. Prendergast, death put an end speedily to his sufferings, and he went to prepare a place for his co-laborer. The remains of both the bishops lay side by side for years. The ravages of the recent war left their burying-place open and unguarded. The Sisters of Mercy removed them to a temporary place of interment in their convent. In 1867 the remains of Bishops Gartland, Barron, and Barry were interred in the cemetery with the most solemn and imposing ceremonies.

In person Bishop Barron was tall, slender, and slightly bent. Having lost his health in Africa and never regained it, his appearance was frail and delicate. He rarely smiled, though his mortified countenance bore the pleasing expression of the interior peace and tranquillity of his soul. His journeys were more extensive than those of the apostle. An exile for the sake of the Gospel, Europe, Africa, and America shared his missionary labors. His faith was so strong and his piety so intense that a medal or any other memorial touched by the blessing of the Church endowed it in his estimation with a value unfelt by ordinary devotion. The fervor or the Mass attended the recital of the Breviary, while prayer and religious duties filled his entire mind, and, like St. Aloysius, there was no room for idle thought to wander. A most efficacious sermon on prayer would be a glance at him while engaged in that evangelical occupation. A martyr of charity, his death was the fitting termination of a life so holy.

Justice demands a brief sketch of the Rev. Edward Quigley in connection with those heroic men whose ministry and labors he shared, but was mercifully spared in the providence of God to toil in his vineyard for the edification of the clergy and the salvation of the people. A link between the past and the future, he is the last living man on whom Bishop England had poured the holy unction of the priesthood. His eulogy can be spoken only after death unseals the lips of silence, for he still is an active and efficient missionary priest. Acts speak louder than words. Like his ministry in the diocese, his name will be found in nearly every chapter of the book.

The Rev. Edward Quigley was born in the County Tipperary, Ireland, and after having studied his philosophy and theology in the Seminary of St. John the Baptist, was ordained in Charleston, together with Father Burke, in 1837, by Bishop England. After his ordination he was stationed on the Sumter mission and its dependencies until 1840, when he was transferred to New Berne and the missions in eastern North Carolina, which he served with great zeal and efficiency until 1844, when he was transferred to Columbia by Dr. Reynolds, after Dr. Birmingham was changed to Columbus, Ga. ; his successful efforts in

behalf of religion will be found in the history of that
church. In 1848, and by his own request, he was moved
to Charleston, where he officiated as assistant in the cathedral, and subsequently under the Rev. Dr. Baker at St.
Mary's.

After the division of the diocese his lot was cast in
Georgia, and in 1853 he was deputed to the charge of the
missions of Macon and Atlanta. In December of that
year he was called to Savannah to build a second church,
and was engaged in that undertaking until interrupted by
the yellow fever, which for years retarded this and many
other zealous enterprises in the cause of religion. Bishop
Gartland fell, all the priests had been attacked, and but one
spared to administer the sacraments to the multitude who
were sick and dying daily and hourly ; this was Father Edward Quigley. He stood to the last, spent and worn for want
of sleep, or rest, or aid. All who could, fled the city of death ;
the physicians perished or broke down ; all trade and activity disappeared ; no ship was seen in the harbor or on
the tawny stream ; no one appeared in the once bustling
streets but the devoted Sisters of Mercy, the priest, an
odd doctor, and the everlasting hearses or death-carts ; to
procure coffins was the labor of the city. Solitude, silence
and death held universal sway. The heroic priest battled
nobly and escaped. If his form does not live in marble, his
memory will be for ever enshrined in the hearts of a grateful people and their descendants. A religious, Sister Mary
Baptist, *née* Julia O'Connell, who also ministered to the
afflicted, was attacked, convalesced, but never entirely recovered, and died in Charleston, at the parent house, some
time after.

Father Quigley ministered in the city and through the
State during the widowhood of the sorrowing diocese
under the administration of Father Barry. He was stationed at Locust Grove in 1856, where he ministered until
the year 1859, when he accepted a charge in the diocese of
Buffalo under Bishop Timon, and has been stationed at
Rochester. He served at various times in nearly all the

missions of the vast diocese of Charleston for a quarter of a century. Of fair complexion, tall, and portly, graceful in manners and dignified in bearing, he was a favorite public speaker and an accomplished scholar; but his labors, his virtues, and his zeal endeared him most to the faithful of the Carolinas and Georgia. The following letter of this distinguished missionary priest, and one of the sainted Archbishop Kenrick, will be read with deep interest by the faithful:

"About the middle of September, 1834, my cousin, Wm. Burke, and myself had the honor of meeting Right Rev. Bishop England at Blackrock Ursuline Convent, Cork. We were then adopted by him as subjects of the diocese of Charleston, and three years and some months after that both of us were ordained priests by him in the chapel of the Ursulines in the same city. This was at the Christmas 'quatuor-tense,' 1837. In the spring of 1838, Sumter District, S. C., was formed into a pastorate, and I was appointed to that mission. After spending two years and six months in charge of Sumter, Camden, Cheraw, etc., I was removed in the latter part of 1840 to New Berne, N. C., and was succeeded in Sumter by Rev. John Guifford. While in Sumter I undertook, by direction of Bishop England, the erection of a church in Camden, which was totally neglected by my successors, and ultimately fell into the hands of one of the building committee, Mr. Villepique, during the episcopate of Dr. Reynolds. From New Berne, N. C., I attended Washington, where there was a neat church, with Plymouth, Edenton, Greenville, Beaufort, etc. Except Bishop England, I was the first priest who ever preached in Edenton, and, without doubt, was the first who preached in Beaufort. I continued in New Berne until the first of January, 1845, when I was removed to Columbia, S. C., and Sumter and Camden, with Cheraw, once more fell to my charge. In the autumn of 1848 I was removed from Columbia by my own request, and became one of the assistants of the cathedral, and subsequently at St. Mary's. In 1850 I visited Ireland, and on my return was sent to take charge of the churches of Macon and Atlanta, Ga. In 1853, about the month of December, Bishop Gartland called me to Savannah to build a church in the western part of the city. The yellow fever and the death of Bishop Gartland, in 1854, both combined to defeat this undertaking, but I had another field of labor opened to me by the fatal scourge. During this dreadful scourge the Rev. J. F. O'Neill was engaged on the mission of Jeckel Island and St. Mary's, and could not prudently return to the city, while Father Kirby, who had been totally unnerved, was speedily prostrated, and on his convalescence ordered to the country by his physicians. Thus the 'burden of the day and the heats' fell upon poor Bishop Gartland, Bishop Barron, who happened to be in the city, and myself. Bishop Barron's feeble health obliged him to confine his labors to hearing confessions in the church. The poor, dear saint succumbed and died of the fever on the 12th of September, 1854. Our own lamented Bishop Gartland survived him only eight days. Both of them fell voluntary victims to their zeal for the glory of God and the salvation of souls, and both of them, I am sure, well deserve to be ranked among the truest and noblest of those Christian heroes who have at any time done honor to humanity, to God, or to his Church, either by the beauty of their lives, the glory of their example, or the manner of their death—a holocaust of the most sublime and unbounded charity.

"In the interim between the deaths of the two bishops I was alone for six or seven days, until at length Father Barry came to my relief from Augusta. I was then visiting from eighty to one hundred sick persons a day, our deaths daily averaging from forty to forty-eight, this last being the maximum, and half of them generally Catholics. For two months at least I neither said Mass nor gave the Viaticum nor Extreme Unction to any one. I was able only to hear confessions, and was sometimes obliged to hear the confessions of husband and wife prostrated in the same bed at the same time, or rather I made their confessions for them in a general way and absolved them, hoping in the mercy of God and their own good dispositions. But this was not all. A storm swept over the city such as has been seldom witnessed. The lower part of the city was submerged; whole blocks were unroofed; the roof of the bishop's house was carried away; and yet I had to sleep in that house, its only tenant, while I snatched my meals from house to house as chance permitted.

"The enclosed letter, which Archbishop Kenrick, of Baltimore, did me the honor of addressing to me soon after, may possibly be regarded by you as worthy of a place in your book and as throwing some light on the history of that time. Possibly your eye may have fallen on a communication from Philadelphia among the *lettres édifiant de la propagation de la foi*. If so, you must put it down simply as the romance of the writer's imagination, a thing that might have happened but most certainly did not.

"In the fall of 1856, on my return from a second visit to Ireland, Bishop Barry appointed me to Locust Grove, where I remained until 1859. My last functions in the ministry of the diocese of Savannah were in the last week of 1859 in the church of Augusta, where I preached the usual course of sermons of Holy Week. I came near forgetting that I made one or two missions to Key West and Tampa in Florida. In Key West I redeemed the church, which was going to be sold, from a heavy debt, and prepared some forty children for First Communion and Confirmation. In Tampa I baptized some twenty-nine persons, both children and adults. I was the first priest who ever administered the sacraments in this latter place. I also visited Fort Brown, on Charlotte Bay, where I spent nearly two weeks, giving some four hundred soldiers the opportunity of the sacraments, etc.

"Ever since I left the South in 1859 I have been stationed in this diocese, and for the last fifteen years in this city of Buffalo. Very affectionately yours,

"EDWARD QUIGLEY."

"BUFFALO, N. Y., April 13, 1878."

"BALTIMORE, September 23, 1854.

"REVEREND DEAR SIR:

"I sympathize with you most deeply in the loss of your excellent bishop, whose death, however, was glorious to religion, as he died a martyr of zeal and charity. The money collected is ready to be sent, but as to-morrow's collections in some of our churches are to be added to the amount, I delay sending it till next week. We have already $400, and will no doubt have the full sum which I anticipated when I wrote last. I presume that the surest way is to buy a draft on Savannah and enclose it to you. I am greatly edified at your exposure of your life in conjunction with your bishop, and at the alacrity with which the vicar-general came to your assistance. The charity of good Mrs. Prendergast also consoles me. Please acknowledge for me the receipt of her two letters, which conveyed tidings sad but in some respects glorious.

"I must beg of you to inform me if the bishop appointed an administrator of the diocese, and whether he left any names to be proposed to the Holy See. Any documents of this character should be forwarded to me at once. I pray that the scourge may cease, although we are threatened with a far greater calamity in the conspiracy so widely spread against our religion and against the Constitution, which excludes religious tests. I also beg to know whether Dr. Barron left a will.

"With great affection I remain, reverend sir,
"Your devoted friend,
"FRANCIS PATRICK KENRICK, A.B.

"REV. EDWARD QUIGLEY."

Right Rev. John Barry, D.D., second Bishop of Savannah,* was born in the County Wexford, Ireland, in 1799, made his ecclesiastical studies in the seminary in Charleston, and was ordained priest on September 24, 1825, by Bishop England, and like the patron of the diocese, St.

---

* Authorities: Personal recollections of the author chiefly. Original sources—Dr. Clark's "Lives of Deceased Bishops," Catholic almanacs.

John the Baptist, he immediately began his course. It embraces for thirty-five years the history of what I continue to designate the diocese of Charleston.

A bishop possesses the plenitude of orders, and all apostolical graces necessary for his mission, suited to every emergency. In the succession of every see, though not in each individual link, we find those wondrous gifts illustrated. One is distinguished for learning, another for prudence; one for heroic fortitude, another for wisdom—all for a virtuous life. Bishop Barry was conspicuous for holiness among priests and bishops; he was by excellence the saint.

He labored on every mission, in every church, and in nearly every town in the three States at one time or another; he was known to every man, woman, and child, either personally or by reputation; he took a part in every Catholic enterprise, shared in every labor, bore every disappointment, nursed every vocation, rejoiced in every good sincerely as if it were personal, and filled every office with positive edification. It would be unjust to claim a negative goodness by affirming that he never on any occasion gave disedification, in private or in public, by word or deed. All his words and acts were animated by a supernatural motive, were virtues in every sense, and preached living sermons to Catholics and non-Catholics alike. The external occupations of the saints surpass the endurance of the most indefatigable worldlings. St. Charles Borromeo, St. Francis Xavier, and St. Gregory the Great, labored more than earthly monarch or conqueror, without the omission scarcely of a devotion, or the undevout distraction of worldly thoughts. Father Barry, by the multitude of his works, never missed a decade of his beads or a week-day Mass, unless from some uncontrollable cause. Slightly over the middle size; perfectly bald, except a tuft of hair over each ear; a pleasing countenance; bloodless, sallow complexion, and emaciated figure, he glowed like a seraph at the altar, and whether in the sanctuary or in the street filled the beholder with religious awe. It was the reputation of his life, his works of charity, the sanctity of his character, the heroism of his missionary labors rather than the eloquence of his sermons that impressed his audience. Only passable as a public speaker, it was in work and deed rather than in word that he excelled.

In 1827 he was appointed by Bishop England pastor of the Church of the Holy Trinity, in Augusta, and attended, besides, one-third of the State of Georgia, a position which he held until 1854; he was also Vicar-General for the State since 1830. In 1844 he was appointed Vicar-General for the diocese of Charleston by Bishop Reynolds, also First Assistant at the Cathedral of St. Finbar, Superior of the Seminary of St. John the Baptist, and Missionary-Extraordinary for all the vacant stations of the Carolinas and Georgia. During his administration he was the working power, the apostolic missionary, of the diocese of Charleston, visiting Augusta only once a month. There will be found mention of his labors in nearly every chapter of this book. Before the arrival of Bishop England the slim congregation was sorely afflicted by the unpriestly behavior of wolves in sheep's clothing, who had crept into the fold and laid it waste.

After years of blameless life, filled with prayer and all manner of good works, Father Barry healed many of the wounds, and restored confidence in the priesthood—a difficult task and an unpleasant position all clergymen must concede who have made the trial. Whenever an unpleasantness occurred anywhere he was always hurried into the gap of danger, to cast oil on the troubled waters, and restore peace. In addition to all these labors, sufficient to occupy the time of a dozen priests, he imposed on himself greater hardship still, which deprived him of domestic rest and left him without quiet or leisure.

In 1832, when the cholera decimated Augusta, and there was no room for the number of patients, he converted his own house into a public hospital for the reception of all the afflicted indiscriminately, Catholic and non-Catholic. In human suffering his charity knew no distinction of rank or creed. He lived amid the sick and dying; he was physician, he was priest, he was nurse, he was sexton; like Tobias, he bore the dead on his shoulders and buried them.

After the destroying angel unfolded his wings and fled away, the cry of the orphans, like the wailing in Egypt, was left in his wake. They were of all ages and of both sexes, uncared for, sick and hungry, bare and wretched, and dying without a mother's compassion or a father's care. The wards that had like biers yielded so many to the graves were immediately readjusted, the hospital was changed into an orphan asylum; sedate matrons were hired to care for the little girls in the absence of the Sisters. He took charge of the male children himself. Like another St. Vincent de Paul, they clustered around him, they clung to his knees, clutched his soutane, learned to stand by the support of his feet. He washed them with his own hands, fed them, clad them, rocked them to sleep, combed their hair, aided by the services of the most grown. It was a wonderful family; he was rewarded even by human love; the children, knowing no other tie, concentrated on him alone all the untold depths of filial affection for both parents. It was returned.

In all that group there was a special favor for each, whether a colored cap, glass button, or the texture of the first pair of pants. His solicitude did not end with their boyhood; they were taught their Catechism and their arithmetic, and fitted by religion and education for future encounter with the world. Nor must we omit to give a due meed of praise to the venerable Father Gregory Duggin, the assistant and sharer of his labors. Both in Augusta and Savannah he established Catholic day-schools, and while administrator he gathered around him and superintended the nursing and raising of the Catholic boys in the latter city. Like the walls of Jerusalem, built with every variety of precious stones, our prelates and priests, living and dead, have contributed to the establishment of the Church in the Carolinas and Georgia, each in his own measure;

but none have excelled or even equalled Father Barry in disabusing the errors of non-Catholics, disarming prejudices, converting sinners, reclaiming heretics and apostates, condemning every vice, inculcating virtue by word and example, and bringing Catholics to the regular and frequent participation of the sacraments. The life of one single-minded priest, devoted to God and his calling, is an apostleship for a nation and a mercy to an age. The fall of such a one into a grievous sin would inflict an appalling injury on the universal Church, more fatal far than the apostasy of Döllinger or Loyson. Father Barry was secure under the shelter of the most intense humility, frequent confession, strict abstinence in food and drink, and devotion to Our Blessed Lady. To sum up all in one word, he was a *man of prayer*, the habit of which he used to say was the end of all meditation, spiritual reading, and other devotional exercises. "The man of prayer will never be lost" was one of his common expressions. Whether the result of austerity, labor, or the severity of the Southern climate, in late years his nerves became weak, which served but to render the performance of public duty more meritorious and his humility more deep.

In 1844 he was Bishop Reynolds' theologian at the sixth Council of Baltimore. In 1853 he was reappointed Vicar-General of the diocese of Savannah by Bishop Gartland. In December of the same year he formed an affiliation of the Sisters of Our Lady of Mercy at Augusta. In 1855 he volunteered to go to Savannah, the scene of death, and passed through the campaign to the end with his usual vigor, and after the bishops and two priests had died by his side. The dart of pestilence fell harmless at his feet, while, like St. Sebastian's arrows, they stuck in the breasts of many beside.

After the death of Bishop Gartland he governed the diocese for two years as administrator, and was, reluctantly on his part, elevated to the see; urged by obedience, he accepted the dignity. He was consecrated August 2, 1857, in the cathedral at Baltimore by Archbishop Kenrick, assisted by Bishops Portier and Newman. Bishop McGill preached the consecration sermon. As bishop he administered the diocese of Savannah two years, made several visitations, and displayed his old fervor and zeal, but without the strength and vigor of former years. His health was broken, and the episcopal dignity seemed to have been bestowed by Providence to give a heavenly sanction before men and a lustre before the angels to a life of unsurpassed piety and grandeur in the American priesthood. He is mentioned among the people rather as Father than Bishop Barry.

The heart of the just is a never-failing fountain of joy and gladness. There can be no real sorrow but sin, because it separates from God, who is joy essential. Bishop Barry was courteous, affable, and entertaining in society at the proper time; he understood the proper time for casting stones and for picking them up again. Everybody expected him to be the forthcoming bishop of Savannah at the time of the appointment of Dr. Gartland. To imagine that he aspired to the dignity would be injustice to his character. He met the new and first bishop in Charleston, and while spending an hour in the afternoon with other clergymen, to dispel, doubtless, the apparent discouragement of the young prelate, the venerable Vicar-General rose and tripped the light fantastic toe in the most approved style of an Irish jig. I just then arrived and saw Bishop Gartland for the first time. Observing my surprise at the scene, a merry laugh, clear as the sound of a bell, rang out over the premises, and the Terpsichorean resumed his seat. It reminded me of St. Philip Neri, who danced before the street arabs on the Corso with affected jubilee for having received the cardinal's hat from the reigning pontiff—a device which released him of the honor thrust on him more efficaciously than expostulation. St. Philip was one of the wisest and most learned men of the day, and the tutor of Baronius; the Church never canonizes idiots or crazy persons.

He visited Europe to seek a restoration of health the

year after his consecration. On his arrival in Paris he repaired to the convent of the Brothers Hospitallers of St. John of God. After a month his exhaustion increased, and death was at hand. He received the utmost care and attention from the religious, and was visited by Cardinal Marlot, the archbishop of Paris. He died November 21, 1859, in the sixtieth year of his age. His remains were buried with due solemnity at Père la Chaise, where they remained until 1869, when, at the request of the faithful of Georgia, they were conveyed by Bishop Persico to the city of Savannah and reinterred with those of Bishops Gartland and Barron.

CHAPTER XVI.

SAVANNAH AND AUGUSTA.

Very Rev. Peter Whelan, V.G., Administrator—Locust Grove—Rev. M. D. O'Reilly—Missions and Edifying Death in New Orleans—A Georgia Priest—The Great Unknown—St. John in the Wilderness—Personal Appearance—Long Journey on Horseback—An Extensive Wardrobe—Administrator—Refuses a Mitre—The Soldiers' Friend—Medicinal Diet—Long Life and Hard Work—A Solid Preacher—Prisoner of War—Living Recompense for Military Service—Death of the Saint—Character of the Georgia Priest—Right Rev. Augustin Verot, D.D., Third Bishop of Savannah—A Long and Prosperous Administration—His Labors, Learning, and Zeal—Identified with the South—His Happy Death—Eulogy by Father Clavreul—Right Rev. Ignatius Persico, D.D.—Resigns after two years—Right Rev. William H. Gross, D.D.—His Labors and Zeal—Institutions—The Sisters of Mercy—Nuns—Benedictine Fathers—Jesuits—Obituaries—Augusta—First Priests—Misses the See—Rev. Drs. Cooper and Brown—A Cholera Hospital—Asylum and Ravages—Rev. Dominic Byrne Lost on the Coast of Florida—A Faithful Priest—Father Gregory Duggan—Hard Sense and Regularity of Life—David and Jonathan—A Great Missionary Priest—Friend of the Needy and Father of the Orphans—Eloquent in Works—A Silent Preacher—Pastor of Augusta—Builds St. Patrick's Church—His Death Universally Lamented—The Last of Bishop England's Priests in the Diocese—Very Rev. John Kirby, V.G.—Labors, Piety, and Zeal—Many Missions—Ministry during the Yellow Fever—Loses his Health—Character—Rev. Patrick Kirby—Missions, Labors, and Death at St. Vincent's—Brother Timothy Kirby, a Cleric—Early Death in the Monastery—Father Ryan—Popularity—Converts—The Pacificator—In Mobile—Vicar-General Hamilton, Pastor of Augusta—Eufaula and Florida—Rev. C. C. Prendergast, Pastor—The Jesuit Fathers—Letters of Father Butler—Increase of Catholicity.

THE Very Rev. Peter Whelan, who was created vicar-general by Dr. Barry, became administrator and governed the diocese two years, until the nomination of Bishop Verot in 1861. He was born in the County Wexford about the year 1800. He acquired a sound classical and mathematical education in his native country, and in early manhood volunteered his services for the diocese of Charleston and devoted himself to her missions. He finished his ecclesiastical course in the diocesan seminary, and was ordained by Dr. England about the year 1830.

He was stationed on the missions in the eastern part of North Carolina in 1831, and about 1833 was transferred to the church at Locust Grove, in Wilkes County.

This district embraced northeastern Georgia, and was a laborious parish. The church at this point was one of the earliest in the diocese of Charleston, and was erected about 1826 by some Maryland Catholics who immigrated to that county. The Thompsons, Semmes, Lucketts, Griffins, O'Neills, and Ryans were the principal families.

One of the first priests was Rev. M. D. O'Reilly, who, with several of his congregation, withdrew to Mississippi, and was for many years pastor of Vicksburg. He retained this position until he lost his health. He retired to the city of New Orleans, where he died about the year 1847, at the residence of Bishop Blanc. He was a respectable priest, accomplished much good, and his memory is venerated by the faithful. He studied in the seminary, and was ordained by Bishop England about the year 1826.

Rev. Peter Whelan was appointed pastor of Locust Grove and the surrounding country for scores of miles, where he officiated until 1850, a period of nearly eighteen years.

In stature he was uncommonly tall, considerably over six feet, whenever he stood straight, with a rugged and fleshless frame, sunburnt complexion, yellow-skinned hands, black and unkempt locks, and stooped in his shoulders. His garments were of an inferior texture, worn threadbare, and short or shrivelled at the extremities. In these days there were no railroads to transport one while asleep to his journey's end. Inch by inch in the rumbling and crowded stage or on horseback must these long visitations be accomplished. Not unaccustomed to the rugged grasp of the plough-handle—for he eked his support from the soil round his cabin—Father Peter unyoked the farm-horse, and, seated on his saddle, all his church articles and wardrobe in his saddle-bags, made his rounds in this humble manner for twenty-five years. A plainer or more unassuming priest lived not in his day.

His countenance was highly intellectual; the thin lips scarcely concealed his teeth; a broad-brimmed hat, worn from time immemorial, would complete the picture. One of the best-educated men in the country, an instructive preacher, a man of great practical sense and wisdom, he adapted himself to the customs of the country in all that was not sinful. None was ever more highly esteemed or more deeply venerated. There could be none more exempt from the degrading weakness of human respect. Calm and self-possessed, like the prophet, he always bore his soul in his hands, and neither felt nor feared the face of man.

As though he had imbibed the spirit of the wilderness, he came in like another St. John the Baptist, and his eloquence, his prudence, and his wisdom wrought wonders in behalf of religion.

As administrator he assisted at the eighth Provincial Council of Baltimore, and, it is credibly stated, was offered the vacant see by the fathers. Father Whelan communicated to Archbishop Kenrick his unshaken purpose never to accept the episcopal dignity, even if urged, which seldom occurs, for the Church has no difficulty in procuring worthy men willing to undertake the burden.

After the appointment of Dr. Verot, Father Whelan for twenty years exercised the duties of the priesthood at the cathedral or as assistant at St. Patrick's Church, or on the out-missions. In his own words, "he lived most of the time on quinine"; yet it generally became his lot to sing last Mass on Sundays so worn and debilitated by ill-health and labors that he rather hung from than stood by the altar.

He wielded a ready and an able pen. His letters to Secretary Stanton after the war, on the occasion of the condemnation of Colonel Wirz, made a profound impression on the public.

During all the time of the war he was general chaplain at all the stations in Georgia from Anderson to Tybee. His name is a spell among the soldiers, especially the survivors of the Anderson stockade, where he was permanently located. It was no difference to him whether the sufferer wore the gray or the blue, all shared alike his ministrations and his pity. He divided with the Federal prisoners all that he possessed, to his wearing apparel and his last cent.

He procured them medicine, fed and clothed them when they were left to perish by the United States, which refused to pay him the money actually spent in relieving the wants of the unfortunate prisoners. His only recompense was an army of millions of vermin and a prison.

While administering the sacraments to the sick at Fort Pulaski the place was carried by assault, and the priest was sent a prisoner to the North with the common soldiers. He was confined some time at Fort Lafayette, and obtained his liberty only after considerable detention. He remained the guest of Vicar-General Quinn until he found an opportunity to return and resume his labors in distant Georgia.

He departed this life February 5, 1871, about the seventieth year of his age, forty of which were spent in the holy ministry, having outlived five administrations in the diocese. His death was holy, worthy of a life so self-sacrificing, and abounding with all consolations, human and divine, and was lamented by all the faithful of the diocese which he had prudently governed and enriched by his labors.

His remains, clad in purple vestments, the color with which the Church decorates her prelates, lay in state in the cathedral, and were venerated by all the faithful. The Requiem Mass and obsequies were celebrated by Bishop Verot, and all that was mortal of the great Georgia priest were placed by the side of his predecessors, the first missionary bishops and priests of the diocese of Savannah.

It is related of this extraordinary man that during his priesthood he never, by his fault, lost a patient unprepared, omitted an office, or missed a Mass, wore on his person an ornament, a superfluous article of clothing, or partook of a second dish at a meal, except to please others. His abstinence from wine was so consummate that the eulogy of the blind poet on the sobriety of Ulysses is not unsuitable: "His cup was always full before him." He had the reputation of having never uttered an untruth or done a foolish act.

Within a year after the death of Bishop Barry, in 1859, the Right Rev. Augustin Verot, D.D., Bishop of Danaba *in partibus*, and Vicar-Apostolic of Florida, was called to govern the diocese, still continuing administrator of the Peninsula. He was the third bishop of Savannah. Until 1870, a period of ten years, he filled this exalted position, and during the arduous times of the civil war, with unsurpassed zeal and great administrative ability. In that year the mission of the first martyr-bishop was created a see by his Holiness Pius IX., of blessed memory, and Dr. Verot translated to it, resigning by his own choice the see of Savannah.

Blessed with the promise of the fourth commandment, his days were long in the land, filled with every good work, and abounding in advantages to the Church of God and the salvation of souls. He built many churches, doubled the number of priests, established religious communities, and received several converts into the fold. None of the interests of religion suffered during the disastrous times that then befell the land.

His vigilance, prudence, and learning brought good out of evil and made temporal losses and adversities the means of establishing the Church and promoting the salvation of many.

He was a cogent and pointed writer and a fluent speaker; all that he spoke and wrote received an additional force from the influence of a holy life adorned with apostolic virtues. His Catechism, after Bishop England's, was the best ever published in the United States, by reason of his admirable chapter on the four marks of the Church.

This single chapter has made converts; it is a summary of the most conclusive arguments on these unmistakable evidences of the truth, refutes all the errors of sectarians, and suggests or furnishes ample matter for an eloquent course of lectures.

The Celtic element is elastic; the French and Irish missionaries readily accommodate themselves to all situations where the honor of God and the cause of religion are concerned. Dr. Verot, like Bishop England, became identified with the best interests of the Southern people. He comforted them in their sorrows, alleviated their crosses, advocated their cause, and shed the light of religion far and wide over the land.

His writings, published in the *Pacificator*, ably conducted by Mr. Walsh, and the appeals made in behalf of the South during the war are familiar to the country. He became dear to the people. They listened to his admonitions, irrespective of party, and hold his memory in undying veneration. A friend in the hour of need a nation never forgets.

Whether as theologian or bishop, we find his presence conspicuous in all the councils of Baltimore for nearly half a century, and at the Œcumenical Council of the Vatican he was one of the prominent fathers.

In person he was under the medium height, with homely features, the embodiment of humility and meekness, without a particle of human vanity or ostentation, such a one as we may conceive the Apostle of the Gentiles to have been, whom he imitated in his zeal, his journeys, and his labors. He spent and wasted himself in the service of his Master, and almost died at the altar, which he adorned by his long and irreproachable life.

I subjoin copious extracts from the merited eulogy delivered by the eloquent Father Clavreul on the occasion of the death of the eminent prelate:

"The melancholy event occurred Saturday, June 10, between one and two o'clock P.M. The bishop was just back from his yearly visitation of the diocese. The fatigues of the mission, although they had been, this time especially, so excessive as to make him feel quite unwell on his return, did not seem, however, to have affected materially his vigorous constitution. It was Friday. In the morning the bishop had said Mass at the usual hour, followed by his thanksgiving. Early in the afternoon he saw Dr. Peck, and then retired to his room. He did not, however, go to bed before seven o'clock, and only after he had recited the Office. Later in the evening, as we insisted upon spending the night with him, he answered he was not sick enough for that, only to put everything ready at hand, that he would help himself, and bade us go to bed. The following day, Saturday, being asked how he had spent the night, he answered in French, and with a smile: '*La nuit est longue à la douleur qui veille*'; and then, as he had not been able to say Mass that morning, he added, in a manner expressive of regret, that it was the anniversary day of his ordination to the diaconate. The bishop all the while, though suffering, did not lose any of his habitual cheerfulness, and was in full possession of his mental faculties. There was nothing that could in the least forebode the impending and tragic issue. At half-past one o'clock in the afternoon, one of the sisters in attendance happened to leave the room to call the servant, in which interval, scarcely for a few minutes, and at the very moment the latter reached the room, the bishop was breathing his last, calmly and without a struggle, as if God, content with the manifold sacrifices of a whole life spent in his service, wished to spare his servant at the supreme hour the pain of even a short agony. His death was sudden, leaving no time for the administration of the last sacraments, but not unprovided, for every day of the saintly bishop's life had been one of continued preparation for that dread moment.

"The news fell upon us as a thunderbolt, filling every heart with sorrow and surprise. All felt that by the bishop's death they had lost a father. Who would have thought when, on Tuesday, the bells from the old cathedral were pealing forth the glad tidings of the bishop's return, that before the end of that week we would be startled by the announcement of his death? Many besides knew the circumstances which had culminated into such a sudden and unexpected death, and this forced upon their minds the conviction that the bishop had died a victim to duty. Of late years travelling through the thinly-settled and yet wild sections of Florida, amidst fatigues and inconveniences to be met with at every step, had become for the bishop, by reason of his advanced age, exceedingly painful, and but two years before had put his life in jeopardy. Human prudence, then, ought to have this time deterred him from the undertaking. But the holy bishop viewed things differently. Duty he held so sacred demanded of him, he thought, this new and, alas! last act of sacrifice and abnegation. Sleepless nights, protracted fasts, exposure, long and interminable rides through roads often impracticable, in wretched and incommodious stage-coaches, together with the discharge of his onerous duties, proved at length too much for the bishop's strength, caused him to lose his appetite, with the impossibility to keep any food on his stomach. Rest and care, had they been resorted to in time, would have no doubt checked the disease. Unfortunately, they were thought of when it was already too late. Thus was the bishop taken away in the midst of the labors of a mission but interrupted, and which he meant to resume that same week by visiting Palatka and other points up the St. John's. Not one day, not one hour, I should say, of his long career that was not full, and which did not see him at work. He had promised to God, as the eloquent Bishop Lynch so justly said, a life-time service, and well did he keep his word.

"Bishop Verot was born at Le Puy, in France, May, 1804. Having finished his classics when hardly sixteen years of age, he went to Paris, where he studied philosophy and theology at the Seminaire de St. Sulpice. He had for professor in dogmatic theology the venerable Mr. Hamon, who died last year Curé de St. Sulpice. The illustrious Mgr. Dupanloup and the great Dominican friar, the late Father Lacordaire, were amongst his schoolmates. He was ordained priest by the saintly De Quelen, then Archbishop of Paris, September 20, 1828, as is stated from the bishop's own handwriting, at the bottom of a humble framed picture he religiously kept for a memorial of this important event. Soon after he became a member of the Society of St. Sulpice. In 1830 he came to Baltimore, where he taught philosophy and theology, together with the higher branches of mathematics and natural sciences, at the Theological Seminary and at St. Mary's College. In 1853 we find him in charge of the Catholic church at Ellicott's Mills, where for six years he remained engaged in missionary duties.

"Possessed by nature of no ordinary talents, with an application that never flagged or grew weary, having had from boyhood the advantage of the best schools, in continual intercourse with men of thought and culture, Father Verot had reached already at that early period that degree of learning that falls to the lot of the few. His manuscripts on philosophy, theology, and Holy Scriptures, would form alone several large volumes. He wrote sermons on all the points of the Catholic doctrine, and, judging from those that have been published or which we heard him deliver, they may, without exaggeration, be pronounced amongst the very best in the English language, thorough, exhaustive, as well as breathing sentiments of the most tender and effective piety. We find also from him notes on physics, mathematics, astronomy, and none could long converse with the bishop and fail to notice how accurate as well as extensive was his knowledge in those matters. Canon law, church history and polity, patrology, rubrics, liturgy he knew with that degree of perfection which made him, whenever consulted, ready to give an answer. Several articles he wrote at this time, as well as other papers he gave to the public before and after he was raised to the episcopate, together with his pastoral letters and his historical and dogmatical lectures on religion, entitle him to a distinguished place amongst the writers of this country. Such attainments in human knowledge, joined to eminent virtue and piety, pointed to Father Verot for the most responsible positions in the Church. So do we see about this time the lamented Archbishop Hughes, who had just founded the Grand Seminary of Troy for the ecclesiastical province of New York, think of placing the humble parish priest of Ellicott's Mills at the head of the new institution, as one whose piety and learning could best insure its success. Providence, however, was to dispose of things otherwise. In 1857, Florida having been erected into a vicariate-apostolic, Father Verot was chosen by the Holy See to rule over the new ecclesiastical district. Four years afterwards (1861), the see of Savannah remaining still vacant since the death of Bishop Barry, Bishop Verot was appointed to replace the deceased prelate. This lasted to the late Œcumenical Council, when Bishop Verot, at his own request, relinquished Savannah for the newly-erected see of St. Agustine.

"We have spoken of Bishop Verot's knowledge and rare ability, of his varied as well as thorough and deep learning, but what the good bishop deemed much more important than the greatest natural talents and all human knowledge, what was the object for which he lived and toiled, what was the prime motor of his every action and thought, and what makes us look upon him to-day with a mixed feeling of love and religious respect is the eminent virtue and piety, I say more, the *sanctity*, of his life, which virtue and sanctity impressed you so much the more as you came in closer contact with him. Men held in estimation by a reverent public, reputed *great*, are rarely thought such by those with whom they are in habitual intercourse, because their virtues oftentimes are but apparent, and cannot stand close inspection. Real merit alone gains by being looked into and scrutinized. Bishop Verot's virtues were of that kind; they were real, and so the more intimately you knew him the more you esteemed and revered the character of sanctity he possessed: as a beautiful picture, which seen at distance presents to the eyes nothing almost but what is common to similar works, but when brought near reveals in the perfection of the details, the harmony of all the parts, the genius of the author.

"The word of St. Paul, '*Justus ex fide vivit*,' is the summary of the bishop's life. The bishop was a man of faith—lived by faith. Faith was the moving principle of his every action and thought, filled his whole being, so the man was lost in the Christian, in the bishop, and he could say with St. Paul, 'I live now not I, but Christ liveth in me.'

"Here was the secret of his tender and affectionate piety, how he loved to spend hours in prayer and meditation, celebrated Mass every day, was seen repairing so frequently to the Church, there to pour out his soul before the altar, inspired him, in fine, with such love for God, the holy mysteries, the ceremonies of the Church—in a word, for all that pertained to religion. The temple where the Divine Victim is daily immolated he would have fitted in a manner worthy of him who, dwelling in light inaccessible, condescends to live and remain therein. Knowing that the ceremonies of the Church are illustrative of our faith, help, piety, and are an essential part of religion, he had them performed with the utmost decorum. The rubrics of the ceremonial he knew in their most minute details, and always enforced their observance. If his humility and child-like simplicity on other occasions caused one to forget he was the bishop, here, whilst officiating, his every feature bore the impress of his dignity.

"Lover of poverty for all that was destined merely to personal use, for the Church he insisted he should have what was best, and no one could fail noticing the striking contrast between the richness, elegance, taste, and finish of the bishop's church vestments, church books, etc., and the poverty of his dress and complete destitution of his wardrobe.

"But true faith only exists where there is compliance with duty; hence, if the bishop was a man of faith, he also was a man of duty, wholly intent upon doing the will of God ; and well could he apply to himself the words of the psalmist, 'That I should do thy will, O my God, I have desired it, and thy law in the midst of my heart" (Ps. xxxix. 9). When, after much reflection and prayer, he had once known what God demanded of him, the personal sacrifices to which his determination, if carried out, would subject him, the opposition on the part of others, human respect, which renders the best men at times irresolute and undecided, never could make him give up or even alter a resolution which he knew came from God.

"Neither did he allow himself to be influenced by passion, whim, and fancy. Everything he weighed in the balance of the sanctuary, doing in the most minute details of common life not what he liked but what duty required ; and where the line of duty was not so clearly marked out, in those moments not taken up by the requirements of his charge, he found yet the means to check the sallies of self-will by the strict observance of a rule of life, convinced as he was of the truth of the maxim, '*Qui regulæ vivit, Deo vivit*'—that to live up to a rule is to live in conformity with God's will.

"Bishop Verot was also a model of disinterestedness, so he could say with the apostle to them under his charge, '*Non vestra, sed vos*'—'It is not your goods but your souls I ask.' Utter contempt of the things of this world, so far as he was concerned, was, I may say, the characteristic trait of the good bishop. Luxuries, superfluities he abominated to the disregard of even the ordinary comforts of life, retrenching on his dress, table, furniture that he might do more for the poor and the Church. His charities, mostly done in secret, are known in a manner only of God and those whom he assisted, yet what we know of it bears us out in saying that they were very abundant, and practised at times in a truly heroic manner ; witness what he did, not once but often, when a priest in the mission of Maryland—taking off his shoes or some other part of his wearing apparel to give it to some poor man he chanced to meet on the road.

"The total disregard Bishop Verot had for riches so far as his own person was concerned could not make him forget his duties concerning the temporalities of the Church. Constituted, in virtue of his office, the guardian of the Church property in this diocese, he owed to God, his conscience, and the Church to defend it. The many and severe annoyances to which he submitted in order to oppose the encroachments of greed and injustice are sufficient proofs of how well he understood his duty in that respect. Head of a diocese well-nigh destitute, he had to provide for his clergy in those localities unable to give the priest a support, to build churches, establish parochial schools, etc. No one, indeed, knew better than he that the maxim of St. Paul, '*Habentes alimenta et quibus tegamur, his contenti sumus*'—'Having food and wherewith to be covered, with these we are content' (1 Tim. vi. 8), ought to be the motto of the priest, but especially of the missionary, than whom none should be found more imbued with apostolic spirit. But he knew also that on the faithful, the beneficiaries of his labors, devolved the obligation of supporting him : 'They who preach the Gospel should live by the Gospel' ; for the people, therefore, to withdraw their offerings from the altar and from those who serve it was a fraud in the holocaust ; that those goods which worldlings spend with such a lavish hand to gratify their vanity and passions have not ceased to be God's own goods and property, and that to him the premises should be offered. The honor of God and the exaltation of his Spouse on earth, the Church—such, then, was the noble, disinterested, and truly supernatural motives which inspired the bishop whenever here or abroad he appealed to Catholic charity in behalf of his poverty-stricken diocese.

"The zeal of the bishop in that direction is known from the fact that whilst the resources at his disposal were barely sufficient to meet his personal wants and those of his clergy, and defray the heavy expenses of far-away and quite inaccessible missions, he found yet the means of spending, within but a few years, from thirty to forty thousand dollars in erecting and repairing churches, school buildings, and convents, buying church furniture, etc. The new and spacious church of Jacksonville, built on the ruins of the one that was burnt in the late war, with its flourishing convent; the church of Fernandina, with Sisters' house and lot; that of Tampa, Tallahassee, with church, extensive grounds, and stately parochial residence; the church of Key West, so materially improved as to appear to-day a different church, and its splendid convent; the several buildings erected in this very place for religious and educational purposes, the considerable repairs and improvements on the old cathedral, are so many lasting monuments of the bishop's indomitable energy as well as rigid economy.

"The temporal advancement of his diocese was, however, but secondary in the bishop's mind; the great, paramount object of his solicitude was the sanctification of souls. He wished to see God better known and more faithfully served; to rear to the Almighty in the hearts of all a spiritual structure, far more splendid and beautiful than mere material churches of stone and wood, the kingdom of his grace; it was after that his truly apostolic sôul constantly sighed, and for that to speak with St. Paul, 'he spent and overspent himself'; for that he undertook with cheerfulness and alacrity the most arduous duties, allowed no difficulties to daunt his courage. The same burning zeal which made him, while yet a priest, travel for several years, afoot and fasting, after a first Mass said in Baltimore to Ellicott's Mills (a distance of eight miles), where he sang High Mass and preached, saw him, when bishop, submit to sacrifices not less severe and painful. And in this great work the least of his flock had the first claim, were his privileged ones. When the time of First Communion or the administration of Confirmation approached, the pains the good bishop would take to instruct the children for the worthy reception of the sacraments were unprecedented.

"Aware of the importance of the visits of the missioner

amongst the Catholics that lived away from priest and church, and of the great good they can effect, he deemed no fatigue, no privation ever too great. The indifference, apathy, and at times the bad dispositions of some lukewarm Catholics could not cool his ardor; and more than once did God reward the intrepid and holy bishop by sudden conversions, so that the very ones that felt least disposed to receive his visits were those most deeply affected when the moment had come for the bishop to leave.

"Such was Bishop Verot; the simple recital of his truly apostolic life constitutes his eulogy. In him we see another link to the golden chain of saintly bishops Catholic France gave to this country, beginning with a Flaget of Bardstown (whose name is associated with that of the patriarch of the Catholic Church in the United States, the illustrious Bishop Carroll), and which was continued in a Maréchal of Baltimore, a Bruté of Vincennes, a Cheverus of Boston, a Blanc and an Odin of New Orleans, and a Portier of Mobile."

The Right Rev. Dr. Moore, consecrated May 13, 1877, is the immediate and worthy successor of Bishop Verot.

The Right Rev. Ignatius Persico, D.D., fourth bishop of this diocese, already mentioned, was translated to the see of Savannah March 11, 1870. His first care was to take measures for the erection of a new cathedral, but although he inaugurated the work, he had to resign in 1872 on account of ill-health. His brief administration is memorable for several good works inaugurated for the interest of religion, which would have matured if his health had continued. But enough was done to exhibit his enlightened zeal, and perpetuate his memory as a high-minded ecclesiastic, generous and self-sacrificing in the cause of religion. After the comparative restoration of his health he again returned to the East. The dwellers on the banks of the Ganges hailed with delight the presence of the former Vicar-Apostolic of Agra. Dr. Persico was of the medium height, with prominent features, very long nose, and stout figure. In his knees he favored the celebrated ex-Bishop of

Autun. In manners he was plain, humble, and unaffected as a child. He loved his clergy, and never sought any other society. He was learned, eloquent, and devout. The latest account that has reached us regarding Dr. Persico is that in the consistory of July 16, 1878, he was appointed to the see of Acquino, in Italy, by his Holiness Leo XIII.

The Right Rev. William H. Gross, C.SS.R., D.D., fifth bishop, succeeded Dr. Persico. He was born in Baltimore in 1837, was professed in 1858, was ordained by Archbishop Kenrick in 1863, and was consecrated by Archbishop Bayley April 27, 1873. His promotion to the see of Savannah was universally applauded.

In the prime of life and the vigor of manhood, he commenced his administration with zeal and efficiency. The new Cathedral of St. John the Baptist, dedicated soon after his consecration, is one of the most imposing churches in the country. The sum of ten thousand dollars was realized at a fair, held in 1878, to pay the debt. About an equal sum still remains due. The Barry Hospital is another monument of episcopal zeal. The Carmelite Nuns, from Guatemala, recently settled in the city. They are refugees from religious persecution, and brought sufficient funds to endow and support their institute. St. Benedict's Church for colored people, the Jesuit mission and house in Augusta, the Benedictine monastery at Skidaway, with many other societies, missions, institutions, and churches, evince the rapid progress of the faith under the energetic bishop. The Benedictine house at Skidaway is a branch from St. Vincent's Monastery, near Latrobe, Pennsylvania.

"ST. BENEDICT'S, SKIDAWAY ISLAND,
  NEAR SAVANNAH, GA., July 13, 1878.
"REV. J. J. CONNELL, D.D., ST. MARY'S HELP, N.C.

"REV. DEAR FATHER: By a letter of Father Herman I am informed that you desire a little history of this establishment. With the greatest pleasure would I comply with your wishes; however, there are certain reasons why you cannot expect much of a history of this place, in sp of my willingness to furnish materials—viz., on account the short time since it was commenced, and to menti other reasons would be superfluous; therefore I commen right away in telling you all that I know about it.

"It was on May 13, 1874, when two Benedictines, the Re Gabriel Bergier, of the Monastery Pierre-qui-vive, in France and the Rev. Raphael Wissel, of the ancient Abbey of Sub jaco, in Italy, arrived in Savannah, Georgia, with the inten tion of devoting themselves to the spiritual interest of the colored population, according to the desire of the Right Rev. Bishop Gross, D.D. They soon collected a congregation, erected a nice little frame church on Harris Street, and opened a parish school. A few young men anxious to join the Benedictine Order were received as candidates, some for the clerical state, others as lay brothers. Under these promising indications Father Bergier gladly availed himself of the kind offer of Dr. Stephen Dupon, at Isle of Hope, to establish a novitiate on a valuable lot which the doctor presented to him, together with a small frame house, suitable for a chapel.

"The assistance of his many charitable friends in the city enabled Father Bergier not only to put up a decent residence for his new religious family, but also to support and maintain it. Nine months had not quite elapsed since the little community occupied their new house at Isle of Hope when suddenly an entire change took place in consequence of the premature death of the superior, Father Bergier, of D. Gregory Enright, a clerical novice, and of J. McDonald, a candidate, who all died within three weeks in September and October, 1876, of the yellow fever.

"The colored congregation in Savannah was given in charge of the energetic Rev. Father Eckert, and the house on Isle of Hope was assigned to the Benedictines of St. Vincent's, in Pennsylvania. These, however, soon after their arrival, which took place March 1, 1877, formed the plan of moving over to Skidaway Island, where the generosity of the Right Rev. Bishop Gross, D.D., provided them with an extensive piece of land, formerly known as the Hampton place (617 acres). This place had been purchased by the late Bishop Barry on May 31, 1859, principally on account of the stately mansion that stood then on the plantation, the dimensions of the main building being one hundred feet in length by fifty feet in width, four stories high, crowned with a beautiful cupola. This magnificent building, the cost of which exceeded the value of the whole plantation, was entirely destroyed during the late war, so that at present not a vestige of its foundations can be seen. This sad accident frustrated the noble intention of the good bishop to locate the male orphan asylum upon Skidaway Island. It is needless to mention here that the Benedictines experienced a difficult and expensive task in establishing themselves on the island, where they found neither shelter nor roof. Nevertheless, faithful to the traditions of their order, they went to work and laid the foundations for a monastery, and in connection with it for an industrial school for colored boys.

"The dedication of this new house took place on June 16, 1878. Now this is all that I can say about it; the house, or rather the community of this house, must develop itself by degrees in the course of time, and with the help of God, for '*Nisi Dominus ædificaverit domum, in vanum laboraverunt qui ædificant eam.*'

"Recommending myself to your pious prayers,
"I remain, yours very respectfully,
"P. OSWALD, O.S.B."

Bishop Gross is an able and eloquent preacher, fervent and persuasive, a wise and prudent administrator. Besides his many other labors, he is also President of Pio Nono College, in Macon. Every part of his immense diocese receives its full share of his episcopal solicitude.

The deaths among the clergy and religious have been extensive, especially in 1876, when the yellow fever desolated the city with the fatality of 1854. The following are furnished by the "Catholic Almanac":

1876—February 17, Rev. John O'Neill at Pio Nono College, just after his ordination.

September 29, Sister Mary Martha Manning, of the Order of St. Agnes, aged twenty-two years, of yellow fever. She had come from Fond du Lac, Wisconsin.

October 14, Sister Mary Berchman Wheeler, a native of New York State.

October 14, Rev. J. B. Langlois, rector of the Cathedral of Savannah. He was a native of Canada, and was pastor of St. Hubert's, Montreal. He became professor of theology at Pio Nono College, and then pastor at Milledgeville.

October 16, Rev. James A. Kelly, at Savannah.

November 5, Rev. Stephen Beytagh.

November 6, Rev. Bernardine Barron, O.S.F.

1877—July 29, Rev. James Murphy, at Macon, in his twenty-ninth year. He was a native of Liscarrol, Ireland, educated at All-Hallows and Baltimore, and ordained January 14, 1877. He was greatly regretted by the people of Macon.

September 21, Sister Mary de Sales, at Fernandina, Florida.

September 22, Mother Célinie, of yellow fever, at Fernandina.

October, Sister Mary Joseph McGrath, of the Sisters of Mercy, Savannah, at White Bluff Orphanage, having contracted the disease at Port Royal.

Other priests and religious died also during those disastrous years whose names have escaped the knowledge of the writer.

Augusta is the second city in Georgia in size and importance, and much healthier than Savannah, which she rivals. In late years it has escaped the scourge of the yellow fever. The city is built on the west banks of the Savannah River, at the head of navigation, and is about two hundred miles from the coast. Surrounded by a fertile country, it is a celebrated cotton market, and possesses many large and thriving factories. Being on the high way of commerce, it is the centre of many railroads.

In 1860 it contained a population of fifteen thousand inhabitants, and at this time may be accredited with twenty thousand. Catholicity has kept pace with its growth, and the number of the faithful is yearly increasing; four thousand may not be an over-estimate. It held the third rank in the diocese of Charleston, and maintained this position until the creation of the see of Savannah, in 1850.

Blessed with edifying priests for many years, practical and edifying Catholics, early scandals were healed, and piety restored among the faithful.

She disputed with Savannah the honor of becoming the episcopal city. An unfortunate event turned the scales in favor of the other city. While the subject was under deliberation, a violent opposition was arrayed against the pastor, Father Barry, in regard to the temporalities of the Church. The timely interference of Bishop Reynolds prevented a schism and restored peace. The prelate was amazed at the unwarranted display of hostility, and immediately decided in favor of Savannah.

The first Catholics were some French refugees from the massacre at San Domingo, and a few Irish immigrants. A schism never existed; but, in consequence of the disorganized state of ecclesiastical affairs, some unworthy priests, early in the century, and immediately after the War of Independence, exercised the functions of the holy ministry. The evils were not entirely removed for many years, and were effaced only by the noble vindication of Catholic virtue, and the sanctity of the priestly character restored in public estimation, by the blameless lives and irreproachable manners of several holy and learned ecclesiastics. Early in the century a square was obtained in the southwest limits of the city, and a small brick church erected, and dedicated to the Most Blessed Trinity. In the course of a few years a transept was added, giving the edifice the form of a cross, and rendering it commodious and good-looking. Close to the church stood the priest's house, serving in after years, and as occasion required, the purposes of hospital, orphan asylum, and academy.

In 1853 we find the convent of the Sisters of Mercy erected on the same lot, and more recently the splendid Church of St. Patrick, one of the most costly and imposing edifices in the State of Georgia.

The priests may be divided into three classes, according to the different periods of their ministrations. The first were not without reproach. The men who followed immediately were in all respects worthy of their calling; they labored long and faithfully and left a favorable record.

Some of them up to this time are held in deep veneration. The learned Bishop Lynch has kindly furnished the names of some from memory. They are all mentioned in connection with Charleston, the same clergyman visiting the out-stations as opportunity or the demands of the faithful required:

Rev. Mr. Keating, 1790.

Another name, unknown.

Rev. Simon Felix O'Gallagher, 1793-1822.

Rev. Robert Brown, O.S.A., 1809, who died pastor of St. Mary's Church, in Charleston, in 1838.

Rev. Mr. Cloriviere, in Charleston, from 1811 to 1819.

The Rev. Mr. Cooper about 1821. He was a native of Maryland, and a convert. He donated ten thousand dollars in 1810 to Rev. Dr. Dubourg, for the purpose of enabling Mother Seton to establish her noble work. He was on the missions in North Carolina in 1829. His fasts and austerities were extreme, and seem beyond the power of human endurance. He visited Europe about 1830, made a pilgrimage to the East, and after his return entered into a monastery in Germany, where he died about 1856. Circumstances popularly deemed miraculous are related of this extraordinary man.

In his person God seems to have vindicated by miraculous interference the character of the priesthood when depreciated in public estimation by the conduct of unworthy men.

The Rev. Mr. Corkery, one of the two priests ordained in Ireland by Bishop England, and who accompanied him to America, was stationed in Augusta about the year 1824.

With him begins the third class of the Augusta priests, the men who were educated for the diocese and ordained for its missions. He died at an early age, and in the course of a couple of years, after having given promise of great usefulness. His death was universally regretted, and his memory is held in veneration to this day. Father Barry, who had been recently ordained, was sent on immediatly by Bishop England, and he remained head of this mission and pastor of Augusta until the death of Bishop Gartland in 1854. His happy administration, works of charity, piety, and zeal, are already mentioned. He more than any other established the faith in Augusta, and over the diocese gained it respect and consideration, and domesticated the Church in the land. Thenceforth nearly all the clergy in the diocese were sharers in his labors at one time or another; the history of this church embraces the lives of all, and is coextensive with the early see of Charleston. The Rev. Dominic Byrne, a native of Ireland, who made his studies in the Seminary of St. John the Baptist, and was ordained in Charleston by Bishop England about 1829, was Father Barry's first assistant. He was a zealous, active young priest, well educated, and a respectable preacher. His sermons were admired for vigor of thought and manly originality. It is related of him that he never made the sermon of another a model for his own. He served faithfully during a year when the yellow fever was most fatal in Augusta.

After the disappearance of the distemper before the first frost, Father Byrne obtained from the bishop leave of absence to recruit his health and to pay a visit of affection to his sister, who lived at St. Augustine. The bishop at first refused the request, and yielded only after renewed and more urgent entreaty. Having embarked on board a schooner, it was dashed to pieces at night by a frightful hurricane near Key West. The priest and all on board were drowned. Their remains were cast on the beach by the waves, and lay unburied until discovered by some fishermen, who gave them the hospitality of a grave on the shore. The voice of many waters from their profound depths sing his requiem, and daily moisten his grave with their incessant weeping.

The following day his untimely fate was currently reported throughout the city of Charleston. It was believed that no vessel on the coast could have outlived the gale, and a well-authenticated fact bordering on the supernatural confirmed the opinion. The sad event suggests the imprudence of acting contrary to the judgment or disregarding the counsel of those through whom God manifests his will for safety and direction.

The Very Rev. Gregory Duggan was born in the County Wexford, Ireland, about the year 1800. He made his classical studies in his native country. Animated with a true vocation and indifferent to the worldly honors that attend the sacerdotal state in Catholic Ireland, he selected the diocese of Charleston, the least inviting of all foreign missions, as the theatre of his future labors. He made his ecclesiastical studies in the seminary, the *alma mater* of so many distinguished clergymen, and was promoted to the priestly dignity about 1830 by Bishop England.

None could enter into that angelic state with a higher appreciation of its privileges and obligations. The bishop in the midst of his trials found deep consolation in the thought that he had imposed hands on so worthy a recipient, and was wont to remark that he was a more efficient missionary than many of the best educated among the diocesan clergy.

He was a man of God, lived by prayer, and in all the events of life was ruled by the maxims of sound judgment, or what may be more aptly termed hard sense. His devotion to the divine office, to the Holy Sacrifice, and all other ministerial duties could be surpassed but by absolute personal holiness. He was the true model of a wise and prudent priest ; a calm, vigilant, self-possessed steward in the Lord's household, free from all extremes and eccentricities; a settled, safe man, whom not even death could move one inch from the path of duty. In illustrating the regularity of his habits, Archbishop Hughes related to the writer that after having sojourned in Augusta for a week in search of health he left Father Gregory at a certain hour enjoying his calumet (his only indulgence), and when he returned, after an absence of several weeks, he found him in the identical position and similarly engaged, suggestive of the idea that he had during the interval unalterably persevered in the same occupation.

A man of consummate prudence, during a long life, and always before the public, he never gave occasion for censure. He is one of the few men who passed through human life without reproach. After his ordination he was sent to Augusta as assistant to Father Barry; but this position was only nominal. He was the co-laborer of the great priest, shared in all his works on the missions, in the congregation, in the class-room, among the orphans, the sick, and the dying. His was the strong arm to labor, the clear judgment to decide, the bright eye to forecast.

Sustained by the same motives, animated by the same spirit, without strife, envy, or jealousy, and free from the selfishness of ambition, they were *two in one*. In mind a closer union could not exist between two distinct mortals. Their friendship, connected by religion and founded on the love of God, was closer than that between Damon and Pythias; they loved one the other as tenderly as David and Jonathan. Whatever of encomium has been passed on Dr. Barry, the same can be claimed with equal justice for Father Duggan. Those who had an opportunity of knowing whispered that the latter was the power behind the throne; and in canvassing their individual merits the laity decided that Father Barry prayed longer, and was frequently moved to tears by the fervor of his devotion, while Father D. could not spare a tear to grace a funeral oration.

Father Duggan, during the entire course of his life, *never sung a High Mass and never preached one sermon.*

He was well acquainted with moral theology, and his counsel was sought in the most critical cases. An assiduous catechist, he devoted his time to impressing the solid doctrines of the Church on the minds of the rising generation, instead of polishing popular sermons to suit the fancy of amateur listeners. Nor did he squander his time in moping over the literary trash of the day. It may be said with little exaggeration that he never read any newspaper except the *Miscellany*. As Omar said of the Koran, whatever is not in it is worthless. Father D. believed the same of the *United States Catholic Miscellany*. All his time was spent in tending, washing, nursing the orphans, in visiting the sick, waiting on the dying, burying the dead, administering the sacraments, and discharging all the temporal duties of the monastic establishment, of which, to use the Georgia term, he was the *wheel-horse*.

His activity as an out-missionary was unsurpassed. He spent the years immediately after his ordination among the laborers on the several railroads then in course of construction in Georgia, and leading from Hamburg to Charleston.

Under the medium height, with a Roman nose and a stout frame like a gnarled oak, his figure was suggestive of Napoleon I., save that a solitary line of softness strayed not over features expressive only of piety to God and benevolence to man.

Seated on horseback, his vestments and wardrobe all in a pair of saddle-bags, and a few biscuits in his pocket, the ample store for the day, this man of adamant, bleached and sun-burnt, traversed the pathless forests of Central Georgia, spent nights in the woods, lived in shanties among railroaders, and visited every solitary Catholic in middle Georgia. Labor and toil seemed only as an encouragement and recreation during the twenty-five years spent as assistant to Father Barry.

Returning from the out-missions, and the crowd of orphans occupying every corner and every spare bed, the toil-worn missionary not unfrequently shared the same couch with the future bishop. By such men and such means was Catholicity so firmly planted on the soil of Georgia and the Carolinas that neither civil war nor domestic strife can uproot it. The Government must first crumble to pieces and sink in the same common ruin.

It can be no depreciation of the services of the many eminent priests, feebly portrayed in these records, to state that the most good has been accomplished by the humblest and least pretentious clergymen, some of them very indifferent preachers and others who never preached at all.

Certainly the Word of God is a power for the conversion of nations, and the gift of tongues an apostolic grace; but the Holy Ghost distributes his gifts differently and as it seemeth good to him. These men excelled in humble works; they were content to gather the sheaves after the reapers, and labored for the preservation of the faith among the Catholic people and its perpetuation among their children.

After the death of Dr. Gartland, in 1854, Father Barry moved to Savannah and Mr. Duggan became pastor of Augusta, a position which he maintained during seventeen years and under three administrations. The years of his pastorate, like those of his whole life, were full of labors, of good works, of piety, of enterprises undertaken for the honor of God and the salvation of souls, and all were successfully accomplished.

The crowning work of his later years is St. Patrick's Church, an ornament to the city and surpassed by few edifices of the kind in the Southern States. The plan was gratuitously furnished by the eminent architect, John R. Nearnsie, now of Baltimore. It is a gem of architectural beauty. Father G. Duggan furnished most of the funds and almost built the church by his own private purse.

It was dedicated by Bishop Verot about 1860, and now raises on high the cross over that beautiful city, memorial alike of man's redemption and of the zeal and piety of that humble, sincere priest, Father Duggan. He was the most honored citizen of Augusta, the father of the orphans, the companion of the sainted Bishop Barry, a devoted priest, and one of the most hard-working missionaries in the Carolinas and Georgia.

He departed this life December 5, 1870, in the seventieth year of his age, of which he spent fifty in the priesthood. He died as he lived, in the friendship of God. His end was peaceful, and consoled by the blessings which he was the means of imparting to others. He was mourned by the entire city, and the Church wept tears of holy tenderness over the honored grave of her irreproachable minister. With him died the last of Bishop England's priests within the diocese. They fought the good fight, established, preserved, perpetuated the faith, built churches, erected asylums, founded schools, converted many, convinced thousands, and left to their successors true men and worthy priests, a Church without a shame, a stain, or a wrinkle, and the aroma of a good name and virtuous example.

So guarded and circumspect was this great priest that during all his years in the ministry he was never known to have sat alone in the company of a female when it was possible to avoid it. Such a scene would have excited the wonder of the beholders, a feature which reminds one of the astonishment of his disciples at finding our Blessed Lord in conversation with the Samaritan woman at the well of Jacob—"They wondered that he spake to her."

The Very Rev. John F. Kirby, V.G., was Father Duggan's assistant from 1854 to 1870. He was a native of County Kerry, Ireland, and was born Nov. 19, 1821. He studied his classics under the auspices of Bishop Egan, whose Masses he served during his boyhood. During a visit to his native country the venerable Father O'Neill received him as a candidate for the diocese of Charleston and placed him in the seminary in 1838. He was my classmate during four years, was tonsured by Bishop England, and ordained priest by Bishop Reynolds May 26, 1844.

After his ordination he was stationed in Augusta during eighteen months, and in 1846 was appointed my assistant in Columbus. He was stationed in Macon the following year, and on the death of Rev. William Burke was sent to Savannah as assistant to his patron and friend, Rev. J. F. O'Neill. On the arrival of Dr. Gartland in 1850 he was created first assistant at the cathedral, and soon after vicar-general, offices which he filled ably during a period of four years and until the death of the bishop.

He was a tall, handsome man, with a fair complexion, and inclined to obesity. He sang well, preached sound, solid discourses, was a matter-of-fact charactered man, and an efficient, respectable priest. In the prime and vigor of life, and devoted to his sacred calling, he became a valuable coadjutor to the bishop, and efficiently aided him in all of his undertakings, especially in the renewal and enlarging of the cathedral.

He bore his share in the labors of the yellow fever crisis, and after the death of the bishop was prostrated; his recovery was for a time doubtful. Although he rallied, his health was shattered and he never recovered his former elasticity and strength. In 1854 he was returned to Augusta as assistant, and aided Father Duggan in all the missions connected with the station, and also in building the new church. He also made a collecting tour and collected some funds to aid in the payment of its expenses.

He was a faithful priest, loved by the faithful, esteemed and respected by all classes for gentlemanly manners, moderation, and clerical bearing.

During the trying time of the war his missionary labors were increased and his health became more enfeebled; his increasing debility admonished him of his early dissolution. Having sought and obtained an asylum at St. Agnes's Hospital, in Baltimore, he ended his days in peace and was fortified in his last moments by all the precious sacraments of our redemption. He died May 4, 1872, in the fifty-first year of his age, of which he was twenty-eight years a faithful minister. His remains now rest in the land of the sanctuary. He devoted all his life and being to the service of his Maker, labored to the end in the trying and exhausting missions of the South, lost his health, and sacrificed his noble life in the cause of religion. Having spent all his strength and borne the heat and labor of the day, he went to receive his reward, immensely great. He slumbers far away from the scenes of his life-long labors, but he will be ever venerated by the Catholic Church as one of the good and true who gave his life for her cause in the land of England, Barry, and Gartland. His name, without spot or reproach, will be inscribed among her honored dead.

The Rev. Patrick Kirby was brother of the former. After spending some time in the diocesan seminary at Charleston, Bishop Gartland sent him, in 1850, to the Propaganda, where he studied for the diocese of Savannah. After having finished a full course of philosophy and theology, he was ordained priest about the year 1856, and after his return was immediately appointed to missionary duties. He inaugurated the church at Rome and served several years at Dalton and the neighboring stations. After some time he was transferred to the missions in Florida. During the war, and subsequently, we find him again laboring in the diocese of Savannah. About 1868 he visited St. Vincent's Monastery, at Latrobe, Pennsylvania, to enter on a prolonged retreat, and died suddenly among the Benedictine Fathers. The solemn obsequies of the dead were performed over his remains, which were attended to their final resting-place by the religious. He was about forty-five years of age and twelve years in the holy ministry. His nephew, Brother Timothy Kirby, was in the monastery, a cleric and under vows, and was preparing for the priesthood. He died about the same time, and he lies buried with his uncle under the walls of St. Vincent's. He was distinguished among holy men for strict observance of the monastic obligations, close application to study, and fervent piety. They share in the suffrages of the community and await in the consecrated soil the glorious resurrection of the dead who die in the Lord.

The Kirby family have given two faithful and devoted

priests to the diocese, and a Benedictine monk to religion, who are all deservedly esteemed by priests and laity.

Towards the close of the civil war Rev. Abram J. Ryan was connected with the church of Augusta, and in the lifetime of Rev. G. Duggan. He rendered signal service to the cause of religion, and received many persons into the Church. He became editor of the *Pacificator*, the most popular sheet published in the Confederacy, and widely circulated because of its strong advocacy of Southern rights. The pointed pen of Bishop Verot and the poet-priest's contributions made it a welcome visitor to every family, and lent it a charm and a fascination which no publication in the South possessed. Father Ryan's exposition and defence of Catholic doctrine rendered it an organ of incalculable advantage to the cause of religion. It was read everywhere, and almost domesticated the faith in every household that wept over the Lost Cause.

Father Ryan in his own sphere was the most popular man in the Confederacy. Lee or Davis, Semmes or Jackson was not more loved than he. He was styled in the land of Burns and of Scott *the best lyric poet of the age*. His strains are heard on the banks of the Boyne and the shores of the Alabama, and his pen has shed as much glory on the lost cause as the sword of Robert Lee. But his notes are sweetest when they breathe the air of the sanctuary, and tell of the unfallen glories of the Church, of Dante and Petrarch, Shakspere and Moore, the only kingdom whose cause is never lost.

Father Ryan was born in Virginia in 1840, and studied at St. Mary's Seminary, The Barrens, Mo. He served some years in the diocese of Nashville. His ministrations among the soldiers are gratefully remembered. He exercised the functions of the holy ministry until about 1870, when he transferred his allegiance to Bishop Quinlan, and is at the present time pastor of St. Mary's Church, Mobile.

Very Rev. W. J. Hamilton succeeded Father Duggan, and was pastor during the administration of Dr. Persico.

He labored zealously in the cause of religion, which prospered in his hands. An accomplished scholar and devoted clergyman, he endeared himself to the congregation and the people in general. He was Dr. Persico's vicar-general, and aided the bishop during his brief administration. About the year 1873 Father Hamilton removed to the diocese of Mobile. His extensive missions in Alabama and Florida afford ample room for his ministerial labors and piety.

The Rev. C. C. Prendergast succeeded, and is now the pastor of St. Patrick's Church. He was born in Savannah, and was deprived of his father at an early age. His mother, who was a woman of tender piety, cheerfully dedicated her only child to the service of the sanctuary. He made his early studies at the Jesuit College at Fordham, and finished his ecclesiastical course in France. He occupied the position of pastor of St. Patrick's Church, in Savannah, until transferred to Augusta by Dr. Gross about 1873. He adorns his office by his piety and fidelity; the cause of religion and the salvation of souls are promoted under his administration.

The Rev. William Faulkner Browne is at this time the able and pious assistant clergyman. Thus, step by step, like the ponderous march of time, the cause of religion steadily advances, and the growing splendors of the Church are daily increasing in the State of Jasper and Pulaski.

In nothing is this progress more manifest than in the introduction of the religious orders. After having converted the hordes of the forest before the Revolution, they kept the light of faith burning on the hidden altars of religion during the dark days of colonial oppression, and watered the soil with the blood of many martyrs. The Jesuit Fathers have entered into the labors of our missions, and continue the work of so many illustrious clergymen, who have left shining names on the brightest pages of our Church history. Before God there is no distinction between Jew and Gentile, nor before his people of regular and secular priest. Engaged in the same warfare, defenders of the faith and soldiers of the cross, they participate in the labors and inherit the same promises.

By their own efforts the Society established a mission and erected a church in the city.

The Church of the Sacred Heart was dedicated by Bishop Gross November 30, 1874; the foundations of the edifice were laid in the beginning of June of the same year, and Mass was celebrated in it for the first time on the first Sunday in October.

The zealous Father Butler, S.J., and another father gave a mission in the city in 1873, on which occasion the bishop informed the people that he intended to create a second parish, and confide it to the care of the Jesuits. In the following April Father Butler purchased the house in which the father now resides and the property on which the church was built. From the month of April to October Mass was regularly celebrated in the parlors of the house, which was converted into a temporary chapel.

The Church of the Sacred Heart is a commodious and handsome building; large congregations attend each of the Sunday Masses. The prudence of Father Duggan, the zeal of Bishop Barry, and the missionary spirit of former priests are all renewed; piety and devotion reign throughout. The railings are thronged with fervent communicants on Sundays. Pious confraternities, temperance and benevolent societies, schools for the education of the youth of both sexes, the academy and convent of the Sisters of Mercy, all mark the progress of Catholicity in a city not inappropriately styled, in a dedication hymn by Dr. Verot, "happy Augusta."

With the Jesuit community, the institution of the sisters, a devoted secular clergy, and an influential body of exemplary Catholics, the entire mass is being leavened and the holy influences of religion are felt throughout the entire community, like the fragrance of the magnolia in the forests of southern Georgia. To crown her happiness, Augusta needs only a mitre of her own; then indeed would she stand the peer of the most favored city on the southern slope of the Atlantic.

Fathers Butler, Heidenkamp and Desribes are the Jesuit Fathers at this time in Augusta.

CHAPTER XVII.

COLUMBUS, CENTRAL GEORGIA, EAST FLORIDA, AND ALABAMA.

Columbus, Georgia—Situation—SS. Philip and James—Extent of Mission—Poverty and Small Number of Catholics—A Poor Priest—Stages—Cradle-rocking—Narrow Escape of a Bishop and Priest—The Apostolic Succession in Georgia Conceded—Talleyrand in a Georgia Saloon—The Parted Glories of the Republic—Rev. James Graham, Founder of the Mission—Early Catholics—Three Slaves—A Bigoted Press—The Crafty Son of Ithaca—An Intrepid Priest—Conflagration—Alpheus Baker and James Ware—Eufaula—The First Mass and Sermon—Albany—The Mission of St. Ignatius of Loyola—A Desolate Mission in the Wilds of Georgia—Hopelessly Lost—Napoleon in the Red Sea—A Man's Reflection at the Hour of Death—Rescued by the Instinct of a Noble Steed—The Human Face Divine—Townspeople—Search for the Lost—Retrospect—Scenery on Southern Rivers—The Gihon and the Ganges—Mission by Secular Priests—Petition for a Church—St. Patrick's Church—Right Rev. John Jaures—First Bishop of Florida—Fathers Louis, Cancer, Tolosa, Carpa, and Companions, Martyrs—Narvaez and Mendosa—The Martyrs of Sebaste—The Cherokees, Creeks, and Seminoles—Once Civilized, and Driven Back by England to Heathenism—Reduced to Slavery—The Blood of Abel a Nation's Crimes—Jealousy of Protestantism the True Cause of the Destruction of the Indian Race—Obstructs their Conversion—Right Rev. Michael Portier—A Great and Cheerful Laborer—A Just Tribute—Bishop Quinlan—St. Peter's Church, Montgomery, Alabama—Bishops Pellicer and Manucy—Fathers Chalon and Savage—Cusseta—A Preacher Enthused—Very Rev. Michael Cullinane—St. Joseph's—The Sisters of Mercy—Rev. A. F. Hewit and the Paulists—Rev. J. Bertazzi—Departure—Prospects for Catholicity, etc., etc.

THE city of Columbus, Georgia, is situated on the east bank of the Chattahoochee, at the falls, and is separated from Alabama by this rapid and majestic river, which is navigable from this point until it falls into the Bay of Appalachicola, in the Gulf of Mexico—a distance of nearly five hundred miles.

The surrounding country is thickly inhabited, fertile, and in a high state of cultivation. The inhabitants are industrious, enterprizing, and liberal-minded, like all Georgians; they are honest, hospitable, and just; they are religiously inclined, and by no means as prejudiced as their neighbors of the Carolinas; to use their own favorite expression, "their religion does not hurt"; they resemble the Western people in manners and habits of thought. There are several factories in good running order, and lucrative, on the falls. The city is built on a flat plain, perfectly level; the streets, like those in Washington, are very long and broad, the residences ornate and commodious, the waters excellent, and the health of the place good.

Macon was added to the district by Bishop Reynolds in 1845, and I was transferred thither as pastor, with Rev. J. F. Kirby as assistant, only for a few months. I held the position during two years, until the return from Europe of my predecessor, Very Rev. Dr. Birmingham, who had gone in quest of health. In territorial extent Columbus was an empire mission, as my readers can readily ascertain by looking on the map and tracing the entire region, embracing nearly 5° of north latitude and 4° of longitude. Montgomery was the western and Milledgeville the eastern boundaries, Monticello the northern and Appalachicola the southern boundaries of this mission. There were more than two millions of inhabitants in this parish, and about two hundred Catholics at most, scattered everywhere, not including Appalachicola, which had a population of nearly seventy-five Irish, employed as shoremen. There was scarcely in all that country a single Catholic who could be called moderately wealthy; they were mostly small storekeepers, mechanics, and laborers. The aggregate value of their property could scarcely exceed twenty thousand dollars, while the priest's salary, derived from all sources, was not over two hundred dollars per year, from which he must also defray all travelling expenses.

On the river I was favored with a free passage on the cotton-boats; the other journeys were by public stage, or on horseback, preferable to the former mode, on account of the crammed condition of the stage, its excessive jolting over bad roads, the intense heat of summer, and the excessive cold of the winter nights. I have seen passengers faint from exhaustion, who were revived only by the use of restoratives. The children were a common care, and each passenger in his turn was expected to become a nurse. While journeying between Milledgeville and Columbus, the stage was upset one frosty night, with Bishop Reynolds and Father O'Neill, of Savannah, as passengers. The former received a severe contusion on the shoulder, and the latter was severely cut in the forehead. After the wound was dressed the venerable missionary preached with a linen bandage around his head; he carried the honorable scar to his grave. Dr. Hoxie, an eminent surgeon in attendance, and a stanch Protestant, playfully remarked that the gash was only an ornament; that one of his predecessors preached with stripes on his back— nothing more becoming a Catholic priest.

Human nature will display its tendencies everywhere and under all circumstances. A closer or better school to study its lessons than a Georgia stage never existed, no less than in the salons of Madame Récamier at Paris or Madame Le Vert at Mobile. The struggle for precedence in anecdote, song, and gallantry, the contest for eminence for a day in the panting or freezing little knot were frequent and amazing. The stage had its etiquette; travelling during many years by this mode, I never witnessed an impoliteness to a lady passenger or a discourtesy to a gentleman. Some one by universal concession became *facile princeps*, often a bishop, or a priest, or some republican nobleman, who governs the subjects of the realm with firm and judicious sway. If there were none competent for the office or too many, the Jehu resumed the reins of government, and no monarch grasped them with firmer hands. Boxes filled with gold, transferred in this manner between banks or for government purposes, were fitted under the seats or scattered over the bottom of the stage, to be trampled under foot. It is doubtful if it would be safe to run the risk at this time, when railroads are boarded and robbed with impunity by masked outlaws.

In the desert ship, heavily loaded with its human and golden cargo, conversation never slackened ; all subjects were discussed, controversy waxed warm, converts were frequently made, and fast friendships formed. There are many to this day who maintain that the glory, honor, and virtue of the Republic died with the last blast of the stage-driver's trumpet.

The distance between Columbus and Macon, the second parish church, was one hundred miles, the road steep and rugged, sandy or clay-bottomed, intersected by many streams and rivers unspanned by a bridge. I have frequently accomplished the journey in fourteen hours on horseback, at the penalty, however, of very shallow genuflections for a week after. The Church of SS. Philip and James was considered out of town and in the commons. It is situated in the southwest extremity, with an entire city square attached, procured by Father Graham, the founder of this mission, and now forming the most eligible church property, situated in the centre of a large city. The church was a plain brick building, erected in 1837, and close by a convenient cottage for the priest's residence. Funds were collected in the cities of the diocese, in Mobile, and New Orleans, by the indefatigable missionary. It was dedicated by Bishop England, and stood like a landmark on the frontiers of the extensive diocese. Among the first priests were the Rev. Mr. Healy, who, having neither church or congregation, was always travelling from place to place without a home. He did not remain to the end, and left for other missions in the North.

Father Graham succeeded, and labored all over this entire country for about seven years, and during the progress of the Brisbane Railroad in Albany, as already stated.

The Rev. Thomas Maloney was sent here about 1840. His mission was limited to the city and Montgomery, Alabama. He was born in the County Limerick, Ireland, made his studies in Canada, was ordained in Charleston by Bishop England in 1838, stationed some time on the missions in North Carolina, and died in Columbus in 1844, after having received the sacraments from the hands of the Rev. Father Coffey.

The Rev. P. J. Coffey succeeded in 1845. He opened a school, and after one year was returned to North Carolina. Father Barry spent some short time here at this period, and also Father Murphy. In 1845 Father Birmingham was transferred from Columbus, South Carolina, to this place, and labored on this mission with his usual fervor and earnestness, until feeble health necessitated a change of climate, and a journey to Italy was recommended.

There were at this time scarcely seventy-five Catholics of all ages, bond and free, in the congregation, and all poor people. The leading members were Toby Howard, a genuine Irish, noble-hearted man, and the very soul of religion and goodness; the brothers Thomas and John McCarty; Patrick Adams, a respectable mechanic, and John Madden, a native of Massachusetts, and a genuine Christian; Mr. Bolter, an Englishman; Mr. Strupper, an Italian; the O'Hara family (truly pious and educated; they conducted the academy); the Matthews of Philadelphia (one of the daughters married James O'Sullivan; she was a woman of tender piety, and was a boarder at the convent in Charleston, quite a little girl, when it was burnt by the mob); the Currys; the Claffeys; Messrs. McCahey, Needham; the Goldens, and two German families—all worthy people, who laid the foundation of the faith in Columbus. The Thompsons and Mrs. Shorter were raised Catholics and professed their religion, but they resided chiefly in the next State; Mr. Rosignol and family were respectable and edifying, but they did not remain in the city very long. There were three edifying colored people, slaves raised in Maryland, who were first in piety and attachment to the faith—Brooks, who led the choir on Sundays; Aunt Lucy, who died in Savannah at my father's residence; and Caroline, with her husband and children.

The number was small, but too large in the eye of jealousy, and we were frequently attacked by wandering preachers, with the connivance of the local ministers, and in the press and pulpit. I wrote a lengthy article to refute a Know-Nothing calumny, "that Catholicity was incompatible with republican institutions." It was my first defence of the faith in the press, and gave me some consideration. Rev. Dr. Andrews, a Universalist minister, published it in his paper. I could get no showing from the Columbus *Times;* its pages were sealed against Catholic questions. The attempt to obtain the insertion of a defence of Catholic principles in refutation of calumnies would be like knocking for admittance at the door of the Temple of Janus during peace.

A preacher on a collecting tour to obtain funds in aid of foreign Protestant missions lectured one night in a church before the assembled wealth and influence of Columbus. In his zeal Dr. Birmingham, with one friend, attended the lecture. It was a tissue of falsehood, misrepresentations, and calumnies against the Church. Towards the end the slender form of the priest rose amid the throng, asking very respectfully and calmly permission to answer. A storm of indignation arose on all sides, which menaced his safety. "Put him out!" "Down with him!" were the mildest expressions of popular indignation. While doing so the little doctor cried out, "If that man received a dollar a lie for every falsehood he has uttered to-night he would have money enough to carry him around the world." The scene that ensued can better be imagined than described. Perhaps the act was not prudent, and was of doubtful advantage. It caused great excitement for some days, some approving and more condemning; the general and final judgment was that he invaded the "religious rights of a community in their church, outraged public decency, and interrupted evangelical harmony." God's saints do many wonderful things which it would be unwise in others to attempt. The blow was a stunner; it slew like a stone from the sling of David, and struck the

Goliath of falsehood in Columbus. Its utterance was never afterwards so boisterous.

It is sad to relate that at this time there was one Irishman, the mayor of the city, who ignored the faith. Perhaps it made him popular for the day, but he was held in detestation by his countrymen and his memory abhorred. Another also shares in the same reproach, one who inherited the name, the faith, and the blood of Gerald Griffin. Like the rich man, they wished to ride to heaven in a carriage, and disdained the companionship of their more humble countrymen on the journey. They are not numbered among the faithful, and their names are no more remembered. The world, its temptations and dangers, are always the same. The Holy Ghost assures us that what has happened before is what will again happen. You will hear of such cases everywhere. Infidelity to obligations among the priesthood and apostasy among the laity are rare occurrences, more so in the diocese of Charleston than anywhere else in America, not excepting the see of a Carroll and a Kenrick.

The Church has lost less and gained more comparatively here than elsewhere in the United States, considering her situation, hampered by slavery and unsustained by immigration. One-third of the city of Columbus was destroyed by fire in the autumn of 1847. It was more fatal in the section inhabited by the Catholics than elsewhere. This calamity, superadded to their previous condition of comparative poverty, reduced them to absolute want. Pecuniary aid was sent to the sufferers from Savannah and other cities. I was appointed chairman of the Committee of Relief, and the most pressing wants of the poor people were provided for. An appeal was made by the distressed congregation to the Catholics of New Orleans. Mr. Charles O'Hara was selected to bear the petition. He received only his pains for his labors. In truth, the Irish of that city, the Eldorado of beggars in olden times, were harassed by the constant calls made on their generosity, and an end must some time come.

In Lumpkin County, and at the principal town, resided one Catholic family. The father, Alpheus Baker, was a native of the New England States, a convert, an educated man, an edifying and enlightened Catholic. While teaching Greek in the South Carolina College, he discovered the inaccuracy of the Protestant translation of the New Testament and the fidelity of the Catholic rendering. This discovery induced him to institute further enquiry, which landed him in the Church. He married an educated Irish lady. They raised a family of six children, who adhered to the faith and illustrated its maxims in their actions and the edifying conversation of their lives. Mr. James Weir, an Englishman, a pious Catholic, and an educated gentleman, resided in the family. They conducted the academy and created a favorable impression towards Catholicity in the whole country.

Eufaula is nearly opposite and on the Alabama side of the river. I visited the town in 1846, when there was but one Catholic, Mr. Colby. He was Irish, of course, an industrious man and much respected. I spent several days in his house and said Mass. He was the only communicant, his wife not having yet embraced the faith, although favorably inclined. Having obtained the use of the Baptist church, I lectured three successive evenings to the townspeople on one subject: "Individual Interpretation of the Bible insufficient as the Rule of Faith." The subject was a new revelation to that intelligent community; it sprung a mine, and in after years a zealous missionary assured me the breach made was never repaired. Continued efforts were made, which tended but to confirm the Catholic arguments in that fundamental point of controversy; most intelligent citizens expressed their convictions of the truth of Catholicity. They intimated a readiness to contribute towards the erection of a church and the support of a priest. Their desires were accomplished; a commodious edifice was soon erected, and there is now in Eufaula a large congregation under the pastoral charge of Rev. W. C. Hamilton, a zealous and distinguished priest, formerly of this diocese.

Before this visit the Word of God had never before been preached to the people.

Albany, situated on Flint River in Baker County, was another station, and distant about fifty miles from Lumpkin. General A. H. Brisbane, his lady, a German family named Mock, a Mr. Silk, and two or three single persons were the only Catholics in this vast wilderness of the Church. Hospitable and entertaining in his family, a visit to the general was a source of much pleasure and literary discussion. He was pious, an enthusiastic admirer of the faith, which he was led to embrace by a miracle, as already mentioned. His railroad did not succeed for want of State subsidy, his inability to pay the hire of his workingmen, and the backward condition of the country. It was too remote in the interior, thinly settled, and sickly. A limestone region, the water is unfit for common use, causing dysentery and other distempers. Rain or cistern water is the common beverage around Albany, the intended terminus. He contemplated the establishment of an Irish Catholic colony, obtaining the services of Father Graham. He appropriated an extensive section of land for church purposes, and erected a missionary cross.

From the causes already specified, and others beyond his control, the infant colony and mission of St. Ignatius, to whom it was dedicated, perished. An attempt to revive it subsequently was equally abortive, and was the cause of unjust blame to all concerned in the project. What alterations in the condition of the country may have taken place of late years I am unable to tell. It was an abiding conviction of the general, was impressed on his mind firm as fate, that St. Ignatius's Mission would rise, flourish, and be a great centre of Catholicity in the diocese of Savannah. I visited Albany three times, preached in the town-hall, or wherever I could procure a suitable place, and was always honored by a large audience. My travelling expenses were never paid. The most wearisome journey of all the mission, the roads were exceedingly rugged, and my vehicle, the old-fashioned sulky, was upset three different times in one day. My route led through Starksville, Americus, Andersonville, afterwards famous as a prison for soldiers, Oglethorpe, Perry, Marion, and ending at Macon, a distance of two hundred miles. I made it companionless, through a wilderness where the sight of every man inspired dread, and there was none to guard but the angel of the way; in his keeping there was no danger to be apprehended. In all that country there was only one Catholic—the priest.

The citizens of Albany on one occasion manifested a deep interest for the preservation of my life. Summoned to administer the last sacraments to a dying Irishwoman, who remained in the country with her family after the work had stopped, and was attacked by the deadly country fever. She resided east of Flint River, along the line of the abandoned railroad, at a considerable distance in a pine forest. After having prepared her for the last journey, on which she entered early the following morning, I started back and refused a guide, confident that I could not miss my way. I was cautioned to make my way directly to the railroad and follow its course westward. An hour's ride on horseback did not bring me in sight of the road; I grew uneasy, it wanted but an hour of sunset, and I was lost. Napoleon, when the tide in the Red Sea stole on him unawares, saved his life by ingeniously directing his companions to separate, striking out in every direction and following the lead of the rider who reported the least depth of water. Single and alone I made the experiment, with a more discouraging result. I had gone deeper into the pathless recesses of the forest; it was dark night, and there was not a star in the heavens to guide me, save the one star of hope, that always enlightens the wanderer whether lost in the wilderness of waters, of woods, or of human life. I turned to Mary and then made another effort for life.

The country is frequently pitted with limestone ponds, dangerous and deep as the dry well of fraternal hatred in the plain of Dothain. The generous steed, the missionary horse of Dr. Birmingham, seemed inspired with my fears, and he became restless and uneasy. I alighted, led him by the bridle-reins, and he reluctantly obeyed. After floundering for an hour over fallen trees and dead logs, like Dr. Kane in the ice-floes of the Polar Sea, I desisted from further effort and abandoned all hopes. Untying the saddle, I placed it at the root of a tree, pillowed my head for the night, resigned to the will of God, always best whether it bring weal or woe. When in imminent danger men are expected to say all the prayers they know; for the want of a better, one poor wretch is said to have recited even the multiplication table. I did not recite all I knew; the task would be interminable, for I had graduated when a boy in the path of paradise, had committed the fifteen mysteries and corresponding prayers of the Rosary to memory, and daily rehearsed the lesson; it is the layman's Office. I made acts of the theological virtues and again prayed fervently to the Blessed Virgin and my angel guardian. After a brief examination of conscience, I reached the safe conclusion of the Methodist on the mourners' bench. Being asked by the exhorter in what state was his conscience, he replied, "In the State of Georgia"; a further discussion was then deemed useless. A wild beast from the jungle, venomous reptiles as common as snakes, or a false step may end life's journey in a moment. Man is generally composed when his danger comes directly from God, without human agency; it is the arm of our brother that we all fear, and not God's; his very stripes are mercies.

My reflections were regret at the idea of losing life so soon. Its worse features were now wreathed with smiles; I discovered I never had an enemy, never tasted sorrow; my missions were but recreations, my friends true as adamant, and the human race disguised angels. I thought I had to die, if not by violence in the night, from the malaria consequent on exposure in that jungle. Death at the hands of a rabble is the most cruel. Our Lord, who exhausted the possibilities of human suffering, gathered solitude and silence around his departing spirit on Calvary. Selim lost his gentle mood, and was not so resigned. He preferred the active life, resolved on locomotion, and expressed his determination by much tugging at the sapling to which he had been tied. I assented, sprung to his side, replaced the saddle, and, like the Knight of La Mancha in search of adventure, determined to follow whithersoever he went. I hoped that perhaps he would make his way to the next stable, like Rozinante. He seemed pleased, the bridle-rein was slackened in coils, lest the slightest pressure should persuade his unerring instinct to yield to the hesitating opinion of man. He conducted me safely, and after midnight I saw a light in the distance. I made directly toward it. It was the abode of man, a log cabin, a fire blazing on the hearth, a litter or bed covering the floor, and the children, fast bound by the chain of slumber, promiscuously scattered around in all directions. This was no den of thieves. At the sound of my voice my German friend, Mock, came to the cabin-door fast by the wildwood. Till then I never knew the full meaning of the phrase, "the human face divine." It was like the first flash of the human face of our Lord blazing on the soul of a good man, after he had passed the dark Valley of the Shadow of Death. The Albanians, good-hearted people, at early dawn organized a thorough search, and set out with rifle, hound, and wood-axe to rescue the missing, if still living, or if dead, recover the remains and solve the mystery. They were rejoiced to learn, after reaching this cabin, that I was safe, and enjoying a sweet sleep after the dangers and fatigue of the night. Village gossip and the press adorned the adventure with a good deal of romance. After thirty-two years I am mercifully spared to relate the simple facts, thank God for my protection, and pray for the faithful who have since tasted the cup of death then passed from my lips.

I reached Appalachicola by the Chattahoochee River in the spring of 1846, on board the steamer *Peytona*, freighted with cotton. The scenery on all our Southern rivers, especially in Florida, is magnificent. The Chattahoochee has its birth in the remote northern mountains of

Georgia and Tennessee. Its aids, obstacles, and obstructions are as numerous as the rugged events found in the chequered way of human life. Until it falls into the Appalachicola, after a journey of a thousand miles, its history is as chequered as the weary life of a patriarch. The many bends give it the appearance of innumerable lakes strung together by an invisible link, and each the apparent end of navigation. The magnolia in full bloom and the bay-tree filling the air with oppressive fragrance, the palm-tree, the cypress, the live-oak, and other trees of great height and gorgeous foliage, drooping over the water and flinging their tall shadows far and wide, would induce fancy to paint each land-locked lake as the source of the rivers of Eden, reluctant to leave the happy bowers, and wander, moaning or sighing or hoarse with weeping, over the entire face of the sin-ruined creation. A pleasing legend relates that the flowers escaped the curse. I would fain claim original innocence for the waters, if it were not disproved by their disorderly lives, lawless acts, and unbridled licentiousness. Always rebellious, nothing short of a divine mandate restrains them from regaining by force their lost empire. They claim once more their ancient possession of the world.

Appalachicola has a cotton-market, and is built on a sand-bed. In 1846 it contained about one thousand inhabitants, one hundred of whom were Irish Catholics. It was sufficiently healthy, if exempt from the scourge of yellow fever, but infested with fleas, exceedingly hostile to strangers, preferring them to the natives, for change of diet. They tormented like the plague of ciniphes in Egypt. Having little communication with the interior, the inhabitants relied on the markets of New York and New Orleans for their supply of provisions. I was accompanied by Rev. J. F. Kirby, who assisted me for a few months on the mission. We preached, said our Mass daily, and exercised other functions of the ministry in the town-hall, which was readily granted as a temporary chapel. All the Catholics approached the sacraments, some children were baptized, and the faithful manifested great zeal in complying with their religious duties. Messrs. Simmes, Brady, and Gibbons were the leading and most influential members. They craved for a resident priest, and pledged their co-operation for the erection of a church. A public meeting was held, suitable action taken, a subscription opened, and a respectable sum promised for the attainment of their laudable object. All was embodied in a formal document, and despatched by mail to the bishop, Right Rev. Dr. Portier, of Mobile, to whose diocese both the Floridas then belonged.

The zealous prelate took action on the petition at an early day; the erection of a church soon commenced. The Rev. Mr. Gibbons, ordained by Bishop Portier, an ex-student of the Seminary of St. John the Baptist, Charleston, S. C., and an Irishman by birth, was placed in charge. He discharged the obligations of the nascent parish with signal zeal and efficiency. He travelled over the diocese, made collections when he could obtain pecuniary assistance, and succeeded after some years in building a large and commodious edifice. It was dedicated in honor of St. Patrick, and is now attended by the Rev. Mr. Hamilton.

Florida was the first diocese established in the United States after the discovery of America by Columbus. It was erected as early as 1527 by the Pope, at the petition of the King of Spain. The Right Rev. John Jaures, a Franciscan and a native of Valencia, was created first bishop. His companions were Fathers Enrique, Austuriano, and another whose name is unknown, and the celebrated lay brother, John de Palos, with several priests besides.* They joined the disastrous expedition of Narvaez, which contained three hundred men. Having landed on Holy Thursday, April 16, 1527, on the coast of Florida, they planted the cross, and said Mass, no doubt, perhaps at Appalachicola, and on the site of St. Patrick's Church, if

* Authorities: Bancroft's "History of the United States," "History of the Catholic Missions," by J. G. Shea, Dr. Clarke's "Lives of Deceased Bishops," and Murray's "History."

an Indian tradition be true, that there will be a church built wherever the first Mass has been offered.

Thirsting for gold and the fabled fountains of perennial youth, they abandoned the fleet and rushed into the interior, contrary to the counsel of the bishop. Having failed in their fruitless search, they again appeared in the light of day at the Bay of Pensacola, decimated by famine and the tomahawk of the Indian; the remnant was worn by fatigue and discouraged by internal dissensions. The few survivors presented the appearance of living skeletons, lacerated by the tangled forests and disheartened by defeat. After constructing four open boats, they reached the Bay of Mobile, and again put out to sea, preferring the terrors of the stormy waters before starvation or the deadly weapon or slow torture of the wily Indian. Only four survived to tell the sad fate of their companions. Those who escaped massacre or death from famine were swallowed up by the waves of the Gulf of Mexico. After having been rescued by the bravery of Narvaez from a watery grave, the bishop, with forty of his co-laborers, was cast on Dauphin Island, where they all perished; some were massacred, and others, who escaped to the woods, died of hunger. The latter, it is believed, was the fate of Right Rev. John Jaures. Thus, like Bishop Eric in New England, died the first bishop of Florida. He gave his life for the faith. In the near future the American Church may petition the Holy See to create him and his companions patrons of the diocese and honor the festival with the office of Bishop and companions, Martyrs. In the ranks of the faithful, both clergy and laity, are many who died in the odor of sanctity, and are worthy of the honors of the altars of religion. All our missionary orders have already furnished martyrs to the American Church, whose beatification is only a question of time. Undismayed by their disasters, and encouraged by their example, other priests entered into missions and continued the labors of the martyred band. Father Louis Cancer and two other Dominican Fathers landed on the shores of the wild Peninsula on Ascension Day, 1549. Father Tolosa, one of his companions, was almost immediately murdered. A few days after Father Cancer received the martyr's crown at Espiritu Santo Bay, June 25, 1549. His last words were, "O my God!"

St. Augustine is the oldest city in the United States. It was laid out by Mendoza, the great Spanish admiral, in 1665. It was called after St. Augustine, and the first Catholic church in our country was here erected. The Franciscans, the Dominicans, and the Jesuits toiled in the new field, and many of them watered the soil with their blood. The countries embraced by the sees of St. Augustine, Mobile, and Savannah formed the scene of their apostolic labors. Father Martinez, the superior of the first band of Jesuits that landed in our country, with two companions, accompanied the expedition of Melandez. While leading an exploring party into the interior, and separated from the ship, the savages rushed to the boat, seized on the heroic Jesuit, dragged him on shore, and beat him with a heavy club until life was extinct. Like St. Stephen, and with uplifted hands, he prayed while consciousness remained. He baptized the soil of Florida with his blood September 28, 1566.

Father Carpa, O.S.F., and three other companions labored among the dusky sons of the South on the Atlantic shores of Georgia. Within two years they received many converts. As in later times among the slaves, their great difficulty and their chief obstacle to the conversion of the Indian tribes was the prevalence of polygamy. Father Carpa died a martyr for upholding the sanctity of the marriage tie. Having reprimanded a young chief, a convert who had relapsed into this crime, the savage sought revenge and determined to silence the tongue that preached a doctrine condemnatory of his loose instincts. He stealthily entered the chapel while the father was at his duties and slew him instantly. Gathering a multitude of young braves, the fiendish chief ravaged all the missions and bestowed the crown of martyrdom on Father Carpa's companions. Like the martyrs of Sebaste, none were missing from the number. These events occurred in September, 1597.

The Franciscans established the monastery of St. Helena at St. Augustine, and from this centre emanated missionaries who carried the glad tidings of salvation to all the tribes inhabiting the Southern region of our country. Numbers of Creeks, of Alabama, the Cherokees of Georgia and the Carolinas were converted, and the portals of salvation were entered by the red man in thousands. Christianity was generally professed, as among the tribes of Mexico. A change soon came; civilization was arrested and a persecution inaugurated by apostate England against Catholicity and the poor converted Indians which swept both from the Peninsula. The English colony of Carolina carried war into the peaceful Indian villages of Florida. In 1703, says a distinguished writer, a body of fanatics ravaged the country, destroyed the Indian towns, slaughtered the missionaries and their forest children, reduced many of them to servitude, and sold others in the slave markets of the West Indies. In 1763 Spain ceded Florida to England, and this was the death-blow of the missions. They were all destroyed, the converted tribes dispersed without a shepherd. The monastery of St. Helena became a barracks, and such it continues to be to the present day. This was private property consecrated to God and devoted to religion and education. Its seizure by England was an unjustifiable act. Our Government ere long will doubtless restore this property to its proper owner, the Catholic Church. The cultivated possessions of the converted natives were seized by England and the owners banished to the wilderness. Deprived of their spiritual guides and of all instruction, they quickly adopted their nomadic life of barbarism, from which Catholicity had reclaimed them. Buried in the pathless Everglades, the Florida Indians took the name of Seminoles, or Wanderers, and having lost the faith, they became the scourge of the whites.

They made powerful resistance during the Seminole or

Florida war, and were finally subdued under General Jackson in 1830, and removed to the Indian Territory. It cost the United States millions of money and many lives to conquer them. At the date of the Revolutionary War England had destroyed every Catholic mission in the country. The uncivilized condition of the Indian tribes and the failure of Protestantism to Christianize them, while they waste millions of money in futile efforts to convert other people's heathens, is a startling fact. It is the result of jealousy against Catholicity, beyond whose pale no heathen nation was ever brought to the light of Christianity. It was the Colonial Government that first obstructed the work of conversion, and the fatal policy, inherited by our Republic, is maintained to this hour with like result. Had it not been for this opposition, there would not exist this day a brave on the war-path nor a savage in the wilderness. Even now the Catholic Church craves permission to begin anew. She engages to end the border warfare, evangelize and convert the red man and fit him for the duties of peace, for any office in the country, from the mechanic's bench to the throne of the bishop or the chair of the President, without the aid of a dollar from the treasury or a rifle from the armory, on one simple condition—to be let alone.

The very savages crave it, but in vain. They are expected to embrace Christianity at the persuasion of a speculating preacher, with a Bible in one hand and a Government grant for their land in the other. Fire-water, the rifle, and legalized robbery are the weapons of *his* spiritual warfare, varied by a barrel of bad meat, a sack of musty flour, and a shoddy blanket, as specimens of evangelical perfections, in mock fulfilment of a violated treaty. In the eternal nature of things, every sin brings its own punishment. The Holy Ghost declares that the sinner is chastised in and by the very things in which he transgresses. The rewards and punishments of a nation must necessarily be temporal; the individual, not the nation, is amenable to the chastisement of another life. Already do we behold the plains of the desert whitened with the bones of our soldiers; the children of the wilderness hunted down like wild beasts; the crime of having wiped out of existence a noble race weighing heavily on the conscience of the nation, and, like the blood of Abel, crying aloud for vengeance, all rendering the country contemptible before the nations of the earth. The blood of the red man and the obstructions to his conversion are not venial sins on the breast of the nation, and demanding but a lustration of water for their expiation. If secure from abroad, the Lord can readily raise an avenging sword at home, which has always been his most severe mode of chastisement. "I will send the Egyptian to fight against the Egyptians."

The Right Rev. Michael Portier, D.D.,* after the long, sad interruption, succeeded the martyr-bishop and other missionaries in their hallowed field of labor. He was created Vicar-Apostolic of Florida in 1825. Alabama and Arkansas were portions of his vicariate. There were but two churches, one at St. Augustine and the other at Pensacola, and a population of three thousand. There were only three priests in this vast territory, and two were lent from New Orleans and Charleston. Without, mitre, crozier, or pectoral cross, he entered on his mission, supported by his confidence in God and an unfailing vein of cheerfulness. Born at Lyons, France, September 7, 1795, after completing his studies at the seminary in Baltimore he was ordained priest at St. Louis by Bishop Dubourg in 1818. He was created vicar-general of the diocese of New Orleans and consecrated bishop at St. Louis by Bishop Rosati, assisted by two priests, by dispensation from Rome, on November 5, 1826. He refused the honor and yielded only to a mandate of the Pope. He died of dropsy in Mobile May 14, 1859, in the sixty-fourth year of his age and the thirty-third year of his episcopate.

He was for many years senior bishop of the American hierarchy; he lies buried in the cathedral. By his strenu-

---

* Authorities: Personal recollections. Original sources—Clarke's "Lives of Deceased Bishops," "Catholic Almanac."

ous exertions he established Catholicity over the region entrusted to his care. Before his death it was divided into three extensive dioceses. He formed a zealous, exemplary, and learned priesthood, several of whom were decorated deservedly with the episcopal dignity. He bequeathed to the diocese twenty-seven priests, a magnificent cathedral, fourteen churches, Spring Hill College, fourteen schools, three academies for boys and the same number for girls, two orphan asylums, one infirmary, and many free schools. He sat in all the various councils of the American Church at Baltimore held to the time of his death, and assisted at the consecration of many bishops. He never made an enemy; he had charity for all. He domesticated Catholicity in Mobile, and endeared himself to all the citizens. His memory is revered by the laity, and no bishop could have been more tenderly loved by his priests. Their sorrows, their joys, their interests were all his own. He was deservedly styled the father of the city of Mobile. He labored on the missions while he was able; as long as strength lasted he stood at the altar. There could not be a more popular bishop. His death was mourned as a universal loss and his last hours were consoled by the prayers and sympathies of a large city, all Catholic in feeling and vastly so in numbers, where he found, thirty-three years back, no church nor priest nor altar to keep the holy vigil by the unknown grave of Bishop Jaures. Bishop Portier was low-sized, slim, and light also, when he rode on horseback from New Orleans to St. Louis to be consecrated. In after years he grew robust and magisterial in person, favoring the Irish more than the French type of the Celtic race.

He was the very soul of kindness; it beamed from his open, candid face, and he delighted to dispense a refined hospitality in the midst of his clergy, the religious, and the strangers who always trod his floor and found shelter under his roof. An honored and toil-worn laborer in the Church of God, his memory burns brightly, as the silver lamp which he hung before the sanctuary in the Cathedral of the Immaculate Conception, and whose light shall not be extinguished in the diocese of Mobile. Having enjoyed his jurisdiction and shared in the honors and labors of his diocese, this just tribute is reverently offered to the memory of a great bishop, a zealous missionary, and a noble-hearted man.

The Right Rev. John Quinlan, D.D., consecrated December 4, 1859, is Dr. Portier's immediate successor. He was born in County Cork, Ireland. The increased number of churches and stations, academies, zealous priests, ecclesiastical institutions, male and female, and the general progress of religion, despite the adverse circumstances of emancipation and the civil war, are the best evidences of his fidelity, zeal, and learning. During the past ten years his administration has been blessed with the most signal success. Calm, discreet, and mild, he enjoys among the clergy the reputation of being a safe bishop. As a preacher he ranks among the first in the land. Called by God to the government of the diocese in boisterous times, his firm and temperate course has won him golden opinions from all classes, and, from his own, love and veneration.

Montgomery, for many years the capital of Alabama, formed the western limit of my mission, and I visited the faithful of that city frequently from Columbus. On the banks of the noble stream that gives its sweet-sounding name to the territory dwelt the Creeks and Seminoles, once Catholic. It is connected with the episcopal city by a regular line of steamboats. St. Peter's Church was one of the oldest in the diocese, and was erected shortly after the consecration of Dr. Portier. As at Sullivan's Island in Charleston Bay, all the clergy at one time or another ministered in the parish, and its reminiscences would embrace the history of the diocese since 1822. Vicar-General Chalon, the bishop's cousin, was pastor at an early date. The congregation was small, but the Duncans, the Crayons, and other Catholics of influence and social eminence, and the piety of all, made Catholicity respectable.

Towards 1845 the congregation had dwindled down to a

few persons, and the church on Capitòl Hill was rapidly falling into decay. A remnant of the Duncan family, P. N. Modigan and family, the O'Connells, who shortly removed to Galveston, and a few others were the only Catholics. There had been no resident priest for a considerable period, but a brighter day dawned, and in after years the first and brightest glories of the Confederacy flung their rays around St. Peter's, and the leading spirits of the new nation worshipped before its altars. A handsome and substantial new brick building was built by Father Pellicer about 1854, and funds collected for the purpose in the republic of Mexico. After having been transferred to the city of Mobile and created vicar-general, Father Pellicer was succeeded by Father Manucy, who exercised the functions of the ministry as pastor until his appointment to the vicariate of Brownsville, Texas. This pastoral charge seems to be an introduction to the highest dignities. The present generation has rejoiced to witness the consecration of two worthy priests and their elevation to new sees, Right Rev. Dr. Pellicer and Right Rev. Dr. Manucy—the first as Bishop of San Antonio and the second Vicar-Apostolic of Brownsville. They are the first natives of Florida who received the episcopal order or the priesthood, descending from the times of the martyred missionaries. They are cousins, about the same age ; were born at St. Augustine about 1822, educated at Spring Hill College, ordained about 1846 by Dr. Portier, and after having discharged all the offices of honor and trust and done their share of priestly work, were consecrated in New Orleans by Archbishop Perché December 8, 1864. Fitted by both language and association for the respective positions, among a population partly English and partly Spanish, a more suitable selection could not be made among all the clergy. Its wisdom was applauded and their appointment was greeted by the universal acclamation of the faithful. Zealous, learned, and devoted to missionary duties, they shine as twin stars on the Southern borders of the domain of the Church, and fling the light of fervor and Catholic discipline far west of the boundary. Bishop Pellicer was among the first band of pilgrims who crossed the ocean and laid the sympathy and veneration of the American Church at the feet of the august prisoner of the Vatican.

At this time Rev. D. Savage is pastor of Montgomery, now containing a large and devout congregation, which in time will increase to thousands after the evils entailed by the civil war and the subsequent maladministration will have passed, and our country becomes happy, prosperous, and Christian. I visited the Thompson family, worthy and respectable Maryland Catholics, and all other members of the faith throughout all the intermediate counties and on the western bank of the Chattahoochee. I prepared for death the sole Catholic who lived at Cusseta, an Irishman of course. The townspeople generously invited me to preach in the Methodist church. At a blast from the horn of the hotel the inhabitants assembled, and formed a numerous and an attentive audience. The minister was a courteous man ; he sat by me while preaching, joined in the Universal Prayer, and during the delivery of the discourse manifested evident signs of deep emotion.

I spent two years on this mission, and the three first years of my priestly life in Georgia. In the fall of 1847, on the return of Father Birmingham, I was recalled to Charleston, and stationed in the Carolinas by Bishop Reynolds. Dr. Birmingham labored within this vast region until the formation of the see of Savannah, in 1850, when he was also recalled to toil to the end in the diocese of Charleston, embracing both Carolinas.

Very Rev. Michael Cullinane, chancellor of the diocese, was pastor of Columbus sixteen years after the departure of Father Birmingham. He was a native of County Wexford, came to Savannah, and was the first priest ordained for the diocese by Bishop Gartland in 1853. He was at different times pastor of Macon, Atlanta, and officiated also in Savannah. Churches and institutions throughout the State of Georgia bear witness to his labors and his zeal. Under his administration the congregation increased rapidly, and religion prospered. The Academy of St. Joseph and the establishment of a branch of the order of the Sisters, day-schools, pious societies and confraternities, and other Catholic enterprises are monuments of his tireless labors and zeal. Though shorn of the greater portion of its former territories, enough was left in Columbus for the exercise of his missionary zeal, and to afford him constant employment. He worked faithfully, and was loved and venerated by all classes, especially by the poor and the orphans, to whom he was a father and a friend. He died at Columbus February 23, 1877, in the fifty-eighth year of his age, of which he was twenty-five years a holy and an honored missionary priest.

The Paulist Fathers, who by their retreats for the city and efficient labors throughout the Carolinas and Georgia advanced the cause of religion, opened a mission in Columbus in 1856. Its success gave a fresh vitality to the Church, introduced a new era for Catholicity; its beneficial results continue to bring forth abundant fruit to this day. The fathers were all converts, eminent for learning and zeal. Their reputation gathered thousands to listen to their elegant discourses on faith and morals. Fathers Walworth, Deshon, and Hewit made an enduring impression on the minds of the Georgia people in favor of our holy religion. Rev. Augustine F. Hewit was at home everywhere in the two dioceses; the faithful to a great extent claimed him as their own priest. He was born in 1820 in Connecticut. In 1839 he graduated at Amherst College. He began the study of theology in East Windsor, and continued it in Baltimore under Bishop Whittingham, who made him deacon in the Episcopal Church. In 1846 he was received into the Church by Bishop Reynolds in Charleston, and was ordained the following year. He joined the congregation of the Most Holy Redeemer, and was professed in 1851. After having labored as a missionary in the order for seven years, he, with Father Hecker and others, formed the Congregation of St. Paul. Since 1858 he has labored in the new institution, on the missions, and more recently as professor of philosophy and theology in the Paulist Seminary, New York. In conjunction with Dr. Corcoran, he edited the works of Bishop England. In various departments of literature he holds a high place among the most distinguished writers of America. But in the Southern States it is as the missionary priest, humble, patient, and mild, that he is chiefly remembered and venerated by the faithful. As a pulpit orator he ranked first among his confrères; the non-Catholic hearers expressed a preference for "the steel-gray preacher." The gathering honors of time and labor clustering on his brow suggested the appellation.

As in all other dioceses, very many of the clergy of Savannah have exercised the functions of the ministry as pastor or assistant in Columbus. The details would be only of local interest, and useless for this generation, who witnessed the labors and shared the spiritual benefits of their priesthood. But the city has been peculiarly blessed by devoted and zealous priests of pious and exemplary lives. Rev. J. Bertazzi holds the position of pastor at this date, and is deservedly esteemed.

The superior health of the city and surrounding country, the number of factories now in operation, and yearly increasing, the great facilities of travel or transportation by water or railroad, and other inducements must render Columbus ere long a grand centre of Catholicity, diffusing far and wide over the confines of two powerful States the light and blessing of the faith.

CHAPTER XVIII.

MACON, MILLEDGEVILLE, ATLANTA, ETC., ETC.

Macon—Milledgeville, Georgia—Church of the Assumption—A Heavy Debt—Catholicity a Disgrace—A Riot Arrested—William B. Watts, a Noble Georgian—Intercession of the Blessed Virgin—The Croghan Family—Early Catholics—An Irish Gentleman—The Capital—a Thorny Road—Sermon in the Protestant Church—A Juvenile Priest not Afraid—A Generous Preacher—Timid Catholics—Sermon at Eatonton—The Penitentiary—An Irish Convert and the Protestant Cup—St. Columbkille in Marietta—A Preacher who Does not Know the Irish Language—Father James Graham, the Founder of the Mission—Tribute from the Rev. C. J. Crogan—Other Priests—Pio Nono College—Bishop Gross—Sisters of Mercy—Marvellous Growth of the Church—Atlanta, Georgia—The Last Battle—Prosperity—New London—Catholic Necrology—Formation of the First Church—Rev. Thomas F. Shannahan—Other Clergymen—Rev. J. F. O'Neill, Jr.—Right Rev. Dr. Whelan—Right Rev. Bishop Feehan, D.D.—Rev. James Hasson—Church of the Immaculate Conception—A Centre of Manufactures—The Academy of St. Joseph and Sisters' House—Greater Progress of Religion in Georgia than in the Carolinas—Causes—South Carolina the Greatest Sufferer by the War—Cromwell in the Land of England and Calhoun—'98 in Carolina—Catholicity in the Carolinas and Georgia—One of the Noblest Triumphs of the Church in the United States—Summary—Churches Free to All—More Priests than were Needed—No Door Collections in the South—A Faithful Priesthood and Devoted Laity—Pelion on Ossa—Slavery—No Immigration—Civil War—Misrule—Emancipation—Loss of Property—Worthless Currency—Destruction of Institutions, etc.—The Truth of the Assertion Established.

FOR many years Macon ranked as the third city in size and population in the State. It was comparatively old when Atlanta sprung into existence, and which not only rivals but now surpasses it in material growth and prosperity. It occupies a central position in the Empire State, is built on both sides of the Ocmulgee River, which, after uniting with the Altamaha, falls into the Atlantic Ocean at Darien. In 1860 the population was over ten thousand.

The vicinity of Macon is noted for a very remarkable event in the history of the Church; the first Christian baptism in North America was administered here. In 1540, while De Soto was marching, it is supposed, near the mounds in East Maçon, two Indians, named Mark and Peter, being assailed by the devil at night, requested to be baptized. They accompanied the expedition as guides, and they said the devil punished them for this reason. They showed the marks on their bodies to the general, who, being convinced of their sincerity, ordered the priests to baptize them, so that the devil could have no power over them (Herrera, "History of America and the Expedition of De Soto," vol. v. p. 313).

Bishop England's first visit to Macon, with Rev. M. D. O'Reilly, was in 1829. He preached three days in the Methodist and three in the Presbyterian churches. A gentleman who entertained him remarked if he remained another week he would convert the whole town.

Macon was my first pastoral charge. I arrived in the city on the Feast of St. Thomas, December 21, 1844.

During the progress of the work on the Savannah Railroad many of the Catholic laborers gathered into the town, and it became an important station about 1835. After the completion of the work the men departed, and scarcely a dozen poor families remained behind. On my arrival the congregation scarcely numbered thirty souls, and the priest scarcely received as many dollars annually for his support. Each member was compelled to work for his daily sustenance, and none had a dollar to spare. The Church of the Assumption was a large frame building, formerly owned by the Presbyterians, but condemned as too far out of town, and at an inconvenient distance for pedestrians. It was situated on a city square, and the entire premises were purchased by Rev. James Graham about 1840. In this manner was acquired what in the course of a few years became the most valuable property in the city.

Rev. Thomas Murphy in 1844 remodelled and embellished the building, and erected at one end a vestry with two rooms, serving the double purposes of robing-room and priest's residence. A debt of seventy dollars remained due, quite a large amount in these times. I made collections abroad and paid it off.

The property was afterwards sold by Dr. Verot, and the proceeds applied to other ecclesiastical purposes.

On Sundays the congregation, scattered over the large, vacant edifice, if collected, would scarcely fill five pews. All the Catholics did not attend the Sunday Mass. Catholicity was branded with the mark of disgrace and its profession a crime. No man or woman having any pretension to social respectability had courage to enter that abandoned, low, Irish church, stationed at the ragged edge of the most disreputable part of the town. If, from curiosity, a gang gathered round on Sunday, unrestrained by public sentiment and the laws of good manners, they ridiculed the divine service, mocked the priest, and insulted the humble but fervent worshippers.

On one occasion a respectable Irish Catholic, indignant at the misdemeanor of a party, expostulated in terms of reproof. The party rudely rushed from the church, and before dark the town was boiling with indignation at an imputed offence publicly offered to a lady, and by such a man and in such a place. Threats of violence, low but deep, were heard on all sides. To quell the excitement I wrote an explanation in an apologetic tone. I did not receive nor did I expect an acknowledgment from "a citizen living in Vineville." However, it produced the desired effect, and the gentleman blamed only his family, who had no business to go to such a place.

There were three men who were prominent in town, and who could have gained us some consideration—a Marylander, a Frenchman, and an Irishman; but they were members of secret societies and hardly ever entered the church.

In so desperate a state of affairs greater credit is due to the faithful few who professed their faith fearlessly and firmly adhered to it when, like her Divine Founder, the church was in the stable, and its members, with some few exceptions, the offscourings of the people. Eminent among these was William B. Watts, a native of Richland, South Carolina, and a non-Catholic. He was a whole-hearted and a generous man, a respectable merchant, and honored with the first municipal offices. He was the most popular man of his day in Macon, and grand chief of the Odd-Fellows. In illustration of the state of society in Macon in early times, he related that on his first arrival in the city he met at a gambling table, accidentally on his part, the mayor, the sheriff, the aldermen, and other high dignitaries of the State Government.

W. B. Watts married a daughter of Emanuel Antonio, of Columbia, South Carolina, who was one of the most pious and devoted Catholic ladies in the State. Her home was the priest's home; he was treated as one of the family; the care and attention extended to him was in a measure a recompense for his privations and for the contempt of the world. Unable to pay their board at a hotel, all the first priests lived in Mr. Watts' family, and sometimes two at a time. They could offer no recompense but their prayers. Father Graham died in the house and was buried from it, Mr. Watts conducting the funeral arrangements.

Bishops Reynolds and Barry, Fathers Murphy, Shannahan, Coffey, O'Neill, Jr., and myself lived with Mr. Watts; in fact, we had no other home.

Deterred by no state of weather, human respect, or other consideration, he was always in his pew, always personally interested in whatever concerned the clergy or the Church, furnishing food and raiment and shelter and vestments to minister at the altar, at which none stood to assist the priest, except the angels of God. He was not as yet even baptized. I shuddered at the idea of his dying beyond the pale of that Church which he more than any other layman had assisted to plant in the heart of Georgia. I made novenas of Masses repeatedly during fifteen years to obtain from our Blessed Lady the grace of his conversion. My life is a living monument of the efficacy of her prayers, and an additional confirmation of the assurance of SS. Augustine and Bernard, that none ever sought it in vain. Such a result has yet to take place in the Church. The event was delayed, but it came at last, sweetly and gently, in our Blessed Mother's good time.

Her Son, who at her prayer changed water into wine, wrought the change in this instance also, elevated natural goodness to the standard of supernatural virtue, and the son of Adam was made the child of God, the co-heir of our Lord and member of his mystic body. He died about 1854, about sixty years of age, fortified with all the aids of religion, lamented by the faithful, and respected by the citizens.

A few years later his beloved wife, the companion of his labors, the solace of his sorrows, the soul that animated his works and inspired his sentiments, was laid by his side at Rose Hill Cemetery, overlooking the broad Ocmulgee. The praise and prayers of the faithful will mingle over their resting-place, combined with the ripple of the waters that in years gone by delighted the spirit of the Cherokee and Seminole. William B. Watts served in the Florida war.

Several children were born to this virtuous couple, most of whom died in infancy and after baptism; others survive. Dr. Alexander Watts studied at Wilmington, Delaware, under Father O'Reilly, and is a respectable and successful physician in his native city. Two sisters survive, who have had their share of the sorrows of human life. In early life they were all trained under the holiest Catholic influences. May they and their offspring prove themselves worthy of their noble parents, from whose hearth the pure stream of Catholicity diffused itself abroad over central Georgia!

The other Catholics were few but fervent. Mrs. Carey was a widow lady, and of the family of Mathew Carey, of Philadelphia. It was while at supper at her father's, in the city of Cork, that the late Dr. Murphy received the Papal bull appointing him bishop of that diocese. Mrs.

Carey was pious, respectable, and intelligent. She departed this life about 1850, leaving one daughter, Mrs. Howland, who still lives, commendable for her piety, virtue, and goodness. Mrs. Howland had one brother, Charles, an accomplished, excellent young man, and a daughter, Martha, who was educated at the convent in Charleston. She was accomplished and devout. She died in 1846, in the first flower of youth and innocence, but she had bloomed only for heaven.

Owen Croghan was a native of County Galway, Ireland. He and his excellent wife were models of fervor and piety. He loved the church and pastor of Macon with an enthusiasm unfelt at home for Catholicity, because of its humility, isolation, and suffering in the land of his adoption. There were several children, who were all animated with the faith and noble sentiments of their virtuous parents. Peter, the oldest, married, brought his wife into the Church, and raised several children, who adhere to their religion. He still lives at Americus, Ga. Hubert, the second son, married in Sumter, where he died in 1855, leaving two sons, excellent young men. Catherine died several years ago. Mrs. Bligh is a widow, and removed to Charleston, where her children now live. Mr. Croghan gave a worthy priest and a zealous missionary to the diocese of Charleston, in the person of his son, Rev. Charles J. Croghan, the pastor of St. Joseph's Church, who, by his learning and missionary labors, has illustrated the name of Catholicity in the diocese.

Owen Croghan died in the fall of 1855, aged about seventy-two years. His wife, Honora Griffin, survived only a few years, and died in Charleston at the residence of her granddaughter, Mrs. Duffy, in November, 1859. Both are buried at the cemetery in Macon, beside the remains of a son and a daughter.

Thomas C. Dempsey was one of the early Catholics, and he is still enjoying the blessing of human life. His father, D. Dempsey, was a respectable merchant in Savannah. A man of sobriety and business habits, he acquired an independence, purchased the Floyd Hotel and other property in the city, which he bequeathed to his only son. He was attached to the faith, approached the sacraments regularly, and edified by the order and regularity of his life. Residing in Savannah, he only visited Macon as business demanded. He died about the year 1850 at a venerable age.

Intelligent, educated, strictly correct in manner and habits of life, and assiduous in the practice of all religious duties, his son was an acquisition to the Church and a consolation to the priest in that wild and prejudiced region. The companion of long journeys, the solace of many a weary hour, and with a mind enriched with the treasures of extensive reading, his recollection is cherished by the writer as one of the most pleasing reminiscences of his Georgia mission. He married a non-Catholic lady, who readily embraced the true faith. Their union was blessed with an offspring of seven children, three of whom are receiving all the advantages of Catholic training in the first institutions; four fled to heaven before contact with the world could brush the baptismal drops from their angelic wings.

He crossed the Atlantic frequently, and on a late visit, after receiving the benediction of the late Pope, the sainted Pius IX., returned invigorated by its influence rather than by the sea voyage.

He is the connecting link between the present and the past of Catholicity in Georgia, exhibiting in his person the true type of the faithful. In those early times the congregation was often honored by the presence of Philip J. Punch, the talented editor of the Savannah *Georgian*. He was a native of Cork, a whole-souled, generous Catholic, an accomplished man and a talented writer. He had a family whom he removed during the war, probably to New Orleans, since which time he has disappeared from the knowledge of the writer. The charms of the company of an Irish educated Catholic can never be realized without spending an hour in the society of such a man as was Philip J. Punch.

Mr. Phelan, the uncle of Father Kirby, a saintly man, taught school one year in Macon, and lived with me at the church. He was not well patronized, and returned to Ireland, where he died about the year 1860.

John P. Gavan, an auctioneer, and his brother, were Catholics. The former raised many children. His mother-in-law, Mrs. McGowan, and the family were truly pious. He received the last sacraments before his death, about 1850.

John and James O'Keefe, brothers, were both attached to their religion, and were not ashamed to profess it openly. It found an able advocate in the former, who was a well-informed man and a classical teacher. He raised a family; the children died young, and he himself died a violent death. He was shot in mistake for another, against whom the assassin cherished a grudge. Doubtless he called on God, for he knew his religion well, and often approached the sacraments. In an emergency a moment is an age before the divine mercy.

Mrs. D'Amour and her mother, Mrs. Tobin, deserve honorable mention for steadfast faith and practical piety. These and the Dacy, Geraghty, and Morrissy families, and a few single men, composed the congregation in 1845.

There lived with me at this time, in the rear of the church, a relative named Michael Cronin. He was a nephew of Father Mathew Horrigan, formerly parish priest of Blarney. He entered the seminary in Charleston in 1840 and remained until 1844, when failing health compelled him to withdraw. He subsequently went to Louisiana, where he conducted a respectable school. He died in Caddo Parish in 1849, fortified with the holy sacraments, and, in the hopes of a blissful immortality, returned to his Maker, who rewards the will no less than the performance. He was twenty-seven years old at the time of his death.

Clinton, twelve miles east of Macon, rejoiced in a good hotel, conducted by an Irishman named Sullivan. He was an elderly man, married a Methodist, and, no wiser than Solomon, adored her gods without having lost his faith in the true Church. This made his condition most unhappy. Yielding to my admonitions, he promised to retrace his steps, and made some efforts in this direction. The children were of course lost to the faith.

I made the rounds of all the up-country as far as Decatur. Atlanta was not yet in existence. In Monroe, Covington, Monticello, and over the entire country, I found but three families permanently settled who were Catholics. The Burns family, all grown people, resided at Covington. There were some laborers on the Monroe Railroad, who left the country after the completion of the work. I collected some money from them, and applied the same to the liquidation of the debt on the Macon church.

Milledgeville was the most important station outside of Macon. It was not known to have been visited previously. It is the capital of the State, had a population of three thousand, a dozen of whom were Catholics. Among these were the brothers Michael and James O'Brien. Louisa, the wife of the latter, became a Catholic. This was a kind and hospitable family. Their house was the headquarters of the clergy, where they were always welcome, were hospitably entertained, and in which the divine mysteries were celebrated and the word of God preached.

The Treanor brothers, John and Hugh, also resided in Milledgeville. They were worthy and enterprising men, and truly Catholic. Father Treanor, of New York, pastor of the Church of the Transfiguration, who died recently, was their nephew. The Shehans, James and Michael, also brothers, intelligent men and much esteemed, were true Catholics. They were single men and dry-goods merchants. There was also a widow, a sister of the O'Briens, whose daughter married Louis Valentine, a Neapolitan. He removed afterwards to Atlanta. It was mentioned among the faithful that I was the first priest who had the honor of offering the Holy Sacrifice in Milledgeville. The event took place in the private room of the Treanors, at the Newell Hotel, in the month of April, 1845.

I preached repeatedly in the Court-house, and generally

obtained a good audience. I preached on the "Absolving Power," and also on "Free Will" and on "The Protestant Rule of Faith, or the Bible alone." I always judged it expedient to sound the alarm of truth among the multitudes who, without thought or reflection, are carried away by the headlong tide of popular error. It is better to assert the truth, warn the multitudes of their danger, and vindicate our rights, and leave the consequences to God. I did so at this place. Attempts were made to dissuade me from this independent course by timid Catholics, who feared their popularity or business interests might suffer detriment in consequence. They refused to procure a respectable place for a lecture. My youth, my inexperience, my Irish accent, were alleged as disqualifications for preaching the doctrines of the Church for the first time before the learned people of Georgia. The attempt to do so was condemned as bold, rash, and inopportune, and must evidently end in a failure. In fact, they were sentimental Catholics, and perhaps it would require only a mixed marriage to wrench them from the Church. In short, they wanted to run me out of town, were ashamed to be seen in my company on the streets, and offered to pay my way back by the return stage.

I had not received the spirit of fear, and, mindful of the admonition of St. Paul to St. Timothy, I determined that no man should despise me on account of my youth. I renewed my efforts, invoked the co-operation of the non-Catholics, and begged for a hall and audience. I formed the acquaintance of the Rev. Mr. Blake, the chaplain of the penitentiary, and also of Rev. Mr. Johnston, the Episcopal minister, and other leading gentlemen in the town. I obtained a large and attentive audience, and, after an hour's discourse, I explained my situation. I complimented them for having vindicated their liberality and intelligence from the imputation cast on both by the timid and cowardly course of a few of my countrymen, who were afraid to be known as Catholics lest they might lose their popularity or the sale of a yard of cloth; in short, that they had judged the people to be so bigoted that they feared to profess the name of our Lord as it is known and professed by nine-tenths of civilization. I concluded by remarking that any Catholic who henceforward feared to acknowledge his faith, to see the minister of the Lord or receive him, was doing an injustice to the community, and proving himself unworthy of confidence or trust.

I took the fortress, and these men made ample reparation. On a next visit they all approached the sacraments, which they had not doné in years before. They persevered to the end, and generously aided to establish the faith at the capital of the State of Georgia.

Parson Blake, who was an Englishman, wished to become a Catholic, and corresponded with Father Barry on the subject. His salary as chaplain at the penitentiary was his only means of support, and this was his only difficulty. On my next visit I received an invitation to preach in the Methodist church, which was gladly accepted. The subject was, "An Explanation of the Controverted Points of Doctrine between Catholics and their Fellow-citizens of other Denominations."

The venerable Father O'Neill accompanied me on a subsequent occasion, and, by invitation, occupied the same pulpit. I read the Universal Prayer, and he delivered an admirable discourse on "Revelation in General." He spoke fully two hours, and this was the only fault of his discourse. I also preached some time after at the Courthouse at Eatonton to a large and attentive audience. I was favored with the honor of being the first who announced our faith in these places.

This is a plain statement of the origin of Catholicity at the capital. My works were zealously continued by the Rev. Mr. Hassan, now of Sing Sing, N. Y., and Rev. Edward Quigley. The number of the faithful increased. We obtained the right to erect a chapel for the convicts at the penitentiary, and accomplished much good for the salvation of souls here and elsewhere on this mission. The succeeding priests, both before and since the war, assiduously attended to this important station. It has grown to be a respectable congregation, with a resident pastor, the Rev. Thomas O'Hara.

Milledgeville was visited in 1847 by Bishop Reynolds, accompanied by Rev. J. F. O'Neill, Sr. The former complained to me of having encountered some difficulty in obtaining accommodations to preach. He baptized and confirmed Mrs. Louisa O'Brien on this occasion. During a long missionary life Milledgeville was the only place in which I encountered Irish Catholics who arrayed themselves against the establishment of the faith and opposed its introduction. There was no objection whatever on the part of the non-Catholics, who were fair specimens of the independence and manliness of the Georgian. But the Catholics speedily redeemed themselves, became active and zealous, and aided in the establishment of the Church.

On one of my visits I obtained from Col. Reding permission to visit an Irish Catholic woman confined in the State prison ostensibly on the charge of vagrancy or some petty offence, but for quite another cause not creditable to the liberality of our half-brothers, the Church of England Catholics. I knew this poor creature well in Savannah. She was thriftless and improvident, and the mother of three or four half-orphans. She lived on the charity of the priest. Previous to the advent of the Sisters, she and her children became objects of special interest to the deaconesses of St. John's P. E. Church. There were tears for their sufferings, food for their sustenance, raiment for their nakedness, and shelter for their heads. In a short time they were placed in an educational institution, and the widow was persuaded to recant and become a genteel matron in a respectable congregation, and trail her mourning weeds by the side of the most fashionable women in the city. All was fixed. A great day was that for Protestantism in Savannah. The reception of a convert from the Irish element of Father O'Neill's flock was announced, and curiosity was excited.

The church was crowded, the Protestant bishop presided,

the ceremony was performed with marked solemnity, and this respectable, well-dressed lady received Communion from the officiating minister. Whether excited by the presence of so many, stung by conscience, or the result of previous indulgence none can tell, but she did not retain the Communion, and expectorated the bread and wine very speedily in the front aisle and in the presence of the *élite* of the city. Suddenly inspired, with arms akimbo, she stood unmoved in their midst, surveyed the assembly with ineffable disdain, and, with a fluency of speech creditable to Cady Stanton, she bitterly reproached them for her perversion, her impiety, her apostasy. She implored that her children might be restored, and begged to be let go. She refuted their doctrines, and pointed to the scene in illustration of the truth of her assertions. The transaction flashed the conviction of imposture and deceit on many a mind; a blush of honest shame burned on many a face, and ignominious defeat was stamped on others. Spectators tittered and smiled in remote corners, and unfortunate Mrs. G—— was forced from the church amid a scene unequalled in the religious annals of the city. She shortly afterwards found herself in a cell in the penitentiary. I administered the blessed sacraments to her thirsty soul, but she was inconsolable for the loss of the children. Why will men, otherwise respectable, practise such deceits, unworthy of the Christian profession and more becoming the Bonzes of Asiatic superstition?

There resided in Marietta an aged man named Molony, a carpenter, who plied his art all over the country for a period of fifty years. He travelled a long distance to receive the sacraments and procure some blessed clay to be placed in his coffin after his death, as he did not expect to be buried in consecrated ground. He possessed a Donay Bible, and probably there never lived a man who knew it better by heart. If not forbidden by reverence, he could converse uninterruptedly in biblical phraseology. I have frequently met such men in the remote settlements who were a living refutation of error, a light to the ignorant, and who, like the Baptist, prepared the way for the coming of our Lord in the person of his minister.

Guarded in manners and circumspect in his intercourse with men, no minister in Central Georgia possessed more moral weight among the people than this octogenarian bachelor from the City of the Violated Treaty. A missionary was advertised to preach in the town, soliciting aid to distribute the Bible in benighted popish countries. Molony was pressed by the people to attend and defend his creed from the menaced assaults. After the usual and disgusting tirade, now grown stale, Preacher Molony, as the wits called him, arose and demanded to be heard in reply. He denied the truth of every statement, denounced the author as a malicious slanderer and an impostor, using a text in each instance, and thus proving the truth of his assertions by authority of Scripture. Georgia being intensely Methodist, this mode of argument was reputed absolutely divine and unanswerable. He continued: "You stated that while in Ireland you found that none prayed to God, but to the Virgin Mary. Irish is the language of the people. Do you understand that language?" "No," replied the itinerant, "my education is deficient in that respect." "Then how can you tell whether the people prayed to God or to his Mother when you are ignorant of their language? How do you stand in French? Of course you understand it: *Parlez vous Français?*" "No sir; I wish to be let alone." "Not until you retract and apologize to this respectable community for the insult offered to their intelligence, and to me for the calumnies uttered against my native country and my God." Molony had many friends, who boisterously sustained him, and the impostor was run out of town. The Georgians are more liberal-minded and republican than the Carolinians. In no community in the latter State would Molony have been so generously sustained. This good man must have died soon after. I never heard a word more about him. He was a hermit, and the defender of the faith for half a century in Central Georgia.

Father Graham was the founder of this mission and church, and also of those of Columbus. I met him in Charleston in the spring of 1842, when he arrived to assist at the Month's Mind for Bishop England. He was above the medium height, fair-haired; his flesh was flabby and his color tawny, like the back of a lion or the clay-banks of Georgia. His clothes flapped loosely on his person, and it was evident that the thirsty fevers of his allotted missionary country, proverbial for their fatality, had drunk up the vital spirits and marked him for an early grave. During the following summer the chills returned with increased severity. He was visited by Father Barry, who heard his confessions, and in three weeks after he was no more. His remains were interred under the old church, close by the altar, where they remained during thirty-five years, until the sale of the property, when they were exhumed and transferred to the cemetery at Savannah.

The following tribute is furnished by the Rev. C. J. Croghan, who was placed in the seminary under the auspices of this distinguished missionary.

V. Rev. James Graham was a native of the County Longford, Ireland, and received his classical education in the celebrated Edgeworth Seminary, of Edgeworthstown, near Longford, where his father was professor. From his earliest years he was thoroughly educated in English literature and belles-lettres, and went through with honor the curriculum of that famous institute. In 1836 or 1837 he was ordained priest in Charleston, S. C., by Bishop England, and immediately afterwards was sent as pastor to Columbus, Georgia, and the adjoining missions. He built the church which still remains there, and in 1840 Macon and nearly all Middle Georgia was assigned him as his missionary field. He purchased a wooden church, which had been used by the Presbyterians as a place of worship, and fitted it up as a Catholic church. It was there I first saw him, in the summer of 1841. I shall never forget his appearance. The gentleman was stamped on his person and actions. His preaching, of an high order, was marked with beauty of diction, and, while ornamented with the imagery of a chaste and refined imagination, was never devoid of close and convincing reasoning. He was thoroughly acquainted with the canons of the best society; for in Ireland he mingled in the most polished circles. Among the few and scattered Catholics of Georgia he found few who were capable of appreciating him. The cultivated and refined among non-Catholics who formed his acquaintance instantly recognized in him the gentleman and polished scholar. Independently of religion, these characteristics have their weight in every clime and country, and in the present instance Georgia was not an exception to the rule. His conversation, always interesting, was rendered most agreeable by the clearness and melody of his voice, and at all times marked not a pedant but a cultivated gentleman.

His mission in 1841 included nearly the whole of Middle Georgia, and his flock was composed chiefly of laboring men who were employed in building railroads and other lowly and irksome duties. We know from sad experience the amount of bodily fatigue he must have undergone. Then there were no comfortable railroad cars in which travellers could recline and at their ease measure space. Miles had to be travelled through interminable forests, under a burning sun or in the cold of winter, on horseback or in a miserable stage. Times and modes of travel have wonderfully changed since. His health gradually gave way, and, under the accumulated weight of bodily and social privations, he died in Macon in the fall of 1842, aged about thirty-four years. His body was interred in the old wooden church, and a few years ago was exhumed and transferred to Savannah, where it rests near those of his old friends, Fathers Whelan and O'Neill, there to await the resurrection. Only the recording angel can give a full account of his labors and works in cities and towns, in the woods, in railroad shanties, seeking and consoling the scattered members of his flock. His name is not forgotten. It is held in respect and benediction by all the old inhabitants, Catholics and Protestants, who had the pleasure and happiness of being acquainted with him.

In the summer of 1844 Very Rev. Thomas Murphy, V. F., was stationed on this mission for some time, together with Rev. P. J. Coffey. Rev. J. F. Kirby succeeded in 1846 for a brief period. The following worthy clergymen exercised the holy ministry in Macon, one after the other, in regular succession, for a period of twenty years, each performing his share of the allotted labor, and all contributing to the establishment of the faith : Rev. Thomas F. Shannahan, Rev. J. F. O'Neill, Jr., Rev. James Hasson ; Rev. James O'Neill, of Sligo, Ireland ; Rev. Edward Quigley, Rev. Louis Bazin, and other clergymen of the diocese. These good priests are mentioned in their connection with other missions. Pio Nono College, after its establishment by Dr. Gross, supplied the parish with learned priests from the staff of the professors. Rev. C. C. Gaboury was its president for some years.

The Right Rev. Dr. Gross now occupies that position, in addition to his many other administrative duties. The college, under his immediate care, has recovered from financial and other embarrassments, with a body of efficient teachers and a patronage of fifty students. It stands high as an educational institution.

The Sisters of Mercy also have an institution with a boarding-school attached in the city, and it is well patronized. The church on Sundays is filled with a large and devout congregation. Macon is at this time the centre of Catholicity in the diocese of Savannah, from which religion and education are diffused over the entire State, and where the Church will flourish and prosper while civilization lasts in the Empire State.

The Catholic Church, from the constant influx of immigration, has made gigantic strides in other localities, but nowhere is her progress more marked than in Macon, where a few years ago the priest was a pauper, a decent person was ashamed to be seen entering the house of God, and the profession of the faith entailed as its penalty a loss of caste in society. This is the severest martyrdom for young and sensitive persons. Among the Hindoos, in China, in Tibet, in far-distant Agra, and all over our Indian missions, this is the most formidable barrier that Satan has opposed to the conversion of the natives. Thirty years back and Catholicity in Macon was the synonym of ignorance, superstition, and vice. The history of the world, of our common Christianity and civilization, made no alteration in the settled opinions of that race of people. The universal conspiracy against truth had triumphed. They unfortunately lived the error, and it died with them. They bore it in their hearts to the grave—innocently in many instances, it is to be hoped.

But a brighter day has dawned. Our community bells not only toll the flight of time and announce our doctrines to an entire city, but they regulate their duties, control their habits, dictate their time for enjoyment, and summon to rest. The chaste, austere features of the Sisters preside in the class-rooms or glide through the streets on their rounds of charity. The Georgian as proudly reverences the mitre of Bishop Gross as the time-honored form of Stephens, of Toombs, and of Colquitt.

Thus the seed sown in sorrow is reaped in joy, and the laborer returns bearing in his bosom the full-eared sheaves of gladness.

Atlanta, now a large and crowded city, a few years ago had neither a local habitation nor a name. Until 1850 it was scarcely known. It was called into existence by the genius of commerce, Southern enterprise, and national progress. As the spear of the conqueror bade cities rise in the desert, American activity has peopled the continent with towns, villages, and cities which within a few years have grown to the importance of the oldest cities in the world, and rival many of them in commerce, education, and prosperity. They need but age to surpass them in excellence.

Towards the close of our civil war Atlanta was the theatre of several severe engagements. The gallant Confederacy made a stand at this point and fought her last decisive battle. The place acquired a historic name and a world-wide notoriety from the stubborn resistance offered by Generals Johnston, Pat. Cleburne, and Hood, with a gallant few against overwhelming numbers. The fall of General Polk, the reluctant retreat of Johnston, and the bravery of the Southern troops shed a halo of glory on the brow of the youthful city which will adorn her while her foundations last. The gate of the Confederacy, she resisted the tide of invasion like a promontory flinging back the turbulent waves of the sea. It was only when deserted and her barriers broken that an army passed through, bringing disaster on a defenceless country and an unresisting people. By an erring counsel, an army never defeated and flushed with victory was directed to retreat. The weapons of war perished, the sword of the conqueror was idly thrown away, and the Confederacy fell after many a well-fought field.

Atlanta in 1860 had a population of ten thousand inhabitants, and possesses fifty thousand at this date. It is a great railroad centre, the highway of commerce and travel between North and South. The surrounding country is of immense extent and unsurpassed for agricultural and mineral wealth. It is a market for Alabama, Central Georgia, North Carolina, and Tennessee. Kentucky, Mississippi, and Arkansas contribute to its prosperity and growth. Numerous railroads either converge or run like arteries from this great heart of trade and commerce. Many factories, foundries, and laboratories of art and machinery already render her the Leeds and Sheffield of the Southwest. The most skilful mechanics, artisans, and able-bodied laborers from the bankrupt cities of New England and her idle workshops find lucrative employment. Unemployed capital from the North finds ready and safe investment, daily increases its prosperity, gives strength to its efforts, and scatters round an air of wealth, contentment, and confidence. Now that the railroad has superseded the ship and the steamboat, it is destined to

CATHOLIC HOUSES CONVERTED INTO CHAPELS. 613

increase more and more yearly, until it becomes a new London for the Southern States.

It is appalling to look over the necrology of our dead bishops, priests, and religious in this diocese during the lapse of twenty-five years—only a moderate period for one administration. All died of yellow fever or other malaria in the doomed city at the mouth of the Savannah River. In former times there was a necessity for concentration which no longer exists.

The prudent consideration of our Provincial Councils may transfer the sees to the interior, unless our prelates wish to adorn the line of the American hierarchy with a number of bishops and their companions, martyrs. Resignations, absence and non-residence, would be released from the suspicion or unjust imputation of timidity or the fear of death. We hail at no distant day the first Bishop of Atlanta. If not a very aged man, his administration will be sufficiently long for the maturing of his plans, and he will wax old with the growth of religion around him.

Catholicity is coeval with the city. Before there stood a brick chimney on its site, and when but two or three shanties, hastily constructed by some Irish Catholics, marked the centre of the future metropolis, Rev. Thomas F. Shannahan, of Macon, offered up the first Mass in one of these. The house of every Irish Catholic is readily and easily converted into a chapel. The furniture is already provided; the crucifix, the Madonna, the beads, are conspicuous ornaments. A confessional chair, a bottle of holy-water, and several children kempt and dressed for Baptism, and two sponsors are waiting for the solemnity. If on a Sunday, and there had been ample notice, every Catholic from Rabun Gap to Dahlonega, the school-master from Murray and the pedlar from Chattanooga, would be gathered round waiting their turn for confession, and fasting. There is already a congregation formed, the Holy Sacrifice offered, confessions heard, Communion administered, a sermon preached, Baptism conferred, and a parish established.

Now, these pioneers of the faith know the precepts of the

Church as well as the ten commandments of God, and they make a collection for the support of the priest. The parting word is, "God bless your reverence; when will we see you again ? Is there any word of a bishop coming to this country?" God never forgets. Perhaps the infant just baptized is already marked in the decrees of heaven to be the first bishop of this place and to consecrate with holy oil the massive granite edifice erected on the spot, and flashing back the rays of heaven's light from the glittering arms of the golden cross.

It would be interesting to ascertain the fact; I am not certain, but I am strongly of the opinion that the first Mass was offered in the dwelling of Patrick Lynch by Rev. Thomas Francis Shannahan, the founder of this mission, who was born in County Kilkenny, Ireland, about the year 1818. He was only a child when he lost his father. The surviving parent, after having made provision for his tutelage, associated herself with a religious community, and after many years died a devout nun. On a visit made by Very Rev. Dr. Baker to his native country in 1837 the youthful aspirant to the honors and labors of the priesthood offered himself as a candidate for the diocese, and accompanied Dr. Baker on his return voyage. After having spent ten years in study and preparation for the duties of his calling, he was ordained by Bishop Reynolds in 1846. After spending some time on the city missions, he was appointed to Macon and Atlanta. He was the first priest stationed in this city, and at a time when it contained only a few scattered huts or shanties, occupied by laboring men, and but a mere hamlet.

With this as his headquarters, the young and inexperienced missionary was required to visit the entire country as far as East Tennessee. Poor, friendless, and homeless, without adequate means of support, his existence for a number of years was rather precarious, living from hand to mouth, and domiciled with the humblest class of his countrymen, in shanties and along railroad routes. He officiated for some time in Macon and on its missions, and domiciled in the family of W. B. Watts, a non-Catholic, on his return from his missionary rounds, sufficiently extensive for the zeal of the Apostle of Japan.

Notwithstanding his poverty and privations, he procured an extensive lot in Atlanta, and erected an imposing and substantial frame church, with a priest's house in the rear. He collected money for this purpose all over the State, in Charleston and wherever he could expect to obtain any pecuniary assistance. He paid all the debt, and the church was dedicated by Bishop Reynolds a short time afterwards.

In this way Father Shannahan inaugurated the church in Atlanta, and was, in fact, the founder of this mission, now loudly claiming to be admitted among the dioceses of the Province; a measure which the importance and position of this great inland centre of commerce and the increasing number of the faithful will reasonably urge on the consideration of the prelates.

After the creation of the see of Savannah Father Shannahan was recalled to the parent diocese. He visited his native land, and after his return was stationed at St. Mary's, as assistant to Dr. Baker. He officiated as pastor on Sullivan's Island, as assistant at the cathedral, and on various stations in and around the city for several years. His health being much impaired after about twenty years spent in the diocese, ten in the capacity of priest and the remainder as student, he retired for some time to the Trappist Monastery in Kentucky. He died in the city of Chicago in the fortieth year of his age.

During his college life his services in the choir were invaluable. He was skilled in music and an excellent singer; his rich, mellow voice was always prominent and leading in the choir, during the High Mass on Sundays, at the Tenebræ Office, and at all the solemn ceremonies of the cathedral.

He was a man of varied literary attainments, extensive reading, and was gentle and harmless, kind and compassionate. He was a fluent speaker. While at the altar and singing

High Mass perhaps he had few equals in America. Like many others, he died early. Looking to his good intentions, may God grant him the accumulated rewards of a longer life in the holy ministry!

Father Shannahan was succeeded by the Rev. Jeremiah Francis O'Neill, Jr. He was appointed by Bishop Reynolds, and served faithfully on this and the surrounding missions, with some brief intervals, until the year 1857, when he expired at the Hospital of St. Agnes, in Baltimore, of cancer of the throat, in the forty-second year of his age, of which he was eighteen years a priest.

The following tribute, extracted from one of the journals of the period, is from the pen of Father Croghan:

"It is with feelings of unfeigned sadness that we announce the death of Rev. Jeremiah F. O'Neill, Jr., nephew of the venerable Father O'Neill, of Savannah. This amiable and accomplished priest breathed his last in Baltimore on the 6th inst., after having undergone a lingering and painful illness, which he bore with Christian fortitude and unmurmuring resignation.

"Last spring, when we grasped his manly hand, and beheld his amiable and beautiful countenance beaming with joy on meeting the friends of his youth, we little thought that the sad duty of recording his death would devolve on us. He had left Atlanta, where he was in charge of a congregation, to visit his uncle, who was then in this city. He complained of a sore throat, and, after a few days, had recourse to medical advisers. Lapse of time seemed but to aggravate his ailment, which was pronounced a cancer of the tongue. After consulting the most experienced medical practitioners and surgeons of Charleston and Savannah, accompanied by his venerable relation, he was placed under the treatment of the most eminent surgeons of Baltimore. A friend writing from there some time since said: 'With certain death staring him in the face, still he is quite patient and uncomplaining, apparently cheerful and happy, and not a murmur ever escapes his lips.'

"The close of his life was in harmony with the past. For the last four or five months he was in St. Agnes's Hospital, Baltimore, where he was tenderly cared for by the Sisters of Charity, and watched over with more than paternal solicitude by that good uncle, whose name shall ever be blended with the name of religion by the Catholics of the Carolinas and Georgia. Strengthened and consoled by the holy sacraments, and by the devout prayers of the faithful and humble servants of God who surrounded his dying couch, he on the 6th inst. gave up his pure soul to him whose distinguished minister he was on earth. His body reached this city on Wednesday, and was escorted by Bishop Persico and the Catholic clergy of the city from the Northeastern to the South Carolina Depot. His brother accompanied it on its way to Locust Grove, where it is to be interred near the remains of his parents.

"Shortly after the birth of Father O'Neill, which occurred in Canada in 1825, his parents settled in Locust Grove, Ga., then a Catholic settlement. Reared by a pious mother with the utmost care, and brought up with sentiments of love and reverence for God and his holy Church, he manifested at an early age an eager desire for the priesthood. His longings were not thwarted. At the age of fifteen years he was received by Bishop England, and placed among the number of young levites who, in days past, used to surround the altar of St. Finbar's, in Broad Street. There he continued and prosecuted his studies, classical, philosophical, and theological, with the exception of a short time passed in Bishop Whelan's seminary near Richmond. In the spring of 1850 he was raised to the dignity of priesthood by the late Bishop Reynolds. Atlanta was then assigned him as the future field of his labors, and for the last eighteen years of his life faithfully and cheerfully did he labor there, in Macon, in Savannah, and in all the out-missions of Georgia. To the truth of this many, very many can testify, to whose sad hearts and troubled consciences he gave peace and tranquillity. During the late war he was unceasing in his attentions to the poor and suffering soldiers. The wearers of blue jackets as well as those of the gray were the objects of his tenderness and solicitude. Many a weary night and cheerless day did he spend in traversing his vast missions, in camps, in hospitals, and in prisons. Would that we could give our readers but even a faint outline of the labors, privations, and the many acts of heroic charity of this amiable and faithful servant of God !

"'Father Jerry,' as he was fondly and familiarly called, was more than ordinarily gifted, and most highly accomplished. To gentleness and amiability of character he united manliness and firmness. Next to his religion his heart was given to literary and its cognate studies. When not engaged in sacred duties he was ever found in his study, poring over the literary treasures of antiquity or the splendid productions of modern European authors. Besides being an excellent classical scholar, he had a good knowledge of Hebrew and could converse in most of the modern European languages. And to those who were present at the consecration of the cathedral and of Bishop Lynch his musical talents must be evident; they cannot but remember the full, musical, and sonorous tones of his voice.' His theological knowledge was extensive and accurate, and his style of preaching in harmony with his refined taste and varied attainments.

"Truly in his case may we exclaim, 'In the midst of life we are in death.' He has been cut down in the meridian of life, with a bright future before him.

"Thus has the diocese of Savannah lost one of her most useful missionaries, and the priests of Georgia a beloved and cherished brother, one who was the ornament of their order. Long will his name be mentioned and remembered by them, as well as by the priests of the diocese of Charleston who were his fellow-students and the companions of his youth.

"May he rest in peace!"

The Right Rev. James Whelan, D.D., O.P., visited Atlanta in 1862, and preached an eloquent sermon in the Church of the Immaculate Conception. The eastern section of his diocese was enjoying the ministerial services of young Father O'Neill, and he cherished him as one of his own priests.

The fewness of clergymen in the diocese of Nashville rendered the attendance on the sick and dying of both armies in the camp and on the battle-field an onerous obligation on the priests. During Dr. Whelan's administration Tennessee was the scene of conflict between the Western armies.

The battles of Chickamauga and Missionary Ridge, under General Bragg on one side and General Rosecrans on the other, were among the most severe contests of the four years' struggle, and actually decided the fate of the Confederacy. The latter officer is a brother of the late illustrious Bishop Rosecrans, of Columbus. Archbishop Purcell, of Cincinnati, was ministering in the Federal Army part of the time, and the Bishop of Nashville toiling with assiduity among the broken ranks of the Southern troops, disheartened, bleeding, and suffering for want of medical care and common army supplies. Bishop Whelan was dear to all that bleeding host; the recollection of his charity and labors is treasured as a sweet remembrance in every heart that escaped the missiles of death. After some time his health suffered from the accumulated burden of missionary duties, camp sickness, and other infirmities; overworked, he needed quiet and rest, and, after having administered the diocese for some years, he retired to his convent at Zanesville, Ohio.

Raised in monastic seclusion, contemplation, prayer and literary pursuits were the chief charm of his life. His "Catena Aurea" and other productions are ornaments to our religious literature. The bishop sustained the reputation of his illustrious order for learning and eloquence, and is worthy of mention with Father Tom Burke and the Very Rev. Stephen Byrne, the zealous founder of the

Dominican Priory in Newark, N. J. Though constantly engaged, together with the devoted clergymen of the youthful community, in giving missions over the North and reviving the decaying fervor of the faithful, Father Byrne composed a valuable treatise on "Irish Emigration," which will be for many years the hand-book of his countrymen, and, like another star of Bethlehem, guide the immigrant to happy homes, where they will meet at the threshhold the Divine Infant, his Mother, and St. Joseph. This volume supplies the greatest want of Catholic literature in our country; it will be a blessing to thousands, and will find its place by the side of the Catechism and prayer-book in the pocket of the emigrant.

Bishop Whelan was born in Dublin, Ireland, in 1823. After having made his studies in the Seminary of St. Joseph, at Troy, N. Y., he was ordained in 1850 by Archbishop Purcell. He was consecrated Bishop of Mariopolis *in partibus*, in May, 1859, and succeeded to the see of Nashville, Tenn., February 1, 1860. He held that position until 1863, when he resigned and returned to his convent. He died suddenly February 20, 1878. His death was lamented by all who knew him.

Right Rev. P. A. Feehan, D.D., a native of County Tipperary, Ireland, succeeded November 1, 1865. He is eminent in our hierarchy for missionary zeal, learning, and all apostolic virtues.

The Rev. Edward Quigley exercised the functions of the holy ministry in Atlanta between the years 1850 and 1853, then Rev. James Hasson succeeded and officiated until about the year 1860, when he withdrew and accepted a position in the archdiocese of New York. Rev. M. Reilly, an able and efficient priest, was next appointed. He spent the prime and vigor of his life in advancing the cause of our holy religion in the city, seconded in his efforts by Father O'Neill, Jr., now in failing health. The lines were extended, new enterprises planned and accomplished. The Church sprung into a new life, assumed more imposing features, and grew into the proportions of an old, well-regulated, and influential parish. The church, the parsonage, the schools for boys and girls, and many religious societies are evidences of tireless zeal and judicious administration. The foundation of the Sisters' house, the introduction of the noble order, the establishment of the Academy of St. Joseph, with its boarding and day-school, are the crowning labors of his useful life.

The task was done, the Church of the Immaculate Conception arose as a queen among the parish churches of the diocese, and she now spreads the blue mantle of her holy influence over the wide area of commerce and industry, like the mild canopy of heaven, calmly resting a summer's evening over the green valleys, golden mountains, and silver cataracts of that famed region, lapped between North Carolina, Tennessee, Alabama, and Central Georgia. Like the throne of his Holiness Leo XIII. on the seven hills, the Catholic Church with her hierarchy, her institutions, and children gives Atlanta all her glory. Break down her altar, and Atlanta will fare no better than Tyre and Sidon, or the cities of old, whose God was gold and their brazen idol Mammon. Their citizens were nobles and their merchants the princes of the earth. In their prosperity they forsook God, and the noise of their handicraft and the din of busy commerce died away; their glory departed, and not a stone remains to mark the site of the world-wide, renowned idolatry. Fathers F. J. Rebman and W. Quinlan are at this time the priests of Atlanta.

In the number of clergymen, institutions, Catholics, and general prosperity Georgia exceeds both the Carolinas. The causes of the superiority are evident to one acquainted with the relative situation and condition of the three sister States. It will be readily conceded that immigration is the foundation, the building up, and the cause of the progress of Catholicity in our country. The agricultural resources, geographical position, and political condition of Georgia offer greater inducements for foreign immigration. The superior enterprise and energy of the citizens have utilized the water-power of the State, and, instead of passing idly along, it turns the wheel for many a factory. Augusta, Columbus, and several other centres are called second Lowells. The number of her railroads in fine running condition, numerous workshops, foundries, factories for all manner of goods and wares, the State works, etc., all employ a great number of operatives, who are chiefly immigrants and Catholics. A vacancy is readily filled, a sufficient number of hands supplied, who find remuneration for their labor, and abundance of cheap and substantial food, comfortable homes, and a healthy country to live in. The streams flow on without interruption. The State is free from foreign rule, the government humane and encouraging. The immigrant finds a new and better home. He meets a priest and a church everywhere, a school for his children, where they may be taught human science without losing the faith. He makes his home in a prosperous country, under a safe government, and under the shadow of God's altar. He soon becomes a respectable citizen of the State, an important member of society, and a stationary member of the Church, with a growing family of Catholic children. The twenty-five thousand Catholics assigned to the diocese of Savannah is not an exaggeration; she will soon possess double that number.

Some of these inducements are offered to the immigrant in the Carolinas, in a moderate degree, while others have been absolutely denied him. While all had their share in the disasters of the late civil war, South Carolina suffered more than any of her sister States. Secession being inaugurated among us, national dislike and even peculiar animosity was entertained against the offending State, and she was doomed to pay the bitter penalty. After Sherman's army crossed the Savannah River South Carolina was devastated by fire and sword, her fields were wasted, the implements of industry destroyed, the cattle and laboring stock slaughtered, private residences burnt. Towns, villages, and cities were reduced to a heap of smoking ruins. The religious institutions were given to the flames, their inmates cast out at night into the blazing streets; colleges, churches, libraries, all ruthlessly destroyed, and the inhabitants hunted away after having lost all their worldly goods. When General Sherman crossed the Catawba he left behind him one wild waste of smoking ruins, famine, desolation, sickness, and death. It is related that he made an excuse by asserting that the North expected him to do so. If so, well has he met the expectation, and faithfully did he inflict the revenge. He has suffered for the execution in the calmer judgment of his countrymen.

Next came the second era, if possible more disastrous than the former, because meaner, longer, and more rapacious. Whoever reads the published letters of Ex-Governor Moses will be astonished that the state-legalized plunder, public and private, which he details could exist in any civilized country in the nineteenth century. An army of greedy, impoverished adventurers, swindling mountebanks, and all the scum of Northern cities, called by the common name of "carpet-baggers," overrun the State like a swarm of locusts, filled all the offices of trust and emolument, and, by utilizing the negro vote, robbed the country of every dollar, sold the lands for bogus taxes, stole the railroads, paralyzed commerce, banished industry, obstructed education. They employed hirelings to provoke resistance, which was called Ku-kluxism, and made it a subterfuge to assassinate the citizens, condemn them to Northern prisons, rob the people of their last penny, and perpetuate their fiendish system. Like Ireland under Cromwell was Carolina under the carpet-bag government. A Carolinian had no home, and the people were compelled to flee from their native soil in thousands. Candidates for the penitentiary were elevated to the high places of the land; iniquity filled the seats of justice, and plantation negroes made laws for the descendants of Sumter, Hampton, and McGrath.

The conspirators deceived the Northern people by false representations, and the Government upheld the iniquitous rule at the point of the bayonet.

Bishop Lynch and other gentlemen addressed the citizens of the United States, appealing against the misrepresentations of the people and the attack made on their liberties. It produced the desired effect; the sober common-sense of the people of America was on the side of justice and truth; the crushed citizens of South Carolina, under the lead of the gallant General Hampton, recovered their long-lost rights; Mr. Tilden was chosen President, and the country saved for the present. Who would make his home in the diocese of Charleston during so hopeless a condition of affairs? Society was upturned from its foundations; the natives were thrown as outcasts on the world, and wandered in search of a home to distant Brazil; the bloody shirt of Morton, like a beacon light streaming from the ocean rock, warned the world that the approach was danger and the contact death.

True, the same obstacle prevailed in other States, but not to the same extent. If States' rights be a political heresy and secession a rebellion, then was South Carolina the front and face of the offending, and dearly she paid for it. It will take some time before she recovers from the sad effects of eighteen years of persecution and suffering.

Georgia, like a young giant, by a strong effort, burst asunder the hateful bonds, and was on her feet soon after the cessation of hostilities; while her sister, like unhappy Erin, the Niobe of nations, pined beneath them for years, and now only is free. During this long period of disaster and disorganization the Catholic Church was all that remained of order, system, and life in the distracted and bleeding country. She comforted and consoled; she sang her songs, like Sion in days of old by the waters of harsh Babylon; took to her bosom the torn limbs of society, breathed hope into its face, and bade it live.

The eloquent author of the "Lives of Deceased Bishops" and the talented writer of the "Popular History of Catholicity in the United States" both justly affirm that the success of Bishop England is one of the noblest triumphs of Catholicity in the Republic. I add, the establishment and preservation of Catholicity in the Carolinas and Georgia is among the greatest triumphs of the Church in America. I fear no contradiction from the impartial reader who has perused what has been already written, or weighs closely the following considerations. An empty compliment can never be the motto of a banner or an epitaph for the early dead in battle slain; it may gratify vanity, but cannot be adopted as the *labarum* of a diocese. Like the survivors of an army on the blood-stained battle-field, let us pause and count our losses and our gains:

DIOCESE OF CHARLESTON.—*Recapitulation.*—Churches, 12; priests, 14; academies, 3; asylums, 2. Catholic population, 10,000.

DIOCESE OF SAVANNAH.—*Recapitulation.*—Churches, 17; priests, 24; churches building, 8; clerical students, 12; chapels and stations, 35; priests ordained since last report, 5; male religious institutions, 3; female religious institutions, 7; female academies, 6; orphan asylums, 3; number of orphans, 130; benevolent and charitable institutions, 4. Catholic population, about 25,000.

VICARIATE OF NORTH CAROLINA.—*Recapitulation.*—Priests on the missions, 7; parochial schools, 4; churches and chapels, 13; stations, 21; female academy, 1; clerical students, 4; female religious institution, 1. Catholic population, 1,700.

The returns are not perfect, and I make supplements in some instances which are approximations.

The summary gives a total: 1. Three bishops (vicariate of North Carolina now vacant). 2. Churches, chapels, and stations, 106. 3. Priests, 45. 4. Clerical students, 20. 5. Religious institutions, male and female, 16. 6. Benevolent and charitable institutions, 4. 7. Literary institutions, 2. 8. College, 1. 9. Asylums, 5. 10. Academies, 10. 11. Several temperance, rosary, and altar societies, etc., etc. 12. Catholic population, about 37,000.

Scattered over an area of 127,000 square miles, and among a non-Catholic population of 3,000,000, verily they are the grain of mustard-seed. Viewed by the side of the reputed 8,000,000 Catholics in the United States, they dwindle into small proportions.

When considered in relation to the difficulties the Church encountered, the obstacles in her way, and the inadequate means of accomplishing her work, the result will convince us of the truth of the assertion. When Bishop England landed in Charleston about sixty years ago there were not then as many Catholics in the three States as there at present in North Carolina; only one or two insignificant congregations, distracted by trusteeism, and one or two priests. Some writers claim a Celtic element in the population of the United States of 18,000,000. According to the authority of Bishop England and others, the number of baptized Catholics that fell away from the faith is enormous, and is asserted to equal the number of the faithful now claimed for the Church in our country. The fault was not hers. Accustomed to defection, she almost converted the world thrice over.

In colonial times hundreds of thousands landed on our shores; their descendants perished under the penal laws that banished their fathers from their native country. The profession of Catholicity was a disgrace, and they became like their neighbors. Hatred against the Church and opposition to her progress were left as a sad legacy by the English Government to the United States after the Declaration of Independence. This evil spirit remains to the present time, more or less modified by recent events. We are not allowed to convert and civilize the Indian because of this satanic hatred to the faith of our beloved Lord. Thousands were lost from other causes. The many Catholic names heard in the ranks of heresy and among the enemies of the Church, like the Indian nomenclature of our rivers, remind us of parted glories, and tell many a tale of ruin. In addition to the above, the chief reasons for the apostasy are in the fewness of the priests, who were incapable of visiting the Catholics scattered in the interior of the country, or meet the spiritual wants of the vast tide of immigration; the want of churches and schools, unworthy priests who gave scandal and created schism, trusteeism, mixed marriages, secret societies, kidnapping children, want of thoroughness in teaching the faith in churches and in our schools, and more recently the charge that "the churches are not free to the poor."* The two last are the only reproaches ever made against the Church in the United States, and are entirely unchristian if true. Now, as in the days of St. Lawrence, the poor are the ornament and the treasures of God's Church, and more especially when the edifice has been built by their hard-earned wages. These are the causes which have shorn the Church of half her numbers in the more favored sections.

They must have produced the same results in the South, but they did not all exist. For the last fifty years there was not a destitute Catholic in the wildest region who was not repeatedly visited by a priest, and perhaps by a bishop, in a stage, on horseback, or on foot. Of the estimated fifteen hundred Catholics comprising the diocese of Charleston in 1821, and their descendants, I have yet to learn that one died without the sacraments by fault of the clergy ; that an infant was unbaptized or a marriage unblessed. Not only the priests but the bishops knew the faithful personally and called them by name ; they domiciled in the huts of the indigent and rested on a litter scattered over the floor. The churches were numerous and the priests unemployed. Instead of repelling a poor Irish Catholic from the door he was praised for his fidelity, and we were rejoiced even when a negro assisted at the service.

The clergymen became school-teachers, even when the attendance was scarcely a half-dozen. Churches, schools, academies were established where needed, or wherever there was a prospect of patronage. In the ranks of the clergy was never found a money-grabber. There never lived since the early ages a more detached body of men. They were homeless, penniless ; often hungry and sick, and naked and unfriended. They were despised by the world, spurned from decent company as heartless

* Murray's "History."

wretches who duped a few ignorant Irish for the purpose of fleecing the last dollar from them, obtained by ditching or fraudulently by illicit traffic with the slaves of respectable people. On the missions it was with this class the priest generally put up, for want of any other accommodation.

The laity imbibed the spirit and teaching of such men, illustrating in their lives and actions all they taught by their words. There were nowhere a more united body; one not only in faith but in mind and sentiment, they were drawn still closer by common suffering, privation, and social exclusion. There were few losses; the laity preserved and imparted their spirit to their children; the priests were true to their last breath. Only one unhappy man of Irish birth abandoned the faith during nearly sixty years, out of more than a hundred clergymen. The children were raised Catholics, strangers received the grace of conversion, and Catholicity grew apace, slowly but surely. The faithful approached the sacraments; went regularly to Mass; more priests were ordained, and religious associations were formed to attend to the wants of the faithful; institutions arose gradually amid poverty and suffering and took deep root in the soil.

Slavery opposed an impassable barrier to immigration, the main cause of the growth and progress of the Church in the free States. An immigrant ship dared not touch our shores; her cargo was as odious and abominable to all decent people as if freighted with lazars from a West India poor hospital, and sick with black vomit. They were ignominiously driven back whence they came from. They acquiesced, enriched the Church and the soil elsewhere, and sent their children back with arms in their hands to avenge the unconstitutional act. The chief difficulty in the free States was to provide churches for their constantly growing numbers and save their offspring. In the South this luxury was never tasted; the labor was different: it was to obtain a Catholic at all. On the one side the labor was to preserve what was already possessed, on the other to create first and then save after.

Some few persons of intelligence and social position had the courage to brave public opinion and profess the faith; but if they encouraged the humble Catholic by their example, their influence in society was limited by universal condemnation; they were branded as crazy people or fools, and would not be elected to fill the most paltry offices of the State.

There was great truth in the battle-cry of the South, that slavery as it existed was the safeguard of Protestantism, the only barrier against Popery. It not only constituted the external breastwork, but it was essentially opposed to Catholicity. The condition of the slaves was, perhaps, morally worse than that of the blacks in the jungles of Africa. Slavery was reeking with all possible crimes except cannibalism. The pseudo Christianity that prevailed among them encouraged crime because of the facility of pardon held forth, and was an incentive of passion and blinded conscience against the first dictates of the natural law. Scarcely any except those owned by Catholics joined the Church. In the universal Mormonism, the convert would pause to select the one out of the plantation seraglio he would now choose to be the companion of his life. But the marriage was dissolved at the whim of an overseer, and the wife of another man substituted for the divorced. Frequently it was with a trembling hand that the priest asked an absolution, and the life of the owner was the sole barrier against the relapse into fetichism.

At the commencement of the civil war many Catholics by industry had acquired some property in slaves. This circumstance was the only redeeming feature of the institution. There was a chapel, a priest, and the Sunday-school; the children were baptized, and all taught the catechism. Catholics were acquiring influence and a better standing in society. The Emancipation Act destroyed this growth, reduced the masters to the former condition of the slaves, and made the slaves legislators and unbelievers. In this way the removal of the leading obstacles to Catholicity became, in the course of time, a detriment, and temporarily retarded its progress. The labor of years was lost for many.

It was not only at home that the Catholic body was depreciated, but abroad, and among their own brethren they were strongly suspected of having lost their moral integrity by the contagion of the institution. Respectable priests declined to accept the mitre worn by the most distinguished bishop in America. Prelates came with deep prejudices, firmly convinced that a reformation was necessary, beginning at the sanctuary, and, with fan in hand, that they must remove the chaff from the wheat all over the threshing-floor of the vast diocese. At present a respectable clergyman would not transfer his labors to some Southern republics where the salutary legislation of the Church is obstructed and her action paralyzed by the infidels and Freemasons, who have seized on the reins of government under the insulted name of Catholics. And such was the reputation of the Catholics of the Cotton States, despite the wisdom and learning of an England, the self-sacrifice of a Gartland, the eminent sanctity of a Barry, and many others no less conspicuous for eloquence, virtue, and apostolic zeal.

Whoever looks back over the long and dreary period of sixty years, and ponders over these and many other obstacles against the establishment and growth of Catholicity in the Carolinas and Georgia, the constant struggle, the ceaseless warfare, the unconsolable labor, the unmitigated poverty, the universal shame and contempt in the terrible disasters of the long and bloody struggle, will be convinced of the truth of the assertion. During the civil war the currency in both sections was plentiful as leaves in Vallombrosa. The fate of war gave value to the greenbacks and ruined the Confederate money; it became utterly worthless. All its millions could not procure a pair of oilstocks to replace those sacrilegiously robbed from the person of the priest in Columbia. Money is a powerful instrument of good. It flowed abundantly in the free States and was lavishly bestowed for ecclesiastical purposes. The Church in the

South was a Lazarus, and its priests and bishops begged the crumbs that fell from the rich man's table.

Slavery and subsequent emancipation, the want of Catholic immigration, the civil war, the subsequent misrule, the universal loss of property, the worthlessness of the currency, the destruction of churches, colleges, and institutions, would reduce the numbers of the faithful in higher regions; they obstructed the faith in the South, and vindicate all that has been claimed for its establishment and preservation.

Many of the laborers who bore the toil and the heats of the day are gone to their reward. On the Southern shores, in Wilmington, Charleston, and Savannah, in the towns and cities and hamlets of the interior, are many graves with crosses. Bishops and missionary priests and religious and thousands of the faithful slumber well beneath the sod. They fought the good fight, they planted and preserved the faith. They form that portion of the Church now before the face of God in heaven. They are still our brethren, and aid us by their prayers. Their work is taken up by worthy successors and will be continued to the end. With hands unshackled, and the shame wiped from the brow of the country by the harsh hand of war, the Church of the Carolinas and Georgia, clad in the habiliments of the confessor and wearing the martyr's robe, enriched by the blood of Juarez and Cancer and Martinez, is now beautiful as the sun rising and like an army in battle array goes forth to conquer souls for heaven, and fight the battles of the Lord against sin, error, and the world. Her fame is bright, her honors fair, and her triumphs greater than those of older establishments.

"*I am black, but beautiful . . . as the tents of Cedar, as the curtains of Solomon. Do not consider me that I am brown, because the sun hath altered my color: the sons of my mother have fought against me.*"

INDEX.

AARON'S BREASTPLATE, 62.
Abbeville, 240, 329.
Academies, Catholic, in the United States, 36.
Adams, Governor James H., 246.
  Mr. Patrick, of Columbus, 573.
Adusto, 178.
"Advertiser," the Cork, 573.
Africa, 95, 179.
  the Apostles in, 140, 146.
Affair, an unfortunate, 252 to 254.
Agenor, 180.
Agnes, Sister, of Valle Crucis, 298.
Agra, Vicar-Apostolic of, 237, 550.
Aiken, S. C., 183, 287.
Aimar, Mrs., 175.
Almars, the, 213.
— Aker, Captain, of Brunswick, 509.
Alabama, 234.
  the, 363.
  the Ursulines in, 278.
Albany, Ga., 120, 577.
— Aldrich, Col., 183.
Alexandria, the school of philosophy at, 43.
Alemany, Archbishop, 420.
Alfred, the sceptre of, 27.
Ali, Hyder, 334.
Allen, Colonel, of Barnwell, 344.
Alt, Brother Alteman, 431.
Almanac, the Catholic, 163.
Aloysius, Sister, 66.
Alphonsus, Sister, 66.
America, discovery of, 23.
  condition of the aborigines, 24.
  Pius IX. and, 22.
  pre-Columbian history of, 23.
  Catholic population in, 21.
  planting the cross in, 24.
  apostles of, 25.
  Catholic republic in, 23.
  conduct of Puritans in, 26.
  female colleges in, 67, 68.
American Church, Bishop England the Bossuet of, 49.
  Revolution, cause of the, 27.
  "   success of due to Catholics, 28.
Amour, d', Mrs., of Macon, Ga., 601.
Anchorite, a happy, 455.
Andrew, St., the apostle, 182.
Andrews, Rev. Dr., of Columbus, 574.

Anderson, 240, 322, 340, 391.
Andersonville, 531.
Angela, Mother, of the Ursulines, 277.
Anthony, St., 34.
Antonio, San, first bishop of, 590.
Antioch, school of philosophy at, 43.
Antonio, Sister Mary, 190, 266.
  Edmund, 199.
Apostles, successors of the, 103.
Appalachicola, town of, 580, 581.
  the mission at, 581, 582.
Archbishops, number of, in United States, 36.
Arden, Miss, 174.
Ardrum, Ireland, 189.
Arkansas, Bishop Byrne in, 121.
  State of, 180.
Army, the Federal, 242.
  the Confederate, 241, 246.
  Sherman's, 159, 199, 241, 301, 322, 334, 428.
Ashapoo Valley, the, 178.
Asheville, 240, 428, 442, 443, 444, 453, 458.
  Church of St. Lawrence, 454.
Assassination, attempted, of Rev. J. J. O'Connell, 491.
Asylums, Catholic, in United States, 36.
Athens, school of philosophy at, 43.
Atlanta, 611.
  defence of, 612.
  population of, 1860, 612.
  the first Mass in, 613.
  Rev. Thos. Shannon in, 613.
  spread of Catholicity in, 613, 614.
  Bishop Whelan visits, 619.
Atonement, Mount of, 236.
Augustine, St., 23, 33, 96.
  city of, 108, 584.
  church of, 108, 127.
  bishop of, 153, 403.
  the cholera in, 531.
  the Jesuits in, 584.
  the Dominicans in, 584.
  the Franciscans in, 584.
  Mother, of the Ursulines, 277.
Augusta, 536, 554, 555.
  Father Barry's school in, 139.
  Sisters of Our Lady of Mercy in, 533.
  the Jesuit mission at, 551.
  the Barry Hospital in, 551.
  Sisters of Mercy, convent of, in, 556.
  Church of St. Patrick, 556, 561.

INDEX.

Augusta, Rev. Mr. Keating, of, 556.
   Rev. S. F. O'Gallagher in, 556.
   Church of the Sacred Heart, 567.
   progress of Catholicity in, 567.
   the Jesuit community in, 567.
Austria, the Emperor of, 235.
Austriaco, Father, of Florida, 562.
Authority, civil, separate from religious, 85.
Averysborough, 159.

Babylon, the plains of, 179.
Bachman, Dr., 58.
   Bishop England's letter to, 78.
Bacon, Rt. Rev. Dr., 186.
Bahamas, the, 153.
Baird, Brother Ulric, 481.
Baily, Judge, of Mount Mitchell, 450.
Baker, Very Rev. R. S., birth, early life, education, ordination, and ministry of, 84, 109, 115, 150, 153, 156, 173, 301, 395, 406, 427.
   Dr., 94, 96, 98, 99, 100, 103, 104, 108, 145, 155, 159, 193, 232, 310.
   Alpheus, of Lumpkin, S. C., 570.
Bakers, the, 322.
Baltimore, 64, 83.
   Lord, in Maryland, 29.
   Provincial Councils of, 74, 127, 517, 238, 533.
   St. Mary's College, 105.
Baptist, St. John the, 85, 124.
   Seminary of, 62, 96, 109, 110, 154, 311.
   Mother Mary, 278.
Baptists, the, 385, 386, 387.
Bartholomew's, St., day, 122.
Bardstown, seminary of, 105.
Barnabo, Cardinal, 158.
Barnwell, 177, 182, 183, 233.
Barron, Rt. Rev. Edward, 126, 509, 522, 523, 524.
   Rev. Bernardine, O.S.F., death of, 554.
Barry, Miss Teresa, 64.
   Father, education and labors of, 83, 113, 146, 182, 231, 241, 357, 454, 476.
   Rt. Rev. John, birth, education, ordination, consecration, and missionary work of, 124, 191, 406, 529 to 535.
   Mother Mary Teresa, 205.
Basket, Colonel John, 200, 201, 202, 226.
Bavaria, the Benedictine monasteries of, 482.
Bayley, Archbishop, 31, 174.
Beale, Harriet, 172, 173.
Beaufort, the mission of, 159, 170, 171, 176, 182, 183, 212, 239.
   district, the, 325.
Beauregard, General, 428.
Becker, Rt. Rev. Dr., 252, 396.
Bedini, Rt. Rev. Dr., 266.
Beecher mob, the, 218.
Belk, Thomas M., 297.
Belton, 333.
Bellinger, the Misses, 181.

Bellinger, Dr. John, 84, 181, 514.
   Edmund, 177, 182, 206, 245, 247.
Benedict, St., 34, 87.
Benedictines, the, 421, 455, 467, 479, 482.
Benton, Captain, 332.
Bermingham, Father, 431.
Berne, New, 401, 405.
   Bishop England at, 406.
   First Mass at, 407.
   Contributors to the church at, 407.
Bergier, Rev. Gabriel, 552.
Bertazzi, Rev. J., of Columbus, 593.
Beytagh, Rev. Stephen, death of, 554.
Bible, Protestant, reading from, 335.
Bieman, Captain, 338.
Birmingham, Very Rev. Dr., birth, early life, ordination, and work in the ministry of, 126, 181, 146, 198, 310, 331, 570.
   Rev. John, ordination and missionary labors of, 145, 201, 231, 241, 296, 302.
Bismarck, Prince, 141.
Bishop, narrow escape of a, 571.
"Bishops, Lives of Deceased," Clarke's, 101.
Blackrock, Ireland, Ursuline convent at, 68.
Blackville, 183.
Blanc, Rt. Rev. Dr., 110, 234.
Blair, General, 272.
Blake, Rev. Mr., of Milledgeville, 602, 603.
Bluff, Mars, S. C., 129.
Bogan, Catharine, 217.
Bogen, Mrs. Johanna, 305.
   family, the, 306, 307.
Boland, George, 324.
Bolter, Mr., of Columbus, 573.
Bollen, C. J., 204.
Borgia, Madame, 83.
   Sister, 120, 277.
Borromeo, St. Charles, 149.
   Seminary of, 224.
Boston, the bishop of, 127, 221.
   Know-Nothing excitement in, 51.
Bowen, Rt. Rev. Dr., 89.
Boyer, President, 72.
Boyle, Father, second voyage of, 24.
Bradley, John W., 217, 218, 239, 297.
   family, the, 218.
Brady, Patrick, of Greenville, 372.
   family, the, Appalachicola, 562.
Bradshaw, Colonel, 416, 441.
Bragg, General, 309.
Brendan, St., 23, 39.
Brett, Miss, 170.
Bretts, the, 180.
Brisbane, General A. H., 119, 306, 577.
Brownson, 31.
Brothers, the Christian, 250.
Brown, Father, 193.
   Rev. Dr., 144.
   Rev. Robert, death of, 556.
   Rev. William Faulkner, of Augusta, 566.
Brownfield, John, 303.
Brownsville, Vicar-Apostolic of, 590.

INDEX.

Brooklyn, St. Michael's Parish, 182.
Bruno, St., 34.
Brûke, Father, 407.
Buckley, Rev. Cornelius, 138.
Budds, Captain, 171.
Burt, Dr., Jr., 233.
Burns family, the, of Covington, 602.
Burke, Rev. William, 108, 508.
  Father Tom, 354, 619.
  Judge, 179.
Butler, 252.
  Rev. T. W., S.J., 567.
Butterfield, Mr., of Charleston, 370.
Byrne, Rev. Andrew, 63, 97, 145, 406.
  Rt. Rev. Dr., 121, 161, 185, 186, 324, 432.
  Rev. Dominic, drowning of, 557.
  Very Rev. Stephen, O.P., 619, 620.
  "   "   work on "Irish Emigration," 620.

Cabot in New England, 25.
Cabarrus, 428.
Cable, Captain, of Greenville, 391.
Cadonal, 143.
Cagney, Mother Veronica, 264.
Cahills, the, of Gaston Co., N. C., 471.
Calhoun, John C., 58, 82, 336, 337.
Calvary, the sacrifice of, renewed, 24,
Calcutta, Vicar-General of, 144, 145.
Calvin, 122.
California, the Jesuits in, 323.
—— Caldwell, Colonel, 416.
  Hon. David, 439.
  Richard, 441.
  Howard Haine, 203, 204.
  Chancellor, 203.
Caldwells, the ancient home of the, 478, 479.
Calumny, a Know-Nothing, refuted, 574.
Callahans, the, of Flat Rock, 444.
Camden, 217, 240, 295, 296, 301.
Canada, 234, 324.
  Fenian raid on, 28.
Cancer, Louis, Father, 25, 584.
Canby, General, 177.
Canty, Jack, the hangman, 91.
Cantwells, the, 209.
Canterbury, St. Thomas of, 34.
Candlesticks, two living, 517.
Carey, Mrs., of Macon, 598, 599.
Carolinians, character of, 59.
Carolina, South, State of, 69, 82.
  missionary ground of, 325, 462.
  first unsectarian institution in, 69.
  Huguenots in, 129.
  Bishop England's work in, 33, 69.
  Catholics in, 82, 212.
Carolina, North, disabilities against Catholics in, 56.
  department of, 146.
  vicar-apostolic of, 149, 310, 396.
  vicariate register of, 1870, 499.
  "   "   recapitulation of, 625.

Carolina, North, missions in, 244.
  Catholics in, 396.
  Know-Nothingism in, 413.
  the English colony of, 585.
Caroduc Family, the, 183.
Carmel, Our Lady of, Church of, 322.
"Carolinian," the, 253.
Carney, Father, of Baltimore, 406.
Carpa, Father, O.S.F., and companions, murder of, 584, 585.
Carroll, Father, first bishop of United States, 30, 36, 142, 167.
  Charles, 326.
Carr, Rev. F. J., 111, 182, 285, 450.
  the brothers, 243.
Case, Mr. John, 100.
Cassidy, Brother Philip, 481.
Cathedrals, mediæval, splendors of, 62.
Catholics in the Revolution, 28.
  persecution of, 81, 82.
  in Washington's army, 28.
  in Maryland, 141.
  in Pennsylvania, 29.
  of New York, 29.
  at the close of the war, 30.
  forbidden to hold office under several State Constitutions, 45.
Catholic laity in United States, 34.
  journalism in United States, 58.
  a, law, 327.
  "Miscellany," the, 59.
Catholicity the foundation of all liberty, 30.
  and Protestantism in United States, 23.
  continent consecrated to, 24.
  destruction of, in the English colonies of America, 26.
  in the Carolinas and Georgia, 27, 629.
  British Government arrayed against, 27.
Catacombs, the, 127.
Catawba River, the, 431, 474.
Catechism, Bishop England's, 540.
Cauble, Captain, of Greenville, 372.
Cavalry, Wheeler's, 333.
Cavenagh, Brian, 305, 306.
Celtic element, the, in United States, 22.
Célinie, Mother, death of, 554.
Cemetery, St. Lawrence, 123.
Charlemagne, 27.
Charleston, diocese of, 37, 61, 87, 100, 106, 107, 138, 149, 393, 304.
  recapitulation, 625.
  population of, 37, 42.
  extent of, 37.
  non-Catholics in, 87.
  Rt. Rev. John England, first bishop of, 37.
  on the arrival of Bishop England, 42.
  character of the people, 43.
  eminence due to Bishop England, 58.
  orphan asylums, 64.
  coadjutor bishop of, 73.
  schools of, 88.
  St. Mary's Church, 87, 103, 104.

Charleston, condition of, at Bishop England's death.
  constitution of the diocese of, 89, 212.
  St. Joseph's Church, 157.
  Hibernian Society of, 142.
  second bishop of, 105.
  first priests of, 145.
  missions outside of, 114.
  first Mass celebrated in, 141.
  erection of the cathedral of, 116.
  theological seminary of, discontinued, 111.
  bombardment of, 125, 326.
  Sisters of Mercy in, 218.
  German church in, 243.
  Seminary of St. John the Baptist in, 431.
  yellow fever in, 431.
Châteaubriand, 143.
Charlotte, 116, 231, 240, 428, 437.
  St. Peter's Church in, 424, 425.
  contributors to the church in, 425.
Champys, the, of Orangeburg, 199, 294.
Charles, Sister Mary, 264.
Charge, a false, disproved, 287.
Chazals, the, 322.
Chatard, Rt. Rev. Dr., 323.
Chattahoochee River, the scenery on the, 561.
Chalon, Vicar-General, 580.
Charity, Sisters of, 34.
Cheraw, S. C., 124, 128, 129, 134, 135, 136.
Chester, 116, 319, 320, 321, 322.
Chicora, 178.
China, missionaries to, 34, 95.
Chicago, 252.
Chickamauga, the battle of, 219, 619.
Chicks, the, of Newberry, 367.
Cholet, the college of, 220.
Choice, Mr., of Greenville, 390.
Choiseul, de, the Count, 445.
Church, Catholic, right to the title, 24.
  the, converts the world three times, 23.
  loss of, in Europe, 24.
  in colonial days, 27.
  progress of, 30.
  of the United States, 31, 32, 77.
  preservation of in United States, 32, 33.
  of United States placed under the protection of the Blessed Virgin, 31.
  the American, 34, 72, 148.
  in United States, needs of, 452.
  orders of the, 34.
  in the nineteenth century, 35.
  a support to republican government, 35.
  in the Southern States, 35.
  hostility to, 22.
  in the United States, 77, 216, 250.
  colonial, the, status of, in the Southern States, 35.
  Irish, the, slavery of, 88, 89.
Cincinnati, archdiocese of, 69, 110, 170.
  cathedral of, 109.
Clancy, Rt. Rev. Wm., 73, 151, 193, 400.
Clare, St., 34.

Clavier, St. Peter, 45, 154.
Claffey, James, 216, 218, 256.
  family, the, 218.
Claffeys, the, of Columbus, 573.
Clarke, Dr. Caleb, 202, 293.
  Miss Emma, 207.
  Sister Ignatius, 264.
  Richard H., 209.
  William, 293.
  Rev. William A., 391.
Clara, Santa, Cal., the Jesuit College, 368.
Clay, 336.
Clergy, religious and secular, 163.
  a submissive, 519.
Cleary, Thomas, 245.
  Rev. Father, at New Berne, 405.
Climate, debilitating influence of, 46, 47.
Clingman, General, 458.
Clorivière, Rev. Mr., 143, 502, 556.
Coffee, Rev. P. J., 109, 188, 189.
Coglan, Hon. T. J., 304, 308.
Coleman, St., cathedral of, 39.
Colonial times, immigration in, 44.
  revival of the intolerance of, 45.
Columbus, 27, 71.
  city of, 384, 569.
  extent of the mission of, 570, 571, 572, 573.
  destruction of, 575.
  Bishop England at, 91.
Columbia, Sisters of Charity in, 112.
  Sister Borgia at, 120.
  cemetery in, 190, 216.
  city of, 190, 217, 240.
  and its missions, 230, 319.
  the Episcopal Church in, 222.
  the Mass said in the jail, 228.
  early pastors of, 230.
  Ursuline Nuns in, 238, 427.
  the sack of, 241.
  opposition to immigration in, 199.
  first Catholics of, 199, 200.
  unworthy Catholics in, 209.
  Academy of the Immaculate Conception, 263.
  destruction of, 268, 269, 270, 271, 272, 273, 274, 428.
  protection of life and women in, 273.
  destruction of the religious institutions in, 276.
Colthurst, Sir Nicholas, 189.
Colony, Catholic, a proposed, 455.
Colby, Mr., of Eufaula, 576.
Collenders, the, of York Co., N. C., 472.
College, St. Joseph's, Philadelphia, 106.
  South Carolina, 144, 221, 223.
  St. Mary's, 216, 220, 241 to 247, 281, 299, 428, 469.
  St. Mary's, Emmittsburg, Md., 299.
  the American, Rome, 299.
  Wooford Methodist, 326.
  the Pio Nono, Ga., 610.

INDEX. 637

Colleges, Catholic, in United States, 86.
Combahee River, the, 178.
Comerford Michael, 216, 807.
" Mrs., 205
Communists in the United States, 32.
Constitutions, State, intolerance of, 45.
Conspiracies, oath-bound, in United States, 82.
Converts, hostility aroused against, 68.
the Barnhardts and other, 489.
Convents, erection of, 67.
Convent, North Presentation, Ark., 188.
the Ursuline, Charleston, 110, 230.
Congaree River, the, 224.
Confederacy, cause of the fall of the, 251.
Conroy, Mgr., His Excellency, Bishop of Ardagh, 190, 823.
Conwell, Rt. Rev. Dr., 517.
Conception, the Immaculate, 95.
Conflagration, a disastrous, 575.
Coosahatchie River, the, 178.
Cooper, Rev. Mr., of Charleston, 556.
Corps, Father, 25.
Cork, 66, 68, 188.
Corkery, Father, 42, 230.
Corcoran, Rev. Dr., birth, early life, education, ordination, and labors on the mission, 111, 124, 147 to 150, 155, 159, 234, 243, 249, 345, 402, 405.
Col. Michael, U. S. V., capture of, 225, 226.
Rev. Dr. J. A., 457.
Council, the Vatican, 34, 148, 160, 237.
the National, 112, 147
the Plenary, 147, 150.
"Courier," Bishop England and the, 56.
the Wilmington, 810.
County, Baker, Ga., 120.
Dooly, Ga., 120.
Early, Ga., 120.
Beaufort, 326.
Oconee, 352.
Cousart, Miss Annie, 297.
Cox, Charles, 331.
Coxes, the, of Gaston Co., 471.
Crayons, the, 199, 230.
Crawfords, the, of Walhalla, 888.
Craft, Mr., and family, 324.
Crews, Mr. Joseph, and family, 328.
Cremation, 436.
Croghan, Rev. C. J., education, ordination, and labors of, 109, 155, 156, 157, 407, 599.
Rev. C. J., letter of announcing Father O'Neill's, J. F., death, 616, 617, 618.
Owen, of Macon, Ga., 599.
Mrs., née Griffin, 599.
Cross, Brother John, 267.
Cromwell, 184.
Cronin, Rev. T. J.
Mr., of Macon, 601.
Crucis, Valle, 69.
Cruise, the Misses, 830.

Cuba, Bishop Reynolds in, 115.
Cullen, Margaret, 205.
family, the, 205.
Cullinane, Rev. John, 164, 414.
Very Rev. Michael, 591.
Cunningham, Alexander and family, 326, 327.
Curtin, the Misses, 204.
Curry, Father, 184.
Currys, the, of Columbus, 573.
Cyprian, St., the martyr, 102, 165.

DALLAS, N. C., 472.
Danville, Ill., 160.
Darien, Isthmus of, Ojéda on, 25.
Datty, Miss Julia, 64.
Dauch family, the, of Walhalla, 338.
Day family, the, of Macon, 601.
Death, a glorious, 521.
Delany, Sister Angela, 68
Mary Joseph, 68.
" Angela, 68.
Bishop, 133, 277.
Dempsey, Lieutenant, 226.
Thomas C., of Macon, 599, 600.
Denman; Mr., 130.
Dent, Sheriff, of Columbia, 235, 237.
Depuy, Miss, 216.
Desribes, Father, S.J., 508.
Devlin, Daniel, of New York, 218.
Devil-worship, 24.
Dillons, the, of Savannah, 511.
District, the Colleton, 180, 401.
Ditch, Cavenagh's, 306.
Doby, Sister Aloysius, 264.
Dolan, Father, of Baltimore, 396.
Dominicans, the, 24.
Domingo, San, 64, 72, 141.
massacre at, refugees from, 555.
Dominic, St., feast of, celebrated in the mountains, 463.
Donoughmore, Ireland, 189.
Doud, Sister Mary Patrick, 264.
Doyle, Rev. A., 53, 405, 509.
Miss M., 206.
Rt. Rev. Dr., 78, 96.
Draude, Brother, 462.
Drowning, narrow escape of the author from, 467.
Dubler, Mr., 175.
Dubourg, Rt. Rev. Dr., 556, 587.
Duelling, 58.
Duff, Rev. Martin, 145.
Duffys, the, of Gaston Co., 471.
Duggan, Father, 118.
Rt. Rev. Dr., 159.
Very Rev. Gregory, 558, 559, 560, 561, 562.
Duhalla, 160.
Dunn, Rev. P. J., 145, 156, 407.
Mother Xavier, 264.
family, the, 325.
Dupanloup, Mgr., 544.
Dupon, Dr. Stephen, of Savannah, 552.

INDEX.

Durland, Mrs., 175.
Durban, Mrs., 212.
Durbaces, the, 211.
Durbec, Mr., of Flat Rock, 445.

East, the Church in, 32.
Ecclesiastical Summary for United States, 1877, 36.
Eccleston, Archbishop, 101, 518.
Edenton, 156, 414.
Edgefield, the mission at, 233, 234, 331, 414.
Edisto River, the, 169.
  Island, 122.
Education, spread of, 30.
  of the masses, 69.
  classical, 58.
  provision for female, 67.
  Catholic, hostility to, 248.
Edward, St., dalmatic of, 24.
Elkeronkrotter, Mr., 176.
Elizabeth, Queen, 122, 414.
Emanuel, Victor, King, 55.
Emancipation, Catholic, 132.
Emigration, absence of, 46.
  Catholic, Very Rev. Stephen Byrne, O.P., on, 620.
England, Protestant, blessings left by, 20.
  suppression of Catholic books in, 51.
  the Church in, 39.
  Mother Mary Charles, 66.
  Miss Honora, 83, 138.
  Madame Augustine, 110.
  Miss Johanna Monica, 42, 87.
  Rev. Thomas, 83.
  Rt. Rev. Dr., birth, early life, education, ordination, missionary labors, consecration, writings, and episcopate of, 37 to 43, 46 to 96, 108, 110, 117, 118, 124, 127, 129, 131, 134, 138, 146, 147, 149, 156, 167, 180, 213, 219, 221, 227, 233, 238, 185, 189, 193, 196, 241, 249, 277, 337, 401, 407.
  Edward, 277.
  Reformation in, 140, 216.
  new sees in, 23.
English, the, priests murdered by, 26.
  monasteries and towns destroyed by, 26.
  penal code, 27.
  Government, the, arrayed against Catholicity, 27.
Engeddi, the vineyards of, 179.
Enright, Father J., 407.
  John, 329, 330, 331.
  D. Gregory, death of, 552.
Enrique, Father, of Fonda, 582.
"Enterprise," the Greenville, 300.
Eric, Rt. Rev. Dr., 23.
Escape, a narrow, 373, 374, 375, 376, 493.
Eulogy, Father Clavereul's, on the death of Bishop Vérot, 541.
Europe, suspended priests from, evil influence of, 46.
  society in, 34.

Europe, Catholic, aids the American Revolution, 34.
Execution, a memorable, 263.
Expeditions accompanied by priests, 24.

Fahey, Mr., of Greenville, 372.
Faith, the United States a sanctuary of the, 22.
  landmarks of the, 25.
  progress of the, 61.
  Irish, 469.
  Protestant rule of, 497, 498.
Fair, Dr. S., 161.
Farrell, Mr. Michael, 156.
  Thomas, 156.
  Rev. Francis, 406.
Father, the Holy, 76.
Fathers, vigilance of the, 31.
Fayetteville, 71, 159, 161, 231, 401.
  missions at, 326, 414.
  church in, 406, 414.
Fear, Cape, 160.
Feeny, Thomas, 305.
Feehan, Rt. Rev. Dr., 620.
Fenwick, Rev. Father, 144, 147, 221.
  Rt. Rev. Dr., 166, 196.
Fernandina, church at, 549.
Fever, stranger's, the, 64.
  yellow, the, devastations by, 46, 64, 148, 150.
Figeraux family, the, 211.
Fillion, Very Rev. Leon, V.G., 153, 154, 157.
Finbar, St., 61, 62, 85, 164.
  cathedral of, 39, 239.
Finola, de, Chevalier Riva, 421, 434.
Fisher, the Misses, of Salisbury, 416.
  Colonel Charles, 438.
  Miss Christiana, 438.
  Miss Frances C. (Christian Reid), 441.
  family, the, 439, 440, 441.
Fitzgerald, Major, 365.
Fitzgeralds, the, 366, 367.
Flanagan, Richard, 217.
Florida, Ponce de Leon in, 25.
  the Indian war in, 119.
  vicar-apostolic of, 108, 540.
  condition of the Church in, 108.
  ceded by Spain to England, 585.
  destruction of the missions in, by England, 585.
Flynn, Father, 111.
  Patrick, 219.
  Charles, 219.
  John, 220.
  Thomas Augustus, 220.
  family, the, 219.
Fogartie, Phil. 211, 256.
Folchi, Father, missionary labors of, 323, 331, 352, 389, 390.
Ford, Joshua, 217.
Fordham, St. John's College, 243.
Fort, Old, 428.
Forsyth, Governor, 58.

Ford, Thompson's, 474.
Forest, pine, the author lost in a, 579, 580.
Foxes, the, 180.
France, executions in, 90.
　aid of, during the Revolution, 29.
　revolution in, 30.
Francisco, San, Catholicity in, 430.
Franciscans, the, 24, 250.
Francisco, the Florentine, 255.
French, natives civilized by the, 26.
　priests, increased immigration of, 30.
Frenchbroad, valley of the, 340.
Freundel, Brother Bartholomew, 481.
Free States free church in, 35.
Freemasons in the United States, 32, 216.
Fryse family, the, 181.
Fulton, Mrs., of Wilmington, 309.
Fuller, Dr., 58.
Fullerton, Rev. Father, of Columbia, 290.

GABOURY, Rev. C. C., of Pio Nono College, 610.
Gallicanism, 74.
Gallagher, Rev. Dr., 128, 304.
　Very Rev. Simon Felix, 142.
Gallitzin, Dr., 239.
Gallon, James, of Greenville, 358, 359.
Gartland, Rt. Rev. Dr., early life, ordination, consecration, and missionary labors of, 26, 113, 114, 191, 233, 512, 517 to 521, 533.
Gardner's Corner, 177.
Gardiner, Hon. James, 205.
Garache, P. B., 208.
Garan, John P., of Macon, 601.
Gaston, 427.
　Judge, 142, 420.
　Hon. William, 427.
　family, the, 141.
Georgia, Bishop England in, 91.
　State of, 103.
　diocese of, created, 113.
　first bishop of, 113.
　Southern, 120.
　Inducements for emigrants in, 121, 622.
　Prosperity of, 622.
　General Sherman in, 622.
　Ku-Kluxism in, 623.
　Carpet-baggers in, 623.
　Political situation in, 624.
Georgetown, N. C., 128, 183.
Geraghty family, the, of Macon, 601.
Germany, the Church in, 83.
Gibbs, Sr., Dr., 253.
Gibbons, Dr., 149.
　Archbishop, birth, early life, education, ordination, consecration, and episcopacy of, 21, 36, 126, 160. 244, 310, 323, 359, 396, 397, 398, 399, 414, 429, 445, 446, 477.
　Rev. Mr., sent to Appalachicola, 582.
　family, the, 582.
Gillick, Rev. Philip, 160, 406.
Gillisonville, 177.

Girard, Stephen, 122.
Gleason, Father, 407.
Goa, 60.
God, St. John of, Brothers Hospitallers of, 535.
Goldsborough, 159, 414.
Goldana, the, of Columbus, 573.
Gore, Rev. James F. M., 155, 164.
Gospel, the, forbidden to teach the negroes, 44.
Government, the Confederate, 177.
Graveyard, Protestant, a modern, 435.
Graham, Rev. James, missionary work of, 120, 572, 595, 608, 609, 610.
　Dr., 173.
Grahams, the, of Blackville, 177, 183.
Grahamsville, 176.
Grasse, de, 28.
Grant, General U. S., 228.
　Captain, 333.
Gregory VII., St., 216.
　XVI., Pope, 456.
　XVII., Pope, 72.
Greenville, missions at, 240, 350, 414, 442, 458, 462.
　a Yankee priest in, 361.
　progress of the faith in, 390.
　new church in, 391.
　Bishop Lynch in, 391.
Greenbrier Co., Va., 243.
Greensborough, 428.
Griffin, Miss Honora, 178.
　E. D., of Raleigh, 411.
Grove, Newtown, 400.
　Locust, Ga., 161.
　"　" principal families of, 357.
　"　" Father Whelan at, 537.
Grover, the Misses, of Charlotte, 425.
Gross, Rev. Mark, 400, 415, 429.
　Rt. Rev. Wm., of Savannah, 400, 451, 452, 453.
　Mrs., 437.
Guards, the Anderson, 332.
Guiana, Vicar-Apostolic of, 74.
Guilford, Rev. John, 296, 484, 475.

HACKETT, Rev. Father, 160.
Hagood, Col., 346, 377.
Halifax, 414.
Ham, the dusky children of, 71.
Hampton, Col. Wade, 207.
　Governor Wade, 183, 247, 251, 287.
　family, the, 254.
Hampshire, New, discrimination against Catholics in, 142.
Hamon, Father, curé de St. Sulpice, Paris, 543.
Hamilion, Very Rev. Wm J., 565, 566.
　Rev. W. C., of Eufaula, 576.
Hand, Mrs., 437.
Hartford, the Bishop of, 108, 160.
Harpers, the, New York, 254.
Harney, Mr., 303.

640 INDEX.

Hartys, the, of Mecklenburg, 434.
Harris, Mother Mary Paul, 264.
Harrington, General, 128, 129.
Happoldt, Dr., of Morganton, 435.
Hasson, Rev. James, 181, 620.
Hawkinses, the, of Gaston Co., 471.
Hayne, 58, 282.
Hayti mission, the, 73.
Hayes, Rev. James, 145.
Heart, Sacred, Brothers of the, 83.
Healy, Father, 165, 573.
    Archbishop, 122.
Heath, Judge, of Edenton, 156, 416.
Head, Cæsar's, 377, 458.
Hecker, Father, 31, 822, 592, 593.
Heidenkamp, Father, S.J., 568.
Helena, St., 297.
    monastery of, at St. Augustine, 583.
Helena, 324.
Henderson, 428.
Hendersonville, 442.
Hennegan, John, 805.
Herman, Father, 551.
Hewit, Rev. A. F., 31, 109, 592, 593.
Hierarchy, the American, 77
Hill, Tunnel, 340.
Hogan, 254.
    Richard, and family, 869.
Hoke, Captain, of Greenville, 872.
Holy Cross, Church of the, 243.
Holden, Governor, 418.
Horeb, the glories of, 62.
Horan, Rt. Rev. Dr., 839.
Hospitals, Catholic, in United States, 36.
Howlands, the, of Macon, 599.
Howard, General, 176.
    Toby, of Columbus, 573.
Hoxie, Dr., of Columbus, 571.
Huet, Father, 117.
Hughes, Mother Antonio, 277.
    Rt. Rev. Dr., Bishop of Gibraltar, 277.
    Archbishop, 31, 35, 95, 114, 148, 159, 161, 182, 186, 871, 413.
    Mary Antonio, 68.
Huguenots, the, descendants of, 129.
Humbird and Hitchcock, Mgrs., 341.
Hunter, William, 322.
    " of Charlotte, 425.
Hurley, Rev. J., 164.
Hynes, Rt. Rev. Dr., 74.

IGNATIUS, ST., the Sons of, 30.
    mission of, 577.
    proposed Catholic colony, 120.
Immigration to United States, decline of, 35.
    Irish and German, 487, 488.
Incident, a remarkable, 185.
Indies, West, the, 141.
    Catholic discipline in, 72.
India, St. Francis Xavier in, 60, 115.
Indians, the Catawba, 392, 393.
    the Seminole, 584, 585, 586, 587.

Infantry, the Seventh United States, 827.
Institute, the New York Literary, 221.
Institutions, religious. prejudice against, 279.
    Catholic, for the sick, established, 57.
Ireland, St. Patrick in, 33.
    executions in, 90.
    bishops in, 108.
    Orange violence in, 183.
Irish immigrants, 64.
    priests, increased immigration of, 30.
Irwin, 184.
Isidore, Sister, 66.
Island, Sullivan's, missions at, 148, 153, 155, 104, 237, 396, 589.
    Morris, 157.
    Hutchinson's, 159, 182.
    Skidaway, 551, 552.
    Dauphin, death of Bishop Janres and companions on, 563.
Ives, Dr. Levi Silliman, 410, 417.

JACKSON, STONEWALL, General, 262.
    Andrew, General, 586.
Jacobins, the, 214.
Jacksonville, the church at, 549.
James, St., Church of, Concord, 421.
Januarius, St., 127.
Janres, Rt. Rev. John, of Florida, 582.
Jelicos, the, 206, 217.
Jerome, Sister, 324.
Jesuits, the, 24, 221, 250.
    missionaries of the, 34.
John, St., 164.
    Bishop, 23.
Johnson, Andrew, President, 177, 357.
Johnson's, the, 183.
Johnston, Joseph E., General, 208.
    Rufus, 258.
    William, Colonel, 258.
    Rev. Mr. of Milledgeville, 602.
Jones, General James, 200, 201, 202.
    Mr., Orangeburg, 294.
Jogues, 25.
Joseph, St., 109, 164.
Joseph's, St., Church, Gaston, 421.
"Journal," the Willmington, 310.
Judas, 104, 219.
Juarez, Bishop, 25.

KEATING, Father, 141, 143.
Keenan, Mrs. Rowland, 217.
Keenans, the, of Nashville, 445, 446, 447.
    the, of Greenville, 857.
Kehoes, the, 217.
Keilly, J. M., 114.
    Mr., in Liverpool, 121.
Keitt, Hon. Lawrence, 203.
    Mrs. Caroline, 208.
    Ellison, and family, 324.
Kelly, John, of Fayetteville, 401.
    Rev. John, of New York, 522.
    Rev. James A., death of, 554.

Keller, Rev. Joseph, O.S.B., 481.
Kenrick, Archbishop, 83, 87, 106, 118, 124, 145, 396, 407, 518.
  Archbishop, letter of, 529.
Kent, Chancellor, 70, 249.
Kenedy, William, 309.
Kenneys, the, 211.
Kilkenny, 96, 220.
Killarney, the Lakes of, 180.
  the cathedral of, 97.
Kinsella, Rt. Rev. Dr., 73.
Kingston, 414.
  diocese of, 339.
Kings, the, of Greenville, 357.
  the, of New Berne, 405.
Kirby, Very Rev. John F., V.G., early life and labors in the ministry of, 109, 111, 113, 138, 139, 562, 563, 564, 570.
  Rev. Patrick, 564.
  Brother Timothy, 564.
Kirby's, the, 243, 564.
Know-Nothingism, 23, 148, 247, 248.
  in Raleigh, 409, 410.
Knott, Dr., 221.
Kohlman, Rev. Father, 221.

LACORDAIRE, Father, 544.
Lafayette, 28, 122.
Lallemant, 25.
Langton, Archbishop, 29.
Landing, Boyd's, 176.
Lancaster, missions at, 217, 240, 296, 300, 337.
  the house of, 229.
Lancasterville, 300, 301, 431.
Langlois, Rev. J. B., death of, 554.
Lawrence, St., the martyr, 308.
  new cemetery of, 115, 165.
  Church, Asheville, 421.
Laurens, court-house at, 327.
Laurinburg, 400.
Leahy, the apostate, 148.
Leary, Thomas, 256.
Learys, the, of Leary's Settlement, 353, 354.
Leader, choir, a slave, 573.
Lecarron, Rev. Mr., 502.
Lee, General Robert E., 298, 363.
  Colonel, of Flat Rock, 444.
Lemercure, Rev. Mr., 502.
Leon, Ponce de, 25, 27.
Leonard, Thomas, 217, 218.
  Mrs., 217.
Leper, Matthew, of Charlotte, 425.
Lepers, the, of Gaston Co., 471.
Leroy, Mrs., of Washington, 156.
Levy, Thomas, 217.
Lewis, Colonel, and family, 294.
Library, the Propaganda, 223.
Limerick, Earl of, city founded by, 28.
Limoslaw, 143.
Lisbon, St. Francis Xavier in, 60.
Little Rock, first Bishop of, 63.
  diocese of, 127, 326.

Liverpool, 121.
Livingstone, 179.
Logue, William, 309.
Longballe, Mr., 178.
London, Vicar-Apostolic of, 30.
  Carolinas included in, 140, 167.
Louis XVI., 143.
Louis, St., 27.
Louisville, diocese of, 106.
Louvain, Seminary of, 163.
Lover, Samuel, the novelist, Father O'Neill and, 515.
Lowther, William P., 217.
Lowe, Sir Hudson, 217.
Loyson, 166.
Lucy, Aunt, of Savannah, 573.
Lynch, Dr., 208.
  Robert, 202.
  Rev. Dr., 99, 111, 117, 194, 247, 308, 402.
  Rt. Rev. Bishop, birth, education, early life, ordination, consecration, and episcopacy of, 23, 69, 124, 125, 126, 127, 128, 134, 150, 153, 164, 178, 192, 220, 234, 235, 278, 401, 403.
  Conlaw, Peter, life and labors of, 128, 132, 133, 135, 136, 164.
  Mrs. Conlaw, Peter, 128, 132, 133, 134, 135, 136.
  Mrs. Eleanor McMahon Neillson, 132.
  Dr. John, of Cheraw, 437.
"Lyon, General," the steamer, 332.
Lyons, 214.

MACARIUS, ST., 84.
MacHale, Archbishop, 354, 398.
MacMahon, Marshal, 132.
Macon, 594, 604.
  added to the Columbus mission, 570.
  first Baptism in North America at, 595.
  Bishop England at, 595.
  hostility to Catholicity in, 596.
  missionary labors at, 604.
  pastors of, 610.
  Sisters of Mercy in, 610.
  Pio Nono College at, 610.
Maden, Father, 243.
Madianito, priest, the, 215.
Magna Charta, the, 29.
Magdalene, Sister, 147.
Magher, Colonel, 162.
Maguires, the, of New Berne, 405.
Maginnis, Rev. John, 430, 431.
Maher, Colonel John, 206.
Majne, Rev. Father, 509.
Maloney, James, 178, 182.
  Rev. Thomas, 189.
  Miss, of the Ursulines, 377.
Maloneys, the, 180.
Mallow, Ireland, 180.
Mallet, Major, 438.
Manly, Judge, 186, 416, 420.
  Hon. M. E., 420, 421.

INDEX.

Mangum, Mr., 219.
Manassas, the battle of, 225, 428.
Manucy, Rt. Rev. Dr., 590.
Mandate, an insolent, 259, 260.
Manning, Cardinal, 93, 116.
  Sister Mary Martha, death of, 554.
Martinez, Father, 25.
  S.J., Father, murder of, 584.
Maryland, Lord Baltimore in, 29.
Marsh, Mrs., 152.
Marsailles, 214.
Martin, John, 217.
Mary, St., Church of, Raleigh, 421.
  St., of Help, Institute of, 467.
  St., Benedictine Monastery of, 430, 431.
Marechal, Archbishop, 105, 144.
Marriage, a South Carolina, 484.
Masons, Free, the, 108.
Mass, idolatry of the, 27.
Massachusetts, bigotry of, 82.
Mathias, St., 104.
Mathelsson, Captain, and family, 333.
Matthew, Father, 311.
Matthews, Mr., 234.
Maxwell, Mrs., 174.
  the Misses, of Charlotte, 425.
  Mr. H., of Charlotte, 425.
Maynooth, College of, 142.
Mayrant, Colonel, 308.
Mayben, Hon. William, and wife, 369.
McBee, Verdry, 361.
  the brothers, of Columbus, 573.
McCarthy, Father, 243.
McCarthys, the, 74.
McCahey family, the, of Columbus, 573.
McCairy, James, and family, Walhalla, 339.
McCarcys, the, 211.
McCloskey, Cardinal, 1, 36, 106, 180.
  Dr., 299.
McColgan, Rev. Father, 162.
McCool, Rev. Jerome, 145.
McDonald family, the, 183.
McDowell, 240.
McDuffie, 58, 262.
McElheny, Miss Susan, 362.
McElrone family, the, 917.
McEncroe, Father, 144.
McFarland, Rt. Rev. Dr., 108.
McGee, Dr., 160.
McGees, the, 160.
McGill, Rt. Rev. Dr., 59, 106, 114, 118, 124, 187.
McGinnis, Rose, 206.
  Ellen, 206.
  Hugh, 522.
McGowan, Father, 326, 407.
  General, 331.
McGrath, Rev. Michael, 146.
  Sister Mary Joseph, death of, 554.
  Governor, 262.
McGuiness, Dennis, 217.
McGuinness, Rev. John, 131, 166, 231, 390.

McGuire, Mrs., of Wilmington, 209.
McGuire, John, 255, 256.
McKain, Mrs., 308.
McKenna, Hon. W., 217, 297, 299, 337, 425.
  the Misses, 219.
  Rev. Thomas, 186.
  Mother Aloysius, 264.
  Patrick, 300.
McKergan, John, 310.
McLane, General, 208.
McLaren, Mrs., 300.
McMahon, Sue, 132.
  Hugh, 132, 133.
  Rev. T. C., 339.
McManus, J. B., 310.
  Rev. Father, 162.
McMullen, Dr., 252.
McNally family, the, 325.
McNamara, Major, 208, 429, 437.
  Sister Agatha, 264.
  Rev. J. V., 415.
McNeal, the brothers, 243.
McNeill, Rev. A. J., early life, education, ordination, and ministry of, 111, 285, 296, 310, 321, 427, 428, 438, 456, 477.
McNeirny, Rt. Rev. Dr., 413.
McPherson, James, of Greenville, 359, 360.
McQuades, the, 234.
Mecklenburg, gold mines in, 421.
Meliapore, 156.
Mercy, Sisters of, work of in the Southern States, 84, 62, 70, 71, 112, 147, 148, 240, 243, 299.
  Sisters of, Our Lady of, 64, 65, 66.
Merrittsville, 873.
Milnes, Mr., of Greenville, 372.
Miles, Rt. Rev. Dr., 109.
Millers, the, of Gaston Co., 471.
Milledgeville, missions at, 602 to 606.
  a, "convert," 605, 606.
  visited by Bishop Reynolds, 605.
  visited by Rev. S. F. O'Neill, 605.
Minister, disgraceful act of a, 175.
Minnesota, 218.
"Miscellany, the Catholic," 47, 57, 59, 100, 117, 123, 148, 213, 347.
Missions, North Carolina, 139.
Missionary centres, formation of, 24.
Mitchell, Mount, 455.
  Professor, 458.
  family, the, 302.
Mittag, J. F. G., 299.
  Sarah, 299.
Mobile, 124.
  Bishop of, 160.
Moch family, the, of Albany, S. C., 577.
Molony, Mother Mary Charles, 68.
  Father Thomas, of Columbus, 572.
  Mr., of Marietta, 606, 607.
Montalembert, 337.
Montague, Charles, 204, 245.
  Agnes, 204.

Montagues, the, of New Berne, 405.
Monastery, the Benedictine, of Our Lady of Help, N. C., 470.
 the Benedictine, Skidaway, Ga., 551.
 St. Vincent's, Pa., 551.
 Pierre-qui-vive, France, 552.
Montgomery, 317.
Monk, Maria, 254.
Moore, Mr., of Greenville, 372.
 Rev. Patrick, 400.
 Judge, 416.
 Rt. Rev. Dr., life and labors of, 108, 111, 126, 153, 265, 550.
Morgantown, 240, 428, 462.
Morierty, Dr., O.S.A., 145.
Morse, Mr., 244.
Morrissy family, the, of Macon, 601.
Moses, Hon. F. J., 308.
 Ex-Governor, of Georgia, 623.
Mountains, the Saluda, 442.
 the Bleak, 458.
Movement, the Oxford, 416.
Moylan, Rt. Rev. Dr., 26, 40.
Moylans, the, 74.
Mulligan family, the, 183.
Mulloney, Rev. Thomas, of Columbia, 209.
Munich, the Society of Missions, 462.
Murphy, Rt. Rev. Dr., 66.
 Very Rev. Thos., early life, education, ordination, and ministry of, 116, 131, 149, 235, 400 to 406, 596.
 Sister Teresa, 188.
 Rev. James, death of, 554.
Murphys, the, 74.
 of Columbia, 209.
Names, Catholic and Protestant, 461.
Napoleon, 55, 236.
Naples, 127.
Nary, Rev. Patrick, 162.
Nashville, diocese of, 619.
Nation, generosity and fervor of the Irish, 59.
 the Cherokee, 186.
 the Choctaw, 186.
Nations, apostate, never reconverted, 449, 450.
Natives, civilized by the French and Spanish, 26.
Nearnsie, Major J. R., 202, 207, 235.
Needhams, the, of Columbia, 578.
Negro, fidelity of a, 333.
Negroes, moral degradation of, 45.
 deplorable condition of the, 421.
 efforts to convert the, 422.
Nelligan, Rev. Father, 153.
Neuse River, the, 160.
New Berne, 141, 326.
 the mission at, 156, 159, 161.
Newberry, 240, 394.
Nice, the Council of, 451.
Nolan, Rt. Rev. Dr., 73.
Norbury, Judge, 846.
Northrop, Rev. C. B., missionary labors of, 104, 181, 294, 297, 300, 301.

Northrop, Rev. H. P., 153, 414.
 Lucius, 181, 302. — — — — — —
 Dr. L., 301.
Northrops, the, 243, 302.
Nullification, the doctrine of, 231.
Nuns, the Ursuline, in Columbia, 277.

O'BRIEN, Miss, 174.
 Richard, 245.
O'Briens, the, 209.
 of Dallas, 472.
 of Milledgeville, 602.
O'Callaghan, Rev. Dr., 189.
Oceanica, missionaries to, 84.
O'Connell, Sister Mary Baptist, 66, 192, 264, 508.
 Mary Antonia, 66, 264.
 Father, 107.
 Lieutenant, 236.
 Trial Justice, and family, 192, 323, 324.
 Patrick, 188, 189, 191, 192, 193.
 Ann Wray, 192.
 Daniel, 40, 41, 76, 182.
 Rev. Dr. Joseph, 281, 289, 332, 342.
 Rev. Dr. J. J., early life, education, ordination, and missionary work of, 109, 188, 224, 235, 239, 245, 290, 297, 310, 342, 428, 477, 591.
 Rev. L. P., birth, education, ordination, and ministrations of, 109, 157, 159, 163, 239, 241, 243, 244, 245, 256, 281, 310, 311, 321, 345, 357, 414, 428, 429, 440, 453, 477.
 Rev. Dr. J. P., life and missionary work of, 111, 182, 187, 245, 252, 266, 267, 310, 321, 428, 429, 438, 440, 453, 477.
 Father Lawrence, 228, 289, 342, 354, 477.
 Rev. Dr. D. J., 190, 273.
 Sister Mary Jerome, 190.
 Mr. P., 211.
 Mrs. Florence, 473, 474.
 Sister Antonio, 508.
 Sister Gertrude, 264.
 Chaplain Major Lawrence, 237.
 Colonel James, of Walhalla, 338.
O'Connells, the, 243.
 the, of Walhalla, 338.
O'Connor, Michael, 170, 171, 172.
 Mary, 170, 171.
 Rt. Rev. Dr., 106, 109, 518.
 Rev. Dr., 139.
O'Connors, the, 331.
O'Donnell, Mr., 172.
O'Donohue, Rev. Francis, 406.
O'Farrell, Miss, 147.
 Thomas, 322.
O'Gallagher, Rev. Dr., 502.
 Rev. S. F., 556.
O'Gora, Father Thos., 358.
O'Gorman, the Misses, 64.
O'Hanlon, Terence, 199.
O'Hara, Mr. Charles, of Columbus, 573.
 family, the, of Columbus, 753.

O'Hare family, the, 322.
Ojéda in Central America, 25.
O'Keefe, Rev. Father, 415.
O'Keefes, the, of Macon, 601.
O'Leary, Jeremiah, 322.
Olives, Mount, Church at, 400.
O'Neale, Father, 63, 86, 92, 97.
O'Neill, Chief-Justice, 179.
    Rev. J. F., Sr., early life, ordination, and missionary labors of, 390, 402, 504, 505, 506, 507, 513 to 517, 605.
    Rev. J. F., Jr., education, ordination, and ministry of, 109, 113, 124, 159, 231, 616, 617, 618.
    Rev. James, 113, 194.
    Rev. P., 126, 139, 151, 152, 166, 171, 309.
    Rev. John, death of, 554.
O'Neills, the, 243.
Onias, the high-priest, 69.
Orangeburg, 240.
Orangemen in U. S., 82.
Order, the Benedictine, 390.
    Presentation, rules of, 64.
    religious, of men in U. S., 36.
    religious, of women in U. S., 36.
    Holy, the sacrament of, 102.
O'Reilly, Father, M.D., 141, 587, 595.
Orleans, New, French Catholics of, 436.
    Ursuline Convent at, 110.
    city of, 214, 234, 240.
O'Rourke, John, of Raleigh, 409 to 413.
Osceola, 120.
Ossory, the see of, 60.
O'Sullivan, Patrick, 305.
Oswald, Rev. P., O.S.B., letter from, 531.
O'Toole, St. Lawrence, 102.

"PACIFICATOR," the Columbian, 231, 563.
Palos, de, Brother John, 582.
Pamphero, Lieutenant, 310.
Paris, 68, 214.
Parson, an opposition, 495.
Paul, Sister Mary, 66.
    St. Vincent de, 34, 216.
Paulists, the, 34, 322, 592.
Peak, Clingman's, 458.
Pedee River, the, 128.
Pedlars and their tricks, 383, 384.
Pellicer, Rt. Rev. Dr., 590.
Pendleton, 335.
People, the Southern, and the negro, 72.
Peoria, 160.
Persecution, a storm of, 253.
Perché, Archbishop, 590.
Perry, Governor B. F., 344, 366, 376, 389.
Periodicals, Catholic, in U. S., 36.
Persico, Rt. Rev. Dr., life and missionary labors of, 62, 183, 237, 512, 550, 551.
Peter, Sister Mary, 66.
    the see of, 68.
Peter's, St., 59.
    Church, Charleston, 421.

Phelan, Mr., of Macon, 601.
Philadelphia, 83, 87, 213.
    the Church in, 28, 146.
    Archbishop of, 149.
Pinckney Castle, 225.
Pickens, Governor, 236.
Pinckney, Mrs., 181, 183.
    Dr., 181.
Pioneer, landmarks of the, 61.
Pittsburgh, first Bishop of, 106.
Pius VII., Pope, 70.
    IX., Pope, sees created by, 35.
    new sees in the U. S. created by, 35, 53, 64, 70, 95, 323.
Pizazi, Joseph, 180.
Plantagenets, the, 24.
Plymouth, 414.
Pocatallgo, 176.
Poincignons, the, 211.
Polycarp, St., 188.
Poole, Mrs., 303.
Pope, the infallibility of the, Bishop England and, 74.
    the, invited to come to the United States, 81.
    Bishop England's works presented to, 75.
Population, Catholic, in America, 21.
    in the Revolution, 28.
Porter, Miss Margaret, 201.
Portier, Rt. Rev. Dr., 114, 124, 160, 476, 582, 587, 588.
Posl, Julius, 245.
Pouncey, Major, 129.
Prelates, Irish, 122.
Preston, Hon. W. C., 221, 309.
    General John S., 246, 277.
    family, the, 254.
Prendergast, Rev. C. C., 511, 566.
Prendergasts, the, of Savannah, 511.
Preacher, a silent, 559.
Priests, education of, commenced, 56.
    suspended, from Europe, 46.
    number in U. S. (1877), 36.
    schools in U. S. (1877), 36.
    disabled, an asylum needed for, 453.
Prisons, the Cork, Father (Bishop) England and the, 90.
Prices, the, 511.
    of New Berne, 405.
Propaganda, College of the, 63, 99, 124, 323.
Prospect, a sad missionary, 329.
Protestantism, converts from, 415, 416, 417.
Publishers, Catholic, in U. S. (1877), 36.
Purcell, Archbishop, 95, 109, 619.
    James, 180.
Purcells, the, 180.
Pulaski, 28.
Punch, Philip J., of Savannah, 511, 600.
Puritans, the, 23.

QUIGLEY, Rev. Father, 164, 241.
    Rev. Thomas, 158, 159, 182, 407, 411.
    Rev. D. J., 146, 299.

INDEX.   645

Quigley, Rev. Edward, early life, ordination, and missionary labors of, 113, 130, 239, 311, 420, 524, 525.
   letter of, 526, 527, 528, 620, 621.
Quigleys, the, 243, 299.
   Rev. W., of Atlanta, 621.
Quinlan, Rt. Rev. John, 589.
Quinn, Vicar-General, of New York, 108, 218, 530.
   John, 182.
   Patrick, 183.

Race, Irish, the, tribute to, 349.
   African, the, 72.
Raleigh, N. C., missions of, 156, 159, 161, 401, 414, 421.
   contributors to the Church in, 408, 413.
Rathburn Gap, 240.
Railroad, South Carolina, 169.
   Blue Ridge, 340.
   the Western North Carolina, 453.
Rodman, Rev. Father, 146.
Revolutions in Ireland, 30.
   in France, 30.
Republic, growth of the, 31.
Reynolds, Rt. Rev. Dr., birth, early life, education, ordination, missionary work, consecration, and episcopacy of, 69, 75, 99, 103, 105 to 115, 188, 122, 123, 124, 126, 138, 146, 148, 153, 155, 161, 164, 194, 215, 220, 224, 233, 243, 249, 292, 308, 326, 364, 456.
Rebman, Rev. F. J., of Atlanta, 621.
Refugees, Catholic, 211.
Regiment, the Sixty-ninth, 225, 228.
Reilly, Bernard, and family, 381, 382.
   Rev. J. J., 405, 414, 415.
"Review, the Quarterly," 149.
"Catholic," 470.
Rice, Judge, 303.
Richmond, 124.
   diocese of, 322.
Richardson, Dr., 308.
Rich, hardships of the, 443.
Rickenbac, Mrs., née O'Connell, 293.
Ridway, William, and family, 381, 382.
Ridge, Missionary, battle of, 619.
Rights, Southern, 444.
Rignolds, the, 211.
River, the Caney, 458.
Roaches, the, 831.
Roanoke River, the, 61.
Robespierre, 214.
Robertson, Senator, 279.
Rochambeau, 28.
Rock, Flat, 442, 458.
   Plymouth, 23.
Rome, School of Philosophy at, 42.
   diocese of, 119.
Romulat, Captain, 333.
Roper, Sallie, 233.
Rose, St., of Lima, 460.
Rosati, Rt. Rev. Dr., 56, 557.

Rosa Salvator, 297.
Rosignol, Mr., and family, of Columbus, 573.
Rosecrans, Rt. Rev. Dr., 619.
   General, 619.
Rouquette, Abbé, 166.
Rouche, Mr., of Salisbury, 433.
   Messrs., of Salisbury, 433.
Royal, Port, 122, 169, 181.
Ruffin, Judge, 420.
Ryan, Captain of U. S. steamer "Huron," 301.
   Rev. Dr. P., 161, 407, 409, 410, 411.
   Col. John, 177, 182.
   Patrick, 177.
   Rev. A. J., 183, 565.
   Rev. A. J., and the "Lost Cause," 565.
Ryans, the, 180.
Ryder, Rev. Dr., 118.

Sacrifice, the Holy, 47.
Sacrilege, the punishment of, 219.
Saints, the Isle of, 64, 158.
   invocation of the, 175.
Sales, de, Sister Mary, death of, 554.
Salisbury, Missions at, 240, 427, 428, 487.
Salvation, exclusive, the doctrine of, 314.
Saltketcher River, the, 169.
Salle, La, 27.
Samaritan, the Good, 531.
Sanhedrim, the, 215.
Santee River, the, 61.
Saunders, Edward, 525.
   family, the, 206, 217.
Savage, Rev. D., of Montgomery, 591.
Savannah, 92, 124, 501, 530.
   Sisters of Mercy in, 65.
   Sisters of Charity in, 112.
   Father O'Neale of, 86.
   new cotton route to, 120.
   the author sent to, 139.
   the diocese of, 237.
   the diocese of, recapitulation of, 623.
   the Nestor of, 505.
   Church of St. John the Baptist, 507.
   Catholic education in, 508.
   leading Catholics of, 511.
   yellow fever in, 521, 522.
   outlying missions of, 508.
Scene, a prison, 237.
Scenery, natural, 379.
Scholastica, St., 88.
Schools, foundation of, 31.
Scholars, pleasures of, 58.
Schacte, Rev. J. O., 104.
Scott, Rt. Rev. Dr., 475.
   family, the, 217.
Sea, the city by the, 58, 114.
Secession unpopular among the poor, 457.
   ordinance of, passed by S. Carolina, 464.
See, the Holy, 25.
Seminaries, theological, in U. S., 36.
Semmes, Mrs. Admiral, 211.
   Senator Thos., 362.

Semmes, Admiral Raphael, 363.
 family, the, 363, 364, 365.
Sennen, Father, 400.
Sepulchre, the Holy, 236.
Servitus, Michael, 129.
Sermons, rival, 369.
Seton, Mother, noble work of, 556.
Settlement, Barker's, 183.
 a Baptist, 385.
Shadler, Rev. Father, 163.
Shannahan, Rev. J. F., 109.
 William, 822.
 James, 822.
 Rev. Thos. F., 614, 615, 616.
Sharp, Senator, of N. C., 847.
Sherman, Gen. W. T., 251, 428, 465, 622.
 at Columbia, 274.
Sheehans, the, of Milledgeville, 602.
Shirt, the Bloody, origin of, 821.
Shorter, Mrs., of Columbus, 573.
Sibb, Madame, 200.
Sickles, General, 117, 182.
Sikes, Dr., 200.
Sims, Dr. Marion, 195.
Simmes, the, of Appalachicola, 562.
Simmis, Gilmore, 129, 182.
Sin, a saturnalia of, 278.
Sinai, the glories of, 62.
Sing Sing, N. Y., 182.
Sisterhoods, establishment of, 57, 66.
Slattery, Rt. Rev. Dr., 73.
Slaves, women, 24.
 condition of the, 44, 71.
 fidelity of, 465.
Slavery, Bishop England on, 71.
 Daniel O'Connell on, 514.
 opposed to immigration, 629.
 the safeguard of Protestantism, 628.
Smith, Fort, 326.
Smithville, N. C., 400.
Smitz, Rev. F. A., 352, 380.
Society, Southern, state of, 108, 377.
Sound, Pamlico, 405.
Spain, friendship of, for U. S., 20.
 bishops in, 140.
Spalding, Archbishop, 31, 100, 106, 310, 306, 416.
Spartanburg, missions at, 183, 325, 326.
Spauns, the, 302, 303.
Spencer, 179.
Spelth, Elias, 170.
Spear, Lieutenant, 327.
Springs, the Warm, 240.
 Chick, 367, 368, 369, 370.
 White Sulphur, 157, 243.
Sports, field, 483.
Station, Green's, 400.
Stations, Catholic, in U. S., 36.
States, Southern, popularity of the Sisters in, 60.
Stephens, Hon. A. H., 210, 389.
Stokes, Rev. Father, 131, 231.

Stokes, Rev. Joseph, 430.
Strother, Mr., 283.
Strupper, Mr., of Columbus, 573.
Stuarts, wars of the, 184.
Students, theological, in the U. S., 36.
Stumphouse Mountain, 340.
Subjaco, Abbey of, Italy, 552.
Sulpice, St., Society of, 544.
Sullivan, Rev. T. J., early life, education, ordination, and labors of, 99, 109, 115, 145, 146, 310, 311, 312, 313, 403, 431.
 Mr., of Clinton, 601.
Sumter, 302.
 Sisters of Charity in, 65.
 churches in, 116.
 Fort, 237.
 first Mass in, 305.
 religion established in, 311.
 Mother Agatha, 437.
Sumterville, 303.
Sumters, the, 302.
Sunamites, the, 131.
Swamp, Whippy, 183.
Swandale, Mr., of Greenville, 358.
Swannanoa River, the, 460.
Sweat, death of, 431.
Swiggins, 822.

TALBIRD, MR., of Beaufort, 371.
Tallahassee, church at, 549.
Tampa, church at, 549.
Tarborough, 414.
Tasmania, 158.
Taylor, Mr., of Columbia, 198.
"Teller, Truth," the, 139.
Teresa, St., 34.
 daughters of, 62.
 Sister, 66.
Thaumaturgus, St. Gregory, 88.
Thébaud, Father, S.J., 174, 243.
Thornton, Rev. D., 124.
 "Preacher," converted, 117.
Thorington, Margaret, 217.
Thornwell, Prof., 808.
Thompsons, the, of Columbus, 573.
Tighe, Mr., of Greenville, 372.
Tillington, 400.
"Times," the Columbus, 574.
Tobin, Mrs., of Macon, 601.
Townsend, Rev. N., 414.
Treanors, the, of Milledgeville, 602.
Trumbo, Miss, 174.
Trumbos, the, 211.
Tudor, 24.
Tute family, the, of Morganton, 455.
Tuigg, Rev. Father, 146.
 Rt. Rev. Dr., 516.
Twitty, Mr., and family, 827.
Tyler, Rt. Rev. Dr., 166.

UNITED STATES, Catholic population in, 1.
 Protestantism and Catholicity in, 23.

United States a refuge for all nations, 22.
　Celtic element in, 22.
　baptized in Catholic blood, 29.
　Constitution of, a Catholic instrument, 29.
　Church of the, 81, 77, 324.
　Catholic laity in, 34.
　ecclesiastical summary of (1877), 36.
　Catholic journalism in the (1877), 36.
　progress of the faith in, 30.
　secular and sectarian press in, 54.
　executions in the, 90.
　Murray's "History of the Catholic Church in," 101, 106.
　difficulties of the Church in, 626, 627.
　sees in the, 107.
Unitarians, claims of the, 144.
Ursula, Mother, 278.
Unction, Extreme, lay, 503.

VALLE CRUCIS, 136.
Valley, Cashier's, 458.
Varella, Rev. Dr. 509, 510.
Vatican, Councils of the, 127.
Verot, Bishop, life and episcopacy of, 126, 538 to 550.
Vestry system, the, 213, 215.
Vendeans, the, 229.
Vigueront, Rev. F. G., 164.
Violence, sectarian, 247.
Virgin, Immaculate, the, 31, 164.

WALKER, COLEMAN, 219.
Walahc, Michael, 245.
Walhalla, 339.
　first sermon in, 339.
　grand celebration at, 343.
Waldron, Father, 361.
Wallace, Rev. Father, 143, 147, 150.
Walterborough, 183.
War, the Seminole, 585, 586.
Wardlaw, Judge, 331.
Washington, George, 142.
　Bishop England on the character of, 58.
　North Carolina, 410, 414.
Watts, Mrs., of Macon, 199.
　Wm. B., of Macon, 597, 598.
　Mrs. Wm. B., and family, of Macon, 597, 598.
　Dr. Alexander, 598.
Wealth, the solitude of, 169.

Webster, Daniel, 336.
　the deserted town of, 350.
Weldon, 414.
Weir, Mr. James, of Lumpkin Co., S. C., 576.
West, Key, church at, 549.
Whealan, Very Rev. Peter, missionary labors of, 131, 161, 407, 536, 537, 538, 539.
　Tim. T., 256, 332.
Whelan, Rt. Rev. Dr., 619, 620, 621.
Wheeler, Sister Mary Berchman, death of, 554.
White, Father, O.S.B., 429.
　John, 217.
　Rev. J. B., 414.
Whitner, Captain, 332.
Wilson, 415.
Wilmington, 63, 220, 252.
　Sisters of Mercy in, 400.
　the Church in, 116.
　yellow fever at, 148, 150, 402.
Wilson, Governor, 128, 129.
Willit, Father, S.J., 407.
Williams, Archbishop, 23.
Williamston, 381.
Wimmer, Rt. Rev. Abbot, 430, 431, 432, 433.
Windsor, 415.
Winnsborough, S. C., 293, 301, 427.
Wirz, Colonel, the condemnation of, Father Whelan and, 553.
Wise, Governor, 389, 413.
Wissel, Rev. Raphael, 552.
Witherspoon, Dr., 308.
Wolf, Father H., O.S.B., 429, 479.
"World, the Catholic," 127.
Wood, Archbishop, 31, 230.
Woodfin, Colonel N. A., 458.
Woodward, Hon. Joseph A., 293.
Wray, Miss Ann, 189.
Wrights, the, of Wilmington, 310.

XAVIER, ST. FRANCIS, 60, 115, 140, 422, 433.

YORKVILLE, S. C., 322.
York, New, diocese of, 231.
　City, 107, 240.
Youghal, Ireland, 180.
Youth, native Catholic, 63.
Young, Father Alfred, 322.

ZACHARY, Pope, 29.
Zebedee, sons of, 104.

www.ingramcontent.com/pod-product-compliance
Lightning Source LLC
Chambersburg PA
CBHW021221300426
44111CB00007B/387